THE TRUE STOF
FROM TRUMAN TO TRUMP

A BABY BOOMER'S
LAST STAND

VOLUME ONE: The First Stand

SECOND EDITION

A Trilogy by Jon Alexander Young

Printed in the United States of America

ISBN:

10 9 8 7 6 5 4 3 2 1

EMPIRE PUBLISHING
www.empirebookpublishing.com

All photos and printed images courtesy of Mershon and Hunter family archives, with special thanks and acknowledgements to Worldwide Publishing and National Singles Register news and photo Archives, S.T.A.R.S. and World Entertainment Archives, Stan Adams, Sheri Determan, Mark Marzouk, Wallace Eagler, Amanda Miles, Paramount Pictures, Los Angeles Times, Los Angeles Herald Examiner, Las Vegas Panorama and Las Vegas Star Magazine, Wolfgang- Gerdes Testa, Henderson News Service, James Bacon, Ralph Parker, World Series of Poker, Las Vegas Sun, Long Beach Independent, KTTV television, KDFW television and The Los Angeles Press Club. All conversations/dialogue contained in this book are reproduced as closely as humanly possible to the original, from the utilization and verification of documented media sources, as well primary and secondary sources.

Table of Contents

PRELUDE TO THE LAST STAND WINTER, 2009 11

BOOK ONE...17

    "MUSIC, GIRLS, AND MEDIA" 17

    1951 - 1969..17

PRELUDE TO THE LAST STAND SPRING, 2009 153

BOOK TWO..158

    "WINE, WOMEN, AND SONG" 158

    1969 - 1972..158

PRELUDE TO THE LAST STAND SUMMER, 2009 267

BOOK THREE 272

    "PUBLICITY, CELEBRITY AND LOVE" 272

PRELUDE TO THE LAST STAND SUMMER, 2009 421

BOOK FOUR 426

    "CELEBRITY, MEDIA AND SEX" 426

    1975..426

PRELUDE TO THE LAST STAND 531

FALL, 2009 531

BOOK FIVE...535

    "MEDIA, DISCO AND COCAINE" 1976-1977 535

EPILOGUE...658

*"Though some may say it's a waste of time
to keep all these thoughts inside
but a life goes by too fast
without memories ya got no past...."*

Lyrics from the song "I Can't Recall Their Names" by JJ Breeze

PREFACE

When setting out to write this "True Story of a Novel Life from Truman to Trump," the theme of baby boomers had already been written about and analyzed extensively in the past, and there is a current trend that is leaving many people today satisfied with the knowledge that it won't be too long before all baby boomers are as extinct as the dinosaurs. The entire *A Baby Boomers Last Stand* trilogy also shows that the old adage of how "History repeats itself" may never apply to the days and experiences of the baby boomer generation with the way the culture has evolved.

As the Proverb in Job:23 was written, many feel the same way today:

> *The womb shall forget him the*
> *worm shall feed sweetly on him*
> *he shall be no more remembered.*

The current culture that leaves many wanting to forget the way things were in the last half of the twentieth century and progress only into the future has left the millennials and current leaders not wanting to hear any more stories about the "baby boomers" and their time on Earth. But it may also show many of those same people how we got to where we are today through the eyes of one particular baby boomer.

From the almost eight billion people on the face of the Earth and billions more who have already come and gone, there are millions of other stories possibly worth telling but are never told. The most important question that goes into the writing of any type of biography or memoir is its purpose, and the reasons why anyone want to read about this particular person, but although some readers may be able to associate with many aspects of this trilogy, most will see there has probably never been a life as unusual or analyzed as fully.

Throughout the last half of the twentieth century and into the twenty-first century, there were probably millions of people who either saw this particular person onstage, read about in the newspapers or magazines, heard or seen being interviewed on the radio or television, and also probably thousands who may have met him or personally thought they knew him themselves. During his unique and his different career choices as an editor and publisher of a groundbreaking national newspaper; a nightclub and party promoter; beauty pageant director: documentary filmmaker; award-winning songwriter and theatrical producer, a well-known gambler and poker player; to even a "sometimes" rock star; he crossed paths and partied with hundreds of world-famous entertainers and celebrities, politicians, sports legends, rock stars and even some notorious mobsters.

But most of those he interacted with never saw any connections between many of those aspects of his life when they might have seen or met him themselves.

It all depended on what name he was using at the time.

In 2017 there was a feature documentary entitled *Legsman69* that was being produced, but when trying to show everything about the different ventures, scandals, near escapes from death, mixed in with other cultural changes that this particular person had been involved in, it was just a sensationalized film that only dwelled on selective aspects that could never describe the entire story. There were too many subjects, events, and important people in his life that had long been forgotten, and stories that could never be explained fully in an under two-hour film documentary.

This book's author wanted to show the story of an entire life with insights and sometimes uncomfortable honesty of just one unique human being who spent his journey living on this planet during a very interesting and probably most important time in the United States' history.

This is the entire story.

Although this book is written in the form of a novel or a type of biographical memoir, every conversation, and details of the subjects mentioned in this book, were documented by actual media coverage or the best personal recollections by those interviewed who were personally and directly involved with this story. Everything in this book is true, and there has never been as much documentation through the media and press archive's, personal artifacts, and interviews with many who knew him personally, to tell the story of those many different aspects of his life that demonstrates the old adage that sometimes the truth is stranger than fiction.

To really explain a life to the fullest and include a journey that explained the step-by-step choices a person chooses that guide him through that life, one *"Book"* wasn't enough. This *"True Story of a Novel Life"* did turn into an over six hundred-thousand-word epic that needed to be broken into three volumes after dozens of interviews, including the subject of this book, and hundreds of hours of viewing archive news footage, video footage, photos, and newspaper stories to document everything that is written on these pages. Everyone written about in this book are real people, and only a few names out of the hundreds have been changed for personal privacy, and everything in this book actually happened as written

Someone once sarcastically said trying to document any particular individual's entire life history in painstaking detail for almost seventy years, and putting it in context with cultural and historical changes over that period, as well as analyzing that history with a touch of the different philosophical principals that everyone considers at various times in their lives, would almost be like trying to rewrite a new version of the Bible. With that in mind, it became much easier of a read by presenting the story in a series of fourteen shorter books included collectively in **Three Volumes** (including the special edition of **The Prologue**), with each book as a separate type of "memoir" told chronologically during the years of 1951-2019 during the presidencies of Harry S Truman and Donald J Trump.

Volume One, "The First Stand" (which includes Books One through Five) could almost be subtitled *Genesis*, covering the birth and creation of a particular baby boomer while living in Hollywood and Las Vegas, then called the modern-day Sodom and Gomorrah, during the transitional 1960s and 1970s and being involved in, and influenced by, the celebrity and media culture of those cities and those times.

Volume Two, "The Second Stand" (which includes Books Six through Nine) could be viewed as a type of *Exodus* as it shows the departure and long journey through the excesses the 1980s subculture of the nightlife and parties when sex, drugs, and rock and roll became the mantra and the lifestyle of a large segment of the American population. And, more press and media notoriety than this particular baby boomer ever imagined.

Volume Three, "The Last Stand" (which includes Books Ten through Thirteen), could be the *Revelation* with how the cultural and social changes from the 1990s to modern-day brought new adjustments and realizations that even though *The Times They Were a Changin'* (to paraphrase Dylan a bit), sex, money, and especially music, was always destined to be part the journey.

There are also "Preludes to the Last Stand" chapters included before each individual Book, which continues the story where **The Prologue** concluded, with each individual Book that follows explaining how he got to that particular point in his life, before the actual "Last Stand" is told in Book Thirteen.

This is just one story of one person's entire life journey not only to show the step-by-step stories that led to *A Baby Boomer's Last Stand,* but a very personal and detailed recollection of the funny, crazy, hedonistic, dramatic, and fateful decisions that probably many can associate at various times in their own journey's. If telling this story can at least bring some smiles and memories to at least those who do remember some of those times, people, places and experiences, it would have all been worthwhile.

Most importantly, by the time this journey has ended, it may give everyone who reads this trilogy some time to examine their own lives and consider its worth.

So, let the journey begin. - *Jon Alexander Young, Author*

8

8

8

VOLUME ONE

"The First Stand"
1951 – 1977

PRELUDE TO THE LAST STAND
WINTER, 2009

It was January 20, 2009, and the seasoned gambler and poker player was watching the action at his table before the betting got to him and saw a young kid on the other end of the table raise the five-dollar blind to fifteen dollars, and then watched one other player call the bet. He also tried not to show any emotion when he finally looked at his own two hole-cards and saw he'd been dealt two beautiful black aces, which although were the two best cards in Texas Hold 'Em, were also the two cards which many professional poker players often joked, "could usually only win a small pot or could also lose someone a big pot."

It all depended on how a poker player decided to play them.

The game was No Limit Hold 'Em with blinds at two and five dollars, with a usual buy-in of five hundred dollars, and although it wasn't the high stakes poker that so many people were currently seeing on television, at that particular casino it was considered the "big game" to most players at the table that night.

Hold 'Em was played with each player being dealt two cards face down called "hole or pocket cards," who would then bet before the dealer would expose five community cards in the center of the table for the rounds of betting. The first three cards the dealer exposed were called the "Flop" which would include another round of betting, the fourth card was called the "Turn" where the players would bet again, and the final card was called the "River" where the players would use their two hole-cards, to complete their best five-card hand of poker and make a final bet.

The seasoned gambler and poker player had about fifteen hundred dollars in chips in front of him, which was a fairly decent stack compared to the rest of the players at the table, but he'd already invested twelve hundred-dollars into the game that night, so was really only about three hundred dollars ahead. He was usually satisfied if he could walk out of the casino every night with a few hundred dollars in profit to keep a normal weekly cash flow and had been planning on leaving the game when the blinds got back around to him, but he also knew if he could win a couple hundred more with his pocket aces, he'd be more than satisfied that poker session.

11

He had also noticed that the young kid who had originally raised the pot looked to be not older than twenty-one years old and appeared to have well over three thousand dollars in chips in front of him and briefly wondered how someone that young, was able to play poker with that much money, knowing that three thousand dollars would have seemed like a fortune when he was that age himself. But the main thing he was thinking about at that moment was how much to raise the pot himself before the Flop, to not only isolate the number of callers, but also make some money at the same time.

Poker was all about making the right decisions, and that all of the decisions that he had made when he was "just a kid" himself were no longer of any consequence, and all he needed to decide on doing these days, was to "call or raise," "bluff or fold," or "keep playing or go home."

Jason Mershon was a professional poker player and nothing else.

After Jason reached down and grabbed some five-dollar yellow chips and raised the pot to seventy-five dollars, "the kid" looked down at his cards again and threw in another sixty dollars and called, while the other player who had called the first raise of fifteen dollars folded his hand deciding another sixty dollars wasn't worth the gamble. That basically satisfied Jason because he knew with holding two aces, he didn't want too many callers who might get lucky on the Flop and catch something crazy that could beat him, and also knew playing one opponent "heads up" gave him the best odds.

The dealer then dealt the first three community cards of a 6 of hearts, a 2 of spades, and a 10 of hearts, which wasn't quite what was known as a "rainbow" flop, but it looked pretty safe for his pocket aces, so after the kid checked his option to bet, Jason bet another seventy-five dollars which was almost half the pot.

After the kid thought for a minute, he loudly announced, "Raise" and pushed two hundred dollars in the pot, which was slightly surprising, but Jason figured the kid probably thought with the junk cards that hit the Flop, the community cards missed whatever two cards he was holding and was making the standard bluff thinking he could make him fold. Jason briefly considered re-raising or going all in himself, but instead, he just decided to smooth call the additional hundred and twenty-five dollars and let the kid bluff off more of his chips, knowing that was how to win a big pot with pocket aces.

The turn card was a 3 of spades, which did nothing to change the board of community cards, but this time, the kid quickly made a three-hundred and fifty-dollar bet, which surprised Jason even more after figuring his last call would have slowed down the betting, but now he had to "think" about what two hole-cards the kid might be holding. He didn't even put the kid on an over-pair like Jacks, Queens or Kings figuring he would have reraised again before the flop, but he also knew when someone bet out quickly as the kid did, it was usually a "tell" that a player was probably on a Flush draw. Jason knew the worst-case scenario would be if the kid flopped three of a kind, but guessed he might just be holding two big Hearts in his hand and was making a "semi-bluff" feeling he had a lot of "outs" to win the pot with another card to come.

He was pretty confident he still had the best hand and Jason decided to just call again, not only hoping a Heart didn't hit the board on the River, but also hoping an Ace of Diamonds would hit, which would give him "the nuts" that couldn't be beat.

The River card was the 2 of diamonds, that paired the board so there were no flush and no likely straight possibilities which made Jason feel more confident. But while he was thinking about what to do, the kid pushed his entire stack of chips in the pot and announced, "All In!"

Jason knew that was the tough thing about No Limit Hold 'Em, and how poker players could lose their entire chip stack in one hand, and naturally, he was against the kid who had a ton of chips in front of him and had no fear of bluffing and now he had to really figure out the hand. He knew if the kid was on a flush draw and missed, the all-in bet would be the obvious bluff, but also considered that he might just have a pair of 10's and was trying to get a better hand to fold. Jason figured the kid probably knew that is what he'd be thinking as well, and if he did have a real hand, like a full house, he might still make that same bet.

He had over a third of his stack in the pot but still had over nine hundred dollars in front of him and needed to decide if he wanted to risk his entire stack of chips on a bluff, but he was also thinking of how doubling up and winning a pot that size would also really make his night.

"Come on old man," the kid sarcastically shouted out, "You going to call or fold?"

Jason half smiled knowing that although he was pushing sixty years old, it did feel strange being called an old man, but remembered when he thought someone his age was an "old man" as well. He was also thinking about how strange it was to feel that calling a nine-hundred-dollar bet was such a big decision for him remembering the days when he was just "a kid" himself, that betting a thousand dollars a hand on baccarat in Las Vegas, or a football game, meant nothing to him. But now, he was playing poker for a living with a limited bankroll and unless he was close to a hundred percent sure, he never wanted to risk everything on a guess and knew it was best to make the other players have to decide on whether or not to call or fold a big bet. Jason had always liked to say that poker wasn't gambling if you played the game right, but now he was gambling, trying to decide whether to call his remaining chip stack.

The kid was also staring at him hard, which was usually a sign of weakness when someone is bluffing, but suddenly Jason didn't want to give the kid the satisfaction of taking the rest of his chips in case he was wrong, and slowly folded his two aces face down and pushed them toward the dealer, deciding to save his chips for another hand.

"I knew you had nothing!" the kid boasted as the dealer pushed all the chips toward him.

The kid then turned his two "hole cards" face up, showing he held the Ace-2 of Hearts, which was a busted flush draw, but he got lucky and got three-of-a-kind on the River. The other poker player who had folded his hand before the flop without calling the first seventy-five-dollar raise then made a frustrated comment Jason had also heard too many times before.

"Damn, I folded a pair of pocket sixes!" the other player said with sarcastic bitterness, "If you guys hadn't raised so much before the flop, I would've stayed in the hand and won the whole pot with a full house!"

Jason felt like saying, "That's why we raised you out of the pot before the flop, you idiot!" but as usual, restrained himself. He always had managed not to let himself go on tilt, or at least never let it show at the poker table, and just said "Good hand" suddenly satisfied when he saw the kids two cards and saw he would have lost if he called.

He also thought to himself that the kid should never have shown his two "hole-cards" to him, and instead of being bothered wondering if he should have called or not, Jason was now happy that he wasn't bluffed and didn't call which would have been just another bad beat story. He was also glad he didn't show that he had pocket aces and let the kid know what a great lay down and fold he made himself.

Jason had been playing poker for over seven hours and was briefly disappointed in himself for not leaving ten minutes earlier while he was still ahead, but was now down about three hundred dollars. He then decided it was a good time to take a break, got up from the poker table, and went to the outside lobby to smoke.

He was at Pechanga Casino in Temecula, California, and the poker room was upstairs in a circular area, that overlooked the casino area and a round bar, but even though it was an Indian casino, it still wasn't like the old days of smoke-filled poker rooms when he could smoke at the table and now, there were only designated smoking areas outside of the poker room.

As Jason took his first puff of his cigarette, he was also still thinking about the last poker hand, and instead of being completely satisfied with his great lay down, he was thinking about how he could have won the hand. He started wondering if he had pushed all-in after the flop, the kid might still have called as he had a small pair and two more cards to make a flush draw. But on the other hand, if he would have pushed his remaining nine hundred dollars in the pot on the turn, the kid may have been less inclined to gamble with only a pair of 2's and only one more card to make his flush. But Jason had already seen how the young players tended to gamble more these days, and with the big stack of chips the kid had in front of him, he might have just wanted to gamble regardless and finally decided that he played the hand right.

The kid just got lucky, just as he had plenty of times in his life, but knew he'd never have the answer and quickly tried to get it out of his mind. Jason also knew that replaying hands in your head could drive poker players nuts sometimes, just as it had been trying to figure out other decisions he'd made in his own life.

He then got distracted by a song barely coming through the PA speaker outside the poker room and focused his attention on the music instead of thinking about the last poker hand.

It was the old Carly Simon song, "Nobody Does it Better," which used to be one of his favorite songs from the James Bond films he'd seen when he was younger. Music always took him back to another time and place, and he always felt it was the music and the songs that kept his memory so sharp. and of the thousands of old songs that had stayed in his head for over the past fifty years, each one always seemed to remind him of something, or someone, who had been important to him at one time.

Jason had often heard the cliché about "popular songs being the soundtrack of your life," especially to baby boomers, but certain songs had always been more than a cliché to him and he knew each old song he'd hear was basically the actual story of his life.

Many of those he played poker with had asked him what he did before becoming a professional poker player, but Jason would always remain vague and just say something flippant like he was a "retired legs man" or "a retired rock star" when he was younger, and although both were true in some ways, he just didn't think it was worth the time to try and explain too much. He knew trying to tell stories about what he once did and all the famous or even infamous people he had crossed paths with in the past forty years would just sound like BS coming from some guy sitting at a poker table. Plus, the culture had changed so much in the past twenty years most of his stories would sound too "politically incorrect" to even mention, and now he was only concerned about the next hand of poker he'd be dealt.

Jason took his last puff on the cigarette and suddenly thought a cocktail sounded good, and although he seldom drank anymore, he figured a Bailey's and Coffee might give him a boost before he went back to the poker table. But when he looked down from the railing to the big Round Bar below the poker area, he saw the televisions around the bar were still showing replays of Barack Obama's Inauguration earlier that day, and except for the bartenders cleaning up, the bar was empty. Jason looked at his watch and realized they'd been closed for almost an hour and had completely lost track of time and knew that in California, they still couldn't sell liquor after two am, even if it was an Indian Casino. He knew it certainly wasn't like his old days in Las Vegas when he'd be coming out of a nightclub at four am with a drink still in his hand, trying to decide where to party or gamble next. But now, this hour was late to him, and this time he really did have to think about whether he should go back in the poker room and try to grind it out for a couple more hours. He also remembered every gambler's most famous motto; "You can't WIN if you don't PLAY and knew there was nothing else to think about.

As he looked down on the mostly empty casino floor and listened to the Carly Simon song end before heading back to the poker table, Jason suddenly remembered the first words of the first James Bond novel he had read over forty years earlier when he was just a kid himself.

"The scent, smoke, and sweat of a casino are nauseating at three in the morning."

BOOK ONE

"MUSIC, GIRLS, AND MEDIA"
1951 - 1969

Chapter One

In 1951, Harry Truman was President, the Korean War was at its peak, and the Republicans were still trying to convince General Dwight Eisenhower to run against Truman in the following year's presidential election to end twenty years of Democrat rule.

The minimum wage in 1951 was seventy-five cents an hour with the average yearly income at three thousand dollars, gasoline was nineteen cents a gallon, and the average cost of a home was nine thousand dollars.

A young prosecutor named Roy Cohen achieved national fame, by being instrumental in the 1951 trial of Julius and Ethel Rosenburg, who would be convicted and later executed for providing nuclear weapons designs to and spying for the Soviet Union. The fear of communism was at its peak that year, and the United States Congress, controlled by the Democrats, would begin its second investigation into communist infiltration in Hollywood by dozens of actors and others in the entertainment industry, with what became known as *Blacklisting*.

Russia had already tested its first atomic bomb, and had increased the "Red Scare" which led the United States to accelerate its nuclear program, and in 1951, the government also moved its atomic bomb test site to a remote area sixty-five miles from Las Vegas in Nevada, where dozens of atomic bomb tests could be visibly conducted as a deterrent to Russia and the Soviet Union.

I Love Lucy also first premiered on television in 1951, as did a wildly popular game show called *What's My Line?* where celebrity panelists tried to guess the occupation of contestants with unusual occupations. The top movies that year were *A Streetcar Named Desire* (which made a star out of the young actor Marlon Brando), *The African Queen*, *The Day the Earth Stood Still*, and the movie that would go on to win the Oscar for *Best Picture of the Year* was the musical *An American in Paris* which featured the music of George and Ira Gershwin. The most popular songs of 1951 were *Too Young and Unforgettable* both by Nat King Cole, *Hey Good Lookin'* by Hank Williams, Tony Bennet's cover of another Hank Williams song, *Cold, Cold Heart*, and Johnny Ray's biggest hit, *Cry*. But there were some other things would become very important in the life of a baby boomer that year as well. It was in 1951 that Cleveland Disc Jockey Allan Freed first used the term *Rock and Roll*, as well as the year author Ian Fleming would start thinking and writing about a new literary character named James Bond and complete his first novel *Casino Royale* the following year, and it was also in 1951 when the first oral contraceptive, later to become known as *The Pill*, began development. In Chicago that same year, a young cartoonist took his first venture into publishing when his book *That Toddlin' Town* was published, which featured a series of risqué cartoons satirizing his observations of "the manners and morals" of those in his hometown of Chicago. After making a small but decent profit off his first book in 1951, that cartoonist, Hugh M Hefner decided to continue in the publishing business and less than two years later, decided to publish an "entertainment magazine for men" called *Playboy*.

Almost sixty years later in 2009, when a certain seasoned gambler and professional poker player thought back to the events of 1951, he knew it was a very interesting year to have been born in, and in many ways, may even have prophesized his own future without him ever realizing it.

Jay Jeffery Mershon was born in Chicago, Illinois, on February 24, 1951, and would be the only child of Richard and Violet Mershon. His parents had married young, with his father having turned twenty-one on the day before he was born, while his mother only turned eighteen five months earlier. Jay remembered very little about his childhood years in Chicago, and the only record or memories of those years, were though what his mother called a "baby book" which she showed him years later about hie early years growing up, as well as a historical record of his ancestry.

The name Mershon descended from the French name *Marchand* and it was traced to Henri Marchand, a French Huguenot who immigrated to the United States in the 1600s to escape religious persecution. Jay's mother's maiden name was Piehl, and her side of the family had German origin and had immigrated in the mid-Nineteenth Century. Jay was also told he was a distant relative of both President Ulysses S Grant and General George Custer whom his mother said gave him a very famous family tree he could talk about when he started to go to school.

Then, there were some things Jay was glad that he didn't remember.

His mother wrote in his "baby book" that he woke up crying around three am and had a fever when he was about two years old, and wrote in those day's doctors were always on call and made house visits even at that late hour. When the doctor arrived, Jay had a fever of a hundred and two and because the big fear in the early 1950s was Polio, it was decided that he should immediately be taken to the Children's Hospital for tests. It wasn't Polio, but it was something just as dangerous at that time called Spinal Meningitis and his mother wrote in the "baby book" that he spent several weeks in the Children's Hospital before he was able to fully recover. She also aways reminded him, "he was lucky he had good parents who took care of him, or he might not be alive." Also, in his baby book were pictures of himself that Jay didn't remember, but his mother had described with notes on the back of the photographs.

One of the photos was Jay's picture when he was around four old, next to a girl around his age sitting on a cut out of a paper moon with the sky and stars as the backdrop. His mother wrote a sentence under the photo that said the little girl was "Jay's first girlfriend Jeannie" and that "*Mr. Sandman* was your and Jeannie's favorite song and you used to like to dance to it together." She also reminded him that the first popular song she tried to teach him to sing was a hit song in 1955 called *It's a Sin to Tell a Lie* by a musical group called *Something Smith and the Redheads* and explained that she took him to a department store in Chicago that had a machine to record voices and still had a recording of Jay trying to sing that particular song.

Jay also noticed that most of the pictures were of him alone, and there weren't any pictures of him with both his parents and just figured that photographs just weren't that common to have in those days. But although old pictures and second-hand stories was all Jay knew about his early years, he did remember some things when his family moved to California when he was almost five years old.

One of the first things he vaguely remembered was he and his parents always seemed to be moving to different apartments and sometimes just pack up and move somewhere new in the middle of the night. Jay always remembered crying because sometimes there wasn't room in the car for everything and he had to leave some of his toys behind. His father also always got mad and yelled at him for crying and just said they'd just get him new toys at their next house, but Jay still cried because he liked the toys he had and hated leaving them behind. The other thing he clearly remembered was that his parents seemed to fight and yell at each other a lot, not only just when they had to move somewhere new, but at least several times a month over different things he never understood. The worst thing he remembered about their fighting was that it was followed by hours, sometimes days, where there was complete silence and they wouldn't even speak to each other, and even he needed to stay silent himself until they decided to start talking to each other again.

With his parents moving so often, Jay also didn't have a chance to make friends with anyone for too long, but would occasionally see some cousins that had also moved from Chicago, but he did remember that most of those family gatherings would normally end up turning into arguments as well. It seemed to him that his mother didn't seem to like his father's side of the family and vice versa, but Jay would usually just play with his younger cousins and try to block out whatever they were arguing about.

Staying in one location for longer than three months was a luxury Jay hadn't experienced before, and he liked it when they did move to a small house in Downtown Los Angeles near the Los Angeles Memorial Coliseum, and lived there for almost two years. He did enjoy going to school and being around different people instead of just spending all of his time with his parents and sometimes wished school lasted longer so he wouldn't have to listen to his parent's fight. He also learned that his father was a Catholic, but his mother wasn't, and she insisted that Jay not be raised as one, which was the main reason he was enrolled in first grade at *Hoover Baptist School* only a few blocks from their house.

Although there was some *Bible Study Time* every day, *Hoover Baptist School* had many other studies that Jay enjoyed learning and especially liked a class where they had group sing-along's every day. All of the kids in his class were given books with lyrics to dozens of songs, and the teachers would have them learn the melody.

Some of the songs Jay already knew like *Mary Had A Little Lamb* and *Twinkle, Twinkle Little Star*, but while he had to learn some religious songs like *Jesus Loves the Little Children* and *Onward Christian Soldiers*, there were also fun songs from Disney films like *Whistle While You Work* and *When You Wish Upon A Star*, American folk songs like *My Old Kentucky Home, Dixie* and *Swanee River*, and patriotic songs like *America the Beautiful, God Bless America* and *The Battle Hymn of the Republic*.

Jay's memories of singing loudly in music class were some of his best when he was young. It was also the first time Jay ever saw his name in some form of the media when it appeared in a printed weekly school newsletter. It read: "The first-grade children are still busy losing their teeth and cutting new ones, and with them, it is a very serious business! Jay Mershon was all day wiggling his loose tooth out and carried it proudly home."

Jay's mother made a big thing about showing him his name in the newsletter and told him he was famous and saved the clipping pasting it in his baby book along with a small envelope with that tooth inside. But he didn't care about that, and mainly remembered stories he'd heard about the *Tooth Fairy* and was eager to put the tooth under his pillow to see it replaced with a quarter the next morning.

But his best memory of those early days was when his parents gave him a new companion, a mixed female golden retriever and cocker spaniel Jay named *"Tinker Bell"* after his favorite character in the movie *Peter Pan*.

When his mother would pick Jay up from school, he discovered that *Tinker*, as he eventually shorted her name, was also a great draw for attracting new friends. Tinker was always in the car excitedly wagging her tail and barking as soon as she saw Jay walking out of the school building, and the other kids would always want to come and pet her. It wasn't long before many kids in the neighborhood would also come to his house and usually ask, "Can Tinker and Jay come out and play?"

Jay didn't really mind that sometimes it seemed his friends liked Tinker more than him and was just happy that they were living somewhere long enough for him to have a larger group of friends. Because he was able to make so many new friends, his parents also decided to host a big birthday party for him and he had over twenty of his new friends playing and celebrating for an entire day. That particular birthday was easier to remember because there were photos and 8mm home movies of the party his parents had filmed that day, and Jay liked that besides himself, all of the girls and boys were dressed in their "Sunday Best" dresses and suits. He also remembered besides getting presents from all his new friends, that birthday was also when he got his own new portable record player as a present from his parents.

His parents always had an older record player and dozens of long-playing records, but smaller *45 rpm records* were what everyone was buying in 1956, and now Jay knew he could start playing the new songs he liked hearing on the radio whenever he wanted to listen to them. His parents also said they'd also buy him at least one new 45 record each week for his birthday that year.

His mother was an Elvis Presley fan and bought his current hits *Heartbreak Hotel*, *Hound Dog*, and *Don't Be Cruel*. She also was a fan of Dean Martin and Nat King Cole and had several of their 45's while his father seemed to like songs by Little Richard, Gene Vincent, The Platters, and Fats Domino. Jay liked all of those songs and artists, but also liked songs like *Sixteen Tons* by Tennessee Ernie Ford, *The Green Door* by Jim Lowe, *The Wayward Wind* by Gogi Grant and talked his parents into buying those 45's as well.

They'd also play some of his parent's full albums by older music stars like Al Jolson, Hank Williams, Frank Sinatra, and instrumental hit songs from the 1940s that featured hit songs from what Jay learned was called the *Big Band* era. The most fun times he remembered was playing all the songs over and over and singing along with them with his parents. When they all sang, their main audience was Tinker, and she seemed to like having songs directed to her, especially when Jay's mother would sometimes pick Tinker up by her front paws and pretend to dance with her while singing *Hound Dog*.

Jay always seemed to have music in his head when he was growing up, and even the movies he watched on television became his favorites because of the music. He never could seem to get *The Little Rascals* or the *Andy Hardy* movie theme songs out of his head and mainly liked watching them just to hear the opening music themes.

There was also a television show called *The Million Dollar Movie* that was on every night that would run the same movie for a week just like in the theatres. The movies that Jay would watch many times during the week were the ones that had soundtracks that stuck in his head or had songs he liked that were featured in the movie. His mother liked the old musicals like *I'll See you in My Dreams*, *Three Little Words* or *I Wonder Who's Kissing Her Now*, and his father liked old James Cagney or Error Flynn movies like *The Roaring Twenties*, *Angels with Dirty Faces*, and the *Charge of the Light Brigade*, so Jay came to like those movies as well after seeing them multiple times during the week.

But it wasn't always fun, music, movies, and parties and sometimes when he came home from school, he was able to see his parents had another fight because they were giving each other what became known as the *silent treatment*. Jay would never say anything and would just go to his room with Tinker, shut the door and listen to records, do homework and find other ways to stay entertained without being bothered by his parent's arguments. His parents yelling also seemed to upset Tinker, so Jay would just sing her the words to the first song he learned, *It's a Sin to Tell A Lie* to drown out the noise and calm her down. Petting and singing the words *"I love you, yes I do...I lo-v e you…it's a sin to tell a lie…"* to his puppy, or listening to his records, always blocked out anything that would concern him about his parents. But he also remembered being yelled at himself when he was young and would get spankings from his father by what became known as *The Belt* at least two or three times a month. Sometimes he would get *The Belt* for getting into trouble at school, throwing rocks and breaking something, or other kid stuff like getting caught playing with matches, but most of the time, he'd get *The Belt* when his father saw him crying.

Jay didn't think he cried a lot and was only if he fell and hurt himself, or saw a sad movie scene or ending like in *Bambi* or *King Kong*. But his father would always get mad and tell him to stop being a "bawl baby" and usually give him four or five swats on his behind with what he always described as "a lesson" not to cry anymore.

The worst swats he remembered, was when they all went to the theatre to see the movie *Old Yeller* and Jay's eyes started to tear up when the young boy in the movie was told he'd have to shoot his dog because he caught rabies. Jay was thinking that Old Yeller looked similar to Tinker and started crying, but his father became angry and told him to "shut up" and said that he was "embarrassing" him. Even though he thought he heard other people in the theatre crying, and even saw tears in his mother's eyes, his father became more furious when Jay couldn't stop crying and made them all leave the theatre before the movie was finished.

During the drive home his mother was yelling at his father saying that Jay was just a little boy, but his father yelled back saying "he needed to learn not to be a bawl baby" and was going to get the belt when they got home.

There were more than four or five swats with the belt that night and harder they had been before which made Jay cry even more, but his father yelled that he wasn't going to stop until he stopped crying. Finally, Jay was able to hold his breath and somehow hold back the crying long enough for swats to stop. His father then angerly left his room and slammed his bedroom door, leaving Jay alone, but he heard Tinker scratching and whining outside the door, and got up to let her in his room.

As his dog was consoling him, he heard his parents yelling at each other from the other room and knew he was in for one or two days of the *silent treatment* again, but after that night, Jay promised himself he would never let his father see him crying and had learned his lesson.

&

By 1958, his father decided it was time to make another move and told Jay that downtown LA was "becoming a bad neighborhood" and decided to move to the suburbs to another city called La Puente, which was about twenty miles from downtown Los Angeles.

When he enrolled at *Nelson Elementary School*, Jay learned one of the problems with moving and changing schools so often in the middle of the school year, was that he seemed to have skipped a half of grade somewhere during his transfers. His mother explained to him that during one of their moves he had been enrolled in one school a semester early and that was the reason most of his classmates were usually a year older than him. Because he was often seen walking to school with Tinker beside him, the other kids would always come over wanting to pet her and as usual, Tinker became his *best friend* maker and he was again able to make new friends quickly which gave him things to do after school while his parents worked.

Jay was never sure what his father did for a living, just that he was in some kind of different sales jobs, and his mother also worked as a food waitress at different coffee shops. They all didn't really didn't spend that much time together except on some weekends, and there were occasions when his parents both ended up working at the same time at night, and Jay would have babysitters.

One teenage girl who babysat was his favorite because she'd always bring over her record collection and because Jay seemed to have a new favorite song almost every week, he and his babysitter would talk about the latest hits and spend hours listening and singing along to the different records they both had. His babysitter was also a big Elvis Presley fan and would always have his most recent songs, including Jay's two favorite current Elvis hits, *A Fool Such as I* and *Hard-Headed Woman* several times in a row, until they both learned the words and tried to sing the songs together.

His baby sitter would then play a game with him, where after singing the songs together, she'd play the record back and pull off the needle in the middle of the song, and then make Jay sing the next line in order to win the game. He got in the habit of trying to learn the words to all the songs he heard on the radio or from his records so he could win the games the next time his baby sitter came over, and remembered learning all the words to songs like *Purple People Eater*, *Sweet little Sixteen*, *Poison Ivy*, *The Great Pretender*, and about a dozen others.

Jay had another baby sitter who also liked playing all the records, but she had a habit of changing the words to certain songs to make them funny. One song she sang that he remembered was Lloyd Prices' *Personality*, and instead of the regular chorus, she'd teasingly sing *"Cause you've got, SPLIT Personality"* instead of the usual lyrics, and also did that with a lot of other songs which always made him laugh.

He thought the babysitters were a lot of fun and was always happy to come home from school to spend time with them almost as much as he did Tinker, but he also thought he baby sitters were cute and sometimes he wished he was just a few years older so they wouldn't think he was just a kid.

Jay already couldn't wait until he grew up and was older.

Chapter Two

During the Spring of 1959, Jay thought it would be fun to join the Cub Scouts which his parents didn't mind because it would keep him busy when he wasn't at school and they also wouldn't have to pay a babysitter as often. Jay already had a couple of friends at school who were in the Cub Scouts and liked wearing his Cub Scout uniform during all of the weekly activities. Plus, he liked it when the Scout Master let some of the kids bring their dogs along on hikes or field trips, so he didn't have to leave Tinker alone too often.

One of his friends in the Cub Scouts was named Tommy who Jay had become friends with, but there was one particular thing he liked about having him for a friend. Tommy had a cute sister named with blond hair named Linda who was a year older than Jay, but she also liked spending more time playing with Tinker than her brother did, so she'd often come to Jay's house without Tommy a couple times a week. The best thing Jay liked about Linda was that she was the first girl close to his age he spent time with alone who didn't treat him like a "little kid" and he started to enjoy spending more time with her than Tommy.

Jay remembered that his mother had told him he had a "girlfriend" in Chicago when he was younger but only recalled seeing her photo and considered Linda his first "real" girlfriend. The other thing he learned about Linda was that she liked to kiss and was the first girl he remembered who kissed him on the lips as a sign of affection. Although they never really kissed a lot and usually just giggled about who could make the loudest "smacking noise" when they did kiss, it did become a part of their playtime together. Linda was also the first girl he remembered going out on a "date' with after Linda invited him to spend a Saturday afternoon together at the local roller-skating rink in La Puente.

Although Jay had "little kid" roller skates he'd use on the sidewalk, he had never tried to gone to a skating rink with "real" roller skates before and talked his mother into giving him a dollar and driving him to the rink to meet Linda to give it a try. Linda was already at the rink and skating with some other kids by the time his mother dropped him off, but she came over when she saw Jay and took his hand to lead him to the skating area. The roller-skating rink was an enclosed outdoor rink with a smooth cement skating surface called the *Vineland Skating Club* and saw that most of the other kids were skating around in circles fairly easily but he was a little nervous trying it for the first time.

Jay saw that Linda was already a good skater, but he felt very awkward and had a hard time not falling as they skated around the rink, but she continued holding his hand and showed him how to slowly take strides and keep his balance without falling. Although he still fell down a couple of times, by the end of the first session Jay was able to keep his balance pretty good, but also knew he would have to learn to roller skate a lot better if he wanted to spend more time with Linda on weekends.

Once summer vacation began and his school year ended, Jay learned the roller rink offered free lessons for beginners, and he was able to talk his parents into letting him take some skating lessons a couple of times a week saying it was a new hobby he wanted to learn instead of continuing to be in the Cub Scouts. His parents didn't seem to mind as it only meant another activity to keep him busy where they wouldn't have to pay a baby sitter during the week. His father also thought it was "cute" that he had a "crush" on a girl and agreed to start giving him an allowance of three dollars a week for doing chores around the house so he could pay for his admission, skate rentals, and some refreshments from the snack bar on his "dates" with Linda.

It only took a few weeks of skating lessons that summer before Jay was able to navigate fairly well around the rink and was spending all of his weekend afternoons with Linda skating at Vineland. Sometimes, their parents would let them stay at the rink on Saturday nights when they featured something called *Moonlight Sessions*, which was mainly for older skaters. In the afternoons, most of the music was piped in organ music, but on Saturday nights, they'd play popular songs that were more fun to skate to and pop music would blast over the speakers much louder than the boring organ music.

Several times during the evening sessions, the rink would feature a special skating segment they called *"Couples Only"* where they would dim the lights, play slower songs where the boys could dance with their girlfriends. Jay and Linda had both considered themselves "boyfriend and girlfriend" by then, so they always liked that part of the session best.

While some of the other couples would just hold hands or dance side-by-side, Linda would skate backward with her arms on Jay's shoulder, and Jay would skate forward with his hands around her hips so they could look at each other while they skated in circles around the rink. With songs like *I Only Have Eyes for You* and *Smoke Gets in Your Eyes* coming from the speakers, it seemed to make them feel even closer, and when the slow songs were over, they'd always look around to make sure no one was watching and sneaked in a quick kiss before the lights came back up.

Although it was the best summer Jay felt he'd ever had and was convinced he was in love, when September came and it was time to go back to school, Linda had some bad news and told Jay that because her father had gotten a job in another city she and Tommy were moving away for "a few months." She also said that although she knew her parents would never let her make long distance phone calls, she would still write

Jay letters every week so they could still be "pen pals" and remain friends until she moved back to La Puente so they could pick up their relationship where it left off.

But a month into his fourth grade at Nelson Elementary School, he still hadn't received a letter a letter from her and never did find out where she had moved.

Jay's parents tried to joke that Linda was just his first "summer romance" and he'd meet plenty of other girlfriends in the future saying it was "just part of growing up" and he probably wouldn't even remember her name in a few years. Even though he did feel like he was experiencing a feeling of being heartbroken, Jay knew better than to ever let his father see him crying over it, but he also definitely didn't like his first experience of "growing up."

‎‎‎‎‎‎‎‎‎‎‎‎‎‎‎‎‎‎‎‎‎‎‎‎‎‎‎‎‎‎‎‎‎‎‎ ‎

Although Linda had moved away, Jay continued spending time at the *Vineland Skating Club* where he liked being around the other kids he had met, plus, there was always something fun going on during the different sessions and roller skating completely replaced his interest in the Cub Scouts.

Usually, at least once a session, they'd have something called a *"Penny Scramble,"* where all the kids would line up against the wall, and then some employee at the rink would throw several hands full of pennies in the center of the skate floor. The kids would race to where the pennies were and got to keep as many as they could gather while the song *Pennies from Heaven* by music group The Skyliners played over the loudspeaker. Sometimes on special occasions, they would mix the pennies with nickels, dimes, and quarters, so Jay would walk away with almost a dollar on some days. But what he really liked was that twice a session they'd dim the lights, play the theme song from the TV series *Peter Gunn*, and place four pylons in a square on the rink floor to make a circular track, which meant it was time for the two daily races around the skating rink.

The first race was only two laps around the pylons, and the second race was four laps around the pylons, with the winner of each race receiving a free popcorn and coke, and the second-place finisher winning a free admission to another skating session. Jay had seen *Roller Derby* on TV and saw the races at the rink were almost just as wild. with a large group of skaters lining up at the starting line, before someone would shoot off a starter's pistol to start the race. It would then become a free-for-all as all the skaters pushed and shoved other skaters as soon as the race stated with half of the skaters knocked down before the first lap was over, with the four or five skaters who were left standing then making a mad dash to hit the finish line first.

It also took Jay many tries, many falls, and many loses, before he started to figure out some strategies.

In the two-lap race, he had to ignore the others and try to get as fast of start as possible to stay away from the pushing and shoving and skating wide while they all fought it out. In the four-lap race, Jay found it was better to lag behind and let the other skaters ahead of him to fight it out for the first couple laps and then just try to pass all the fallen skaters and try to slide by the others up front who were still pushing and pulling at each other during the last lap. He didn't win every time, but he did manage to finish first or second several times, which also got the attention of one of the rink managers who approached Jay after one of the races he'd won.

The rink manager explained that *Vineland* had a speed racing club that competed in races throughout California every month and introduced Jay to a coach who suggested that he join their skating club and learn how to "become a *real* speed skater" and win something more important than a box of popcorn. He explained that *Vineland* was a member of the *"USARSA US Olympic Association, Amateur Athletic Union"* and that the monthly competitions called *"Meets"* that led to a State Championship, and then to a National Finals in different states each year.

When Jay mentioned it to his parents after they picked him up from the rink, his father at first said it just sounded like a way to get him to "buy expensive roller skates" and pay for lessons, but decided to talk to the coach himself and make sure "it was legit." After just a few days of discussions and making Jay promise he wouldn't get bored with roller skating the way he did the Cub Scouts, his parents agreed to put out the money needed for new speed skates, lessons, and memberships.

The speed skating lessons and training were two hours each, three times a week in the early evenings so that it wouldn't interfere with school, and Jay's parents would always make sure one of them was off work to make sure he made it to practice. He also found out the competition season would begin the following February, so he had only a few months to be ready for the first "skating *Meet*."

Between going to school and his skating, Jay didn't spend that much time at home, and not wanting to be away from Tinker that often, the coach agreed to let him bring her to most of the practices, but after she started chasing Jay when she first saw him racing around the pylons, she needed to start wearing a leash. Jay and the other kids would always spend time sitting and petting her when they weren't practicing so she wouldn't feel left out, and the coach started to joke that Tinker was almost like the team mascot with all the attention she was getting.

As usual, Jay saw that Tinker always made him more popular whenever she was around. He also immediately learned the races in real competitions were going to be a lot different than the ones he was used to, and there was no pushing or bumping, and all the skaters pretty much had to stay in their lanes when circling the pylons. He was also trained on how to get faster starts from the starting line, navigate all of the turns around the pylons to save the most ground, how to use different strides for speed at different levels of the race, how to swing his arms properly while racing and even how to breathe during the race. Because the Vineland rink was built on a smooth concrete surface, which was different from the wooden floors at other skating rinks where he would be competing, the coach also explained that training on the concrete surface would help him skate even faster on the wood floors.

It was a lot more complicated than he'd thought, but he was having fun.

Jay also found out that he would be competing in a group called the *Juvenile Boys Division*, which was for nine and ten-year-old skaters and there was another boy his age named Milton Butler, who liked to be called Jake, who he'd be competing against in the different *Meets*. Jake had been skating about a year longer than Jay and was considered the best speed skater in his age group, but the coach considered them both teammates and was training them to mainly win against the speed skaters from other skating rinks throughout California.

There were around thirty kids, both boys and girls, in the skating club who were always at practice, and they ranged in age from about eight to fifteen years old many of them would attend the Saturday evening *Moonlight Sessions* at the rink just for fun after a hard week of practice. Most of the parents would also spend Saturday evenings at the rink socializing, including Jay's parents who were always in a good mood when they were around other parents even if they had a fight that week, and were giving each other the *silent treatment* at home.

The kids at the rink and also seemed to like the social activities at the skating club and some of them had become "boyfriend and girlfriend" and would always skate together during the evening sessions. Jay still missed Linda but had also become friendly with a girl his age in the skating club who he thought was cute and reminded him of Darla from *The Little Rascals*.

Her name was Deanna, but had the nickname "Peanuts" and was the first girl since Linda he asked to skate with him during the one of the *Couples Only* dance segments. Jay showed her how he used to skate with Linda, with her hands on his shoulders and his hands around her waist, but his time because he was now a better skater, he would skate backward and let her follow him.

Although "Peanuts" didn't gaze into his eyes the way Linda did when they skated together during the slow song, Jay decided when the dance was over to lean in and give her a quick kiss to let her know he liked her, but instead of kissing him back, she pushed him away and skated over to her mother, crying, "Jay tried to kiss me!"

Deana's mother got furious and ran over to Jay's parent's saying what a "bad-boy" he was, and to "leave her daughter alone!"

Although his parents acted like they were concerned in front of Deanna's mother, Jay was surprised they didn't get mad at him, and they even kind of laughed about it during the drive home that night. But Jay also decided that from then on, he'd just make sure the girls liked to kiss before asking them to dance with him again.

❧

His parents did seem to like socializing with the new groups of friends they made during the past two months and Jay liked that during the entire Christmas holiday's they didn't even have one fight for over two weeks. Although he usually needed to be in bed by ten pm, on New Year's Eve of 1959, his parents also let him stay up until midnight and he sat with Tinker on his lap to watch *Guy Lombardo's New Year's Eve Special* on television.

When midnight came, and his mother started singing along with the music on the television screen, *"Should auld acquaintance be forgot, and never brought to mind?"*, Jay immediately knew he liked the melody of that song and wanted his mother to teach him the words so he wouldn't forget them. He decided *Auld Lang Syne* was going to be his new favorite song that week, and for some reason, he felt that learning and remembering the words would remind him about how happy he was that he had met Linda even if he didn't see her again. He figured that she was at least somewhat responsible for how he'd become a competitive roller-skater and all the new friends he met that year, but he did hope that she'd still move back to La Puente someday.

As he sang the closing words with his mother of *"We'll take a cup of kindness yet, for Auld Lang Sane*, even though Jay still didn't have a girlfriend, he was confident that 1960 was going to be his best year ever and couldn't wait for it to begin.

Chapter Three

The first competition *Meet* was in Bakersfield, California the following February and conducted over an entire weekend, so Jay's parents found a room at a motel that allowed pets so they could bring Tinker and make it felt like a real vacation for them all to enjoy together for the first time.

Vineland was strictly a speed skating club, but Jay discovered there were other competitions he knew nothing about and there were over two hundred other skaters from different rinks throughout Southern California who were competing in categories like *Figures*, *Freestyle*, and *Dance*. Jay was surprised there were the same types of events as those he had seen before as part of the *Ice Capades* and *Ice Follies* and that roller skating wasn't just all about speed racing.

For his competition, Jay just wore shorts over black leotards and a shirt that was designed to represent the Vineland rink, but he also saw other boys, many of them his age, dressed up in tuxedos and elaborate costumes with very bright coloring and sequins. He also noticed that the girls all wore makeup and lipstick and very short skating skirts and costumes, which made them look as pretty as the blond fairy *Tinker Bell* in the movie *Peter Pan*. Even though he saw some of those girls smile at him, he felt completely underdressed in his speed skating uniform and was too embarrassed to approach or talk to them.

When it was finally time for his race, all the speed skaters had about ten minutes to warm up while they set up the pylons on the floor, and the officials also sprinkled powdered rosin around the curves for better traction. Jay did notice the wood floor did seem slippery compared to the concrete floor at Vineland and he tried to adjust to it during his practice laps. He also felt his knees shaking as he lined up with the other skaters to start the race and took a deep breath, trying not to act nervous.

When the starter's pistol sounded, he got a slower jump than he wanted and was only in the middle of the pack as they skated around the first turn and could also see that Jake had started well and was leading. Jay skated wide after the first run along the course's backside, hoping to make a sharp inside move on the second turn around the pylons as his coach had taught him figuring he could pass some other skaters on the curve and move up to get closer to Jake.

As he had hoped, three or four skaters went wide around the second curve, and Jay cut inside sharply to try and pass them, but it turned out to be too sharp, because coming out of the curve he was unable to straighten his skates and ended up losing his balance and falling hard. He did jump up quickly, but all the other skaters had already passed him, and he dejectedly crossed the finish line behind all of them.

As he skated off the floor, he saw his teammate Deana giggling as he skated by her, and she pointed down to his knee and said, "Your stocking is torn, and your knee is bleeding."

Jay looked down, and there was a big hole in his leotard exposing his bleeding knee and hadn't even noticed it till she pointed it out, but now besides feeling embarrassed and dejected, his knee started to burn. He also started to feel tears starting to well up in his eyes, but then he saw his parents coming toward him he quickly tried to rub them away knowing what would happen if his father saw him crying. When they walked over, he told his father he thought he had some rosin in his eyes, and just acted like that was the only thing that was bothering him. Although his parents looked disappointed, they didn't seem that mad at him once his coach joined them and said he liked "the move he made around the curve" saying he'd work with Jay during the next practice to correct the mistake that he made.

He felt much better when he saw that everyone wasn't that mad at him for losing and tried to enjoy the rest of the day watching his teammates compete. But during the drive home from Bakersfield, his parents did seem to give each other the *silent treatment* being upset about something, but Jay was just anxious to start practice again wanting to do better, and figured that would at least get his parents in a better mood next time.

The following week at the next practice, all of the skaters who had won trophies brought them to the rink to be displayed in a glass case for that month and Jay's coach assured him that he'd eventually be able to win some trophies himself before too long. His coach also spent time showed Jay some different techniques on how to keep his balance coming out of curves, and he spent the next month practicing to make sure he didn't make the same mistake and fall down again.

The extra practice did help and Jay and he did better at the next two monthly *Meets* staying competitive throughout the races without falling, but he still didn't win a trophy for finishing in the top three. He did come close with a fourth-place finish that got him a certificate, which was at least something to show for his improvement.

There was an important *Meet* coming up in May at a rink in Escondido, California, where the top three finishers in all of the competitions would qualify for the State Finals to be held in June. Those finals had been what everyone had been working toward for the past five months, and when Jay managed to finish third in the qualifier, it made everything he had practiced for worthwhile.

Besides winning his first trophy, Jay and the other qualifiers were excited about seeing their names in the local paper when they went back to Vineland for the next practice mentioning that they were all advancing to the State Finals. Jake's name was at the beginning of the story along with the other skaters who finished first, and toward the end, it named the other skaters who qualified for the State Finals, including another skater from their club named Guy Mosley, who finished second, and then in print at the bottom of the story, *Jay Mershon, nine years old, third place.*

Their coach had made copies of the newspaper story for all those mentioned and told Jay when he gave him his copy, that hopefully would only be the first of many more stories to come.

Jay hoped so too, because it was fun seeing his name in the newspapers for something special besides just losing a tooth.

&

The State Finals was at a large skating rink in Hollywood on Sunset Boulevard, and as school was out by then, it was easy for the kids from all over California to attend. The *Juvenile Boys* division wasn't scheduled until Sunday morning, but Jay's parents still got a motel room on the Friday before to make another fun weekend and again were able to bring Tinker with them. His parents had also become friends with the parents of many of the other kids in the club so skating had turned into the main part of their social life as well, and they did seem to have fun at a big Friday night welcome party at the Hollywood skating rink.

After spending Saturday morning at the rink to watch some of the other competitions, Jay and his parents, along with Tinker in the car, took a drive up and down Sunset and Hollywood Boulevards sightseeing. Besides stopping at *Grauman's Chinese Theatre* to see all the famous footprints in cement, they also drove around Beverly Hills looking at all the expensive homes which his father said were probably worth over twenty-five thousand dollars and only could be afforded by movie stars or celebrities. Jay had his head out the window with Tinker most of the time looking to see if he could spot any movie stars, but was disappointed that he didn't see any famous faces. His mother did say that some of the women they saw on the street *"probably were movie stars,"* but because so many of them wore heavy makeup in the movies, they didn't look the same when they just walked around in public.

After a day of sightseeing and having dinner at a Denny's on Sunset Boulevard, his parents left Jay and Tinker at the motel around eight pm and went out with some of their friends and told him to go to sleep early so he'd be rested for the races the next day. Jay had almost forgotten he was in Hollywood for a serious competition, and not just for fun, and started thinking about the rules for the State Finals his coach had explained.

What was different about the State Finals was that in previous meets there was only one race, but for the State Championships, there were two races for each division that included a *220-yard* race that was twice around the pylons, and a *440yard* race

34

that was four times around. There were points for each of the top three finishers, and the skater with the most points after both heats was the winner.

Jay liked that because he remembered the two different races they had on Saturday afternoons at Vineland, and he felt he was better at longer races, and as he was starting to fall asleep, he envisioned himself passing all the skaters at the end of the race and finishing first and hoped if he kept picturing it happening in his head, then maybe it would.

The next morning, the referees gathered all the boys about a half-hour before their first race explaining the rules and told them to introduce themselves to each other and be good sports. Jay already knew Jake and Guy, so he just introduced himself to the others and was surprised when several of the other speed skater's he'd be racing against said they'd "already won medals the day before" in other events like dance, figures, and freestyle, and nonchalantly admitted that "speed skating wasn't as important" to them as their main skating talents. Jay liked hearing that and it made him realize the two skaters who finished ahead of him the previous month, Jake and Guy, would probably still be his main competition and the other skaters wouldn't be trying as hard to win.

When the first *220-yard* sprint began he appeared to be right, as Jake broke out fast and took the lead like he always did, with Guy in second and Jay in third. But on the first turn, some other skater cut sharply inside of Jay and Guy trying to move into second place but in doing so, collided with Guy, knocking him down. Jay managed to avoided them both and moved into second place and stayed solidly behind Jake and was gaining on him during the second lap, but the finish line came too soon, and Jake won by a few paces, and Jay was second.

Their coach was cheering for them both as they skated off the floor, but reminded them they had still had to race the *440* in about an hour and stay hydrated but not to drink too much water, before going over to console Guy, who was crying uncontrollably after having finished last.

When Jay went over to his parents, his father was pleased that Jay was really gaining on Jake in the race and cheerfully said he'd get him in the *440*, but then he looked over to where Guy was crying and disgustedly said, "Look at that bawl baby!"

Jay was also suddenly glad his father had taught him to not cry and knew he didn't ever want to look like a "bawl baby" and embarrass himself like Guy was doing just in case he had fell down himself, but he was mainly thinking about how he could do better in the next heat and actually finish ahead of Jake.

About an hour later, as all the speed skaters in Jay's division lined up for the 440-yard second heat, Jay could see that Guy was composed but had an angry look on his face. Guy's anger showed at the start of the race as he started out sprinting as fast as he could, and took a big lead into the first turn with Jake in second and Jay behind a few other skaters in fifth place. But by the end of the second lap, it was apparent that Guy was tiring, and Jake passed him on the third lap, and Jay passed him at the start of the fourth and final lap. Jake was still ahead, but Jay was moving up and was right on his heels as they rounded the final curve, but even though Jay went all out with his arms swinging and legs moving as fast as they could towards the finish line, Jake was still the fastest and again finished a couple paces ahead of Jay.

Jake and Jay's coach was again cheering wildly as they both skated off the floor and heard him yelling, "Another Gold and Silver medal for Vineland," but even though he was disappointed for not finishing first, Jay realized that second place wasn't that bad already knowing that Jake was a faster skater and it could have been a lot worse.

As he skated over to his parents, he saw his father was again looking at Guy in disgust who was also again crying uncontrollably, but also saw they were both very happy that he had done so well in his first State Finals and was actually going to win a medal.

Jay knew the drive back to La Puente would be a lot more fun this time.

࿋

At the big awards ceremony later that night, after Jay got his trophy with the *Silver Medal* attached, everyone was starting to talk about the National Finals that were going to be held in Levittown, New York, the following month. All the skaters who won gold medals had qualified, but Jay was surprised when he found out that Jake wouldn't be going to the National Finals, even though he had finished first.

"My old man won't fork out the money for me to go to New York," Jake said, using the popular term *old man* to describe his father as most of the other kids his age regularly did.

Jay and his parents discovered there were only a couple skaters from Vineland, mainly two of the older teenagers, who were going to make the trip to New York with "the money and cost of the trip" or "the parents not being able to get off work" being the main reasons they weren't competing in the National Finals. The Vineland coach also spent more time talking to Jay's parents that night, telling them that because Jake wasn't going to the National Finals, Jay qualified as the "runner-up" and they should consider going to New York because "Jay's getting better every month" and "may have a *real* shot" at winning a national medal.

During the drive home from Hollywood, Jay heard his parents talking about how the National Finals could also give them a good excuse to visit Chicago on the way to New York to see their own parents who neither of them had seen in years. Jay vaguely remembered meeting his grandparent's years earlier when he was younger, but

36

couldn't even remember what they looked like. Jay also knew there wouldn't be any more skating competitions in California till early the next year and liked the idea of completing once more time in what was actually the main purpose of entering the competitions in the first place. He also liked that his parents didn't want to leave Tinker alone for over three weeks and said they'd bring her along to keep him company in the back seat and when they stayed in motels.

Jay was more excited than he could remember and couldn't wait to tell all of his friends he was going to New York and started thinking about how lucky he had been to meet Linda a year earlier, and how fun his life had become since then.

But even though he still missed not having a girlfriend, he also knew he really didn't miss her as much as he had six months earlier, and decided that trying to becoming a champion speed skater, and seeing his name in the newspaper's occasionally, would be good enough for now.

Chapter Four

Jay's father had a fairly new car, but the air conditioner seemed to go out often and the car would overheat when they drove through the desert along Route 66. They had to drive with the windows rolled down most of the time, which seemed to make it even hotter, while Jay sat in the back seat with Tinker, who didn't seem to mind the heat, except when they had to stop every few hours to "let her do her business," and he could tell she didn't like the hot desert sand on her paws.

His parents also constantly turned the radio dials to find radio stations that came in clear, but it seemed they'd lose reception every half hour, so most of the time they would turn off the radio and just sing by themselves. One of Jay's favorite songs that summer was *Wild One* by Bobby Rydell, and he knew all the words, so he'd sing it many times during that trip. His father would only occasionally join in on some songs like *Row, Row, Row Your Boat, Side by Side,* or the song *Route 66* which was a new song Jay learned the first day. His mother also would try to teach Jay some of the songs she liked when she was younger, like, *I Wonder Who's Kissing Her Now, As Time Goes By,* or *It Had to Be You,* which were some of the songs he knew from watching old movies on *The Million Dollar Movie* each week. Jay always liked learning new songs even if he didn't have the record, so he'd have his mother sing many of the old songs repeatedly until he could remember all the words.

The trip across the country seemed fine when they were singing, but he also thought the drive was a little scary at times. Most of the drive was along two-lane highways, and his father would get mad whenever they got stuck behind a big truck or a slower driver that he couldn't pass and would yell things like "C'mon you asshole, either shit or get off the pot!" even though he knew the driver in front couldn't hear him. Every time he did try to pass and pulled back quickly because another car was coming from the opposite direction, his mother would get mad and yell at his father to slow down which always caused them to start yelling at each other and they ended up driving in silence for several hours.

There were other times when everything seemed fine, but his father would suddenly start pounding his fist on the steering wheel without saying anything, which was also a sign that they needed to drive in silence, so Jay just sat quietly in the back with Tinker, who would just rest her head on his lap seeming to sense when it was time to be quiet as well.

It was a relief to finally get to their first stop in Chicago, where they ended up staying with Jay's grandparents, who were from his father's side of the family, along some other aunts, uncles, and cousins Jay was meeting for the first time.

His grandfather would tell stories about what Chicago was like when he was younger himself, and tell stories about the "real" *Roaring Twenties* and explained to Jay that he drove a taxi cab in the 1920s and did meet several "real gangsters" back then. Although he said he never met Al Capone, he did say he was acquainted with one gangster named, "Machine Gun Jack" who he had driven around Chicago several times, and was rumored to have been involved in the *St. Valentine's Day Massacre*. His grandmother also said she once had a handkerchief with John Dillinger's blood from when she went to the *Biograph Theatre* after he was shot to death and she and some of her friends soaked up his blood for a souvenir.

Jay's time in Chicago did turn into a lot of fun and his parent's showed him where they used to live when he was a baby, went to an amusement park called *Riverview* which had a lot of fun rides, took him to the *Prudential Building,* Chicago's tallest structure where he got to play on the elevators, rode on the subways, and he also got to try his first taste of Chicago pizza.

After three fun days in Chicago, it was back on the road to New York, which they drove straight to without stopping, except for a couple of pit stops for Tinker.

Jay was having fun traveling and again feeling lucky that he had qualified for the national finals and thought about what he might have missed if he hadn't.

❧

The skating rink where the National finals were to be held was in Levittown on Long Island and wasn't set to begin for two days, so Jay and his parents had a chance to sightsee in New York City as well. Jay was mainly interested in seeing the Empire State Building because he knew it so well from the movie *King Kong* and wanted to see the building the giant ape fell off of. He also had fun riding the subway and stopping by Times Square where he had watched the New Year's Eve celebration on television the year before.

The night before the competitions were to begin, there was also a welcome dinner that all families and skaters were invited to attend, and it gave Jay and his parents a chance to look around for other kids and their parents that they knew or met in California. They saw a couple of people from Vineland with whom they really hadn't become that acquainted or friends with, but they did see others they had become friendlier with at early *Meets* in California and the State Finals.

One was a lady named Mickie Paxton, who brought her daughter Joyce to New York to compete in the Nationals. Jay recognized Joyce from other *Meets* in California and was surprised how much younger she looked out of her skating costume without all the makeup and lipstick she wore in the competitions. He remembered that she the same age as he was when they met a few months earlier, but found out that she was actually about eight months older and had recently turned ten years old. Joyce also wasn't a speed skater and strictly competed in figures, freestyle, dance, and her skating club was in Buena Park, about twenty miles from Vineland in La Puente.

Jay also discovered that Joyce was supposed to compete in two events that she had won gold medals at the state finals in Hollywood, *Singles Freestyle* and *Couples Dance*, but her skating partner in the dance wasn't able to come to New York, so she was only competing in her individual *Singles Freestyle* competition.

They all socialized together during the welcome dinner and although Joyce didn't go into details, she just mentioned that her father had died and she just lived with her mother. Jay was also starting to like Joyce and found out she was also an only child, so they had something else in common besides skating they could talk about. Although Jay and his parents left early, as his races were scheduled to start early the next morning, his parents made plans to get together with Mickie and Joyce in New York City once the nationals were over. Jay's parents had seemed to be getting along fine since they left Chicago, but things changed quickly as they all were driving to the Levittown Skating Rink the morning of the first qualifying heat of Jay's speed skating competition. His father said they were running late that morning and thought they could make it to the rink without buying gas, but they didn't.

"You dumb son of a bitch!" Jay's mother began yelling at his father, "I told you to stop and get gas!"

Jay's father didn't say anything, but his face got red and again began pounding the steering wheel with his fist. After exiting the car, his father suddenly slammed his fist into the driver's side window, which cracked the glass and also caused his hand to immediately start bleeding.

"Look what the fuck you made me do!" his father began yelling at his mother, "It's all your fault for taking so long to get ready this morning!"

Jay sat quietly in the back seat while they argued before his father got a gas can out of the trunk, threw a quarter at his mother, and told her to find a gas station while he tried to get his hand to stop bleeding. It took about fifteen minutes for Jay's mother to return to the car with the gas can full, but by the time they put gas in the tank and finally got to the skating rink, it was only about fifteen minutes before his race was to begin, and Jay barely had time to warm up. There were also thirty other boys competing in the *Juvenile Division*, so there were three 220-yard heats with ten speed skaters in each one, with only the top three finishers advancing to the 440-yard finals later that day.

The few minutes of Jay's first national speed races also wasn't as memorable as he hoped, and although he thought he raced well enough, and skated just as fast and skilled as he did in the State Finals, the other boys seemed much more experienced and faster, and he ended up finishing fifth which didn't qualify him for the next heat.

As he glided away from the rink, Jay observed his parents' ongoing anger towards each other, as well as their disappointment in his failure to qualify. Despite feeling disheartened and vulnerable, Jay made a conscious effort to mask his emotions and reassure his parents that he would strive to do better in the future. But his parents seemed to act friendlier when Mickie Paxton came over to say hello and tried to encourage Jay by saying that he'd get better with more experience.

Jay was glad that his parents never showed their anger with each other when other people were around and was also glad Mickie invited them all to stay and watch Joyce skate in her competition later that afternoon instead of immediately leaving the rink so soon after he had lost. He was disappointed that his opportunity for winning a medal was over but he also didn't want to have to go back to the motel and spend the rest of the day going through the silent treatment until his parents decided to make up again.

His father did seem to get in a better mood when they were around other the parents socializing for the next couple hours waiting for Joyce's competition to begin, and the argument his parents had earlier seemed to have been forgotten.

Jay also saw how Joyce looked older again with her makeup, lipstick, and fancy sequined skating skirt she was wearing in her competition, which he thought made her look at least twelve or thirteen years old. All of the figure and freestyle skaters had a special piece of music in which they skated their rehearsed routines, and Jay thought it was unusual that Joyce's music she began her routine with, started out sounding like a loud siren that was similar to the weekly air raid tests in California that warned of an atomic bomb attack. But he did like the music and asked his mother why there was an air raid siren at the beginning. She explained to him it wasn't a siren, but a musical instrument called a clarinet making the sound, and that the music was a famous classical piece called *Rhapsody in Blue*.

Jay saw that Joyce was a very good skater as he watched her glide around the rink during her routine as she performed her jumps and spins in synchronicity with the melody, and also noticed that everyone was applauding much louder at the end of Joyce's performance and the other freestyle skaters than they did for the speed skaters. It was obvious to him that audiences seemed to like those skaters more than they did the speed skaters and his father explained that audiences thought those events were "classier" than just watching the skaters racing around pylons.

After Joyce ended up winning a silver medal and they all attended the awards ceremony together, as they had planned, they met Mickie and Joyce for dinner a pizza restaurant after his parents said they wanted to compare the New York pizza with their favorite Chicago pizza.

They all sat in a lounge area of the pizzeria, and his parents and Mickie also ordered pitchers of beer, which they even let Jay and Joyce try a sip from their glass. Both Jay and Joyce giggled about it thinking they were doing something only grownups did.

Mickie was still mad and complaining about Joyce's roller-skating partner for not coming to the National Finals and said the boy's parents were "too cheap" to spend a couple hundred dollars to come to New York for a few days.

"Joyce could have probably won another medal," Mickie complained, "All those months of practice and meets and he acted like it was no big deal."

Besides talking about skating, Mickie and Jay's parents also started talking about the upcoming presidential election coming in November which was also in the news that week because of the Democrat Convention had just ended.

Jay had already learned that his parents were Republicans and previously had supported the Eisenhower/Nixon ticket against the Democrat, Adlai Stevenson in the last election, and were now supporting Vice President Nixon against John Kennedy that year. His parents had explained to Jay that they had grown up in very bad times with the Democrat president Franklin Roosevelt, and things had gotten much better in the 1950s with President Eisenhauer as President.

"We don't need a damn Catholic in the White House anyway," Jay listened to Mickie complaining about the Democrat candidate John Kennedy, "We'll end up having the Pope running the country."

As Jay listened to parents agree with Mickie and talk about national and world issues about Khrushchev and the possibility of Kennedy being too young to prevent starting an atomic war, his mother could see that Jay and Joyce weren't enjoying the conversation about politics, so she gave Jay a quarter to find some songs in the jukebox to give them something else to listen to. She also told him to play her favorite new Elvis' song, *It's Now or Never*, and then said he could pick out his other two favorite songs. Mickie also gave Joyce a quarter as well, and they went to the jukebox, which was in front of a small dance floor.

Jay found the song his mother wanted to hear and then picked out two other songs he currently liked *Wild One and Please Mr. Custer*, while Joyce chose *Itsy Bitsy Teenie Weenie Yellow Polka Dot Bikini* and another popular song called *A Summer Place*, before asking Jay if he wanted to dance. Although he had only somewhat "danced" with girls before on roller skates, he figured he'd give it a try.

Joyce then showed him how to move around to the songs, spin her around under his arm during the fast songs, and take different steps while holding her closer during the slow songs. When they were slow dancing to the song *A Summer Place*, Jay was having fun and was really starting to like Joyce even more and even thought about giving her a kiss, but he remembered how it turned out the last time he kissed someone without asking and decided not to push his luck.

While they were dancing through all the songs on the jukebox together, Jay also noticed his parents and Mickie seemed to be in a deep discussion the entire time and when they finished dancing and re-joined their parents, Jay found out what else they had been talking about.

"I don't want Joyce going back with her same skating partner when we get back to California," Mickie said with irritation before smiling, "You both seem to get along well, and looked cute dancing together so how would you like to try and be Joyce's new skating partner, Jay?"

Mickey added that they had over six months before the next series of *Meets* began again in California and they'd have plenty of time to learn the same routines as Joyce did with her previous partner. She also mentioned that because Jay was still nine years old, they could re-enter the *Juvenile Division* which Joyce had won medals in that year because she had a new partner.

"Joyce has been skating for three years now and is already known as the best skater in her division," Mickie added, "So you'll have a big advantage having Joyce as your partner because she's already known as a champion."

Jay saw his parents seemed to like the idea of him trying to learn something new as well and said it might also keep him from getting bored with roller skating as he did with the Cub Scouts. Jay was also thinking that his parents probably wanted him to just try something "classier" than racing around the pylons, but he liked when he saw Joyce smile at him and suddenly liked the idea of spending more time with her.

"I think that might be fun," Jay smiled as well.

૭

During the drive back to California, Jay's parents explained what it meant if he wanted to become Joyce's skating partner, including practicing at Joyce's rink in Buena Park, which was about a half-hour drive from La Puente in a different area called Orange County, and required a trip over a two-lane mountain road called Highway 39. Because Jay would be starting fifth grade at Nelson Elementary School in less than two months and both his parents still had their jobs in La Puente, they explained it wouldn't be possible to move to Buena Park that year and they need to commute several times a week if he changed skating clubs.

Mickie had also suggested his parents that he should also take figure and freestyle classes saying the *Couple Mixed Pairs* competition was another event Jay and Joyce could compete in together the following year. They said that would require Jay to take private skating lessons to learn the techniques of the different events and said private lessons from a good professional was expensive. They added that Mickie had told them it cost up to "five dollars an hour" for private lessons so he needed to be certain he would take it seriously if he really wanted to skate in different competitions.

Jay assured them that he'd try "real hard" and said he couldn't wait to start.

Besides those new plans, the drive back from New York turned into another new adventure when his parents decided to make a quick stop before going to California, and spent time in a city that Jay had heard his parents talk about, but said they had never seen, Las Vegas, Nevada.

His parents drove down the Las Vegas Strip, and Jay saw all the famous names on the marquee's and all the flashing and neon lights, and they also went to downtown Fremont Street which they said was easier to stop and go into a casino. They didn't want to leave Tinker in the car for long, so his father parked in front of a casino called the *Nevada Club* that had an open front area they could just walk inside and keep an eye on Tinker in the car at the same time.

Jay watched from the street just a few feet away, and saw his parents buy a few two-dollar rolls of nickels, and watched as they put the coins in the slot machines and pulled the handles which spun the reels. It only took his mother about five minutes before she excitedly said she "just hit a five-dollar jackpot" and saw a bunch of nickels fall into the tray. Jay thought the slot machines were the "neatest" thing he'd ever seen, and seeing he was just a few feet away from the slot machines they were playing, his father discreetly let him put some nickels in the machine and pull the handle himself. It only took Jay three pulls before got two cherries in a row which caused five nickels to spill out to the bottom tray. His father scooped out the nickels and gave them to Jay telling him it was a good time to stop, and sarcastically added he could keep them, and "at least go home a winner for something."

Although they spent less than two hours in Las Vegas, Jay was starting to realize what he liked best about roller skating. Aside from the competitions, which only lasted a few minutes each month, it was everything else associated outside the competition including the practicing, preparation, the traveling, and all the socializing that came with it, that was the most fun. It was almost midnight before they made it back to La Puente from Las Vegas, and Jay and Tinker were both exhausted by the time they got home and were both sound asleep on Jay's bed within ten minutes after they arrived. But when he woke up the next day, Jay was also a little sad that his adventure was over.

He wasn't that excited about just being home and was ready to start all over and do it all again.

Chapter Five

While they were still in New York, Mickie had told his parents that it would be a few more weeks before she and Joyce would be back in California because they were going to visit relatives in different states. During that time, Jay and his parents traveled to the Buena Park rink to meet with coaches and rink officials to talk about getting Jay getting a membership in that skating club and find out when he could start taking lessons.

The Buena Park skating rink was called *The Rollertorium* and was nationally known for producing many national champions, as well as being known to have some of the country's best coaches and professional instructors. Although *The Rollertorium* was mainly known for their figure, freestyle, and dance skaters, they also had a small speed skating group, which meant Jay could continue his racing as well.

It was also a couple of weeks before Jay was able to go back to Vineland and tell his friends about his adventures traveling across the county, as well as telling them that he was going to be switching skating clubs.

Jake Butler didn't seem too impressed with any of Jay's stories about his trip to New York and just said that he was "sure he would have won the Nationals" if he would have gone, and just said it "wasn't worth spending all that money" to even bother trying. Jay remembered someone telling him once that trying hard was sometimes more important than winning, and tried counter Jake's remark saying he would "never know because he didn't even try" and he at least went to New York to represent *Vineland* and California.

"I'm still the state champ and you only went because I didn't want to," Jake just laughed, "I always win when we race against each other and no matter how hard you try, you'll still only be second best."

Jay also noticed that his other teammates at Vineland weren't as friendly after learning he was changing skating clubs, and even though he told his friends that he'd still be living and going to school in La Puente and was sure they'd all still see each other often, they pretty much stopped talking to him after learning he wasn't going to be on their team any longer.

His mother told him they were just jealous because they knew Buena Park was a "more famous skating rink" and not to let it bother him, but Jay was still a little disappointing after seeming to have lost their friendship just because he was going to change skating clubs.

It was also during one of the visits at *The Rollertorium* when Jay and his parents were shocked to learn that Mickie and Joyce had been involved in a head-on car crash in Arizona on their way back from New York and were recovering in a hospital in Phoenix. Hearing that news also put any plans about changing skating clubs on hold until they found out more news about the accident.

After several weeks Mickie and Joyce were able to return to California and Jay first heard the horrible news that Mickie had her leg severed in the crash, but although Joyce was also injured, she didn't suffer anything as severe as her mother, but had several serious cuts and bruises when she'd hit the windshield.

Jay remembered he had met an uncle who had one leg, who would sometimes walk around with a wooden leg that he would attach to his torso and remembered how his uncle would pull that leg off when he sat down and shake it at Jay which always scared him. He even remembered having nightmares about the wooden leg chasing him, and wondered if Mickie would get a leg like that too. But he was also worried that his plans to be Joyce's new skating partner was in jeopardy and he might not be joining the Buena Park skating club and have to go back to *Vineland*.

It wasn't until around Labor Day before Mickie and Joyce felt they could be seen in public again, and *The Rollertorium* skating club planned a type of "welcome back" party for them which Jay and his parents attended. The club manager at the rink canceled the nightly skating session for that night and set up tables with food and refreshments, along with having someone also set up a large stereo and speakers in the center of the rink to play popular music to give it a party atmosphere.

When Mickie and Joyce arrived, Joyce was pushing her mother in a wheelchair, and everyone tried not to notice her missing leg and cheerfully greeted them. Mickie was trying to act cheerful like it was nothing unusual and was laughing and saying how comfortable the wheelchair was and how it was "the only way to fly," similar to the TV commercial for *Western Airlines*, and also joked about how she was glad she had "less weight to carry around."

When Jay first approached Joyce, she seemed a little shy and timid towards him, and saw her face still had some red welts and lines from where some stitches had been removed, but was surprised when the first thing she asked him was, "do you still want to be my skating partner?"

He could see that Mickie had tried to cover her red welts up with makeup and he just said "Of course I do!" and assured Joyce that he was already planning to take skating lessons on how to learn dance and freestyle routines and would be ready to start practicing with her as soon as she was ready herself. Jay could also tell Joyce was still uncomfortable with the welts on her face and quickly added that she "still looked pretty" which she seemed to like, and they both cheerfully joined everyone else in the center of the dance floor for the party.

The skating surface of the rink was being used as a dance floor that night, and the disc jockey who was playing the records called the entire crowd out to the center of the rink and shouted out, "Okay, everybody, take off your shoes and get ready cause here we go!"

The disc jockey then turned up the volume on the speakers and played the record that was the hottest song in the country, *The Twist* by Chubby Checker and everyone then took off their shoes and started trying to "Do the Twist" in their stockings.

Jay was trying to give it his best try with Joyce and he even saw his parents dancing along with all the other parents. Someone else rolled Mickie out in her wheelchair and was balancing her on the back two wheels, moving her around to make her feel like she was dancing and Jay could see she was laughing and having fun as well. There was nothing sad or depressing about the party that entire evening and everyone wanted Mickie and Joyce to know that everything was going to be alright.

When Jay and Joyce said their goodbyes that night, she added that her doctor told her that the red lines on her face would go away in a couple of months, and that she should look completely normal by the time the competitions began the following February. Jay was also pleasantly surprised when Joyce took his hand, leaned over, and gave him a quick kiss.

"I really still want you as my partner too," Joyce smiled as she gave him a second longer kiss.

Jay immediately like that she was the one who instigated the kiss first and it made him feel that everything was going to be alright as well.

❧

Since the welcome back party for Micky and Joyce, and after his parents deciding that Jay would still change skating clubs, they were driving over the hill from La Puente to Buena Park every few days and Jay was getting to know every curve and turn on the route over Highway 39 called Turnbull Canyon Road.

Because his father mentioned it would cost him a lot more money in gas, taking him back and forth, they always looked for gas stations that had the cheapest prices. Jay saw that gas was around twenty-five cents a gallon, but sometimes they had "Gas Wars" where stations would lower their prices to compete with a gas station across the street. If one station lowered its price to twenty-three cents, a station across the street would lower their price to twenty-one cents, which was where Jay's parents would end up getting gas.

His parents also found out they needed to buy him different roller skates with "precision wheels" if he wanted to learn how to compete in other events, because the wheels on his current skates were strictly for speed racing. But they didn't seem to mind because his parents liked the atmosphere at the Buena Park rink and commented it was much nicer and cleaner than Vineland was. They had also become friendly with quite a few of the parents they had met of the party for Mickie and Joyce and felt they "had more style" than the crowd at Vineland, or as his parents also used to say often, "it was classier."

During the time that Joyce was recovering from the accident, Jay had started taking some group lessons on the basics of figure skating at the Buena Park Rink, and after less than a month, the club manager decided he was ready to start taking private lessons from one of the resident pro instructors. His coach was a former National Champion skater named Ronnie Fitzgerald from New York who was always telling Jay to "Arch his back," and Jay and the other kids would always make fun of the way he said it with his strong New York accent. Ronnie was teaching Jay all sorts of jumps called the Mapes, the Toe Flip, the Axel, the Loop, the Salchow, the Lutz, and spins called the Camel and the Jackson and he had plenty of bruises and cuts from all the falls he took learning those jumps and spins. He would also spend hours just practicing his footwork and posture while gliding around the skating rink, and then the next session, spend hours working on his spins, jumps, and landings.

Jay immediately liked being a club member at *The Rollertorium,* and besides all the new friends he was meeting, he noticed that the girl skaters were much prettier and dressed up regularly in cute skating skirts, and seemed like movie stars compared to the girl speed skaters at Vineland.

One of the girls Jay had seen at other skating meets was named Carol Knudsen who he guessed was at least thirteen years old and she always wore a tight one-piece leotard which made him start to notice her figure a lot more than the girls his own age. The roller skates had always made all the girl's legs look much longer, and the outfits they wore always seemed to emphasize that, but Carol's one-piece body suit also emphasized something the younger girls didn't have.

Carol had *boobies,* as Jay and all the other boys would call them.

When Jay and other boys would watch Carol practice skating, he learned another word called "sexy" they used when describing Carol and started using it himself. He thought she looked especially "sexy" when she skated to some music in her routine that had a little musical coda at the end where she would slowly sway her hips back and forth and swing her arms suggestively as she spun.

The way she moved her body to the music, especially the musical coda at the end, made Jay realize he had a new favorite song and asked Carol what the song's name was, but she said she wasn't sure and was just some music her coach had picked out for her.

The coach later explained to Jay that it was some instrumental music from an opera called *Porgy* and *Bess,* and Carol's routine was a track called *I'm On My Way.*

He was surprised when his mother told him later that the composer of *Porgy and Bess* was the same one who had written *Rhapsody in Blue* that Joyce skated to which she had already bought Jay the record. She also added that a song she taught him when they drove across the country called *Summertime,* was also from the movie version of *Porgy and Bess* and was written by a composer named George Gershwin.

"Can you get me the record from that movie too?" Jay asked his mother, "It's my new favorite song this week and I'd like to hear the whole thing."

He actually just wanted to remember the way Carol made those sexy moves during the coda of that one song, and even if he wasn't seeing her move to it in person, he could imagine her "sexy" skating style every time he heard the music.

๛

Jay's parents also liked spending more time at the skating rink socializing with the other parents and would drive him after school at least twice a week for private lessons on weekdays and two days on the weekends. He did like that they were usually able to bring Tinker along like they had at Vineland, and also liked that they didn't seem to argue as much as before and liked that he was becoming a better skater. When the coaches decided Jay was ready to start practicing with Joyce as his partner, it was also decided that besides Jay having individual coaching for himself, they would have Ronnie Fitzgerald give Jay and Joyce private lessons on their dances together, as well as their "Couple Mixed Pairs" freestyle routine.

Jay learned that because he was competing in the *Juvenile Mixed Pairs* division with Joyce, they only needed to do single jumps and mainly concentrated on the footwork and spins they would need to be scored by the judges. The dance routines they needed to learn together for the *Juvenile Couples Dance* competition without the jumps and lifts, seemed to be a lot easier with Joyce, because she already knew the dances well from competing in those events with her former skating partner. Aside from the private lessons with Ronnie, Joyce led Jay and showed him the dance moves when they skated together during the regular skating sessions.

Music was also very important for their routines and Ronnie chose music that would help synchronize and have dramatic accents in certain parts, for the jumps and spins that were required in the routine. For their couples dance event, Jay and Joyce needed to skate the "waltz" and danced to a record called the *Blue Danube Waltz* by Johann Strauss, and also danced the "tango" to a record called the *Blue Tango* by Leroy Anderson. Besides those two titles, Joyce was still skating her *Singles Freestyle* routine to an edited version of *Rhapsody in Blue* and Jay thought it was funny how so many songs had the word "Blue" in the title.

Along with the dance music he was skating to with Joyce, Ronnie had chosen music called "Conquest" which was from the soundtrack of a movie called *Captain from Castile* for Jay to skate his *Singles Freestyle* routine, and for the *Couple's Mixed Pairs* Jay and Joyce would perform to, Ronnie chose a song called *Granada* which was one

49

of Joyce's favorite pieces of music because it was by Percy Faith and his Orchestra, who also recorded her favorite song *A Summer Place*.

Besides practicing at the rink, Ronnie suggested Jay should watch old musicals on *the Million Dollar Movie's* shown on TV for the entire week, especially movies that featured dance routines by Fred Astaire and Ginger Rogers. He told Jay to pay attention to Fred Astaire's posture and the smooth manner in which he held Ginger Rogers during their dances together and said it would not only help with his individual performance but his routines with Joyce as well. Even when they weren't at the skating rink, both Joyce and Jay would take their music with them to listen to on Jay's portable record player to memorize each part so they'd remember and visualize all of their skating moves.

Even though Joyce's mother Mickie was usually confined to a wheelchair, she did occasionally use crutches, and because she was no longer able to work a regular job, Mickie said because she was a seamstress and had always made Joyce's skating costume's she could make costumes for Jay to wear in their competitions as well. Although Jay did think that some of the costumes were a little bright and funny looking, Micky assured him that bright costumes were a big part of making him stand out, and the judges liked "showy" costumes.

"Putting on a good show is the most important thing to remember and always let everyone see you're having fun out there," Mickie as well as the coaches always emphasized, "Even if you miss a step or a jump, never show that it bothers you and always keep smiling."

Jay saw his parents were also enjoying spending more time in Buena Park and would also attend parties with other parents of skaters at Mickie's house, including an aunt of Joyce's named Joannie who would always bring what she called "adult beverages" to the parties, while Jay and Joyce would always need to go into Joyce's bedroom with Tinker and do their homework when their parents would socialize. He usually tried to do some of his homework during the drives back and forth between La Puente and Buena Park, but although Jay knew he still needed to get passing grades at school and managed to get "B's and "C's" in almost every class, he sometimes felt there weren't enough hours in the day to have fun and sometimes wished he didn't even need to go to school.

He did get a "D" in *Math* his first semester at *Nelson Elementary School*, which was his first class of the day and never felt like he was fully alert that early, but he also got an "A" in *Current Events* which made up for that one bad grade and kept his parents from getting mad at him. Jay's parents had the *Los Angeles Herald Examiner* newspaper delivered to their house each day and he always read it knowing that *Current Events* was his best subject and always made sure he followed the news.

The Presidential Election that year was the first one Jay had at least halfway followed, and although his parents, and most of those at *The Rollertorium*, were disappointed that Nixon had lost to Kennedy, everyone pretty much stopped talking about politics after the election and switched their attention to more fun subjects like movies and television, but mainly, about skating.

Jay did see some of his former teammates from *Vineland* at school, including Jake Butler, but because he was busy traveling to Buena Park on a regular basis after his classes, any socializing with them as he had in the past had disappeared, and they rarely would even say "hello" to each other any longer. But he was completely satisfied spending his time with his new friends, and mainly with Joyce, because all their time together wasn't just all about skating practice.

She had also become his *girlfriend*.

Joyce had already explained to Jay that because they were skating partners, it meant that they we were "going steady" and weren't allowed to dance with any other skaters during the regular sessions at *The Rollertorium*, which he didn't mind at all because he liked Joyce, and liked the idea of having a regular girlfriend again. He also liked how Joyce had taught him how to kiss longer with their lips together, without making the "smacking sound" like Linda had, explaining that the smacking was just "kid stuff" and not the way boyfriends and girlfriends were supposed to kiss.

She also said because they were "going steady" they were was supposed to give each other a present at Christmas, but even though Jay's father had increased his allowance to four dollars a week after he finished second in the state finals earlier that year, between the money he spent on comic books, candy, and refreshments at the skating rink snack bar every week, he didn't have enough money left over to spend on a present for Joyce. Instead, he just gave her one of his 45 records that his parents had bought called *Mule Skinner Blues,* which was a song he didn't like very much, and in return, Joyce gave Jay her 45 record of the song *A Summer Place*, which impressed him because he knew it was one of her favorite records. She also said that *A Summer Place* was an "important song" because it was the "first song they danced to together in New York" and that whenever they played the record, or heard it on the radio, they should always remember to call it "our song."

By the time there was the New Year's Eve party at *The Rollertorium* that year, because all the kids were still out of school for the holiday vacation, almost all the other skaters were allowed to stay at the party until midnight and celebrate with the adults. Besides being able to celebrate New Year's Eve with a large group of his friends for the first time, Jay mainly liked that he had Joyce to kiss at midnight while everyone in the rink was singing along to one of his favorite songs, *Auld Lang Syne* He also heard someone mention that 1961 was actually the official beginning of the 1960s because "new decades always started with a *one* and not a *zero*" which did seem confusing to him, but he did like that even though he felt 1960 had "officially" been his best year ever, he also felt that 1961 was also going to be even better.

Jay felt his life was perfect.

Chapter Six

By the end of January in 1961, all of the practicing and lessons had made Jay comfortable about how his practices were going and the coaches told his parents that he had learned very quickly and would have no problem being ready to compete in his individual freestyle event, as well as his two events with Joyce the following month. He still wanted to compete in speed skating, but with everything else he had to learn the past four months, he'd been to only about five practices for speed skating.

The Buena Park Skating club was still mainly known for its *Dance* and *Freestyle* skaters and had less than ten other kids who signed up for the speed skating events and had only one class a week. But Jay felt he already knew enough to be competitive once the *Meets* began, and had focused most of his attention on learning the other events.

At the first couple warn up *Meets* that year, the results turned out as good, if not better than the coaches, his parents, and even Jay and Joyce had hoped for, finishing first or second in both their *Couples Dance* and *Mixed Pairs* freestyle events together, along with Jay picking up a second and third place in his individual *Singles Freestyle* event. His only disappointment was that he never finished better than fourth in his *Speed Skating* in the *Sub-Novice Boys* division, which both he and Jake were required to move up to that year.

As usual the *Vineland* speed skaters won most of the speed events, and also as usual, even though they were in an advanced division with more competition, Jake still finished first in all the warm up meets well ahead of Jay.

Jake and Jay had normally had a friendly rivalry in the past, but now Jake and his old friends at Vineland still seemed mad at him because he had joined a different skating club, and even though he had won trophies in other events, they said the other events were for "sissies" and they seemed almost happy to see him lose in speed skating.

Just as there was at *Vineland*, there was always a party at *The Rollertorium* the Tuesday after the weekend *Meets* and all the club members were always there with their trophies they had won. The rink had some glass display cases where they'd exhibit all the trophies the club members won that month, and another that showed all of the local newspaper clippings, mentioning the names of the skaters who won trophies at the *Meets*. All the club members always flocked to that display case to see their names in the newspapers and made a big thing out of it, but although Jay thought it was "neat" seeing his name listed for winning trophies in *Singles Freestyle*,

Couples Dance and *Mixed Pairs,* he wasn't happy about not seeing his name listed for *Speed Skating*, which did take away some of his excitement about having won in the other events.

He also didn't like being called a "sissy" by his old friends, but his mother again just said they were jealous and not to let it bother him.

The qualifiers for the State Championships were coming up the next month and Jay decided he'd put some extra effort into his speed skating because he knew he hadn't been practicing as hard as he had when he was at Vineland. His coach at Buena Park had already mentioned that a lot of the older boys in the *Novice* and *Intermediate* speed skating divisions had started using new advanced wooden wheels to get better speed on the floor surfaces. He explained that Jay's roller skates he'd had since he'd been at Vineland had been good "starter skates" when he was in the *Juvenile Division*, but because he was now skating in the *Sub-Novice Boys* division, he suggested that Jay might want to give those a try himself.

After his parents agreed to buy the new wheels, Jay also decided to spend more time practicing after his coach said the wooden wheels might take some time getting used to, but also felt with confidence that he might have a "secret weapon" to use the next time he raced. He also didn't want to just qualify in the "sissy events" and wanted more than anything to make sure he qualified for the State Finals against Jake for a rematch from the year before. By the time of the qualifier *Meet* for the State Championship, Jay and Joyce had no problem qualifying as they won both of their events together and Jay finished second in his *Singles Freestyle,* but his best moment of that meet was when he almost caught Jake in the speed competition and finished a close second behind him which did seem to surprise Jake.

"I knew I was going to win so I wasn't even trying that hard," smiled Jake, "I was just saving my best for the finals next month, you'll see."

Jay felt the wooden wheels had made him skate faster himself and was anxious to practice even harder the next few weeks. He also talked his parents into letting take a couple Friday's off at school so he could practice a full day by himself on his speed skating and singles freestyle, and then just practice with Joyce on the weekends.

He was confident he'd pass all of his classes at school, and even if they weren't all A's or B's, he knew winning gold medals at the State Championship and qualifying for another National Finals, was more important than one report card that year.

Mickey volunteered to let Jay stay at her house on weekends and also said he could bring Tinker along which Jay liked even more. He also didn't mind being away from his parents on those weekends, and actually felt more relaxed not being around them knowing they still went through the "silent treatment" a least a couple times a month when they were at home alone which was never fun.

Mickie had also made special costumes to wear for the State Finals, and although Jay thought the bright orange sequenced matching costumes he and Joyce were wearing, along with a bright purple jumpsuit she designed were a "little loud," Ronnie Fitzgerald convinced him as Mickie Paxton had, that showmanship was important, and the costumes would help him "stand out."

"Just make sure you smile at the judges often and look like you're having fun out there," Ronnie again emphasized constantly that month, which Jay already knew would be no problem, but he was also focused on winning that year.

❧

At the State finals in Northridge which were held over Memorial Day weekend, Jay's events with Joyce and his Singles Freestyle routine came after the speed skating competitions, which Jay had been especially focused on for the past month, and was confident he was ready for his rematch with Jake. During the final lap in the first heat of the 220-yard sprint, he and Jake were both in the middle of the track almost side by side, fighting it out towards the finish, and Jay managed to barely pull ahead of him as they crossed the line. Unfortunately, while they were both fighting in out in the middle of the course, another skater from Bakersfield slid through on the inside and passed them both with Jay finishing second and Jake in third. After they crossed the finish line, Jay and Jake just looked at each other with a surprised look, and neither of them could believe there was someone faster than them both.

In the second heat, the 440-yard, the kid from Bakersfield easily took first place again, with Jay second even further this time ahead of Jake in third, but even though he didn't finish first, Jay was somewhat satisfied that he had beaten Jake as he had picturing doing for the past month. He also found out after the race that the kid from Bakersfield was planning to compete in the National Finals which meant Jay wouldn't be able to compete as the silver medalist as he had the year before when Jake didn't go to New York. With having accomplished his first goal of finishing ahead of Jake, it did make Jay more motivated for his other events the second day of the State Finals, and was confident that just having to follow the music and display his "showmanship" for his singles competition and routines with Joyce, would be his only focus if he wanted to win gold medals and be able to travel to the National Finals.

Jay's confidence was even higher, although he knew he was a little lucky, that the kid who finished ahead of him at the state qualifier, slipped coming out of one of his jumps and fell, which gave Jay the gold medal in his individual *Singles Freestyle* event. After Jay and Joyce also won gold medals in both their *Couples Dance* and *Couples Freestyle* events, Ronnie Fitzgerald, Mickie, and especially Jay's parents were ecstatic with the results and were already talking about the national finals.

Although he was only slightly disappointed that he wouldn't be able to compete at the nationals in speed skating, and still felt a little lucky he had won a gold medal in his *Singles Freestyle*, Jay still felt great knowing that in only his second State Finals he

55

had qualified in multiple events and could now be called an actual "California State Champion" and not just a "runner up" at the National Finals.

For the awards dinner and trophy presentation, Jay's parents bought him a new suit and tie to wear so he'd look like a state champion when he accepted his trophies and medals. Jay figured his lucky weekend was continuing, because before the awards were handed out that evening, the officials had a raffle for some prizes, and Jay's name was called as the winner for something he'd wanted for a long time. His prize was a new transistor radio and almost liked winning that prize more than the trophies and medals he would be presented that night, knowing he could now listen to the popular radio stations and his favorite songs wherever he went.

He did feel that he was very lucky that Memorial Day weekend.

During the awards ceremony, as Jay kept bringing the trophies over to his parents, his mother happily laughed, "I don't know where we're going to keep all these trophies because you're winning so many!" Jay also saw his father liked being congratulated by everyone else from *The Rollertorium* and hadn't seen him smiling and laughing that much in a long time.

Jay was standing with Joyce, trying to play with his new radio trying to get reception when the night's final award was being announced which was an annual award for the skater of the year, and just about everyone knew who was going to win it. Another champion skater from Buena Park named Dennis Pollard who was four years older than Jay, had won the same award the past two years and had gone undefeated in all of his events at the State Finals that year. Dennis had also won gold medals at the previous two National Finals and was already famous for being one of the top skaters in the country and both Jay and Joyce had already figured that Dennis was a cinch to win the award again as the emcee was about to announce the award.

"And now," announced the emcee at the awards podium," The winner of the most versatile skater of the year for 1961 is ...JAY MERSHON!"

Jay thought he heard his name and looked up from playing with his transistor radio and saw Joyce with her mouth open excitedly applauding. He saw his parents with shocked but happy expressions also applauding, and then noticed everyone else was looking at him smiling and applauding as well. Joyce finally pushed Jay towards the stage and he walked towards a lady who seemed to be waiting for him as she handed him a huge trophy that he could hardly hold in both hands. Although he was completely surprised and didn't actually know what the word "versatile" actually meant, he knew that it was special.

As he walked back to give his parents another trophy to take home, he also saw that some of his former teammates from Vineland, including Jake, were politely applauding him as well.

He still didn't like being enemies with his old friends, so before he left that night, instead of bragging about all the trophies he'd won, he walked over to the Vineland group and said, "Hey guys, look at this neat transistor radio I won!"

Jay didn't want people to think he was "too cocky" even though inside he knew he was.

❧

The week following the State Finals was the craziest week Jay had ever experienced and from the moment he and his parents arrived home, it seemed the phone was ringing nonstop. Not only were all of their friends calling to offer congratulations, but sportswriters from the *Los Angeles Herald Examiner* and other local newspapers wanted to come to their house to get pictures of Jay and his trophies to put on the newspaper. When the reporters and photographers came to the house, Jay didn't know what to say to them when they asked him how he felt winning such an award as *The Most Versatile Skater of the Year,* and he was only able to answer with a meek, "Fine" and let his mother do most of the speaking for the interviews.

He'd had his name in the newspapers before, which the kids at his school always made a big deal about, but now that his picture was added along with stories about him, it seemed even the other skaters at *The Rollertorium* started acting like he was a movie star.

Jay's trophies, picture, and news clippings were the main focus in the display case at the skating rink and there were many who had copies of the newspaper stories and asked Jay to sign his name by them, while others had some programs from the previous skating meets and asked him to sign his name in those too. Even Dennis Pollard and many of the older skaters who acted like he was just a kid before, now they seemed happy to be friends with him and Dennis even lightly teased Jay about winning the award, which kept him from winning it three years in a row.

"Well, kid, you dethroned the *King,*" Dennis said half teasing. "You know, I took three gold medals too, but that silver you picked up in speed is what gave you the points to win this year."

"Well, you never enter any of the speed events, so I guess that means I'm more *vers-tille*, than you, "Jay tried to halfway joked before adding, "But I guess I am lucky you didn't because you probably would have won it again."

"It's pronounced *verse-it -tile* not *vers-tille*," Dennis joked back, "You can't call yourself a versatile skater until you learn how to pronounce it right, but at least this year you're the best so congratulations."

Jay knew Dennis had been skating years longer that he had, and was more experienced and still a better skater than he was, but he wasn't jealous of Dennis because of that. He was mainly jealous of Dennis because his skating partner in *Couple Dance* and *Couples Mixed Pairs* competitions was Carol Knudsen.

Even though Jay was the center of attention that week and had won the trophy for *The Most Versatile Skater of the Year*, he was still envious that Dennis had what Jay started feeling was even a better trophy.

He had Carol Knudsen as his girlfriend.

❧

The National Finals were being held in Livonia, Michigan that year, and after the car accident the year before, Mickie Paxton decided she didn't want to drive cross country again, and instead arranged for Joyce to fly back to Detroit with her Aunt Joannie. Jay was a little envious because he had never been on an airplane himself and thought it would be more fun than driving cross county with his parents. But when he asked his parents why they couldn't just fly like Joyce was doing, they just said, "It would probably cost well over a hundred dollars for all of them to fly on an airplane, and that they weren't "millionaires" and could only afford to drive.

The drive back Chicago, where they again spent a couple of days with his grandparents before continuing to Michigan, where his mother's parents lived, and they also stopped to visit, was similar to the year before with some singing and the usual arguments between his parents.

His mother would still yell at his father whenever he tried to pass a big truck screaming, "Remember what happened to Mickie and Joyce last year, God Dammit!" which would always get his father yelling "Shut the fuck up!" and the silence would begin for the next several hours. Jay was glad they brought Tinker with them again and could at least pet and talk to her during the drive which helped him not be bothered by his parent's arguments.

There were also some more arguments between his parent's each time they left both of his grandparent's homes and it still seemed that his mother and father still didn't like each other's parents. Jay felt much more relaxed when he got to the skating rink in Livonia and was reunited with his *family* of the other skaters from *The Rollertorium*, which also kept his parents in a better mood when they were around them.

Joyce was already there and they met the day before the finals to practice their routines and dances, but there was also one big thing he noticed about Joyce that was starting to change. He'd noticed that since the time they started skating together about eight months earlier, she had grown to be about an inch taller than he was, and she seemed to be getting bigger in other ways.

When they competed at the State Finals, even though they won, he first noticed it was becoming more difficult lifting her during their freestyle routines, but when Jay

58

had mentioned to Joyce that she seemed to be getting "a little bigger", she got mad and shouted, "I am NOT!" and skated away from him.

Although she did come back a few minutes later and gave him a kiss, saying that she'd just "scoot down a little" so he'd still look taller than her when they skated their routines together, Jay didn't want to say it out loud, but it wasn't just her height he was concerned about.

When the National Finals began, his worst fears came true when he ended up dropping Joyce during one of the new lifts Ronnie Fitzgerald added to their routine for the Nationals which kept them from winning a medal. Joyce was angry that Jay had dropped her, but when they did finish second in *Couples Dance*, winning a Silver Medal she didn't seem as mad.

Jay also fell during his *Singles Freestyle* routine, trying to complete a harder jump he'd been practicing for weeks, but Joyce did win another Silver Medal in her own Singles Freestyle competition.

The other Buena Park skaters also did very well with Dennis Pollard and Carol Knudsen both winning Gold Medals in their couple's competitions, along with several other older skaters who also won medals to take back to California. Jay's parents seemed disappointed that after doing so well in California, he had nothing to show for it nationally except one second place medal.

Jay was also disappointed he couldn't call himself a National Champion yet, but he still had his title as the best skater in California and was looking forward to going back to Buena Park where he was still a champion.

But he also knew he had some work to do if he wanted to keep that title the next year.

᪣

The drive back to California was mostly quiet, with only with only a few stops for Tinker and meals, after Jay's father decided to drive straight through to Las Vegas from Michigan, and took turns diving with his mother.

His parents decided to stay in Las Vegas longer on that trip and got a motel for two days where they let Tinker stay in the room while they went to different casinos. Jay again got to watch his parents play the slot machines, and they also let him put some nickels in the machines when no one was watching, but it was when they woke him in the middle of the night to go with them to what they said was a "special party" that was the most memorable.

They all went up to a rooftop at a hotel on Fremont Street where there was a large group of people dancing to the music of a band and looked like they were still drinking liquor. Jay thought it was crazy that so many people could still be awake and having a party at that hour, but then, right as the sun was starting to come up, the band stopped and everyone started walking towards the edge of the roof and were looking out at the sky.

Suddenly, there was a bright flash of light in the distance and everyone started cheering, and Jay's father pointed out where the flash came from, to what looked like a puff of smoke rising in the distance, and said, "That's the Atomic Bomb going off!"

Jay had remembered the movies called *"Duck and Cover"* that his teachers had shown at his schools, and the weekly air raid drills that they'd always practice, but seeing the atomic bomb going off in person that morning didn't seem nearly as bad as he thought it would, and actually thought it was kind of neat.

He knew he'd have lots of things to tell his friends when he got back home, but the main thing he thought about was getting back to *The Rollortorium* to have fun with his family of friends there.

Chapter Seven

Jay's parents decided only a few weeks after coming back from the National Finals that it was time to make the move from La Puente to Buena Park so they wouldn't need to keep making the drives back and forth. They had been looking for a while, and now that Jay had finished his year at school, they figured it was a good time. and moving to Buena Park turned out to be more fun than Jay imagined.

It was still summer, and with skating *Meets* over until the following February, and with serious skating practice not due to start till November, there was time for many other activities until after Labor Day when school started up again.

The year earlier, Jay seemed to have missed summer vacation completely because he had started skating practice almost immediately when they came back from New York, and he felt like it was the first real *free time* he had in quite a while.

Their new house was close to Knott's Berry Farm and Jay and his skating friends could walk over to the park whenever they wanted, to spend a day and ride all the attractions like the old-fashioned stagecoach and the steam engine train, that both always got robbed by bandits each time they rode it, as well as seeing the "old-time melodrama's" at the *Birdcage Theatre*. Plus, Disneyland wasn't that far away either, so his parents took Jay and Joyce there, along with her Aunt Joannie because Mickie didn't want to go in her wheelchair or try to use crutches.

His parents seemed to like living in Buena Park much better too and had made a lot of friends from the skating rink that they would spend most weekends socializing with, but the skating club was still the center of Jay's universe, and even though the competitions and training were on break, almost all the skaters in the club regularly spent time at *The Rollertorium*.

The skating rink operators had regular parties and special events like "hayrides" on weekends to make sure all the skaters stayed together like a family, and regularly had themed costume parties like "Hillbilly" nights, "Bum's and Tramp's" nights, and "Cowboy and Indian" nights, where Mickie and Jay's mother would always dress Joyce and Jay up in crazy costumes trying to win the five-dollar best costume prizes.

Jay won the prize when his mother glued a mustache and goatee on his face, dressed him in weird shirt and pants, and had him wear sunglasses while he walked around acting like he was in a daze, playing bongos for the "Beatnik Night" party.

He won another prize when they had a costumed lip-sync contest, where the kids would dress up and sing along with a record they liked, and Jay's mother thought it would be cute to dress him up as a minstrel in blackface, and have him lip sync to the

Al Jolson song *Mammy* that Jay had already memorized the words. The crowd thought it was hilarious seeing a little kid like Jay singing along to an old song like *Mammy*, and the other kids said they wish they had worn blackface as well saying "it looked really neat."

For the last big party of summer on Labor Day weekend, the skating club had a big *Sadie Hawkins Party* that started with a daytime hayride and ended at the rink with another costume party that evening. They had also set up a kissing booth, which they said was a benefit to help pay for the party, and some of the cute older girls, the fourteen and fifteen-year old's, were giving kisses for a quarter.

But the main rules for Sadie Hawkins Day was that the girls would have to ask the boys to dance.

Jay had become very popular representing *The Rollertorium* as the *California Skater of the Year* and with the news clippings, trophies, and pictures of him displayed prominently around the rink, it wasn't unusual that a lot of the girls his age would ask him to dance with them.

Joyce would become furious at the girls when they did, and always let them know she was "going steady" with Jay and he would reluctantly turn down the invitations even though he thought some of those girls were cute and would be fun to dance with. But that night, because it was a Sadie Hawkins party, Joyce said it would be okay for him to skate with other girls and even said it would be okay if he donated a quarter for the party benefit and kissed an older girl, joking that Jay was "too young for them anyway.

The night of the party, Jay still skated most of the dances with Joyce but a few other of the younger girls also asked Jay to dance, but saw that most of the older girls were all asking Dennis Pollard to dance because he was still the best and most famous skater from Buena Park. He also saw that Carol Knudsen was skating with some of the older boys as well, so it was obvious to him for at least that night, none of the couples were "going steady" with each other.

After Jay had just finished dancing to another song with Joyce, she went to the refreshment stand to buy each of them a coke, which she said was also a custom that night, and he stood at the railing around the rink to wait for her as the disc jockey at the rink started the song *Stardust* by Nat King Cole

Jay heard a voice behind him shout out "Hey, you c'mon, we haven't danced yet and I haven't skated to a slow song tonight!" and saw it was Carol Knudsen, who was reaching out to take Jay's hand to lead him on to the skating floor and he didn't even hesitate.

Stardust was one of Jay's favorite songs, but it was a hard song to dance to because it was so slow, and also because Carol was over a head taller than Jay, rather than skating closer together as he had with the other girls. they were mainly coasting in circles around the rink holding hands.

Jay was glad that Carol finally started a conversation to break the monotony of just skating in circles.

"So, you ready to start practice's again?" Carol Knudsen cheerfully said as they slowly glided around the floor.

Jay said he was, but then quickly changed the subject, saying he thought Carol "should have been one of the girls" working in the kissing booth.

"Nope," she said, "They asked me, but I didn't want to stand behind a booth all night and wanted to enjoy the party."

"Well, I think they would have made a lot more money for their benefit if you were in the booth," Jay tried to say as a compliment. "Heck, I would have even spent a couple of quarters myself."

Carol just smiled and gave a slight laugh.

"So, you wanted to kiss me, huh?" she laughed. "I thought you got enough kisses from Joyce when I saw you two going at it on the hayride today."

"I just thought it would be fun to see you in the kissing booth," Jay tried to say as if his suggestion was no big thing, "Joyce even said because this is a Sadie Hawkins party it would have been okay."

Carol was still smiling about his last comment as they skated around the rink and finally said, "Okay, I'll tell you what, Jay, you give me a quarter to put in the benefit box, and I'll give you your kiss."

Jay saw Joyce was still at the refreshment stand talking to some friends and again didn't hesitate when she led him off the skating floor toward the front door and outside the rink.

Carol stood in front of him as Jay leaned back against the wall as she cupped her hands softly against his cheeks and smiled.

"All right," she said, "Here's your kiss, just open your mouth a little..."

Jay briefly pulled back when he felt her tongue in his mouth, but when she said "It's okay; this is a 'French kiss' and it's how you're really supposed to kiss," he tried to relax and let her give him a kiss that lasted for several seconds that gave him a funny feeling, but actually wished had lasted longer.

Carol finished the kiss with a smack on his lips, and cheerfully said, "Okay, give me your quarter, and I'll put it in the benefit box."

Jay gave her the quarter he had in his pocket before they skated back inside the rink as the song *Stardust* was just ending, and he saw no one even noticed that they had gone outside. When the song did end, Jay skated back toward Joyce, who was still at the refreshment stand when a song they both liked, *Only You* by the Platters, was starting, so Joyce told him it was their turn to dance again and she led him back to the skate floor.

"I saw you skating with Carol Knudsen the last dance," smiled Joyce, "I know you like her, but you know she's too old for you, right?"

Jay didn't say anything, and just smiled as he held Joyce's hand as he led her around the rink during the song, and was too busy wishing he had some more quarters to think about that.

☞

Once the party season was over that summer and Jay went back to school, he only would go to *The Rollertorium* on weekends until the practices for the 1962 skating season would begin in November. Jay had also heard some rumors from a few of his friends at the rink as to why a few of the top skaters at the club had suddenly quit roller skating and had moved away.

One story he heard was that one of the coaches at the rink had been fired for supposedly being "too friendly" with one of the teenage girls in the skating club and that her parents also decided to make her quit skating and didn't want her around other coaches. He heard about other skaters whose parents were going through a divorce and moved away, including one story about the mother of the skater had returned home with her daughter from practice early one night, and saw her husband and another man naked in their house.

"She found out her husband was a *queer*," laughed one of the older boys who told Jay the story, "After she told one of her friends, all the other parents at the rink found out about it, and she decided to just move away from Buena Park too."

Jay didn't know the skaters who had quit that well, but was glad that his parents had never talked about getting a divorce themselves, but even though they did seem to fight and argue a lot, they never did in public so he was also glad there weren't any rumors about them.

Because the skating club usually did lose a few of their top skaters each year for one reason or another, they were always trying to recruit new skaters to join the club to keep their roster full for the different divisions in the competitions.

The Rollortorium had gotten a new rink manager shortly after Labor Day who wanted to have a big promotion to attract new skaters to the skating club and decided to produce a roller-skating revue called *"Rhythm on Wheels"* similar to the *Ice Capades* and *Ice Follies*, that would feature the champion skaters from their club. The new manager also said he had some Hollywood contacts and would be able to invite some celebrities to see the show that would help attract a big crowd and get a lot of publicity for the skating club. He wanted to showcase the best skaters from all the different age ranges who were "State and National Champions," along with the professional instructors who were also going to be featured in the show.

Because Jay was still known for being the "Most Versatile Skater in California" that year, he was chosen to be the representative for skaters his age, and six other champion skaters including Dennis Pollard and Carol Knudsen represented the other divisions and would just need to perform a "showy" demonstration of their skating routines as part of the show. Joyce was a little disappointed she wasn't chosen to skate her routine, but the rink manager assured her and all the other skaters who weren't chosen for solo spots, they'd all be part of an "Introduction of All Champions" during the finale.

"Two of your gold medals at the state finals last year were with me," Joyce reminded Jay, "So don't get a big head just because you were chosen as the only ten-year-old in the show."

Jay was a little cocky that he was chosen over Joyce, but just told her that most of the other skaters were girls, and besides Dennis Pollard and a few of the coaches, they probably just needed another boy to even it out.

He didn't want Joyce to think he was conceited.

The rehearsals were a lot of extra work during the week after school, but Jay thought it was fun, and he especially liked practicing with Carol Knudsen on those nights they would all practice. Neither of them mentioned the time they kissed but always smiled at each other in a knowing way, and Jay liked that it was like they had their own little secret between each other.

There were pictures of Jay, Dennis Pollard, and Carol Knudsen along with some of the other stars of *Rhythm on Wheels* in the newspapers and magazines advertising and promoting the show in January of 1962 and the kids at Jay's school always made it a big deal out of it, and always tell him, "You're famous!" each time his name or picture appeared. Although Jay liked the attention, he was getting used to seeing his name in the newspapers, and it wasn't as exciting as the first few times he saw it, but he was excited about how big the night of *Rhythm on Wheels* turned out to be.

The rink manager had rented searchlights that were illuminating from the front of the Rollertorium, and there was a long line of people standing outside the rink watching the celebrities who were walking on a Red Carpet that led into the rink and were giving autographs to the crowd.

Jay recognized some of them but didn't know all their names, but he did know Richard Crenna, who played *Luke* on one of his favorite TV shows, *The Real McCoy's*, and thought it was neat that the actors would actually come over and have their pictures taken with Jay and the other stars of the show on the Red Carpet.

Once the show was ready to begin, Carol Knudsen gave Jay a quick kiss on the cheek and said, "Break a leg" which seemed to motivate him even more to put on a good show that night.

The performances went as smoothly as their dress rehearsals and they all were featured in solo variations of their competitive routines, but more *showy* than *difficult* because they didn't want anyone to fall trying to complete a strenuous jump. There was also a group comedy routine they had rehearsed, where his coach Ronnie

Fitzgerald, Dennis Pollard, and a couple of other older skaters, dressed up as clowns used Jay as a prop. The four older skaters would each toss Jay to each other while skating, and pretend to almost drop him a couple of times before one of the other skaters would catch him before he hit the floor. Jay saw that the audience was laughing and clapping each time they managed to catch him at the last minute and was glad he was chosen to be part of that routine.

During the grand finale, when all of the champion skaters from the Buena Park Club were being introduced, and the crowd was loudly cheering and applauding, Jay was thinking that *performing* in front of an audience was actually more fun than *competing* in front of an audience.

He also liked that instead of just "being famous" to the kids at school, he actually felt like a "celebrity" himself that night and Jay couldn't have asked for a better way to start out 1962.

Chapter Eight

Jay couldn't believe what a disaster 1962 was turning into for him and not the way he had pictured it was going to be.

It was less than a month before the State Finals that year and Jay was practicing with his second different skating partner in *Couples Dance* and *Mixed Pairs* since he and Joyce had split up earlier that year.

The problems started when Jay again started mentioning to Joyce that she had grown another inch taller than him and was also getting even heavier to lift than the year before.

"It's just taking you too long to grow up!" she had snapped back before adding "You're just not as strong as the other boys."

The other thing Jay noticed that wasn't going well between them, was that Joyce seemed to be getting moody at times and wasn't as fun to be around. There were times each month when Joyce seemed to get mad at Jay for no reason at all and sometimes wouldn't even talk to him for three or four days.

Jay's mother tried to explain to him, that Joyce and some girls her age, always went through certain "girl things," and he shouldn't worry about it and that Joyce would be better soon. He didn't really understand what she meant, and although Jay never spoke swear words out loud, he sometimes thought them in his head, and after Joyce had another one of her moods and stopped talking to him, he started thinking to himself, "Joyce is turning into a bitch!"

Ronnie Fitzgerald noticed the problems Jay was having lifting Joyce during the practice and sat Jay and Joyce down for a talk. He explained that the Sub Novice Division they'd be competing in that year required more complicated jumps, spins, and lifts, because Joyce was "growing faster than Jay," they should both consider different partners for *Couples Freestyle* and just concentrate on *Couples Dance*, which didn't require lifting.

Joyce wasn't that happy about having to give up *Couples Mixed Pairs* freestyle together, but she decided to compete in *Couples Dance* with Jay and her own singles freestyle event and only compete in two events that year. But Jay on the other hand, had no problem finding a new partner. He was still the reigning State Champion, and he found several girls his age who wanted to be his partner.

Jay finally decided to choose a girl named Christine Blackford, who was almost a year younger and at least a head shorter than him. Plus, besides being very easy to lift, Jay thought it didn't hurt that he'd always thought she was also really cute.

Christine was already a good freestyle skater and had actually finished ahead of Joyce a couple of times in the warm up skate *Meets* in their division the year before and finished second to her at the State Finals of 1961.

Jay also wanted to skate a new routine with Christine to a different song than *Granada* that he and Joyce had skated to and had listened to other music tracks on the Percy Faith album *VIVA-The Music of Mexico* and heard another song he liked that he thought would be perfect. The song had a very dramatic opening and a fun part in the middle with a lot of other parts that would fit with their jumps and spins. It also had a name Jay couldn't pronounce, so he brought the record to his coach. It was called *Zandunga; Jesusita En Chihuahua* and was subtitled (*The Dancing Donkey*), so Jay just called it *The Donkey Song* and was happy when the coaches agreed it was a perfect song for them to skate their routine.

After a month of spending half his time with Christine and the other half with Joyce, Jay actually began to like having two different skating partners, which besides being fun, he figured it was good for his image as a "versatile" skater.

Joyce also reminded Jay that even though he was skating with Christine in that one event, it didn't mean that she and Jay weren't still "going steady" as they always had. But Joyce had started becoming so irritable to be around, even though he still liked her, she just wasn't as fun as before.

It was after one of the last practices before the start of the first monthly *Meet*, Joyce angrily skated over to Jay. She had tears in her eyes and shouted. "I saw you kissing Christine after practice!"

Jay had kissed Christine a couple times when they were alone together and did briefly think it was fun having "two different girls to kiss" as well as "two different skating partners," but he saw it wasn't as easy as he thought. He was also getting tired of Joyce's outbursts and shouted back, "That's because you don't seem to want to kiss me anymore, and she DOES!"

"That's it then and I'm done skating with you!" Joyce cried out before adding, "Get Christine to be your new dance partner too because I don't want to skate with you at all anymore!"

"You would never have won your versatile skater award without me," she snidely added as she left practice, "So let's see how you do on your own!"

When she skated away, their coach came over and asked Jay what happened, but Jay just shook his head and said he didn't know, but that was the end of his partnership with Joyce. He actually wasn't that upset because he felt Joyce had been becoming a "bitch" since the first of the year and Christine had been much easier to get along with

Jay's father seemed more upset about his break-up with Joyce, because he said it might affect his parent's friendship with Mickey as well, and angrily said Jay should have "started lifting weights" if Joyce was getting too heavy to lift.

Christine did agree to be Jay's new partner in *Couples Dance*, and although they won their *Couple Mixed Pairs* event at the first warm up meet in February, with only a couple weeks to practice their dance routines together, the only finished third in their *Couples Dance*, but the coaches said they were confident they be better prepared by the time of the State Qualifiers in May with more practice.

Jay had also finished third in his own Singles Freestyle competition and only fourth in his speed skating event after having practiced more with Christine as his new partner and not as much on his individual competitions. He was mainly surprised that some of his old friends from Vineland told him that Jake had quit roller skating altogether after learning that Jake's parents had also moved away from La Puente to another city that didn't have a skating club. Jay was mainly disappointed that he wouldn't be able to have a chance to race against Jake again at the *Meets* that year, because finishing ahead of Jake had been his main goal the year before and the speed skating didn't seem as much fun without that competition.

Instead, he was now mainly focused on winning his events with Christine so he could show Joyce that he could still win without her at the State Finals. But just as Jay was getting confident with Christine as his new partner and planned on spending more time on his individual events to make up for lost practice's, there was another problem that came up after the second monthly *Meet* in March.

Christine's mother informed Jay's parents that her husband had been awarded a trip to Hawaii for is entire family at his job, and the trip was the same week as the National Finals that year, so even if Christine and Jay won the State Championship, she wouldn't be able to attend the nationals.

Jay was surprised that Christine didn't seem that upset, and told him that even though she "enjoyed skating and everything," she mainly entered the competitions because "that's what her parents wanted her to do," and she "didn't really care" if she went to the Nationals or not. But Jay did want to go to the Nationals, and now he had to find another skating partner who would help him qualify for the State Qualifiers that were coming up in May.

His coaches tried to help Jay find a girl his age who was experienced enough to learn the freestyle routines and dances with a limited amount of practice time but most of the top girl skaters already had partners. There was one girl, Cheryl Ridgeway ho was a year younger than Jay who was a top *Singles Freestyle* skater in the juvenile division, but had never competed in *Couples Dance* or *Couples Freestyle*. Ronnie Fitzgerald felt Cheryl was a good enough skater to be able to at least learn enough basics for the State qualifier, and then they'd have more time to practice for the State Finals. But most importantly, her parents said they would take her to the Nationals if she qualified so Cheryl became Jay's third skating partner that spring.

Jay also knew he'd been distracted earlier that year feeling he had two girlfriends and thought Cheryl was cute, but he had no interest in even thinking about looking at her in that light and wasn't planning on even trying to kiss her, and was going to keep the next several weeks of practice strictly business to make sure he qualified for the State Finals that year.

Jay's parents, and Cheryl's parents, had let both take Friday's off at school during those weeks so they could get in some extra training and the extra practice did help them qualify for the State Finals as well as for both of their individual freestyle competitions. But Jay had only managed to finish fourth in his speed skating event which meant he'd only be competing in three events at that years State Finals.

He knew it was going to be tough to be named the "Most Versatile Skater" of 1962 and knew he needed to really depend on Cheryl looking and skating as good as Joyce had the year before if he was going to have a chance.

Jay was trying to stay optimistic, but he just didn't feel as confident as he had the year before.

❧

A few weeks later, even with all the distractions he'd been through that year, Jay was halfway satisfied that he managed to win two gold medals at the State Finals, one in his *Singles Freestyle* and another with Cheryl in *Couples Dance*, but it was disappointing only winning a bronze medal in *Couples Freestyle* knowing he'd have no chance of being named the *Most Versatile Skater* again.

Dennis Pollard regained his *Most Versatile Skater of the Year* award and teased Jay that next year they'd see who would break the tie between them if Jay settled down to thinking about "skating more seriously" instead of how many "different girls" he could skate with.

Cheryl had also won a gold medal in her *Singles Freestyle* event over Joyce which meant that Joyce wouldn't be competing in the Nationals that year. Although Jay didn't want to gloat about how he'd qualified without her to her face, and act *conceited*, inside he was satisfied that he had.

Jay's parents also seemed satisfied he had at least qualified again for the National Finals, because the National Finals were being held in Harvey, Illinois that year which wasn't that far from Chicago and they had already planned on taking the trip and visiting Jay's grandparents again.

About ten days before they left for Chicago, the speed skating coach from their skating club asked Jay's parents if they could do a favor for someone.

A twelve-year-old girl named Judy Beaumont who was a member of their speed club and whose mother had recently died, also said she didn't have a father, so she

70

was temporarily living in a foster home and didn't have any way to attend the National Finals that year. They all felt very bad and thought it would be good for her, and maybe make her feel better, if someone could take her back to Illinois for the Nationals and let her know she still had a family of skaters who supported her.

Jay knew Judy, and they had practiced speed skating together, but he didn't know her that well because she was always very quiet and usually just came to speed practice and went home. Judy seldom attended any of the events or parties at *The Rollertorium*, but Jay did know she was a fast skater and usually won her speed events at the *Meets*.

His parents did agree to bring Judy along with them on their trip to keep Jay company, but he was disappointed when his father said it would be easier to just leave Tinker at the kennel for the two weeks they'd be gone, saying there wouldn't be as much room in the car with Jay and Judy in the back seat. Jay wasn't happy about leaving Tinker alone for two weeks, but also felt having Judy along would keep his parents from arguing knowing they didn't like to fight in front of other people.

The first day of driving was a light and friendly time of everyone getting to know each other and although Judy was quiet at first, she loosened up after singing songs together that played on the radio, and then group sing-alongs when the radio lost reception. Jay and his parents had also made a point not to mention anything to Judy about her mother or family, and they just talked about skating and some of the other skaters they both were friends with.

Jay did like the way Judy laughed and giggled during some of the tongue twister songs like *Mairzy Doats,* and trying to remember all the different repeating verses to *She'll Be Comin' Around the Mountain When She Comes,* and by the second day of driving he felt like they were already good friends.

Judy hadn't been to Chicago before, so they all again went to the *Prudential Building* to ride the elevators and rode on the subways like Jay had done his first time there and liked having Judy along which made it more fun than just being with his parents.

They then drove about a half-hour to the city of Harvey, to check out the rink where the Nationals would be held and see who else had arrived from their skating club, and saw that many of their friends were already there, including Cheryl.

They all spent some time practicing and also stayed for the regular skating sessions to get familiar with the skating surface, but besides skating with Cheryl during the session, Jay also skated with Judy a couple times. Cheryl wasn't his girlfriend so he wasn't concerned about skating with another girl in front of her and wanted Judy to know that he liked her.

Judy's speed skating event was scheduled the day before Jay's competitions, so Jay and his parents went down to cheer on the speed skaters from Buena Park. and everyone from their skating club cheered the loudest when Judy ended up taking first place and the Gold Medal in her speed event.

Everyone knew about Judy's mother dying and cheered loudest when she ended up winning, wanting to let her know she still had her family of skaters who cared for her. Jay was also surprised when Judy rushed over to Jay and his parents immediately after winning and gave them all hugs thanking them for bringing her and almost acted like she was celebrating with her own family.

Over the next two days the other skaters from the Buena Park club would again have a lot of success, with Dennis Pollard again winning gold medals in his *Singles Freestyle and Mixed Pairs* event with Carol Knudsen and a silver medal in his *Couples Dance* with her. There were other skaters from their club who also won medals at the Nationals, but Jay wasn't as fortunate in his two events.

During his dance routine with Cheryl, their roller skates got tangled on one of the turns during the Tango, and Cheryl almost fell, and although Jay caught her before she did, it did kill their chance for a medal. And then, during his *Singles Freestyle*, the event he felt he had the best chance to win a medal, Jay fell while trying a double Lutz he had been practicing for a month just to perform at the Nationals.

Cheryl also fell during her *Singles Freestyle* routine, which her parents insinuated was Jay's fault for taking up so much of her time the past two months, and said they weren't sure if they wanted Cheryl to continue being Jay's partner when they went back home.

Jay knew his parents were as upset as he was at having nothing to show for his Nationals that year, but they didn't want to show it in front of the other parents. His father just tried to joke to them that at least by bringing Judy, they'd leave Illinois that year with at least "one gold medal" so the "time and money" wasn't completely wasted.

During the drive back to California, because Judy was with them, they decided to make it like a "real family vacation" and stopped at different tourist attractions and not be in a rush to go home. They visited places like the *Lake of the Ozark's* which reminded Jay of all the Hillbilly parties that he'd attended, *Abraham Lincoln's Grave and Memorial* in Springfield, Illinois, *The Dalton Gang Hideout* in Kansas, the *Meteor Crater* in Arizona, and many other attractions they'd see posted on the roads.

The best thing he liked was that they stayed in several motels along the way, and Jay and Judy stayed in their own room together, which he liked that a lot more than staying in the same room as his parents. They also spent another night in Las Vegas, and it was there when they were in their room alone, that Judy finally started talking about her mother.

When Jay asked her how her mother died, he really didn't understand her answer when she told him that "Some man stuck a needle in her arm" and just thought her mom was sleeping in her bed for several hours before discovering she wasn't alive.

Jay figured Judy just didn't really know how her mother died, because he had shots in his arm before when he went to the doctor and he didn't die, but also decided not to ask her too many other questions. They had been having fun together for two weeks and Jay's didn't want to talk about anything depressing, especially on the last night they were spending together before their "family vacation" was coming to an end.

Before they drove Judy back to her foster home in Buena Park, Jay's parents told her that she could come over to their house whenever she wanted and even spend a couple of nights a week there during the rest of summer vacation.

Jay did feel like the first half of 1962 hadn't been very good for him and was anxious to find way to make up for it during the second half of the year.

Chapter Nine

Jay felt like Judy had become his best friend during the summer they spent together and there was even some talk about her becoming Jay's new skating partner. Jay also liked that Judy and Tinker got along great and saw she did seem to enjoy being somewhere besides her foster home and did start spending a couple nights a week sleeping with Jay and Tinker in his bedroom.

"Now you can see what's it's like having a sister around part time," his mother teased Jay, "You always asked why you don't have a brother or sister so now you can see what it feels like."

Jay had asked his mother a few years earlier about "why?" he was an only child and his mother also teased him by just saying, "Once I saw you, I decided one was enough, and made sure they tied my tubes so I wouldn't have to go through that misery again."

"I definitely couldn't have handled having another one like you," she sarcastically added.

Jay never really missed not having a brother and sister, but he also didn't want Judy to feel like a sister and was starting to like her in other ways.

He thought Judy had very pretty eyes and although she never wore makeup because she was just a speed skater, Jay could imagine how much more attractive she'd be wearing the short skating skirts, and making herself up with makeup and lipstick like his other skating partners had.

Jay figured that Cheryl was only temporary and was sure she and her parents wouldn't mind if he changed partners and just told them he'd be "going in another direction" when the practices and training would start up again after Halloween. He also wanted to be the one to decide to change partners before her parents said anything definite.

Cheryl didn't seem that bothered, but Jay did notice that Joyce and Christine always stood together and gave Jay dirty looks when they'd see him spending all of his time, or dancing with Judy, at one of the summer parties The Rollertorium would host for the skaters. He didn't mind the "dirty looks" from them because he figured he'd already tried being partners with them and it was *their* fault that they weren't still together.

Plus, he had a good feeling about Judy.

It was when he had taken Judy to a "sock hop" party at the rink, and while they were dancing to what they both said was their current favorite song, *Slow Twistin'* by Chubby Checker and Dee Dee Sharp, that Jay started to notice how "sexy" of a dancer Judy actually was. He even saw she moved her arms and hips in the same manner as Carol Knudsen had, and was even more optimistic about how good they'd look together as skating partners.

It was a week after the sock hop, when Jay and Judy decided to sneak into the swimming pool at one of the motels on Beach Boulevard to cool off from the August heat while his parents were both at work, and as usual, Jay had brought along his transistor radio so they could listen to some songs by the pool while they swam.

Since they had traveled to the National Finals, Judy also started to like singing along with Jay to the songs on the radio and there was a new song they both had fun singing together recently called *"I Remember You"* by Frank Ifield. That particular song was fun to sing along with because it had a "yodeling" part they both thought sounded funny.

While Ifield sang the title, they'd both try to yodel the *"I remember you...ooooooo!"* verses together in the same high-pitched manner and just laugh at their unsuccessful attempts. Jay kept his transistor radio next by the pool while they swam so they could hear when the song came on the next time, and they could again sing along and try to yodel.

The disc jockey on *KFWB* had also been playing that particular song at least twice an hour that day since he had reported that Marilyn Monroe had been found dead earlier that morning after apparently committing suicide.

"This is for you Marilyn," the disc jockey would announce each time he played that song, "and I'll always remember you."

Judy said she thought it was sad because she couldn't understand how someone as "pretty and famous" as Marilyn Monroe would ever want to kill herself, but by the second verse of the song, they both started trying to yodel the *"I remember you-oooooo"* part of the song again and not be bothered by the news.

Jay had also started to notice how cute Judy looked in her swimsuit that day noticing she was even starting to get boobies like Carol Knudsen and started explaining to her about how the girls all wore makeup and lipstick and told Judy she could be "just as pretty" and probably "look like Marilyn Monroe" if she tried that.

Judy said she was still a little nervous because she didn't have any experience in anything but speed racing, but Jay assured her how fast he learned when he was just a speed skater himself, and said he could help her the same way Joyce had helped him. Jay also saw that Judy had seemed to like comparing her to Marilyn Monroe, so he figured it was a good time to let her know the other "rules" that Joyce had taught him.

"You know," Jay tried to say naturally, "Once we become skating partner's we also become boyfriend and girlfriend and kind of go steady."

Jay liked it when he saw Judy smile and knew it was time for him to make his move.

"And," he tried to say with charm, "We get to do this…"

He cupped his hands around Judy's cheeks the way he remembered Carol Knudsen had done with him and leaned in to kiss her, but was surprised that Judy's mouth was already half open and they did almost end up having a *French Kiss*. Jay was thinking to himself that even though Judy didn't have any experience in dance and freestyle skating, he liked that she obviously had some experience in kissing.

When he pulled away, Jay saw her eyes were still closed and was waiting for him to kiss her again, but just as put his arms around her and started to kiss her, they both suddenly heard their favorite song begin to play again on the transistor radio and started singing together instead.

"I remember you…ooooooo!" they both sang out to the song deciding that trying to "yodel" was *almost* as fun as kissing.

After that day at the swimming pool on the day that Marilyn Monroe died, Jay was even more anxious to start practicing for his *comeback* with his new partner, and his new girlfriend, and was confident the next year was going to turn into his best year yet.

Unfortunately, it was around Labor Day, when Jay and his parents learned that a social worker had located a distant relative of Judy's and that they had agreed to raise Judy themselves back in Kansas.

With everything else that had gone wrong that year, Jay had been getting used to disappointments, but after losing both a girlfriend, and a new skating partner, he didn't know how things could get much worse and knew his luck had to eventually somehow get better.

❧

When Jay began his school year in September, he knew the practices and training at *The Rollertorium* weren't scheduled to begin again until November in order to give the kids a couple months to get adjusted in their new school years. Jay wasn't that excited about having to ask Cheryl or Christine if they wanted to try and be his skating partner again, but he hoped he might be able to find someone new in the next couple months. But it was towards the end of October of 1962, a couple weeks until Jay needed to make his decision, when everyone in Buena Park, as well as across America were distracted by something that was more important than roller skating.

Jay had already read in the newspaper, and heard on the television news about how the Premier of the Soviet Union, Nikita Khrushchev, had installed atomic missiles in Cuba, and President Kennedy was threatening to retaliate by attacking the weapons sites unless they were removed.

Everyone seemed to be afraid there was going to be an Atomic War between the United States and Russia and there were even more air raid drills at school, learning how to "Duck and Cover" if a bright flash appeared in the sky, and the neighborhood air raid sirens were also being tested every couple day's rather than the usual once a month.

When Jay was walking home from school on the day of what the news was calling a "Naval Blockade" of Russian warships heading to Cuba, he noticed that a lot of people were packing boxes with canned food into their cars, and even saw a small airplane parked in the driveway at one of the houses on his block. Jay saw that everyone was getting ready to leave in a hurry if the air raid sirens began sounding when there wasn't a test scheduled.

When Jay got home, he saw his parents were also packing boxes into their cars, but it looked like they were taking everything out of the house and packing a lot more items than his neighbors.

Jay's mother just coldly told him, "We're moving, and I've already packed your things, so see if there's anything else you want to take before we leave today."

He saw his father also quietly carrying out boxes to put in the car and just said, "Go get Tinker, we're leaving in about twenty minutes."

Jay tried asking his parents why they were moving, but they kept saying, "Don't worry about it, just do what you're told."

When he tried to tell his mother that he was supposed to start his skating practice the next weekend she just coldly said, "You won't have to worry about practice next week."

He could tell his parents had been fighting by the looks on their faces and by the silent treatment they were giving each other as they continued putting items in the car. Jay knew he wasn't supposed to talk, and after carrying Tinker to the car and getting in the back seat, he sat quietly with Tinker's head on his lap as he waited to drive away from their house.

It wasn't until they were blocks away from their house that his father quietly tried to give Jay an explanation about what was happening, but his mother remained silent and didn't say anything.

"Kennedy is probably going to get us into an atomic war," his father quietly said, "And we need to move away further away from Disneyland."

His father started explaining that when Nikita Khrushchev was visiting California a few years earlier, he got mad because from a distance, Khrushchev saw the "rocket

77

ship ride" that was prominently visible, and wanted to know what was inside the *supposed* theme park.

"They wouldn't let him visit Disneyland," Jay's father added, "So the Russian's probably think it's a secret military base, and will more than likely drop one of their first atomic bombs there."

Jay didn't think that made sense, remembering that the atomic bomb he saw explode in Las Vegas seemed to be as far away as they lived from Disneyland and knew they didn't get hurt then and shouldn't have seemed that worried. He also didn't know why his parents would be giving each other the *silent treatment* over something like an atomic war, and knew there had to be something else going on they didn't want to talk about. But neither of his parents wanted to talk about it anymore and just continued driving in silence as Jay was starting to wonder where they were moving hoping that it would at least be close enough to ride his bicycle back to Buena Park.

He was also hoping that there wouldn't really be an atomic war and everything would get back to normal quickly so his parents might get in a better mood.

Jay didn't want a stupid war to ruin his chance to have fun again the next year.

Chapter Ten

"You've got to stop moping around the house!" yelled his father as Jay was lying on his bed with Tinker reading comic books. He'd heard the same thing from his mother numerous times in the past six weeks, but felt he had good reason to be *moping*. There was never an atomic war, and Jay didn't understand why they had to stay in their new house and away from Buena Park any longer.

"Why can't we just go back to our old house?" Jay argued at least twice a week and unable to understand why he wasn't allowed to roller skate anymore

HIs father had tried to convince him that three years had been long enough for Jay to enjoy as a hobby, but it wasn't anything that would be beneficial to continue with as he got older.

"Roller skating still isn't as popular as ice skating and it never became part of the actual Olympics," his father said, "It's fun for kids as a hobby on a smaller level, but there really isn't any type of long-term career in it for you."

"Besides, you probably wouldn't have found a partner as good as Joyce was this year anyway and should have just stayed with her," his father had added with slight bitterness, "You've already hit your peak with roller skating so it's time for you to just find a new hobby."

Jay didn't like that his father had insinuated it was his fault he had to have different skating partners that year, and also never looked at skating as just a hobby. He was still a state champion in two events and knew he would be able to get even better with a partner he could practice with full-time the next year. But his parents both insisted Jay was done with roller skating and to just get used to it.

He could also never understand why he wasn't even allowed to call any of his old friends, at least by the telephone, but his mother claimed that because they now lived in Los Angeles County which had a different area code than Orange County, it was a long-distance call and argued it would be too expensive to make phone calls out of their area, and forbid him to make any calls to them.

Jay knew better than to cry about it, so he just took to yelling like he always heard his parents do, and then as they also did, he started with his own *silent treatment*. His parents called it *moping*, but he called it, *letting them know* about how he felt about everything.

"Why don't you go outside and just meet some new friends?" his mother would often yell at him as well tell him to stop "moping" around, but Jay would just snidely reply that he "didn't have any friends anymore" which was basically true.

They had moved to Lakewood, California, which was a suburb of the larger nearby city of Long Beach, and Jay always thought it was only temporary, but when his parents both said they had new jobs there and told him he was going to have to attend a new school, he wasn't happy.

He had to enrolled halfway through the first semester at his new school and it was too late to sign up for many of the activities other kids had already signed up for and felt like a total stranger. He usually just came home from school and spent time in his bedroom alone with Tinker doing his homework or reading comic books and had kept pretty much to himself for the past two months.

Because his parents both worked, and because he was old enough now to not need a baby sitter, sometimes after school, Jay would just ride his bicycle to a record store called *Wallichs Music City* close to his house which had free listening booths where he could listen to a wide variety of song's he liked without having to buy the records. He still liked to practice learning all the lyrics to his favorite songs and would spend hours in the listening room at that record store.

His father had always said he was self-employed and worked different types of jobs from selling photo albums, frozen TV dinners, and other products, but once they moved to Lakewood, he started working more hours and also would spend a couple weekends a month in Arizona where he said he was also trying to sell land lots in Lake Havasu, so Jay never saw his father that often. His mother was also working two part-time jobs, one as a food waitress and another working at *See's Candy* in a big shopping mall called *Lakewood Center* which was directly across the street from *Wallichs Music City*.

Jay also saw almost every time his father came back into town from working in Arizona, there would be another argument, and there would still sometimes be two or three days when no one would talk to each other at the same time. Jay thought it was weird, but his mother never seemed to get over her fights with his father, until she somehow also managed to get angry with him over something. It almost seemed she liked to have arguments, and when she got angry at Jay, she found ways to punish him that she knew would hurt him without using "The Belt."

She wouldn't spank him, but she knew it would bother him even more if she broke one of his records or threw away something else that he really wanted to save. They didn't speak for almost a week when she threw away his entire Superman comic book collection that he'd been saving since he was seven years old.

His mother then told his father that Jay shouldn't get an allowance that week because he was "being a brat" by not talking to her, which then started period of the "silent treatment" between Jay and his father. It seemed rare when at least one of the three of them weren't talking to each other at the same time.

Jay eventually started trying to find ways to stay away from the house so he wouldn't have to be around his parents that often, and decided to get a job as a paperboy delivering the Herald-Examiner's afternoon editions. Tinker would usually run along beside him while he rode his bicycle during his route, which besides being fun, was also making him some extra money so he wouldn't just depend on his parents for his allowance.

He didn't like it when he had to collect money from the neighbors for the papers the first and couldn't understand why they wouldn't come to the door when he tied to make his collections. Sometimes, he even saw the curtains in the windows drawback, so he knew that someone was home, but they never answered their doorbells. Other times, he'd have to sit on the curb with Tinker for over an hour waiting for someone to come home from work so he could collect their monthly bill that would only earn him about ten or eleven dollars a month. Also as usual, it was Tinker who eventually helped Jay meet some new friends in Lakewood.

When he'd take her for walks, or they'd see her running alongside Jay on his paper route, some of the neighborhood kids would want to pet her, and sometimes they'd have some balls that Tinker would chase after. It wasn't too long before some of the neighborhood kids started coming over to Jay's house to ask if Tinker could come out to play.

As Jay started to make new friends, his parents didn't seem to argue as much, and there were even some weeks when they all tried to do some things to try and get along better. He reluctantly would play cards with them on nights they weren't arguing and they would all occasionally would go see movies together.

One thing Jay did start liking, was right after Christmas when they started going to the horse races at Santa Anita Racetrack in a city called Arcadia. Along with his allowance and the extra money he made from his paper route Jay was usually able to take at least ten dollars to the racetrack and have his parents make some bets for him, so he started learning how to bet on the races to try and win some more.

He found out that betting to "Win" was the most risk, so he'd usually just bet two dollars to "Show" on the horses that were favored to win and that way, he'd still win money if they just finished first, second, or third. Although he'd only get a small profit of sometimes less than a dollar each race, it sometimes it added up to four or five dollars after all nine races, which Jay thought was pretty good.

A couple of times, he did lose over four or five dollars, but he kept track of his earnings and was usually a few dollars ahead by the end of the month by keeping his betting system.

They had also attended a few NFL football games near where they used to live near the LA Coliseum to see the Rams play, but although they would make the drives to Los Angeles or Arcadia, they still would never would take him back to Buena Park.

Coincidentally, during that winter, the *Million Dollar Movie* was showing *Porgy and Bess* with Sidney Poitier and Sammy Davis Jr the entire week on television which Jay watched once with his parents, and three more times on his portable television set alone in his bedroom with Tinker that week.

He liked seeing some of his favorite songs by George Gershwin come to life in that movie, and always looked forward to the sad finale where Sidney Poitier as the crippled *Porgy*, decides to have his goat pull him on a cart for a thousand-mile journey to New York City to find *Bess* and rescue her from Sammy Davis Jr's character *Sportin' Life*.

Jay would always look forward to hearing the closing coda to the song *I'm On My Way* which had always his favorite part, but just as the movie's ending was sad, watching *Porgy and Bess* and listening to the closing coda, also seemed to be much sadder each time he heard to it.

But he also never wanted to forget it.

∞

Jay finally accepted that he would never see his old friends again and decided he'd try to find something new to make him happy. By early 1963, and around his twelfth birthday, the second semester of school was starting and he was looking for some of the classes and activities he could join that might be fun.

One course at *Bancroft Junior High School* that interested Jay, was a beginning band class with the only requirement was that each student would have to rent or buy their own musical instrument. He asked his parents if they would buy him what he needed to join the class for his birthday present, and said they would as long as it wasn't' expensive like a piano, so he decided on an instrument that wasn't that big or expensive.

Jay remembered that the clarinet was the instrument used in the opening solo of *Rhapsody in Blue* and he wanted to learn how to play the music instead of just listening to it. Even though he didn't have his *old friends* anymore, he still had the music in his head that wouldn't let him forget them, or his time as a competitive skater.

Jay's music instructor at Bancroft Junior High School was named Mr. Peters, and he was very patient with all of the beginning musicians. There were about thirty students in the class trying to learn almost every possible instrument and luckily Mr. Peters knew quite a bit about the clarinet, so he could spend time with the three other clarinet students in the class, showing them the basics on how to bite down on the reed and mouthpiece while holding the different spaces on the clarinet to hit certain notes.

The first songs they were taught were almost all kid songs that Jay had learned growing up, *Mary Had A Little Lamb*, *Twinkle, Twinkle Little Star*, and *Hot Cross Buns*, and the main studying was spent on how to learn read all the notes and sheet music.

It was going to be harder than Jay thought because he didn't realize that there would be even more homework added to what he already thought was a heavy workload at his new school. But his clarinet did become Jay's main focus, and after a full semester, he was actually able to learn some more difficult songs and was learning how to read music fairly well.

During summer vacation, Jay spent most of his time practicing the clarinet and had his list of songs to practice during summer, but after a while, he felt he learned them and needed something new to practice.

During that time, Jay's favorite song was called *Those Lazy-Hazy-Crazy Days of Summer* by Nat King Cole, so he started trying to learn it "by ear" on his clarinet, but trying to guess and hit certain notes without reading music made his clarinet squeal and screech quite often. Tinker used to always stay with Jay in his bedroom when he did his homework, but when he practiced his music, she'd usually start whining or barking and leave his room.

Jay's mother would also get irritated when he was trying to learn that new Nat King Cole song when the squeals and screeching became more frequent and there were numerous times his mother would yell, "Jay, stop trying to play that god damned song, you're hurting Tinker's ears!" His parents finally decided it would be better if he practiced somewhere besides their house, so they arranged private lessons at a *Wallichs Music City*, which also had music instructor's twice during the week.

There was one other weekend during the summer of 1963, that was memorable to Jay when his parents decided to go to Las Vegas again, but even though he didn't see another atomic bomb go off because above ground atomic testing had been banned earlier that year, he did get to see his first Las Vegas show at the *Sands Hotel.*

It was the Dean Martin show, and although he liked seeing a movie star and famous singer in person, Dean Martin's performance wasn't what he liked best about that night.

A large group of showgirls also danced while he sang his songs, and Jay's eyes got wide when many of them took off their tops. Jay was a little embarrassed because he hadn't seen naked breasts in person before, and only in some magazines his friends had shown him, but the main reason he was embarrassed was that he had to sit with his parents while he watched.

He heard his mother whisper to his father that "maybe they shouldn't have brought Jay" to see that show, but his father was watching too, and just told her that "Jay was getting older" and it would be all right.

Jay knew he would have enjoyed it much more if he could have watched the ladies with their tops off alone, but he also knew he was too young to do many of the things he liked by himself and looked forward to when he was older and could go places, and enjoy things, without his parents.

He still couldn't wait until he was a "grown up" and would be able to make his own decisions.

Chapter Eleven

The private lessons on his clarinet helped Jay improve much faster than he'd been able to in his classes, and he was confident he was now beginning to feel like a real musician and had even learned a few melodies "by ear" of songs he remembered growing up that didn't have that many notes to play. He was able to learn by himself, the opening theme music from *The Little Rascals*, and also a song from the movie *The Roaring Twenties* he'd seen many times and already knew the words to, *It Had to Be You*.

Jay did like that the clarinet was featured on a lot of the songs from the old music albums his parents had, and movies he had seen when he was younger, and when the new school year started that September, Jay had joined the intermediate band classes and felt he had a good head start on the other students in the class.

Being a band and not an orchestra, the class mainly learned music with the brass and woodwind sections and included marches and patriotic music, a few popular variations of big band music from the 1940s, and a few jazz tunes from the 1920s and 1930s. Jay especially liked that the musicians would also have a monthly contest to decide who the best on the instruments of their group.

Each instrumentalist would compete against their group on the last Friday of each month, and the best player would be named "First Chair" for their particular instrument.

Jay liked the idea of competition again and felt he had become good enough to win the *First Chair*, but another clarinet player in his group won the first two months of the competitions and it always irritated him because the other clarinet player would always gloat about "how much better" he was than Jay, and how "Jay would never beat him" and be *First Chair*.

By the third month of his school year, Jay was almost obsessed with trying to win *First Chair* and took his clarinet with him everywhere, trying to practice harder. The next competition at school was going to take place a week earlier than usual that month, because the actual last Friday was Thanksgiving weekend when the kids would be out of school.

Mr. Peters always would pass out a song to all the musicians they would have to play in the contests the week before each judging, and the clarinet players were given a Hawaiian song called *Sweet Leilani*. Jay spent hours that entire week practicing each note where he almost knew that song by heart without reading the music.

When the competitions were completed that Friday, the clarinet player who always won the first chair had his usual cocky smirk on his face again, expecting his name to get called as the winner, but when Mr. Peters made his announcements and said, "First Chair for Clarinet this month is Jay Mershon," his expression quickly changed.

The class was obliged to applaud each winner while they stood and moved seats to sit in the *First Chair*, and when Jay switched seats with the clarinet player who thought he'd never have to give up his seat, Jay was more excited and satisfied than he had been in a long time.

He was a winner again for something else besides roller skating.

Jay also couldn't wait for his class to end, so he could tell everyone he knew at school that he had won *First Chair* in music and was the best clarinet player that month. But it was immediately at the end of his band class around eleven am, when there was an announcement over the loudspeakers for all students to immediately report to the school auditorium.

Jay was still beaming with excitement and joking facetiously to his friends that they would probably announce that he had won *First Chair* to the entire school. But when the principal standing onstage in the auditorium announced that President Kennedy had just been assassinated in Dallas and all the students were being sent home for the day, everyone's mood changed and weren't interested in hearing anything that Jay had to say.

When he walked home alone that day carrying his clarinet case, it seemed quiet everywhere, but instead of being concerned about the assassination, Jay was mainly getting mad at President Kennedy again. First, Kennedy was the reason they had to move away from Buena Park a year earlier when his father said he was going to start an atomic war, and now, he was the reason that no one seemed to care that he had won *First Chair* on his clarinet.

Jay always remembered that November 22, 1963, was a bad day for him.

෴

There were a lot of changes in the coming months, which quickly seemed to make everyone forget about the Kennedy assassination, particularly in February of 1964, when *The Beatles* appeared on *The Ed Sullivan Show.*

Jay also turned thirteen years old that same month, but also ended up getting braces on his teeth as his "birthday present" that year, which made it hurt for over a month and more difficult when he tried to bite down on his clarinet's mouthpiece.

He was excited that he was finally a teenager, but after seeing how all the screaming teenage girls got excited watching *The Beatles* perform, and seemed more interested in rock and roll music than the music he played on his clarinet which had become difficult with his braces, so Jay decided to switch to playing drums in the band class halfway through his second semester at school.

Jay knew he was going to miss playing the clarinet, but figured he had already become the best player in the class and it was time to try something new. He also noticed that none of the girls he met at school seemed that impressed that he was a "great" clarinet player anyway, so he thought being a drummer in the band might seem more interesting to them.

He was still a little self-conscious about talking to girls, especially with the braces he had to wear on his teeth, but was mainly disappointed that he never did get to learn the opening clarinet solo to *Rhapsody in Blue.*

It was also over Memorial Day weekend in 1964 when Jay's parents said they were going somewhere that surprised him. They were spending a day back in Buena Park, but it wasn't any type of reunion with old friends and instead, they were going to a political rally at *Knott's Berry Farm* for Barry Goldwater who was running for President that year.

His father said he had met Barry Goldwater a couple times in Arizona and they were supporting him for President and volunteering to work on his campaign. Jay had heard his father often say that first President Kennedy, and now President Johnson had been "pussy-footing around" in a country called Vietnam and that Goldwater knew how to end the conflict without dragging it out and turning it into a major war like the Korean War had been.

While they were at the rally, Jay tried not letting his parents see him looking around to notice if he could see any of his old friends there and although he didn't see anyone he recognized, he didn't know what he would have said to them anyway. The almost two years since he'd seen any of them seemed to have been in the distant past and now almost seemed like it had just been a dream to him.

Jay was a little bored with all of the speeches everyone was giving that day, but he did have fun after the rally when they got to shake hands with all of the movie stars who were there that were supporting Barry Goldwater for president.

Besides shaking hands with Goldwater, Jay also got to shake hands with John Wayne, who Jay thought was the biggest movie star in the world and starred in one of his favorite western movies, *The Man Who Shot Liberty Valance.*

There was also an actor he met named George Murphy who had been famous in the 1930s and 40s for making movie musicals, but was currently running for the US Senate seat in California that year, and he also shook hands with Efrem Zimbalist Jr, the star of the television show *77 Sunset Strip*. which Jay mainly liked because of the catchy theme song from that series. But Jay thought the "neatest" famous person he met that day, was the actor Ronald Reagan, because besides being a movie star he'd seen on both television and the movies, instead of just shaking Jay's hand, Reagan actually spent a few minutes personally talking to him and asking him about himself.

Jay was surprised that a "movie star" was interested in what he did, and when Reagan asked him what he did for fun, not knowing anything impressive to say, just said he "went to school" but quickly added that he "used to be a champion roller skater" a couple years earlier.

Reagan told Jay that he was impressed by that, and mentioned how important sports was to him when he was growing up, and had played football, baseball and basketball himself when he was Jay's age. He added that Jay's schoolwork was important, but told him to keep playing sports because the competitions involved would be important for other lessons he needed to learn about as he got older.

"Keep playing sports, study hard and also remember to tell your friends at school to tell their parents to vote for Barry Goldwater and George Murphy this year," Reagan smiled to Jay before saying good bye and good luck.

They shook hands again, and Jay promised him he would.

Jay was still thrilled driving home with his parents, thinking about how he couldn't believe that a famous movie star actually took the time to stop and talk to a kid his age that night, and made his return to Buena Park more fun than if he'd just seen his old friends again.

He also decided that Ronald Reagan was definitely going to be one of his other favorite movie stars from now on.

❧

By the time summer vacation from school that year began, Jay got tired of trying to collect money from customers on his newspaper route but he still liked making the extra money each month, especially because he and his parents were going to the horse races fairly regularly at another racetrack called Hollywood Park.

Jay started thinking of other ways to make money during the summer and thought he came up with a brilliant idea.

Everyone knew about the "Ice Cream Man" who drove through the neighborhoods every day, but the kids all thought the ice cream truck driver named Mac was creepy, and they didn't like buying ice cream from him. But seeing Mac was the only ice cream man in their neigborhood, they usually had no choice.

Jay's plan was to rig up an ice chest on the back of his bicycle, pack it with dry ice, and then buy ice cream bars from the wholesalers, and ride around the neighborhood on his bike before Mac usually did his route. He figured he be making a five to seven-cent profit off the different ice cream bars and if he could sell thirty or more bars a day, he'd probably clear almost ten dollars a week instead of ten dollars a month.

After he talked to his parents, they thought it was a funny, but also a good idea and agreed to help him give it a try. Some friends helped Jay get his bicycle rigged with an ice chest correctly, and then his parents drove him to the *Carnation Dairy* warehouse, where they bought blocks of dry ice, and ice cream bars wholesale. Jay just bought the most popular bars, the Sidewalk Sundaes. Fifty/fifty Bars, Drumsticks, Ice Cream Sandwiches, and also got a wide variety of Popsicles because they had a higher profit margin. He then put a makeshift sign on the front of his bike that said "JAY'S ICE CREAM," along with cowbells on his handlebars to let everyone know he was coming down the street.

Jay knew what time Mac usually drove his route, so he would start about a half hour before he did, and also let Tinker run along beside him during his route, because he knew all the kids liked her and would also come running outside when they saw her.

After only a few days, everyone in the neighborhood knew Jay was in business and started waiting for him to ride down the street on his bicycle with Tinker beside him, and in his first week of being the new "Ice Cream Man," Jay did clear almost ten dollars. By this fourth week he never cleared less than twelve dollars and was already picturing how much money he'd have saved up by the end of summer, but it was also shortly after his fourth week of being in business, when Jay and his parents got a knock on the door while they were having dinner.

It was Mac, and he started angrily threatening Jay's father about the "illegal business" Jay and his parents were "trying to get away with" that was costing Mac money.

"Either he stops his ice cream route or I call the police and get you all into a lot of trouble," Mac threatened Jay's father, "It's against the law to sell ice cream without a business license and vender's permit."

There was some arguing between his father and Mac, and all Jay heard was a "Fuck You!" when his father slammed the door on Mac and then said to Jay, "We'll show that bastard!"

The next day, his father took Jay down to get his Social Security card and business license from the State Board of Equalization under the name *Jay's Ice Cream* and made sure that all the licensing was in order. After that, there was nothing Mac could do, and Jay continued his route throughout the summer and had been able to open a new savings account with almost a hundred dollars that he'd saved that summer.

When he did go back to school, Jay continued working on weekends and decided he'd try to keep adding at least five or ten dollars a month in his savings account and was really starting to feel like a businessman.

He also liked that he didn't have to depend on his parents for money.

Chapter Twelve

Since he had been to Barry Goldwater's political rally at Knott's Berry Farm, Jay had started paying closer attention to the presidential campaign that year, especially when he watched a nationally televised speech by Ronald Reagan with his parents a week before the election that year in support for Goldwater.

Reagan was speaking in defense of what the Democrats were calling Goldwater's extremist views, especially about Vietnam and how he said America shouldn't get involved in a prolonged conflict in that country, and should instead, just go in with overwhelming strength and end any possibility of a real war.

President Johnson had campaigned that he would "never send American boys nine or ten thousand miles away from home to do what Asian boys ought to be doing themselves" when talking about how Goldwater would escalate the war in Vietnam, but it was a particular television commercial that Johnson used against Goldwater that had gotten the most attention that year.

That one political advertisement featured a little girl alone picking flower buds as a voiceover that sounded like a missile launch countdown leads to a nuclear explosion that evidently kills the little girl as just an "atomic mushroom cloud" is seen on the TV screen. President Johnson's voiceover is then heard saying, "These are the stakes, to make a world that all of God's children can live or to go into the dark. We must either love each other or we must die…" before another voiceover announced, "Vote for President Johnson, the stakes are too high for you to stay home."

Jay did see how that one commercial did receive widespread news coverage the week after it ran on television, and with the publicity it received, the Democrats began referencing its message by describing Goldwater as someone who was "mentally unstable" and as someone who would start a nuclear war if he was elected president.

With everyone in the county still nervous about how close the United States went to war with Russia two years earlier, Johnson's supporters were trying to convince the public about what might happen if they voted for Goldwater. One magazine ran a headline that claimed over a thousand psychiatrists said that "Goldwater is psychologically unfit to be president" while others claimed that Goldwater "has the same pathological make-up as Hitler, Castro, Stalin and other known schizophrenic leaders." Martin Luther King also was quoted as saying "We see dangerous signs of *Hitlerism* in the Goldwater campaign,"

Jay had read and saw on television. that the Democrats campaign tactics comparing Goldwater to someone like Hitler was also receiving widespread criticism for introducing divisive, negative and scare tactics against a particular candidate that had never been used as blatantly before, saying it was a "dangerous path to destroy an opponent's character with unproven innuendoes just for the sake of politics."

Jay's parents also complained that it was the "dirtiest presidential campaign" they had ever seen, but the negative advertising and comments did seem to work that year regardless, and Lyndon Johnson ended up winning the November election in a landslide over Goldwater.

It also became big news that the former actor George Murphy, and not an established politician, did end up winning the election for the US Senate in California, and there were many who started mentioning that with the widely praised speech Ronald Reagan had made for Goldwater that year, that he might make an excellent politician himself.

Jay thought 1964 had been an interesting year, both with some of the people he met, as well as his first experience of being self-employed, but he was mainly looking forward to finishing his final year of junior high school in 1965, and finally becoming a high school student the following September.

He knew once he started high school, he would be fourteen years old and be in his second year as a teenager and wouldn't feel like "just a kid" any longer.

&

Even though he had tried to ignore his braces for the past year and a half, Jay still felt self-conscious around people he talked with, especially the girls.

He had started getting new feelings about girls ever since he had seen Ann-Margaret onscreen in *Bye-Bye Birdie* a couple years earlier, and actually went back several times just to see her sing the title song at the very end of the movie when she was onscreen by herself singing and suggestively shaking her skirt as she smiled into the camera. Jay thought she was the "sexiest girl" he'd ever seen and often fantasized about how exciting it would be having a girlfriend like her, but by the time *I Can't Get No Satisfaction* by The Rolling Stones was blasting on everyone's radio during the summer of 1965, Jay felt that song could apply to him. He hadn't had a girlfriend or even kissed a girl since he'd lived in Buena Park and had almost forgot what it was like.

Although he did meet girls and talk with them, it seemed he had nothing interesting to tell them about himself, and had already discovered they certainly didn't want to hear about how he was a great roller skater when he was a ten or eleven year old kid.

Jay was thrilled when he learned he would be able to get the braces off his teeth before he started his first year of high school because didn't want every girl's first impression of him to be "the kid with braces" on his teeth.

Shortly after he had graduated ninth grade at *Bancroft Jr High School*, there were orientation meetings with different counselors at the nearby *Lakewood High School* for classes to sign up for the following September. He also learned he was required to take certain classes in high school that he wasn't that excited about, especially the Algebra and Chemistry classes, and was also required to take the standard History, English, Civics, and Geography courses. High school students were also required to learn a foreign language, and while most students were signing up for Spanish, Jay decided he'd learn French, which he thought sounded much more romantic, and thought about "how cool" it would be to talk to girls in French. He also signed up for a class called *Creative Writing,* which the counselor's explained was good practice to learn how to "think out" original thoughts and creative ideas which could be beneficial for a variety of different professions when he got older.

Although Jay had once thought playing in the school band was special and something the girls would be impressed with, he discovered that playing in a high school band was becoming known as "dorky" to the *cool kids*, so he decided to get more involved with sports and signed up for the "Bee Football" team that the Physical Education coach said would give him extra credit and an automatic "A" in his gym class.

Football had become his favorite sport after attending so many Rams games at the Coliseum. Plus, he had played flag football in PE Classes in Junior High and with an Intramural football team at one of the recreational parks in Lakewood the year before.

The other students who signed up for football were told they needed to sign up and practice a month before school started to be ready to play when football season began, and when Jay signed up that summer, he also knew what position he wanted to play and told his coach he wanted to be a quarterback.

He was a fan of Rams quarterback Roman Gabriel and had seen how everyone always talked about the opposing quarterbacks the Rams would be playing against. Jay also always looked forward to seeing Johnny Unitas, Bart Starr, Fran Tarkington, and other star quarterbacks when they came to town to play against the Rams and knew they were the most famous players on the teams.

The football practices were scheduled to begin in early August 1965, but were postponed for over a week when a riot broke out in the city of Watts, which was less than fifteen miles away from Lakewood.

Th riot had started after a black man had resisted arrest for drunk driving and there was a mob of onlookers nearby who started arguing that the police were using too much force trying to subdue him and began throwing rocks and bottles at the police as they were trying to arrest him. That led to more police units being called to the scene, as well as more groups of blacks gathering in the streets who also began fighting with the police. During that night, hundreds of more blacks became involved and began looting and starting setting businesses on fire which ended up turning into a full-blown riot involving thousands more the following day.

Jay and his parents watched on television what looked like a war going on after the California Governor Pat Brown had called in the National Guard after the Los Angeles Police Chief William Parker said fighting the "negro rioters" was comparable to an insurgency by the Viet Cong" and needed the military to confront the "guerrillas and gangsters."

Seeing Army tanks and armed military vehicles engaging in gun battles on the streets of Los Angeles while dozens of buildings were in flames, made Jay almost feel like he was watching a scene from a movie, or a war in another country. But although there weren't many negros he'd ever seen in Lakewood, the riots did start spreading to neighboring cities close by, including Long Beach, so everyone in Jay's neighborhood was warned not to journey too far from their own homes for over a week.

By the time the riots were finally under control by the middle of August, it still wasn't until a week later before the football coach said football practices would start. He also said that everyone trying out for the football team would need to spend two times a day practicing, once in the morning and later in the afternoon to make up for the time they'd lost because of the riots.

Jay had also decided to give up his ice cream route during that time to concentrate on football, but he was also starting to feel that riding around on his bicycle selling ice cream bars to kids wasn't a *cool image* to have now that he was going to be a sophomore in high school. He was satisfied that he had managed to save over two hundred dollars in his bank account in the past year from his ice cream route, but was ready to try something new that could be more fun.

Jay was a little concerned that he was still almost a year younger, and not quite as big as the other players trying out, because of the half year he jumped ahead in school years earlier, but he still wanted to prove to his coach that he could play quarterback that year.

When the practices started in late August, it was hard work because the weather was still hot, and learning to run plays in full uniforms and helmets was brutal. But it was more brutal when Jay learned he wouldn't be the starting quarterback when the school season began in September.

The head coach was named Mr. Ford, whose assistant coach Mr. Gilles was in charge of the Bee Football team and he designated Jay and another boy who tried out for quarterback as back-ups rather than naming them "second or third string."

Coach Ford said the boy Mr Gilles named starter just excelled a little better at practice, but told Jay and the other *back-up*, he was sure Coach Gilles would give them both "plenty of playing time" and to stay motivated.

Jay's father told him he should have started lifting weights a few years earlier so he would have been a big as the older boys on his team and seemed disappointed that he wasn't the starting quarterback. Although Jay still felt it was his father fault for moving so often that caused him to jump ahead a year at school which always had made him younger than anyone in his class, he still felt he could play as well as them if he just got the chance.

The Lakewood Bee football team was good, and they had won their first two games to start the season, but Jay had still been sitting on the bench and hadn't even played in one series during those games. But it was when they were playing against their third team that season, and had a big lead in the fourth quarter with only about five minutes left in that game, when he heard Coach Gilles yell out. "Mershon, you're up!"

Jay jumped up and put on his helmet and ran over to Coach Gilles who told Jay to run the plays he'd send into the huddles after each play. He was happy that the first play was a pass, but it was just a short screen pass he threw to a running back, who ended up gaining about five yards. He felt good that he completed his first pass as a quarterback, but after that one pass play, his coach kept sending in running plays to just run out the clock.

With only about a couple minutes left in the game, Jay turned after the snap to again hand off the football to the running back, and although he wasn't sure which one of them had gone in the wrong direction for the handoff, he saw the running back run by him without the ball.

Without thinking, Jay spun around, still holding the football, and started to run himself and instantly had visions of the pro quarterback Fran Tarkington, who was famous for being known as a *scrambler*, and thought about how *neat* it would be if he could run it in for a touchdown himself. But before he could even get back to the line of scrimmage, Jay saw two big defensive players almost flying in the air toward him and the next thing he knew, he was on the ground with a sharp pain in his left leg.

He got to his feet and limped off the field in pain as he heard Coach Gilles calling for the other "back-up" quarterback as if nothing had happened.

Back in the locker room after the game, some of the other coaches put ice on his swollen leg and said if it got worse to have a doctor look at it.

Jay ended up just limping home, hoping he could just walk it off, but he found out the next day it was broken. The doctor put a large cast up past his knee on his left leg and gave him crutches to use, and told him to stay off the leg as much as he could for the next couple months.

Besides knowing that his football season was over, and knowing he'd only be able to watch his football team while standing on crutches from the sideline for the rest of the games that year, Jay was mainly upset that he didn't get to be a star quarterback, or even score a touchdown to at least impress some of the girls at school.

That bothered him even more than having a broken leg.

❧

The next couple of months consisted of Jay's mother driving him to school and then picking him up to go home and nothing to do except homework, watch television, or play an occasional game of Pinochle, Gin Rummy, or Draw Poker with his parents on nights everyone was getting along.

Jay's father seemed upset that he had broken his leg the first time he was hit in a football game and again said Jay "should have been lifting weights" to make up for being younger and smaller than the other players, but Jay never argued back knowing it would probably just start a fight and more of the "silent treatment" which his parents still had at least a couple times a month.

Most of the time he spent while his leg was in a cast was in his bedroom with Tinker and reading a lot of books he'd been assigned to read in his classes.

His English class always assigned different books to read and write book reports, so he had plenty of time to handle those assignments while he recovered from his football injury. For history classes, Jay was also assigned historical books like *The Rise and Fall of the Third Reich* or biographies on historical leaders like Napoleon and Julius Caesar. Sometimes his teacher would let him choose his own favorite biography subject and explain why they were an influence on him, and one of the first subjects Jay chose to write about was George Gershwin. Besides *Porgy and Bess* and his classical music, Jay had learned almost all of Gershwin's popular songs when listening to different albums at *Wallich's Music City,* and was interested in learning more about Gershwin's life himself.

For Creative Writing, it was mainly fiction books he was assigned to learn the different writing styles of famous authors and read the books *Moby Dick, The Call of the Wild,* and *The Catcher in the Rye.* But aside from the books he needed to read for his classes, Jay had also started reading some of his parent's paperback books they had in the house.

One book he really liked was *Knock on Any Door,* which he'd also seen the movie version of starring Humphrey Bogart and an actor named John Derek who played a gangster named Nick Romano who often used the catchphrase "Live fast, die young and have a good-looking corpse." Jay had also brought that book to school, telling some of his friends they should read it because it also had some "good sex stuff" in it that wasn't in the movie.

Jay had some friends from Lakewood High School he had known since they were at Bancroft together, but mainly hung out three new friends that year named Dan Kittridge, Lee Volpe, and Reese Brisbane because of their shared interests in music, and most importantly, girls. He loaned the book *Knock on Any Door to* those three friends and it wasn't long before "live fast, die young and have a good-looking corpse" became a light, joking phrase amongst the four of them.

There were some other books his parents read that he found lying around the house with the book titles *A Stone for Danny Fisher*, *79 Park Avenue*, and *The Carpetbaggers* by an author named Harold Robbins that had even better "good sex stuff" that he started reading that year and would also share with his friends.

One of the main things Jay learned during his first year in high school was that Harold Robbins was his new favorite author, and it seemed his parents liked him too because there'd usually be a new Harold Robbins book every few months that he'd always find to read.

Unfortunately, those books only again reminded Jay that he hadn't met a girl he could even kiss in almost three years, but besides wanting to at least kiss a girl again, he also knew he wanted to eventually try to do some of the other things that were written about in those novels.

It was fun reading, but he knew it would be a lot more fun trying.

Chapter Thirteen

Even though his leg was completely healed from the year before, Jay had decided that he wouldn't even try to make the football team again the following year. Things had seemed to completely changed by early 1966, and even the athletes or "the jocks" as they were being called, were starting to be considered "not hip or cool," with a lot of those at his school.

Ronald Reagan also announced that he was going to run for Governor of California in early 1966, and Jay's parents said they were going to volunteer and work weekends passing out literature for Reagan like they had for Barry Goldwater, and Jay also decided he would help his "favorite movie star" and hand out bumper stickers and lawn signs to his neighbors as well.

He was mainly excited when he turned old enough in 1966 to get a "learner's driving permit" in California, and although he still couldn't drive a car until he was sixteen, he could drive a limited power motorcycle until then. His father helped him find a used *Honda 90* motorcycle that they could buy for less than a hundred dollars and agreed to pay half of it if Jay paid the other half with his money in his savings account.

It wasn't a full blown "motorcycle" like he had pictured in his head, but he was still thrilled that he finally had some *wheels*. He also wasn't allowed to take the motorcycle on the freeway or drive too far from home, but he did ride it to school every day and to all of his friends' houses.

Although he briefly thought about attaching an ice chest on the back of his "new wheels" to start an even bigger ice cream route to save up more money for an actual car when he'd turn sixteen in 1967, he again decided that being an "Ice Cream Man" seemed "dorky" or "not hip" and decided on another way to start making some extra cash.

The one place Jay did start to ride his motorcycle regularly that was about a fifteen-minute ride from Lakewood, was Los Alamitos Racetrack, which had quarter horse racing instead of longer thoroughbred races, but he was still able to make the same bets as the other racetracks he'd been to.

He wasn't old enough to be admitted without showing an ID, so he'd park his motorcycle over by a fence on the side of the racetrack, and then climb the fence to get inside. Jay also always wore sunglasses and a hat to try and hide the fact that he looked too young, and when he went to the cashier's window to make his bets, he'd try to speak in a lower voice and say, "Two dollars to show on number six," or whatever horse he was betting.

Jay started going there after school a few times a week before his parent's came home from work and was usually able to bet on the last three or four races of the day and sometimes was making an extra four or five dollars a week at the races. He would also usually exaggerate to his friends at school and usually say he was always winning over ten dollars a week at the races, which got his friends more interested. and were impressed that he was making "that much money" by just betting on horses.

When he explained that the minimum bet was two dollars each race, some of his friends at first said they couldn't afford it, but after seeing he always had more cash in his wallet than they had, a several of those he knew at school tried to pool fifty cents or a dollar between them and share in bets together and asked Jay to start making bets for them.

Each morning before he went to school, Jay started buying the *Daily Racing Form* and hid it amongst his books until he could show his friends during lunch which horses running that day, and find out who they wanted to bet on. His friends also didn't know how read the past performances of the horses the way he did, so they would all just pick out a horse by their name. He also saw they didn't know about the *Win, Place,* and *Show* betting, so they always just bet the horses to *Win*.

Jay noticed that some of the horses they picked out were real longshots and had very little chance to win, so he started only betting the horses that were five-to-one odds or less, deciding to keep the money for their bets on the "real longshots" for himself. He knew if they got lucky and won with a longshot, he'd have to get money from his savings account to pay them, but fortunately that never happened on the days he went to Los Alamitos and started pocketing an additional five or six dollars a week for himself along with any money he'd win by betting to *Show*. Jay wasn't getting rich, but it was fun and it was giving him enough money for gas and always have money in his pocket, and if he had a good week, he'd try to put some cash away in his savings account.

He was able to follow the routine of sneaking into the racetrack and make bets for several weeks, but there was one time when a guy in a suit approached him and pulled out a badge and asked to see Jay's driver's license. When Jay tried to just say that he "left it in his car" and couldn't prove he was twenty-one, the plain clothes officer, ended up escorting Jay from the racetrack and said, "Don't let me see you here again!"

Jay only waited about a week before trying to go back to the racetrack, but he remembered what the guy with the badge looked like, and would just be more careful and always look around before he made bets.

There were a few times when he did see that same guy again, and their eyes even made contact a couple of times, but Jay would just take off running and hop the fence back to his motorcycle and always get away.

But after several more times of going to the racetrack and managing to avoid getting caught, it was while he was in line to make a bet on the last race of the day and was looking down at his racing form when he felt a strong grip around his shoulders.

"Got ya this time *rabbit*!" he heard the voice say as he realized he'd been caught.

This time the plain clothes officer led Jay to a private office and called the police who took him to the Los Alamitos Police Station. The police had to call his mother at work to come and pick him up, but Jay noticed they were all kind of laughing with his mother as they let him out of a small jail cell after only about an hour.

Jay could see that the police were only half-serious when they said, "We're letting you go this time, but don't let us see you here again, or we'll charge you with gambling which is a serious crime!" Even Jay's father half laughed about it when he came home that night, but did tell Jay to wait until they all went to the racetrack together.

Although he decided not to try and sneak in to Los Alamitos Racetrack again, he was satisfied that he had "earned" back over half of the money he had paid for his motorcycle and had been able to put it back in his savings account.

For one of his assignments in his creative writing class that year, the teacher instructed the class to write an original story about an unusual experience they personally had, that was unique and be different from what the other students in the class may have experienced. Jay decided to write about his experience at the horse races and titled it *A Funny Thing Happened on the Way to the Racetrack,* and after writing about why he loved horse racing and gambling, he wrote a funny narrative about the one day he was arrested at Los Alamitos

Jay concluded his story by writing that "even though he was arrested" that one day, and knew he'd need to be more careful in the future, he liked "winning money too much" to let it ever deter him from betting on the horses again. He facetiously wrote that Hollywood Park would be opening soon and he'd "try that racetrack" next time, but it was the last line of his narrative that his teacher especially enjoyed, and wrote "Very funny and marvelous ending" on his paper when gave it back to him along with an "A+" for that story.

The last line was, "What's that? You think I'm a compulsive gambler? I'll bet you five bucks I'm not!"

❧

Throughout the rest of the school year and into the summer, Jay also continued passing out literature for Ronald Reagan's campaign for Governor, and just as he'd told his friends at school to tell their parents vote for Barry Goldwater two years earlier, he continued to do the same thing for Reagan.

Most of the others his age, weren't that interested in politics, and those who were considered the "hip kids" at school, were more into the popular music scene and were always talking about how cool the "hippies" were who they'd see on television that had started gathering in San Francisco and Hollywood. Some kids at his school tried to dress and grow their hair long like "hippies," but there was a strong dress code and they were often sent home to get their hair cut, along with the girls who tried to wear mini-skirts, which had also become "hip" to wear, but not allowed at his school.

Jay wasn't really interested in being a hippie type, except for his interest in the hippie music and what the hippie girls were calling their new attitudes about what was being called *Free Love*. The most important thing Jay felt he learned from the Harold Robbins novels he read, was that women loved sex as much, if not more, than the men in those books, and he knew all he needed was the opportunity.

He did like that some of the girls at school liked taking rides on the back of his motorcycle, but although the girls were always friendly, just giving them rides wasn't how he pictured becoming involved in romances like he'd read about in the Harold Robbins novels. He knew he'd have to wait until he got an actual car to drive after he turned sixteen before he would have that opportunity. Jay also felt that those at his high school seemed to be more like "fake hippies" who talked more about it than actually acted out the lifestyle, and it did seem like Lakewood was boring compared to what he'd see was happening in Hollywood.

Although it was less than thirty miles from Lakewood to Hollywood, Jay hadn't been there in over five years, and he knew he'd never want to ask his parents to drive him there and wouldn't be able to enjoy "the scene" with them. He also knew he wasn't allowed to ride his *Honda 90* that far away from home.

Jay did have a new friend he met that summer named Frank who had an older sister named Lynn who was eighteen years old, and who actually did consider herself a *real* hippie. She would always tell Jay and Frank how "groovy" it was in Hollywood and mentioned that she'd spend most weekends cruising Sunset Boulevard and going to nightclubs that always featured "bitchin' bands" that were great to "trip out" to. Lynn also offered to take Jay and Frank with her some weekend if they wanted to experience the "groovy scene" for themselves.

After Jay's parents said it would be alright as long as he was home by midnight, Jay jumped at the opportunity, and it was on a Saturday night when Jay took his first trip to Hollywood with Lynn and Frank. He also saw that just driving to Hollywood was an experience by itself.

Lynn would usually stop whenever she saw some cute hitchhikers who were also going to Hollywood, and by the time they arrived on the main drag of the Sunset Strip, their car would be filled with people that Lynn had given a ride to "join the

100

party." Lynn and almost all of the hitchhikers in the car would always talk about music, and how Bob Dylan, The Beatles, Joan Baez, and The Grateful Dead were the modern-day poets and philosophers, and how their music all had such deep meaning. They'd also talk about Timothy Leary, and how going on what they called "trips" had opened up their minds. Jay would always try to agree with them, so he'd seem more in tune with the hippie culture, and not just seem like a square high school kid.

Driving down the *Sunset Strip* was also always like a party, and music would be blasting from everyone's cars, while everyone was yelling and waving to each other as they leaned out of their car windows while they drove. They'd cruise past one car that was blasting *19th Nervous Breakdown* by the Rolling Stones and another, Bob Dylan's *Rainy-Day Women*, or another, *Hold On, I'm Comin'* by Sam and Dave.

Because Jay loved all the music that had been playing on the radio for the past couple of years, choosing a favorite song was impossible, so whatever song he usually heard, he'd always yell out to the car next to him, "That's my *favorite* song!"

He at least wanted to let everyone know he was "hip" to the new music scene.

Jay's first experience in Hollywood only lasted for a few hours because he needed to be home by midnight, but Lynn said if Jay's parents would let his stay out longer, she'd drive him up there again sometime.

Because it was still summer vacation that year, Jay was able to talk his parents into letting him stay out longer, at least on Saturday nights, and extended his curfew until one am on Saturday nights only. Although Lynn didn't take Jay and her brother to Hollywood every Saturday night, she'd usually take them at least once and sometimes twice a month on the nights she said she didn't have a date.

Because Jay was able to stay in Hollywood longer, Lynn had also tried to sneak Jay and her brother into a couple nightclubs where she hung out called the *Whiskey-a-Go-Go* and *The London Fog* which admitted eighteen-year-olds, but although they were able to sometimes "sneak in" without being noticed, someone would eventually ask for their identification, and they got kicked out. Fortunately, there were also two other places on the Sunset Strip where they didn't need ID's that Lynn liked to hang out called *The Fifth Estate* and *Pandora's Box* which was where they'd usually spend their Saturday nights when they weren't cruising.

The Fifth Estate was just a coffee house and always seemed to be playing the song *Season of the Witch* by Donovan, almost every time Jay was there with Lynn and her friends. Lynn explained *Season of the Witch* was a "good acid trip song" and also explained there was a nearby basement that had padding on the walls, where people could legally "drop LSD" and not hurt themselves, in case they did have a "bad trip."

But *Pandora's Box* was Jay's favorite spot because it had live bands playing where even those under eighteen years old could be admitted and also had a lot of "hippie girls" who were always there.

The big thing he noticed, was that the girls in Hollywood didn't look like anything like the girls he knew in Lakewood, and most wore mini-skirts, lips-stick, and makeup, which Jay again thought made them look sexier. He did talk to some of those girls and even danced with a few of them at *Pandora's Box*, but they always seemed disappointed after asking him where he lived.

Jay had heard the "hip crowd" at school always call their parents "my people," so when he told girls that he still lived with "my people" in Lakewood, they seemed to lose interest. But regardless of not meeting any new girlfriends yet, Jay still hoped that he eventually would with his frequent trips to Hollywood.

There were a few nights when he didn't get home till after one am, but his parents didn't seem to mind because it was a weekend, and they were usually asleep when he got home. Jay preferred not having to see them after a fun night out and was happy that it was only Tinker who would always be anxiously waiting at the front door for him and wagging her tail, no matter what time he got home.

He also knew Tinker was still the only reason he was ever anxious to come home at all.

Chapter Fourteen

When summer vacation was over that year and Jay went back to school, his parents did say that as long as he was done with his homework and kept his grades up, he could continue to stay out till one am on Saturday nights, but after only a couple months, and a few more trips to Hollywood, Lynn told Jay and her brother that she had some "bummer" news.

She said there had been complaints about the noise and the crowds from the businesses in Hollywood, and the police were going to start enacting a ten pm curfew for anyone under eighteen years old. She added that because she didn't want to leave "the Strip" that early on Saturday nights, she wouldn't be able to drive Jay or Frank to Hollywood any longer.

But surprisingly, it was less than two weeks later, and the Saturday after Ronald Reagan had won the election for Governor, when Lynn cheerfully called Jay with some exciting news.

Lynn started describing to Jay about what she called a big *"Happening"* in Hollywood that night, which was going to be a protest over the ten pm curfew and a plan to close down Jay's favorite nightclub, *Pandora's Box*. She said there'd probably be hundreds of kids under eighteen years old showing up who decided to protest in front of *Pandora's Box* for their own *Civil Rights*, the way the negros had been doing for the past couple years. She added that even though her brother Frank couldn't go, because he was on "restriction' that weekend, Jay was welcome to come if he wanted to hitch a ride with her.

He told Lynn he definitely wanted to come along and wanted to protest with everyone, especially if they could convince the police to drop the ten pm curfew and he could start going to Hollywood again. Plus, Jay's parents had already told him they were going to a victory party that night for the volunteers who had worked on the Reagan campaign, and said they wouldn't be home until late that night themselves.

Jay was at least happy that Reagan had defeated Governor Pat Brown in the election earlier that week, even though the Democrats and Brown had tried to use the same tactics that had worked against Barry Goldwater two years earlier. They had also tried to claim Reagan was "mentally unstable" as well as a "right-wing extremist" who would turn California into a police state with his "law and order" ideology. But it hadn't worked that year, and Reagan had won the governorship in a landslide regardless. When Jay found out that Reagan wouldn't personally be at the victory party his parents were going to and he wouldn't be able to meet him again, he had no interest in attending it with his parents and knew it would be more fun to go to Hollywood that night with Lynn.

Jay was already waiting in the driveway when he saw Lynn wave to him from a different car than he'd been used to seeing, and saw that she was with a new boyfriend who would be driving them to Hollywood. As he got in the back seat, he was briefly irritated when he heard her boyfriend start to complain about having to drive "a kid" with them, but Lynn assured him that Jay was "cool" and wouldn't be a problem. Jay also didn't like that after he mentioned that his parents had gone to a victory party for Ronald Reagan that night, Lynn's boyfriend started calling Reagan "a fascist" and how California was "going to suck" having him as Governor. Jay decided not to argue with him knowing that it might cost him his ride to Hollywood, but did see that her boyfriend wasn't like the usual fun people that he had traveled to Hollywood with before and already didn't like him. It was after eight pm by the time they got to Hollywood, and they had to park several blocks away from *Pandora's Box* because the streets were so jammed with people, as well jammed with the police.

As they all walked down Sunset Boulevard towards *Pandora's Box*, it seemed every other song Jay heard coming from the cruising cars that night was *Last Train to Clarksville* or *96 Tears*, and even when they stood outside *Pandora's Box* with the several hundred other protesters, those two songs seemed to be playing regularly with other rock songs which almost made the protests seem like a party.

It was shortly before ten pm when Jay saw some problems were starting to begin after the police started using a megaphone to announce the curfew was about to go into effect, and everyone under eighteen had to disperse from the area. Before then, it was a fairly peaceful protest, and everyone was just walking around with signs, chanting, singing along with songs that were coming from passing cars, and just generally having fun.

After the police made that announcement, everyone started booing and Jay heard Lynn's boyfriend yell, "Fuck the Police" which made everyone else start yelling "fuck the police" as well.

It wasn't long before dozens of more police officers started to arrive and started trying to push back the crowds and started attempting to arrest some of them. Several the cars on the street also started to stop in front of *Pandora's Box* with their horns honking, and some people started getting out of their cars to join the crowd of protesters who were starting to fight with the police.

It was after Jay heard some glass breaking and heard someone yell, "TEAR GAS!" when several groups started running away from *Pandora's Box*, and not seeing either Lynn or her boyfriend, Jay started running with a group down Sunset Boulevard who were now being chased by the police themselves. He was thinking how he didn't want to get arrested and have to call his parents to get him out of jail again, so he broke away from that group and ran to a side street off Sunset, far enough away where he hoped he wouldn't be found.

Jay was concerned about being separated from Lynn and her boyfriend, but could see there was a still a big commotion going on towards where *Pandora's Box* was and didn't want to go back and try to look for them and take the chance he'd be arrested.

It was after eleven pm before he wandered back onto Sunset Boulevard, but figured he'd never find Lynn and forgot where her boyfriend had even parked his car, but was getting more worried about how he was going to get home that night.

Jay decided he'd walk down Sunset Boulevard in the opposite direction of *Pandora's Box* hoping that Lynn and her boyfriend would see him walking, but by the time he got to a restaurant called *Ben Franks*, he pretty much knew he was stranded and started trying to figure out what to do.

He didn't want to hitchhike along Sunset Boulevard where the police might see him, so he started asking people in the parking lot who were leaving *Ben Franks* in their cars, if any of them were going anywhere toward Lakewood and would be willing to give him a ride. It did take almost an hour of asking, but he did finally meet a girl who said she lived in Bellflower, a city that bordered Lakewood, and cheerfully said she'd give gladly him a ride all the way to his house.

Jay was relieved when they drove away from Hollywood and all the police activity, and although he was briefly concerned that Lynn and her boyfriend were still looking for him, he was just glad to be heading home.

After he found out the girl's name who had given him a ride was Angie, he listened to her start to complain almost non-stop how that night had turned into a "bad trip and a bummer" and how angry she was that the cops had to ruin such a "groovy happening." But she also cheerfully added how "bitchin" it was to meet Sonny and Cher in person earlier that night when she was protesting herself and fighting with the police in front of *Pandora's Box.* Jay was slightly disappointed he didn't see Sonny and Cher that night, but figured he must have been too busy running.

Jay also learned Angie was eighteen years old and had graduated from Bellflower High School earlier that year, and had taken six months off to have some fun before she was planning on attending Long Beach City College in February when a new semester would begin. Jay decided to fib a bit and said he'd be "graduating high school the next year, but hadn't decided on which college to attend yet.

He thought Angie was cute and had interesting look, but not quite as sexy as some of the other girls he saw in Hollywood. She had straight blond hair and wore pink-colored glasses, but she had a nice smile, and he liked her bubbly personality.

As she was speeding down the freeway heading back toward Long Beach, and after she turned up the radio full-blast when she heard what she said was her favorite song *Last Train to Clarksville* start playing again, Angie reached in her purse and grabbed a cigarette. But, when she lit it, and the aroma filled the air, Jay immediately knew what it was. He hadn't seen or smoked marijuana before, and when she handed a joint toward him to offer a *hit*, he just said, "No thanks, I already had one tonight."

Jay was still trying to act *hip* but was mainly worried that he might get arrested with her if they got pulled over because she was driving so fast, but he continued trying to act relaxed and just listened to Angie talk about the different bands she'd seen in Hollywood and they talked about all of the favorite new songs they both currently liked. She also talked about how some friends of hers were going to another protest in a couple of weeks against the Vietnam War, and she couldn't wait to go.

"That fucking Johnson keeps sending more troops to Vietnam, and we've got to stop him," she bitterly said.

Jay wanted to sound knowledgeable and added, "Yeah, if Goldwater would've won the election a couple years ago, he'd have won the war by now, and it would be over."

He had already seen on the news how some of the older "hippies" had started protesting the selective service draft and refusing to be sent to Vietnam, the country "nine thousand miles away" that President Johnson promised never to send "American boys" to fight. Jay didn't want to say anything to disagree with Angie that might cause her to not drive him home, and even though most of his friends, as well as his parents supported the war in Vietnam, he didn't mention it.

When Angie finally pulled off the freeway on Del Amo Boulevard to drive toward Lakewood, she casually put her hand on Jay's leg and started rubbing it.

"So, do you want to ball?" she smiled, "I was kinda hoping that I might get laid tonight but the cops ruined those plans."

Jay knew the hip crowd said "ball" instead of "screw" or "fuck" and he wasn't about to let her think he wasn't *hip*, and although he was slightly nervous, he casually said in his same deeper voice he had used at Los Alamitos Racetrack, "Sure, but where can we go? I still live with *my people*.".

Angie just pulled into the Lakewood Center Shopping Mall, which was empty at that hour, and said just as casually, "We can just do it here," as she parked her car in a dark area and started to take off her top.

"Just don't come inside me," she added as she leaned back on the bench seat of her car as they started to kiss.

Jay knew how important it was to make Angie think he knew what he was doing and act as confident as the characters that were in books that he'd read. He also knew he'd practiced enough by himself for the past couple years and had been waiting for this opportunity for a long time and was ready to go. But although he immediately had to "pull out" less than a minute after being inside of her, he saw that Angie liked that he didn't lose his erection afterwards and was immediately ready to "do it again" and continued for over ten more minutes more before having to "pull out" for a

106

second time. He could also tell by Angie's moans that he had done alright and knew he was finally experiencing the best night of his life.

When Angie told him how good it felt and wanted to "do it again" after she took a couple more puffs off her marijuana cigarette, Jay realized he was finally an *Adventurer*, just like one of his favorite characters in a Harold Robbins novel he had read earlier that year.

It had taken him a few years, but he was excited that he finally was going to have a *real* girlfriend.

❧

Jay discovered the next morning that Lynn's boyfriend had been arrested the night before and she had been at the police station all night waiting for him to be released from jail, but said she was relieved that Jay had make it home okay. He didn't go into any details with her, but although he hadn't liked her boyfriend and was glad that he got into trouble, Jay also appreciated that he was somewhat responsible for how he had experienced "the best night of his life."

He had also given Angie his home phone number after she said she didn't have a telephone and was excited when she had also called him the next day saying "how much fun" she had the night before. Angie also excitedly told Jay that there was going to be another protest on the *Sunset Strip* that night, and asked Jay to join her and volunteered to pick him up at his house later.

Jay knew that Sunday was a school night and there was no way his parents would let him go to Hollywood, but besides not wanting to possibly get in trouble or arrested himself, he still tried to sound cool not wanting to disappoint her.

"I have school tomorrow and I need to stay home with *my people*," he said before adding with excitement, "But I can see you next Friday and Saturday night!"

He noticed Angie was silent for a few seconds, but finally asked, "Tell me, Jay, how old are you really?"

Jay decided to be honest with her and figured if they were going to be seeing each other regularly, he'd eventually have to tell her the truth.

"Well," Jay tried to say with confidence, "I'll be sixteen in a few more months."

There was brief silence again but heard her sigh, "Wow…fifteen…."

Angie quickly said that even though the night before was fun, that "maybe he should stick to girls his own age" and said a quick "Bye" before hanging up.

Jay wished he could immediately call her back, but knew she was calling him from a payphone and that she didn't have a home number. He didn't even know Angie's last name or where she lived in Bellflower and suddenly was very unhappy that he told her the truth and wished he'd lied to her about his age. But at the same time, he was still feeling very happy about the night before, and still hoped that she liked how he had performed and would eventually call him back.

But she never did.

Over the next two weeks, Jay started playing another popular song on his record player regularly, *Wouldn't It Be Nice* the latest single by *The Beach Boys*, and kept thinking how true the lyrics were about what he wished he could have said to Angie.

He remembered how Joyce Paxton had once said the song *A Summer Place* was "our song" and thought how the lyrics in *Wouldn't It Be Nice* about how "nice" it could be when *they were older, could stay together*, and eventually *live together*, might have become his and Angie's song if he could have just seen her a couple more times.

Jay finally accepted that he wouldn't be seeing Angie again, and in early 1967, another song would come out by the band *Buffalo Springfield* that was inspired by that night Jay was in Hollywood called *For What It's Worth*. The singer and composer Steven Stills said he had written that song to describe what he saw that same night at what had become known as "*The Riot on the Sunset Strip.*"

Every time Jay heard the chorus to stop and listen to "that sound" and to look at what was "going down" in that song, he knew it would be one of his favorites of all time. He also knew that *For What It's Worth*, along with *Last Train to Clarksville* would be two songs that would always remind him of that night and Angie.

Jay just hoped that she would at least think of him once in a while when she heard one of those songs as well.

Chapter Fifteen

With the curfew in Hollywood having never been lifted, as well as Lynn deciding to move to a city called Berkeley with her boyfriend, Jay hadn't gone back to Hollywood since that one night, but it wasn't long after he turned sixteen years old, when he was very excited about something else that became more important to him. Jay was now old enough to drive a car, and after he was able to sell his *Honda 90* for almost the same price he paid for it, his father said he'd help him find a reasonably priced car to buy. Because his father said turning sixteen years old was an important age, he agreed to pay cash for a used car not more than six hundred dollars, as long as Jay would pay him back half of the price to learn how to start paying bills himself and learn about responsibility.

Jay did get a part-time job after school at an *Orange Julius* restaurant where he'd earn enough to pay back twenty-five dollars a month over the next year and also have enough money left over to pay for gas to drive around having fun. The car Jay found in his price range that he liked was a used 1964 Chevy Impala convertible that the owner had originally asked seven-hundred and fifty dollars for, but said he'd take six hundred and fifty if his father paid him cash. The car also had over sixty thousand miles with a couple dings on the bumper along some small tears in the convertible top, but although his father had said that cars with over fifty thousand miles were usually "shot" and ready for the junkyard with that many miles on it, when he looked at the Impala with Jay and saw it still "drove okay," he said it should be good for at least "a couple more years" and agreed to pay cash after he'd talked the owner down to six hundred dollars. His father had spent almost the past two years working with someone Jay had often seen on television named *Madman Muntz*, and his father said he'd been making "real good money" selling the new stereos people were beginning to install inside their cars called "tape decks" that could play entire music albums, so he said paying for the car in cash was no problem. His father also said he'd install a new tape deck in Jay's car as an additional present. Jay was mainly excited that he was able to actually have his own car before any other of his friends and couldn't wait to take them for a drive. But the first one to get a ride in his "new car" was Tinker, who although was getting older and heavier, never hesitated when Jay said "wanna go for a ride?" and always ran as fast as she could to jump in the car and ride along with him.

When Jay did start driving his friends like Dan, Lee and Reese to school, he did think the Impala drove fine except it did seem to overheat a couple times a week and Jay would regularly need to stop at gas stations to put water in the radiator. His usual command to the gas station attendant was, "Give me fifty cents worth of regular, wash the windshield, check the air in the tires, and put water in the radiator."

Jay and his friends would laugh when the attendant didn't take the radiator cap off slow enough, which caused the hot water to shoot out like a volcano, and always make the attendant fall backward. There also seemed to be a problem with the muffler because it sometimes often backfired, but Jay and his friends found a way to turn that problem into something that was fun.

They discovered that while they were driving, they could turn off the ignition and coast for a few seconds, and the Impala would let off a loud backfire when they turned the ignition on back on. The more they did it, the louder it became, and Jay and his friends had fun watching people jump when they'd drive down the street, leaving loud explosions. Sometimes his friends would hold their arms out the window, pretending they were aiming a rifle at someone, and watch people dive for cover when they heard the loud explosion and see a glimpse of someone apparently aiming at them. Some of people would yell at them and shake their fists, but after a while, some of those in his neighborhood knew to just to hold their hands over their ears when they saw Jay driving down the street, accepting that although it was irritating, it was funny at the same time.

Another big benefit of owning his own car was that Jay and his friends could go "cruising" like the older teenagers, but knowing they were still too young to go to Hollywood, there was another "cruising" strip along nearby Bellflower Boulevard in the same city where Angie once said she lived. Although Jay at first wondered if he'd ever see Angie cruising along the same strip, he finally decided it would be more fun to find someone new, and someone who hadn't "dumped him" just because of his age.

All of the older teenagers would mainly spend all night driving back and forth along Bellflower Boulevard, showing off their cars, and trying to look cool when they made eye contact with cars full of girls they hoped to "get lucky" with, which was the term they used for meeting someone who wanted to have sex. They also would try to show what kind of image they wanted to convey by the songs and music they'd blast from their car radios.

From some cars, songs like *San Francisco (Be sure to wear some flowers in your hair)*, by Scott McKenzie, *Get Together* by The Youngbloods, or *White Rabbit* by Jefferson Airplane would be playing loudly insinuating they had the San Francisco "peace and love' hippie mindsets, while others would be blasting Wilson Pickett or Aretha Franklin songs like *Mustang Sally* or *R-E-S-P-E-C-T* demonstrating their interest in "soul" music.

110

The girls in the cars would act less aggressively and play mellower songs, like *Groovin'* by The Rascals, *There's a Kind of Hush All Over the World* by Herman's Hermits, or *Never My Love* by The Association.

Jay would turn up the volume on the radio when he heard some of his current favorite songs like *Light My Fire* by The Doors, *I Think We're Alone Now,* by Tommy James and the Shondells, or *Gimme Some Lovin'* by the Spencer Davis Group, but mainly played his collection of albums on his tape deck.

His favorite album was currently *Green Grass and High Tides*, which had most of The Rolling Stones greatest hits, so when he cruised by a carload of girls, *Get Off My Cloud, It's All Over Now, Play with Fire* or *19th Nervous Breakdown* would usually be the songs blasting from his car.

If the girls didn't respond to their taste in music or show interest in them when they cruised by, Jay's friend Dan would usually just say, "Those girls are probably all *on the rag*" which the term the guys were calling girls on their *periods*, or Lee would sometimes stick his butt at them and pretend he was going to "moon them" and one time actually did. His friends would usually just encourage Jay to leave a loud backfire from his muffler to scare the girls who ignored them, before cruising to the next carload of pretty girls.

Because Jay's friends Dan, Reese and Lee all liked Tinker, they'd sometimes bring her along the cruise strip, figuring she'd also be an attention-getter to meet more girls and whenever they'd park and order food at the *A&W Root Beer Drive-In* on Bellflower Boulevard, it did seem to work and the girls would always want to come over at pet Tinker when they saw her in the car.

But besides just cruising, they'd sometimes go to the Long Beach Pike amusement park to meet girls, as well as another nightclub that was similar to *Pandora's Box* in Long Beach called *The Cinnamon Cinder*. Because that nightclub didn't serve alcohol, even teenagers under eighteen were allowed to attend, and that was where Jay met some girls he started asking out on "dates" to usually go to the drive-in movies.

Most of the girls he'd take on dates were actually a year or two older than him and he did decide to make a couple changes to his appearance to make himself appear older. Jay started to let his hair grow a little longer and went to a barber who gave him a new look which involved blow drying his hair and styling it in place with hair spray and also always added a year or two to his age figuring they'd believe him because he had his own car. But he also saw some girls were disappointed that he didn't have any "pot" to smoke, or even what some of the girl's called "reds" which was the name of the prescription drug "Seconal" that they seemed to like, especially if Jay expected them to make-out" on their dates. Although Jay wanted nothing to do with "pot" or "pills" that he knew could get him arrested, the girls would always ask Jay to at least bring along some beer or *Boone's Farm Strawberry Hill* wine so they could "get high" together when they went to the drive-in movies or parked by the beach.

Before he picked any of them up for dates. Jay would just stand outside liquor stores and patiently wait until some older person, who was over twenty-one years old, would agree to buy some liquor for him, and once he was able to secure beer or wine for the night, the girls always became friendlier and more romantic.

Jay was slightly disappointed himself, that although the girls did like to "make-out" and kiss passionately when they drank the beer or wine together, his first few dates only turned into what was known as "dry-humping" when the girls either claimed they were still virgins, or were afraid of getting pregnant, and would never go "all the way" as he had with Angie.

Although it was still pleasurable, and he was always able to have orgasms on the outside of their panties, that was as far as any of those girls would go. Jay did hope that one of them might turn into a regular girlfriend and eventually go "all the way" but when they learned that Jay still lived at home with his parents, they seemed disappointed and his dates that summer usually just turned into a one-night encounter in the back seat of his car.

1967 was known as the *Summer of Love*, but even though Jay still hadn't had what he considered a real girlfriend who had "gone all the way" since Angie, Jay knew that even with the "almost sex" he was having with several different girls he met that year, he was gaining the experience that was starting to make him feel like a real *Playboy*, not only like the ones in that particular magazine, but like the ones in the books he still read as well.

෨

When Jay started his senior year at Lakewood High School, the studies were more demanding, and term papers were required in several classes in order to get passing grades to graduate the following year in 1968.

During his first semester in English that year, his class would be studying what his teacher called "Romantic Heroes in Literature" and would be required to write a lengthy-term paper profiling their own personal favorite literary character which would determine their first semester grade.

At the beginning of that semester his class had group readings of literary characters his teacher explained were considered *romantic hero's*, such as Jay Gatsby from *The Great Gatsby*, Rhett Butler from *Gone with the Wind*, Jean Valjean from *Les Misérables*, and Cyrano de Bergerac from the book of the same name.

Jay liked that he was chosen to read the lead role of Cyrano de Bergerac during the class reading because he had seen the film a few times on *The Million Dollar Movie*, and figured he could "ham it up" and be funny the way he remembered the actor Jose Ferrer acted in the movie. He was never interested in the secondary roles and remembered how disappointed he was when he wasn't chosen to play the lead role

112

Chapter Sixteen

It was in January 1968 when Jay and his parents started noticing that Tinker was having difficulty walking, and although she still seemed happy, she was starting to drag her hind leg and Jay would have to lift her to sleep in bed with him each night.

Jay and his parents took her to the veterinarian several times trying to get medicine and treatments to help her leg get better, but after the vet told them Tinker had a "type of cancer" and may need an operation to cure her disease, his parents told the vet that they'd do "whatever it took" to make her better, and immediately made plans for Tinker to have surgery within a week.

Jay would spend all of the time with Tinker when he wasn't at school for the next week, and saw she still seemed fine and happy whenever she was lying down with him and just hoped that she wouldn't have to limp anymore after the operation.

On the night before Tinker was scheduled to go to the animal hospital, he stayed awake in bed until after midnight, petting her and assuring her that "everything was going to be alright," and told her he'd see her when he came home from school the next day.

The operation was scheduled in the morning while Jay was at school, and during the lunch break, he immediately went to a payphone to call home to see how everything went. It was also raining hard that day, and he was already wet from standing in the phone booth impatiently waiting for his mother to answer the phone, and when she finally did, Jay immediately asked how Tinker was and if she'd be home when he finished school that day.

After a brief pause, his mother said in a very soft voice he could barely hear, "Tinker died....," before she just started crying into the phone.

Jay didn't want to believe what he'd just heard and quickly hung up the phone hoping what his mother had said was a mistake. He also didn't want to call her back and hear her say that again, but suddenly, Jay's chest felt like it was about to burst and he felt like he couldn't breathe, as he stood at the payphone for several minutes not moving and just trying to catch his breath.

He kept thinking there had to be something he could do to make it not be true and also was starting to hate himself for not going to the animal hospital with her so he could have made sure nothing like that would have happened to her. Jay also didn't even think about going back to school and just got into his car and started driving.

The pain in his chest was pounding as he drove in silence and he started breathing even heavier thinking about how she had always been the most important thing in his life, and he didn't want anything except for her to be in his bed like always that night. Jay also didn't even want to go home without seeing Tinker there, and just started driving not wanting to believe that he'd never be able to talk to her again or tell her how much he loved her.

Jay tried listening to the radio and turned it to the oldies station *KWIZ* to clear his mind with music, but because it was raining, one of the songs the DJ was playing was *Raindrops* by Dee Clark, which only caused Jay to associate the lyrics with his feelings about Tinker, and how "a man wasn't supposed to cry" as he just drove in silence. There were other old songs he'd hear like *Take Good Care of My Baby* by Bobby Vee, that only caused Jay to associate the lyrics as if it was his prayer for someone in Heaven to take care of Tinker, or as he was really praying, to "bring my baby back home to me."

He didn't know how long he had been aimlessly driving, but it was well after dark, and it was still raining before Jay finally went home that night. The house was completely silent with only a couple of lights turned on, and when he saw his parents sitting on the couch, they didn't, or couldn't, say anything to him as he walked in.

Jay could see his mother with a handkerchief wiping her eyes and knew she had been crying, and even saw that his father's eyes were red and watery, but there was also nothing they could say to each other, so Jay just walked directly into his bedroom and shut the door.

As he sat on his bed just staring at where his dog and always slept next to him, he kept breathing deep breaths trying to make the pain go away, but he knew what was causing the pain, and that was what was bothering him the most.

Although he had never felt any type of sadness in his life as much as he was feeling then, he just couldn't let his tears flow and it was hurting him even more that he couldn't cry for his *Tinker Bell.*

∾

The following month was very somber and Jay couldn't go to school or work for several days, and when he finally did return, he had no enthusiasm or interest and didn't even want to spend time with his friends.

He always tried not to return home from school until after dark for several weeks because he couldn't bear going home to what he felt was like an empty house and there was also only short, polite dialogue with his parents, with none of them wanting to speak about anything that would remind them of the loss they all felt. Jay never asked, and really never wanted to know if Tinker had died during the operation, or if his parents had just decided to put her to sleep knowing that she couldn't be cured. He also couldn't bring himself to attend the funeral his parents had for Tinker at a pet

116

cemetery they had arranged, and didn't want to see his dog in any type of casket being buried knowing how much that would hurt him again. He decided he wanted just remember her as when she was alive and not think about her death, but everything had changed since then, and he felt that nothing would ever feel normal again. Jay thought it was weird, but what finally seemed to bring along some type of normalcy after the long period of mourning, was when his parents started to fight with each other again. He had always learned how to ignore their arguments, but since Tinker's death it was getting different and even more bitter.

Although he'd seen both of them start conflicts in the past, he began to notice that his mother would always try to escalate the arguments until it would turn into a full-fledged fight. She had also become even more bitter during the arguments and even started trying to get Jay upset with his father by revealing some of the reasons his parents had always fought. She said the reason they had moved so much when he was younger, especially sometimes in the middle of the night, was because his father had never made enough money to pay the rent and they always had to move before they were evicted.

"Your father always thought he was a *hot shot* salesman and could always make enough money for us," she'd sarcastically say to Jay in front of his father, "But why do you think I've always had to work for all these year's?"

"The reason we had to move so often when you were young is because your father always had bill collectors after him," she snidely added, "That's why we always had to leave in the middle of the night when no one would see us leave."

"If I hadn't worked for all those years, you could have never even started your roller skating or taken those trips across the county each year," she'd snidely add, "It was always my money that helped pay for everything."

Jay's father would usually just sit in silence drinking a beer or cocktail with an angry scowl on his face trying to ignore what she was saying

"At least he has a decent job now and is finally making good money," she'd add with more sarcasm, "But we'll see how long that lasts."

Jay would usually hear his father finally start to say, "That's enough Violet! That's enough Violet!" louder each time, but she'd keep on yelling until he'd sometimes throw a glass or something else against a wall in anger and breaking it.

They didn't even try to go into their "silent treatment" when Jay was around any longer, and they would loudly scream and swear at each other until one of them angrily left the house and get in their car and drove away for several hours.

It was also during one of their fights, when it also came out that the Cuban Missile Crisis and the concern about an atomic war breaking out, wasn't the *real* reason they had to leave Buena Park in 1962. His mother again escalated one of the arguments by snidely telling Jay that the reason they left Buena Park so quickly was because she had discovered that his father had "a thing" going on with Joyce's aunt Joanie and his mother had insisted they had move away and not communicate with anyone there again or she was going to divorce his father.

His mother obviously wanted Jay to blame his father for being the reason for any disappointments he'd had, from having missed a half year at school, to having to had quit roller skating and losing contact with all of his friends from back then.

But also, now that he was older, there was something else that Jay knew about.

He knew when his parents' wedding anniversary was, and knew his math and biology well enough to realize that he was born less than six months after they were married and it was obvious to him now, that they were forced to get married because his mother was already pregnant. Jay also knew enough about sociology and knew when his parents had been growing up and younger themselves, an unwed mother who had what was known as an "illegitimate child" was basically shamed and shunned, as was the child who was labeled a "bastard" if it was discovered the parents weren't married when they were born.

Jay never talked to his parents about it and always kept it to himself, but he was certain they knew he had figured that out by now. He guessed that they probably had never really loved each other in the first place and had only stayed together because of him, and was probably the main reason they had argued and fought with each other for as long as he could remember.

There had never been affection between his parents that Jay could remember, and he couldn't recall ever seeing them kissing, hugging, or even saying "I love you" to each other, but Jay also couldn't remember doing any of that himself either.

Almost all of their affection for as far back as he could remember always went to Tinker, and she seemed to be the bond that made them a family and the one they would always show the most affection.

But without Tinker, they weren't really a family anymore, and with her gone, it seemed there was no affection for any of them left to give.

Chapter Seventeen

Jay still wasn't in the right frame of mind to pursue a "social life" and all he wanted to do over the next few months was finish up his last year in high school, go to work and sleep.

In the early spring of 1968 to avoid spending that much time at home with his parents, Jay also decided to get a second part-time job working a graveyard shift from at a *Der Wienerschnitzel* drive-through restaurant from midnight till six am a few nights during the week. Although he had to go to school almost immediately after he finished those shifts at *Der Wienerschnitzel*, he decided to start taking a couple of *No-Doz* caffeine pills that were in his parent's medicine cabinet, along with starting to drink coffee at work to stay awake when he went to school.

Jay only had about three months until graduation, so he figured he could handle the workload till then and mainly went home to sleep after school when he had the graveyard shifts, and worked his other job at *Orange Julius* on the days after school when he hadn't worked the night before. His main plan for the rest of that year was to save enough money so he could move out of his parent's house by the time he turned eighteen years old in 1969.

It was also in the spring of 1968 when Jay decided he didn't want the name his parents had given him and wanted to feel like a new and different person, so he had announced to his friends at school he wanted to start being addressed as *Jason Mershon* from now on. Having a new name did help change his frame of mind, but although there were some memories of being *Jay* that he wouldn't forget, there were many others he preferred not to remember.

1968 was also a presidential election year and having still been following politics since he had once joked to his friend's that he had "helped Ronald Reagan win the governorship" by passing out buttons, bumper stickers, and lawn signs in 1966, Jason was following the presidential campaigns as another diversion from everything else he'd been thinking about that year.

President Johnson had surprised everyone in the country when he announced that he wouldn't be seeking re-election at the end of March, when it had become obvious that a majority of those in America blamed his policies for the civil unrest in the country. Before Johnson had started his term in 1965, there had been less than four hundred US soldiers who had been killed in Vietnam, but in the three years since he'd been re-elected president, there were over thirty thousand Americans who had been killed in the war.

The television news stations had been broadcasting stories almost nightly about various conflicts in Vietnam that were killing more American soldiers, as well as protests and demonstrations against the war that were occurring at college campuses and in major cities across America.

There were several candidates from both political parties who were using "ending the war in Vietnam" as their main campaign issues including a Democrat Senator from Oregon named Eugene McCarthy who had been President Johnson's strongest critic. But since Johnson announced he wasn't seeking reelection, John F Kennedy's brother Bobby Kennedy, who was now a Senator from New York, had also decided to run for the Democrat nomination as an "anti-war" candidate against McCarthy, even though many had blamed President Kennedy for having first become involved in Vietnam when he was still in office.

On the Republican side, Richard Nixon who most everyone thought was finished in politics after losing the presidential election to John F Kennedy in 1960, and then even losing the election for Governor of California to Pat Brown in 1962, and famously saying to the press, "You won't have Nixon to kick around anymore," was again running for the Republican nomination against the Governors of New York and Michigan, Nelson Rockefeller and George Romney. There was also one other Democrat who had actually run against President Johnson in the 1964 primaries named George Wallace from Alabama, who had formed a new political party called the *American Independent Party*, after complaining that "There's not a dime's worth of difference between the Democrat and Republican parties." Wallace was also critical with the way Johnson was conducting the war in Vietnam, but was mainly opposed to Johnson's civil rights policies and was campaigning mainly on "States Rights" regarding segregation of negros without interference from the federal government, which had also been causing division in America the past decade, but even more so in 1968.

Jason was working the counter during one of his after-school shifts at *Orange Julius* on April 4, 1968, when he first heard a bulletin on the radio reporting that Martin Luther King was shot in Memphis and was dead, but also saw one of the customers at the counter of *Orange Julius* seemed unconcerned and just said, "It's about time someone took care of that Martin Luther *Coon* for riling up all the colored people the past five years!"

He figured the customer was trying to get a laugh, but Jason had already heard some kids at school and others call him Martin Luther *"Coon"* instead of "King" so many times before it had gotten old by then, and only a couple customers in the restaurant laughed his attempted humor that day.

Jason had already seen that most people were becoming more afraid of offending the black people by 1968, when militant groups like the *Black Panthers* had formed after the Watts Riots in 1965, and along with other groups like the *Black Muslims*, and another black leader named Stokely Carmichael, were encouraging all black people to enact their "Second Amendment Rights" and begin arming themselves with guns to fight with what they said was a coming race war against "white" America.

Almost everyone had also stopped using the term "Colored people" or "Negros" any longer, and were just calling them by their preferred term of "Black" since the slogan "Black Power" had started being used a couple years earlier by civil rights groups.

With all the threats of violence and some other "race riots" that had occurred in the United States the past couple years, there were a lot of people who had been moving away from the downtown areas of cities that had large black populations that were known as "high crime areas" and "bad neighborhoods" just as Jason's father had once said was a reason they had moved from downtown Los Angeles when he was younger.

After riots again started to break out after the assassination of Martin Luthor King, the owners of both restaurants where Jason worked, hired armed security guards for the entire week after it was being reported on the news that "white businesses and white people" were again the main targets of the rioters and looters.

The riots and looting were even more violent and destructive than the Watts Riots were a few years earlier, with fires and looting being shown non-stop on television from almost every major city in the country, which many also calling it the beginning of a second "Civil War" in America.

President Johnson not only called on the National Guard to assist the police in fighting the mobs, but also invoked the federal "Insurrection Act" and had actual soldiers from Army to fight against them after they came within two blocks of the White House, and also had the Marines set up machine guns in front of the US Capital ready to fire on them if they tried to attack. In some other major cities, mayors like Chicago's Richard Daley encouraged law enforcement to "shoot to kill" any rioters who were engaging in destructive acts, and Jason did see that it was again starting to look like the television war coverage in Vietnam.

Although there never was any major rioting or destruction near to where he lived and worked, after what was also called the *"Black Insurrection"* came under control in less than a week, Jason saw that those at his school still weren't nearly as concerned about being affected by the racial violence as they were about the war in Vietnam.

Jason had already heard about some students from Lakewood High School who'd graduated in the past couple years that had already been killed in the war, and while some of his friends were pro-war and couldn't wait to go to Vietnam and "whip some commie ass!" there were others who were completely against the war and were siding with those presidential candidates who were calling it a "dirty war" that could never be won.

Even though Jason and his friends knew they wouldn't even be able to vote until they were twenty-one, there was so much happening in in the county it was almost impossible not want to be involved with was happening in the United States in some way. Because it was also another diversion from just going to school and working, and also because he was still the only one in his group of friends who had a car, Jason did decide to attend some political rallies that spring. Different presidential candidates from Richard Nixon, Eugene McCarthy to George Wallace were coming to Southern California almost every week to campaign for votes in the state primary which would probably decide who the nominees would be that year.

It was around Memorial Day 1968, when there was news that Bobby Kennedy would be flying into Long Beach Airport near Lakewood, to greet supporters and give a speech while he was campaigning in the California Primary, so Jason and a large group of students from high school, and a few of his friends, went to the airport early to get a good spot to watch Kennedy's speech that day.

While Kennedy was speaking to a mostly cheering crowd, there were occasional "boos" from some who didn't support him, and when Kennedy was speaking and asking the question "Why should we send our boys to be killed in some foreign war thousands of miles away that doesn't concern our interests," one of Jason's friends who was a supporter of the Vietnam war yelled out, "So we won't be considered *chicken shits* like you!"

Kennedy looked irritated as he glanced over and made eye contact with Jason's group for a moment, but his supporters drowned out that comment with loud "boos" towards his group as Kennedy continued his speech.

During the drive home after that rally, his friends was joking about "how they got Kennedy to look at them" and were anxious to tell their friends they were "famous" that day because they "*personally* interacted with Kennedy" during his speech.

It was also day after he'd been to the Long Beach Airport speech by Bobby Kennedy, when between classes at school, Jason heard a friend shout to him, "Hey Jay, you're famous!"

First, he was annoyed that some of his friends still refused to call him "Jason", but secondly, hearing the phrase, "You're famous" was something Jason hadn't heard in a very long time, and had no idea what his friend was talking about.

Jason's friend showed him the front page of a newspaper that had some photographs of Kennedy at the Long Beach Airport the day before and then pointed out one particular picture and excitedly said, "Look, there you are with Bobby Kennedy!"

Jason looked at the photograph and only saw Kennedy leaning over and shaking hands with supporters, but then his friend pointed out what he was talking about. In the background of the newspaper photo, he saw the spot where they were watching the speech the day before, with Jason and his friends just sitting on a wall watching Kennedy speak to his supporters.

"See," said his friend, "You're in the picture with Bobby Kennedy in the newspaper and that makes you famous!"

Jason remembered how the little kids in La Puente and Buena Park got excited when they saw their names in newspapers from roller skating and they all thought that made them famous, but he couldn't believe friends his age would get that excited about seeing a photo as inconsequential as that one.

Jason handed the newspaper back to his friend and said, "You're not famous unless your name is mentioned for something you've done, not for just being in the background of somebody else's picture."

His friend didn't seem to care and asked Jason to sign the newspaper just "for the heck of it" and even though Jason thought it was stupid, signed it for him anyway.

As Jason was walking away, he briefly thought about weird it was that people thought it was impressive to have someone else's autograph and had always wondered why people just didn't try to go out and do something themselves that would make them feel famous. But he also knew the term "different strokes for different folks" and figured there were just some people who were completely satisfied living their lives though someone else's glory and was at least glad he wasn't one of those people.

It was about a week later, while Jason was getting ready to go to his graveyard shift at *Der Wienerschnitzel*, and watching the California Primary election results on a small TV set in his bedroom, when only a few minutes after hearing Kennedy finish his victory speech after having won that primary, another bulletin came on the screen announcing that "Senator Kennedy has just been shot!".

Jason was going to tell his parents but knew they were both asleep, but as he was leaving his house, he saw his father was on the living room couch tossing, and figured his parents were fighting again and weren't sleeping in the bedroom together that night. Seeing his father wasn't completely asleep, Jason said before he left that he just heard "Kennedy had been shot," but his father didn't even look up and just said, "Good, now go to work."

Jason grabbed a couple of *No Doz* from the medicine cabinet and left for work, knowing he'd be graduating high school in a couple weeks and wouldn't need the pills after that. He was mainly thinking about how bad the first half of 1968 had been in so many ways, and was anxious to finish high school and summer vacation to begin, so he could think more about his own future without any other distractions.

He was just hoping that he'd be able to think about what he could do that would actually make his own life better in the last half of that year.

Chapter Eighteen

Jason picked up more hours to work that summer and was putting most of the money he was earning into his bank account, hoping to have at least five hundred dollars saved up by the end of the year. He had already paid back his father the three hundred dollars for his car, but was also concerned that the Impala wasn't running as well when he first bought it, and mainly was just driving it to work.

Most of Jason's classmates he had graduated with were also turning eighteen years old that year and knew they were going to have to register for the Selective Service Draft, and knew that unless they went to college to get a student deferment, they would probably be drafted into the Army and end up going to Vietnam.

Jason's parent's views about the war had also changed that year and wanted him to get a college deferment as well, but Jason knew he wouldn't be turning eighteen years old until the following year and wasn't immediately concerned. Even though most of his friends had already signed up to begin classes at Long Beach City College or Cal State Long Beach the following September, Jason decided he didn't want to sign up for college until a new semester would being in February and decided to continue working more hours until then, instead of "just going back to school" so soon.

He also wanted to be living on his own by the time he started college and also wanted to try having fun again that summer by having some new experiences.

Jason's friends Lee and Reese had both gotten new cars as graduation presents from their parents, and with both of them planning to begin their first year of college in September, they told Jason they were planning separate road trips in August to "break in their new cars" and asked Jason if they wanted to join them.

They were taking separate road trips because they both wanted to go to different destinations, and because they didn't want to travel alone, they said Jason would only have to chip in for gas and pay for some of his own expenses.

Jason hadn't taken a trip to different parts of the country since he was a roller-skater and after having spent the entire year working, he arranged to take a few weeks off work in August for what he hoped would be a new adventure traveling to different parts of the country with his friends rather than his parents. He knew he had enough money in his bank account to easily cover the expenses, but also knew because he wasn't going "back to school" himself in September, he'd be able to make most of it back by the end of the year.

During his first eight-day road trip with Reese, they drove southeast through Arizona and New Mexico, to El Paso Texas where they also spent a few hours in Juarez, Mexico, and then traveled to San Antonio to attend the 1968 World's Fair before driving back north through Dallas. They both wanted to see *Dealey Plaza*, the famous location where JFK had been shot in 1963 which had been continued being discussed because of different conspiracy theories about his assassination. After spending the night in Dallas, they then picked up *Route 66* in Amarillo to drive back to California.

It was less than a week after being back in California before Jason joined Lee on his trip through the Midwest states to a city called Waterloo Iowa, where Lee said he had lived when he was younger himself. After spending a few days in the Midwest, Lee then planned on driving back through the Rocky Mountains to stop in *Yellowstone* and *Yosemite* National Parks before driving back home.

The one common theme was that whichever of his friends Jason was traveling, they both enjoyed blasting the rock and roll radio stations like Wolfman Jack's show on *XERB*, the *Mighty 1090*, along with another high-frequency radio station called *KOMA* out of Oklahoma City that they could always get reception when they were driving at night.

It was once again fun cruising along the highway and singing along to the current hits like *Born to be Wild* by Steppenwolf, *Jumpin' Jack Flash*, by The Rolling Stones, or *Hello, I Love You* by The Doors, and during each of the individual road trips, Jason had more fun than he ever did traveling with his parents, especially because there weren't any arguments or long stretches of the *silent treatment*.

It was while Jason and Lee were in Waterloo Iowa the last week in August, when Jason heard about a big *"happening"* in Chicago that was only about three hundred miles from where they were. Jason didn't have any desire to visit any of his relatives that still lived in Chicago, but instead saw that thousands of college students had gathered to protest the Vietnam War at the Democrat National Convention and thought it might be fun to join the protests, or even possibly get inside to at least watch some of the candidates speak. Lee was still all for the Vietnam War and didn't want anything to do with the "hippie" protestors, but after Jason convinced him that it would also be a good place to "meet some hippie chicks" who were looking for "some free love" after the protests, Lee agreed to take the less than four-hour drive from Iowa to Chicago.

It was just getting dark when they arrived in downtown Chicago, and it took a long time to find a place to park because several streets were blocked off by dozens of police cars with flashing lights, but once they parked, Jason and Lee just followed the dozens of others walking in groups who said they were "going to the Hilton Hotel" where the convention was being held, and where the main protests had already started. Jason also saw there were dozens of police officers on almost every block, who were wearing masks and holding their Billy Clubs in a threatening manner after someone in the group he was with would yell out "Pigs" as they passed groups of officers on each corner.

After almost a half-hour of walking, they could see they were getting close to the larger group of what looked like over a thousand demonstrators in front of the Hilton Hotel, surrounded by even more police in masks, when suddenly there were a couple loud explosions with large puffs of smoke starting to rise only about a half block away. After those in crowd in front of Jason and Lee's group yelled out "Tear Gas" and turned and started running back toward them, he also saw police starting to tackle some of those running, so his group immediately turned around and started running back in the direction they had just come from.

Jason started thinking that it was turning out the same way it did when he was in Hollywood a couple of years earlier, as he was trying not to fall with the running crowd away from where most of the conflicts were taking place, and after running for what they felt was at least two miles, Jason and Lee could see they were far enough away to be safe.

Lee just sarcastically said to Jason, "Well, this was a great idea!"

Jason was mainly disappointed all they had done was walk and run rather than participate in at least one demonstration, and it was obvious that the crowd in Chicago wasn't anything like the "hippies" or "peace and love flower children" he expected to meet.

After they went back to the car and drove away from downtown, they stopped at a pizza shop to eat and decided to just leave Chicago that same night and just find a cheap *Motel 6* somewhere further away from the city, before heading back west to continue their *adventure*.

Later that week, after they had left *Yellowstone National Park* and were driving through the Rocky Mountains on their way to *Yosemite*, the disc jockey on the radio station they were listening to, was excitedly announcing that the two newest songs from The Beatles had just been released on a *45 record* that day, and decided to play those two songs back-to-back continuously during the two hours they had reception on that radio station that night.

The first song was slower and called *Hey Jude* with the flip side sounding more rock and roll and titled *Revolution,* and after hearing both songs multiple times during those two hours, Jason had almost already memorized the lyrics and thought both songs were "catchy" and liked them immediately. He was also thinking about how appropriate and timely the lyrics to the song *Revolution* were not only because of his time in Chicago earlier that week, but also with everything else he'd seen going on in America that year. Jason already agreed with the "former hippies" he'd met a couple years earlier who always preached that rock and roll musicians were the "modern-day poets and philosophers" but also liked the messages by so many rock songs, especially about wanting to *"feel free"* or just to *"live for today"* as so many song's lyrics often preached.

The past few weeks of just traveling on the open roads and listening to music had felt so peaceful and serene to Jason, he hadn't even been thinking about his life and responsibilities, and wasn't looking forward to his adventure ending or going back to Lakewood where he didn't *"feel free."*

He knew he'd be turning eighteen years old in about six months and had a lot of decisions to make until then.

❧

Over the next few weeks after he went back to work and his ordinary life, it wasn't too much fun being back at home with his parents after experiencing his big adventure by himself, but at least by having not as spent as much time together that year, they had been at least been getting along better and there had been polite civility between them.

Jason's father was still selling car stereos and equipment working with "Madman Muntz" which Jason saw had obviously been successful for him because he had been buying a new car for himself every year and usually paying it off quickly, explaining that in his profession as a salesman, "it was important to always look successful" to those he did business with.

It was less than a month since he'd been back in Lakewood, when his father said he was planning on buying a new *Oldsmobile Toronado* "like Madman Muntz" drove, and already seeing that Jason's *1964 Impala* was on its "last legs" he said he'd give him a deal on his current car, a *1967 Ford Galaxy.*

Jason's parents still wanted to make sure he attended college the following year to avoid being drafted into the Army, and his father he'd give Jason his current car as a "late high school graduation present" as long as he promised to attend college the next year and get his student deferment.

Jason knew how important that was as well, and had already started thinking about what courses of study he was planning on taking in college and gladly agreed to that "deal" and promised that he would.

His father had also encouraged him to take some ROTC classes in college so in case he did have to eventually go to Vietnam, he'd be able to "enlist as an officer" in any branch of the military which would put him in a safer position if he had to fight in that war. Jason instead told his parents that he had decided to study to become a lawyer which was a profession that he'd learned could pay over twenty thousand dollars a year.

He had also been a fan of the *Perry Mason* television series since the late 1950's, not only because he always enjoyed hearing the theme song that started each episode, but because each show had different story and never seemed boring like an ordinary job.

He also knew that almost all politicians had started out as lawyers, and thought if he ever decided to get into politics himself, that was anything but ordinary, law was the best profession to learn.

Jason also knew he still had several more months to enjoy his *freedom* until he needed to start college and still didn't want to feel his extended "summer vacation" was over just yet.

As he joked to his friends who did start college that September, he wanted to enjoy the "last days of his youth" a little bit longer.

Chapter Nineteen

Having a "new car" without mechanical problems gave Jason a new freedom he hadn't felt before, especially because he now could drive further away from home without worrying about his car breaking down. He was also able to switch his graveyard shifts at *Der Weinerschnitzel* to longer afternoon shifts and was able to quit his other part-time job at *Orange Julius* now that he'd be earning the same amount of money at just one restaurant. But he mainly liked having his nights free without worrying about getting up early for school the next morning or going to work in the middle of the night.

With the schedule he'd worked that year, Jason had almost forgotten what it was like to have a social life and wanted "to start feeling like himself again" and have some fun with his new freedom. Although he was still seventeen and knew he didn't want to take a chance of getting pulled over by the police in Hollywood where there was still a curfew, there were other *cruise strips* besides Bellflower Boulevard, where teenagers usually hung out on weekends, including Firestone Boulevard in Downey, which was less than ten miles from Lakewood.

Jason did meet finally meet someone new at a drive-in restaurant called *Harvey's Broiler* on Firestone Boulevard who did make Jason start "feeling like himself" again, and who had become more than a "one night encounter" in the back seat of his car.

Her name was Jackie Madison, a tall pretty brunette who said she was a former cheerleader at her school in Downey, but although she was the same age as Jason, Jackie was still a senior in high school and only allowed to go out on dates Friday and Saturday nights. Jason also saw that like the other girls he'd known, she'd always wanted him to get some *Boone's Farm Strawberry Hill* to drink together on their dates, and also like the other girls, she'd always became more romantic after they finished the first bottle. Jackie had also told Jason that even though she wasn't a virgin, she only had sex with her former boyfriend a couple times and was still afraid of getting pregnant, so most of their first dates consisted of the same *dry humping* when they'd park or go to a drive-in movie together.

After month of dating, she did let Jason go farther than he had with other girls, and although she still wouldn't let him go "all the way," she did start to let him "put in *the tip* in a little" as long as he always made sure that he never "came inside her" which Jason was happy to promise and always made sure that he did. But it was after they had been seeing each other for almost two months and went to the drive-in

130

movie to see the new Steve McQueen movie *Bullitt*, when Jackie surprised Jason saying she wanted to take the next step in their relationship.

While they were in the back seat of his car kissing and grinding against each other passionately, Jackie breathlessly whispered to Jason, "Tell me that you love me and promise to pull out in time and I'll let you go all the way tonight."

Jason didn't really remember seriously saying the words "I love you" to anyone before except for his dog Tinker, and although he did like Jackie, he wasn't sure if he really "loved" her, but at that moment he did say those words, knowing it would make her happy, but mainly knowing how happy it would make him feel that night.

Over the next few days, Jason thought it was strange that even though he now had a regular girlfriend he could do things with he'd always wanted, he was feeling a little uncomfortable thinking that he had somehow made a commitment by telling Jackie that he loved her, and felt that she might start thinking that their time together was supposed to be more than "just having fun."

Fortunately, Jackie didn't bring up what they'd said the first time they had "real sex" together in their normal conversations, and the only time those words were spoken after that first night, was during the times they had sex.

Jason was glad they both were still having fun without getting "gushy" or too serious, knowing he still had a lot of things to think about in the next few months about his own future and definitely didn't want things to get complicated or too distracting until then.

He had already visited Cal-State Long Beach to look at the schedule of classes he might be interested in the next year to make sure he got a college deferment from the Selective Service Draft, and Jason's parents said they'd pay his tuition at Cal-State Long Beach as long as he continued working part time to pay for his books and other expenses.

Jason still wasn't that excited about staying in Lakewood like his other friends who were already enrolled in college and still living at home with their parents, but he also felt like he was still on his "extended summer vacation, and with it still being the fall of 1968, he knew he still had at least three months to figure things out.

He still wanted to enjoy "the last days of his youth" until then.

∼

With Jason only working one job, he usually had two consecutive days off during the week, and because he had so much fun traveling that previous summer and also had a more dependable car to drive, he decided to take his own shorter "one-day road trips" when he was off work, and while Jackie was at school, instead of just staying at home.

He decided to start visiting somewhere he had only been with his parents that wasn't costing him too much money to travel and could enjoy having some fun by himself.

Las Vegas was only about a four-hour drive from Lakewood and although he knew he needed to be twenty-one years old to get into casinos, Jason knew the same thing when he had snuck into Los Alamitos Racetrack for the horse races and wasn't going to let it deter him. He was still able to get gasoline for around thirty cents a gallon which made his round-trip drive cost only about ten dollars, so along with another fifteen dollars he'd bring to have some fun, it was worth it to just get away by himself.

Although the drive was usually a little scary when he made the trip at night driving along the winding two-lane mountain highway through the El Cajon Pass and other two-lane winding roads on his drive to Las Vegas, he did enjoy the freedom he felt just driving along the open highway and blasting the music from his eight-track tape deck, but mainly he enjoyed being away from Lakewood even if it was usually for less than twenty-four hours.

When he was in Las Vegas, Jason always wore suits and ties as well as sunglasses just trying to naturally act like he was already twenty-one years old, and was always pleasantly surprised when he saw that he never seemed to have a problem playing the nickel slot machines, or other casino games like Craps, Blackjack and Keno where he could make one-dollar bets. He sometimes won enough to enjoy some of the ninety-nine cent "all you can eat" buffets he'd seen in the casinos, and there were even a couple times when he won over ten dollars and decided to stay overnight in one of the six-dollar motels, so he wouldn't have to drive back at night which was the scariest time to drive the two-lane road home alone.

At the *Nevada Club*, the casino he remembered visiting when he was "just a kid" with his parents, Jason was also surprised that the cocktail waitresses would even offer him free beers or cocktails without asking for his driver's license or showing his ID. He also thought it was fun that the *Nevada Club* offered free souvenir photos of customers in front of the slot machines, and had several photos of himself inside the casino holding a beer or cocktail which he'd then show to his friends in Lakewood, to brag about "how cool" Las Vegas was, and all of the things he was able to get away with just by confidently acting older than he was.

On one of his road trips, he was at the *Horseshoe Casino* on Fremont Street, when a pretty girl in a short mini skirt came and sat next to him in the Keno lounge while he was drinking a beer and asked him in a friendly voice if he was winning.

When Jason told her "Nothing yet," she didn't seem concerned and just continued being friendly, asking him about himself, before adding that she was "working her way through school" at a small Las Vegas college named *Nevada Southern*.

Jason was surprised learning there was a college or even schools in Las Vegas and had always thought that that entire city was mainly a "Disneyland for Adults" and

132

didn't think that anyone actually lived normal or ordinary lives there. But he was more surprised when she suddenly smiled at him and casually said, "I'll give you some *head* for twenty dollars."

When she saw Jason looked confused, she said, "Head, you know a *blow job*."

She then added that she had a hotel room, and they could just "go upstairs for a few minutes to do it," and it was then Jason realized she was a prostitute offering sex for money, but was mainly finding it hard to believe a young and pretty girl like her could actually be one.

After Jason tried to sound natural and polite by just saying "No thanks" she then lowed the price to ten dollars which he also declined. Besides knowing that he only had enough money on him to pay for his gas home that night, and to stop for a hamburger at the *Denny's* Barstow or the *Summit Inn* at the Cajon Pass, Jason thought it was crazy to have to pay that much money for just a few minutes of sex.

After she just smiled and said "maybe next time" as she walked away, Jason did briefly think about how it might have been exciting to get some *"head"* from her, because that was something the other girls he'd met said was "disgusting" and something they'd never do. But he also never wanted to consider himself that "hard up" to actually need to pay for sex.

Jason had been keeping track, and Jackie was the fifth girl he had sex with, and although less than half of them had actually gone *all the way*, he still considered *dry humping* as sex, because they all ended with an orgasm.

He was also satisfied that all the girls had enjoyed it as much as he did, and besides telling him how good he felt, they also said he was a "great kisser."

Jason sarcastically thought if anything, that prostitute should have offered *him* money to have sex because of how *experienced and good* he'd became by then, in same way he remembered Dax had been paid for sex when he briefly worked as a gigolo in the novel *The Adventurers.*

During his drive back to Lakewood later that night, Jason was thinking about how much more exciting and fun Las Vegas was than anywhere he'd been in California, but besides also still thinking about the girl who had offered him some "head," he was also thinking about how she mentioned there was a college in Las Vegas which was really starting to make him *think*.

Jason liked that there was never any talk about the Vietnam War, assassinations, protests, or demonstrations in Las Vegas, and everyone he met there was always just enjoying themselves and having fun.

He wasn't sure if the Nevada Southern college that the prostitute had mentioned was a *real* college where he could actually take classes to get a student deferment, but he did decide that the next time he drove up to Las Vegas, he 'd try and find out.

Jason didn't know if it was really possible, but he was starting to think about how much of an adventure it would be if he could.

It was while Jason was having Thanksgiving dinner with his parents when he first discussed what he'd learned on his last "road trip" to Las Vegas.

Nevada Southern was a legitimate college and was actually planning on changing its name the following year to the *University of Nevada in Las Vegas* and had the same classes as Cal-State Long Beach that he had been planning to enroll in there. Jason also learned that the costs for each class was only fifty-five dollars per unit, which was about half of what each class at Cal-State Long Beach was costing, and pitched his parents that with units he was required to take for his student deferment from the military, it would be saving them almost eight hundred dollars a semester.

He had already told his parents he wanted to get his own apartment when he started college and assured them because it was only four hours away from Lakewood, he wouldn't really be that far away from home, and was confident he could just get another part-time job in Las Vegas to cover his expenses in the same way as if he went to Cal-State Long Beach.

"I've got over four hundred dollars saved up from working at my jobs for the last year and a half," Jason confidently told his parents, "With that money, along with a part-time job to pay for an apartment and expenses, I don't see any difference from going to college there instead of here."

His mother at first said she thought it was a "stupid idea," but after they eventually said they'd let him attend *UNLV* as long as he took his required classes and made sure he got a part-time job so he wouldn't be asking for more money, Jason was feeling more excited than he could ever remember.

But there was someone else who wasn't nearly as excited as he was.

"What going to happen to us if you move to Las Vegas?" Jackie Madison almost cried when Jason gave her the news, "I thought you loved me!"

Jason also tried to assure her that Las Vegas was only four hours away and they could still see each other when he came to visit his parents in Lakewood during any holidays or any weekend trip's he might be able to arrange.

"We can still see each other but just not as often," Jason tried to justify, "But you know I need to go to college to keep from being drafted, plus it's saving my parents a lot of money to go to college there."

Jackie still wasn't happy, but after Jason assured her that he wasn't "breaking up with her" and they would still stay in touch until she graduated from high school the following year, she seemed to accept his explanation.

Jason still wanted to continue having fun with her for the next couple months, but even though he didn't say anything to her, he was actually more excited about starting a "new life" in Las Vegas, and wasn't sure how much he'd really be able to see her once he did move away.

He figured he would try, but he didn't want to make any promises.

Chapter Twenty

Jason's friends had been telling him "How lucky" he was that his parents were letting him go to college in Las Vegas and although Jason knew he'd miss hanging out with them on a regular basis, he also told all his friends he'd make sure he'd see them whenever he came back to visit. He did feel somewhat lucky about finding what he thought was the "coolest college" to attend, but it was less than a week after New Year's Eve, and only a few weeks before he was planning to move to Las Vegas, when Jackie told Jason there was a problem that they needed to talk about which made him feel that his luck might have run out.

"My period is almost three weeks late, and I'm worried that I might be pregnant," she nervously said, "My parents will kill me if they find out and I don't know what to do."

Jason knew he'd always been careful to "pull out" in time with Jackie, but she said because he always immediately "put it back in" after his first orgasm to keep going for a second time, he may not have completely finished and there may have been some "drops" that went inside her. Even though Jason felt that was unlikely with how careful he'd been, he knew it was possible, especially with how much time he had spent with Jackie "getting lucky" over her two-week Christmas vacation when she was off school the previous month.

Jackie mentioned that if she was pregnant, she at least wouldn't have the baby until after she graduated high school, and started asking Jason about what they should do if she actually was.

"I don't even want to think about getting married until after I graduate high school," Jackie said, "but if I am pregnant, I can tell my parents that we're engaged so they don't freak out too much."

Jason tried not to show how "freaked out" he was by how Jackie sounded so casual about "what they should do" and had felt they had just been having a good time without nothing about marriage had ever been discussed, but was also feeling like his entire future he'd planned for that year was in jeopardy.

He didn't want to be a jerk and accuse Jackie of anything, but he had heard stories from his friends about others they'd known who'd been in similar situations about how some girls said they were pregnant when they thought a boyfriend was breaking up with them, or in his case moving away. One of Jason's friends said he actually knew someone who did end up marrying his girlfriend after she told him she was pregnant, but who also found out afterward she really wasn't and had lied just to get him to marry her.

Jason didn't feel like Jackie was that kind of girl and could tell she sounded serious about the situation, especially when she brought up another option when she saw he wasn't that comfortable about telling her parents they were engaged to be married.

"I know a girl who got pregnant in high school and knew a doctor who was able to take care of it," Jackie quietly said, "She said it cost around three hundred dollars, so if I am pregnant and you aren't ready to get engaged yet, that's something else we might have to consider."

Neither option sounded good to Jason knowing that getting engaged to get married when she finished high school was probably the same thing his parents had been forced to do, but he also knew that paying out three hundred dollars to "take care of it" would take away almost all of the money he had saved, and wouldn't leave him with enough to move to Las Vegas.

Jason felt dejected that his plans about starting his "new life" might be over, but because he knew he was somewhat responsible, he reluctantly told Jackie he'd do "whatever she wanted to do" if she was pregnant.

Fortunately, it was only about a week later when Jackie called him to say she had started her period, but besides feeling like he had dodged a bullet, Jason still felt uncomfortable about how serious their conversations had been, and wasn't sure if Jackie thought it meant that he was considering a real future with her once she graduated high school.

Although he did feel a little guilty about leaving town so soon after the issue they'd just been through, Jason did promise to exchange letters with Jackie at least once a week and did say he'd see her when he came back to California, but after the brief scare that he had just gone through with her, he wasn't sure if he was even that anxious to have sex with Jackie again anytime soon.

But he also knew he couldn't have picked a better time to leave town and wouldn't have to decide about anything like that for a while.

❧

It was the week Richard Nixon was sworn in as the thirty-seventh President of the United States after winning the election by saying he had a "secret plan" to end the war in Vietnam and vowed to "bring the country back together again, and also only a month before his eighteenth birthday, when Jason had finally packed all of his belongings for his move away from Lakewood that same week. He knew he had to register for college courses before the new semester started the following month to get his military deferment before he turned eighteen, and also needed to find an apartment and part-time job before he started his classes.

Jason's parents were standing in the driveway as he loaded his last box into the Ford Galaxy, but even though there had been many conflicts between them the past, they all knew they had to at least act like they were going to miss each other.

His father even slipped him what he said was a "lucky fifty-dollar bill" reminding Jason that Ulysses S Grant was his "seventh" cousin which he also said was a lucky number, telling Jason to always keep it in his wallet and only use it in an emergency.

It still seemed a little awkward because they never had been an affectionate type of family, and their goodbyes seemed more businesslike than melancholy, as Jason just shook his father's hand and gave his mother a slight hug, all promising to "stay in touch" but that was it.

As Jason drove away to begin his "new life" in Las Vegas, he didn't feel any sentimentality about the decision to leave his "old life" behind him, and instead, put his eight-track tape of the greatest hits by the rock group *Cream,* and waited for one of his favorite songs from that tape to play on his car stereo.

As he sped along the 605 freeway away from Lakewood, he turned up the volume when song *I Feel Free* finally began and loudly and optimistically sang along with the chorus.

He was ready for his new life as *Jason Mershon* to begin.

BOOK ONE PHOTO GALLERY

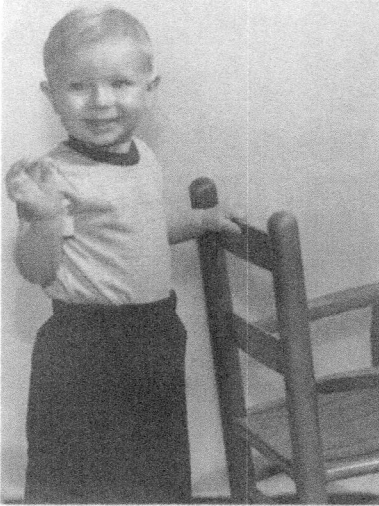

Two photos Jay's mother saved in his "baby book" from his early years in Chicago - 1951-1955, including a photo with who she said was his first girlfriend, "Jeanie" who he like to dance to the song "Mr. Sandman" with.

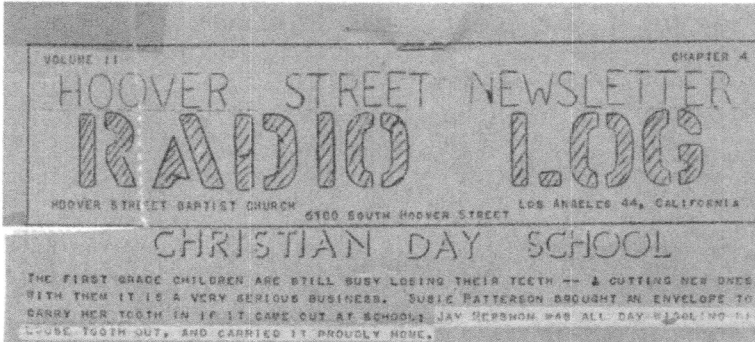

Another clipping from Jay's "baby book" that his mother saved of the first time his name was ever seen in any type of news publication. She said it made him "famous" that week.

Richard and Violet Mershon, Chicago, 1950.

Jay's fifth birthday party, Los Angeles, 1956.

Jay and his dog Tinker, 1957.

Jay alone with his father, taken during a period of "the silent treatment", circa 1958.

Bassett Skaters Win in So. Calif. Speed Contests

BASSETT — Speed skaters from the Vineland Skating rink in this community this week returned from a Southern California tournament at Escondido with ten trophies, the Herald learned.

The trophy winners, all of whom qualified, are to participate in state competition in Hollywood next month.

Skaters, and the places they won, were listed as follows:

First place winners were Deana Manouse, 8, (called "Peanut" by her teammates) and Milton Butler, 9.

Lonnie Butler, 12, second; Judy Jones, 11, second; Sharon Kears, 12; Guy Mosley, 8, second, and Gary Reynolds, 16.

Robert Miranda, 11, third place; Paulette Mosley, 10, third; Jay Mershon, 9, third.

Competing, but not qualifying, for the local rink was John Kears, 16.

(Left) Jay after joining the Cub Scouts in 1959, shortly before joining the United States Amateur Olympic Roller Skaing competitions at Vineland Skating Rink in La Puente, CA in 1960. (Right) Jay's first newspaper clipping for finishing third in the juvenile boys speed racing competition.

Jay with his trophy and silver medal at the California State Championships in Hollywood, CA, June, 1960

AYE CHAMP—Jay Mershon, 10, of La Puente, took three firsts and was named Southern California Skateland Championships at Northridge May 20-21. He was the most versatile Southern California roller skater of 1961.

SKATE CHAMP — La Puente's Jay Mershon, 10-year old member of the Olympic Skating Association, displays trophy he won as most versatile roller skater of the year at Southern California Championships at Northridge Skateland.   —Tribune Photo

Jay got his first big experience with the media when he was named the top skater of 1961 and won the "Most Versatile Skater of the Year" award.

The Buena Park Skating Rink had regular events and parties for all of the members of the skating club, including the above hayride. Joyce Paxton seen in center while Jay was preoccupied playing with another girl's ear with a piece of hay (far left).

Parties included a "Raging Redskin Night" with Jay (left) dressed as an "Indian Brave" after his mother darkened his skin with makeup, while on the upper right, Jay and Joyce won best costume for "Beatnik Night."

Jay in the kissing booth at "The Rollertorium's" Sadie Hawkin's party where he had the chance to kiss the older teenage girls for 25 cents a kiss.

(Above left) Carol Knudsen and (right) Jay's skating partner Joyce Paxton, who both gave him his first interest in George Gershwin's music from the music they skated to in their competitions. Jay also noticed by the end of 1961 that Joyce was growing and not as easy to lift as his partner.

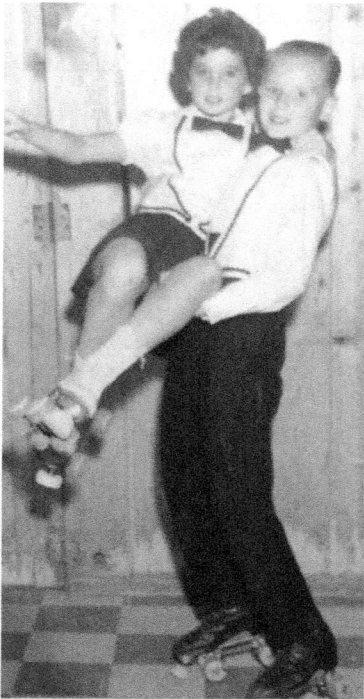

Top left: Jay (center) with two of his speed racing competitors including Jake Butler (Jay's right). Top right: Jay's first skating partner Joyce Paxton, 1961. Bottom: Jay's other two skating partners in 1962, Christine Blackford (left), and Cheryl Ridgeway (right).

FEATURED SKATERS from the "Rhythm on Wheels" show presented by the Buena Park Skating Club are, left to right: Linda Palmiere — U.S. & Calif. State Champ, Carole Ewald — Calif. State Champ, Carol Knudsen — U.S. & Calif. State Champ, Dennis Pollard — U.S. & Calif. State Champ, Margaret Miller, Sheri Byrd, Jay Mershon — Calif. State Champ and Debbie Ewald — Calif. State Champ.

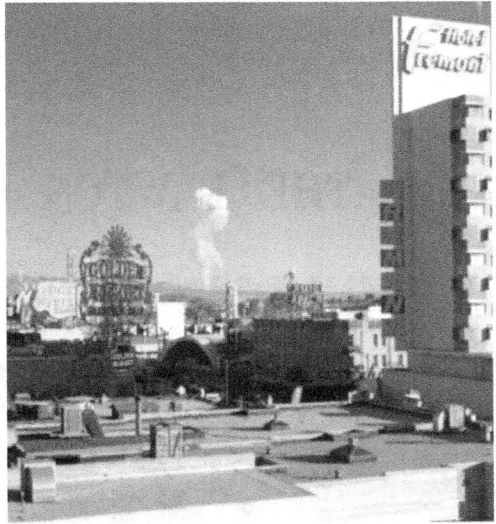

Top: Newspaper clipping of Jay (far right) starring in "Rhythm on Wheels" show with Dennis Pollard and Carol Knudsen (center), 1962 Bottom left: Jay with both his parents during trip to 1962 National Skating Championships in Harvey Illinois. Seated next to Jay in mock antique car is Judy Beaumont who Jay was planning on being his new skating partner in 1963. Bottom right: The view from the roof of a downtown Las Vegas Hotel of the Atom Bomb explosion during the above ground testing period. Jay observed an Atom Bomb test in 1961, and also thought was the reason he was forced to discontinue his skating competitions during the Cuban Missile Crisis in October, 1962.

147

Jay with some of the Hollwood celebrities who attended the "Rhythm On Wheels" show (including Richard Crenna (right), was excitedly anticipating his 1963 skating competitions with a new partner and a new start.

THE LAWTON CONSTITUTION

RUSSIA SAYS BLOCKADE 'STEP TO NUCLEAR WAR'

OAS Backs Up Soviet Servicemen
Plans To Curb Discharges Halted,
Cuba Buildup All Leaves Canceled

The "Cuban Missile Crisis" and the fear of nuclear war in October of 1962 was the reason Jay's parents told him they suddenly needed to move away from Buena Park, and he needed to "retire" from roller skating.

After his forced "retirement" from competitive roller skating, Jay's next goal was learning to play the clarinet in his junior high school band. He mainly wanted to learn the opening solo in George Gershwin's "Rhapsody in Blue." Unfortunately, the day he won "first chair" in his clarinet class was November 22, 1963, which ruined "his glory."

Jay's report card from Bancroft Junior High Schoo in intermidiate band in January, 1964, which he had to quit shortly after getting braces on his teeth which made him switch to drums.

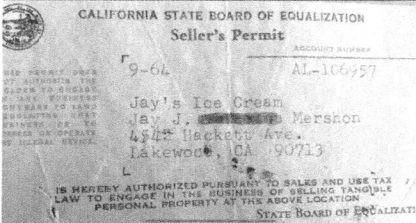

Jay's first self employed business, Jay's Ice Cream, 1964.

Jay's short-lived career as a high school quarterback (number 19) in 1965.

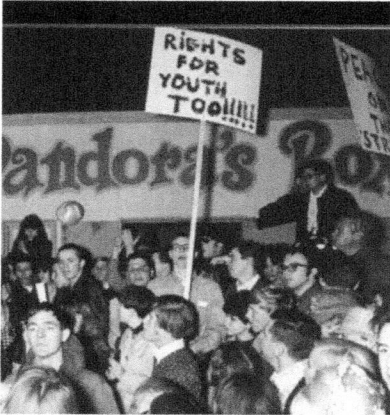

Jay had a memorable time protesting the 10:00pm curfew and the closing down of his favorite nightclub Pandora's Box in Hollywood, 1966.

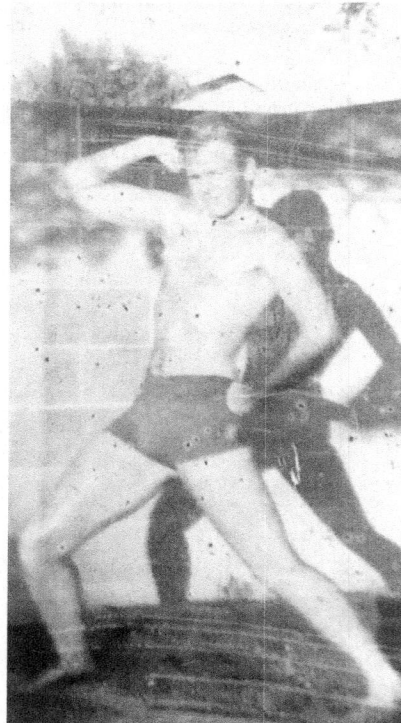

After his experience at the riot and protest in Hollywood, Jay took a "vanity photo" (right) trying to appear older and more desirable to the "hippie chicks" he met there.

150

Jason (far left sitting on wall) at a rally with Bobby Kennedy (right) greeting supporters at Long Beach Airport in 1968.

High school graduation photo, 1968.

After visiting Las Vegas numerous times, Jason decided to move to Las Vegas and attend the University of Nevada, Las Vegas (UNLV) in 1969.

PRELUDE TO THE LAST STAND
SPRING, 2009

The seasoned gambler and poker player and walked in and looked around the Commerce Casino's tournament area to see who was there that he knew and one of the first poker players he recognized when he sat down at his tournament table was Jerry Buss, the owner of the Los Angeles Lakers.

The seasoned gambler greeted him, "Hi again, Jerry," he said as Jerry sat next to him.

"Hey, Jason," replied Jerry, "Good to see you again."

Jason had met Jerry Buss about five years earlier in another poker tournament and discovered that they had mutual acquaintances with two girls Jason had become friendly with in Palm Springs, Puppy and Veronica. Although Puppy and Veronica had never actually been legally married to Jerry, they both filed multi-million-dollar palimony lawsuits against Jerry and continued to add the name "Buss" as their own last names. Once Jason learned how much money it cost Jerry to settle those lawsuits, he never brought up Puppy or Veronica's name again when they played poker together.

He was also surprised that Jerry Buss always remembered his name because "Jason" was such a common name these days.

Jason remembered how he used to joke to one of his girlfriends that the reason the name 'Jason" became so popular was his doing because of all the press and publicity he received in the 1970s and '80s for almost everything that he was involved in. He could laugh about how dumb it must have sounded back then and that he probably did seem a little egotistical, but he always thought having a healthy ego was a good thing.

Nowadays, if he said something like that, with all the new terms and labels being thrown around, it would probably be another reason for somebody just to call him a narcissist. It seemed to him that no matter what people said or did these days, some doctors always have some new label that defined them, and everyone seemed to think they were an expert at psychiatry.

Jason and Jerry Buss were both at The Commerce Casino for a tournament series called the California State Poker Championships that always attracted the major professional players and celebrity poker players. The actor Ben Affleck had won the title of California State Champion a few years back during the "poker boom" which helped draw even more interest in poker.

It seemed there was some type of poker show or tournament being aired on television almost every day, but Jason didn't like playing in tournaments as much as he did years earlier, and now mainly focused on cash games to earn money daily.

Jason had been on a winning streak at Pechanga Indian Casino and had built up his bankroll enough in the past month to give this tournament a shot and thought it might be fun to be a California State Poker Champion.

The championship tournament he was entering was a smaller three hundred dollar buy-in event, but first place was over thirty thousand dollars. Jason lightly thought about how three hundred dollars had once been enough money to live on, pay all of his bills for almost two months, and now seemed like such a small amount of money. Plus, he liked that the smaller three hundred dollar buy-in was a "limit" tournament and not the usual "no limit" because Jason always felt it took more skill in a limit game, instead of everyone just pushing chips and saying "All-in" like many players did.

No limit was a whole new game with different skill-sets that only became popular when the "poker boom" began in 2004.

Jason and Jerry Buss drew the same tournament table and were seated next to each other, waiting for the tournament to begin. They had played a few tournaments at the same table together before and Jason was always surprised that Jerry played in such low buy-in tournament when he was already so wealthy.

"I just like the competition," Jerry always said.

Jerry Buss had once been at his table when Jason was involved in the wildest "no limit" poker hand everyone at the table said they had ever seen. It was at a big tournament at the Bicycle Casino a few years earlier, and after Jason had raised a pot, he was then was re-raised by another player and Jason decided to move all-in with a pocket pair of nines, and the other player instantly called with his pair of aces.

Jason stood up knowing he was beaten, but the dealer flopped a 2-9-9, and the table started yelling with disbelief and laughter because it looked like just another bad beat for the player holding aces. Then, it was the other poker player who stood up to leave after seeing Jason's four 9's knowing he was beaten, but when the dealer turned an Ace on the turn and another Ace on the river, the table really started yelling in disbelief. It was very rare to see quads over quads in big poker tournaments.

Jason ended up getting beat, but he remembered Jerry Buss saying, "You'll never see a board run out like that again in your lifetime, it's a zillion to one shot!" and he and Jerry had discussed that poker hand often when they had played together since then, and it was now just a great "bad beat" story to laugh about.

But now that the tournament was starting, Jason didn't want to be labeled a "bad beat storyteller" tomorrow, so he started just focusing on winning the current tournament. He figured he was destined to win one of these bigger tournaments eventually and hopefully, tonight was the night.

He wanted just to play patient, solid, and stay focused.

Jason had been sitting next to Jerry Buss for most of the early part of the tournament and saw him get eliminated after about three hours when Jerry was low on chips and missed a flush draw. It was a long tournament with the blinds starting out low and increasing each hour. Almost five hours after Jerry Buss was eliminated, only about thirty players were remaining from the over four hundred who started.

Jason felt good about still being in the tournament and having already "made it into the money" and sharing in the total prize pool that only the top ten percent of the total players who entered were eligible for. He did manage to win some good pots with some big hands, and even managed to bluff a couple of nice pots on the river.

"A little bluffin' never hurt anybody!" Jason always liked to say.

After a short break, the remaining thirty players drew seat numbers to move to the final three tables in the tournament and Jason was in seat one next to the dealer which was a seat he liked because he could easily observe the players and the community cards in the middle of the table.

Sitting directly across from him at the table in seat four was a well-known poker pro he had played against a few times named Paul Darden. Paul had been one of the first "poker celebrities" when the poker boom began and was featured a few times on the World Poker Tour television show. The commentator on the World Poker Tour, Mike Sexton, had often said that next to Phil Ivey Paul was the best-known African-American pro poker player, but that was at least five years ago, and Jason figured Paul must have fallen on hard times to be playing in such a low buy-in tournament.

Jason also saw that Paul recognized him as well, and they both gave each other a friendly nod as the tournament resumed.

The dealer started dealing the cards at the new level and the blinds were increasing to one thousand and two thousand with a three hundred chip ante. Jason figured he had around twenty-five thousand in tournament chips left in front of him, which was only fair because even though he saw that many players had much smaller chip stacks, there were also quite a few who had twice or three times the amount of chips he had.

He could be fairly patient, but not overly because each time the button moved around the table, with blinds and antes, it would cost him fifty-seven hundred in chips and he knew that if he wanted to at least make it to the final table where the tournament payouts were the highest, he'd need to at least triple or even quadruple his chips to have a chance.

When he looked down at his two hole-cards and saw pocket Queens on the first hand he was dealt, he saw he wouldn't have to be patient for long. Everyone at the table had already folded when the action got to him, and Jason announced "Raise" and made the bet four thousand. After the button and the little blind folded, it was then it was up to Paul Darden to fold or call.

155

Jason wouldn't mind if Paul just folded because just picking up the blinds and the antes would be okay with him for the first hand at that level, but Paul reached down and announced "raise" himself, and put in four thousand in chips.

Jason knew in No Limit, it was easier to make a move from the blind with a larger bet, but only having to call two thousand chips more wasn't going to get any player to fold. That's why Jason decided just to call the two thousand instead of re-raising knowing Paul would call another single raise and decided to see what cards came on the flop. But he definitely didn't want to see an Ace or a King on the flop because then he'd have to make his own decision about calling if Paul bet again, knowing that most players would only re-raise with at least one strong Ace or King in their hands.

The dealer spread the flop of a 3, 7, and a Jack of different suits and with no flush or straight draws, as well as no over cards to his pocket queens, Jason thought it was a perfect flop.

Paul Darden pushed in a bet of two thousand chips without any hesitation, which Jason figured was a standard bet because it didn't look like the flop helped Jason if Paul figured he was holding big cards himself, but he did hope that Paul did have a Jack and was betting, thinking he had the best hand. This time Jason raised to four thousand and re-raised again when Paul made it six thousand and after having already invested over half of the chip's he'd started the hand with, Jason decided if an Ace or King didn't come on the turn, he was fully committed to his pair of Queens.

The dealer then turned over the 9, which didn't seem to change anything.

Paul looked over at Jason's chip stack and said, "How many chips you got left?" and Jason moved aside his hands so he could see.

When Paul bet four thousand, Jason raised and then committed the last of his chips when Paul put in one last raise.

"Okay, turn over your cards," said the dealer as it was customary for the players to show their hands before he dealt the river card.

Jason was confident his Queens were best but quickly saw Paul turn over a pair of Kings but neither of them said anything because there was still one more card to come. Jason still knew although it was a longshot, there was still two Queens left in the deck and immediately started hoping for a "River Miracle."

The dealer quickly burned a card and turned over another 9, and that was it, Jason was out of the tournament. Paul just said "Good game" as the dealer pushed him the pot, and Jason just said, "Good luck everyone," as he turned and walked away from the table to collect twenty-seventh place money.

His payout for twenty-seventh place was only eight hundred and seventy dollars, a far cry from the thirty thousand he'd hoped to win, but even though he was disappointed, Jason knew that was the deal with tournaments and either you win a lot, you win a little, or you win nothing at all. But this was now his profession and always tried to accept that "any win is a good win" and at least on that night, a big win just wasn't in the cards.

As he walked outside to the Commerce Casino's front to get some fresh air, Jason heard an old song by the music group Bread playing from a car in the valet parking area and it briefly made him think about a girl he once knew over forty years earlier who lived in Downey, the next city over from the Commerce Casino. He was also only about ten miles from where he had grown up in Lakewood, a city he had never gone back to visit in forty years, but also knew so many things had changed since those days, it may as well have been a hundred years ago.

While he waited for his car in the valet parking area, Jason started thinking that in the old days, he would have gone back inside the casino and taken one of the cocktail waitresses or some other girl he knew to the Hyatt Hotel that used to be across the street from the casino, or to some party, and boned her for a couple of hours to get over a tough loss at the poker tables.

Sex and romance had always been something that kept him in a positive frame of mind through other losses or disappointments in his life, but then he sarcastically thought to another new label that was being attached to everyone, and figured he probably would have just been called a "sex addict" these days with the attitudes he had about romance back then.

He remembered how someone once told him that "money and sex" were the only things that mattered in life and how that person actually ended up being right.

For Jason's entire life, it seemed sex was his main priority, but those days were over, and sex wasn't a priority any longer. He really didn't care that he hadn't had a girlfriend in years, and these days it was only about the money, and tonight, all he wanted to do now was go back to the house he was staying to be alone with his cat he had named Lucky.

Times had changed a lot.

BOOK TWO

"WINE, WOMEN, AND SONG"
1969 - 1972

Chapter One

In 1969, Richard Nixon was President with his platform of "Wanting to bring people together," but the Vietnam war was still dominating the nightly news and millions were marching in protest across America. *The Vietnam Peace Moratorium* motivated students at most large universities to stage student strikes, violent protests, demonstrations, and even attempts of student takeovers of entire campuses.

The minimum wage in 1969 was a dollar and sixty cents an hour, with the average income around six thousand dollars a year and while gasoline prices hadn't changed that much and averaged thirty-two cents a gallon, the cost of a new home had increased to around fifteen thousand dollars.

Rowan and Martin's Laugh-In, Gunsmoke, Bewitched and The Beverly Hillbillies, were the top-rated TV show that year, while in the movie theatres, *Butch Cassidy and The Sundance Kid, Easy Rider* and *The Love Bug* were the top films of 1969, along with the first X-rated film to win an Academy Award for Best Picture, *Midnight Cowboy*. It was also the year when the film *On Her Majesty's Secret Service* introduced a new James Bond, George Lazenby, when Sean Connery decided against playing the role again The popular songs that year were *Honky Tonk Women* by the Rolling Stones, *Suspicious Minds* by Elvis Presley, and two songs from the controversial Broadway musical *HAIR, Aquarius/Let the Sun Shine* by The Fifth Dimension, as well as the title song, *Hair* by The Cowsills. It was also in 1969 when Mario Puzo released his best-selling novel, *The Godfather.*

There were many other memorable events that year, including Neil Armstrong becoming the first man to walk on the Moon, The Beatles performing their final concert on a rooftop in London, and Ted Kennedy's car accident on the Chappaquiddick Bridge which caused the death of Mary Jo Kopechne. But the peace and love ideology of the hippies that had peaked with Woodstock in 1969, was starting to be replaced by the image of violence with the deadly Rolling Stones concert at Altamont, and the Sharon Tate murders by a hippie cult led by Charles Manson.

While racial riots for civil rights by the blacks had subsided somewhat in 1969, a huge disturbance that started after police raided, and tried to arrest, groups of homosexuals and transvestites in a New York City bar called *The Stonewall Inn*, led to weeks of violent riots and protests by homosexual and lesbian groups demanding the right to exhibit their sexual orientation without the fear of being arrested.

159

A new organization called the *Gay Liberation Front* was created in its aftermath and other organizations formed using the term *GAY* for the first time to describe their lifestyle, which they wanted to replace the term *homosexual,* and those organizations carried out protests and demonstrations in cities across America demanding the same civil rights as the blacks had demonstrated and rioted for in the past decade.

America was still in the midst of unrest in most major cities across the county which definitely made Jason Mershon glad he decided to attend a "not so activist" smaller university like UNLV, in a smaller city like Las Vegas that was mainly known as a place to have fun.

When Jason moved to Las Vegas in 1969, it only had a population of around 120,000, and even the entire county had less than 250,000 full-time residents, but the tourists always gave it a big city feel when Jason was on *"The Strip"* or cruising on downtown Fremont Street.

On his earlier trips to Las Vegas before his permanent move, he had gotten his paperwork and the listings of the classes that would be available for him to start college when the new semester began in 1969. UNLV was still a very small university with less than three hundred graduate students each year combined between Associate and Bachelor Degrees, but Jason was mainly concerned about signing up enough required classes before he worried about which degrees he was going to achieve.

When he turned eighteen, Jason was also required to register with the selective service and applied for his Student Deferment at that time, but he would be required to be enrolled, and pass, fifteen and a half college credits each semester to avoid being drafted into the Army and made sure he signed up for sixteen units to be covered.

Jason decided that he did want to study to possibly become a lawyer, so he signed up for classes that would be preliminary requirements that were required if he ever wanted to go to law school. He also noticed that most of the classes had *"101"* attached to the courses like Criminal and Civil Law and Law Enforcement studies, as well as Political Science. He also signed up for some other *"101"* courses that interested him, including Journalism, History, Philosophy, and Psychology.

He also knew he'd need to find a job he could work around his studies, and he found one at a small barbecue restaurant in the *Wonder World Shopping Center.* called *Johnny Reb's* which was very close to the campus on Maryland Parkway. Jason liked that job because it paid thirty cents more an hour than what he had been paid in California, and would earn a minimum wage of a dollar sixty an hour now that he'd turned eighteen years old.

Because he was going to classes full time, he was only able to work part-time during the week, but his boss gave him eight-hour shifts on weekends which he figured would give him enough money to live on, and also liked that his boss said he'd be allowed to eat a couple meals each day at *Johnny Reb's,* which he figured would save him at least ten dollars a week.

Jason also found a place to live he could afford, at least until he made some more money from his job during the summer when he could work full time, called the *Strip Hotel*, that only cost sixty dollars a month. It wasn't actually on the strip, but a couple of blocks off Las Vegas Boulevard between Sahara Boulevard and Downtown and was more like a motel. It also didn't have a private bathroom, so Jason had to share a community bathroom and shower in the hallway with other tenants, as well as share a community pay telephone in the hallway. He knew he couldn't afford a private phone yet, but he didn't mind and was just happy he had his own "apartment" and was just excited to be living in Las Vegas on his own. Jason also still had over three hundred dollars after his move as back up, so he figured he'd have plenty of money to at least be comfortable for the first several months of living there.

One big concern he did have, however, was that the name on his driver's license still said Jay Mershon. He definitely wanted his new Nevada License to have the name Jason, so before he went into the Nevada DMV, he took a razor blade and scratched off the "Y" on his name on his California driver's license, and crumpled it up a bit make it appear it had been damaged.

When Jason went to the motor vehicles department to get a new Nevada license, the young female clerk at the counter seemed preoccupied at her typewriter after she gave him the paperwork he needed to complete for a new license. As he walked away, the clerk casually said, "Oh, if you're not twenty-one, you'll need to show your birth certificate."

Jason immediately knew that she had gotten the requirements backwards and just quickly said, "No problem, I just turned twenty-one a couple months ago," to see if she noticed. While he was filling out the paperwork, he decided to try and damage his California license even more and scratched off the piece that showed *1951* as the date of his birth, and changed the birthdate on the paperwork to *1948* before he walked back and handed it to the same preoccupied clerk.

When she looked at his damaged California license, she sarcastically said, "What happened to your license, did it get run over by a bulldozer!?"

Jason tried to sound natural as he told her "His wife" got it caught in a washing machine along with his credit cards, which he hoped would also make him sound older.

The clerk basically just ignored his California license and set it aside while she just typed the information from the paperwork he had filled out. When she handed him his temporary Nevada License and asked him if he wanted his old license back, Jason was relieved when he saw her cut in in half and throw it in the trash when he said no.

A few weeks later, he received his actual Nevada driver's license in the mail and was amazed at how lucky he got. So many of his friends in California had always tried to get fake ID's so they could buy beer or get into places where they had to be twenty-one, but now, "*Jason Mershon*" appeared to "*legally*" be twenty-one years old with a Las Vegas address, and he felt like he had become reborn into a new life.

He knew even more now, that he was going to love Las Vegas.

❧

Some of his classes at UNLV were fun, but others were boring and it usually depended on who the instructors were. One of the fun classes was *History 101*, and on the first day of class, the professor let the students know "things were going to be different" in college. He told them that semester, they would be learning something they never learned in high school, and he would explain some of the juicy stories about the sex lives of Benjamin Franklin, Alexander Hamilton, Thomas Jefferson, and other early statesmen.

"The founding fathers loved spreading their seeds to a variety of women and were very accomplished cocksmen of their day," the professor said with a smile.

That got a good laugh from the entire class, and Jason knew that that course would be fun.

Another class Jason enjoyed was *Criminal Justice 101* and his instructor was named Jim Santini, who was the current Clark County Public Defender, but taught classes on law as a side profession.

On his first greeting to the class, Santini explained how important every detail of the law was and needed their full understanding and he gave an example by talking about a previous class he had taught when explaining the legal definition of rape.

Santini said he explained to his previous class that "*any penetration*" constituted a criminal violation of rape and had noticed that a young female student hadn't been paying very much attention and was reading something else in the class. Santini said he decided to get her attention and asked, "Miss Butler, I'm sure you have been following everything I've been saying carefully, so could you please share with the class the amount of penetration that is needed to constitute a legal crime of rape?"

Santini explained with a laugh, that as she looked up and nervously thought about it for a few seconds, she answered, "About six inches?" which Santini said he immediately retorted to her, "I wasn't asking about the definition of *pleasure*, Miss Butler!"

That, of course, got his class laughing as well, and Jason knew he'd have fun in Jim Santini's course.

Jason liked the lighter classes where the professors would have a sense of humor while teaching and not be so monotone about the subjects.

162

In those classes, Jason had problems staying awake, but he knew he had to study knowing he wasn't ready to get drafted and go to Vietnam, but he was also trying to work as many hours at *Johnny Reb's* as he could between his college classes, to make sure he made enough money to pay his bills without draining his reserve money.

The owner of the restaurant Jason worked was named Frank Reich and had moved to Las Vegas from North Carolina to open his own restaurant, but he also worked as a craps dealer at the *Sahara Hotel*. Frank said he still had to work a full-time job that bought in a steady income until the restaurant became more profitable.

Jason liked Frank's southern drawl and attitude, and also that he was very easygoing and flexible about Jason's work schedule. Frank liked that Jason was always on time for work and never missed a shift, and also said he hoped that Jason might consider becoming a "full-time assistant manager" eventually after only working there for three months. Jason also became friendly with his new co-workers as well, including two of them he worked with on weekends, Tom Casey and Rhonda Talbot, were the same age as him, but still had their senior years to finish in high school.

Tom was planning on attending UNLV and said he'd probably be taking some of the same classes as Jason, because his father was in the FBI, and he wanted the same profession when he graduated.

"You can't get into the Bureau without a degree," Tom added, "So we'll probably be in some of the same classes at *UNLV* after I graduate from high school."

They had all become good friends, so Jason trusted them and told them the funny story about getting his driver's license at the DMV, and how he was now able to go anywhere in Las Vegas without worrying about being carded. Both Tom and Rhonda thought Jason was lucky because they both wished they could go anywhere as well, so Jason told them both he could probably sneak them in with him sometime using his ID as "the adult" accompanying them.

His first few months in Las Vegas was like Heaven to Jason, and he was already happy with all of his new friends and knew he had made the right decision about leaving California.

He felt at home.

❧

Jason didn't really consider himself still "going steady" with Jackie Madison, but they were still exchanging letters at least a few times a month, so he wasn't really feeling that guilty when he decided to start meeting new girls on weekends.

He had a friend he met in one of his classes who lived in a city just outside of Las Vegas called Henderson, and who said the "Henderson girls were more fun and friendlier" than the ones who cruised on Fremont Street, and that he always met different girls every weekend, so that's where Jason decided to start spending some of his Friday and Saturday nights.

The teenagers in Henderson cruised in cars down the main drag called Water Street in the same style he remembered from Bellflower Boulevard, with the main hangouts being the *Polar Queen* and *Artic Circle*.

Jason did meet a few girls in his first month of hanging around Henderson who were still in high school, but not really that much younger than him, plus they seemed much older and experienced than any of the girls he' known in his high school, especially when it came to sex.

None of the girls he met in Henderson were virgins, but because they were still in high school, Jason always let them know he was really only eighteen years old and was actually only about a year older than they were, but they did like that he had a driver's license that allowed him to get beer and wine with no problem, which was the one similarity that all of the girls he'd known had usually shared.

The girls he met also liked that he had his own "apartment" at the *Strip Hotel* and Jason saw they probably considered it a luxury not having to spend their time "having fun" in back seats of cars or in secluded parks, but even though the girls said he could just "pull out" like he always had, saying they liked feeling the "real thing" inside them instead of just *rubber*, after the experience he had with Jackie earlier that year, Jason decided to start wearing a condom even though it wasn't as nearly as pleasurable.

He did like that the girls he was seeing were just happy having him as an occasional fling a few times a month without talking about anything serious or having a steady relationship, but even though Jason now had a couple new girlfriends he was seeing fairly regularly, he'd still answer Jackie's letters every week just as he promised.

But each letter was also increasingly becoming like a chore to him, and his new life in Las Vegas was starting to make everything from California seem only like a distant memory that he wanted to forget.

He loved his "new life."

Chapter Two

The biggest news in Las Vegas in the summer of 1969 wasn't about any of the turmoil or protests around the county, but that Elvis Presley would be making his concert comeback at the new *International Hotel* that had just been built off the Las Vegas Strip.

Rhonda Talbot was as huge of an Elvis fan as Jason was, so he told her with his ID he could probably be able to take her with him, again lightly adding it would be all right seeing she'd be with an *adult*. But getting reservations seemed impossible when they were told that every Elvis show was full, and almost gave up until Frank Reich offered to help, saying he "knew some pit bosses" at *The International Hotel*.

Frank seemed as pleased with himself, as much Jason and Rhonda were, when he told them he had secured reservations and proudly added, "You're going to find out you can get anything you want when you have some *juice* in Las Vegas."

Jason was also happy that the reservations were for the midnight show rather than the dinner show, which was more expense and cost fifteen dollars per person, compared to the midnight show that was half that price and in their budget. Plus, the seven dollars and fifty cents it cost for the midnight show also included two cocktails, so both Rhonda and Jason figured it was worth spending that much money.

When they were both asked for their ID's when they ordered cocktails in the showroom the night of the concert, Jason gladly showed his driver's license and casually said, "My wife left her purse in our hotel room," the waitress didn't even question Rhonda, and they were both were served cocktails with no problem.

"See?" smiled Jason to Rhonda, "It's all just acting like it's no big deal, and they always believe you."

The showroom's audience was restless, but polite, for the opening comedian Sammy Shore but started going wild when he completed his act, and the lights dimmed for Elvis to begin his show. And then, suddenly there he was, right in front of them singing *Blue Suede Shoes*, which wasn't easy to hear at first, because of all the screaming from the women in the audience.

Jason didn't speak more than a couple of words to Rhonda and was focused on watching Elvis singing almost all of his earlier hit songs during the first half of the show. He'd seen several concerts with some famous bands in California, but this was *Elvis Presley*, and just seeing him perform in person made it much more than a concert.

Jason's favorite segment was when Elvis didn't even sing, and instead just talked to the audience for about ten minutes about his early life, time in the Army, and all the movies he had made in the past ten years. But in the second half of the show, Jason was surprised that Elvis decided to sing hit songs by other artists, including the Beatles, instead of his own hits, and guessed Elvis just wanted to show he was hip to the new sounds and not just an oldies performer.

By the time Elvis concluded with what he said was a new song that would be released in a couple of weeks called *Suspicious Minds*, and a rousing version of the Ray Charles hit song *What I Say*, he concluded his show with one of his biggest hits from the movie *Blue Hawaii, Can't Help Falling in Love*.

It was an experience enjoying not only a legend like Elvis, but he also liked being seeing a show where he didn't need to be accompanied by his own *adult* parents.

Although he knew the shows at the hotels were expensive, because there were so many other names on the marquees that he wanted to see, Jason decided to ask Frank Reich for another night shift at Johnny Reb's so hopefully he'd be able to see a major act like Elvis at least once a month.

He knew he was in Las Vegas to mainly go to college, but he also wanted to have some fun whenever he could.

҉

When Jason started his second semester at UNLV that September and managing to pass all of his earlier required classes, he was still spending at least one weekend night trying to enjoy his social life, and had recently met a girl met a girl from Henderson named Nancy Silver who he started seeing fairly regularly.

On the first night he took Nancy to his room at the *Strip Hotel*, she also said "a rubber didn't feel like "real sex" and preferred the "real thing." She also assured Jason that because she knew her menstrual cycle very well, she knew when it was the safest time to have sex without getting pregnant, and only wanted to have sex on those nights so he wouldn't need to wear a condom.

Even though they only had "real sex" on the nights Nancy said were *safe*, Jason still made sure he "pulled out" in plenty of time on those nights as well and still didn't want to take any chances.

But Nancy also explained the way they could still have fun even when it wasn't safe.

"If I know I'm ovulating or if I'm on my period, I'll just blow you," Nancy nonchalantly smiled, "Besides, I love giving *head."*

She then demonstrated the other way she "loved to have fun" that he never experienced from Jackie or any other girls, which immediately made her his "favorite Henderson girl" that he was seeing.

Although Jason started spending at least one night a week with Nancy that fall, because she looked even younger than the seventeen-years-old she claimed to be, he

166

could never take her to the casinos or the showrooms because she didn't come close to looking or acting as mature as Rhonda Talbot had. Most of their weekend dates were at drive-in movies, or "all age venues" where she never needed to show an ID.

The major "all age venue" in Las Vegas was called the *Ice Palace*, which was an ice-skating rink that was converted when needed, to be a concert venue that regularly featured famous rock bands.

Jason had also met Mike Tell, the promoter of all the concerts at the *Ice Palace*, when he came in for lunch at *Johnny Reb's* a few times, and besides talking about different bands and the upcoming shows that Mike was producing at the *Ice Palace*, he also offered Jason a pair free tickets and an occasional backstage badge for passing out flyers or posters at UNLV or other places he would frequent around town. Jason was more than happy to do that fairly regularly and liked that he was saving the four of five dollars that the concert tickets usually cost.

The Doors was one of the concerts that Mike was producing in November of 1969 that Jason was looking forward to attending, and did pass out several hundred flyers at UNLV and was excited that Mike had also given him a backstage badge for that concert.

But a week before *The Doors* were scheduled to perform, the sheriff of Las Vegas Ralph Lamb, and the District Attorney George Franklin, had been threatening not to allow Jim Morrison to perform due to his recent obscenity arrest and reputation for inciting violence at his concerts. Both Lamb and Franklin said the concert would have a large police presence, and if Morrison made one obscene move or gesture, he would stop the concert and arrest him on the spot.

When Jason and Nancy Silver arrived for the concert, it was filled to capacity, but there were also uniformed police officers were surrounding the stage which Jason hoped wouldn't turn into another riot where he'd have to take off running again.

There was a long delay and some were worried that the concert had been cancelled, but when concert did finally begin, Jason immediately recognized the opening keyboard notes of *When the Music's Over*, which was one of his favorite *Doors* songs, but he also saw that when Morrison stepped to the microphone, it didn't look like Morrison, even though Jason halfway recognized his deep baritone voice. The guy at the microphone looked heavier than Jason remembered and he was just standing completely still, smoking on a fat cigar. Plus, he was singing in a monotone style when he began the vocals with no emotion or any of his trademark screaming.

The crowd tried to be enthusiastic at first, but when Morrison just stood completely still smoking on his cigar during the long instrumental sections of the song, they became less thrilled and someone yelled out, "That's not Morrison!" and "Bring the real Jim out!" as half of the crowd started booing, and others were shouting, "Let them play!"

But what was even worse, was that everyone was becoming bored and restless because the band never seemed to end the first song, and after over a half hour of just jamming to *When the Music's Over*, *The Doors* not only ended the song, but ended the concert without playing anything else and just walked off the stage.

The crowd was both booing and yelling for more as the lights came up, and the police started leading everyone to the exits, while Jason and Nancy headed backstage to avoid the exiting crowd and deciding to use his backstage badge to meet the band.

He already knew where the dressing room was and decided to take a peek inside, but when he opened the door, he saw the three musicians, Ray Manzarek, Robbie Krieger, and John Densmore, quietly packing up their gear, and across the room, he saw Morrison hunched over in a chair by himself with his head lowered.

"Good show," lied Jason trying to be friendly.

The band members didn't say anything and just nodded silently while Morrison never looked up. Jason saw they weren't in a social mood, so he and Nancy made their exits, while still talking about was a crappy show it was, and decided just to head back to Jason's room.

At least Nancy told Jason her "cycle" was safe, so the night wasn't going to be a total waste.

Ș

It wasn't more than a couple of weeks after *The Doors* concert when Jason dropped off another "Henderson girl" at her house that he was dating occasionally and was heading back home to Las Vegas, but while he was driving down Lake Mead Drive a few minutes later, he suddenly heard a loud pop and saw what looked like a flashbulb going off to his left.

Jason looked over and saw a car swerving towards his car, and quickly made a sharp right swerve himself, as he heard another pop and saw a flash coming from the car next to him. While his car started spinning as he hit the dirt path off the highway, all he could see was dust, and although he didn't understand what was happening, he was relieved that when his car finally came to a stop, that he hadn't hit anything and was glad he didn't crash his car.

When the dust was clearing, his heart was still pounding from the near accident, and looked around to see where the other car was, but Jason didn't see anything except another motorist who had pulled off the highway and raced toward him to see if he was alright.

"I think that guy was trying to shoot you!" the other motorist yelled as Jason got out of the car.

Jason had no idea about what that guy was talking about, but then he saw the hole next to the driver's door of his car and looked up Lake Mead Drive to see if the other car was still around, but it was nowhere in sight and obviously sped away. After

168

looking for any other damage to Jason's car, the other motorist saw a police cruiser driving by and flagged him down.

After Jason told the police officer's he had no idea about what just happened, they asked him to follow them to the Henderson Police Department to make out a report. He was in a daze still not knowing what happened, but Jason was a little nervous when they asked for his driver's license and was relieved when they didn't seem too concerned with his ID and just were asking him about the shooting. The police detective did seem suspicious that Jason couldn't describe the vehicle or couldn't tell them why someone would want to shoot him, but after almost an hour of questioning, they finally let him go home.

During his drive home, his mind was racing, trying to figure out what just happened, and he had no idea who would want to shoot him. There had been two other girls from Henderson besides Nancy that he'd been seeing for the past couple months, and besides his friend in one of his classes at UNLV, they were pretty much the only ones he knew in Henderson and couldn't figure it out.

The next day, he got a phone call from his classmate from Henderson while he was working at *Johnny Reb's* with some news he really didn't want to hear.

"Hey, *you're famous!*" he sarcastically said, "Your name is on the front page of the newspaper."

When Jason's friend read the headline in the local newspaper, "*Shots Fired at Man on Lake Mead Drive*," he started to cringe, but he did halfway smile when his friend continued reading the first sentence of the newspaper story.

"A 21-year-old Las Vegas youth, Jason Jeffery Mershon was shot at twice as he drove his car down Lake Mead Drive last night," his friend started reading the story.

While Jason listened to his friend continue reading, for some reason he liked that the newspaper story not only mentioned his name was *Jason*, but also that his age was *twenty-one years old*, which made him feel that he wasn't going to get into trouble with the police and seemed to make his name *Jason* and his age completely legitimate. It wasn't quite the way he expected it to be, but he at least had his first newspaper clipping as *Jason Mershon*, and was anxious to get a copy on the newspaper himself so he could prove to anyone who ever questioned him, that his name was legally Jason, and also prove he *was* twenty-one years old.

It was printed in a *real* newspaper which he knew would prove to anyone that it was true.

Frank Reich and his other friends at *Johnny Reb's* just kind of joked about the shooting with Jason when they saw the newspaper story and would sarcastically ask him "whose wife he screwed" or "who he pissed off," but Jason had also tried to be light about the experience and explained that it all had to have been a mistake or a case of mistaken identity.

169

Tom Casey told Jason he should never have started hanging out in a sleazy area like Henderson because it was an area known for having a lot of "juvenile delinquents" who were known to sometimes have weapons and there really might have been a jealous boyfriend to targeted him because of that.

Jason still couldn't believe that someone had actually tried to shoot him the night before, and that his pretty blue Ford Galaxy had a bullet hole in its side, but he also learned there was another repercussion later that afternoon when Nancy Silver frantically called Jason at work.

"My Mom won't let me go out with you anymore!" Nancy almost cried into the phone, "She read about you in the newspaper and said you're probably a dangerous person and even lied about your age and older than you told her!"

Jason was trying to work and just told her he'd call her later, but it wasn't long before she called back again and said she had a brilliant idea.

"I'll just tell my mom that we're engaged, and then she'll have to let me go out with you, right?" Nancy desperately tried to suggest.

Jason sternly told her not to consider saying "something stupid like that" or making up some ridiculous lie and tried to calm her by telling her just to wait a couple of weeks "till things cool down" and then they could decide what to do. He also guessed it wouldn't be too long before the other girl's parents would probably end up saying the same thing, but he suddenly wasn't that concerned about seeing them again.

Even though Jason did want to feel the shooting may have just been something random, or even done as a prank, and did think it was crazy that some people may have thought he was *dangerous*, he was still somewhat concerned.

A couple of days later, Frank Reich brought a box to work and told Jason he had something he was planning on selling for a higher price, but would sell to him for a lot cheaper. Jason was surprised when Frank showed him it was a "38 revolver" pistol and said it was just one of several guns that he owned. Frank also said it was one of his "old guns" he was planning on selling for twenty-five dollars, but he'd sell it to Jason for twenty dollars.

When Jason just laughed and said he didn't want to spend twenty dollars for a gun, Frank told Jason that seeing he lived alone, he should at least keep some kind of protection "just in case" anyone was actually planning on targeting him in the future, or if anyone ever tried to break into his room.

"It's just something that can give you some peace of mind and you can just keep it a drawer and know that it's there," Frank tried to convince him, before adding with a lighter tone, "The truth is that you probably never will need it, but if you ever do, it'll probably be something you only use one time in your entire life and either end up shooting someone who's coming after you, or getting shot yourself if you miss."

Jason knew several people in California who had bought guns for protection, especially after all the riots by the blacks in Los Angeles during the past several years, but never thought about owning one himself, After Frank said he'd give Jason a raise to two dollars an hour and add a few hours to his weekly schedule to work as an *assistant manager*, he added that he'd just take five dollars a week out of his next four paychecks to make it "nice and simple" to pay for.

Although he still really didn't think he needed a gun, Jason did like that his raise and extra hours at work would basically pay for it, and agreed to buy it.

At least for Frank's reason of, "just in case."

When Jason went home that day and put the gun in a box in his nightstand drawer, he had made some other decisions about what else he needed to do.

First and obviously, he knew he was going to stay away from Henderson and not even talk to the girls he knew there. He also figured Nancy and the other girls would forget about him in a month or so, already knowing that they weren't the type of girls who would be alone for very long. Secondly, he needed to find a new place to live, and not just because whoever had shot at him might know where he currently lived, but because it was time to move out of what was really like a motel room and find someplace nicer now that he would be making more money each month. And lastly, the newspaper story had said he was twenty-one years old, and now it was time for him to try and start acting like it.

There weren't going to be any more teenage girls for him.

Chapter Three

After deciding it might be a good idea to move away from the *Strip Hotel*, Jason found a studio apartment down the street from the *Sahara Hotel* where Frank Reich worked, called the *Park East Apartments* near Paradise Road on Sahara Boulevard. His rent did go up to eighty-five dollars a month, but he was a little closer to work and college, so he figured he'd save a little in gas The gas prices were still only about thirty cents a gallon in Las Vegas, but there was a gas station called *Terrible Herbst*, which was usually two or three cents less and usually bought his gas there. Jason also felt he had "moved up in the world" because he now had his own private bathroom.

He had been working more hours at *Johnny Reb's*, and with his classes at college, he did cut down on his social life for a period, but there were some shows he felt he had to see.

The big show people were talking about in late 1969 was when *The International Hotel*, the same hotel he saw Elvis Presley, was bringing *HAIR: The American Tribal Love-Rock Musical* to Las Vegas.

The District Attorney George Franklin and Sheriff Lamb were again threatening not to allow *HAIR* to play in Las Vegas, not only because of its "subversive messages" but because it featured "full frontal total nudity," which Franklin considered obscene, as opposed to just women's breasts which were everywhere in Las Vegas. Franklin wasn't able to stop it from opening, but with all the publicity he gave *HAIR*, it became the hottest show in town next to Elvis.

Jason just bought tickets for himself to go alone to the opening night premier because at seven dollars and fifty-cents a ticket, without including any cocktails, his friends, including Rhonda said it was too much money to pay with the Christmas holidays less than a month away. But even though Jason didn't have a date, he ended up enjoying it more than almost anything he had ever seen before, but it had nothing to do with the big *naked scene*, and it was all the music, dancing, and energy that made it two hours of non-stop fun. Especially, when the cast brought the audience members on stage to dance and sing *Let the Sunshine* during the finale, and it felt like everyone was actually part of the show and joining a party as part of the cast themselves. The entire experience made Jason think about how fun it would be to do something like that every night, and knew he'd be coming back to see it again just to be a part of the party.

After the show, Jason was surprised to run into his Criminal Justice professor Jim Santini in the casino lobby.

"I had to come and see the show my old friend George Franklin couldn't shut down," Santini joked, "And in case someone got arrested, I wanted to be here to defend them."

Santini then introduced Jason to his wife with a subtle tease.

"Honey, this is one of my famous students I'm teaching in class, Mr. Mershon," he smiled to his wife, "He can sometimes be seen on the front page of newspapers, so maybe you might want to get his autograph."

Then he lightly added to Jason, "Dodge any bullets lately?"

Jason was still a little embarrassed whenever that subject came up, but it was worse when he went to his classes after the shooting in Henderson, which obviously most of those in his law class had read about in the newspaper. Many Las Vegas police officers were required to take Santini's classes on Criminal Justice to be eligible for advancements in the department, and they always looked at Jason with suspicion after his name was plastered on the front page since then.

Jason talked with Santini and his wife for a few more minutes about how great *Hair* was, and after Santini said he'd see Jason in class and to "stay outta trouble," he gave Jason his business card with his home phone, and jokingly told him to call if he ever got "shot at again" or had any other problems.

Although he never did find out what happened that night in Henderson, or who would want to shoot him, Jason just started trying to make light of it to everyone as if it was "no big thing" and probably just some girls "jealous boyfriend" trying to scare him. But he did still occasionally get nervous whenever a car did pull up next to him at a stoplight and he did always to look around carefully to see who was next to him.

Just in case.

❧

Frank Reich had a brother named Johnny that Jason had met and became friendly when he worked at *Johnny Reb's*, who was married to a country-western singer named Kay Adams who'd actually had a hit county song called *Little Pink Mac* along with a couple of other hits on the radio and was very well known in Las Vegas.

He liked Kay, and she always spent time talking with him when she stopped in Johnny Reb's, and Jason would joke how she had the same name as the main female character in the book he was currently reading, *The Godfather*. Kay said although it was a common name, it sounded more *country-western* than being known under her married name of *Reich*. Jason was glad that his name was unique, and he hadn't met anyone else with that name since he changed it, plus everyone he met had usually said it was a "cool name" and it definitely made him easier to remember.

Kay said she regularly sang at a very popular country-western nightclub on Boulder Highway called the *Nashville Nevada* and invited Jason to come and watch her show on weekends. She also added that there were always a lot of pretty girls who went there and one's he'd like a lot more than the "school girls" he was used to.

Jason hadn't been to a real nightclub for twenty-one-year old's where he could drink alcohol, and although he knew approaching "older women" in a bar was going to be a lot different than just cruising in his car on Fremont or Water Streets, Jason liked that he at least had a regular place where he could practice and convince himself that he was an adult.

The first time he went to the *Nashville Nevada*, he dressed in a suit and tie like he had when he went to the hotel casinos to appear older, even though he noticed that most others were dressed in jeans and cowboy hats.

When Kay saw Jason standing alone at the bar by himself and drinking from beer bottle, she joined him during her break and mentioned another way for him to appear more attractive to *older* women when he was at the bar.

"Honey, the girls in the bars, are usually attracted to men with cocktail glasses in their hands, instead of the *typical old redneck beer guzzlers* who drink from the bottles," Kay described her *secret hint* in her southern drawl, "You look good in your suit, but you'll look a lot more attractive and sophisticated holding a cocktail glass instead of a beer bottle."

He decided to order a more sophisticated sounding cocktail called "Scotch and Soda" and even started to enjoy its taste, but even though he felt more confident after a couple drinks, he still just stood at the bar "posing' holding his drink and smoking a cigarette, hoping that someone would just ask him to dance so he wouldn't feel embarrassed if he asked them and was turned down. Jason still wasn't that comfortable asking some of the older girls, who he knew were actually at least twenty-one years old to dance, until he looked like he fit in being in a bar.

But after Jason's first few trips to the nightclub, even the doormen and bartenders had gotten to know his name, and because they saw he was a friend of Kay's, they didn't even bother asking for his ID any longer. He also did start being approached by "older women" who did ask him to dance, but although he still hadn't met anyone he felt comfortable asking out on a date, he knew he was "getting there" and it wouldn't be too much longer.

❧

Over Christmas vacation, Jason told his parents he would come home for a visit, plus he also wanted to pick up his record collection now that he lived in a bigger place and had some room for a stereo.

Jason had someone put what they called *"Bondo"* in the bullet hole, and then used touch up paint over it, so his parents hopefully wouldn't notice and didn't feel he needed to share the *Henderson story* with them.

Since he had moved away from California, his parents had moved from Lakewood to a townhouse in Los Alamitos, after saying that Lakewood was starting to become not as nice of neighborhood" as it once was.

Jason had dreaded the thought of going back to his old house in Lakewood as well, and was actually relieved he didn't have to go back to a place he felt he no longer had a connection.

His visit with his parents was friendly and cordial, but Jason knew he didn't feel at home when he was with them and the main subjects they discussed were work and college. He did learn that his father was now involved with some new business that he called "computer dating," which Jason thought sounded weird. His father tried to explain how it all worked, but he had a hard time staying focused on another project his father was involved with, after having heard he about so many different businesses before.

Jason had still been reluctantly exchanging letters with Jackie every month, so he told her that he was back in town for a few days, and said they could have dinner together one night. He was also trying to figure out how to tell her it was time for them to stop writing to each other.

When he did meet Jackie, she had already made some special plans for what she called their "reunion" and had purchased tickets at the *Whiskey-a-Go-Go* for a new band that she liked called *Bread*. The "Whiskey" was also where they had gone on one of their dates the year before to see another new group that made it big since then called *Three Dog Night*.

Jackie was acting like they'd never been apart and were going to be picking up where they left off now that he was back in California, but although Jason really didn't want to give her false hopes that they were still going steady, because Jackie was acting so sweet and almost overly nice that night, he didn't want to ruin her special plans and tried to be enthusiastic. He also hadn't had sex with anyone for almost two months, and besides feeling somewhat obligated to Jackie, he didn't mind renewing that part of their relationship in the back seat of his car after their date. But he was also very careful he "pulled out" in time, and made sure he didn't repeat the words "I love you" back to Jackie when he heard her whispering those words to him.

Even though the current number one song in the country that had been playing in his head all week that kept repeating the chorus *"Na na na na, Na na na na, Hey, Hey, Goodbye…,"* Jason knew it wasn't the right night to tell Jackie goodbye, or that he wanted to move on permanently from her, and decided he'd either write her a letter or call her from Las Vegas after the first of the year.

During his entire time in California, Jason just didn't feel comfortable and couldn't stop thinking about getting back to his *real home* to Las Vegas, and in many ways, actually didn't care if he ever returned to California again.

175

Chapter Four

Jason was happy to be back to work a couple days before New Year's Eve, and Frank Reich said he'd pay him on the thirty-first so he had enough money to celebrate the beginning of 1970 with his friends. Kay Adams was also performing New Year's Eve at the *Nashville Nevada*, and that's where Jason decided to celebrate.

He told his friend Tom Casey that he could likely sneak him into the nightclub that night, as he had some "juice" there, and added that the bouncers always seemed to let pretty girls in without asking for their IDs, so Tom's date shouldn't have a problem being admitted. Jason added that "just in case" the bouncers did ask Tom for his ID, Jason would just let him use his driver's license because the bouncers already knew him and stopped asking for his.

"Plus, the Nevada licenses haven't got photos on them like they do in California," Jason added, "So the bouncers will probably just look at the birthdate and not even notice the name."

Tom said it sounded like a good plan and thought it would be fun taking his girlfriend to a *real* nightclub for the first time. His girlfriend was named Shannon King and was the daughter of the well-known Las Vegas entertainer Sonny King, and Tom had been dating her since they were juniors in high school in 1968. Tom had also already told Jason that besides having a famous father, Shannon's *"Godfather"* was Vito Genovese, the famous mafia gangster who had recently died.

After the book *The Godfather* became so popular, everyone liked dropping the names of some *gangsters* they knew, especially in Las Vegas, but Tom assured Jason it was true that Genovese was actually her Godfather, and wasn't just name-dropping.

"Shannon's dad knows all those old mob guys from all the nightclubs he performed at for the last twenty years," Tom had smiled before adding, "My dad is in the FBI and knows some of those guys too."

Jason didn't currently have a regular girlfriend so he decided to go stag, hoping he'd meet someone at the *Nashville Nevada* to "get lucky" with after the New Year's Eve party. He had also tried to set up his apartment where it would appear to be what he heard described as a "cool bachelor pad" to make it seductive as possible if he did bring a girl home. He had put a red light in the lamp next to his bed that would illuminate the room dimly when he entered and hit the wall switch. He also used the same wall outlet so his record player would begin playing music at the same time.

Jason didn't want rock and roll to be blasting, and instead had an album that featured Henry Mancini's greatest hits ready to start playing more mellow music that he knew would set the mood when he turned on the light switch, which he felt would also make him appear more *mature* and *sophisticated*.

Tom and Shannon discovered Jason was right, and they had no problem attending the *Nashville Nevada's* New Year's party as the doorman just waved them inside when they saw Jason. They also thought it was " cool" that they weren't asked for ID's when they all ordered cocktails at the bar.

Kay Adams was already onstage singing, and everyone was in a celebratory mood with the dance floor packed with partygoers, with the band backing up Kay, mixing county music with a lot of fifties rock songs by Chuck Berry and Jerry Lee Lewis, while Jason and Tom took turns dancing with Shannon the first hour.

It was almost eleven pm when Jason was watching Tom and Shannon dance and sipping on his scotch and soda when someone approached him at the bar.

"Hi," she said, "My name is Anne, and I really like this song, do you want to dance?"

Jason didn't hesitate as she led him to the dance floor, and had already noticed her sitting with some other girls earlier. He also thought she was one of the sexiest girls in the bar that night, and saw the way she styled her blond hair reminded him of a lot of Nancy Sinatra. Jason was mainly pleased that she had actually asked him to dance first, without having to approach her himself and risk being turned down.

Kay was onstage singing *Stand by Your Man*, the song Anne said she liked, and Kay smiled approvingly at Jason when she saw him slow dancing with her in front of the bandstand. Although they didn't speak while they were dancing and listening to Kay sing, Jason did immediately like how good Anne felt in his arms and especially liked the perfume she was wearing.

"It's called *Jungle Gardenia*," Anne answered after Jason complimented her on "how nice she smelled."

After the dance, Jason bought her a drink and introduced her to Tom and Shannon while they stood at the bar and all talked during the band break.

Her full name was Anne Sanderson, and said she had just started to attend cosmetology school to be a beautician, and also worked full time at *Fletcher Jones Chevrolet* as a receptionist until she graduated. Jason told her that he was going to UNLV to become a lawyer and also explained he was a part-time an assistant manager at the restaurant Kay Adams' brother-in Law owned until he graduated himself. Anne also joked that she was actually only twenty years old, but said she never got carded at the nightclubs, so Jason decided to tell her that he was twenty-one years old "just in case" his real age might turn her off as it had Angie, without letting her know he was still in his first year of college. He knew he didn't want to lose *this one* before he even had a chance to get to know her better.

At least for that night.

Anne stayed at the bar with Jason, Tom, and Shannon, and they'd alternate dance partners for some songs when the band started again, but Jason and Anne always danced together for the slow ballads when Kay Adams sang Patsy Cline's *Crazy*, or another song by Brenda Lee called *Johnny One-Time* that Kay had lightly dedicated to Jason that night, obviously trying to help him get Anne more interested in him by insinuating that he was a well-known and popular customer at the bar.

As midnight was approaching and everyone was gathering on the dance floor, Jason grabbed Anne's hand and had Tom and Shannon follow him to be near the front of the stage as Kay was starting the countdown with "FIVE-FOUR-THREE-TWO-ONE!" before screaming out, "HAPPY NEW YEAR!" which led the band to immediately start playing *Auld Lang Syne*. As everyone sang along with the first verse, *"Should old acquaintance be forgot, and never brought to mind?"* all those on the dance floor proceeded to kiss their partners as well as anyone else who was nearby.

Jason gave Shannon a quick kiss, then Kay leaned over from the stage, and he kissed her, before turning to Anne to kiss her as well. When Anne cupped her hands on his cheeks and gave him a kiss that was longer than he expected, and then gave him a hug and pushed her body against his, Jason felt confident that he was going to "get lucky" with someone even sexier than he had hoped.

They all danced to a few more songs before Tom said he'd take Shannon home in a taxi, when he saw Jason wanted to stay longer and spend time alone with Anne.

Anne's friends that she came with that night were also leaving around the same time, and after she asked Jason if he could drive her home, he again didn't hesitate, and said, "no problem."

As they drove away from the *Nashville Nevada* shortly after two am, Anne explained that she still lived with her parents, so Jason casually asked her if she wanted to stop by his apartment and have one more drink before he drove her home. He was happy when she didn't hesitate and said, "Sure, but I do need to work tomorrow at noon, so as long as I'm home before dawn" and Jason casually just said again, "no problem."

When they walked in Jason's apartment, he turned on the light switch and the Henry Mancini album began playing softly in the dimly lit room, and after he mixed them both a cocktail, he knew he wanted to say something romantic to start the conversation. Before he handed her the drink, he took the back of her hand and kissed it saying. "I'm glad we met tonight because I think I'm really starting to like you," and although he was afraid it sounded corny, he immediately felt better when Anne said she liked him too and kissed him back. But he felt even better when after a few minutes of passionate kisses, Anne leaned back on his bed and pulled him toward her saying, "And don't worry about anything, I'm on the pill."

Besides knowing he was going to be having sex with his first *woman* who wasn't a teenager he'd have to worry about "pulling out," Jason also thought it was a bit ironic

178

that the Henry Mancini song playing on his stereo as he started to undress her was titled *Mr. Lucky,* and started feeling that 1970 was going to be his luckiest year yet.

&

Jason had always known about the term "love at first sight" and thought it was ridiculous to think he was in love after just one night of great sex, but after thinking about how long and the number of times they had sex the night before, along with how passionate and romantic it had felt, he also felt something with Anne that he'd never felt with any other girl before.

With the practice he had with "pulling out" with the "teenage" girls he'd been with, and how he had learned to keep going for a second time without going *soft,* he saw that Anne got turned even more with him not stopping even after she felt him come inside her the first time, and always breathlessly moaned with pleasure each time she said she was having another orgasm herself.

Besides thinking how it had been be best night of sex he ever had, Jason was also thinking about a mature way he should contact her again and let her know how much he enjoyed himself and not letting her think he considered the night before just a New Year's Eve fling.

He distinctly remembered because he never got up to change the record that had been playing in his apartment, the needle on his stereo just kept returning that side if the album and Jason remembered how the Henry Mancini song *The Days of Wine and Roses* been playing softly when they enjoying their first after-sex cigarette together, as well as Anne commenting about what a pretty song that was. After hearing that same song play at least four more times before he took her home that morning, he decided to let the lyrics of that song be his message to Anne with what he thought would be a classy and romantic gesture.

Jason knew she was working her job at *Fletcher Jones Chevrolet,* so while he was also working at *Johnny Reb's* later that afternoon, instead of just calling her on the phone, he went to the florist during his lunch break, ordered a dozen roses, and also included a bottle of wine he bought to be delivered to Anne at work with a message handwritten by him.

Without even signing the card, Jason just wrote the line, *"For the memories of the golden smile that introduced me to the days of wine and roses... and YOU!"* hoping she'd remember the song as he had, and know it came from him.

Anne's reaction was even better than he hoped and she called him at *Johnny Reb's* that same day saying she'd be over to open the bottle of wine with him when they both got off work, and *personally* thank him herself.

After his second romantic night with Anne, Jason also knew it was time to write Jackie a letter saying he was sorry, but he had met someone he'd become *serious* with and told her not to plan on him coming back to California.

It was a hard letter for him to write, but it was the end of the 1960s and Jason needed to put his past in California behind him, and knew future was definitely going to be in Las Vegas.

Chapter Five

They both knew with Jason going back to his classes at UNLV and Anne to cosmetology school, as well as both of them working at their jobs, they'd probably only be able to see each other on weekends. But their sexual attraction for each other made it impossible to wait that long, and Anne would usually visit him for a few hours at least once or twice during the week at his apartment.

Although Jason had always held on to the fifty-dollar bill his father had given him a year earlier, and had kept hidden in a book in his apartment, after he started seeing Anne regularly, he had to break it and now only had a twenty-dollar bill stashed away to use for any emergency. He also needed to ask Frank Reich to work a few extra hours a week at *Johnny Reb's*, so he could afford to take Anne on "adult dates" and to some of the lounge acts in Las Vegas were within his budget.

The lounge shows at the casinos had no cover charge and only a two-drink minimum, which meant even with the tip, they could see some great performers for less than ten dollars for both of them which Jason felt was affordable.

The *International Hotel* lounge shows regularly featured acts like Ike and Tina Turner, Redd Foxx, Gladys Knight, and the Pips, Bobby Stevens and The Checkmates, Jerry Lee Lewis, Frankie Laine, or Little Anthony and the Imperials, while the *Flamingo Hotel* lounge shows would have acts like Fats Domino, Billy Joe Royal, Wayne Cochran, and the CC Riders, The Mills Brothers, or The Platters. But it was at *The Sahara* where his boss Frank worked, who with his "juice," was able to get Jason and Anne "comp'd" to see acts in the main showroom like comedians Buddy Hackett and Johnny Carson.

After the shows at *The Sahara*, they'd usually stop at the craps table where Frank was working and Jason would place some bets on the "Field" or the "Hard Way" numbers, figuring that that because the show was free, he'd gamble five or ten dollars to see if he could double his money. Whenever he did get lucky and win what he considered "free money," he'd then take Anne to one of the casinos that regularly offered Prime Rib dinner specials for only a dollar and ninety-nine cents.

It was difficult, but Jason managed to go to his classes, try to work almost thirty hours a week to keep his bills paid and have enough energy to go on fun dates with Anne on the weekends and keep her entertained.

Although they had met at the *Nashville Nevada* and would occasionally go back to see Kay Adams perform and listen to county music, Jason would always play *The*

Days of Wine and Roses at least once on the way back to his apartment after they both agreed to start calling it *"Our song."*

But there was something else Jason discovered they coincidentally shared together that was really making him feel that he'd met his perfect match.

It was while Jason and Anne were at a movie together watching the previews of coming attractions, when Jason saw the movie version of the novel *The Adventurers* would be coming to that theatre in the future, and was pleasantly surprised when he also discovered that Anne had read several Harold Robbins novels herself, and also thought *The Adventurers* was his sexiest.

Because Anne believed he was actually twenty-one years old, he wanted to make sure it sounded like his high school days were well in the past, even though he'd just read that book a few years earlier.

"When I was just a teenager years ago," Jason smiled to Anne, "I learned more about sex in Harold Robbin's books than I ever did in sex education at school, especially *The Adventurers.*"

"But besides Dax, I really liked the character Sue Ann Daley," Jason lightly added, "I remembered how sexual she was and always remembered a line she said in that book when grabbed Dax's dick and screamed *'Get it in there!'* when she couldn't hold back how much she wanted it, and I always fantasized about meeting a girl who was always horny like that when I was *just a kid."*

Anne thought that was funny, and said because she vaguely remembered that line in the novel as well, she joked she'd make his fantasy come true and *"Get it in there!"* became her own "romantic" demand" to Jason when they were in bed together.

Romantically, they had the song *The Days of Wine and Roses*, but sexually, Jason did feel like he was Dax and felt that he had actually found his Sue Ann Daley.

For what Anne still thought was Jason's twenty-second birthday in February, she decided to surprise him and treated him to a dinner at the *Golden Steer* restaurant for what she said was famous for its Prime Rib and "definitely better than the dollar ninety-nine Prime Rib casino specials" they'd been on previous dates. She also treated him to see Ella Fitzgerald in the main showroom act at *The Flamingo Hotel*, who Jason said he liked because she sang several George Gershwin songs, whose music Anne also liked.

Jason had already discovered that they both had a wide range of taste of all music and entertainment and Anne also liked his assortment of eight-track tapes, which would always be playing on his car stereo as they drove to the various lounge shows on the Las Vegas Strip.

Anne said her favorite song on Jason's tapes was by the group *Rare Earth* called *Get Ready* and said that she loved how sexy the singer's voice sounded when he sang the lyrics about "getting ready to make love to you" and *'Get Ready cause here I COME!'* and joked that it really made her feel like saying "Get it in there!"

"I'm not like a groupie or anything," Anne smiled," But when I hear singers like that, along with ones like Tom Jones and Elvis, it always turns me on."

Jason had already seen that Anne never had a problem with getting turned on when it came to sex, but her comment did make him think of another fun way to show her he wanted to be her fantasy as well.

He knew it would be something crazy that he'd need some practice, but also thought that if it did add "anything extra" to their relationship, he'd at least give it a try and give her his own surprise.

Jason already knew about an amateur talent contest the *Nashville Nevada* nightclub had each week, and although he already knew the lyrics to some country songs that the house band regularly played for the contestants, he wanted to learn something more rock and roll that he could practice in advance so he wouldn't look *too much* like an amateur.

There was a student his Criminal Law class with Jim Santini named Paul Kirby who Jason had become friends with, who he also learned was also a guitar player and interested in eventually starting a surf rock band in the style of *The Ventures*.

Paul hadn't performed anywhere in stage yet either, but did think entering a talent contest and performing in front of an audience, would be a good way to "work on his chops," as he liked to call it, and agreed to practice at Jason's apartment a couple nights a week where they could also work on their homework together for their criminal law class.

Jason knew he wanted to surprise Anne with his "performance" but also knew his vocal range wasn't strong enough to try any songs by Tom Jones or Elvis, who were Anne's fantasy singers, so Jason told Paul he wanted to sing something that just "looked and sounded cool" onstage.

After they started practicing different songs to learn together, Paul let Jason know what songs were out of his vocal range, and which songs were acceptable to try and perform live. The one thing that surprised Paul was all the song lyrics that Jason seemed to know by memory without having to learn them, but Jason explained it was just something that came naturally to him when he listened to music, and he'd always sing along with the eight-track tapes or songs on the radio when he was driving.

Jason knew that Anne also thought Mick Jagger was sexy, and Jason thought Jagger's vocals were more within his range, so they practiced the songs *Play with Fire*, and *Under My Thumb*, but the song Paul said Jason sounded the best and was more upbeat, was another old Rolling Stones song called *It's All Over Now*.

Paul also said it was an easy song with simple chords that the band at the *Nashville Nevada* could follow along with, and because Jason had already sung along with that song so many times in his car, he also felt it was one he sing with that "Jagger style and attitude" that Anne said "turned her on."

He also decided on the perfect night to give Anne her surprise.

183

Both Jason and Anne had been eagerly anticipating the opening in Las Vegas of the movie version of the book, *The Adventurers*, and Jason had chosen the night for them to finally see the movie, on the same evening a talent contest would be held at the *Nashville Nevada*.

The Adventurers were playing at a theatre inside the *Bonanza Hotel and Casino*, on the corner of Las Vegas Boulevard and Flamingo Road, so Jason figured he could just cut down Flamingo Road to Boulder Highway after the movie and make it to the *Nashville Nevada* in plenty of time for the contest which wouldn't begin until after ten pm.

Anne and Jason were both excited when the movie began because it was starting out just like the novel, with Dax as a young boy witnessing the bandoleros attacking his family. But what bothered Jason immediately was the onscreen graphic in the very beginning, showed the place and timeframe of the movie as "CORTEGUAY 1945", knowing that at least a third of the book took place before 1945, and was wondering how the movie was going to tell a cohesive story with that much of the timeframe missing.

Although he thought it was great seeing his favorite characters come to life on the big screen for almost three hours, when the movie was over, both he and Anne were disappointed that although many of the scenes in the book were similar in the movie, it didn't really tell the entire story, and the characters portrayed in the film weren't nearly as exciting or sexy as they were in the book.

But Jason had more important things on his mind than just the movie that night.

He had told Paul Kirby earlier that day to meet him at the *Nashville Nevada* and sign them up for the talent contest before he would arrive, and had also invited several of his friends to come to his "performance" that night not only to make it look like a "little party" he was taking Anne to after the movie, but to also have a cheering section for the audience applause judging which was how the contest was decided.

Because Tom Casey and Shannan King had been to the nightclub a few other times since New Year's Eve with Jason, the doormen had gotten to know them and weren't ever asked for their ID's. Jason had also invited Rhonda Talbot who he knew the doormen would let in with no problem, as well as another mutuel friend of Tom's named Victor Consuela who'd Jason met several times when he came into *Johnny Reb's* and had become friends with as well.

Victor always liked telling a story about how his family had escaped from Cuba on a small boat after Fidel Castro had taken over Cuba, but Tom had already told Jason that Victor had actually just flown into the United States well before then and just made up that story to impress girls.

Because it was Victor's first time to the *Nashville Nevada*, Jason just let him use his driver's license knowing he wouldn't need it himself and also told his friends not to mention that he'd actually be singing in the contest and wanted to keep it a surprise.

184

His friends were all there when Jason and Anne arrived after the movie, and while they were socializing and watching the first two performers in the talent contest, Jason saw the surprised look on Anne's face when the emcee announced, "And our next contestant tonight is Jason and his guitar player Paul!"

As Jason stood on the stage as Paul told the house band members, "The key of G," and the bass line and tempo the band could accompany them, he felt his right knee trembling a little, almost like the first time he raced in a roller-skating competition, and decided to take the microphone off the stand and try and sing the while he moved around the stage so he wouldn't look nervous.

As soon as Paul started the opening riffs to *Its All Over Now* and the band joined in, Jason saw Anne cheering with his friends, but he was mainly concerned with not embarrassing himself, while still trying to look cool and sexy at the same time.

As he sang Jagger's lyrics about how he used to love a particular girl who treated him badly but decided to dump her and had no regrets about moving on, Jason knew it wasn't the most romantic of songs, but it still basically conveyed the kind of cocky attitude he wanted to project.

Jason started feeling more confident as he strutted back and forth across the stage singing the chorus of how he *"used to love her, but it's all over now,"* and tried to sing with swagger whenever he made eye contact with Anne, but was relieved when he finally concluded the song feeling that he at least had hit all the right notes and was satisfied that at least his friends were applauding and cheering.

Tom Casey joked that even though he could see that Jason was having fun up on stage and thought he sang okay, he sarcastically added that he "shouldn't quit his *day job* at Johnny Reb's just yet." But it was Anne's reaction that he liked best, and after she excitedly told him "How sexy he looked onstage" and whispered she couldn't wait to tell him to "Get it in there!" when they went back to his apartment.

Jason smiled and told Anne hearing her say that line made up for not hearing it in *The Adventurers* movie that night.

They didn't win the twenty-five-dollar first prize, but Jason and Paul did finish third out of the seven contestants thanks to all of his friends cheering them in the audience applause judging, and they did win a ten-dollar bar tab which Jason used to buy drinks for his friends for their support. He was just satisfied he at least *done it*, and knew hearing Anne say how much she enjoyed seeing him sing, was worth more than twenty-five dollars anyway.

But it was later that same night while Jason and Anne where in bed together with seemingly even more passion than usual, when Jason learned his first night of singing a song onstage was more memorable for another reason.

As they were passionately kissing, Jason heard Anne whispering words to him and although he was sure he heard her correctly, he asked her to repeat it.

"I love you," she whispered again.

Jason felt like an idiot for asking her to say it again, but then a warm feeling started coming over him like he'd never felt before. It was the first time the words "I love you" had been spoken between them, and hearing it from Anne, gave him a completely different feeling than when he had heard it from Jackie. He held her tighter and closer, and felt even better when he said, "and I love you" back to Anne.

They both excitedly kept repeating the words with each kiss until it seemed Anne was almost crying, and he knew hearing the words "I love you" from someone he loved as well gave him more passion that *"Get it in there!"* ever did.

The next day Jason was back at the florist sending Anne a dozen roses and a bottle of her favorite perfume, *Jungle Gardenia*, but this time wrote a message with the words; *"I never met a girl who makes me feel the way that you do, so get ready cause here I CUM!"*

Jason decided to use some of the lyrics to the song *Get Ready* that Anne said always turned her on, deciding to add the sexual innuendo so he wouldn't sound too gushy, but this time he closed his note with the words "I love you" wanting her to know he really meant what he'd said the night before.

1970 wasn't even half way over, but it had already turned into his best year ever.

Chapter Six

Now that Jason and Anne had both admitted they were really "in love" with each other, they did also occasionally talk about what it would be like being be married "someday" in the future, but with Jason still in college studying to be a lawyer, they both felt they needed to wait until both their careers were established and were able to afford raising a family together. Anne had also always said she loved his name and would often repeat it, saying, "*Jason Mer-shon, Jason Mer-shon…,*" and Jason liked that she was just imagining what her last name might be someday.

They would even sometimes fantasize about what they'd name their children if they ever did decide to get married, and Jason said he wanted original and unique names for any children and decided that if he had a daughter, he wanted to name her Venus or Aphrodite after the goddesses of love and sex, and if he had a son, he'd like to name him after himself, because the name Jason was still so unique. But although he couldn't picture himself being married for quite some time, he knew he'd found the perfect girl to plan his future with, and wanted to continue to keep everything exciting with Anne until them.

Jason wasn't trying to kid himself into thinking he was a great vocalist, but after seeing how much Anne had enjoyed, and especially reacted to seeing him on stage, he also discovered that he loved singing all the songs he had in his head to a live audience.

He figured as long as he could carry the tune without embarrassing himself, he wanted to continue singing in the talent contests, so Jason and Paul started practicing other songs that Jason liked to sing, including Johnny Rivers versions of *Memphis* and *Seventh Son*, as well as a couple of Beatles songs Jason had always liked, *I'll Follow the Sun.* and *I Feel Fine* which he wanted to dedicate to Anne.

When Jason's friend Rhonda Talbot from *Johnny Reb's* said she wanted to try and sing in a talent contest with Jason, he added the Nancy Sinatra/Lee Hazelwood duet, *Summer Wine.* to his practice sessions. *Summer Wine* was a song that Jason originally tried to get Anne to sing with him because he thought she looked so much like Nancy Sinatra, but Anne didn't like singing onstage, so Jason stuck with singing that duet with Rhonda.

Jason was also learning how to cover his limited vocal range by graveling certain notes he couldn't reach or just speak/singing them and just wanted to show confidence and showmanship and make sure he looked good onstage.

"Hey, Dylan and Jagger aren't great vocalists," Jason would often joke to his friends, "It's all in the attitude, man."

The house band at the *Nashville Nevada* was *Mike Franklin and The Common People*, and Jason had noticed that Mike Franklin sometimes liked changing a lyric or two to some of the popular songs he'd sing, to give it a slightly dirty but funny meaning.

The audience always laughed at the innuendoes, so Jason would usually change a lyric to a song he was singing to get a laugh from the audience to cover up any of his limited singing ability and decided it was better to have them laugh at an innuendo rather than have him think they were laughing at his singing.

The talent contests at the *Nashville Nevada* became a regular night out for Jason, Anne and his friends, but Jason wanted to turn it into a twice a week "party" when he learned another country-western bar, *The Lariat*, had a talent contest on a different night than the *Nashville Nevada*.

Victor Consuela was also usually the only one who could join Jason and Anne for the talent contests at *The Lariat* after Tom Casey said going out twice a week on school nights was too much for both him and Shannon, as did Rhonda Talbot.

Victor had also given Jason something he said was better than *No-Doze* for staying alert at college called "white crosses" which Jason did take occasionally when he felt he was getting too tired in his classes or at work, which he definitely didn't want to interfere with his love life and the fun he was having.

As Jason began to get more confident in his singing ability while he was "working on his own chops," he still wanted to sing songs that Anne liked and spent three weeks practicing with Paul to a new song that he wanted to sing to her at next talent contest at *The Lariat*.

They both liked the lyrics to the song *Let It Bleed* from *The Rolling Stones* latest album of the same name, and Anne joked that the lyrics about how "you can *cream* on me" was something else besides "Get it in there!" that sounded sexy to say when she wanted sex.

Because it wasn't a popular song that had played on the radio and he knew the band at *The Lariat* probably hadn't heard before, Paul said he'd just start the song with his acoustic guitar in the talent contest and hope the bass player and drummer could follow him and join in after a verse or two.

When he sang *Let It Bleed* for the first time at *The Lariat* club, he saw Paul was right and the house band, *Bobby Douglas and the Conspiracy*, had never even heard about that song before and just tried to follow Paul's lead guitar.

As Jason sang the first verse about having *"someone to lean on"* the band seemed uninterested about what he was singing, but when he sang the second verse about needing *"someone to cream on"* Jason noticed that Bobby Douglas glanced questioningly at the other band members.

By the time Jason sang the last verses about needing *"someone to bleed on"* and finally about *"someone to cum all over me"* Bobby abruptly stopped playing and said, "C'mon man, you can't sing that kind of trash up here!"

Jason tried explaining it was just a song by The Rolling Stones, but Bobby said "those kind" of songs weren't allowed and was surprised when Bobby disqualified him from the talent contest. He couldn't understand it because he'd seen how comedians like Redd Foxx, Buddy Hackett, and even Johnny Carson, were popular in Las Vegas for their "dirty" or what was called "blue" comedy shows, but Jason at least was satisfied that Victor, and especially Anne, liked his performance and thought it was funny,

Victor just laughed after they left *The Lariat* that night, saying they were just "boring country western *hicks* at that bar" and *Let It Bleed,* was his favorite song he had heard Jason sing, while Anne just whispered her new favorite line about how Jason could *cream all over her* when they got home that night. Jason also liked how Victor and Anne teased him about being the "bad boy" of the talent contest that night, so he figured he'd continue to add sexy humor to some of the songs he sang in the talent contests by just changing a few lyrics without being too dirty, hoping it might be something that could make him stand out to the audiences and at least make them laugh.

Jason and Paul never did finish better than second place in any of the talent contests they were entering, but Jason was still planning to keep "working on his chops" sarcastically joking to his friends that "next to sex' singing was now his "second favorite hobby."

He also felt his life was perfect and almost couldn't believe what a great year he was having.

☙

Almost three months had passed since he had written Jackie Madison his last letter, and Jason was surprised when her response came in a large envelope addressed to him.

She had sent him the new album by the pop band *Bread* that they had seen at the *Whiskey- A-Go-Go* on their last date together the previous December, and Jackie included a short note telling Jason to listen to a particular song from that album and think of her whenever he heard it.

The song was called *It Don't Matter to Me,* and although Jason thought it was one of the prettiest songs he ever heard, the lyrics made him feel it was also one of the saddest songs at the same time. Especially, the lyrics at the end that mentioned there would always be an *"empty room"* and *"open heart"* that would be waiting for him if his search for happiness ever brought him back together with her.

Although Jason did feel a little guilty about how he had ended his relationship with Jackie, he did it was interesting how she wanted to convey a goodbye message to him, in the same kind of classy way he had decided to start a relationship with Anne by using the lyrics in a song. But any guilt he did feel, was overshadowed by how happy he was *really being in love,* and hoped she'd realize it had just been a "teenage romance" and would eventually move on as he had.

It was also the last communication Jason ever had with Jackie.

Chapter Seven

It was less than a week after the *Kent State* shootings in Ohio, where four student protesters against the Vietnam war were killed by the National Guard in early May, when Jason picked up the phone at *Johnny Reb's* while he was working.

"You stupid son of a bitch!" he heard his mother's voice scream into the phone, "With all the fucking around in Las Vegas you're doing, you've lost your college deferment and now you're going to get drafted and have to go to Vietnam!"

Before he could say anything back, she hung up the phone, but was immediately concerned and went outside to use a payphone to call his mother back, knowing Frank Reich had already asked him not to make long-distance calls from the work phone, but also not wanting to talk about any problems in front of anyone at *Johnny Reb's.*

Jason already knew how his mother always had a bad habit of showing her anger by taking the phone off the hook after one of her rants, and only got a busy signal when he called her back, but he kept redialing her number from the phone booth, now worried that the letter he'd been dreading had finally arrived from the draft board.

When he had signed up for the Selective Service when he turned eighteen, Jason was still was using his parent's home address, so any letters from the Draft Board would still go to that address and now he was in a panic to find out what his mother may have received in the mail.

After Jason was finally able to get through to his mother, he was relieved that it wasn't his draft notice ordering him to report for duty, but just his reclassification to 1A stating he was now only eligible to be drafted.

"You didn't pass enough units for your deferment last semester," his mother snidely yelled into the phone, "That means you're going to be drafted this year for sure!"

With all of the different things he was involved with since New Year's that year, Jason had ended up receiving an "Incomplete" grade in his early morning class after skipping quite a few classes the past semester on the weeknights he'd stayed up late with Anne. He hoped that because he had passed all his other classes and didn't actually *fail* that class, and it was just *incomplete,* the draft board wouldn't make a "big deal" over just a half of unit or that he had only passed fifteen units instead of the required fifteen and a half.

But he quickly realized that they obviously had.

Jason did contact the local selective service office to assure them that he'd make sure he passed all of his required classes the current semester that was ending in June, but they explained because he was now classified *1A*, his deferment was invalid and couldn't be reinstated, as well as telling him he could now receive a draft notice from the Army at any time.

Besides being angry at himself for letting his deferent lapse, he was also pissed and frustrated that the government was able to control him and keep him from just enjoying his life. But he also didn't want to regret anything that he had done that year, which he felt had been the best five months he'd ever experienced.

Jason had mainly been hoping he wouldn't receive an actual draft notice until the new "Draft Lottery" that President Nixon had created the year before would take place, so he could have some more time to decide what to do. He had already investigated everything he could about how the lottery worked and what his odds were if he waited.

In the first "Draft Lottery" the year before, Jason learned that only the first couple hundred birthdays they drew randomly were actually drafted, and with Nixon having promised to continue reducing the number of the troops in Vietnam, he'd read that number would probably be even lower that year. He knew that gave him close to a fifty-fifty chance or better, but he also had to decide if he wanted to bet his life on a coin flip. He also knew that year's "Draft Lottery was still a couple of months away, and now that he'd been reclassified *1A*, he wasn't sure if he had that much time.

Jason began talking to everyone about his other options to keep from going to Vietnam if he did receive his draft notice before them. He knew he'd never consider escaping to Canada to avoid the draft like he'd heard a couple of friends from high school had done, and was just trying to find a way to stay in Las Vegas.

Victor Consuela told Jason he had some friends who were planning on signing up for the *Air National Guard* at *Nellis Air Force Base*, and also that the waiting list wasn't as long in Las Vegas to sign up for the reserves as it was in some other cities.

The *Air National Guard* did sound like the best option that would allow him to stay in Las Vegas, but it was also a six-year commitment, and he'd still have to leave for basic training for six weeks, and then spend a weekend a month "playing soldier."

But it would also mean he'd be assured of not having to go to Vietnam.

Jason did go with Victor friends to inquire about signing up for the *Air National Guard* and after they filled out some forms, they were told they'd be assigned a time to come in for a physical once they signed their paperwork to enlist.

The officer in charge explained it would be best to sign up that day, because after the draft lottery, "everyone and their brother" would be trying to sign up and there wouldn't be as many openings after that.

Victor's friends signed their enlistment papers, but Jason said he wanted to wait a while longer to think about it, and had other concerns before he made a final decision.

The 1970 "Draft Lottery" had also been well-publicized as being drawn for all those born in 1951, and with all of the decisions on his mind, Jason felt strange thinking that his biggest concern was having to let Anne know that he was only nineteen years old and eligible for the draft that year.

They had recently celebrated Anne's twenty-first birthday, and she made a joke saying she'd finally caught up with Jason and was now "legally" twenty-one years old herself. Jason had sent her flowers again and got her a *Tom Jones Live in Las Vegas* album he knew she liked, but the best gift he found was a musical jewelry box that played the chimes of the song *The Days of Wine and Roses* which he also bought her.

Jason knew he had to eventually tell Anne his real age, but because he was now in love with her, he didn't want her to think he was "just a kid" or "a liar" and spoil it, so when he did tell her, he just lightly explained that because he didn't know he'd be falling in love with her when they first met, he didn't think his age would matter.

Anne was surprised, but Jason couldn't have been more relieved than when she just laughed it off and said it didn't matter to her.

"You don't act like a kid and you're certainly more romantic than any older guys I dated," Anne just laughed before adding with a tease, "Besides, I think it's cool to have a younger lover, and I can just tell my friends that you're my full-time *gigolo*!"

"But I love you, and your age doesn't bother me at all," Anne said more seriously.

Hearing that made up his mind, and Jason knew he didn't want to leave Anne for even the six weeks of basic training in the *Air National Guard*. He knew if he his birthday was drawn as a low number in the "Draft Lottery" he would definitely be in the first group to be drafted into the Army, but was also thinking about an old Frankie Laine song he'd always liked called *The Moonlight Gambler*, and decided that because he was in Las Vegas he was going to gamble and hoped he'd draw a high number.

For the next month, Jason was wishing harder than ever, that the lyrics Frankie Laine sang in that particular song about how he had *"gambled for love and lost"* would be wrong, and this would be a gamble he would win.

❧

The week before the July 1st "Draft Lottery" drawing, Jason told all of his friends he was having a party when the drawing was completed, and it would either be a celebration party or a possible going away party, depending on how it turned out.

The day before the lottery, Jason also read that only the first *"150"* out of the *"366"* birthdays drawn at random would be called for the draft that year, but those whose numbers were as high as *"215"* would still be *"on call"* for the next few years. A number over *"215"* was the only way to become immune from ever having to serve in the military under Nixon's new selection process.

July 1st fell on a Wednesday, and Anne called in sick for work to be with Jason when they began drawing numbers on television that morning and decided he'd be happy if his number was at least over *150*.

On the TV screen he saw there was two large bingo type of machines on the stage filled with what looked like Bingo or Keno balls with all possible birthdates, and the other with numbers *1* through *366*, as Jason waited patiently and nervously to hear them call February 24th and the corresponding number that it was matched.

Finally, the person drawing the numbers said, "February 24..." and Jason's heart was pounding as he heard the announcer say, "Number two...." and then, "...hundred and thirty-six."

Both Anne and Jason quickly looked at each other with their mouths open, wondering if they heard it right, but then another voice confirmed it, *"February 24th, number two hundred and thirty-six."*

After the screaming and cheering, they went out and got beer, wine, liquor, and food for what Jason said would be the best celebration party in his life for the party with his friends later that night.

Jason invited Tom Casey and his girlfriend Shannon King, Victor Consuela, Rhonda Talbot, Paul Kirby, and three other girls he worked with at *Johnny Reb's* named Jane, Arleen, and Mary Lou as well as Frank Reich and his wife, to all come to his apartment, and although it wasn't a huge party, it was lively.

The music was loud, and although a few residents in his apartment building occasionally came to Jason's door requesting he turn down the music, as soon as they left, Victor would turn the volume back up full blast, and they'd all sing along with the songs on the stereo.

One of the best things Jason remembered about that party was kissing Anne passionately and only stopping occasionally to join everyone in singing the chorus of what he kept saying was his new favorite song, and currently the number one song in America that week, *Mama Told Me Not to Come.*

Jason wanted to remember that Three Dog Night song and always remember to associate it with one of the best nights of his life, along with the Cream song *I Feel Free* which he felt was actually finally true now.

The next day, Jason and Anne called in sick to work again and spent the entire day in bed recovering from the best hangover he'd ever had and did feel like he was definitely *Mr. Lucky* for real.

Chapter Eight

With all the money Jason had spent on his celebration party, he was around forty dollars short for his rent that month and even needed to get an advance from Frank to cover it. He'd already discovered that year that it wasn't cheap trying to have a good time in Las Vegas by just living paycheck to paycheck.

He was also still a little concerned about Anne learning he was only nineteen years old, as well as having her know he still had several more years of college to attend before he graduated, and with September approaching, he knew he needed to make an important decision as far as returning to UNLV and started trying to rationalize the benefits of continuing to try and become a lawyer.

Spending one more semester just to get an *Associate's Degree* seemed like it wouldn't really accomplish that much, and also knew he wouldn't be able to get his *Bachelor's Degree* for almost three more years, and then have to go to Law school before he could even really become an attorney.

It was still summer break from UNLV, and with so much off his chest about the draft, Jason started thinking more about his other future plans. Besides wondering how long he would continue just living paycheck to paycheck, with all plans he had discussed with Anne about their possible future together, he didn't want her to feel like she was waiting for him to "grow up" or that he was still just a college kid working a part-time job for three more years.

Jason knew the necessity of going to college for a student deferment in the draft was over, and after figuring he wouldn't be able to start making decent money as a lawyer until he was almost thirty years old, that began to sound like forever to him, and he wanted to start making more money now.

His parents were a little disappointed with his decision to drop out of UNLV but said he should do whatever he thought was best and it was his life. Anne was supportive, even though she was a little disappointed that Jason decided against becoming a lawyer, but said she just wanted him to find something that would make him happy.

Frank Reich had already told Jason that even if he made him a full-time manager and gave him more hours, two dollars and twenty-five cents an hour was the maximum he could pay for now, explaining that the restaurant was only making a small profit, and that's why he had to work nights as a crap dealer at the *Sahara Hotel*.

Jason had often heard Frank mention that casino dealers made great money in Las Vegas mainly because of the tips, and casino workers sometimes made two or three times more than their paychecks just in tips alone, and it assured them they would always have cash in their pockets.

Unfortunately, as *Johnny Reb's* only offered counter service, no one ever left tips, but although Jason didn't want to leave the restaurant because he knew it was a solid job and was receiving well over the minimum wage, he also liked Frank and enjoyed working there with his friends. But working as a casino dealer also sounded good and Jason asked Frank if he could help him get at least a part time job at one of the casinos to learn the business.

Frank said he'd check around and see if there was any casino that was training dealers while he continued to work at Johnny Reb's full time, but the only position Frank was able to find for Jason without having experience was at a smaller location that at least was on the main Las Vegas Strip.

The Castaways Hotel and Casino was in between *Caesars Palace* and *The Frontier*, and almost directly across the street from *The Sands*, and also one of the five hotels and casinos that Howard Hughes owned in Las Vegas.

Frank joked to Jason that if he went to work at *The Castaways*, he could always say he worked for Howard Hughes, and it would look great on a resume. Frank also explained that "Just getting his foot in the door" at any location on the Strip was important if he wanted to start in the casino business.

Jason was a little worried about getting the Casino License and Sheriff's Card required to work in a casino, but was pleasantly surprised when his Nevada Driver's license worked again with no problem. He saw how lucky he got when the Nevada DMV clerk made her mistake, and although not quite legally, he was now officially a twenty-two-year-old casino worker approved by the Las Vegas Sheriff Department.

He was also satisfied that with a full and part -time job, he'd now be making almost twice as much as he ever had.

Because he also wanted to show Anne that he was "doing well for himself" and making more money, in the summer of 1970, Jason found a furnished one-bedroom apartment in a much nicer complex called the *Royal Shadows* that was directly behind the *International Hotel*. Even though Jason's rent went up to one hundred and twenty dollars a month, with the extra money he was making he could afford it.

Another big change that occurred at the end of summer was that his friend Paul Kirby would be returning to the law classes at UNLV, and was tiring of just playing guitar at talent contests. Paul said he wanted to "work on his chops" as a solo guitar player and concentrate on playing instrumental music.

Jason felt he had advanced from the talent contests as well and because he was friendly with Kay Adams and Mike Franklin at the Nashville Nevada, they'd sometimes just let him come onstage and sing a couple of songs as a so-called guest performer.

He'd sing some country or fifties rock tunes he knew the band regularly played, and knowing the lyrics to dozens of songs, Jason never had a problem singing along to songs like Hank Williams *Hey Good Lookin'* or *Kaw-Liga*, Chuck Berry's *Sweet Little Sixteen*, or Kenny Rogers and the First Edition's, *But You Know I Love You*.

Jason liked that he felt more of a part-time entertainer in Las Vegas rather than just a guy in a talent contest, but his main satisfaction was still Anne, and he wanted to show her that he was more of the *adult* now and not just a *college kid*.

Although Jason learned he'd need to start at the bottom and take a position as what was called a "Shill" or "House Player" at *The Castaways*, the pit boss who was his supervisor, also offered to give him training as a craps dealer during the slower hours of his shift. His main duties would require him to sit at empty Blackjack tables or stand at empty craps tables and make minimum bets until other players would come to those tables, after the pit boss explained that most gamblers didn't like playing at empty tables, and he was mainly acting as a *prop*.

The casino would supply Jason with a stack of chips, and he would always just bet a dollar on the Pass Line on Craps, or a dollar on each Blackjack hand and was also instructed to never "hit on a bust hand" on Blackjack. He did think it was boring at first, but at least he was getting a start in the casino business and earning extra money each week.

The pit boss he worked with at *The Castaways* was named Jimmy, and after six am when the casino slowed down, he would let Jason "work the stick" at the craps table for practice. Jimmy also showed Jason how to "stack and cut" chips and watch how the dealers worked at the crap tables.

Jason was learning how to handle the dice with the stick and yell out like a carnival backer, "Comin' out, bet the Seven or Eleven, bet any Craps, the Hard Ways, or the Field!" and he also learned to always say *"Yo-leven!"*, instead of *"Eee-leven."*

He was getting practice as a dealer but was still officially a shill, which meant he still couldn't share in any of the tips the dealers received, but Jason did find a way to earn extra cash at his job.

During the time in the breakrooms, he noticed that several dealers would be playing Gin Rummy against each other, trying to play as many hands as they could on their breaks. They were only playing *Seven-Card Gin*, which made the games go faster, and would gamble with the stakes being one dollar for "knocking" and two dollars for a *"Gin."*

After a couple of weeks, Jason asked if he could join in, and they didn't seem to mind as they figured he was a rookie and would be *easy money*, but Jason had become a pretty good Gin Rummy player when he was younger from playing cards with his parents, and then later with friends.

The other dealers were always surprised when Jason would sometimes walk out five or ten dollars ahead after each shift and Jimmy said he "got a kick" out of watching a young guy like Jason consistently beating all of those older dealers at Gin Rummy each night.

Jimmy would also often talk about Las Vegas and what a good opportunity this was for Jason by starting at a young age, and would always tell him that he was going to find out there were only two things that mattered in life and Las Vegas offered them both.

"*Money and sex* are all that matter," Jimmy would always mention to Jason when they talked during the slow early morning hours at *The Castaways*. He would often point out the attractive girls who were sitting at the bar and let Jason know those were the "working girls" who were prostitutes, and then point around to the gaming tables and back to the girls again, saying, "*Money and sex* are all you'll ever need in life."

Jason must have heard him say *"Money and sex,"* at least a dozen times like he was trying to implant it in his head, but although Jason knew he had his sex with Anne, he still wasn't sure if he was making *enough* money yet.

But he was confident he would eventually.

$$\approx$$

Jason worked three nights a week during the graveyard shift, two am till eight am, and arranged to work the afternoon shift at *Johnny Reb's* following those days so he could sleep for a few hours in between jobs. He also occasionally had a Friday or Saturday night off at *The Castaways* when they didn't need "Shills" which allowed him to spend those nights with Anne.

There was another nightclub almost directly across the street from *The Castaways* called the *Pussycat A-Go-Go* that Jason and Anne frequented a few times before Jason started his graveyard shift at *The Castaways*.

They had gone there to see a popular Las Vegas band called *Stark Naked* and the *Car Thieves*, and Jason liked that it was a rock and roll club instead of country-western bar, and they had several bands that played throughout the night as well as some female *Go-Go Dancers* on different stages.

The Pussycat was known as the trendiest nightclub in Las Vegas, but Jason didn't have any *juice* there like he did at the *Nashville Nevada*, and always had to pay the one or two-dollar cover charge. Plus, the drinks were more expensive than the other bars he'd been, but Anne liked going there because it was the place that most major entertainers on the Las Vegas strip frequented, and she was always hoping Tom Jones or Elvis might pop in some night.

Because he worked different graveyard shifts at *The Castaways* and sometimes did need to work on at least one weekend night, Jason and Anne tried to spend time together around his schedule.

If he had to work at two am early on a Saturday morning, they'd spend the early evening together and then go to the *Pussycat* around midnight to hear some bands and then Jason would just walk across the street to *The Castaways*, leaving Anne his car to go back to his place. She'd then pick him up at eight am, and they'd go back to sleep for a few hours and "fool around" until he had to go to work at *Johnny Reb's*.

On one of those early Saturday mornings around one thirty am, Anne was walking Jason out the front door of *The Pussycat* as he was leaving for work, when someone who was just waking in the bar called out Anne's name.

"Hey baby!" he said, walking over, "The band *Chase* is starting in about a half an hour, you're not leaving yet, are you?"

Chase was the most popular band that played the Pussycat, but they weren't starting until two am and Jason needed to be at work.

"Johnny, this is my boyfriend Jason," introduced Anne as they shook hands.

Although Johnny was addressing them both, his attention mainly seemed to be on Anne, and Jason immediately noticed that he seemed like one of the "trendy guys" that frequented the *Pussycat*.

Jason had never felt inferior to other people they met, but this "Johnny" guy was good looking, tanned, and dressed a lot sharper than he was, and he figured the gold chains around his neck probably cost more than Jason's entire wardrobe.

"You two should definitely stay for Chase," Johnny said. "They're a band that's going to make it big time, and you probably won't see them in clubs this small again."

Jason wanted to show he wasn't concerned about the "Johnny" guy and told Anne she should stay and see the band if she wanted while he was at work, but was a little relieved when Anne told Johnny that they both had to leave and would see the band some other time.

When Jason asked Anne who that "*Johnny guy*" was, she just casually said his name was Johnny Russo, and everyone at the *Pussycat* seemed to know him.

"I think that he's *connected*," she smiled as she rubbed her index finger across the side of her nose.

Jason had learned that rubbing the index finger across the nose's side was a type of signal that someone was connected to the mob in Las Vegas.

Anne said she'd met him "a couple of times" at the *Pussycat* while she was waiting for Jason to get off work, and then quickly added as if to assure Jason he had nothing to be jealous about, "I met his girlfriend too and she's really beautiful."

When Anne picked Jason up at work at eight am and went back to his apartment, he let her know he'd take her back to the Pussycat to see *Chase* when he had a free night, not wanting her to feel like she was missing out on any fun with the hours he was working.

Jason was making more money than he ever had, but he was also working over fifty hours a week between his two jobs, and he felt like it was starting to affect his time he wanted to spend with Anne. But he figured once he was trained as a full-time dealer, he'd eventually just be able to work one job and have a normal schedule where he could he and Anne could feel the plans about their future together could be a possibility.

Although they had only hypothetically discussed getting married in the future and raising a family, neither of them felt they were ready to make that commitment and weren't in a good enough financial situation to ever consider it currently. Jason knew he'd probably have to have at least twenty-five hundred dollars in his bank account, along with a great paying full-time job before he'd even ask Anne to marry him and figured that was still at least a couple years away.

But there was something else that Jason had been thinking about as well.

Most of the dealers Jason played Gin Rummy with, all complained that the money and tips weren't that good at *The Castaways*, and said they were just working there until they could get a better job dealing at one of the bigger casinos on the Strip. Some of them also said they'd been waiting for several years and that "you needed a lot of juice" to be a dealer at the bigger hotels.

They told Jason if he was patient, *The Castaways* was a good place to learn, and if he was lucky, in a couple of years he might be ready to go to work at a major hotel.

Jason didn't like hearing it would take that long and made him feel like he was still in college, plus Jimmy had told him it would probably be at least six months before he could become a full-time dealer at *The Castaways*. He also figured that even with the money he was making, it would be a long time before he had twenty-five hundred dollars as back up money and was also concerned if he'd ever get rich working at *The Castaways*.

One of the dealers mentioned to Jason that he should consider driving a taxi if he just wanted to make good money without working two jobs.

The dealer said it's "not the most glamorous job," but told Jason that he heard some drivers were making almost two hundred dollars a week between their salary and tips and Jason decided if he could make that kind of money with only one job it would be great.

He was also starting to realize it wasn't easy trying to keep his split shift love affair going with the hours he was working and told Anne he was going to investigate the taxi job as soon as he could. Jason assured her it wasn't really a career he was planning in the long run, but sounded better than what he was doing now

Jason didn't know if it was really going to end up making him rich, but it was at least worth giving it a shot.

Chapter Nine

Jason met Gene Maday through a gambler named Gus he'd become friendly after meeting him at *The Castaways*, and who Jason occasionally went across the street with, to bet on the horse races or football games at the *Churchill Downs Sports Book* between the Sands and Desert Inn hotels.

When Jason mentioned to Gus that he was interested in driving a taxi, Gus said he "knew some people" and would ask around, and it was less than a week later, when Gus introduced Jason to Gene Maday at a small casino Maday owned on the Strip called *Little Caesars*.

Besides owning that small casino, Jason learned that Maday also owned the only non-union taxi cab company in Las Vegas, *Checker Cab*.

"Gus told me you want a job that makes good money," Mayday said to Jason after they introduced themselves, "Well, you can make as much as you want if you put in the work and the time."

"I like that you're wearing a suit and don't look scruffy like most of my other drivers," Maday continued, "And you seem to have a good attitude and personality which you'll need to build up some regular and repeat business."

"Just treat the job like it's your own business, and you'll be happy with the results," Gus also added to Jason during the brief meeting.

Jason was surprised that it took less than ten minutes for Maday to tell him he could start for *Checker* as soon as he got his Taxi permit.

It turned out the Gus had been friends with Maday for years, and proudly told Jason his job request was "pretty much taken care of" in advance, and again reminded him how good it was to have "juice" in Las Vegas.

Jason had no problem getting his taxi permit and then met with his new supervisor, who said, "Just call me Prado," and who also explained how Jason would get paid along with the company rules.

First, because Jason was a new driver, Prado explained he'd be on what was called the *extra board*, which meant Jason could come in whenever he wanted, put his name on a waitlist, and then just hang around the garage to wait for a taxicab to become available to drive. He said Jason's pay would be fifty percent of what his taxi meter showed at the end of his shift, plus he could keep "all of his tips" and didn't have to share them like the dealers at the casinos. Prado also said not ever to tell anyone how much he made in tips, not even him.

The fact that Jason could choose his own hours and was somewhat self- employed was something he thought was perfect. He also learned that working the eight pm till four am shifts was when he'd make the most money, but was the hardest shift to get to the top the extra board.

Jason was assigned the number 669, which would be his ID number for the dispatcher to call him on the two-way radio and check in on his location if she got phone calls for a pick up in the area he was driving. He was also told he could park and wait in the cab lines at the Strip Hotels and would get most of his fares from those locations. But Prado also explained that because *Checker Cab* was non-union and not part of the Teamsters Union, there were a few Strip Hotels including *The Rivera* they weren't allowed to park at the cab stands or pick up passengers and emphasized that Jason didn't want to piss off the other union drivers or the Teamsters Union and never park in line at those hotels.

There was another major policy that Prado told him about that was very important.

"If you pick up any fares who want a ride to the *colored* part of town, you need to call in a code," Prado began explaining. "Especially If you pick up any blacks who want a ride out there."

"You call from your radio and say, 'This is *669 Purple'* and give the address you are driving to on the west side," Prado continued seriously, "There's a designated route that you'll need to take, and the dispatcher will contact a Las Vegas police unit who'll follow you to the destination."

The west side of Las Vegas was the "colored part of town" Prado was talking about, and he explained several taxi drivers had been robbed, and one was even murdered there. Prado said that since then, *Checker Cab* and the other taxi companies had a policy of using a code when he contacted his dispatcher about his destination. Jason learned the word "Purple" was the word that would let the dispatcher know he had a black passenger.

"Most drivers say they just avoid picking up any black passengers at all," concluded Prado, "They say it's just too much of a hassle and are shitty tippers anyway."

After learning all the rules and being told he could basically work as many hours as he wanted, Jason planned on working as many hours as possible the first month to gauge the potential income he could expect to earn.

Jason also felt some regret that he was going to need to give notice those he had become friends with that he was giving up his other jobs.

It wasn't as bad letting Jimmy know he was going to be leaving *The Castaways*, because he agreed that Jason would probably make more money driving a taxi, and as usual, Jimmy again reminded Jason how important it was to remember that "money and sex" were all that really mattered in the long run.

But Jason did feel bad telling Frank he was leaving *Johnny Reb's* and saying goodbye to Tom, Rhonda, and his other friends who worked there he'd been seeing regularly for well over a year.

"I promise I'll always stay in touch with all of you," said Jason before adding with a laugh, "And it'll always stop in for visits no matter how rich I get from driving a taxi!"

He wanted to get rich, but he also wasn't going to let it change him or forget his friends.

➴

Jason came into the *Checker Cab* garage around five pm each day, and usually got a taxi by eight pm and quickly realized he'd made the right decision. After only a few weeks of driving, he discovered he'd made more money than he had in almost a month of working his previous two jobs combined.

He also improved his wardrobe and decided to wear better suits and sports jackets when he drove his taxi so he'd stand out from the other drivers. As Maday had described, the other drivers always seemed to dress shabbily, and Jason didn't want to be an *ordinary* cab driver. Jason also had *Checker Cab* business cards where he'd write his name and number *669*, and always ask his fares to call for him personally when they needed a taxi.

By the end of his second month, he ran into Gene Maday, who was very happy with Jason and told him "He'd turned in more money from his meter" than any other driver that month. Maday also told Jason he'd make sure his name would be on top of the *extra board* anytime he wanted to come in and drive and added that he wouldn't have to "sit around for three hours or four hours" to get a taxi anymore.

He was surprised that Maday paid that much attention to how he sometimes had to sit around waiting for a taxi, but besides loving his new job, Jason also liked that he actually felt like he'd made some *juice* with the company's owner with the hours he was putting in.

Jason did pick up some interesting fares while sometimes driving up to ten-hours a shift, including some famous Las Vegas entertainers. Although he didn't get the "big tippers" like Frank Sinatra, who other drivers said gave huge tips, he also didn't get the "cheap ones," like many drivers had described Johnny Carson.

Most of Jason's fares left decent tips, and he always figured the way he was dressed as one of the main reasons, but the best tippers turned out to be the ones who Jimmy from *The Castaways* had described as the "working girls" that Jason would pick up during his shifts.

Jason would drive them to different hotels where they'd sit at the bars waiting for "tricks", and usually call his taxi company and ask for *669* when they were finished and ready for another ride

But there was one "working girl" in particular that Jason got along with best, named Terri Larson, who became a regular nightly fare.

Terri said she was originally from Southern California but had moved to San Francisco to "become a hippie" in the late 1960s and told Jason she just recently came to Vegas to make some easy money. She always tried to explain and justify why being a hooker was no big deal and said, "all men paid for sex one way or the other," and she was just a "sure thing" who was always available.

Terri said she really didn't worry about venereal diseases because most of her "tricks" were married and just wanted some "strange pussy" while they were in town. She also claimed she wasn't a *"whore"* like some of the other girls, because she never turned more than *"three tricks"* in one night.

Jason always thought Terri did seem the classiest of the working girls he knew, but was disappointed that she still lived in a cheap motel with her black pimp.

He had met her pimp, *Johnny*, a few times when he picked up Terri from her motel, and Johnny would also use Jason as his driver, when he needed to go to the *west side* of Las Vegas to "pick something up", as he always described.

Johnny also told Jason that he knew all about *"Code Purple,"* and told Jason he didn't need to use it when he drove him to the west side. He said he had "plenty of juice" in that part of town, and that no one would "fuck with him" if they knew he was with Johnny. Jason was still always a little apprehensive about driving to the west side but never did have any problems. Plus, he liked that Johnny always gave him an extra ten dollars each time he drove him there.

He did see that most of the other "working girls" were very attractive and said they liked not only the way Jason dressed, but also liked his attitude and personality, and teasingly told Jason it was fun having a young, handsome driver who seemed more like a *limo driver* than a typical cabbie.

Candy, Tracy, Brandi, or Tiffany seemed to be the usual names they used, and they always tipped him well when they had a good night, and a couple of them would sometimes even take him to a late dinner when they were finished "working" for the night before he drove them home.

On Sunday Nights, there was a restaurant called *The Flame* that offered free spaghetti dinners for all the cab drivers in Las Vegas after midnight. The restaurant set up long buffet tables and for twenty or thirty of them at a time, and the drivers always looked forward to their free dinners. But instead of joining the other drivers, Terri or one of his other "working girl" fares would occasionally take Jason to *The Flame* on those nights and buy his dinner.

Jason would walk in the restaurant wearing his suit and tie, accompanied by a sexy looking girl, and sit in one of the booths away from the other drivers and order a steak or prime rib. He would just smile at the other drivers waiting for their free spaghetti dinner and liked that he wasn't hard up for a *free* dinner as they all seemed to be.

He had heard that some of the other drivers resented him for always getting praise from Prado and Maday for having the biggest totals on his meters, and that Jason seemed to be *flaunting it* when he went to *The Flame* for those Sunday night dinners and appeared to be *showing off* his success. But he also didn't want to act like he was "above them" and instead tried to show some camaraderie with the other driver's when he sat with them in the Checker garage waiting for a taxi.

Because some of them had seen him at *The Flame* with one of his "fares" a couple times, he just tried to make up some funny stories he could tell them about the half dozen or so "working girls" who had become his regular customers.

One of the jokes he liked to tell involved the time during the city election season that year, when the local politicians, including the Sheriff wanted to make sure the public saw they were doing their jobs and got some publicly. Jason had heard from Tom Casey that it was usually just a stunt to get some press in the newspapers, but a couple weeks before the election, the sheriff announced a "crackdown" on prostitution at the hotels, and for an entire weekend, uniformed officers stood at the entrances at the casinos to turn away some of the "obvious" working girls who normally sat at the bars inside the casino to solicit their *tricks*.

Because that "crackdown" did receive a lot of publicity, Jason made up a story he tried to tell seriously to the other drivers so it sounded believable, but was actually only half true.

"So, I'm driving this hooker up and down the strip, and back and forth from the Sahara to the Tropicana during the crackdown, as she's trying to get inside just one so she can work that night," Jason started his *story*, "She told me to just keep my meter running each time we stopped at a hotel entrance, but each time she got turned away and after over almost two hours of driving her around, she decided to give up and told me to just take her home."

Jason knew that part of his story was true, but then added his own sarcastic ending and explained with a straight face that once he got to her apartment "the taxi fare was up to over thirty dollars" and she tried to offer him a deal on the money she owed him by suggestively lifting up her skirt and asking from the back seat, "You know, I didn't make any money tonight so do you think you could take the cab fare out of this?"

He then added his punch line to those who were listening to his "true story" and said he looked back at her as she was spreading her legs toward him and just said with a straight face, "Sorry lady, you got anything smaller?!"

That got all the drivers in the garage laughing loudly and Jason knew it was always good to have them laugh along with him instead of feeling any resentment for his success. He wanted to stay friendly with them and didn't need any enemies, but at the same time, he figured they were all basically self-employed, and if they worked as hard as he did, they'd have nothing to bitch about.

By December of that year, Jason had built up a nice group of regular customers and very rarely had to sit at the hotels with the other taxis waiting for a fare. He also had managed to save almost five hundred dollars in cash from his paychecks and tips, and even finally got a telephone installed at his apartment.

He'd always given the number at *Johnny Reb's* as a contact, or had used payphones for the past year and a half, and felt for the first time since he was in Las Vegas, that he wasn't struggling for money.

Jason felt like he was starting to get rich.

&

The only thing that was bad about Jason's job was that by trying always to work the eight pm to four am shifts, and some nights even longer, he couldn't see Anne on those nights and tried to make up for it by sometimes taking three days off in a row so they could at least spend more time together.

Now that he had some extra money, Jason took Anne to some of the better restaurants in town and to more main headliner shows like Frank Sinatra, Liberace, Tom Jones, Duke Ellington and also Elvis Presley again. Jason wanted Anne to see how successful he was with his new career and how much more fun they could have with all the extra money he was now earning.

On New Year's Eve of 1970, Jason took Anne out to a restaurant she liked, the *Aku Aku* at the *Stardust*, and then decided to celebrate their one-year anniversary at the *Nashville Nevada*. Kay Adams was performing and let Jason sing a duet with her during the song *Summer Wine*, and then when midnight came, Kay invited Jason and Anne onstage to celebrate with the band and join in singing *Auld Lang Syne*.

For Jason, he felt like it was his best New Year's Eve yet, but when they were in bed later and enjoying their usual after sex cigarette, Anne mentioned something that made him start thinking.

"You know, it's funny", she said as she took a drag from her cigarette, "A year ago when we met, you were going to college to become a lawyer and even managing a restaurant part-time, but now here you are, driving a taxicab for a living."

"It's strange how some things work out sometimes," she said before adding, "Do you ever think about what you'll be doing five years from now?"

Jason leaned over and kissed her and said, "Well, hopefully, I'll be here in bed with you."

Although he felt he was doing great in Las Vegas, he knew what Anne meant and wanted her to know that he was still planning his future with her.

"I'm just trying to get some more money saved up right now, but I'm not planning on being a taxi driver forever," he said, "But hopefully by this time next year I'll have at least a couple thousand dollars saved up from my taxi job and then I can figure out what I'm going to do next."

Jason had made having two thousand dollars in his bank account after paying all his bills as his main goal for 1971, and figured once he had that much money saved up, he could think more about a future career.

But what that was, he wasn't really quite sure yet.

Chapter Ten

Jason knew when the dispatcher called through the two-way radio, "669...pick up at the *Regent Motel*," it would be Brandi, or when she called, "669...pick up at the *Blue Angel Motel*," it would be Terri. He had at least a dozen regular customers who would call him each night, including a few other semi-regulars he'd become friendly with.

One semi-regular was Jim Parker, who wrote a column for the weekly entertainment magazine *The Panorama*, but was best known as *The Vegas Vampire* and hosted a weekly television show on Channel Five called *Shock Theatre*.

Jason usually would drive him to his office at the *Panorama Magazine* at least once a week, or to different hotels for shows he was reviewing for his column, and had also driven him to his television station a couple times in Henderson for his Friday Night television show.

Because Jason didn't want to seem like just a boring taxi driver to Jim Parker, he would exaggerate and say he was also a singer, and just driving a taxi as a second job for some extra money. Jim also had said he'd be glad to help Jason out sometime and give him a call if he ever got a regular gig, so he could put a "blurb or photo" of Jason in his weekly *Panorama* column.

Another semi-regular was Ricardo Villasenor, who owned the *Las Vegas Star* magazine, and like Jim Parker, they'd swap funny stories about some of their funny experiences in Las Vegas and Jason would always include his "Sorry lady, you got anything smaller?" joke to them, as well as other fares he knew had a sense of humor.

Ricardo told Jason that besides the magazine, he arranged junkets for groups from Mexico to travel to Las Vegas each month, and said the junkets were actually more profitable than the magazine.

"I only charge a quarter for my magazine," said Ricardo, "But because the *Panorama* is free, they've got a lot more readers, and it's tough selling ads trying to compete with their circulation."

After hearing Jason's "Sorry lady..." story and about some of the girls he drove around in his taxi, Ricardo also mentioned he liked to arrange for his groups from his junkets to "meet some girls" when they were in town, and told Jason if he knew any "classy but not too expensive" working girls, to give him a call.

"Hey, I just *drive 'em* and don't *pimp 'em*," Jason half laughed to Ricardo, "And you know as well as I that you don't need my help with finding *working* girls in Vegas."

Ricardo said he was just trying to offer Jason a chance to make "a little extra money" and to not worry about it.

Ricardo also said that if Jason had any good stories about driving a taxi involving celebrities or something else interesting to give him a call saying he was "always looking for good stories" for his magazine.

Jason had collected at least a dozen business cards and figured he was acquiring a little *juice* in Las Vegas himself if he ever needed it, and was having more fun driving his cab and the people he was meeting, that he ever could remember.

It was only a few days into the New Year, when Jason heard a call from his taxi dispatcher asking if anyone was in Henderson's vicinity, and he quickly answered into his radio, *"669"* wanting to be the first driver to respond. He had just dropped off a fare on Boulder Highway and was ten minutes away from Henderson, but after the dispatcher gave Jason the address, he sped up trying to make it there in five minutes.

Two long hair guys dressed in jeans and leather jackets came out to get into the cab, and when Jason saw one was carrying what looked like a guitar case, he figured they were musicians, and after one of them said to "Take us to the Pussycat-A-Go-Go," he knew they were musicians for sure.

The guitar player said his name was *Tommy Starr*, and the other guy called himself *Alvin Vegas* and said he was a keyboard player, but also joked that whenever he had a gig in LA, he just changed his name to Alvin *Hollywood*.

After they started talking about their gig that night, Jason found out there were three other guys in their current band and Alvin said their shows at the Pussycat were mainly just "pick-up gigs" that didn't pay much money, but was a good place to be seen. Tommy added that they also played with some other musicians at other nightclubs besides the *Pussycat*, and kind of considered themselves "floaters," but that he and Alvin usually always played together. He said that unless they had a *"house gig"* it was common for a lot of the bands in Las Vegas to have interchangeable musicians. He added that because most musicians had other full-time jobs and weren't always available, and Tommy and Alvin could sit in with just about any band.

Tommy said that he also worked with Hollywood agents who'd call him regularly to come to LA to sit in with other bands that paid better money and said he even backed up Chuck Berry once.

"The money is pretty good when we get a chance to play with *name bands* when they needed another guitar or keyboard player," Tommy added, "But winter is pretty slow so we're just waiting to get some calls for some of those gigs later this spring."

Jason again exaggerated and said he was also a *singer* and not just a *cab driver*, and also somewhat of a "floater" himself, and added that he'd sung at "different nightclubs" in Las Vegas.

He knew that along with the times he'd sang songs at the *Nashville Nevada*, he had also sung once at *The Lariat*, so he felt he wasn't exaggerating *too much*.

"I haven't had a chance to sing that much lately with my job taking up so much time," Jason said, "But I still like to *work on my chops* whenever I get a chance."

Tommy then casually mentioned that they hosted a regular "jam session" with other Las Vegas musicians every Sunday afternoon at their house, adding that they could always use another vocalist, and that if Jason was interested, he was welcome to come and sit in with them.

He immediately liked their offer, and after they arrived at the *Pussycat-a-Go-Go*, Jason said because they were "fellow musicians" he was "comping" their ride, and after giving them his business card and exchanging phone numbers, he also offered to give them a comp'd ride back to Henderson after their gig. He'd already made enough in tips that night not to worry about leaving his taxi meter down and paying for the fares himself, and with his percentage of the meter, it would actually only be costing him half of the amount.

Jason felt Tommy and Alvin had been his "luckiest fare" that week and was now going to be able to have fun with something else he loved besides the "money and sex" that Jimmy had always tried to emphasized, and couldn't have pictured a better way to have started out 1971.

 ❧

It was less than a week after meeting them, when Jason decided to take Tommy and Alvin's offer to "sit-in" with them at their *jam sessions*, but although he did feel a little apprehensive because he knew he wasn't really a professional vocalist, he hoped he'd be able to fake it good enough if he didn't try to sing anything difficult.

There were around ten different musicians at the jam session that day, and Jason discovered just as Tommy and Alvin had told him, most of the musicians weren't committed to always playing in the same bands together and would often change members based on whoever was available for certain gigs at different live music clubs in town.

Being the lead guitar player, Tommy was also the leader of the *jams* and played and sang along on just about every song and encouraged Jason to just join in on the songs that he knew.

When he first joined all the musicians who were there, they were already practicing two new songs that were currently popular on the radio, *After Midnight* by Eric Clapton and *One-Man Band* by Three Dog Night. When Alvin asked him if he wanted to sit in and sing along, Jason knew those songs were probably out of his range, and he couldn't pull off *harmonies* like Three Dog Night. He just wanted to sing something that would sound good the first time they heard him and just sang back-up with Alvin or Tommy on easy songs he knew like *I'm So Glad.*

Alvin preferred the *Deep Purple* version of that song as it began with a long keyboard prelude called *Happiness*, which showcased Alvin's keyboard playing and

Jason knew *I'm so Glad* basically had just one verse, and mainly kept repeating the chorus of the lyrics "I'm So Glad," so he just tried to look cool when he had the microphone and sang along. He eventually asked the other musicians if they knew *It's All Over Now,* and felt more confident when they said they did, knowing that was the song he sang best by himself and was in his range for a solo.

"It's in the key of G," Jason decided to add, remembering it would make him sound more professional, and as he had done before, just tried to sing it in the same style as Mick Jagger who he had the easiest time with matching the vocals. He also liked being upfront surrounded by professional musicians who were even better than the ones at the *Nashville Nevada* and was enjoying just having the opportunity to sing with them.

Jason was satisfied when Alvin said it "sounded good," after that song and Tommy said they did another Rolling Stones track called *Stray Cat Blues* that he could try. Jason had the eight-track tape of *Get Yer Ya-Ya's Out* by the Rolling Stones and had sung along with the song *Stray Cat Blues* enough times in his car to feel like he knew the words well enough to try it.

He also liked that Tommy played the slower and bluesy version of the song from that album, and had always liked the way Jagger lecherously sang the sexy and nasty lyrics about inviting supposedly innocent young girls upstairs to his bedroom to seduce by singing, *"it wasn't a hanging matter or a capital crime."* Especially, when he sang about how the supposed innocent girl's mother would be surprised at how experienced they actually were in bed, and how they *screamed with pleasure* as they *scratched his back,* which always had reminded Jason of some of the "Henderson girls" he once knew.

Jason also was satisfied when the band seemed to enjoy his take on *Stray Cat Blues* and he was starting to feel more comfortable singing on more songs that day.

The only thing Jason didn't like about the jam session, was that they'd all sit around smoking joints between all the songs deciding which one to try and play next. Marijuana was just something Jason never liked and wasn't a high that interested him, but he'd still accept the joints when they passed it to him so he'd at least look *cool,* but he never inhaled and was good at faking it, and instead just drank four or five cans of beer during the jams to get his own high.

Several of the other musicians joked while they were sitting around *getting high,* that Jason still had a "baby face" and reminded them of the actor Christopher Jones who played a rock star that became the President of the United States in the movie *Wild in the Streets.*

"You look a lot younger than twenty-two years old and you're lucky Las Vegas hasn't aged you yet," Alvin sarcastically joked, "But keep hanging around here for a couple more years and you'll be able to get that *burnt out* look like all the rest of us have."

Even with Jason adding three years to his real age, he learned he was by far the youngest musician at the jam sessions after learning Tommy was twenty-five years old, and that Alvin was twenty-six, and they were themselves considered the youngest musicians after him.

Tommy then mentioned that because Jason actually did remind him the rock star who Christopher Jones portrayed in the movie *Wild in the Streets*, he said he could play one of the hits from that movie called *Shape of Things to Come* and suggested that Jason try and sing it with them.

Jason had seen that movie and knew that song, but also thought it would be great to try and be as cool as the rock star character *Max Frost* was in that movie, so *Shape of Things to Come* was another song he knew and enjoyed singing that day.

He liked the camaraderie and feeling that he was a *fellow musician*, as well as working on his "stage presence chops" and decided to mention that if any of them ever needed a taxi, to call *Checker Cab* and ask for number *669* and he'd "take care of them" as far as the fare. He was making good money, so anything it might cost to comp their taxi fares would be well worth it to keep the camaraderie going amongst them.

By the end of the first Sunday jam session, Jason did get to sing lead or back up on at least ten songs during the three-hours he was there and felt good when all the musicians said, "they'd see him next week" and Jason decided that was going to be where he was going to start spending his Sunday afternoons from now on.

After a few weeks of jam sessions, and seeing Tommy and Alvin in his taxi several times a week, Jason became pretty good friends with them both, and liked spending time with them talking about music. It was when Tommy mentioned that a lot of the musicians at the jam sessions would also occasionally "sit in" with them when they performed at the *Pussycat-a-Go-Go*, Jason decided to get bolder and asked them a favor.

Jason said although he knew he wasn't "as experienced and professional" as some of the other musicians, he'd really like to join them onstage and sing a couple rock and roll songs at the Pussycat eventually. He'd learned that the Pussycat had become Anne's favorite nightclub in the past couple months and she sometimes went there with friends on the nights he was working the graveyard shifts, and knew how impressed she'd be seeing him singing there.

Although Alvin said the *Pussycat* wasn't as easy as the *Nashville Nevada* when it came to allowing "amateur" musicians to sit in with the bands, Tommy added because Jason was their friend, after a month or two more of rehearsals, they'd figure out a song or two that he sang best and try to arrange something.

Jason liked that "working on his chops" was starting to pay off, and he would have a chance to show Anne that being *just a taxi driver* also was starting to pay off which would let her know he was still thinking about his future.

It wasn't even a month old yet, but 1971 was turning into another lucky year for him.

❧

Jason was sitting with Anne in the lounge at *The International Hotel* waiting for Bobby Vinton to begin his midnight show and as usual, Jason had slipped the maitre d' five dollars to make sure they had a good table next to the stage.

He was also telling Anne about the different band members he'd met and how much fun he had *"jamming"* with them, and also excitedly told her he felt his singing was getting good enough where he might eventually be able to sing a few songs with them onstage at the *Pussycat-A-Go-Go*.

Anne did seem as excited as he was and said she'd love to come down and see him jam sometime when she wasn't working herself.

When Jason started to order his usual Scotch and soda from the waitress before Bobby Vinton started his show, Anne casually mentioned that her friend *"Gee-on-Eee"* was also a scotch drinker and had told her the only Scotch to drink was *"Che-fece"* and suggested Jason should try it.

The waitress didn't understand and asked, "Do you mean *Chivas*? That's the name of the good Scotch."

Jason laughed and told Anne, "It must be good if you can't pronounce it."

The waitress also laughed and said, "For costing over a dollar more than the regular scotch, it's gotta be good."

"Who is *Gee-On-Eee*?" Jason asked Anne as they waited for their drinks.

Anne said her friend pronounced his name "Johnny" but it actually was spelled "G-I-A-N-N-I," so she just liked to tease Johnny when she occasionally would bump into him somewhere, and pronounced it "*Gee-On-Eee*."

Anne took a business card from her purse and showed Jason his name, and casually mentioned that Jason had met him before at the *Pussycat-a-Go-Go* when Jason was still working at *The Castaways*.

Jason looked at the name *Gianni Russo* and started to remember who the "*Gee-On-Eee*" guy was. It was the supposedly "connected" trendy guy with the gold chains and tan, Jason remembered meeting once, and was slightly irritated he had a *cool* name that Anne seemed to like in the same way she did *Jason*.

He tried not to sound concerned by it but casually said he didn't realize that Anne had become friends with *"that Johnny guy."*

Anne sounded reassuring when she said they weren't really friends, but just ran into him a few times and they mainly talked about business. She said when she had casually mentioned to *"Gee-On-Eee"* that she would be graduating from cosmetology school fairly soon, he then mentioned to Anne that he was thinking about opening some beauty salons in Las Vegas and might have a job for her managing one of his

213

salons. She added that "Gee-On-Eee" was already a very successful businessman in Las Vegas also and owned a few jewelry stores and told her she could even work at one of those stores until she got her license as a hairstylist.

"I'm bored with my job at Fletcher Jones anyway," Anne also added, "Plus, it would also pay me more money than I'm making now."

Jason tried to sound encouraging as he said, "it sounded good" and started feeling better, realizing it was just business they talked about. He figured the guy was too old for Anne to be interested in anyway, and remembered she had also mentioned that "Gee-On-Eee" already had a "beautiful" girlfriend.

"Well," Jason told Anne, "In about ten years when I'm as old as *Gee-On-Eee*, I'll probably have some business of my own too."

Anne casually just answered, "He's twenty-seven."

The lights were dimming, and Bobby Vinton was starting his show, so Jason just tried to get any concerns out of his mind, and after the waitress had brought them their cocktails, Jason also started thinking that if this *Gianni Russo* guy had any redeeming qualities, it was that he was right about the Scotch, and it did taste better.

At least he had a new drink he could start ordering.

While Bobby Vinton was singing one of his hit songs, *There I've Said It Again*, and sang the words *"I love you. I will till the end"*, Jason took Anne's hand and kissed it wanting to remind her *again* himself, and let her know that there was always a love song that he associated with her.

But he was also looking forward to his birthday the following month so Anne wouldn't have to feel like she was dating a teenager anymore.

214

Chapter Eleven

It was around two am during one of his shifts when Jason got a call from the dispatcher telling him he had a pick up at an address he wasn't familiar, and he had to look on his map to find the directions. But when he pulled up to the darkened house, he saw Terri Larson standing out front, and was carrying something when she got into the back seat of his taxi.

"Just hurry up and take me to *The Dunes*," Terri said sounding like she was out of breath.

Jason sped off, but then looked in his rearview mirror and saw Terri had a portable television set in the seat next to her.

"What's with the TV set?" Jason asked as he headed back towards *The Strip*.

"I need you to keep this for me until tomorrow," she said, "I know someone who'll probably give me at least fifty bucks for it."

Jason was a little concerned and asked her what she was talking about, but Terri just said the "trick" she was just with was an "asshole" who didn't pay her and she had just grabbed hip portable TV as her payment.

"Jesus Christ Terri, you stole it?!" Jason said now even more concerned.

"No, I didn't!" she argued back, "He owed me."

"I worked on that guy for over an hour trying to get him to *come*," Terri started to complain, "He was too drunk to even get hard, so when I told him I was done trying and he needed to pay me for my time, he wouldn't pay up so I just took the TV from his bedroom."

"Don't worry about it," Terri then casually said. "Do you think the asshole is going to call the police and tell them a *prostitute* he didn't pay stole his TV?"

"It's all cool," Terri added like it was no big deal.

It was less than a minute after she said it was "no big deal" when Jason got a call over his radio from the dispatcher saying, "*669…please call in from a private phone.*"

Jason knew that wasn't a *good call* because the only time the dispatcher told drivers to call from a payphone was when they had messages they didn't want heard over the airwaves.

"I hope this isn't about you," he told Terri with some irritation as he pulled into a closed restaurant on Maryland Parkway where he knew there was a payphone.

"Look, Jason, I called you because I trusted you, so if it's anything about that guy, just tell them you already dropped me off at one of the hotels," she tried to say calmly before sounding more concerned, "Johnny will beat the shit outta me if I get into any trouble over this, so please don't say anything about me."

215

Jason got out of the cab and called the dispatcher operator from the payphone who immediately told him that "the fare he picked up had robbed the man she was with" and he wanted the cabbie to "bring her back to his house" or he was going to call the police.

Jason hesitated for a second and then tried to sound surprised.

"What!?" he answered in a shocked tone, "Damn, I just dropped her off at the Sahara not more than five minutes ago, and I'm not even sure if I remember what she looked like."

Jason heard the dispatcher put her hand over the phone and heard the muffled sound of her talking to someone.

"Prado wants you to come in right now," the dispatcher said when she came back on the line, "He needs to talk to you."

Jason hung up the phone and rushed back to Terri, who seemed more concerned with putting on her lipstick than the phone call.

"They know about it!" Jason said with urgency, "The guy just wants you to go back and give him his stuff, and they want me back at the garage right now."

"Fuck that!" Terri said, getting out of the taxi, "He's probably already called the cops."

She pulled out a five-dollar bill and handed it to Jason.

"I'll just flag down another taxi, and you can go stash the TV for a couple of days until things cool down," Terri tried to say calmly, "Just make sure you hang on to it, and I'll give you twenty bucks when I sell it."

Jason was pissed as Terri started walking down Maryland Parkway and wave down another taxi leaving him alone, but was more pissed thinking that she would even think he cared about making twenty bucks from a stolen TV.

He knew gotten himself in the middle of this by lying to the dispatcher, and was now mainly interested in not getting in any trouble himself, but he also saw the TV set was still sitting in the back seat of his taxi. Jason knew he had to get rid of it before went back to the garage, and then thought about someone who lived close-by, and quickly sped to that location before going back to meet Prado.

Jason was trying to remember which bedroom window to look for, as he slowly walked towards the back of the darkened house carrying the small TV, and quietly tapped on a window until Victor Consuela finally opened the sliding glass frame.

"What the fuck, Jason," said Victor still half asleep, "What time is it?"

"Listen, this is really important, so just do me this favor and I'll explain everything tomorrow," Jason said as he started to hand Victor the portable TV through his window, "Just keep this hidden till you hear from me and don't tell anyone about this until I call you."

Jason was relieved when Victor took the TV without asking any questions and knew he was the type that wouldn't make a big deal out of it. But with that problem solved, Jason now had to focus on acting innocent with his "baby face" when he met with Prado.

He knew he just had to keep his story short and simple.

"I didn't see her carrying anything and had never seen her before," Jason was trying to explain to Prado after he'd driven back to the garage, "She just got in the back seat, and I dropped her off at the *Sahara*."

Prodo told Jason the dispatcher said the "fare had called in for *669* personally," and he must know who the hooker was, but Jason kept insisting that he gave out hundreds of his cards to different people all over town and that he really didn't know who the girl was. Jason had also learned from Prado that Terri's *trick* was supposedly someone who had *juice* with the Las Vegas Police Department and "definitely wanted the hooker" arrested and had already called the police telling them a driver from *Checker Cab* driver was involved.

"Well, the police may still want to talk to you," said Prado. "But you're done driving tonight, and I'm suspending you for a week until I talk to Maday."

Jason tried to act pissed that they would even *think* that he'd do something illegal like that, but he also knew it was too late to change his story and he had to stick with it.

He decided a week's suspension was better than getting fired, so he just hoped everything would cool down by then and would just have to live with it for now.

ॐ

Jason hadn't been able to fall asleep till nearly six am and figured he'd sleep till at least noon, but he was awakened by a loud knock on his door at eight am and saw there were two plainclothes detectives holding badges when he answered, asking if he was Jason Mershon.

"We want to talk to you about the *whore* you picked up last night," one of them said as they just walked in and started looking around his apartment suspiciously.

Jason rubbed his eyes, trying to wake himself up and tried to look calm at the same time.

They both immediately told Jason that being "an accessory to a robbery" was a serious offense, and they just wanted Jason to be "straight with them."

"All we want is the name of the *whore*," one of the detectives said, "You won't get into any trouble if you just tell us."

Jason kept sticking to his story that "he had no idea" and just thought she was one of the "dozens of cocktail waitresses" he usually picked up around that hour. He just kept trying to play dumb and innocent about everything they asked him, and insisted he didn't even pay attention to the girl, and usually never even talked to his fares.

"I just pick them up and drop them off," Jason kept saying.

Jason couldn't believe they were making such a big deal over a lousy portable TV, but he also knew from what he had learned in his *Criminal Justice* classes, not ever to change his story or add any information they were looking for to try and *throw him off.*

The two detectives only stayed about fifteen minutes, and although they still acted suspicious towards him, one of them just gave Jason his business card and said to call the station if he decided to change his story.

"You should seriously consider calling us if you have anything you want to add before we have to come back here again," one of the detectives seriously said before he left, "You'll be in a lot more trouble if we find out you aren't telling the truth."

Jason locked his door when they left, suddenly wide awake, and felt his heart pounding while thinking about what to do.

The first person he needed to contact was Victor, and Jason felt better when he reassured him that he wouldn't say anything and keep the television set hidden in his closet until Jason told him anything different.

He then thought of someone else he could call and dialed another number.

Jason knew his former instructor at *UNLV* would be the best person to call for advice because Santini was still the Public Defender of Clark County, and they had always gotten along well in and out of his classes. Jason felt he could trust talking to him and although he still played innocent when he told Santini about what the detectives had said, and how they threatened him with being an accessory,

"Do you think the cops care about a lousy TV set?" Jim Santini half-laughed after Jason told him his situation, "They could care less about that."

Santini said that they also probably could care less about arresting him, and all they really wanted was the girl. He explained that a lot of the hookers who were "trick rollers" were usually "heroin addicts," and their "pimps were usually pushers" and the vice squad was just trying to see if they could get information from Jason about that.

"That's just the *MO* of the vice squad and they just play hard ass to try and scare someone who they think will rollover and snitch," Santini said, "But if you didn't do anything wrong, you've got nothing to worry about."

"But if I was an expensive fifty dollar an hour lawyer representing you, I'd just say, don't talk to anybody, lay low, and maybe just disappear for a week or so," Santini lightly added, "If there aren't any warrants out for your arrest, it's not like you're evading arrest or anything, and they can't hassle or try to scare you if you're not around."

Santini told Jason he'd quietly ask around and let him know if he heard anything about "a stolen TV" but could pretty much guarantee "that the whole thing would blow over" in a week, and the cops will move on to something more serious than just a "trick roller."

Jason felt more relaxed after he spoke with Santini and then decided he'd better call Terri at her motel, and let her know what happened. He especially wanted to tell her what Santini told him about "laying low for a week," so she wouldn't do anything dumb.

He knew Terri could tell he was still pissed about what had happened the night before, and she tried to apologize for being "so stupid," but she claimed it happened so fast, she just wasn't thinking straight. She also said she'd take some time away from *"working"* in case the cops had a description of her, and promised she never mention Jason's name to anyone if anything did happen.

Jason then thought about what Santini said about disappearing for a week or so and started thinking it might be a good idea to leave town for at least a few days, especially as he wouldn't be able to work for a week.

He also wanted to call Anne, but didn't want to tell her that he was suspended for a week because he figured he'd then have to tell her the whole story, which he didn't want to have to explain.

Anne had recently started a new job at a jewelry store during the day, and it had been tough seeing her as often the past two weeks with their different work schedules, and Jason usually didn't call her till after six pm. When he finally called her, he decided just to tell her that he would visit his parents for a few days and maybe start looking for a new car at the same time. He had already mentioned to Anne that he was thinking about trading his Ford Galaxy for something newer, so it sounded like a good story, and she seemed to accept it without question.

Jason also called Tommy and Alvin to let them know he wouldn't be at the *Jam* or even driving the taxi for a week and just hoped, as Santini said, everything would get back to normal by the time he came back home in a few days.

He also remembered some other things he had learned in Jim Santini's criminal law classes, about how hard it was to convict anyone of murder unless the body was actually found, and how it was also true when it came to stolen property.

Jason knew what else he needed to do.

The next day, as he was getting ready to drive back to California, Jason stopped at Victor's house to retrieve the television set when he knew Victor's parents wouldn't be home, but was irritated that Victor seemed upset when Jason said he was going to just "get rid of it" and tried to talk Jason into letting him keep it for himself.

"That's a nice little color TV, and it's a shame just to get rid of it," said Victor. "It's probably worth well over a hundred dollars and I promise I won't tell anyone if you just let me keep it."

Jason didn't even bother answering him, as he put the small television set in the trunk of his car and started his drive out of town.

After driving for over an hour and crossing the state line, when Jason got to *Zzyzx Road* outside of Baker, he pulled off the highway and parked next to an open desert area. He then took out the television from his trunk, along with a hammer he'd brought along, and proceeded to pound it into pieces until it was unrecognizable.

Jason never wanted to see or think about that television set again and wanted to make sure it was dead and would never be found.

Chapter Twelve

It felt strange being back at his parent's townhouse in Los Alamitos and sleeping in the guest bedroom, but Jason felt more relaxed than he had in two days and slept for close to ten hours the first night he was there. He also didn't feel any need to tell his parents why he suddenly visited them, but they seemed happy that he did.

Jason's only friend from high school that he stayed in contact with was Dan Kittredge, who came over the second night he was there, and his mother cooked dinner for them all saying that it would seem like the "good old days" when they were all living in Lakewood a few years earlier.

Dan had fallen in love with a girl he met just after graduating high school, who Jason had met her a few times before he moved to Las Vegas. Dan also mentioned that his girlfriend was pregnant, but said they both planned on waiting to get married until the baby was born. He also said if it was a boy, he was going to name him after Jason because it was such a *cool* name.

Jason just thought it was funny because he thought Dan was way too young to have a family, and even though Jason was *in love* himself, he knew that he and Anne weren't ready to take that step yet and was lucky that Anne religiously made sure she took her birth control pill every day.

During dinner, Jason's father mentioned that he had started his own business selling used newspaper vending machines for a profit to distributers of daily newspapers like the *LA Times, Herald Examiner* and the *Long Beach Independent*. He also said he was thinking of creating a specialty newspaper himself to sell to the newspaper distributors that would be a type of *spin-off* of the *computer dating* business he had been involved in the past year so he could sell even more news racks. His father said the newspaper would have personal ads for dates, and he'd only charge a small fee to place an ad, but it wouldn't cost anything to respond to a personal ad.

"It's not going to be anything like computer dating services at all," Jason's father said, "Computer dating clubs charge for everything, and this is just a way people can meet each other for free."

His father added that when was involved with computer dating, he saw there were a lot of people who were actually looking for serious relationships, and he'd make sure the personal ads were "straight and clean" to cater to that market, instead of the "swinging singles" who bought those other newspapers.

Jason had seen tabloid newspapers with personal ads like the *LA Free Press* and some in Las Vegas, but they had always seemed to be *pretty kinky* that were mainly for sex or escorts.

"Mainly it'll be another newspaper for the distributors can put in the news racks that I sell them," his father added, "Plus I'll make additional money from each issue they sell just like the daily newspapers do."

His mother didn't seem that excited about his father's idea and mainly teased Jason about how he had "followed in his grandfather's footsteps" and was driving a taxi in Las Vegas.

"I hope you're not planning on doing that for the rest of your life," his mother sarcastically said.

"The money has been great and I'm making over twice as much as I did last year," Jason said enthusiastically, "I'm sure I'll figure out something else in the next couple years, but for right now, it's a great job."

After dinner that night, and because Dan was there, his mother said it would be fun to play some card games together like they had when both he and Jason were still in high school. Jason also wasn't that anxious for Dan to leave and be alone with his parents and also agreed it would be fun as well as to get his mind of any problems he had in Las Vegas.

While they were playing different poker games they had sometimes played together in the past, Jason's father again started talking about his idea for a newspaper and what he should name it, so everyone started lightly throwing out different names about what they thought sounded good.

Newspaper names like the *Dating Examiner* and *Singles Times*, where some of the first names they were suggesting, but when someone mentioned *Meet Market Place*, Jason laughed and said that it definitely sounded like a "swinging singles" name, and that it sounded too much like they were talking about "M-E-A-T," and the word *Meet* was quickly eliminated. After someone mentioned *Singles Register*, his father wrote it down on a yellow legal pad with the other names that sounded the best and said he had a good list to consider over the next couple months.

Everyone was having fun and laughing together while they played cards, and Jason was just happy to get his mind off the problems in Las Vegas, but after less than an hour of playing cards, his mother made some sarcastic remark that his father didn't like about how he always seemed to have "get rich" schemes that never worked out for more than a year or two.

His father just said, "That's enough, Violet!" but when she made a snide remark back to him, he abruptly threw his playing cards down, said, "That's it!" and got up from the table to sit on the couch in silence, and turned on the television.

When his mother said, "Stop being such an ASSHOLE Richard!" His father responded with a "FUCK YOU!" Jason and Dan knew the reunion of the "good old days" was over.

Dan just laughed about it as Jason walked him out to his car, saying nothing had seemed to have changed between his parents. Dan had seen it plenty of times before when he visited Jason at his house when they both were still in high school, and always would just joke, "They're crazy!"

Jason just laughed with him as he always had and just sighed, "Yup."

The next morning, Jason's father had already left the house, and he could see his mother was in her usual foul mood that always followed the arguments.

"Your car looks like shit!" she immediately started yelling at Jason as soon as he came downstairs, "Don't you ever wash it?!"

She then added, "And make sure you make your bed and clean up your room because I don't want to have to pick up after you like I always do!"

Jason couldn't believe that she was talking to him like he was still in high school and still living at home. He also knew there would be the *silent treatment* for the remainder of his stay and realized he should have just stayed at a motel instead of thinking anything would ever be different with his parents.

He was disappointed at how fast their moods changed the night before after they seemed to be getting along fine, but then again, Jason knew that some things never changed.

&

Jason waited three more days before he decided to call Jim Santini again, and was anxious to get back to Las Vegas.

Santini said he knew one of the detectives who came to Jason's apartment and had actually once been a student in one of his classes at *UNLV*. Santini also said the detectives just laughed about the case when he had spoken with them, and said they got "more satisfaction" out of threatening the guy that Terri stole the portable television with being arrested himself for solicitation.

It turned out the guy that Terri robbed was a well-known local politician, but no one in the police department had ever liked him and the detectives lightly told the politician, "That's what he got for bringing *whores* to his house."

Santini said the detectives said it was more fun "busting the balls" of the politician, than if they would have arrested the hooker, and also said they didn't care about the cabbie and were just trying to scare him.

"They said it's basically a closed case and just another trick roller wasn't anything they planned on pursuing," Santini assured Jason, "But try not to keep getting yourself into weird situations anymore, because you might not be as lucky the next time."

After hearing the good news, Jason couldn't wait to get back to Las Vegas, and just left with a quick "See ya" to his parents, after leaving their townhouse within an hour of talking to Santini. He felt good and was confident once he was home again, everything could get back to being normal.

Jason had called Anne regularly while he was gone and had made plans to get together with her as soon as he was back, but first, he wanted to stop in and see Prado at the *Checker Cab* garage and let him know that there were no problems with the police, and he was anxious to get back to work.

"We've decided to let you go 669," said Prado, not even addressing him by his name after Jason had gone to the garage.

Prado told him that he and Maday had talked to some of the other taxi drivers, and they all said Jason was "well known" for driving the "wrong kind of girls" around town and had been almost working like a pimp himself.

Jason immediately started regretting the times he had those "working girls" take him out to dinner at *The Flame* and knew he had no one else to blame but himself for acting cocky around the other drivers. He tried convincing Prado that it wasn't as bad as they thought, but he knew the circumstances weren't in his favor and finally accepted the fact that he really was fired.

Jason was angry at himself but was especially angry at Terri for having started the whole chain of events, but when he called Terri at her motel to yell at her for what she had caused to happen, he ended up getting angrier when the desk clerk told him she'd checked out of the motel and didn't leave a forwarding number.

He was mainly angry because he didn't get the satisfaction of telling Terri of all the damage she caused and to "fuck off!" and knew with her leaving without even calling to see how he was, she beat him to the punch and got to say "Fuck You!" to him first.

Jason then realized that the bitch was just another *whore* after all.

Chapter Thirteen

The only thing Jason felt fortunate about, was that he had saved up enough money from driving his taxi not to have to worry about his rent or bills for at least three months, and figured he'd be able to find another job by then.

He knew he could always go back to *Johnny Reb's* for a few months, but that seemed depressing to him because he wanted to move forward and not backward and wanted to find something that sounded even better for a possible career and hopefully make as much money as he had by driving a taxi.

Jason was relieved when Anne didn't seem that disappointed when he told her he was leaving *Checker Cab* to find a new profession without going into the details about how he was actually fired, and Anne just said she hoped he'd find something he liked.

He had collected plenty of business cards when he was driving his cab and started looking through them all to see if he could get any ideas about what kind of job or profession that he actually might like to pursue.

Jason had often been out and about in Las Vegas at the different showrooms and nightclubs with Anne since he'd been driving a taxi, and he started thinking how Ricardo Villasenor once said he was "always looking for good stories in his magazine," and decided to give Ricardo a call.

When Jason set up a meeting with Ricardo to talk about going to work for the *Las Vegas Star*, he was excited when Ricardo offered him a job writing a column for his magazine. He had always liked his writing and journalism classes in both high school and at *UNLV* and were always ones Jason enjoyed most and usually excelled, but he wasn't thrilled when he found out that the magazine column wasn't how he would get paid.

Ricardo explained a magazine column would mainly help Jason sell advertising for *The Las Vegas Star*, and he would pay him commissions on how many ads he could sell each issue. Ricardo said it would be easier by having a column in the magazine because Jason could write something good about his clients that bought advertising and also explained how much the business owners liked having "blurbs about themselves or their business" in entertainment and nightlife columns more than the actual ads themselves.

"It makes them feel like their business is *famous*," Ricardo smiled, "They usually don't mind paying for an ad if they see there's some publicity that comes with it."

Jason was a little apprehensive about not getting paid a regular salary, but when Ricardo explained the potential commission earnings along with some of the comp's he'd receive for writing reviews for shows and restaurants as a "member of the press" it started to sound more attractive. He also told Jason he could write other articles or interviews with personalities if he wanted to do work on his "journalism chops" and learn more about the magazine business.

The biggest benefit Jason felt was that he'd again be working his own hours and still basically feel self-employed, which was something he'd really come to like. He also liked that he wouldn't have to work a graveyard shift, which had been causing him to spend less time with Anne and told Ricardo he'd give it a try.

Jason figured the *comps* could be just as good as the money and he'd be able to take Anne out on more fancy dates once he got himself established as a real *journalist.* Plus, working for a magazine had more status than anything he'd done yet, and might be something that would be fun for a real career.

Although he wasn't sure he'd be able to make as much money as he had with *Checker Cab* right away, he knew he hadn't been planning on doing that forever, and decided that he was just moving forward a little earlier that he had planned.

Just as he had learned in some of his philosophy classes at UNLV, he wanted to feel that everything happens for a reason.

It was less than a week after Jason decided to start working at the *Las Vegas Star* and came up with a title for his column, *Neon Lights, and Nightlife,* that Anne said she wanted to talk with him during her lunch hour away from Gianni Russo's jewelry store she was now working at full-time.

Jason's birthday wasn't for another week and he figured Anne wanted to talk about how they would celebrate him "not being a teenager anymore" and finally would be turning twenty years old.

Anne was already sitting in a booth at *Foxy's Deli* across from the *Sahara Hotel* when he arrived, and he immediately sensed that something was wrong when she seemed to be nervous about something.

"I think we need to take a break from seeing each other for a while," Anne quietly told Jason after they both ordered lunch. "It just hasn't felt the same the past couple of months."

Jason didn't understand what she was saying at first, and optimistically tried to tell Anne about how much more fun they were going be having now that he was going to be receiving some comp's for reviewing shows and different restaurants in his new column.

"It's not that we don't always have fun," Anne continued quietly, "But I just don't think I can try to continue having a relationship with you."

Jason couldn't believe that Anne was actually talking about breaking up with him, but then she said something that started to bring tears to her eyes.

"I've been with someone else," she quietly whispered.

226

Jason was hoping he hadn't heard her correctly, but knew he had when she started crying.

"It just happened during that week you were in California," she cried lightly, "It wasn't anything that was planned, but I just feel different now."

Any hurt that Jason expected to feel was replaced with anger and betrayal as he sarcastically asked, "Is it your friend, *Gee-On-Nee?!*"

When Anne didn't say anything and continued to cry, Jason suddenly began getting a sick feeling in his stomach, picturing Anne having sex with an *old guy* like Gianni Russo, and also suddenly became disgusted imagining her saying "Get it there!" to someone else besides him.

But he also had a feeling inside that he hadn't felt since his mother told him that "Tinker died" and he knew he just needed to get in his car and drive away from *Foxy's*.

As Anne continued to lightly cry, Jason didn't know what else to say and just stood up and threw five dollars down on the table towards her to pay the bill before their food even came and said with disgust, "You're just another fucking whore!" and angrily stormed out of the restaurant.

Jason stood outside of *Foxy's Deli* for at least five minutes, walking back and forth on the sidewalk, immediately regretting what he said and thought about going back inside to apologize for what he called her, but then angrily thought he had nothing to apologize for. Anne was the one who fucked someone else and not him and he wanted to make sure she felt as bad as he did.

But he also doubted that she did.

As Jason drove aimlessly around Las Vegas trying to understand what had just happened, he felt completely empty and couldn't believe that after how committed they had been to each other for over a year, Anne would just suddenly want to end their relationship. He briefly wondered if she had actually ever felt comfortable with their age difference, as it had been with Angie when he was "just a kid," but that had just been *sex* and *love* wasn't even involved back then.

Jason was also thinking about that since Angie, Anne was the first one who was ending the relationship, instead of the way he had just decided to break off his other relationships, and didn't like feeling that he was the one who was being *dumped.*

He always tried to feel that he was lucky and everything was going to work out, but he couldn't stop feeling that he was a loser that day.

1971 had already turned into his worst year ever.

❧

Although his phone rang several times over the next two days, Jason refused to answer it and eventually just took it off the hook. He guessed that one of the calls might have been from Anne calling him to say that she changed her mind and wanted to get back together, but Jason knew that things between them could never be the same. She had sex with someone else, and no matter how much he would try not to think about that, it would always be in the back of his head and knew it was something that would be impossible to forget, knowing he could never feel the same way about her again.

It was easier to have everything end quickly as it had at *Foxy's Deli*.

Jason didn't want to talk to anyone else or even try to work that day, and just wanted to be alone to think, but while he sat on his couch and listened to his records as a distraction, he started to realize he was only making himself more depressed by continuing to listen to particular songs, especially a song that he had been playing multiple times on his stereo.

His favorite song for the past month was *Isn't It A Pity*, which the disc-jockeys would regularly alternate with *A-side* of George Harrison's current number one hit single *My Sweet Lord*. Jason had told everyone he thought that Harrison's *Isn't It a Pity* was better than *My Sweet Lord,* and just as beautiful than anything *The Beatles* had ever recorded, and called it a "musical masterpiece" since the first time he had heard it. But now, Jason only was associating the lyrics with his own situation, and he couldn't get that damn *masterpiece* out of his head, after having continued to play that song over a dozen times in the past two days.

Continuously hearing the lyrics about what a pity it was *how people seemed always to break each other's hearts,* wasn't helping Jason's attitude, and instead of associating "love songs" with Anne, he was associating "break-up" songs with her, and was realizing how many more songs were written about bad relationships and heartbreak, rather than relationships that lasted forever.

He also found himself playing a song from his *Rare Earth* album, remembering how Anne said the lead singer's voice sounded *so sexy,* but instead of listening to the song *Get Ready*, Jason would play one of the other *Rare* Earth hit songs *I'm Losin' You,* and could feel the emotion in the lead singer's voice when he sang the lyrics about how it was *all over her face,* that *someone had taken his place,* seemed too appropriate as far as exactly the way Jason was feeling.

But the more he was associating every song he was listening to with his own "break-up," Jason was also beginning to feel awful about how he had shown his emotions so openly the last time he saw Anne, and was especially mad at himself for discovering he even had such negative emotions that could get him angry enough to call her a *whore.*

He also started remembering how Jackie Madison responded when he had broken up with her, by sending him the song *It Don't Matter to Me*, and wondered if Jackie had felt as bad as he did now. He had always thought that Jackie's way of sending a positive song that she associated with their relationship was a classy way to say goodbye, and Jason knew that the last words he spoke to Anne weren't *classy* at all.

228

He was not only sad, but he was also embarrassed that Anne's final memory of him was that he acted like just another *wimpy and jealous teenager*, who instead of acting mature, had just called her a *"whore"* and didn't want that to be the way she remembered him.

The next day, Jason finally decided to call Anne to let her know he didn't mean what he had said and was sorry he called her that name. Anne apologized as well and said she felt terrible that their relationship had to end the way it had.

But there was no reconciliation, and they both knew their relationship was over.

Jason tried to act mature over the phone, and told Anne he'd always be glad for the times they had, and told her whenever he heard *The Days of Wine and Roses*, he'd always think of her. But at the same time, he silently thought he never wanted to hear that song again and needed to keep those memories out of his head.

That thought made him sad as well, because *The Days of Wine and Roses* had always been one of his favorite songs and was going to miss listening to it, but he also never wanted to feel as hurt and depressed as he did that week again.

The title song of George Harrison's solo album, *All Things Must Pass* was the same attitude Jason wanted to associate with from now on.

Chapter Fourteen

Jason spent his twentieth birthday with Tom Casey and Victor Consuela at *Macayo Vegas* Mexican restaurant and they gave him a couple new eight-track tapes, including *The Rolling Stones* new album *Sticky Fingers* as a birthday present, joking that *Brown Sugar* or *Can't Ya Hear Me Knockin'* might be songs he could sing in the future. Jason also knew he didn't want to show any signs that he was depressed or look like a *wimp* to his friends about his break up with Anne and wanted to show the same light and philosophical attitude that Tom and Victor had both exhibited when they had broken up with their previous girlfriends.

Victor had already been through three girlfriends he had said he "was in love with" since Jason had known him, and had never seemed bothered by break-ups.

"The next ones were always better than the ones before," Victor joked instead of acting upset about a relationship ending, "and some new pussy is all it takes to get your mind off the last one."

"There's plenty of fish in the ocean to ever be upset about losing just one," was the cliché Tom also used after his over two-year relationship with Shannon King ended.

Jason remembered how unemotional Tom had acted when he said that "Shannon met some jerk from Beverly Hills" who she thought had a more exciting future planned for himself in "show business" than Tom was planning when she decided to break up with him.

"Fuck her," Tom had said, "I'm planning on being an FBI agent, and if Shannon thinks some *Hollywood type guy* is more exciting than me than that's her problem."

"It was fun while it lasted with Anne," Jason also tried to sound somewhat positive and philosophical, "But as they always say, nothing lasts forever."

As Tom and Victor toasted to Jason's comment, as well as his birthday, Jason quietly knew that although he had once hoped other things could have lasted forever, the reality of his statement was true.

Jason also knew he needed some other things to keep him positive that week and knew there was something else that he was *still in love* with that would keep his time occupied.

When he arrived at the Sunday *jam* and casually told Tommy and Alvin that he had broken up with his girlfriend, they teased Jason and said maybe they should all just jam to some songs about break-ups that day, because evidently, "Jason ain't gettin' *no sugar tonight!*" which led to Alvin start playing his keyboard and singing the chorus from the popular song by The Guess Who, *No Sugar Tonight*, but changed some lyrics to having "No sugar to *SLEEP* with me" instead of *"RUN* with me" to give it a cute meaning and keep everything light.

"Hey, you're a rock and roller like us!" Tommy also teased, "Chicks are fun for a while, but ya never want to spend all your time with just one anyway."

All the other musicians at the jam still thought Jason had just celebrated his twenty-third birthday, and he didn't want them to see him as a wimpy kid worrying about just one girl and said he was just planning to go out and "get laid with a couple new girls" to see what he'd been missing by "wasting his time" with just one girl for over a year.

Jason had always liked the song *No Sugar Tonight/New Mother Nature* and did already know all the lyrics, so he told the musicians to start the song from the beginning, and he'd sing it, and wanting to show he had a rock and roll attitude more than usual. He also joked about one of the other new songs from the Rolling Stones *Sticky Fingers* album about how "love was a *Bitch"* was another song they should try to learn at the jam.

After Jason started singing a few of his other usual songs like *I'm So Glad, Shape of Things to Come* and *It's All Over Now* that helped erase *Isn't it a Pity* and *I'm Losin' You* out of his head, Jason thought about a regular feature in *Reader's Digest Magazine*, and how it needed to be revised to include *Laugher (and "Singing") is the Best Medicine*.

Although it had hurt him as much hearing "I've been with someone else" as much as when he heard, "Tinker died," singing with his friends almost seemed to magically make his pain go away. It had hurt, but it hadn't killed him, and although he really wasn't interested in going out to "get laid with a couple girls" and just having sex again, he knew he needed to keep making money and get back to work, and that was going to be his main focus for now.

It had taken Jason a couple of weeks without making any money before selling his first ads for the *Las Vegas Star*, but even then, he saw he wasn't making close to what he had been making as a cab driver and barely as much as he had at *Johnny Reb's*.

He had been using his home number as a business phone, but could very seldom reach the right people in charge of advertising and when he tried to reach someone at the major hotel and casinos, he rarely received callbacks after his first pitch. Jason decided that it would be easier to hit the streets and just pop into smaller businesses where the owners were usually working themselves, and always got his foot in the door by telling them he was mainly interested in "doing a story" on their business, and didn't even talk to them about buying ads until after interviewing them.

During the time he talked with the business owners without trying to sell them anything, Jason built up a good enough relationship, where they almost seemed happy about "putting out a little extra money" and buy an advertisement.

"It naturally will give readers more information about your business to go along with the story I'm writing in the same issue," Jason always assured the business owners.

The independent businesses didn't have the major hotels and casinos budgets and usually bought smaller ads, but Jason figured the volume would eventually make up for it.

"*Volume* is where it's at!" Ricardo always stressed, "And eventually, it'll all start to pay off for you."

Jason liked having printed business cards from the *Las Vegas Star* with his name and title of *Entertainment Reporter*, rather than saying he was an advertising salesman, but besides making hopefully enough money that would pay his bills, he also liked that he was going to be a writer, and at least in a small way, be a respected member of the press and give him some more status.

He also wasn't interested in trying to meet another girlfriend immediately and instead would invite Tommy, Alvin, or some other friends to join him when he received *comps for two* for dinner, or to attend an opening night show at a casino to write about in his column.

Jason would often run into his old taxi fare Jim Parker from *The Panorama* magazine in the different showrooms and Jim introduced Jason to other Vegas columnists and reporters like Ralph Pearl, Forrest Duke, Joe Delaney, and Sig Sakowicz. He liked the camaraderie he shared with the other columnists by having his own *Neon Lights and Nightlife* column in the same way he had with the other musicians at the jam sessions and was starting to feel much better than he had as a cab driver, even if he wasn't making as much money.

Tommy and Alvin were particularly excited that he was writing for the *Las Vegas Star* and besides enjoying all the "comp's" he was inviting them to, also asked Jason if he could write about them or put their pictures in his column in the future if they got any "special gigs."

As Ricardo wasn't paying him a regular salary, he at least gave Jason free reign for his column's content, so Jason was glad to help out his friends with a little free press and publicity and did mention their names a couple times in his column.

Jason still thought it was funny that some things never changed, and everyone still wanted to see their names or pictures in a newspaper or magazine. But he also knew that how else would anyone ever know they were famous unless they saw it in the press?

❧

Although there was a new song that was being played on the radio constantly by The Jackson Five called *Never Can Say Goodbye* which did still make him think about Anne occasionally, he had made peace with himself that his last conversation with her had been somewhat positive even though it was a final goodbye.

Jason hadn't talked to Anne since their last phone call, but thought she may have called a couple of times when he answered his phone, only to have the caller hang-up, but he also was surprised at one phone call he received he wasn't expecting.

"Jason, it's Terri," he heard her say, "I'm sorry I didn't check in to see how you were doing, but I ended up leaving town fast."

"I tried calling you a few times," she added, "But I ended up not knowing what to say and just hung up."

At first, Jason was disappointed that it was Terri who'd probably hung up on him so often, but let her explain why she was finally calling.

Terri explained she was back in San Francisco because of a big fight she had with Johnny after telling him the police might be looking for her "because of that fucking TV set" and that after Johnny had "beat the shit" of her again, she decided to get away from him and Las Vegas for good.

Enough time had passed, and his other circumstances caused Jason not to be as mad as he was before but did somewhat bitterly explain the problems "that fucking TV set" had caused.

"There were some other problems I had that I never told you about," Terri tried to apologize, "and I wanted to try and straighten them out before talking to you again."

"But I feel terrible about causing those problems for you because I did consider you a friend," she added, "I wish there was something I could do to make it up to you, but maybe I can in the future if we can stay friends somehow."

"We can at least talk by phone sometime," Terri suggested, "and maybe we can just laugh at some of the adventures we had someday."

After Terri said she was going to "get out of prostitution" and possibly go back to school to straighten out her life, Jason did reluctantly decide to stay in touch with her occasionally. He figured keeping at least one friend from that weird period in his life might actually be something he could laugh about in the future and would remind him of all the adventures he had when he was *still a teenager.*

"Without memories ya got no past," Jason decided to sound somewhat philosophical instead of angry, "so hopefully things can turn out better for us both somehow."

He also decided that the *"fucking TV set"* that he once felt had ruined his past life might have actually led him to what he had now decided was going to be a better future and staying in touch with Terri by telephone was at least better than another final goodbye.

Jason didn't know if he ever could, but he did hope he could just laugh at his teenage adventures someday.

Chapter Fifteen

During one of the music jams around Memorial Day, Tommy and Alvin mentioned to Jason that they had some exciting news. They had another booking at the *Pussycat A-Go-Go* coming up and a couple of agents from Hollywood they'd worked with on bigger gigs were coming to Las Vegas to see them perform and talk about another gig they wanted to hire them for later that year.

Alvin called it an audition, but Tommy said it was mainly to talk business because they were pretty much already friendly with the agents and had hired him for other gigs a few times before. Tommy said the agents were looking for musicians to fill in spots for some well-known *"sixties bands"* they represented who were changing band members.

He said the agents represented groups like *The Zombies, The Animals, Iron Butterfly, The Grass Roots,* and quite a few others, and were planning on booking what they called a *"Sixties Music Revival Tour"* with some of their bands. Tommy continued explaining that some of those groups had members who had left the original band and the agents just replaced those members when they went on the road to perform their hit songs to live audiences.

"Sort of like the way we change musicians here in Vegas," Alvin added.

Tommy and Alvin were excited because the agents needed both a guitarist and keyboard player to play with the band *The Box Tops*, which meant they both might get a great gig together on the road for a few months.

"That's something you can write about in your column!" Alvin excitedly told Jason, "Plus, it'll be a good steady income for Tommy and me for the a few months we'll on tour."

Jason knew who *The Box Tops* were, although he never knew the names of any of the band members, and had the eight-track tape of their greatest hits, and was familiar with all of their hit songs. Their biggest hit song was *The Letter*, which was a huge hit when Jason was still in high school, but his favorite *Box Tops* song was *Neon Rainbow* because Jason would often play it and sing along while driving around Las Vegas. He had always associated Las Vegas with the song *Neon Rainbow* and thought he probably chose the name of his column, *Neon Lights and Nightlife*, because of that song.

Tommy and Alvin explained how they were able to be called *The Box Tops* without having the original singer and only two original members of the band remaining, and Jason was learning how strange the concert business actually was.

Alvin explained during the time *The Box Tops* were recording hit records; they changed band members so often that different musicians often played on different hit songs. Tommy said because they weren't a group like The Beatles, The Doors, or The Rolling Stones, where everyone knew who all the band members were, the public just knew the name of the band, and that was the selling point to the audiences.

They both explained that because so many of those rock groups from the 1960s broke up or always changed band members, booking agents or managers "somehow got the rights to own or use the name of those bands" and "somewhat legally" put versions of those bands together. They said the agents always tried to have at least some original members who played on the records, but if not, it came down to having at least "someone who played with someone" who had been once really been an "original member" that made it somewhat legitimate.

"As long as the bands aren't advertised like Diana Ross and the Supremes or Gary Puckett and the Union Gap and claim to have those singers," Alvin added, "it's still the band the audiences are mainly familiar with and as long as they hear the hit song's they're happy."

"Most of the old bands who had hits in the fifties have been doing that for years," Tommy explained," so some of the bands who had hits in the sixties are starting to do it now too."

When Tommy also casually mentioned during the jam that the agents might also be looking for some lead singers for some of the other groups, Alvin said he was disappointed that he wasn't going to be able to audition to sing in *The Box Tops* and they only needed him as a keyboard player.

"I like it when I get gigs where I get to sing too," Alvin said, "But the keyboard player in the Box Tops wasn't the lead singer, and they want to make sure we're a five-piece band so they want someone else to be the front man."

Jason surprised himself and didn't know what possessed him, but suddenly decided to be a little bold and half-seriously asked Tommy to find out if the agents were still looking for a lead singer because he knew all *The Box Tops* hit songs and casually said he "wouldn't mind trying to *audition* with them" if they were interested.

Tommy and Alvin seemed a little surprised, and both just smiled, because they really hadn't seen Jason perform on stage before and only at the jams.

"We've talked for months about me possibly singing a few songs with you at the *Pussycat*," Jason continued trying to convince them he was at least half-serious, "Just ask the agents if they would at least consider listening to me as a favor to you guys when they come to Vegas."

236

Jason also suggested Tommy should also tell the agent that he wrote an entertainment column and could put some blurbs and even some reviews, that would give all the different groups the agents managed some good free press and publicity whether he got the gig or not. He remembered that Ricardo Villasenor had told him could write other articles, so he figured Tommy passing on that information to the agents couldn't hurt.

"I'd just like to try it," Jason said, "And at least I could finally sing with you guys at the *Pussycat* at least once before you leave town."

"Well, we do owe Jason a favor for all the shows and dinners he's taken us out to for free," Alvin smiled to Tommy, "And the agents already know us and plan on hiring us anyway, so it might not hurt to just let him sing a few songs."

Tommy agreed with Alvin that Jason did come across like a cool front man, and decided that if they all worked on a few showcase songs for Jason to perform for the agents, he might be able to pull off *at least* an audition.

"Whether or not you get the gig or not," Tommy said, "It would be a good experience for you, but I've still got to check with the agents and see if they're still auditioning singers."

Jason assured them he'd be able to pull it off, and whatever happened, it would be fun to at least give it a shot. He also tried to make it sound like a just a fun idea and facetiously joked "how cool it would be" if they all ended up getting the same gig.

After Tommy called the agents, he told Jason they did seem to like the "press and publicity angle" because any news clippings always helped when they sent out press kits to promoters who were booking the concerts.

"I did exaggerate a bit and told them you were a well-known rock and roll columnist and would include some positive stories about all the shows they promoted," Tommy smiled, "I also told them you sat in with different bands here in Vegas did seem to like that and said they'd come and check you out when they come to the Pussycat and see if you're right for the gig."

"You have sat in with members of different band members at the jam sessions," Tommy added, "So that's just stretching the truth a bit."

Jason had just wanted to sing at the *Pussycat-A-Go-Go* at least one time, but although he was a little apprehensive, he was also excited that he was now going to be auditioning to be the new lead singer of a famous band.

"Now," Alvin laughed to Jason, "We just have to make you look like a pro."

Tommy and Alvin said they'd spend the next few weeks getting Jason ready to perform a "great set of four or five songs," and arranged for the bass player and drummer who would be playing with them at the *Pussycat-A-Go-Go* come to all rehearsals with Jason.

"Just a short and sweet set," Alvin lightly mentioned, "We'll just call you up on stage in the middle of our usual set as a guest singer, so it won't even seem like an audition."

"We'll just do a few of the best songs you sing at the jams and work on a Box Tops song or two," said Tommy, "We want to make sure we nail those songs to sound just like the record."

"You just need to sing in a gravelly voice like the original singer of *The Box Tops* does on the records," Tommy added, "Fortunately, the original singer Alex Chilton wasn't a household name, so most people don't remember what he looked like, but you at least want to try and sound like him."

They did spend the most time during rehearsals, trying to nail down the sound and Jason's vocals, to get as close to the original records as possible. Even when he wasn't at rehearsals, Jason would play those songs in his car and constantly try to match the way Alex Chilton sang in his gravelly voice. He took the rehearsals more seriously than anything he could ever remember, tried not to have any doubts, and tried to show complete confidence that he could get this gig.

Or, at least be good enough not to embarrass himself.

Tommy and Alvin also mentioned that to look more professional, Jason should have a good publicity photo printed with his name to give the agents when they met him and said they knew a photographer who could do it fast and didn't cost that much money.

Jason didn't waste any time and immediately set up a photo shoot, which he figured was worth the twenty-five-dollar investment. He posed holding a microphone and positioned himself as if he were performing, and did try to look similar to the *Max Frost* character in the movie *Wild in the Streets*. Several band members at the jam sessions had always told Jason he had a similar look to the actor Christopher Jones in that movie, so Jason felt he'd pose in a similar way.

After choosing the photo he liked from the proof sheet, Jason decided to print the single name "*JASON*" on the bottom of the print, thinking how cool it would look just using his first name. He then thought of something else that would make him appear professional when the agents met him for the first time.

He knew it would be great to have some press for himself to show the agents when they came to see him and adding a press clipping would add legitimacy to the fact that he was a well-known lead singer in Las Vegas. But Jason also knew it would look *fake* if it was seen in the magazine with his column inside.

Jason then remembered what Jim Parker had once mentioned when he was still a taxi driver, about putting a "blurb or picture" of Jason in *The Panorama*, and decided to see if he could call in a favor.

The Panorama was the most famous entertainment weekly in Las Vegas, and Jason knew he would immediately appear to be *famous* if he could talk Jim Parker into at least running his photo and include a caption saying "*Jason*" could be seen performing at several nightclubs around town.

He was happy when Jim Parker told him he would be glad to do it but was surprised when Jim said it would cost Jason another twenty-five dollars. He explained that Jason "should know by now," as he was a columnist himself, how to use his column to make some extra money. Jim also remembered that Jason said he had once taken law classes at UNLV, and joked that *everything* in Vegas is *quid pro quo*.

"Do you think I could make a living just by writing a column once a week?" Jim laughed, "The column just gives me the juice I need to make money in a lot of other ways."

Jason realized he was basically doing the same thing the way he wrote blurbs for the advertisers when he sold them ads, so he didn't object and figured it was worth the money. He just wanted to make sure that the photo would be in *The Panorama* before the agents arrived in town, and also told Jim to just use the single name of "*JASON*" for the caption, deciding it sounded flashier than using his entire name.

He briefly thought about letting his friends know when he'd be performing at the *Pussycat*, but then decided that it might be too much of a distraction to have them there and wanted to remain focused. Besides, he knew most of them didn't really take him that serious when he told them he had an audition to become the lead singer of a famous band.

Victor Consuela wasn't even familiar with *The Box Tops* and just asked, "Aren't they a black group?" and Jason had to explain that it wasn't *The Four Tops,* and tried singing a little of the song *The Letter* to remind him. But Victor was more familiar with the Joe Cocker cover version of the same song, which became a big hit the year before.

Tom Casey just thought it was funny because he never took Jason's singing seriously and just sarcastically wished him good luck, while Frank Reich said nothing Jason did surprised him, and said he always figured Jason would end up doing something *unusual or wild*.

Jason also called Terri in San Francisco, who sounded the most excited for him, but he also decided not to call Anne to let her know and figured she would probably see his picture in *The Panorama*, and that would be good enough to show her how famous he'd become since they had broken up.

He also hoped she'd see that he had always been thinking about "what he'd be doing five years from now" like she once asked, and wanted her to see that he was doing well without her.

But he was also hoping there was a chance that he actually could get the gig, because singing with Alvin and Tommy had at least helped him get over the somewhat empty feeling he'd had since they broke up.

Singing had become his best medicine

Chapter Sixteen

The two agents from Hollywood were sitting at a table near the stage at ten pm, waiting for Tommy's band to begin their early set at the *Pussycat-A-Go-Go*, and there were less than fifty people in the bar at that hour.

Jason saw one of the agents was dressed well and seemed serious and businesslike, but the other guy looked like a slob. Alvin joked that the other agent seemed more interested in wanting to know "If his drinks were comp'd" or if the girls sitting at the bar were "working girls or free agents."

Tommy gave the serious-looking agent a copy of *The Panorama* that featured Jason's picture, while Jason just stood next to the bandstand as the band went onstage to begin the set.

What they had all rehearsed was that about twenty minutes into the set, Alvin would start with his long keyboard solo of *Happiness*, which led into the *Deep Purple* version of *I'm So Glad*, and when the bass player and Tommy's guitar riff to the song started after the keyboard solo, Jason would walk up on stage with no introduction and just begin singing the opening lyrics. Tommy told Jason it would also give him a natural and dramatic looking effect for his entrance.

Tommy and Alvin also agreed that it was a great and easy song to open that Jason sang well, plus the song had a lot of back-up vocals to make it sound strong and full.

"When you walk to the microphone, have that *'Jason attitude'* and look like a rock star," Tommy constantly emphasized.

When the cue for Jason to walk to the stage did begin, any nervousness he was concerned about was gone once he began posing, and singing the opening chorus of *"I'm so glad, I'm so glad, I'm glad, I'm glad, I'm glad…"*

Jason knew it was a ridiculously simple song to begin his set, but it was easy enough to get him relaxed and show his *'Jason attitude"* which was what he mainly wanted to convey.

The second song was the one they all knew Jason sang best, It's *All Over Now*, and the next two songs were Jason's chance to show what Alvin and Tommy called his "Box Tops chops" and what they had spent the most time rehearsing.

Jason made sure he sang the opening lyrics to *The Letter* in the same gravelly-voiced style as Alex Chilton and emphasized the lyric about getting a ticket for an *"aero-plane"* instead of *"airplane."* He has also originally wanted to sing *Neon Rainbow* for his fourth song, but Tommy said *Cry Like a Baby* was the second biggest hit by *The Box Tops* and that Jason's vocals fit that song better. Jason hated the lyrics to *Cry Like a Baby,* and also didn't like that if by some small chance Anne Sanderson had been it the audience that night, it would be a wimpy sounding song for her to hear him singing about *"crying like a baby"* when thinking about their former romance. He didn't really want to sing a song that would make him sound like a *bawl baby,* but after seeing that Anne wasn't in the audience that night, he felt more comfortable singing it as they rehearsed.

After singing the first four songs, Jason felt good when he saw Tommy and Alvin give him positive nods and even heard Tommy whisper "nailed it!" after the two *Box Tops* songs.

The final song to his short set was another song Tommy and Alvin said Jason sang best was *Shape of Things to Come* which they told Jason to channel his best "Christopher Jones/ Max Frost" attitude, and come across like a real rock star by showing his *swagger.*

After *Shape of Things to Come* ended, Tommy just yelled out, "All right, let's hear it for *JA-SON!"* as he casually walked off stage to let the band finish their complete set.

The whole *audition* seemed to go by in a flash, but he felt great that even though the bar's audience was small, he got a decent round of applause. Jason tried not to make eye contact with the agents and just walked over to the bar like it was *just another gig* and ordered a double Chivas on the rocks.

When the band set was finished, Jason stayed at the bar while watching Tommy sitting with the agents and talking, but after about twenty minutes, Tommy walked over to him with a disappointed look on his face.

Jason knew that although he had tried to act confident the past few weeks, he was mainly having fun playing a *rock star* at the rehearsals and onstage that night, and didn't want to show any disappointment if it didn't happen. But when Tommy broke into an excited smile and said, "Believe it or not, you got the gig!" Jason was at first excited, but then suddenly realized what he had gotten himself into.

He started wondering what he was supposed to do now.

❧

It was around three am the same night. Jason, Tommy, and Alvin were sitting in the lounge on top of *The Landmark Hotel,* having celebratory cocktails, listening to the rock songs playing through PA system, and listening as Tommy explained everything he talked about with the agents.

"It's a good thing they know me, and I've got some *juice with them,"* Tommy proudly boasted to Jason, "I convinced them you'd sound just like the records when the shows start and be a cool front man as the fifth member of the band."

Tommy then added that the agents said that Jason looked good on stage and had the right look for *The Box Tops*, but suggested Jason comb his hair down and forward, so he didn't look so much like a Vegas singer.

Jason was just happy that changing his hairstyle was all they were concerned about and satisfied with his vocals.

"Those agents don't really care about who the *pick-up* members of the bands are anyway," Alvin sarcastically said, "Just as long as they sound almost like the original bands and will work for cheap enough money."

Tommy then let Jason know that the agents would only pay him fifty dollars a show because it would be his first gig with them.

Jason really didn't even care that much about the money and was just thrilled he would be going on tour and become a lead singer of a famous band. When Tommy also added that the agents would be booking at least four and sometimes five shows a week and pay travel expenses, Jason figured he'd make at least enough to cover all of his bills.

Tommy said that because this was going to happen, "There's a lotta shit," they had to get started on quick. He explained that the agents told them they'd only need to perform about a half hour set because they'd be performing with some other *Sixties* bands, and they only needed to play the songs the audiences already knew. He added that once that the agents had all their bands assembled, they'd start booking a tour that would start in the fall.

"This should be a piece of cake," Alvin smiled. "We've already got two songs down, so we only have to learn about five or six more."

"Oh, by the way," Tommy added, "They're hoping you're able to get them some good advance press clippings about the different groups when they do get the tour booked and include some photos in your column."

Jason was surprised the agents were so interested in having him write something in the *Las Vegas Star* because he figured a tour with so many famous rock and roll bands wouldn't have any problem getting press, but then he found out the reason the press clippings were so important to the agents and becoming a rock star was different than he imagined it would be.

He discovered that most of the other bands that they would be touring with were also in a similar situation as *The Box Tops* without having all the original members, and even the "headliners" they would be opening for on the tour, no longer had the original lead singers, which was why the booking agents were so interested in press clippings with positive slants. The agents mainly used the news clippings to send out to potential venues they booked the shows, to add legitimacy to the bands performing in their *Sixties Rock and Roll Revival Tour*.

Tommy told Jason not to worry about it and just print the stories the agents supplied, because as Tommy said, "a little BS never hurt anybody" and justified it by again saying there were so many bands from both the 1950s and the '60s who were still touring with a different lead singer than who sang on the record, it was "no big deal."

Tommy also said he was going to use a different name on this tour and because he'd used *"Starr"* with some other bands that he played guitar, he said his new stage name with *The Box Tops* was *Tommy Gunn*. Alvin decided as Tommy wasn't using the name *"Starr"* he'd be *Alvin Starr* for this tour. Jason thought it was strange how they could easily change their names, but they explained that the musicians in many famous bands were so interchangeable, they sometimes just used different stage names for different gigs.

Jason also discovered why Tommy and Alvin used different names when they changed gigs because they didn't want to lock themselves into a name associated with some of the bands they performed with in the future. In all the time he'd known them both, Jason never found out what Tommy and Alvin's real last names were, but he was having fun and wasn't going to let the fact that it didn't seem real ruin it for him.

Alvin also mentioned that because Jason was writing his columns as Jason Mershon, and because the first name *Jason* was so unique, it would look like he was writing good reviews about the band he was in himself, which would look fake and Tommy and Alvin suggested Jason should use a stage name as they were themselves.

"The agents said you're not *Elvis* and really shouldn't try to go by just the name *Jason*," Tommy laughed, "So they said not to try and make it sound like you are."

Jason liked his name but Tommy said that *Jason Mershon* didn't sound *rock and roll* like *Tommy Gunn* or *Alvin Starr* and also said that having the same name on his column that showed *Jason* as being the lead singer of *The Box Tops* wouldn't look good either.

They all threw around some different names the same way Jason had with his parents when they were thinking of a name for the newspaper his father was starting and all finally decided Jason's first initials *"JJ"* something or other might be good.

Jason immediately thought of using the name *"JJ Bond"* mainly because recently he and Victor Consuela had gone to see the filming of the new James Bond movie *Diamond Are Forever*, which was being shot in Downtown Las Vegas. They both went to Fremont Street and stood in front of *The Golden Nugget Casino* to watch a car chase scene involving James Bond, which was being filmed around four am.

As the cars in the scene being filmed by the camera crew raced by them several times, Jason and Victor tried to get as close to the front of the crowds as they could, hoping that they might be seen in the background and could always joke they were in a *James Bond movie*. Plus, it was also a James Bond movie, *You Only Live Twice*, that had originally given Jason the idea of changing his name from *Jay* to *Jason*.

Alvin thought the name *JJ Bond* was cool, but Tommy said it sounded too much like a clothing store or a type of business and kept throwing out some other names.

When they asked Jason what his current favorite song was, to maybe get an idea, Jason said he liked the song *Born to Wander* by the group *Rare Earth* because it had the attitude about being cocky and not bothered by any women who ever try to tie him down.

The song *Born to Wander* was actually a song that Jason had started singing to himself since his break-up with Anne that he decided was really the new attitude he wanted to convey to himself so he wouldn't ever feel as badly as he had again.

"That is a cool song," said Alvin as he started singing the lyrics about the *"wind being his mother,"* the *"highway being his brother,"* and how he was *"Born to Wander."*

"Those are great lyrics for a touring musician," Alvin smiled as they all started playing with some wind and highway type of names.

"JJ Breeze," Tommy suddenly said, "That sounds really cool and had a ring to it."

"Yeah, JJ Breeze," Alvin agreed, "It does sound like a musician's name and sounds perfect."

Jason walked over to the lounge's windows on top of the *Landmark Hotel* which looked over the entire city of Las Vegas and was a little disappointed he wouldn't be using his real name because no one would ever know that it was actually him singing. But after he lit a cigarette and looked at the city lights, he was thinking that *JJ Breeze* did sound kind of cool, and the name really wasn't that important as his performance would be.

Tommy and Alvin came over to the window and excitedly pointed out that the song playing on the speakers in the lounge was "almost a sign" that the name they had chosen was the right choice.

"They're actually playing the new song by the band we were just talking about," Alvin lightly joked about the coincidence, "That's gotta mean something!"

Jason did hear the hit song *I Just Want to Celebrate* by *Rare Earth* playing over the speakers and Alvin started singing along with the chorus of that song, encouraging Jason and Tommy to join him, acting as though they were as a jam session rather than in the lounge of the *Landmark Hotel*.

"Okay, JJ Breeze, it is!" laughed Jason, "Let's celebrate with some more drinks, and they're on me the rest of the night!"

As they all sang along with the closing and repeating chorus of the song *I Just Want to Celebrate*, not concerned with looking weird to the others in the bar, Jason was thinking about how lucky he'd become by just being a cab driver that led him to meet Tommy and Alvin. He was also thinking that maybe this was the reason he was meant to come to Las Vegas in the first place, and it just took him a couple of years to figure it out.

He was going to be a rock star.

Chapter Seventeen

Tommy said they needed to get some new publicity pictures that were similar to the outfits that *The Box Tops* wore on the album covers so they would look more *authentic* to the audiences. He also said they needed to be individual and not group photos because the agents already had pictures of the drummer and bass player who were the only two remaining "original members" of *The Box Tops* who would be performing on that tour. He said those two original members of the band already knew the songs, and they'd meet them when the tour started, and it wouldn't be any problem not playing as a group until then. Tommy did have a drummer and bass player who had played at the jam sessions to rehearse with them in Henderson, but there already was a prearranged setlist that the two original members of *The Box Tops* also were furnished, so when they all met on the tour, they could quickly run through the setlist at the soundchecks without actual rehearsal time together.

"The bass player and drummer from the actual Box Tops will just have to follow Alvin and me," Tommy explained, "We just need to play the songs like they sound on the records, and a quick rehearsal after we meet them and during the sound checks is all we'll really need."

Jason thought it was weird that they wouldn't be rehearsing with the other two actual Box Tops members and that the three of them would be just joining them once they were on the tour, but he wasn't going to question anything and figured Tommy and Alvin were used to always working that way.

Between rehearsals, Jason went with Tommy and Alvin to the *Goodwill Store* in Las Vegas for the wardrobe they'd need on the *Sixties Rock* and *Roll Revival Tour* to look authentic. The agents wanted them all to look similar to how the original *The Box Tops* dressed on their record albums, which included some bright colored shirts and jackets.

Tommy chose a couple of bright shirts that looked like they'd been out of style for years but told Jason they needed the "authentic 1960s look" when they posed for more publicity photos. Jason chose both a bright colored orange shirt along with a bright purple silk shirt with a sixties- neckerchief which Alvin said looked almost exactly like a shirt a band member wore on an early *Box Tops* album cover. He also reminded Jason wear his hair combed forward and down, instead of combed back for the publicity photos so "JJ Breeze" would look alright to the agents.

Even though Jason was still a little apprehensive about whether he could actually pull off trying to be a "rock star" so quickly, things did seem to be moving forward, but even before the tour dates had even all been set up, there was a blip that came up.

Because he needed to give up his full-time job selling advertising for the *Las Vegas Star* while he was rehearsing for the tour, Jason knew he still needed to have enough money to live on and pay his bills for the next couple months until the tour started. Fortunately, Tommy was able to give Jason three hundred dollars cash which he said was Jason's share of the advance money the agents had given them. Tommy also said once the tour started, he would still be getting fifty dollars for each concert they had booked.

Jason figured that would give him more than enough money for now, but the other blip that was his main concern was that by not working at the *Las Vegas Star* he wouldn't be able to continue writing his *Neon Lights and Nightlife* column.

Tommy said it really wouldn't be a deal-breaker as far as keeping Jason as the singer, but it was always a good thing to keep his *juice* with the agents and follow through with some press clippings in an actual magazine or newspaper.

Fortunately, Jason found a way to at least keep his end of the bargain rather quickly.

His father had recently printed his first copy of the newspaper, which he did end up naming the *Singles Register*, but when Jason saw the first issue when it was mailed to him in Las Vegas, he wasn't too impressed. It was only a sixteen-page tabloid that didn't have much content except for ten pages of personal ads for dates, and only a few generic articles that came from a news service. But his father said he wasn't as concerned with the content of the *Singles Register* as much as selling the newspaper vending machine racks, which he said was "where the money is for now" and considered the newspaper "just a *vehicle*" to sell the news racks. He also said newspaper was at least being sold in almost two hundred newspaper racks around the Long Beach area, and had some visibility on the streets in a few other cities, so Jason figured the Hollywood agents would at least consider it a legitimate publication.

Jason's father also seemed more impressed with him becoming the lead singer of *The Box Tops* than his mother, who only sarcastically said, "We'll see how long that lasts" and had thought that because Jason had so many different jobs in Las Vegas that he never took anything seriously. He had never shared or explained the reasons he changed jobs with his parents, and didn't really want to, but he did need a *"vehicle"* himself to get his column published, and asked if he could include a column in the *Singles Register* that would cover the music scene. Jason felt better when his father said it would be fine, and he'd include the column somewhere in the next issue.

Jason decided to name his new column *The Rock, Roll, and Soul Scene*, and included photos and a story from a press release the agents had sent him, including photos of all the bands performing on the *Sixties Rock and Roll Revival Tour* who besides *The Box Tops* included *Canned Heat*, who had some hit songs and had played at Woodstock, *The Seeds* who were mainly known for having one big hit called *Pushin' Too Hard* and *Spirt*, who also had a big hit song called *I've Got A Line On You, Babe.*

Jason was satisfied he at least followed through on some press he told the agents he could supply by sending them clipping of the stories in the *Singles Register* and would be able to just focus on what he hoped would be his new career.

He was still a little apprehensive, but with the way everything had seemed to "fall in place" to keep moving forward, he was confident he was going to be able to pull it off and really become a rock star.

è

It was over three months since his audition at the *Pussycat-A-Go-Go* and although Jason was trying, he really didn't feel like a rock star.

After Jason, Alvin and Tommy were all flown into Phoenix, a tour bus was supplied to drive them and musicians from the three other bands who would be traveling together to cities in the Southwest and Midwest to act as the opening acts for various other bands who would alternate as the "headliners" at each concert in different cities. Those bands included *The Zombies, The Grass Roots, The Animals* or *Iron Butterfly* who would travel separately to each concert, but before the concert tour even began, Jason discovered the two original members of *The Box Tops* who were supposed to be joining them on the tour, turned only into one member, when the bass player quit and was replaced with another "pick up" musician who Tommy suggested to the agents. The only "original" member who would be traveling with them was the drummer Tom Boggs, who Jason learned wasn't actually the actual original drummer, but had joined *The Box Tops* after *The Letter* had become a hit and had played drums on a couple other Box Tops hit songs, so technically he could be called an original member.

Jason was disappointed that they weren't booked in bigger cities or famous venues like the *Whiskey-A-Go-Go* and *The Troubadour* in Hollywood, or even in Las Vegas at the *Pussycat-A-Go-Go*, and most of the concerts were booked at smaller venues, colleges, and an occasional old movie theatre that had been converted into a concert hall.

The bands traveling on the tour bus would just meet the different headliners at the soundchecks who alternated in different cities and although none of those bands had the original lead singers, with the exception of Eric Burdon who had been well known as the singer of *The Animals* and not part of the *New Animals* on that tour, Jason had never been that familiar with who the original lead singers of the other "headliner bands" they were opening for.

Jason did see how interchangeable band members had actually become when the new lead singer of *Iron Butterfly* Mike Pinera, one of the other bands they opened up for, had actually been the singer of the group *Blues Image* just the year before and had his own big hit song, *Ride Captain Ride* which Pinera didn't even sing during the concert.

Both Alvin and Tommy used Mike Pinera as an example, and assured Jason that *JJ Breeze* was now the *somewhat official* lead singer of *The Box Tops*, and teasingly said that he was lucky he never had to spend years "working on his chops" to become a rock star and was able to have hit records to perform with the first band he was ever in. But Jason did see that the audiences did all seem to just enjoy hearing the well-known songs not seemingly that concerned with the particular singers as long as they *acted* like they had always been a part of the particular band who was performing.

Regardless of all the different circumstances, Jason was still trying to having fun but was also a little disappointed that although he was still the "front man" and somewhat official "lead singer" of *The Box Tops* shouting out the phrases like "Are you ready to rock and roll!" and "Is everyone having a good time?" to the different audiences, Jason learned he'd actually only be singing half of *The Box Tops* hits songs at the concerts and would share the lead vocals with Tommy and Alvin.

"It's the band and the songs the audience knows," Tommy again explained, "So it's cool to break it up and just have you sing the songs you do best and have Alvin and I sing a couple songs too."

After singing the first three songs in the set, *Cry Like a Baby*, *Soul Deep* and *Neon Rainbow*, Jason would introduce "lead guitar player Tommy Gunn" to the audience who would sing the Box Tops songs, *I Met Her in Church* and *Choo Choo Train*, before he would then introduce "the keyboard player Alvin Starr" who would also sing two songs, *Sweet Cream Ladies* and *A Whiter Shade of Pale*.

Jason was especially disappointed he wasn't singing lead vocals on the song *Sweet Cream Ladies (Forward March)* because the song lyrics were a light tribute to prostitutes and the services they provided. Jason had joked that he could associate a little bit with those lyrics, but Alvin sang lead, and Jason just sang back up on a few lyrics to that song.

A Whiter Shade of Pale had been a big hit for another group called, *Procol Harum*, but *The Box Tops* had included a cover version on one of their albums and was a well enough known song that Alvin wanted to sing and showcase his keyboard abilities.

Alvin would then finally introduce Jason by shouting "We've got one more song for you tonight so let's hear it again for JJ Breeze!"

Aside from his brief introduction before he sang the closing song *The Letter*, it did seem that the band members were just an afterthought and the audience wasn't really paying that much attention to any of their names.

Although *The Box Tops* sets were less than thirty minutes, Jason was happy with the audience's responses and felt like he had pulled off his act as *frontman*, he did sometimes wonder if he was only along on the tour as a hired hand that Tommy hand convinced the agents to add him along as a favor, and if Tommy was paying him out of his own pocket.

The tour manager always paid Tommy the money after each gig to pay the other band members in *The Box Tops* privately including Jason's fifty dollars a show, and although the other band members never talked about how much money they were being paid themselves, Jason guessed it was probably a lot more than he was making.

But he also knew better than to even be concerned and just felt lucky that he was being accepted as "one of the guys" by the other musicians on the tour.

There was another major bump in the road when only three weeks into the tour, Tom Boggs who Jason had started to become friends with, decided to quit the band as the other "original" Box Tops bass player had done.

Tom Boggs said that he originally had hoped that the new version of *The Box Tops* might eventually go back into the recording studio to record some new hit songs, but when the agents said just as the other bands on the *1960s Rock and Roll Revival Tour* were, "The Box Tops weren't a recording band anymore" and "strictly a touring band," Tom said he could make better money doing something else for a living back in Memphis.

Jason was worried with Tom leaving it would also be the end of the tour for *The Box Tops*, but was surprised that Tom leaving the band had no effect when the agents immediately flew in another drummer to fill in and continue on the tour.

It did seem to Jason that most of the time was spent traveling on the tour bus and staying in less than desirable motels rather than performing, and he also tried to get used to all the pot smoking almost all the other band members indulged in on the bus and before the concerts. He did his usual faking it when a joint was passed to him without inhaling and mainly just drank several beers before the concerts to have the same "stoned attitude" most of the other band members had onstage to keep in the "1960s rock and roll spirit" to the audiences. But the biggest reason that all the other musicians enjoyed being on tour was for the obvious reason of the groupies they would sometimes meet after each concert.

"The *road whores* are the best thing about touring," Alvin would often joke, "The money might suck, but so do they."

Jason did it was funny at the number of cute girls who would always want to go back to his motel as soon as the concerts were over because they just wanted to have *sex* with a *lead singer* of one of the bands. He didn't mind the occasional one-night stand, knowing that enjoying a night of sex together wasn't a *"capital crime,"* as he remembered singing in the song *Stray Cat Blues*, and it was just part of his act of being *JJ Breeze*, the rock star.

Although he did meet a few that he thought could have been girlfriends under different circumstances, Jason had no current interest in being with "just one" as Tommy had once said, and wanted to continue being a *"rock and roller"* like the others were on the tour.

After the final show of the tour ended and all the other musicians were preparing to fly back to their home cities, although Jason was looking forward to more shows in the future, he started getting concerned that his time as *JJ Breeze* might only be a one-time-deal.

The bass player and drummer started talking about joining another famous band the agents managed who were getting more bookings and being paid more money than *The Box Tops*. And, members of the other famous bands were also talking about the "next gig" they were working on.

Even Tommy and Alvin decided to go to Hollywood to "try and gig" with some other bands before going home to Las Vegas, but Jason also got concerned when he found out that there was another band touring as *The Box Tops* on the east coast that the agents also managed.

Tommy explained the agents decided to work with the other Box Tops band back east to save money on expenses. They let Tommy know the *JJ Breeze* version wouldn't be needed for a while but would call if they ever did. Even though Jason had tried not to think of himself as just a temporary hired hand to help make the agents some money, he basically knew that's what he was.

Tommy and Alvin always just said, "enjoy the ride" and just be happy for the experience and fun, because "nothing lasts forever."

Jason was well aware of that expression but was still a little sad when it ended. He had also learned so much during that time about how the music business and agents worked, and discovered it wasn't nearly as glamorous as he thought it would be.

JJ Breeze had played a rock star on stage, but Jason Mershon still really didn't feel like a rock star and he also suddenly realized that his *"fifteen minutes of fame,"* the catchphrase that Andy Warhol had talked about a couple of years earlier, might be over.

Chapter Eighteen

Jason was back at his apartment in Las Vegas, and for the first time, in a long time, he felt completely alone. It was also the first time, in a long time, he could ever remember having nothing to do.

The tour had given him so much action and excitement for the past three months that nothing else sounded fun.

Although he still had some money in the bank to hold him over for a couple of months, he felt that any type of *ordinary* job would feel like he was going backward again. Jason couldn't motivate himself enough to go back to work for Ricardo at *The Las Vegas Star* just to sell advertising and felt he needed to do something more exciting than just an ordinary job.

He knew it would also be embarrassing to let his friends know that his days as a rock star were over, so Jason decided to tell them was "just on a break" until he started the next phase of his music career. Jason also called his parents and let them know he was "just on a break," but let them know he still wanted to continue writing his music column in the *Singles Register* and figured at least he could keep that connection to the music business and might still be able to get some comps for writing about something or someone.

After Jason mentioned he wasn't planning on looking for another job right away in Las Vegas and was going to take a few more weeks to decide his future, his father then suggested something that surprised him and said if Jason was interested, he might want to consider working part-time as an editor for the *Singles Register*, and he'd pay him "a little extra money" until he decided what he wanted to do.

His father said all of his time was being spent on distribution and selling the news racks, but the newspaper itself wasn't selling very well for the distributors. He also said that because Jason had spent time at the *Las Vegas Star* and had always liked writing, he may have "some good ideas" to make the *Singles Register* more interesting to readers.

Jason didn't like the thought of working on a project with his parents, because although they were getting along, it was mainly because they very seldom saw each other. He knew how things usually turned out when they spent too much time together after living with them for eighteen years and wasn't about to kid himself into thinking it would be any different.

He just wanted to be polite and told his father he might be in California for a couple of days to "check on his deal with the band" and said he'd stop by their townhouse to talk about it. He still wanted to sound positive about possibly re-joining another version of *The Box Tops* but also knew he'd need to start earning some type of income in the future and decided playing a *part-time editor* on the side might be fun as well until he got another gig.

But he was still hoping that his singing career wasn't completely finished yet.

Tommy had given Jason a number for what he called his *answering service* where he could leave a message, and then he'd call back and let Jason know where he and Alvin were staying. Jason hadn't seen either of them since the tour ended over a month earlier and called the answering service to let Tommy know he was coming to California to visit.

After Tommy called back and gave him the name of a motel they were staying at in Hollywood, Jason decided to drive to LA to find out if there was any shot continuing with a music career, or if he should move on and accept that he wasn't going to become the next Mick Jagger.

He figured he could also visit his parents. to at least find out what the deal was with the *Singles Register* newspaper.

Jason had nothing better to do, but knew he needed something.

ॐ

Jason was sitting with both his parents at their townhouse in Los Alamitos looking over the monthly issues of the *Singles Register* that had already been published, and although he didn't say it, he still wasn't impressed.

It was still only sixteen pages and still looked more like a monthly newsletter than a newspaper, with only some weird art design on the cover, and the block lettering *"Hundreds of Singles to Meet"* under the title *Singles Register*.

The typeface throughout the newspaper looked cheap, with the only photos being some of the ones Jason had supplied from his *Sixties Rock and Roll Revival* tour.

Almost all of the content inside was still just personal ads from supposed people who were looking for dates, and his mother said that most of those personal ads were "made up and only fillers" to interest people in buying the newspaper.

His father said that decent money was coming from selling the newspaper racks to distributors, but it wasn't helping that the distributors weren't interested in buying more racks unless the sales from the newspaper started to increase.

Jason's mother made a sarcastic comment about how his father was "just a *salesman*" and didn't know how to run anything like a newspaper. When she added how she "knew that the newspaper was a bad idea," Jason could see by his father's face that another argument could be brewing and tried to change the subject.

"If it's going to be called a *newspaper*, it needs some current articles of interest that makes it readable," Jason said trying to sound knowledgeable, "The first thing I'd do would be to make the cover and content inside more attractive because, besides my column, there isn't much to read."

Jason at least wanted to show his parents he had some knowledge from working with the *Las Vegas Star* and wanted to give friendly suggestions.

"Fifty cents is a lot of money to pay when all the other newspapers only cost a dime or a quarter," Jason also mentioned, "and who will buy the paper again if the personal ad's they respond to aren't real and never get a response?"

"It's obvious that if more people bought the paper for the content," Jason added, "eventually real people will actually pay money and place a real personal ad themselves for dates."

"Well, I'm positive that once more people start buying the paper for the content, and actually start using the paper for dating," his father said, "this concept can start making money on its own and not just from the news racks I sell."

"I do know some columnists in Las Vegas who might contribute some articles," Jason said, "And I might be able to write a couple of articles or a new column to make it more interesting for single people around town."

When they both asked Jason if anything like that might interest him, he said he still needed to meet with his other band members to see if there was possibly another tour being set up soon. He also told his parents he'd talk to them again before he left town and think it over, but he still had to give being a rock star one last shot.

Jason decided to drive to Hollywood around three pm the next day and wasn't impressed when he saw the cheap motel on Sunset Boulevard where Tommy said he and Alvin were staying.

Alvin seemed still half asleep when he answered the door, and he saw Tommy was still sleeping in one of the double beds in the room.

"Hey man," Alvin said, groggily as Jason walked into the room, "We didn't think you'd be here till later."

Tommy didn't even wake up, and Jason apologized for coming that early and then noticed what was on the nightstand next to the beds. It was syringe sitting next to a Zippo lighter and a spoon that was obviously blackened by the lighter.

Jason suddenly felt like he didn't want to accept what he was thinking and tried to look away, but when Alvin saw that Jason saw the syringe, he just nervously laughed and blurted out, "Oops, BUSTED!"

"It's no big thing," Alvin tried to say while picking up he syringe to put in a drawer, "It's just some stuff one of the guys on tour turned us on to, and we just decided to give it a try."

"It's actually a pretty cool high", Alvin casually added as if it was nothing for Jason to be concerned about.

"Heroin?" Jason asked without trying to sound shocked.

Whenever Jason heard himself or someone else say "*Heroin*," he always flashed back to the little girl he once knew who said, "My mommy died when a man stuck a needle in her arm" when they were both too naïve to know what really happened.

"We're not hooked or anything like that," Alvin said nonchalantly, "It's just something to party with once in a while."

Jason looked at Tommy, still snoring on the bed and suddenly just wanted to get out of there.

"Listen," said Jason, "Let me give you guys a little more time to get ready, and I'll just grab a bite to eat and call you later."

"That's cool," Alvin answered with some relief, "It'll be fun to hang out in Hollywood tonight."

"And it's great seeing you again, Jason!" Alvin added as Jason walked out of the room.

When Jason was walking back to his car, he already knew that he wouldn't be calling them later and would just leave a message on their answering service and say he had to get back to Las Vegas.

He suddenly wasn't even thinking about being a rock star and wasn't sure if he even wanted to play *JJ Breeze* again.

Chapter Nineteen

As Jason was driving back to Las Vegas, he felt like he had a million thoughts going through his head, but he was mainly thinking about the conversation he had with his parents the day after he visited Tommy and Alvin at their motel.

When Jason had told them, he decided to "pass for the time being on a music career" and was going to think about a new career; his parents again brought up the *Singles Register*.

Jason was surprised that talk about him becoming the editor was mentioned again, as well as at the apparent business arrangements they began discussing along with the possibility of him moving back to California, which he had never considered doing. His father decided he was actually more in need of a full-time editor, who could accomplish some of the things that Jason had talked about, as far as turning it into a *real newspaper.*

"If you'd think about moving back to California," his father began, "There's already a small office with some staff you can work with on the newspaper."

"You'll get paid two hundred dollars a week to start," his mother quickly added, "And that's probably more than you could make in Las Vegas."

Jason exaggerated and told his parents that the money had always been great in Las Vegas, and said it would "cost him a lot" just to pack up everything and suddenly leave.

He was surprised even more when his father told him he'd give Jason enough money to cover moving expenses back to California, and enough to get set up in his own apartment. Jason figured his parents must have discussed the idea amongst themselves after he'd left the other day, to have a plan like that already in place because it was surprising to suddenly hear an offer like that come out of nowhere.

Although his mother tried to be light, when she half gloated that she "knew she was right" and Jason "wouldn't be successful as JJ Breeze," she also tried to be encouraging at the same time, saying that becoming a newspaper editor "might fit his talents a lot better."

Jason was irritated about his mother's partly negative tone because even though his time as *JJ Breeze* had ended, he did think it was a success that he at least accomplished it, even if it was only for about three months.

He also still didn't like the idea of working with his parents, and his father must have sensed the same thing, the way he continued discussing the possibility.

He added that Jason would mainly be "working on his own" with the staff at the office, and his father would always be "in the field" selling news racks. He added that his mother would be handling the mail and personal ads at their house, so it would be rare if they even saw each more than a few times a month.

"The newspaper itself could be your own business," his father said, "And after a year or so of seeing if you like it, and can build it into a newspaper that sells, you'll be able to share in the profits."

"You'll basically be the owner of the newspaper along with us," his mother added.

His father also added that being a newspaper editor may turn into "something he liked doing" and might turn into something "very profitable" in the next couple of years.

Jason was trying to decide if his parents just felt sorry for him for not making it as big as he expected as a rock star or if they thought he could actually be a benefit to the newspaper.

But he was continuing to be surprised as the offer got even better.

His father also mentioned that he had switched to leasing cars and would give Jason his current 1972 *Lincoln Mark 1V* he'd had for only six months, to drive as a company car and would just lease a new Cadillac for himself because he saw that Jason's 1967 *Ford Galaxy* was on its final legs.

Hearing a sudden business offer from his parents was that furthest thing he'd been thinking about, and although he tried to not be rude and brush it off, Jason did tell them he needed some more time to think about it, and didn't want to commit to anything that day.

As Jason continued thinking about everything during his drive back to Las Vegas, he occasionally would hear a song on the radio that some band members on the tour bus would constantly play from a new album they liked called *Hunky Dory* by David Bowie.

Jason didn't care much for that album, except for one song that was currently popular on the radio called *Changes*.

That song made Jason think about an expression he heard or read somewhere before about how *"only the dead never change,"* and thinking about how it applied to him currently.

He was also starting to think about what was really keeping him in Las Vegas.

It was a fun city, but he didn't have a girlfriend or even a great job that was keeping him there. Jason knew if he stayed in Las Vegas, he'd either have to start selling advertising again for the *Las Vegas Star* or find another job.

He also knew his thoughts of being *JJ Breeze*, the rock star, were pretty much over, and staying in Las Vegas doing the same old thing, would almost be embarrassing after everything he had told his friends about his future plans as a singer.

"*Ch-ch-ch-ch-changes…,*" Jason was singing to himself along with the song on the radio, as he felt a change actually coming over him.

Jason had thought long enough and had made up his mind.

രൂ

Less than a month after being back in Las Vegas, Jason's apartment had been emptied, and his car was packed with everything he owned and the only thing Jason decided he was going miss were his friends he'd made in the past three years.

He had spent that month saying goodbye to all his friends but assured them he always be back visiting Las Vegas and seeing them.

Frank Reich said he'd "be pissed" if Jason didn't stay in touch with him and laughed that "one of these days" he hoped he'd be hearing that Jason was "doing something great" that would make him proud for knowing him when he was young.

"But knowing you," Frank also joked, "I'm sure it'll be something wild and crazy so just try to stay out of trouble."

Tom Casey and Victor Consuela both assured Jason that they'd visit him in California, and also said they'd always stay in touch. Tom also said Jason could use his home address in Las Vegas if he wanted to keep his "special driver's license" when it was time to be renewed.

Ricardo Villasenor thought it was great that he was going to be an editor and said he could always call him if he needed any help or advice, and Jim Parker said the same thing, adding that if Jason needed a Las Vegas column to call him. Jason even called Jim Santini and let him know that he was getting a "respectable job" and thanked him for the things he had learned from him.

He also called Terri in San Francisco to give her a number she could reach him in California as well as a couple or the musician friends he'd jammed with, but he also heard that Tommy and Alvin got gigs and were back on the road and was only able to leave a message on their answering service.

Jason knew they were probably still embarrassed from the last time he had seen them, and felt sick that his two friends would even consider trying heroin, but he did hope they'd eventually become themselves again and re-connect.

He briefly thought about calling Anne Sanderson to let her know he was leaving, but a long time had passed, and knew she probably didn't even care what he was doing anymore.

As Jason drove past the Nevada State line into California, he felt melancholy in many ways but was happy about one thing in particular. Although he had decided to keep his driver's license that said he was three years older, Jason had finally turned twenty-one years old a few weeks earlier and wouldn't have to pretend he was an adult any longer.

But he was also reflecting about his actual first twenty years and wasn't sure if he'd ever experience as much as he already had in his life. He had already achieved a certain amount of fame before he was even a teenager, and he certainly knew he had his share of drama, but he had also experienced love and heartbreak which was making him feel he had done it all and wasn't sure what was left to him to experience.

Jason didn't know if he could ever repeat some of the thing's he'd been through in his first twenty-one years, but he was going to try.

PHOTO GALLERY

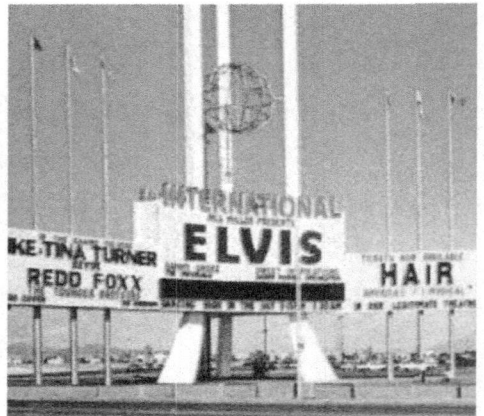

Top: Two views of the Las Vegas Strip in 1969. Bottom: Jason and Rhonda at Elvis Presley's concert at the International Hotel and Casino, Las Vegas, 1969.

Two Shots Fired at Man On Lake Mead Drive

A 21-year-old Las Vegas youth, Jason Jeffery Mershon, was shot at twice last night as he drove his car down Lake Mead Drive near the Ivy street intersection, according to Henderson police.

Officer Carl Anders and Det. Bob Matheny investigated the incident which occurred at 7:15 p.m.

According to Mershon, he heard two shots which sounded as if they came from a vehicle beside his car. He slammed on the brakes, almost losing control of the car, and the suspect vehicle continued on eastward on Lake Mead Drive without lights. Mershon could give no description of the vehicle or its occupants.

One of the shots apparently hit the car about one inch under the rear window and police were searching for the bullet. Mershon told police he could think of no one who would shoot at him.

LAMB INDIGNANT

The Doors Will Open After All

The Doors will open on schedule Saturday night at the Ice Palace, but they will not have the blessing of Sheriff Ralph Lamb.

Lamb wanted to close The Doors before they ever opened by not issuing the hippie-styled entertainers a business license, but the district attorney's office said that legally he couldn't do this.

The sheriff said the group's leader James Morrison, was a "sickening entertainer" who was run out of several other towns because of his lewd actions while on stage. "I just didn't feel our teenagers should see such entertainment. If there is one thing lewd at that show Saturday night they'll be singing the rest of the act in the county jail."

The show is being produced by Mark Tell Productions. The Doors caused near riots in Miami and Los Angeles when they played there. Five people were arrested in Florida and six federal warrants were issued.

Top: Jason was more satisfied seeing his "new" name and age in the above front page headline, than he was concerned about being shot at. Bottom left: Although Las Vegas had a reputation as "Sin City", the local Sheriff and District Attorney both tried to ban the rock musical *Hair*, as well as Jim Morrison and The Doors from playing in Las Vegas. Bottom right: Jason's criminal law and political science professor at UNLV, Jim Santini. Santini would go on to become a Republican United States Congressman, before losing the election for U.S. Senate to Democrat Harry Reid in 1986.

261

JOHNNY REB'S
LEXINGTON
BAR-B-QUE

— Has —

Hickory Smoked
PORK — BEEF — RIBS

BAR-B-QUE SANDWICHES

With Johnny Reb's Special Bar-B-Que Sauce & Slaw

PORK, Chopped 69c
PORK, Sliced 69c
BEEF, Sliced 69c

HOT DOG SPECIAL!
hili, Mustard, Onions & Slaw 35c

TWO SANDWICH SPECIAL !
rk or Beef and One Hot Dog
ecial, Plus Baked Beans 98c

SIDE ORDERS
NCH FRIES .25
PUPPIES .25
ON THE COB .35
BEANS .25
.20

Special !
BAR-B-QUE PLATES
With Slaw, Hush Puppies
And Baked Beans

PORK, Sliced 1.25
BEEF, Sliced 1.25
SPARE RIBS 1.75

COMBINATION PLATE
Pork, Beef, Spare Ribs,
Baked Beans, Slaw and
Hush Puppies
2.50

Golden Fried
APPLE PIES
20c

**ALL ITEMS CAN
BE MADE TO GO**

DRINKS
PEPSI-COLA

PEPSI
DIET PEPSI — ORAN
TEEM — ROOT BEE

NASHVILLE
NEVADA

NASHVILLE
NEVADA
CLUB

Home of WYNN STEWART
OPEN 24 HRS

DANCING
CASINO
HO OF
WYN STEWART

Top left: The menu at Johnny Reb's in 1969, where Jason worked while studying at UNLV. Many thought sixty-nine cents for a sandwich was expensive, because McDonalds had recently introduced its new sandwich, the "Big Mac" for only forty-nine cents. Top right: Kay Adams, a popular country western recording artist, and the sister-in-law of Johnny Reb's owner Frank Reich, first invited Jason to the Nashville Nevada nightclub where she would regularly perform. Bottom left: The Nashville Nevada Club nightclub where Jason would first sing in talent contests in 1970. Bottom right: The stage at the Nashville Nevada Club nightclub.

262

RESULTS FROM LOTTERY FOR MEN FACING THE DRA

The lottery drawing held July 1, 1970, determined the order in which men be called to report for induction into the military.

How to read this chart: This chart shows all the birth dates in a given year and the assigned to those dates. Read this chart like a multiplication table. At the top a months of the year. On the far left are the dates of the month. The numbers in the lottery numbers. For example: To find the lottery number assigned to July 15, loo until it matches up with the number "15" on the left side of the table. The corres the middle is "273." This means that all men born on July 15, 1951, were as number 273.

The highest lottery number called for this group was 125. All men assigned that any lower number, and who were classified 1-A or 1-A-O (available for military se to report for possible induction.

Lottery Numbers, by Birth Date, for Selective Service Lottery Held Jul

	Jan	Feb	Mar	Apr	May	Jun	Jul	Aug	Sep	Oc
1	133	335	014	224	179	065	104	326	283	30
2	195	354	077	216	096	304	322	102	161	19
3	336	186	207	297	171	135	030	279	183	13
4	099	094	117	937	240	042	059	300	231	26
5	033	097	299	124	301	233	287	064	295	16
6	285	016	296	312	268	150	164	251	021	0
7	159	025	141	142	029	169	365	263	265	1
8	116	127	079	267	105	007	106	049	108	0
			278	723	357	352	001	125	313	

Top right: Jason and Anne Sanderson in a showroom at The Flamingo Hotel and Casino, February, 1970. Middle right and Bottom left: The televised Draft Lottery on July 1, 1970 selecting those who would be drafted into the military by the numbers drawn matching the birthdays of those born in 1951. Bottom right: Jason celebrating with Anne Sanderson that he drew number 236 in the draft lottery, which meant he no longer need to be concerned with being drafted or going to Vietnam. Behind Jason and Anne is Paul Kirby who played guitar for Jason in the talent contests at Las Vegas nightclubs.

The Castaways Hotel and Casino in 1970 where the Mirage Hotel now stands.

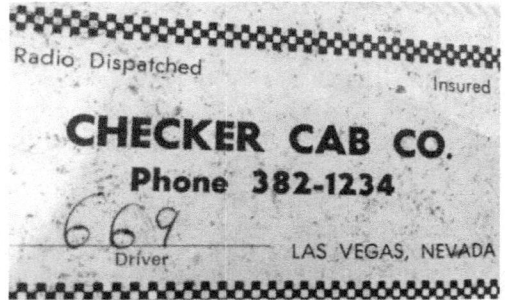

One of the actual business cards Jason would distribute when he drove for Checker Cab with his number, 669.

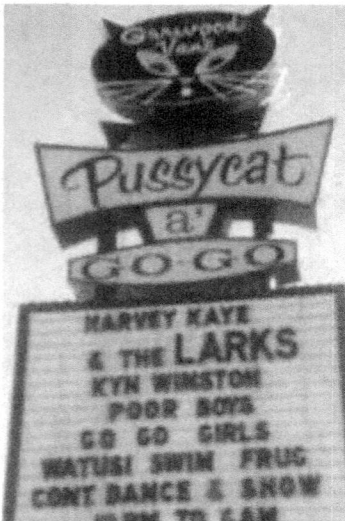

The famous Pussycat A Go-Go.

Jason and Anne Sanderson, December 1970.

Left: Jason's first newspaper clipping as a "rock singer" in the *Las Vegas Panorama Magazine*, 1971. Top and Middle right: Jason's first publicity photos as "JJ Breeze", during Jason's first stint with The Box Tops in 1971-72, which would be revived again twenty years later. Bottom right: The *Las Vegas Star Magazine* where Jason briefly wrote his "Neon Lights and Nightlife" entertainment column, before he began writing another column in a small California tabloid called the *Singles Register*.

Preregistration

2009 World Series of Poker

TOURNAMENT BUY-IN RECEIPT

$ 275 STS

SINGLE TABLE SATELLITE

JASON MERSHON - 0013500124456

3,849

Cash:	$275.00	Wire Transfer:	$0.00
Chips:	$0.00	Cashier Check:	$0.00
BIC:	$0.00	Other:	$0.00

Total Buy-In: $ 275.00

two hundred seventy-five and xx / 100

Tournament Date: 05/26/2009

Received By: K Calcaro

June 17, 2009   6:55 pm

PRELUDE TO THE LAST STAND
SUMMER, 2009

It was a typical hot summer day in Las Vegas, and Jason was sitting in the Keno Lounge at the Rio Hotel and Casino where the World Series of Poker was now being held after being moved from the Horseshoe Casino several years earlier. He didn't feel like taking the long walk back to the poker tournament area, and didn't want to spend an hour trying to find his friend he had agreed to meet amongst the thousands of poker players competing in the various preliminary tournaments.

His friend was another poker player from California he knew named Paul Gilbert, who had a second house in Las Vegas and spent each summer at the World Series of Poker and Jason decided to call Paul from his Blackberry and suggested they met in the Keno Lounge, which would also give him some time to play his favorite Keno ticket while he waited.

"Hey!" Paul excitedly said after he arrived and sat in a seat next to Jason, "I just saw Phil Ivy and Doyle Brunson playing in one of the tournaments just now!"

"And yesterday I saw Daniel Negreanu and Phil Laak," Paul continued, "I was standing the rail next to Jennifer Tilly watching them play."

Jason knew Paul was a decent poker player but he could never understand why he just watched the various events instead of playing in some of the World Series tournaments himself. Jason had never liked being just an observer and always wanted to be part of the action.

"That's nice,' said Jason without much interest.

He was still amazed at how so many people got excited by seeing a poker player that they saw on television and considered them a celebrity, but these days, it seemed everyone was already a celebrity anyway.

Jason had seen with the Internet, YouTube, and especially Reality TV, some form of the media seemed to be making everybody famous in some way. He had also played against so many of the "Celebrity Players" from all his years of playing poker in Las Vegas and Los Angeles that it wasn't a big deal to him. He actually remembered playing against many of the so-called "poker stars" when they were still playing low limit cash games and how some of them almost cried if he beat them out of a fifty-dollar pot. But in the past several years, because of online poker, the poker boom of 2004, and almost non-stop coverage of poker on television, many of those he had played poker with in "the old days" had used the media exposer to their advantage, and many of them had become millionaires because of it. But Jason was never jealous of their success and was always involved with something else, with poker being just a hobby to him back then,

He had always tried to make his "millions" in other ways.

"Are you going to play in some satellite tournaments?" asked Paul, "You should really try and win a seat into the Main Event this year and win a few million!"

"Nope, not interested in the Main Event," said Jason. "If I win some satellites, I'm just going to sell the tournament chips and pocket the cash."

Jason liked the satellites because they were smaller single table tournaments with only ten players that took less than a couple hours to complete. He also had no interest in paying the ten-thousand-dollar entry fee and playing against six thousand players for over a week to hopefully make it "into the money in the Main Event. Only about six hundred players would actually win any money in the Main Event, and beating over five thousand players just to double his entry fee didn't seem worth the effort. Jason knew he'd have to make it even deeper into the tournament and make the top one percent of the entries before the payouts even seemed worth it.

"The odds are just too tough to even cash in the Main Event," Jason just smiled, "Much less make the final table."

"Besides, at almost every final table these days, it's hard to find anyone over thirty-years old," Jason added with a touch of sarcasm, "The 'internet kids' seem like they are taking over the game, and it's gotten tough for us old-timers."

"Yeah, but Jerry Yang won it a couple of years ago," said Paul, "and he's not a kid."

Both Jason and Paul had played with Jerry Yang at casinos in California prior to him winning the Main Event in 2007 and were surprised as everyone else when he won. Jerry Yang was a good player, but Jason and Paul had finished ahead of him quite often in the tournaments they competed against each other at Pechanga or Lake Elsinore Casino.

"Well, Jerry also had a lot of luck," said Jason, "and I'd rather use the ten thousand dollars for cash games than risk it one tournament."

Jason then decided to change the subject and looked at the Keno board to see if his two-spot ticket he bought had hit. He had been betting on the same two numbers, twenty-one and sixty-nine, for as long as he could remember, and for some reason, he had always had a lot of luck with those two numbers. He also knew the odds were better picking less numbers and was happy to get a twelve-to-one pay out back on his investment instead of trying to win tens of thousands by betting more numbers.

"Damn sixty-nine hit but not twenty-one," said Jason as he stood up to go back to the Keno window, "Hang on Paul, I'm going to try them both again next game."

Jason gave the Keno writer another twenty dollars, and bet the same two-spot, and then walked back where he was sitting.

"You know, I always thought you were a very good poker player and probably better than Jerry Yang," said Paul as Jason sat back down, "I remember when you used to always have your picture in the poker magazines for tournaments you were winning and it's a shame you took those years off from playing right when the poker boom was starting."

"Well, I had my reasons," is all Jason said not wanting to talk about that.

"If you could just make the 'November Nine' this year," continued Paul, "Think of how great that would be."

Jason didn't really care for the new concept of the "November Nine" that the World Series of Poker officials had started, which involved having a four-month break in the Main Event for those who made the final table. The WSOP officials and ESPN figured the hype and excitement of making the final nine players more well-known and turn them into "poker celebrities" would give them higher TV ratings.

"I always heard you were kind of a celebrity back in the seventies and eighties," said Paul, "So besides the money, think about how famous you might be again."

Jason always laughed whenever Paul mentioned he thought that Jason wanted to be a poker celebrity, become "famous" again.

"That was years ago", said Jason, "I have no interest in being famous, and I'm just trying to make a living and win enough to pay my bills."

Jason knew he had enough of being known as a so-called celebrity, especially whenever he thought back to how he once thought that everything he was doing was so important and meaningful. It usually just made him cringe when he thought about how "young and dumb" he actually was back then and how nothing he had previously done even mattered to him anymore. Especially, anything from the 1970s and 80's which he now looked at it as a complete waste of time.

"Let all the kids try to become famous on television," Jason said, "But I'd prefer to have nothing to do with the having the press or media publicizing anything about me anymore."

Jason was looking at the Keno Board when they began calling numbers for the game and saw that both twenty-one and sixty-nine had hit this time.

"Yes!" Jason shouted out with satisfaction, "There's a nice little two-hundred-dollar profit that'll almost pay for my first satellite today."

Jason collected his money from the Keno window and started to walk back with Paul to the tournament area. He also asked Paul if he wanted to play in a satellite with him but knew before he answered what he would say.

"No," said Paul, "I'm just gonna go watch some more tables and see who else is playing."

Jason just laughed and started walking by himself to the satellite section of the poker tournament room and stopped to grab a cold bottle of Starbuck's Frappuccino from the gift shop. He never liked the Red Bull or other energy drinks that most of the other players drank, but he knew he wanted something to stay alert and focused during the poker satellite.

As he was walking out of the gift shop, Jason heard someone calling out his name and saw it was another poker player he'd played poker with on occasion years earlier, but whose name he couldn't remember."

"Hey, Jason, it's Sammy!" he excitedly said. "I figured I'd see you up here for the world series this week. How ya doin'?"

Jason was glad Sammy mentioned what his name was so he wouldn't act like he'd forgotten.

"Hangin' in there," Jason smiled as he shook his hand, "How about you, Sammy?"

"I'm doing great, but I'm getting low on cash today, and I wanted to enter a satellite," Sammy smiled, "But I'm about sixty dollars short and was hoping you'd help me out."

Jason actually trusted the poker players he known, even more than some of his other friends he'd known for most of his life, and didn't mind helping a fellow poker pro out,

The poker players had always paid him back.

As Jason pulled out three twenties and handed them to his friend, Sammy then noticed that Jason had purchased a Frappuccino.

"You need coffee drinks to keep you going now, eh?" Sammy lightly laughed, "Not like the 'old days' when we had something better that kept us going all night!"

"That was a long time ago," Jason half laughed back, "It's not as fun as it used to be."

"Yup," said Sammy, "Times have definitely changed."

After they both said their "see you later" and good luck wishes, Jason saw he had a few minutes before his poker satellite would start, so he had time to hit the bathroom.

Inside the men's room, he couldn't help but notice other poker players rushing in, trying to discreetly smoke a quick cigarette while standing at the urinals, or guzzling a quick beer before they rushed back to the poker tournaments they were playing in the main room. There was no smoking any longer at the poker tables, and they always tried to get a quick fix while taking a pee so they wouldn't miss too many hands in the tournaments.

Jason smiled to himself as he thought about all those who thought being a professional poker player was such a glamourous way to make a living, and that drinking, pissing, and smoking, is really how most of them all spent their time during the long gambling sessions.

270

As Jason sat down at the poker table to try and turn his two-hundred and seventy-five dollar buy-in into over a two-thousand-dollar profit in the next couple of hours, he started thinking about something else that suddenly popped into his head.

He was thinking about how he'd spent almost all of the past twenty years involved with music and briefly regretted he wasn't writing any more songs, because "drinking, pissing, smoking, and gambling" could be funny opening lyrics to a song about poker. He also lightly thought if he won a few of these poker satellites, it might be something to try that at least might be fun.

Jason had forgotten what that was.

BOOK THREE

"PUBLICITY, CELEBRITY AND LOVE"
1972 - 1974

Chapter One

In 1972, Richard Nixon was president and would win re-election in a landslide victory against anti-war candidate George McGovern which was helped by a new term called the *"October Surprise"* when Henry Kissinger announced "Peace is as hand" regarding Vietnam's war shortly before the election. That same year, the word *"Terrorists"* also became part of the world's vocabulary when a Palestinian group called *Black September* took eleven Israeli athletes as hostages at the Munich Olympics before murdering them. But fortunately, the violent protests, demonstrations, and race riots that had been so dominant in the USA just a few years earlier had subsided somewhat, and it seemed to be a much more peaceful and quiet year.

The average income in 1972 increased to around seven thousand dollars a year, gasoline was staying steady around thirty-six cents a gallon, but the average cost of a home had increased to twenty-seven thousand dollars.

The top television shows that year were *All in The Family, Sanford and Son, The Mary Tyler Moore Show,* and *M*A*S*H,* while top songs in 1972 were *American Pie, I Am Woman, Papa was a Rolling Stone, The First Time I Ever Saw Your Face, A Horse with No Name,* and Chuck Berry's only number one single, *My Ding-a-ling. The Godfather* was also released in movie theatres in 1972 and would go on to win the Oscar for Best Picture, winning over the other top films of that year, *Cabaret, Deliverance,* and *Last Tango in Paris.*

1972 was also the year *Jesus Christ Superstar* and *Grease* would become huge hits on Broadway, comedian George Carlin was arrested for obscenity for reciting his *"Seven Words You Can Never Say on Television,"* and the Supreme Court agreed to reconsider arguments in the case, *Roe V Wade* regarding on whether or not to restrict laws on abortion.

It was on June seventeenth in 1972, when the *Washington Post* editor Ben Bradlee, would run a short news article about a break-in at a hotel called *The Watergate,* but it was also during that same month that Jason Mershon was establishing himself as a newspaper editor himself and was working on what he felt was a *real* career.

The *Singles Register* office was in the city of Paramount, which was only about five miles from where he grew up in Lakewood, but Jason knew he didn't want to live near the same area as he had lived with his parents in the 1960s and instead moved to the top floor of a high-rise apartment at 8440 Sunset Boulevard in West Hollywood called the *Park Sunset Plaza*. He also decided he wanted to live somewhere that made him feel like he was close to the action, as he had in Las Vegas.

There was always a doorman on duty at the *Park Sunset Plaza* who would park his burgundy *Lincoln Continental*, and Jason would only usually have to tip him fifty cents or a dollar as he had done with the valet runners in Las Vegas. Jason also liked that his Lincoln had a better stereo system than he'd ever had before, and besides listening to his eight-tracks, he could get great reception on the popular FM radio stations, *KLOS* and *KMET*, that played all rock and roll music with fewer commercials than the AM stations.

Jason had spent most of his money in his bank account, along with the over six hundred dollars in moving expenses his father gave him to furnish his new apartment. His monthly rent did skyrocket to two hundred and forty dollars a month, but with his steady salary of two hundred dollars a week, he figured he could afford living in an *upscale* location to go with his new title of a newspaper editor.

He was especially glad he had his driver's license that showed he was twenty-four years old, so those he was now interacting with in Hollywood wouldn't think he was just a kid and too young to have that title.

Jason's twenty mile commute each way from West Hollywood to the office in the small city of Paramount would only take about a half-hour unless Jason hit a little traffic, which was rare. The office was small, and only had a few employees, including a typist who worked on a *Compugraphic* typesetting machine, and a couple of others who had already showed him how to use *Exacto* blades and a waxing machine to cut and paste a copy on flat boards to get each issue ready to go to the printer.

Jason's father still always said the newspaper was just a vehicle to assist him in selling news racks, but as far as the news racks that he was selling, the large majority of them were in the Long Beach area and surrounding cities around the office in Paramount. His father said he was planning on selling more news racks in larger population areas soon, including a large percentage closer to where Jason lived in Hollywood, but his mother seemed more interested in getting future income from any personal ads and subscriptions that were generated from people who bought the *Singles Register*. And, as his father mentioned, she worked from home handling all the mail and collecting the checks that came in from those sources so Jason never saw her at the office.

But Jason also saw that before anyone would want to subscribe to the *Singles Register*, let alone pay fifty cents for it in the news racks, he had a lot of work to do.

He still thought the *Singles Register* just looked like a local sixteen page throw away circular, but knowing he now had no other current obligations, Jason seriously wanted to focus all his attention for the next several months on creating a *real newspaper* almost from scratch. Jason had already spent time thinking about the things he needed to accomplish making the newspaper appear more attractive in the news racks and make it more readable for those who did pay fifty cents for a copy.

The big obstacle for Jason was that besides his parents not wanting to spend any cash advertising in any outside media to promote the *Singles Register* as a dating publication, there also wasn't a budget to pay any writers. He figured he'd just find other ways to get the *Singles Register* more well-known once the newspaper looked better to help establish it as a *real* newspaper. He also decided to write a new column titled *Chasin' with Jason*, which covered a wide array of subjects including music, entertainment, hot spots to see and be seen around Hollywood, and anything else he could write that might make the newspaper look more current.

Although he'd taken journalism classes in both high school and college, and knew the basic concepts of creating a readable newspaper, before he left Las Vegas, Jason had also talked with Ricardo Villasenor for any suggestions on improving the *Singles Register*. Ricardo had explained that when the *Las Vegas Star* went from monthly to biweekly, his profits increased and saw the concept of having a new issue every two weeks had a huge advantage in increasing his readership. That was one idea that Jason had to clear with his parents, but they agreed it made sense. Although it would double the cost of printing, it would also double the revenue from any newspaper sales and personal ad advertising, and would also make the newspaper seem more current and newsworthy, rather than just seeing the same issue sitting in the news racks for an entire month.

Ricardo had also said that Los Angeles and Las Vegas had one big thing in common as they were both entertainment capitals, and audiences liked reading about celebrities and different articles they didn't see in the daily newspapers.

"Celebrities always sell, and it'll at least get them to buy a copy of the paper, and maybe eventually, they might decide to subscribe or advertise for dates," Ricardo added, "It hasn't hurt tabloids like the National Enquirer and just having a celebrity photo on the cover always helps."

When there were finally news racks that sold the *Singles Register* on almost every street corner in Hollywood, with such high visibility the Hollywood crowd enjoyed seeing anything written about themselves in an easily accessible newspaper, When Jason started socializing around Hollywood at different nightspots, looking for interesting copy for his *Chasin' with Jason* column, he did end up meeting publicists, agents, and managers who were looking for "some press" for their clients.

He ended up personally meeting with several celebrities he'd been asked to interview, including a young actress who'd recently moved to Hollywood from New York named Stockard Channing, and a theatre director named Tom Moore, who was bringing a new musical to Los Angeles that had opened on Broadway earlier that year called *Grease*.

After seeing different celebrities being featured on the cover of the *Singles Register*, which was now seen in news racks in different areas in Hollywood every two weeks, Jason began getting press releases, invitations for advance movie screenings, opening nights of different stage productions, as well as dozens of new record albums from the record companies that they hoped would be reviewed. He always wrote the articles and reviews himself deciding to use different pen names so it would look like he had more writers, but he mainly liked that he had projects that always kept him busy, and there was never a day where he had nothing to do.

He mainly liked that he was involved in the business's creative and promotional end and wouldn't have to worry about selling that much advertising himself, but Jason did like that besides receiving fifty percent commission for any cash ads he sold on top of his regular salary, his father told him he could work out any trade outs with businesses for himself personally. Jason decided that along with along with just personal use, he'd also award a dinner for free two each issue, for one of the personal advertisers who could use it for a date they met through the Singles Register to entice more readership.

His father had previously tried to hire salesmen to sell commercial advertising in the *Singles Register*, but most of them were having a hard time selling ads to businesses in a newspaper that had nothing but classified ads for dates and still wasn't that well known.

Although Jason did manage to sell enough advertisements to some small business for around fifty dollars each for smaller "business card" sized ads, which usually covered his monthly salary, he also decided to approach some restaurateurs in Hollywood and arranged to put bigger advertisements and blurbs in his *Chasin' With Jason* column in trade for a monthly tab of at least a hundred dollars for himself at those restaurants. He always pitched the restaurant owners on the idea of how singles always went out to dinner more often than married couples, and were looking for great places to have dinner with people they met through his newspaper.

He also assured them he'd regularly mention their restaurants in his column along with their names and certain standout employees by name as well.

One restaurateur Jason was able to work a big trade out with was Bernie Tohl, who owned four restaurants on La Cienega Boulevard, *The Captain's Table*, *The Blue Boar*, *The Lobster Barrel*, and *The Islander*, along with another restaurant that was owned by the well-known Hollywood personality, which he named after himself, *Nicky Blair's*.

Nicky Blair was the friendliest of the restaurant owners he'd met, and Nicky also supplied Jason with photographs of celebrities who frequented his restaurant to use in his *Chasin' with Jason* column, which Jason also figured would add status to the newspaper by having those celebrity hang out restaurants included as his advertisers.

Jason ended up with a nice tab of trade-outs that he could use for his own social activities each month, and also knew the articles and blurbs he wrote were at least getting him some juice in Hollywood as it had in Las Vegas. He saw that everyone still loved getting press in almost any publication, even if it was only a dating newspaper for singles, but with almost half of the newspaper now filled with editorial copy rather than just personal ads, as well as increasing to twenty-four pages, it was starting to look like a real newspaper.

By the end of the summer in 1972, Jason was also able to find another salesman to work on a fifty percent commission to spend more time selling ads than he wanted to do himself, so he could spend more time being in charge of making the *Singles Register* bigger and adding more than the twenty-four pages it currently was.

Jason knew he still had some work to do as far as making the newspaper more readable and not just a dating service, and that was going to be his main focus for the remainder of 1972.

But he also decided he was going to have fun doing it.

Chapter Two

Jason felt his social life at night was also part of his work routine and because he was always looking for stories and personalities he could feature in the *Singles Register*, he knew just being out and meeting people while telling them about the newspaper was good promotion.

Tuesday nights were always the opening nights at *The Troubadour* in West Hollywood and that's where Jason would be every week as he was always comp'd on those nights to review the shows. The biggest names in rock music always performed at *The Troubadour* and he loved seeing them up close and not in some arena or stadium, and also liked all the musicians, famous or not, who would always be at the bar before the shows began.

He had often hoped that he'd run into Tommy or Alvin during one his nights at *The Troubadour*, but he never did. Jason had left his new phone number on Tommy's answering service, but the last time he had called him, the answering service operator had said they weren't taking his messages anymore.

When Jason first started going to *The Troubadour* regularly, he tried to show some comradery between the well-known musicians he talked with and casually mentioned that he "once was lead singer" of *The Box Tops*, but he quickly saw that wasn't anything special that impressed them.

Jason was talking in the bar with Kenny Loggins and Jim Messina who were performing that night, and whose current song, *"Your Mamma Don't Dance and Your Daddy Don't Rock & Roll"* was a big hit on the radio and casually mentioned that he was formerly the lead singer and toured with *The Box Tops* a year earlier, but Loggins just said, "Alex Chilton was the lead singer of *The Box Tops*," without missing a beat.

Jason discovered that the famous musicians were much better acquainted with who Alex Chilton was than the general public was.

When Jason reminded them that "Alex didn't sing with The Box Tops anymore," Messina also sarcastically said, "Yeah, and Jim Morrison doesn't sing with *The Doors* anymore either."

Since Jim Morrison had died the year before, even Jason knew *The Doors* would never be able to continue as a band without Morrison, but he also saw that "JJ Breeze" wasn't the one with the juice and stuck to introducing himself as "Jason Mershon, editor of the *Singles Register*" newspaper from then on.

Another favorite place Jason spent time was *The Rainbow Bar and Grill*, which had only recently opened, but quickly became another major rock and roll hangout for musicians and had quickly become friendly with two regulars who were always at *The Rainbow*, and who always sat in the same booth in front of the fireplace. One was Art Laboe, who was known as *"Mr. Oldies-But-Goodies"* for records he distributed and a radio show he hosted, and who also owned a nightclub named after himself, directly across from Jason's apartment on Sunset Boulevard. The other was Bill Gazzarri, who owned one of the most famous rock and roll nightclubs on the Sunset Strip, he also named after himself, *Gazzarri's*.

Jason would often sit with both of them at *The Rainbow*, along with drinking his Chivas on the rocks, telling them about the *Singles Register* and hearing them tell wild rock and roll stories about the famous bands they'd worked with over the years. When Jason would also stop by their nightclubs occasionally, they always comp'd his drinks, and Jason would always write "blurbs" in his *Chasin With Jason* column when they had something they wanted to promote.

Next to Art Laboe's nightclub across from his apartment, another new club had recently opened up called *The Comedy Store*, which Jason learned was owned by the comedian, Sammy Shore. Jason had first seen Sammy when he opened for Elvis Presley at the *International Hotel* in 1969, but met him personally in Las Vegas when Sammy performed by himself in the lounge at the International, and had also once given Sammy a ride in his taxi.

Because it was also right across the street from where he lived at the *Park Sunset Plaza*, he stopped in at least two or three times a week to see the comics who were also waiting to make it big in show biz, and after having become reacquainted, Sammy and Jason saw each other often, and soon he was on the comp list at *The Comedy Store* as a member of the press.

Jason regularly would include blurbs in his *Chasin' with Jason* column about Sammy, as well as the many new comedians who were performing at *The Comedy Store*, and along with the other places he started frequenting during the week, "Quid pro quo" became Jason's lifestyle, and not just an expression.

Even though Jason felt good about having the title of a *newspaper editor*, some people still looked at the *Singles Register* differently, and most of those he had recently met considered the main aspect of the newspaper of "advertising for dates" was a "lonely hearts" method for "losers" who couldn't meet any other way. Also, because all of the content was geared to "clean and non-swinger" personal ads from older people looking for serious relationships and not just sex, many people he met in Hollywood just thought the *Singles Register* was what they often called "square."

As the *Singles Register*'s main guy, Jason was always defending the concept and telling everyone how it was just a smart and modern way to meet other singles who were seriously looking for relationships. Although Jason did somewhat feel the same about "advertising" for dates, mainly because he'd never had a problem meeting any girls himself, he always tried to sound convincing when defending the concept of personal ads after already learning that "a little bs never hurt anybody" and knowing it was just good business. But he was at least satisfied that besides the personal ads, people were also starting to enjoy most of the articles he was writing under his different "pen names" each issue, along with a couple other writers he had found who just wanted to get their articles and "names in print" in a newspaper for the exposure

Jason still didn't have a budget to pay any well-known columnists, but in the fall of that year, Sammy Shore mentioned he was friends with a famous writer he knew named Sydney Skolsky and took Jason to lunch as *Schwab's Drug Store* on Sunset Boulevard to meet him.

Sammy had already told Jason that Sidney was a legendary Hollywood columnist who'd been around since the days of Hedda Hopper and Louella Parsons and was respected and known by everyone in the entertainment industry. Jason immediately knew that having a regular column by a celebrated personality like Sidney would definitely add status to the *Singles Register* and add important readership from those in the entertainment industry themselves.

After Jason and Sammy sat down for lunch at the counter with Sidney at *Schwab's*, Jason quickly saw that Sidney was a talker like he was, and they swapped a lot of stories. Jason first joked about how *Schwab's Drug Store* was directly across the street from where *Pandora's Box* once stood and told the story of how he had to escape from the police the night of the riot on the Sunset Strip, which gave Sidney a good laugh saying he remembered that night well, and had a good first-hand view of the protests from *Schwab's*.

Jason also learned that Sidney had also been the producer of one of Jason's favorite movies, *The Jolson Story*, and he let Sidney know that he'd been a fan of Al Jolson since he was a little kid and had memorized the lyrics to most of his songs. Sidney also laughed when Jason told him about the time he dressed up like Jolson in blackface and lip-synced the song, *Mammy*, when he was only ten years old, in the same manner the actor Larry Parks had lip-synched Jolson's voice in the movie.

"Larry Parks did an incredible job imitating Al Jolson and even won the best actor Oscar," smiled Sidney, "Larry had a great future in front of him until he got backlisted as a communist sympathizer and his career never recovered from that."

"It's a good thing we're over that witch hunt stuff now," Sidney added, "Those were bad times back then and they ruined a lot of peoples careers with just some wild rumors."

Jason was mainly happy that he and Sidney seemed to hit it off in the hour they spent talking, and they actually seemed to become friends in that time. That made it easier when Jason explained that although he'd love to have Sidney writing for the *Singles Register*, he didn't have a budget yet to pay his writers.

Sidney laughed and said he had already had made money in his career and just wrote his column those days to b keep active. He also added that he'd do it on the condition that Jason "*personally pick up his column*" at *Schwab's* every two weeks and always have lunch together so they could swap more stories. He added that he'd also spread the word about Jason's newspaper and if it got big, then he could pay him something, but if not, he didn't to worry about it.

Jason excitedly shook his hand and told Sidney they had a deal, and besides liking that he'd actually become friends with a Hollywood legend, he really started feeling that the newspaper was becoming his business and he was doing his part as one of the owners of the *Singles Register*.

Jason also eventually found other columnists, including Jim Parker in Las Vegas, who agreed to write columns for free, and a couple others who were just happy to be published in what now was beginning to look like a real newspaper in Southern California. He figured as Jim Parker did that the other writers would be able to use their fame as a published writer, find a way to use their columns for their own *juice*.

He was learning about business a lot quicker than he thought he would and was satisfied he'd found his real destiny.

Chapter Three

Jason realized that his two hundred dollars a week salary seemed like much more because of all the freebies, trade outs, and comp's he was getting as a "respected" member of the press. He also noticed that he was treated even better than he had in Las Vegas when he was seen around town because, as an editor, everyone respected the main guy in charge instead of just a lowly hack writer. Although many were surprised that someone in Jason's position was so young, he never had a problem saying he was twenty-four years old rather than twenty-one and if they ever questioned him, he had the ID to prove it.

He also didn't miss having a steady girlfriend and could usually find entertaining companionship on his nights out in Hollywood, but It seemed that almost all of the girls he'd meet since he lived in Hollywood claimed they were *actresses* or *models*, even though he mainly knew most of them as *cocktail waitresses* who worked at many of the nightspots he frequented. He discovered that almost everyone in Hollywood was waiting to "make it big" in show biz in some form or the other.

Jason also liked going to parties at the hotel next to *The Comedy Store* called the *Continental Hyatt House*, nicknamed *"The Riot House"* because of the wild parties like The Who, Led Zeppelin, The Rolling Stones, and others became known for having at the hotel.

Jason didn't have the opportunity to be at a Rolling Stones party but finally got to see them perform live at the *Los Angeles Forum* during their tour that year.

As Jason and his date watched Stevie Wonder perform the opening set, he was glad that Nicky Blair introduced him to a regular at his restaurant named Alex Henig, who was known as *"Mr. Tickets"* and well known as a ticket scalper.

He paid Alex thirty dollars for his Rolling Stones tickets with a face value of only ten dollars, but Jason saw the extra expense was well worth it, and Jason and his date were sitting center stage in the second row which was close enough to see the sweat on Stevie's forehead when he performed his current hit song, *Superstition*.

When the Rolling Stones finally started their set, from the opening song, *Brown Sugar*, to the closing song *Street Fighting Man*, Jason couldn't help but momentarily wish he was on stage himself again as he saw Mick Jagger strutting and posing throughout his entire concert.

He was a little disappointed Jagger didn't sing some of the songs that he sang himself, like *It's All Over Now* or *Let It Bleed*, and mainly showcased songs from their new album *Exile on Main Street*. Jason also thought Jagger didn't put too much effort into his vocals and sounded a little sloppy on some songs, but regardless, it was still great, and it was still *The Rolling Stones*.

With all the work and entertainment, his social life was limited to casual flings, but because he was always going someplace fun to write about in the *Singles Register*, he was becoming known as a "great date" with the girls he met.

Jason had comps at some of the best restaurants and nightclubs in Hollywood, and his dates always liked how Jason just signed his tabs after a night of partying without even looking at the bills. They also seemed impressed with how he would always casually leave an impressive ten-dollar cash tip to his servers.

His dates would usually end with a night in his apartment, and they were always impressed with what he considered his *penthouse bachelor pad*. Jason had furnished it with a bright orange sofa and love seat, which seemed to light up the room, and the music from his stereo would always be playing softly. His top-floor apartment also had great views of the Sunset Strip directly below his front living room windows, and his bedroom window had a clear view of the skyline of downtown Los Angeles which was less than ten miles away.

Although he had been in several flings since he had broken up with Anne Sanderson, the "I love you" words had never been spoken since. The "actresses and models" he was meeting also always assured Jason they never wanted a pregnancy to interfere with their careers and either used the birth control pill or an "intrauterine device" they called IUD's so they could enjoy sex without worrying about consequences. There were also a couple of girls who said now that *Roe V Wade* had been approved by the Supreme Court, getting an abortion was "no big deal" and that was another choice they could choose if they did get pregnant that wouldn't cause them to give up any of their future ambitions.

There were a few girls Jason saw on a semi-regular basis and even grew close with some of them, but none seemed to give him what he now called "The Thunderbolt," the term he'd picked up from the book and the movie *The Godfather*. He knew it was just another term for *love at first sight*, but Jason preferred using what the book and movie called the "Sicilian" term.

But besides remembering the term "Thunderbolt," there was something else he would remember about the first time he went to see *The Godfather* at the movie theatre that year.

While watching the film, he couldn't help but keep thinking he recognized the actor who was playing the role of *Carlo Rizzi*, but he couldn't remember from where. Jason had to wait for the final credits to roll to see if he recognized any names besides the main actors, and half smiled in surprise when he saw the actor who portrayed Carlo was Gianni Russo.

He couldn't believe that "Gee-On-Eee" had ended up as one of the stars of such a great movie, and would go see *The Godfather* a couple more times that month. It wasn't because Jason got any pleasure in seeing the Carlo character get garroted by Clemenza, and his feet smashing through the windshield during his painful death, but because he immediately knew it was one of his *"favorite movies"* of all time.

Jason was enjoying being a Hollywood bachelor, but did hope there would be a time when *"The Thunderbolt"* would hit him again as he felt it had when he with Anne Sanderson, but he had also convinced himself that his previous relationship with Anne, and even his short stint as a *"rock star"* was just *kid stuff*, and tried not to even gave it a second thought any longer.

That was all in his past, and felt his current life is what he was meant to be doing all along.

ℒ

In the middle of October of 1972, Bill Gazzarri called Jason to let him know there was going to be a big press party at his nightclub. Bill explained that the party was also featuring a beauty contest to publicize an upcoming event at the *Beverly Hilton Hotel* called *The Artist and Models Ball* and added the producer Gary Berwin, looking for some interesting judges who would also give him some good press and publicity in the media.

"I immediately thought about you," laughed Bill, "And there should be some nice *talent* if you know what I mean."

Jason smiled to himself, knowing that when Bill Gazzarri mentioned "nice talent," he was talking about beautiful girls.

He told Bill that he "was in" and would definitely be there, figuring it would be fun to judge in a beauty contest, and might even meet a beauty contestant or two, who'd be more interesting than the typical actresses and models he'd been dating lately.

When Jason arrived at Gazzarri's a few nights later, Bill introduced him to Gary Berwin and another judge, actor Dennis Cole, who Jason recognized from a TV series called *Felony Squad* he used to watch when he was still in high school.

A food buffet was set up and an open bar that Gary Berwin joked about, saying that he never had a problem "getting press" when they found out he was offering free food and drinks. Jason didn't want to look like just another a mooch *press hack* and stayed away from the buffet and just ordered a double Chivas on the rocks when he sat at the judge's table.

The beauty contest was to name a *Queen* for Gary's *Artist and Models Ball*, and the contest itself only took about fifteen minutes as the contestants only made one walk across the stage in evening gowns. Dennis Cole and Jason had voted for the same contestant, another young "actress" named Polly Middleton, who was crowned the winner.

Several press photographers took pictures of Polly, and Jason felt a little awkward that he didn't have a staff photographer present to take pictures for the *Singles Register*. It was a press party, and Jason knew he was expected to give Gary some "press and publicity" for being invited.

Jason approached a photographer who was taking most of the photos to see if he could get some extra prints to use himself for his newspaper.

"Hi, I'm Jason Mershon with the Singles Register," he told the photographer, "My photographer got tied up on another assignment tonight, and I was wondering if I could get a couple of prints from the party tonight so I can run them in my next issue."

Jason didn't want to sound like an amateur who didn't have a regular photographer at his newspaper.

"I'm Stan Adams, and I'm the *official photographer* for the Artist and Model's Ball," said the photographer shaking Jason's hand, "So that shouldn't be a problem."

Jason exchanged business cards with Stan, who said he'd be developing the photos the next day at his studio in Sylmar and told Jason could stop by and pick out some prints he liked. Stan then said he wanted to get some pictures with the contestants and judges and had Jason pose with Dennis Cole and the winner.

"That one will look good in your paper," said Stan after taking several photos. "You and Dennis look like you could be brothers."

Both Jason and Dennis had blond hair and similar features, but Dennis was taller and older and Jason just laughed at the idea. But he didn't mind the comparison that much, because Dennis was known as one of the most handsome actors in Hollywood and just figured it was a compliment.

As the party at *Gazzarri's* was dying down, Jason was sitting with Dennis, Bill, and Gary Berwin talking about the upcoming *Artist and Models Ball*, and Gary mentioned he'd have all of them on his VIP guess list.

Jason learned that the *Artists and Models Ball* was the biggest annual Halloween event that was well established as one of the year's biggest celebrity parties and Gary said he was expecting over two thousand attendees for that year's *Ball*. Jason was also telling them how the *Singles Register* was expanding its circulation and how he would give Gary Berwin some good press, but again, he found himself trying to justify why advertising for dates wasn't just a *"lonely hearts"* concept.

"It's mainly for those who are actually looking for a serious relationship," Jason tried to say with conviction, "and not just a one-night-fling."

"Well, you won't get too many advertisers here in Hollywood," laughed Bill Gazzarri, "Everyone in this town considers *volume fucking* as its number one sport."

"And a great sport is," Gary Berwin joined in lightly laughing, "There's so much *talent* to choose from."

Jason also laughed, knowing that he was starting to feel the same way, but he still wanted to sound like he was serious and believed in the newspaper that he was an editor.

"*Volume fucking* is fine for a while," Jason continued to say with conviction, "But eventually everyone wants to find that one special person and that's the market for the Singles Register."

"Well, it is hard finding a serious girlfriend in this town," Dennis Cole joined in the conversation, "Between the *starfuckers* who just want to screw you because you're a celebrity, and the other chicks who hope you'll do something for their career, it's hard to take any of them seriously."

"Well, I guess we'll have to suffer through the *auditions* until the right one comes along," Bill smiled facetiously.

After the party, as Jason was driving down Sunset Boulevard back to his apartment, he was trying to decide on which "actress or model" he knew to invite to the *Artist and Models Ball* the following week. He then thought of a sexy willowy blond waitress he'd recently met at the *Palomino Nightclub* in the San Fernando Valley, and thought the famous *Artists and Models Ball* would be a great place to take her for a first date.

Or, as Bill Gazzarri called it, an "audition."

Jason was also still smiling to himself about the term "volume fucking" that Bill had used and lightly thought how they called it the "number one sport" in Hollywood.

He knew that Las Vegas had always been called *Sin City,* but also started to realized that Vegas had nothing on Hollywood, and was an even better town for certain *sporting events.*

Jason tried not to even think about *"The Thunderbolt"* and was just enjoying having fun.

Chapter Four

The first person that Jason recognized when he walked into the *International Ballroom* at the *Beverly Hilton Hotel* was Stan Adams, dressed in a clown costume and running around taking everyone's photos in their elaborate costumes.

Jason decided to dress in a 1920s gangster costume, and his date Lynn Everest, the waitress from *The Palomino*, was dressed as a sexy saloon girl in a skimpy outfit and fishnet stockings that mainly highlighted her long legs and Stan immediately greeted them and started taking photos of them. Stan also said he had been taking a lot of photos of celebrities in their costumes that Jason could also use in the *Singles Register* for free, as long as he got photo credit and mentioned that he was the "official photographer" of the *Artist and Models Ball*.

Jason was also meeting many other media members who were covering the *Ball* and exchanged business cards with several other writers and press photographers, including an Egyptian reporter and photographer named Mark Marzouk who said he was a member of the *Hollywood Foreign Press*. Mark mentioned that in a few months he would be attending an even bigger "celebrity party" in that same ballroom, *The Golden Globe Awards* and he'd mail Jason some press photos from that awards show and party he'd be taking himself.

Jason saw that Ricardo was right about people wanting to read about celebrities and had been gearing the *Singles Register* to that type of content which seemed to be working, because his father had told him the newspaper been selling a lot better the past two months.

As Jason and Lynn stood at the bar and watched the crowd, he had the *Three Dog Night* song "Celebrate" playing in his head, about it being the night of a "*Celebrity Ball*" and smiled at how appropriate it sounded to him at that moment. Jason briefly thought he should request for the band play that *Three Dog Night* song, but then realized it might make him appear *un-sophisticated* about being overly impressed, or star stuck, with all the celebrities at the party.

He finally found Gary Berwin and Dennis Cole in the crowd as Stan Adams gathered around them to take more photos, and Jason was also impressed with Dennis Cole's costume as a World War Two *German SS Officer*, which he said he rented from *Western Costume*, the company that supplied the movie studios with wardrobes for many of their films.

"The one good thing about the Nazi's," Dennis smiled, "Is that they had great looking uniforms."

With Dennis' blond hair, he definitely looked the part, and even though Jason had originally thought that he and Lynn had "cool" costumes, he felt underdressed and a little embarrassed he hadn't put more effort into an elaborate costume for himself. He also decided that if he ever went to another big costume party, he'd look for something similar after seeing how many compliments Dennis was getting from everyone at the party about "what a great costume" he was wearing that night.

Jason did see many other faces he recognized from television and films while he danced with Lynn, and was a little overwhelmed at the wild costumes that the majority of the party-goers were dressed. Jason figured they must have spent a fortune on their costumes, and he also overheard some of them saying how they had "been planning for months" to find the perfect costumes to wear to the *Artists and Models Ball.*

The main highlight of the *Artist and Model Ball* was the different categories of the *Best Costume Contest*, which was awarded over fifteen hundred dollars in cash prizes to the winners at midnight, and Jason was impressed that Gary Berwin was offering such a huge amount of prize money, and was obviously the reason so many people had been "planning for months" to choose their costumes.

Although he wasn't interested in entering any costume contest and was mainly trying to make future business contacts and dropping the *Singles Register's* name whenever he could, Jason was also still trying to be an entertaining date to Lynn Everest.

He thought Lynn was just as sexy as the other *actresses* and *models* posing on the dance floor and encouraged Lynn to enter the *"Sexiest Costume"* category herself to try and win some of the money being offered, but she declined after seeing some of the other girls were wearing costumes that barely hid their nipples and pubic hair.

""I'd have to take off my costume and just wear my fishnets even to have a chance against those other girls," Lynn smiled, "But I'm glad you think I'm sexy enough to at least have a chance, but I'm not ready to have you see me get that naked yet."

Jason liked the way she flirtatiously said, "get that naked *yet*," and was already looking forward to the party continuing later at his apartment.

They left the Beverly Hilton before one am and went to *Dino's Restaurant* on Sunset Boulevard, where Jason knew was always a great place to go for a late breakfast after a night of drinking, as well as only a few blocks from his apartment where he planned on the night ending up. But during breakfast Lynn said she needed to be home by two am to take care of her baby sitter and couldn't go to his apartment that night.

He had already learned that Lynn was a single mother and had a two-year-old son she'd had with a previous boyfriend, but although he was slightly disappointed that he needed to drive back to her apartment in Canoga Park, instead of his apartment a few blocks away, Jason assured her he'd get her home on time.

It was almost two am when they parked outside of her apartment building and Jason figured he'd be invited inside to spend the night after her babysitter left, but Lynn said she didn't want to take a chance of waking up her baby that late.

"I had a great time," Lynn said, "It's too bad I had to come home so early."

Although Jason was again disappointed, he decided that they'd just get together some other time, but then Lynn leaned closer to the driver's seat and gave him a long passionate kiss and started rubbing his leg.

"You know that TV commercial that always says a mind is a terrible thing to waste?" she whispered as they continued kissing, "Well, your *thing* reminds me of something else right now."

Jason knew that commercial and catchphrase *"A Mind is a Terrible Thing to Waste"* for the *United Negro College Fund* that was constantly being shown on television but was more interested in Lynn's sudden passion.

"An *erection* is also a terrible thing to waste," Lynn smiled invitingly as she leaned back in the long front seat of Jason's *Lincoln Continental*, "Let's just do it in the car."

When he was driving home about an hour later, Jason was smiling, thinking about the funny pun Lynn had used and started thinking of a funny line he could use himself if any girls ever asked him if his *"thing"* had a nickname.

Jason smiled, thinking about how he'd tell them he called his penis his *"mind,"* and if they asked him why, he thought of a great punchline.

"I'm not really sure," he would casually say before adding, "By the way… do you wanna *blow my mind?"*

Jason also sarcastically started wondering if he was hanging around *The Comedy Store* too much.

❧

Since their first date, Jason started seeing Lynn fairly regularly and even took her to his old friend Dan Kittridge's wedding when Dan asked Jason to be his *Best Man.* They had been good friends in high school, but Jason rarely saw Dan any longer and was surprised that Dan would still consider him to be his *best friend* after so many years. Jason guessed that seeing Dan been with his girlfriend since graduating high school, he hadn't had an opportunity to meet that many new friends and seemed satisfied to continue living in Lakewood. He also learned Dan did end up having a son born before deciding to marry his wife, and did end up naming him *Jason.*

"I still don't know anyone else with the name *Jay-San*," Dan teased Jason remembering how he came up with the name, "So hopefully no one else will have that name when my son gets older too."

289

Jason decided that seeing Dan had been nice enough to still consider him his *best friend*, he arranged for Stan Adams to be the photographer as his wedding present.

He knew the contacts he made in the past few months could be beneficial to the *Singles Register*, especially Stan, and knew having a regular photographer to add more photos in the newspaper always enhanced the content and appearance.

Stan was in his forties, but Jason thought he had a fun personality for an *old guy*, and they had become good friends since they'd first met at *Gazzarri's.* But Jason also saw that Stan really wasn't making that much money and was still trying to make a name for himself and build up his photography business.

Jason had noticed that Stan always liked calling himself the *"official"* photographer" of something or other, so since Jason told him he wanted him to be the *"official"* photographer as a "personal favor" at Dan's wedding, he also told Stan he could be the *"official"* photographer of the *Singles Register* newspaper.

Jason had explained to Stan, as he had to Sidney Skolsky, that he really didn't have a budget for a staff photographer but would always give him photo credit in the *Singles Register*. Stan said that was fine and mainly liked the idea of being a photographer for a newspaper that was widely seen in news racks throughout Southern California.

"It'll just enhance my portfolio and legitimize my reputation as a top Hollywood and Beverly Hills photographer," Stan smiled, "Plus, having regular photo credits in a newspaper should help me add ten dollars an hour to my usual rate."

When Dan Kittridge saw Stan also taking several photos of Jason and Lynn, who were also formally dressed at the wedding and reception that day, Dan teased Jason and asked if he would be "the best man at Jason's own wedding" anytime soon.

Jason just shook his head and laughed at Dan's suggestion knowing marriage was the farthest thing from his mind with Lynn and just considered her his current girlfriend.

Even though he was having fun with Lynn and they had been having a passionate romance since they'd met, he knew Jason wouldn't ever be struck by *"The Thunderbolt"* with her and that their relationship would never be permanent.

He knew he could never be comfortable being married to a girl who had someone else's baby, and "just having fun" was all he was interested in for now with Lynn. She was one of the wildest girls sexually he'd been with lately, so Jason was just enjoying their time together regardless of how long it lasted.

Jason also decided to take Lynn to Las Vegas for New Year's Eve, knowing she'd be the most fun date to celebrate the start of 1973, and the fun began even before they got to Vegas that weekend.

During the drive, when they were between Barstow and Baker, Lynn decided she wanted to "put on a show" for the passengers on a Greyhound bus that Jason was passing on Interstate 15.

"This will probably be a better show than anything they'll see in Las Vegas on New Year's Eve," Lynn smiled after telling Jason to continue driving slow in the lane next to the bus, "I think you'll like it too."

She then immediately lowered her head onto Jason's lap so the passengers could see her *pleasuring* Jason while he drove.

"You are crazy," Jason laughed as he tried to continue driving naturally while Lynn took care of her business, "But you sure are fun."

Jason did enjoy being with Lynn that weekend, but he was mainly looking forward to seeing his old friends again to show them how successful he'd become as a newspaper editor in the past year. He had brought several issues of the *Singles Register* to Las Vegas to show everyone and mentioned he'd put some blurbs about them in his next *Chasin' with Jason* column and make them all *famous*.

"But I don't want to be famous!" Tom Casey sarcastically laughed when Jason said he'd write something about him in the next issue.

Tom was still studying at UNLV but also had a federal grant, which allowed him to become a part-time police officer with the Henderson Police Department. He said it would be a good experience to help him get into the FBI once he graduated, but didn't think a *blurb* in a singles newspaper would *"enhance"* his law enforcement portfolio.

"Well, I am writing about this weekend in Las Vegas in my column, so I'll probably mention your name somewhere," Jason teased Casey before facetiously adding, "I'll just write about how you're keeping Water Street in Henderson safe from all the *Jaywalkers*."

"I'll make sure I include that blurb when I apply for the FBI," Casey again facetiously joked back.

Victor Consuela had gone into business with his father and opened a combination jewelry and men's clothing store and loved the idea of getting a mention in *Chasin' with Jason* and said to mainly make sure Jason "spelled his name right" in the column.

Jason was also able to reach Jim Santini, who was now a District Court Judge in Las Vegas, and who also seemed happy that Jason was doing well.

"I'm just glad I won't have to see you standing before me in court," Santini joked, "Or read about someone taking potshots at your car."

Jason took Lynn to have lunch at *Johnny Reb's* and was also eager to see Frank Reich again. He told Frank even though his newspaper wasn't sold in Las Vegas, he'd mention how great of a restaurant *Johnny Reb's* was for tourists, and would mention that Frank was *world-famous* for his original barbeque sauce.

Frank just laughed but said a press blurb might actually help him because he was thinking about getting investors to open up other locations of *Johnny Reb's*. Frank also seemed the happiest that Jason was doing well as a newspaper editor.

"I always saw you had a lot of ambition and would make a lot of money," Frank smiled, "Hopefully, we'll both be very rich soon."

Jason didn't want Frank to know he wasn't making much more than he had when he was in Las Vegas, but he liked that it at least appeared that he was.

He also stopped in with Lynn to see Ricardo Villasenor, Jim Parker, and other friends he hadn't seen since he left Las Vegas, and even visited some old friends at *The Castaways*, telling his old pit boss Jimmy that he'd write something good about *The Castaways* as well.

Although he knew most of his old friends probably didn't care and weren't impressed about getting any blurbs about themselves in his column, Jason at least wanted them to know that he hadn't forgotten them and still appreciated the friendship they'd shared in Las Vegas.

Jason also decided to drive to Henderson, hoping to see Tommy and Alvin, but their neighbors said they had both moved "somewhere near San Francisco" and was still disappointed that he never heard from either of them since the time he popped in on them at their motel in Hollywood. But so many things had changed in his life since he'd last seen them, Jason knew he no longer had anything in common with them and nothing he had done in Las Vegas had really led to anything positive in the long run.

It was fun being back in Las Vegas, but after being away for almost nine months, he was surprised that he now agreed with a familiar motto; *"It's a nice place to visit, but I wouldn't want to live here"* and was more than happy with his new home in Hollywood and his *new life*.

On Jason and Lynn's last night in Las Vegas on New Year's Eve, while they were in a passionate moment, Jason heard Lynn begin whispering the words he wasn't planning on ever hearing from her.

"I love you! I love you!" Lynn began saying even louder as she was reaching her climax.

Even though it had been three years since he had felt *"The Thunderbolt"* for the first time, Jason knew better than to even reciprocate those words to her when he didn't really mean it and have her feel he was committing himself to her.

Lynn was fun, but he couldn't see himself being with her in five years.

Fortunately, nothing serious was discussed about *love* after that, and Lynn joked it just felt good to say "those words" once in a while, and made it easier for her to "cum" when she had sex. But although he still didn't think Lynn expected their relationship to get more serious, he did know that the opening words to the song *Auld Lang Syne* they sang together earlier that night, would eventually ring true sooner, rather than later.

But he also started wondering if he'd ever really feel *"The Thunderbolt"* again and ever want to say those words again himself.

Chapter Five

Even though he was trying to have an active social life, Jason still commuted to the *Singles Register* office at least five times a week and sometimes on Saturdays to oversee the copy and production lay-out for each upcoming issue and most of his time was spent designing interesting cover stories, headlines, and photos that would catch people's eyes when they walked by the news racks on the street.

Besides the entertainment and "show biz" columns, Jason also found writers that would include articles about relationships, dating tips, how to attract the opposite sex, and even some health and wellness articles to keep with the theme as a specialty singles newspaper.

Jason discovered that almost everyone he met was just happy to just have a column or photos with their name attached, published in a real newspaper rather than being paid, and knew most of them were using their "press" for *juice*, just as Jason was doing with his own column.

It was a pretty easy process putting the newspaper together once he learned the mechanics and would just collect all of the articles and copy from his writers every week and would then spend hours proofreading or editing before giving a copy to the typesetter to print on the typesetting machine. Jason would then proofread a second time, after the typesetter supplied him with the camera-ready galleys, and then the girls would run them through a wax machine to cut and paste on the cardboard sheets called *flats*. He also decided to break up all of the pages of personal ads with photos and articles of interest so it wouldn't look like just another classified ad type of publication like the *Penny Saver*.

Stan Adams photography "studio" was just a dark room he had set up at his house in Sylmar, where he lived with his wife and three daughters, but he did share an office in the 9000 Building on Sunset Boulevard with a modeling agent named Ron Smith who owned a business called *The Performing Artists Guild.*

Jason always arranged to pick up any photos from Stan he needed for the *Singles Register* at that office so he wouldn't need to drive to Sylmar, but did need to outsource the photos into half-tones to make them camera ready before he could "cut and paste" them in the different articles.

His mother would drop off the copy for the personal ads she received in the mail on the Friday before each deadline, and Jason also noticed that there were now actually a good number of *real* personal ads coming into the post office box each day, which did show that more people were buying the *Singles Register* in the news racks.

Once all the galleys were pasted and rolled on the flats, they would be assembled by page numbers and be ready to go to the printer. Most of that work in the office was usually done the last four days before the deadline, so Jason always had time in between issues to keep trying to improve the content.

After over nine months of working as the editor, besides his father being happy about the distributors telling him the newspaper was starting to sell much better, his mother was also happy that more *real* personal ads were coming in the mail and he was satisfied that he had created a *real* newspaper and felt like a *real* editor.

Jason had discovered that being the editor and publisher of a singles publication during that year turned out to be very lucky timing. With *No-Fault Divorce* becoming law in California, making it easier to get divorced, the women's movement pushing the concept of women not needing husbands for success, and *Roe V Wade* legalizing abortions, which made "having to get married" a thing of the past, suddenly being and staying single was turning into a popular lifestyle.

Newsweek Magazine had run a cover story on the growing "Singles Market and Craze," and other national magazines were writing stories about how more people were choosing to remain single and Jason felt he was now a big part of the hottest business market and industry in America.

He regularly read the *LA Times, Herald Examiner,* and weekly news magazines, wanting to stay educated himself with the current issues and show enough knowledge as a journalist when he spoke with others about his newspaper's philosophy and the growing singles market. Jason also wanted to make sure if any publications wanted to write stories about the *Singles Register* in the future, he'd be informed enough to make sure he was sounded like a singles expert and legitimate editor and publisher when he spoke. As he had always done since he was younger, Jason continued reading one or two fiction or non-fiction books a month, but now began reading more books about the culture and relationships.

Although the *Singles Register* had mainly been pushing the concept of meeting someone to marry, Jason began showing both sides and mixed in articles about the positive side of staying single and just having fun. He still used different *pen names* for many of the different stories about dating and relationships he'd write himself, so it looked like he had a bigger staff of writers. But because he didn't want to discourage readers from placing personal ads for dates to meet that someone special, he pushed the idea without making it sound like he was encouraging being any type of a *swinging single.* Jason tried emphasizing that advertising for multiple dating partners was actually more fun, and how important it was to date a variety of possible matches before even considering getting married. He'd write that it also gave everyone an opportunity to meet someone they may not have met in their geographical area that may turn out to be their perfect soul mate.

There were also more people contacting Jason, who wanted to write articles in the *Singles Register* and even had authors who were writing books on the singles lifestyle that wanted to have exposure by writing a column or excerpts from their books.

As the editor and publisher, people were reaching out to him now, wanting to be a part of his newspaper instead of Jason having to find ways to fill the pages on his own, and he was soon able to add eight more pages to each issue.

He finally considered himself the *real* owner of a *real* newspaper now

Jason also figured the newspaper itself was beginning to become profitable, and although he wasn't exactly sure how the business end of everything was supposed to be handed with the money that came in as one of the owners, he was doing fine with his salary, and all the other perks he was getting from the newspaper. He knew it was still only his first year in business, but he was already starting to think about how much better he could make it and how much more money he could make in five years.

By early 1973, with all the new features Jason had added, the *Singles Register* had become a thirty-two-page newspaper and wasn't looked as just a "dating service" any longer. Jason had changed the entire look of the *Singles Register* had managed to get enough copy to regularly include articles of interest to singles about relationships and dating, restaurant, movie and record reviews, and a regular *Calendar of Events for Singles.*

He had been keeping himself busy enough in Hollywood to think about his previous life in Las Vegas and sometimes it already seemed like a dream that had never even happened.

꙰

It was shortly before his twenty-second birthday, when Jason got a phone call from someone else from his past who was in Los Angeles that week. It was Terri Larson saying she'd flown in from San Francisco to visit her family and said she'd only be in LA for a couple days and thought it would be great if they could get together and talk about "old times."

Jason had stayed friendly and in touch with Terri by phone for over a year and any anger he'd once had for her about "ruining his life" had diminished, and thought it would be fun to see her again and show her how well he was doing.

His relationship had cooled off with Lynn Everest since New Year's Eve and although he had no interest in having anything "romantic" with Terri, he didn't mind having her as a friend.

Terri's parents seemed very reserved and proper and nothing like he expected and lived in a very upscale home in the expensive area of West Los Angeles, and she cheerfully introduced Jason as "an old friend from Las Vegas" when he first arrived to pick her up for their reunion. Terri also introduced Jason to her younger brother Mark, who said he was "hoping to get into show business" and had an audition to become a regular dancer on *Dick Clark's American Bandstand.* Jason mentioned that if Mark did get hired, he'd put a blurb about him in his *Chasin' with Jason* column, making sure he also mentioned that he was the editor of the newspaper and didn't want her family to think he was an old *"trick"* of Terri's, or a *"pimp"* in case they knew anything about her past.

He had decided to take Terri to dinner at one of the restaurants he liked and had become friendly with its namesake, *Alan Hale's Lobster Barrel* on La Cienega which was also was one of the restaurants he had a trade-out with in the *Singles Register*.

Terri was thrilled because *Gilligan's Island* was one of her favorite TV shows when she was young and was impressed that Jason was going to introduce her to *"The Skipper."* Jason also told her he'd call his photographer to stop by after dinner so Terri could have her picture taken with Alan Hale.

"I wish I could have gotten photos with some of the famous tricks I fucked in Las Vegas," Terri lightly giggled, "But I'm glad I don't and I want to forget about those days completely."

Terri seemed nothing like the girl he remembered, and after seeing how proper and well off her family appeared to be, Jason wondered how she ever ended up being a hooker living in a cheap motel in Las Vegas.

"It was the heroin," said Terri as they talked during dinner, "I know I should have known better, but once you get on that shit, being a hooker seemed like no big deal."

When Jason mentioned how two of his close friends may have fallen into the same lifestyle and might be living somewhere in San Francisco, Terri just said, "good luck ever seeing them again," because she explained that, once you get started, "smack becomes the only thing important in your life."

"I've been clean for over a year now and don't plan on making that mistake again," she said before adding with a slight laugh, "But without memories you've got no past and at least I can look back at it as a wild adventure I experienced when I was young and dumb."

Jason joked that he probably was "young and dumb" with some of his own adventures he'd had in Las Vegas, but agreed with her and now just looked back on it all as a learning experience and was glad they both had moved on to a better life.

Alan Hale did join them at their table, and for about twenty minutes told Terri old stories about his days on *Gilligan's Island*, which helped turn their reunion into a much lighter mood. Stan Adams also did stop by to take several pictures of Alan Hale and Terri, which Jason said he'd put in his *Chasin' with Jason* column and mail to her.

"That would be great," smiled Terri, "My friends in San Francisco will think I'm famous if they see that, and It'll definitely remind me how much better my life is without heroin."

When Jason dropped Terri off at her parent's house, he promised to visit her in San Francisco looked forward to always staying in touch. But as he drove home and listening to the FM station *KLOS*, Jason was also listening to the lyrics of the popular song currently playing on the radio, Neil Young's, *The Needle and the Damage Done*. He sometimes surprised himself about how he always managed to hear a song that seemed to be appropriate to something that was happening or happened in his life, but although he figured it was just a coincidence, he did think it was strange regardless.

Hearing Neil Young singing about how he'd seen *"the needle and the damage done"* was a bit depressing that night, feeling he'd seen that as well, but he also felt lucky he'd never experienced anything like that first hand.

Jason knew no matter how bad he had felt at certain times in the past, it could have been a lot worse, and that was something he always wanted to try and remember.

Chapter Six

Stan Adams was using his own new juice as the "Official photographer" of the *Singles Register* and invited Jason to meet him at a new nightclub on Rodeo Drive in Beverly Hills, which he was also hoping to become another *"Official"* photographer for. Stan said the location was formally a famous spot called *Romanoff's*, which had closed a couple of years earlier, and was now being re-opened under a new name, *McInerney's*.

He explained to Jason that it was going to be an exclusive *"members only"* private nightclub, and should become the new in spot for the trendy Beverly Hills and Hollywood crowd. Stan also emphasized that it was considered a major *status symbol* to have a membership to those "private" nightclubs.

Jason was familiar with some of the *trendy* private nightclubs in Beverly Hills like *The Candy Store* and *Pips*, but wasn't a regular member and only went to those clubs a couple of times as a guest. Many of those private clubs had yearly memberships that varied from two hundred and fifty dollars up to a thousand dollars and were considered to be mainly for *millionaires* or *movie stars*.

Stan knew neither of them could afford that kind of money for a membership to a nightclub, but told Jason he had offered the new owner his services to be the *"official photographer"* for *McInereny's*, in exchange for a membership.

"I requested not only a membership for me," Stan half laughed, "But I told him I also needed another VIP membership for the editor of the *Singles Register* who would give *McInerney's* a ton free press and publicity each month."

"The private nightclubs need publicity like everyone else," Stan told Jason. "How is anyone going to know about all the millionaires and movie stars that were at their club without seeing it in print?"

Jason laughed at how Stan liked using his "official photographer" title for some additional benefits but was glad to see he was starting to feel like he was a part of the *Singles Register* and thought about helping Jason get some additional benefits as well.

After the owner, Mike McInerney, did agree to give Stan and Jason VIP memberships to his new nightclub, Jason was looking forward to having a new and fun nightspot to hang out a couple of nights a week.

Jason felt like he was ready for a new hangout and knew that change was always a good thing to keep things fresh.

It was only Jason's third visit to McInerney's since he got his membership and was sitting in a booth talking with Mike McInereny and Rudolf Wanderone, who was better known as *Minnesota Fats*, the legendary pool shark who was immortalized in the movie *The Hustler* and starred Paul Newman with Jackie Gleason as Minnesota Fats.

Stan was, as usual, taking photos as Mike was anxious to have photos of celebrities who were at his nightclub show up in Jason's newspaper or column.

After about twenty minutes, Jason had heard enough stories from *Minnesota Fats* and decided to walk around the nightclub and socialize with some of the talent he noticed on the dance floor.

The women he saw dancing were dressed much nicer and sexier than places like *Gazzarri's, The Rainbow* or *The Troubadour,* and it did remind him more of the trendy crowd he'd often see at the *Pussycat-A-Go-Go* and the Las Vegas showrooms.

Jason had seen someone he thought was very sexy, who had been dancing and posing by herself on the dance floor, and was now standing alone at the bar.

"Hi, I'm Jason Mershon with the Singles Register," he said, reaching out his hand to greet her, "And I'm just looking for some interesting singles to write about in my column."

"Edy Williams, and I'm not single," she said before lightly adding, "But you can write that you saw me here if you want." Jason then recognized who she was.

He had recently seen a nude photo layout of Edy Williams in *Playboy* magazine and remembered seeing her in a movie called *Beyond the Valley of the Dolls.*

Edy did seem to like that he was a member of the press and added, "But I am separated from my husband if that counts for anything."

She was fun to talk with, and Jason eventually offered to interview her for a cover story.

"I mean it's not *Playboy,*" Jason tried to justify, "But it is in news racks all over Southern California, and you'll be seen by a wide audience."

Edy said that "any press is good press," and they exchanged phone numbers to set up an interview at her house the following week.

Jason figured Edy would sell a lot more issues of the Singles Register than Minnesota Fats and was already enjoying his new VIP membership at his new hangout.

"Edy Williams!" Stan laughed when Jason told him he needed him to come to the interview to take some photos, "She's got quite a reputation, and hopefully, you'll make it out of her house alive."

"Hey, I'm just a journalist," Jason joked back, "And whatever it takes to get a good story, I'll just have to make that sacrifice."

But Stan was excited about shooting a photo that would be on the cover of the *Singles Register* and agreed to accompany Jason to the interview.

Although Edy had separated from her husband, the famous producer Russ Meyer, she was still living in their mansion on Mulholland Drive.

Jason liked the house, especially a smaller pool inside the house with a passageway that allowed swimming from the living room to the main swimming pool outside.

Although he wanted to write some things about Edy that she'd be happy talking about and reading about herself, Jason wanted to focus at least a part of his interview with the *Singles Register's* main theme, which was being single and advertising for dates. He also knew it would be nice to have a celebrity support the classified dating concept that he was always trying to defend himself.

After he interviewed Edy about her career and future plans, Jason then mentioned that he wanted a good quote he might be able to use for the cover for his singles market.

Jason was picturing how a great headline like *"Edy Williams says; There's Nothing Wrong with Advertising for Dates!"* or *"Classified Dating is the Way to Go in the 1970s!"*, would be perfect for the cover.

He didn't get those exact quotes, but did get Edy to talk about classified dating, her thoughts on relationships and circled different quotes he might be able to use as he wrote on his yellow legal pad.

"Well, I am technically single again myself," Edy whispered in a sexy voice she seemed to like speaking, "And I enjoy dating a wide variety of men and not really interested in getting married again for a long time."

Edy added there was nothing wrong with "staying single", and how fun it was to "just date new and different men" and just having a good time.

She also wanted Jason to include in the interview and emphasize that although she came across in public as very sexually promiscuous, especially after posing in *Playboy*, when it came to relationships, she was just the opposite, and added that she was "very choosy" when it came to men.

"I don't want to come across like a *whore* in the story," Edy half laughed as she decided to speak her normal voice, "Or sound like I'm screwing every guy I meet, so maybe tone down that part about *dating a lot of different men all the time."*

"Don't worry, I definitely won't make you sound like a whore," Jason smiled back, "I'll write it so you come across a very sexy, but very sweet lady."

"I mean, that what I saw the first night I met you," Jason added in a complimentary tone.

Edy seemed to like that comment and then continued talking about dating.

"But if people are seriously interested in finding that one special person," Edy smiled, knowing it might be a quote Jason was looking for," I don't see any problem with advertising for dates in a newspaper like the Singles Register so why not try it?" After the interview, Jason, Stan, and Edy spent over an hour with the photoshoot.

Jason liked that Edy couldn't help but look sexy as she posed for dozens of photos in different outfits that Jason thought would look good, but acceptable on the cover.

The other issue that Jason had to often justify about his newspaper was that besides being sold in news racks next to the *LA Times* and *Herald Examiner*, the *Singles Register* was also surrounded by news racks that sold the *swinger* and *pornographic* types of tabloids.

The *"Pornos"* always had sexy and scantily clad girls on their covers, and that was the reason Jason stuck with celebrity photos or clean headlines, to differentiate the *Singles Register* from those newspapers.

Jason liked the story and how he geared the interview with Edy towards singles issues and chose a photo that was sexy, but not too suggestive.

Even though the *Singles Register* was sometimes considered "square," he knew what everyone in the business knew.

"Sex sells!", was the catchphrase in everyone's vocabulary.

"Well, I don't like the idea of putting Edy Williams on the cover," said Jason's mother after he had met with his parents to tell them about his next cover story, "Especially if she was just in *Playboy*, and it'll make us look like just another *porno* newspaper on the street!"

Jason would usually go over to his parent's house at least twice a month to mainly talk about what he was doing with the *Singles Register*, but it never seemed like a family get-together and always involved business.

"Jeez, it's no big deal and just a cover story that a lot of people may want to read," argued Jason, "And because she was *'just in Playboy,'* seeing her name on the *Singles Register* cover should catch people's eye when they're walking by the news racks."

"The personal ads for dates are all that matter in the paper," his mother argued, "And those advertisers could give a shit about anything else you're writing about!"

"Don't be such a prude," Jason tried to add lightly, "Besides, she won't be posing semi-nude or in a bikini like the covers of the porno's and it'll be a nice classy photo."

Jason knew all his father cared about was selling more issues so he could sell more news racks, and hoped he'd agree with his point.

But Jason also figured his parents must have had another argument recently because they seemed to be in their *silent treatment* routine with each other.

"Having well-known people on the cover, especially one who gives classified dating a type of endorsement, is what was making the *Singles Register* readable and sell better," Jason argued, "I've been the editor for a year now, and I think the stories and articles are what's selling the paper and not just the same old *'Looking for Dates?'* headline on every cover."

"Well, do whatever the fuck you want!" his mother half-shouted, "But all that celebrity shit you're putting in the paper, isn't what's bringing in the money."

Jason was always frustrated that his mother could never associate that what he was doing to improve the reading content went hand in hand with increasing the revenue.

"You're up in Hollywood and Beverly Hills hanging out with the *big shots* and having a good time," she continued arguing, "Why don't you just sell some advertising and do something worthwhile?"

"We're here doing all the work that does bring in money!" his mother snidely added, "I don't see you bringing in any checks from what you do."

Jason didn't say it, but he wondered what she thought she did that was *"bringing in the money"* every month.

He knew he still went to the office every day to work on the layout and production as the editor. He was still always looking for new writers and articles to improve the content and always pushing the *Singles Register's* name with everything he was doing.

His parents never wanted to spend any money advertising the newspaper, and his father said the news racks were all the advertising they needed.

Jason remembered Ricardo Villasenor once told him, "The only thing that makes money without advertising is the US Mint," but with his parents refusing to give him an advertising budget to promote the newspaper, he needed to find other ways to get the name of the *Singles Register* out there.

All his mother seemed to do was collect the checks for ads that came in the mail and forward the letters from people who were answering the personal ads for dates.

He knew the amount of mail she was bringing home from the post office had at least tripled in the past few months, along with the number of real personal ads in each issue.

Jason also knew the paper was selling good because his father had said he now had news racks distributed throughout Los Angeles, Orange County, the San Fernando Valley, and even Palm Springs. He also figured they had to be bringing in good money for themselves, and he felt his efforts were a big part of the *Singles Register's* growing success.

He always got angry whenever they tried to say they were doing all the work and wondered if they even wanted a *"real newspaper"* or just a *"vehicle"* to get quick cash in their hands and was tired of trying to explain that the promotion he did away from the office was just as important. Jason never liked spending too much time talking about business with his parents because it always seemed to turn into an argument, but also didn't want to waste any more time arguing, and was anxious to finish his business meeting, and headed back to Hollywood after about thirty minutes.

Jason decided to run the story with Edy Williams on the cover, whether his mother liked it or not.

Three weeks later, he felt completely vindicated when the *"Edy Williams Cover"* ended up being the largest selling issue of the *Singles Register* to date. His father told Jason the distributers said if future issues started selling as well as that issue, they'd definitely be interested in buying more news racks and might even start placing them in cities like San Diego or San Francisco.

Jason knew he probably couldn't get a celebrity to talk about "the singles angle" each issue, but did start thinking about another idea.

He was constantly meeting very sexy and beautiful *"actresses* and *models"* every week in Hollywood and Beverly Hills, and although those girls weren't *celebrities* yet, Jason knew they would look great on the covers, and he could gear stories about them with the singles angle like he had with Edy. keep the cover photos "clean but sexy

Jason decided a new highlight of the *Singles Register* would be to feature a great cover shot of some of the most eligible single girls in Southern California, who would love posing for just publicity and not worry about being paid modeling fees. But he knew he'd also would keep the cover photos "sexy but clean" so he wouldn't have his mother bitch about putting more girls on the cover, and rather than "Playmates" as *Playboy Magazine* did, he'd call his cover girls the "Bachelorettes of the Week" to fit it with the singles angle.

He also knew Stan Adams would be more than happy to add some more photo credits to his *resume* each issue and knew a new gimmick to begin his second year as editor was just the change that he needed to keep him motivated.

.

&

Edy Williams was also very happy with her cover story and Jason had become good friends with her during that time. They also had mutual friends in Sammy Shore, Nicky Blair, and Sidney Skolsky, and they'd spend time at *The Comedy Store, Nicki Blair's Restaurant* or have lunch at *Schwab's* with Sidney when Jason picked up his column for the *Singles Register*.

Edy was invited to some incredible parties almost every weekend and seemed to know just about everyone in show biz, and with Jason having a trade out with a limousine company, they attended several parties together. He also discovered that being a member of the press allowed him to fit in with almost every social situation as someone who *belonged there* and wasn't considered an outsider.

Jason and Edy were at an after-concert party that Led Zeppelin was hosting, but it wasn't at the Continental *"Riot"* House where they had been banned, but at a downtown Los Angeles Hotel. He wasn't really a huge Led Zeppelin fan because he always thought Robert Plant's voice got annoying after a while, but he knew the band threw good parties, and he'd probably find something to write about in his column or as a feature story.

He also noticed that the dozens of groupies surrounding Robert Plant and Jimmy Page were definitely better quality than the groupies he met when he was on the road with *The Box Tops*, and although Jason tried to talk to Plant and Page to see if they were interested in being interviewed in the *Singles Register*, they were both too preoccupied with the groupies to talk business. There was also a lot of stuff he saw going on at that party that he knew he could never write about publicly in his newspaper but he did enjoy meeting and talking with other musicians, including Johnny Rivers, who was also at the party. Jason had sung many of Johnny's hit songs when he had entered talent contests in Las Vegas and was happy when Rivers agreed to be interviewed for a future issue of the *Singles Register.*

Jason knew that just a few years earlier, he would have been starstruck by all the celebrities he was now meeting but also knew he needed to act more sophisticated and come across as a mature journalist.

It seemed that everyone he met seemed to enjoy having their names included in his *Chasin' with Jason* column, or having a story written about themselves, so everyone always seemed happy to talk with him.

Jason felt fortunate that his social life was basically his business life and that everything he did away from the office did involve something he was writing about in his column or including with promoting the newspaper. He also had no problem finding potential *Bachelorettes of the Week* everywhere he'd spend his nights out, and the old adage about mixing business with pleasure not only allowing him to have fun, but was allowing the name of the *Singles Register* to become more widely known, and people were beginning to notice.

Edy Williams always introduced Jason to everyone at various events and parties as the *"Editor and Publisher"* of the Singles *Register,* and had told Jason it sounded classier and would give him the image of a *"Young Hugh Hefner"* type. Although he first laughed at her comparison and had never thought about adding the title "Publisher" before, he did start to think that it had a ring to it.

Although Jason's parents took care of most of the business as far as paying the bills, working with distributors, and the printer, neither of them had ever wanted to have their own names listed on the newspaper's masthead and had always said they preferred staying in the background.

After Jason did mention the possibility of adding the title to is father said because Jason was basically now "the face" of the *Singles Register,* and was always representing the newspaper in public, he agreed that "Editor and Publisher" would look better on the masthead, and that title was added to the new issues.

When Jason would sometimes bring up what his father had told him about sharing in the profits for building up the newspaper after "a year or so," he'd just say they'd "work something out later," but did give Jason a fifty dollar a week raise saying the paper was becoming profitable.

Jason decided the raise and the new title would satisfy him for the time being and didn't want to sound greedy or start any arguments that would keep him from enjoying the life he was living and didn't want to change anything that would complicate that.

With the extra fifty dollars a week salary, Jason also decided to spend a weekend in San Francisco to visit Terri Larson after she had invited him to stay at her new apartment and meet her "new and respectable" boyfriend.

Jason was with a new bachelorette he'd met named Annette Steward, and although he still hadn't had what he considered a full-time *girlfriend* since he'd been with Anne Sanderson, since then, he never had a problem at least enjoying casual romances without them ever turning into another "I love you" type of relationship. He didn't feel like he was volume fucking, but he did like all of the opportunities that always seemed to be available.

While Jason, Annette, Terri, and her new boyfriend, were all enjoying the great view of the San Francisco skyline while they were having dinner at *Ondine's Restaurant* in Sausalito, Terri said she had some "crazy news" to tell Jason.

"Guess what I'm doing for a living now?" Terri asked.

Jason just hoped it wasn't "hooking" or selling heroin, but before he could say anything, she broke out laughing.

"I'm driving a taxi!" she laughed, "Can you believe it?!"

"I may not be *'Mr. Editor and Publisher'* like you", she joked, "But just give me a few more years!"

Jason did think it was ironic and how so much had changed in the just the two years since he drove a taxi, and also sometimes thought about where he'd be in five more years as Anne Sanderson had once asked him.

But he was certain that he was at least on his way up, and that the sky was the limit as to what he could possibly do in the future and was very satisfied with his life.

Chapter Seven

Jason walked into *McInerney's* alone to see if any of his friends were around, but it was still too early, and there were only about twenty people in the bar, but did see Mike McInerney in a booth sitting with a very attractive young blond and decided to join him for a couple of drinks until more people arrived.

"Jason, this is Lori Wagner," Mike said as he introduced them to each other, "Jason is the editor and publisher of the *Singles Register* newspaper and he's always looking for pretty girls to be his Bachelorettes of the Week."

"I've already been a *bachelorette*," Lori lightly laughed as Jason sat next to her, "I was on the Dating Game television show."

Lori started explaining how she appeared as a contestant on the TV show *The Dating Game* and won a date with David Cassidy when he chose her, and although Jason thought she had a great laugh and was immediately attracted to her bubbly personality, he wasn't about to start flirting with Mike's girlfriend. He decided to act more businesslike and let her do most of the talking, but he still found himself enjoying her smile and outgoing attitude.

It was only after about fifteen minutes before more people starting to arrive in the disco, and Mike decided to greet a few celebrities he noticed and left Jason and Lori alone in the booth.

"So, Lori," Jason casually asked, "How long have you and Mike been together?"

"We're not dating, and we're just friends," she smiled, "It's nice knowing the owner, so I don't get jumped on by the horny old guys that always come here looking for fresh pieces of meat!"

Jason laughed with her and could see that she was the one that everyone would always be hitting on. By far, she had the best look and attitude of anyone he'd met at *McInerney's*, or anywhere else in a long time.

"Well, don't worry," Jason just laughed at her comment, "I'm not a horny old guy."

He didn't want to appear like all the other guys she probably met there and didn't want her to think he was just looking to get laid.

"So, you're an editor and publisher of a newspaper, eh?" she asked, "You look kind of young to be in that position, how old are you anyway?"

Jason gave his standard three years older answer and said, "twenty-five years old," and let Lori volunteer her own age.

"I'm twenty-one," she said, "But I've never had a problem getting into clubs since I was eighteen."

Jason decided to get a little more information and asked how things worked out with her date with David Cassidy.

"We dated for a while and are still friends," Lori said, "But he's on the road a lot doing concerts, and always busy with the *Partridge Family*, so I hardly see him much anymore."

Lori then laughed and added. "Are you trying to find out if I'm dating anyone?"

Jason felt a little embarrassed that he was so obvious but liked it when she added. "Well, I am currently single if that's what you wanted to know."

"No, it wasn't that," he lied, "But I did have two tickets for the *Dorothy Chandler Pavilion* to review Jon Voight and Faye Dunaway in a stage version of *A Streetcar Named Desire* tomorrow night."

"I just found out tonight that the girl I was going to take has to work and can't make it," Jason added nonchalantly, wanting it to sound like a casual invitation and more about his job. "It would be a shame to waste a ticket on such a great show and was just wondering if you're free tomorrow and might like to join me?"

"Wow, I've wanted to see that play, and I'd love to go!" Lori excitedly answered, "But I live with my father near Palos Verdes and work till five pm if you don't mind picking me up there?"

Jason didn't hesitate to say he'd pick her up by six pm and casually added that they could even grab a late dinner afterward. He also reminded himself to call the girl he would take to *A Streetcar Named Desire* and come up with a good excuse to break their date.

When he was driving home later that night, he couldn't get Lori off his mind and was suddenly more excited than he had in a long time about going out on a date with someone.

But he also felt a certain rumble coming on that he hadn't felt in a long time as well.

❧

Jason and Lori were having dinner in the private upstairs booth at *The Islander* restaurant on La Cienega, where he had another trade-out and always received VIP treatment by the staff there. He always gave *The Islander* great press, and often mentioned many of those who worked there by name, and knew it would be the perfect place to take Lori after the play for an impressive and romantic dinner.

"STELL-AHH!!" they were both laughing and mimicking to each other, while they were comparing Jon Voight's stage characterization of Stanley Kowalski to Marlon Brando's same role in the movie version of *A Streetcar Named Desire*.

Jason had ordered special drinks that were served in hollowed-out coconuts called a "Coco-Loco," and both he and Lori had a nice buzz well before their dinner was even served.

Lori had already told Jason she was currently studying at *Brooks Fashion College* in Long Beach and was also working part-time at *John Robert Powers* modeling agency saying she was thinking about modeling or acting but really wanted to be a singer. He also learned she loved the same types of music from George Gershwin to the Rolling Stones, and also discovered that like himself, she always sang along with songs she heard on the radio and knew the words to dozens of songs. They also laughed and talked about the many things that had in common, including not only had she lived in La Puente when she was around the same age as Jason but was also an only child, and also remembered her parents always fighting while she was growing up, but unlike Jason's parents, Lori's parents had divorced. They also discovered they knew several of the same people in Hollywood had even frequented many of the same nightspots and were shocked that they had never met before.

"I think we were probably destined to meet eventually," laughed Lori.

Jason surprised himself but felt he wanted to be completely honest with Lori and told her things about himself he never talked about with his other dates and even told Lori that his parents were "a little involved" with the *Singles Register*, and never tried to make her believe he'd started it all by himself. But he did want her to know that he was definitely one of the owners of the newspaper, and was definitely the one in charge as the editor and publisher not wanting her to think that he just worked for his parents or hadn't been responsible for the newspaper's success.

"Family businesses are sometimes best," said Lori, "You can always trust your family more than you can other business partners."

Jason even told her how he got his driver's license in Las Vegas and was only twenty-two years old and explained that he didn't want everyone who met him as an *"Editor and Publisher"* to think he was "just a kid" and just casually added that, "A little BS never hurt anybody."

Lori laughed at that expression and admitted that she was only twenty years old herself and wouldn't be twenty-one until August.

"I can't believe everything we're telling each other on our first date," smiled Lori, "But we do seem to have a lot in common," smiled Lori, "I think if I had been the one choosing on who to go out with on *The Dating Game*, I definitely would have picked you."

Jason felt that that there had been an immediate attraction between them that night, but because Lori had already said she to attend her classes at *Brooks College* the next day, he didn't even want to consider taking her back to his apartment after dinner and act like another "horny guy" who just wanted to have sex.

During the drive back to Lori's father's house, it actually had seemed like they had known each other for years and had definitely made a connection, especially the way she sat close to him so he could put his arm around her while he drove.

Lori was singing along with the current Helen Reddy hit song called *Peaceful* that was playing on the radio as they drove, and did seem appropriate as there was no traffic by midnight on the 405 freeway. When another popular song came on the radio, Stevie Wonder's *You Are the Sunshine of My Life,* they both started singing together and Jason joked that someday they might end up calling that particular tune their first "our song" if their future dates were as fun as that night. But even before he dropped Lori off at her father's house and made another date for that weekend Jason already knew what had happened.

He'd been struck by *"The Thunderbolt."*

꙳

Although Lori Wagner seemed to have a school and work schedule as busy as Jason, they did try to see each at least twice a week over the next month, but ever since she had spent the night the night at Jason's apartment on their third date, it did seem like *"The Thunderbolt"* had struck them both and they had become "boyfriend and girlfriend" almost immediately since then.

Stan Adams told Jason that he could see an immediate change in him the first time he saw him with Lori and could tell that Jason had met what Stan called *"The One."*

"It's about time," laughed Stan, "You need to stop having so much fun with all those other girls you've seen for the last six months."

"You need to settle down with just one," Stan sarcastically added, "So you can have a nice, boring and miserable life like I have."

Stan was having problems in his marriage and often mentioned that he wished he was single again himself.

Besides Stan Adams, Lori liked almost everyone else in Jason's circle of friends but said she wasn't really a fan of Bill Gazzarri, Gary Berwin, or Dennis Cole and said she knew about their reputations as *"volume fuckers"* and wasn't thrilled that Jason still seemed to spend time with them in Hollywood.

Jason didn't go into details about how many flings he'd actually had himself the past year and explained that "those friends" were mainly introducing him to girls who they thought would be good for the cover of the *Singles Register,* and it was just part of his business. He had already told Lori some stories about his time in Las Vegas but mainly tried to keep everything current and positive about how he planned on continuing building up the *Singles Register.*

Lori said she understood that Jason had to meet other actresses or models to feature as a *Bachelorette of the Week* and wasn't jealous, but also said he should still be careful.

"Most of the girls in Hollywood are the type that will jump all over you the first chance they get," Lori half laughed, "And I don't want you bringing back the crabs or something to me when we're together."

Jason just laughed and told her she had nothing to worry about, and lightly assured Lori she was more than enough for him sexually.

"After the nights I spend with you and how much you drain me," Jason joked, "I wouldn't have enough energy left anyway."

Jason meant what he said to her and discovered that when it came to sex, Lori was the most passionate lover he'd ever been with. He knew if he'd once thought Anne Sanderson was his *Sue Ann Daley* from the book *The Adventurers*, Jason discovered Anne wasn't even half as sexual as Lori was.

On weekends, they'd go to Jason's regular hangouts, *The Comedy Store*, *Nicky Blair's*, or *The Rainbow*, and have late night breakfasts at *Dino's*. But their favorite dates were attending the rock music clubs like the *Whiskey-a-Go-Go* and especially *The Troubadour*, where they'd spend every Tuesday night together, attending the opening night concerts of all the great recording stars who regularly performed there.

When Jason discovered Lori liked horse racing, he took her on dates to both Hollywood Park and Los Alamitos Racetrack, and she'd also join him for other special openings or events he'd be covering for the *Singles Register*. But they would always spend at least one night a week returning to the location of their first date, *The Islander*.

What they both liked best about *The Islander* was the lounge that had live entertainment by a duo named *Pearl and the Shell* that normally played Polynesian music, but the piano player also knew some popular standard tunes and let members of the bar crowd sing along with them occasionally.

Jason hadn't an opportunity to sing on stage since his Box Tops tour and liked being able to "sit in" with actual musicians to try and sing some different types of "old songs" he remembered his mother had taught him years earlier.

Although Jason and Lori preferred singing rock and roll and current pop songs to each other while they were driving, they both liked that they had an opportunity to sing live to each other, and any small crowds who were in the bar at *The Islander* and Jason was surprised Lori knew the lyrics to several old song standard herself.

Jason was able to pull from his memory some of the old romantic songs like *It Had to Be You* or *Embraceable You*, he learned when he was young. Lori, in turn, would sing romantic songs she remembered like *As Time Goes By* or *The Man I Love*. They eventually discovered other piano bars in Hollywood and Beverly Hills, where the piano players had a wider variety of romantic songs by Gershwin, Cole Porter, or Irving Berlin; they could both pull from their memory or learn.

Jason liked that he was able to at least sing again occasionally in some bar or lounge, and found the perfect match with Lori, who enjoyed music and singing as much as he did.

They had often joked about how one word could change the entire song, meaning to take the *gushiness* out of some of the songs and not look like they were so serious to any audiences in the piano bars. Lori would sometimes change one word to the verse of the song *As Time Goes By* and singing, "And when two lovers *'screw'*, they still say I love you…" while Jason also sometime changed the words to George Gershwin's *Embraceable You*, by singing, "I love all the many charms that I see…above all I want your *'legs'* around me…"

They both knew the feelings they had for each other but still wanted to keep it fun and fresh without getting too gushy after having just started their relationship. They both had come to agree they wanted to always feel that they were still *courting* each other and it was best to make *each date,* feel as important as their *first date* so it would never get boring.

Lori's continued to mention how her main fantasy was to be a singer like Carly Simon, and hopefully sing at clubs like *The Troubadour* and the *Whiskey-a-Go-Go* herself someday. Her favorite current music album was *No Secrets* by Carly Simon, so Jason bought the eight-track tape, so Lori could sing along with it while they drove in his car.

Jason lightly joked how he'd once pictured himself as the next Mick Jagger and would sing along with Lori to Carly Simon's hit song *You're So Vain*, in which Mick Jagger sang back-up vocals. Lori also always liked lightly singing the lyrics to the title song of the Carly Simon album about how *they had no secrets* from each other and *told each other everything*.

"I feel like this is the most honest relationship I've ever been in," Lori always smiled.

Lori's comment reminded Jason of the first song he ever learned and used to sing to Tinker with the lyrics about *always being true* when saying the words *"I love you"* and how *It's a Sin to Tell a Lie.*

Jason did love sharing all of his thoughts and plans with Lori and loved that she shared hers with him as well. He also saw that Lori liked to be philosophical about love and relationships, especially on the nights they'd spend looking at the stars and the ocean on late nights they'd spend on the beach. They both agreed about how rushing into marriage was a mistake, as they saw the consequences of their own parents marrying young, as well as others they personally knew.

"We need to accomplish everything we want individually," Lori would often say while they looked at the stars, "Before we can even consider sharing our lives with someone else permanently."

"Besides, you can't make another person happy unless you're completely happy with yourself," she repeated often, "And, you can't *truly* love someone unless you love *yourself* first."

Jason had heard so many variations on that subject from people he met in Hollywood about satisfying your own ego first and how people without healthy egos could never successful, it was almost like a mantra.

"There's nothing wrong with feeling somewhat egotistical about yourself and showing confidence to people," Lori said, "Plus, it gives you a positive attitude that'll keep you motivated."

"It's kind of like that song *You're so Vain,*" Lori lightly added, "Carly Simon is singing about how cocky and vain that guy in the song is supposed to be, and how much she supposedly hates that attitude."

"But if that's a real person she's singing about," Lori half laughed, "It's obvious that she really does still like his cocky attitude, and that's why she wrote a song about him."

"That's what I like about you," Lori smiled, "You're a little cocky and have a positive attitude that comes across a lot older than a typical twenty-two-year-old."

"Well, like I said before, I need to come across like a *mature* and *successful* editor and publisher," Jason facetiously joked, "I don't want people to think I'm over my head and not take me seriously."

"Well, we're both ambitious, and I think we'll both be successful when we are actually twenty-five or thirty years old," Lori confidently said, "And then we won't have to fake it."

Lori also said she thought thirty was the best age to get married.

"If a person doesn't make their fantasies come true, by the time they're thirty," Lori half-joked, "Then it will probably be too late ever to be happily married."

Jason basically agreed with much of what Lori would say and did feel they both needed to accomplish what they personally wanted before settling down to what they both called an *"old married couple."* They did agree that it was destiny that bought them together because of so much they had in common, and did sometimes lightly discuss what it could be like in the future if they did eventually get married and Jason brought up a couple of things he had once only talked about with Anne Sanderson.

When he mentioned if he ever had a son, he'd probably name him after himself, Lori agreed because she, like almost everyone he met, thought "Jason" was a cool and unique name but she didn't like Jason's idea for a name for any daughters.

"Venus or Aphrodite!?" Lori sarcastically laughed, "You give a girl a name like that, and the poor girl will probably end up a stripper!"

Jason just laughed and told Lori if they ever did get married, and after they were both satisfied with their own careers, she could choose any of the girl's names.

When they did both finally say the "I love you" words together in bed after two months together, Jason not only knew that Victor Consuela had been right about the "next one" being better than the *first one*, but came to appreciate the Frank Sinatra song *The Second Time Around* even more and realized how true it was.

With his personal life as perfect as could have hoped, Jason knew he also wanted to work even harder on making the *Singles Register* a completely respected and established newspaper that would last for hopefully years and be something he could always feel that he had started from scratch.

Then he knew he'd be completely happy with himself.

Chapter Eight

The agent that Stan Adams shared an office in the *9000 Building* on Sunset Boulevard, Ron Smith, was also sometimes a source for assisting Jason with a *Bachelorette of the Week* to feature on the covers of each issue.

Ron's business, *The Performing Artists Guild*, had beautiful girls in his office daily, hoping to sign with his agency. Because Stan was increasing his business as a photographer as well, and wasn't available on some occasions, Ron introduced Jason to a couple of other photographers, Wally Eagler and James Mares, who would also photograph his *Bachelorettes* and be happy with just photo credit in the *Singles Register*.

Gary Berwin had his office near where Ron Smith and Stan shared their offices, also on Sunset Boulevard, and said he could always assist Jason with interesting *Bachelorettes* mentioning was always auditioning girls to be in his next *Queen of the Artist and Models Ball*.

Gary's beauty pageant was even televised locally, giving more exposure to his actual *Ball* each year and said as soon as one *Artist and Models Ball* ended, he'd immediately begin preparing for his next *Ball*, because keeping it famously known as the main celebrity party of the year took a lot of work. Gary also explained the *Ball* was "very, very profitable," and he made more money off that one event than some people earned in a year.

Stan Adams was always telling Jason that he should try to get the *Singles Register's* name attached to the *Artist and Models Ball* in some way, and said all the free press and publicity the newspaper could receive by having it associated with such a famous party that attracted so many celebrities, would make the *Singles Register* look like a real hip and big-time publication.

Jason was amused how Stan was always impressed by everything that involved celebrities, but he knew that being in Hollywood and Beverly Hills constantly almost made it a required subject matter. He also knew Stan had a point, and it could help attract readers who were more familiar with the *Artist and Models Ball* than they were with the *Singles Register*.

When Jason started talking with Gary about his next *Ball*, Gary mentioned he was going to move it to New Year's Eve that year because he had started a new business buying and selling "fixer-upper" houses in Hollywood and Beverly Hills and hadn't been able to spend as much time on promoting his Ball in time for Halloween.

Gary was also impressed with what he'd been reading about the growing "singles craze" and always said Jason "had a goldmine" in having the only newspaper in Los

Angeles that specialized in that market. When Gary said that he was also thinking of adding an additional promoter to assist him with his *Ball* that year because he was spending so much time with his houses, Jason decided to take a shot and pitched to him that as far as additional promotion and press, he could offer Gary a lot of free publicity in the *Singles Register* if Gary would include the newspaper as a co-sponsor of that year's *Artist and Models Ball*.

He pitched that because the *Singles Register* featured many entertainment articles about the Hollywood scene, and with the "huge circulation" his newspaper had, it might be the "right vehicle to sell a ton of tickets" without Gary having to take too much time away from his real estate business.

Jason really didn't know what the Singles Register's actual circulation was and left that part of the business to his father, who handled all the distribution. His father had told Jason to include on the covers, a subtext that read "Over 100,000 Singles Will See Your Ads!" so Jason always used that figure when talking about his circulation.

"Well, singles are the biggest part of the crowds at the Artist and Models Ball," Gary said after thinking it over, "So that actually might be a great tie in."

Gary agreed fairly quickly that the *Singles Register* would be a good co-sponsor, and told Jason how he could help as a co-promoter himself.

"See if you can set up a couple of press parties for next month, and I'll do the rest," Gary said, "I'll figure out what percentage of the ticket sales I can offer you once everything is set."

"Basically, we'll just do the same thing I did last year at *Gazzarri's*," Gary added, "Just find some fun locations, and I'll supply some celebrities, some contestants from my beauty contest, and I'll get my other press contacts to attend."

Before Jason left that day, Gary also casually mentioned that he was going to start taking investors in his real estate business, and if Jason had an "extra ten thousand dollars to invest," Jason might want to consider getting a "piece of his company" as an investment in the future.

Jason knew that everyone thought with his position as an editor and publisher, he had to be rich already, and that amount of money was nothing to him. Jason didn't want to let on that he considered ten thousand dollars a fortune, and just told Gary it would be something he'd consider, but mainly wanted to focus on his newspaper at that time. But Jason did say he'd start working on setting up some press parties immediately and was just thrilled that Gary agreed to include the *Singles Register's* name as a *co-sponsor*.

Jason had always been giving free press and publicity to everyone else but now, the *Singles Register* would be getting a ton of free press and publicity itself. He also found that using the name of the *Artist and Models Ball*, along with the *Singles Register*, opened up a lot of doors, and everyone wanted to be involved in some way.

Sammy Shore said he'd get a couple of big-name comics to perform at a press party, so Jason decided *The Comedy Store* would be a fun place for one of the parties, and for the other press party, Jason decided it would be fun to set something up at Hollywood Park Racetrack, where they featured night harness racing and reserved areas for special groups.

The officials at Hollywood Park were thrilled to play host to a press party announcing that years famous *Artists and Models Ball* after Jason assured them that he'd have celebrities and beauty contestants at their racetrack.

Jason had learned that during the nightly harness races, the racing officials would sometimes name certain races after special groups or businesses during their program and also mentioned he'd run a full-page story with photos from the *Singles Register's* press party and wanted a couple of races named for both *The Artists and Models Ball*, and another called *The Singles Register*.

When the Hollywood Park officials said that would be no problem, Jason let Gary Berwin know that everything was set.

Gary said both places were great and laughed that he'd make sure the "freeloading press" knew that there'd be food at both events.

Jason was glad he was always looked upon as being above just a member of the "freeloading press" and liked being known as the *one in charge* of the newspaper and also *somewhat in charge* of helping promote that year's *Artist and Models Ball*.

It reaffirmed his belief that everything he was doing now was what he was meant to be doing all along.

ॐ

The Comedy Store was an easy location to make it appear the first party was packed with a big crowd with well over one hundred people crammed into the small bar that only had seating for about seventy-five people, and it looked like many had to be turned away at the door.

Besides Jason and Gary Berwin acting as cohosts, those in the crowd included Dennis Cole, Ron Smith, Mark Marzouk, Art Laboe, Edy Williams, Nicki Blair, Bill Gazzarri, and over a dozen beauty contestants and past and potential *Bachelorettes of the Week*.

Sammy Shore had celebrity comics including Redd Foxx and another young comic named Gabe Kaplan.

Redd Foxx had always been one of Jason's favorite comedians and had seen his act several times in Las Vegas before becoming the star of the hit television series *Sanford and Son*.

Gabe Kaplan told Jason he had recently appeared on *The Johnny Carson Show*, and lightly suggested that Jason should start featuring a *Bachelor of the Month*, and he'd gladly pose for a cover story himself.

"I wouldn't mind being known as one of the most eligible bachelors in Hollywood," Gabe joked, "Or auditioning some more of the talent that might like seeing me on your cover."

Jason still smiled at how everyone just referred to all the girls in Hollywood as the *talent* when describing the one's they wanted to have sex.

Sammy Shore also sarcastically joked that he'd also be a good *Bachelor of the Month* because he was going through a divorce with his wife Mitzi, and would soon be single himself.

Jason also met Sammy's daughter that night, Sandi Shore, who was working the front door and said it was the best party she'd seen at *The Comedy Store*.

There were writers and photographers from most of the LA media who all received press releases announcing the *Artist and Models Ball* was changing its date from Halloween to New Year's Eve. And, the press release also reported that California's largest singles newspaper, the *Singles Register*, would be the co-sponsor of this year's *Ball*.

Jason knew that he'd be including a big story with many photos in the next issue the *Singles Register* and made sure Stan Adams and Wally Eagler shot a ton of pictures.

There was another celebrity Jason met named Bill Ballance, who Jason remembered as a disc jockey on *KFWB* radio that he'd listen to on his transistor radio when he was still roller skating.

Bill currently had a very popular radio talk show and mentioned he might want to interview Jason on his radio show about the "growing singles craze" and wanted to know more about the *Singles Register.*

Jason was mainly having fun playing the host, greeting everyone present, and knowing he was making some great contacts, but Lori seemed to attract the most attention. She was the current *"Bachelorette of the Week"* on the cover of the *Singles Register's* issues that Jason was passing out to everyone, and the men were disappointed when they learned Lori was Jason's girlfriend.

Almost all the men were constantly telling Jason, *"What a lucky bastard"* he was to have a girlfriend like Lori, but Jason would just smile and tell them they could meet some great women themselves just by using the *Singles Register.*

Although he knew most of those at *The Comedy Store* had come to the party because of their interest in the *Artists and Models Ball*, Jason dropped in the name of his newspaper every chance he could.

The name *Singles Register* did appear in some of the daily newspapers, including the *LA Times, Herald Examiner*, and the *Long Beach Independent*, when the press party's stories appeared over the next few days, and he knew no matter what his parents had said, Jason still knew publicity in more well-known publications was worth more than just seeing the *Singles Register* sitting in a news rack.

The next press party at Hollywood Park Racetrack was even more packed than *The Comedy Store.*

A large buffet was set up in the Turf Club area reserved for their group, and Jason liked that the different locale attracted even more press and was a change of pace from the usual party scene, and everyone seemed to enjoy a party where they could also gamble on that evening's harness races.

To differentiate this press party from the last, Gary said he would be announcing his top finalists for his *Queen of the Artist and Models Ball* and introducing his celebrity judges who would make the decision.

The actual *Ball* was still three months away, so he wouldn't name a Queen until his televised Pageant in December.

Gary had made up sashes inscribed with the *Artist and Models Ball* logo for the twenty-five contestants to wear over their gowns. Although Jason was a little disappointed there was no room to add the *Singles Register's* name, he knew the *Ball* is what was really attracting the press and was just happy being mentioned as the main sponsor.

Jason and Lori were sitting with a group deciding which horse to bet on the upcoming race that was named *The Singles Register* when one of the girls wearing an *Artist and Models Ball sash* came and introduced herself.

"Hi, I'm Annie Gaybis," she said, "I understand you're the editor and publisher of the Singles Register?"

"I'm not really a contestant in the beauty contest," Annie then half laughed, "But Gary Berwin asked me to wear this sash and said it would be good publicity.

"And," she added with a smile, "he said you'd probably put my picture in your newspaper from the party tonight."

Jason just half laughed himself at her motive and said he probably would include a photo of her if she'd join him and Lori in the *winner's circle* after the next race.

He figured Annie was cute and having a picture in the winner's circle with Lori, who was a *Bachelorette of the Week*, having another girl representing the *Artist and Model's Ball,* would look good in the *Singles Register* and continue to tie his newspaper to the Ball.

Annie sat down at the table with Jason and Lori and explained she had recently moved to Hollywood from New York, after being named *Miss Broadway* by the New York media, and was also a singer and an actress.

Annie said her agent had told her about the *Artist's and Model's Ball* and *Singles Register* party that night, and also mentioned she heard that Jason was always looking for interesting bachelorettes for his cover.

"I am single," Annie laughed, "So if you need a bachelorette, I'm your girl!"

But Jason was slightly surprised when Annie added, "Oh, and I've already met your *brother.*"

Jason and Lori immediately gave a quizzed look at each other, but Jason was also wondering if she thought Dennis Cole was his brother that night.

"My brother?" Jason laughed, "Dennis Cole isn't my brother."

"No, not him," laughed Annie as she pointed to a group of people, "Your brother, standing over there."

Jason had a surprised and very uncomfortable feeling come over him when he looked and saw his father standing with a group of party-goers, knowing he was the last person he expected to see. His father had never shown any interest or even mentioned that he was thinking about being at that night's party.

He didn't want to say anything to Lori, who looked confused, and just excused himself and walked over to where his father was standing.

As Jason approached him, he heard his father introducing himself to one of the celebrities at the party, actor Peter Brown, who was standing with another group.

"Hi, I'm Dick Mershon with the Singles Register," his father was cheerfully greeting Peter Brown and the others.

His father always introduced himself as *"Dick"* rather than "Richard," and Jason was wondering what his father was even talking to them about.

When he saw Jason and the surprised look on his face, his father tried to act excited and natural.

"Ah, Jason, I was looking all over for you," his father cheerfully said, "I wanted to talk to you about something, you got a minute?"

Jason could see that his father wanted to explain his presence in private and told him "Sure" as they stepped away from the group to speak alone.

"Hey buddy," his father tried to lightly say, "I'm sorry for just popping in like this, but I just thought I'd stop in for a few minutes to see how it was going."

Jason didn't want to act rude and just said he was surprised and wished his father would have given him some advance notice. They had always managed to keep their positions with the *Singles Register* separate, and now Jason started feeling that his father was crashing his way into *his world.* His father also explained he decided to just say he was Jason's brother as to make Jason seem older, and not have people think he was just running his father's business.

"But actually, the reason I stopped by," his father explained, "I was with some guys tonight who are thinking of buying a lot of news racks, and I thought it would be kind of impressive showing them a Singles Register party."

"You don't mind, do you?" his father added, "These guys I'm with get impressed with celebrity parties."

Jason said he didn't mind and tried not to act bothered even though he knew he was.

"But I do have to spend time with some other people here tonight," said Jason, just wanting to get back to his friends, "So let's just talk tomorrow sometime."

"Sure, no problem," said his father, "We'll talk tomorrow, and by the way, great party!"

Jason was still feeling uncomfortable knowing his father was there but tried to act like everything was fine when he rejoined Lori and Annie with the rest of the group.

"Who was that?" Lori suspiciously whispered, "I thought you were an *only* child."

"I am," whispered Jason back to Lori, "I'll just tell you about it later."

The race named after the *Singles Register* was beginning, and Jason wanted to enjoy that moment and not have to explain anything just then.

After posing in the winner's circle with Lori and Annie Gaybis, Jason took Lori aside and told her "that was my father," and that he had no idea why he was telling people he was his brother.

Lori said it really "sounded weird" but was mainly upset that Jason didn't even introduce her to him.

"I am your girlfriend, and I can't believe you didn't introduce me to your father," she said with irritation, "I think that was kind of rude."

Lori did seem upset and confused, so Jason looked around the turf club when they went back upstairs, but he didn't see his father and figured he had already left.

Jason told Lori she could meet his parents some other time, but the whole incident made him upset that it seemed to make Lori bothered the rest of the party and he couldn't believe that just his father's brief presence had managed to start an argument between himself and Lori.

The last thing he ever wanted was to have his parent's *argumentative aura* ever rub off on him, but somehow it managed to happen that night.

Since they'd been together, Jason had already taken Lori to Las Vegas to meet his friends, including Tom Casey, Victor Consuela, and Frank Reich, as well as having introduced her to all of his friends in Hollywood, but after that night at Hollywood Park, Lori was still bothered Jason had never introduced her to his parents.

Jason had already tried explaining the distant type of relationship he'd always had with his parents, and how as long as he could remember, they really never felt like a typical family. He explained he had gotten used to never having close family ties and had always considered himself closer to his friends than with his parents.

"That's terrible, and you shouldn't feel that way about them," Lori argued, "They're your only family."

"It's no big deal," Jason tried to explain lightly, "We still manage to get along without having any major arguments, as long as we keep our relationship businesslike, and don't try to pretend we're a family."

"Well, you need to start trying to have a closer relationship with them," she said, "It's not healthy not being close to your parents."

Jason didn't like being psychoanalyzed by Lori but didn't want to start arguing and tried to laugh it off.

"Well actually, I feel much healthier keeping my distance from them both," Jason lightly said, "Family life is way over-rated and usually seems to lead to problems, so the less close we are, the less chance there are for arguments."

Lori added that she'd had "plenty of arguments" with her parents when she was growing up but still loved them.

Jason just tried to sarcastically joke that he did "like his parents sometimes," but he never thought there was any "real gushy love" between them when he was younger.

"Well, I hope you don't start feeling that way about me," said Lori.

"Of course not, I love being close with you and my friends," he tried to laugh, "Just not my parents."

"That's why I've got so much love for you, baby," he continued to try and joke to Lori, "I've just been saving it all for you."

Lori didn't like what she called his "cavalier attitude" about his parents, and because Jason knew it would stop them from arguing, he did reluctantly agree to plan a meeting with his parents to introduce them over dinner in the next week or so.

Jason said he wasn't happy about it, but he'd do it for her.

&

It was two weeks after his party at Hollywood Park, and Jason was sitting uncomfortably in the private booth upstairs at *The Islander*, listening to Lori laughing and carrying on conversations with his parents. For the past year, it was rare when he'd be with both of his parents at the same time and most of his interactions with them had always been separate and mainly involved the business. It did seem whenever the three of them had been together, more times than not, it seemed his parents had been in a *silent treatment* mode with each other, and he didn't want anything like an argument to somehow start again that night.

Jason had introduced his parents to Lori by their first names Vi and Dick, as he normally had been doing for years, and actually couldn't even remember the last time he ever addressed them as Mom or Dad, but guessed it had been well before he moved to Las Vegas in 1969.

He wanted to appear he was having a good time as well, but he also knew it would be more bearable if he were a little medicated, so Jason decided to have a couple extra Coco-Loco's to help him relax and feel more at ease.

Although his parents thought they were telling funny and sarcastic stories that were making Lori laugh, Jason still was uncomfortable listening about how they were supposedly one big happy family when he was growing up.

His parent's kept sharing stories with Lori about when he was younger and how "little Jay" did this or "little Jay" did that which was the first time they had really discussed anything prior to 1969 in a very long time.

Jason tried laughing along with the stories, he really didn't like them, reminding Lori that it wasn't that long ago, and that they still seemed to talk and think of him as just "little Jay" that night. But Jason also felt that without his parents realizing it, some of the things they were trying to joke about had a negative tone, especially the way they mentioned, "All the money they spent" trying to show "little Jay" a good time when he was growing up.

"I put out good money paying for Jay's roller-skating lessons and traveling around to all the skate meets," his father tried to lightly say, "But he was too young to know how much it cost and always thought everything was just fun."

"But he did become a real good skater and won a lot of trophies," his father added, trying to sound more positive, "And all the little girls wanted to skate with him and be his partner because he was so good."

His father also told Lori about the time they took Jason to Las Vegas to see an atomic bomb go off and joked about how when they took him to go see Dean Martin in Las Vegas, "how wide Jay's eyes got" when he first saw topless dancers in that show.

"I'm sure Jay always remembered that night more than the atomic bomb," his mother joked, "And that was probably why he liked going to Las Vegas so much when he got older."

But Jason also noticed his mother was getting a little irritated when his father was talking about Jay's days as a roller-skater, and she quickly changed the subject.

His mother started joking about all the different things Jason tried doing when he was younger, like playing the clarinet, selling ice cream on his bicycle, and even playing football, but never really stuck with one thing too long, and how it also just ended up "costing money," because Jay got bored easily and was always was looking for some other adventure.

"But he was always ambitious and did work hard," his mother added, "Even when he was in high school, he worked two jobs and finally started earning his own money."

Jason was briefly glad his mother said something a little positive without talking about "how much he cost them" when he was young, but then she also tried to sarcastically joke how even though Jay once said he was going to be a lawyer and get into politics, she knew that when he went to college in Las Vegas, it would be too distracting for him to take seriously.

"And then after he dropped out college," Jason's mother continued to sarcastically joke to Lori, "First he was going to get into the casino business, then he was a taxi driver, and then out of nowhere, he told us he was going to become a rock star!"

Jason had never even discussed with his parents the reasons he'd tried so many different things during his time in Las Vegas and didn't like that she was making him sound like he had failed at everything he tried when he lived there.

"When Richard and I decided to start the Singles Register a few years ago, I knew that Jason always liked writing, so it seemed like a natural for him," Jason's mother said again, trying to sound positive, "And he also has natural promotion skills that have done very good things for the newspaper."

"He's done a great job as editor building up the Singles Register in the past two years," his father added, "And I think Jason has found his niche."

"At least he got that idea of trying to be a rock star out of his system," his mother half laughed, "He always liked singing, but I knew it wasn't the right career choice."

"Well, Jason still likes to sing, and we go to piano bars all the time," Lori cheerfully joined in, seemingly not even noticing the negative tone as much as Jason had, "I can't believe all the old songs Jason knows by heart, along with all the rock and roll songs we sing together when we're driving."

"Well, I taught him all those songs when he was still a little boy," his mother proudly said, "I always knew a lot of songs too, and would sing to him when he was a baby."

"And then we'd always sing songs when we'd drive across the country to his national roller-skating meets," his mother continued, almost boasting, "I taught Jason the words to all those songs, so that's where he got it all from."

Jason was glad they were at least now calling him by his right name, but even though he was trying not to show it, he was starting to getting irritated hearing his parents explain to Lori how they were responsible for everything in his life.

He had always tried to feel his real-life began in 1969 when he moved to Las Vegas and had mainly told Lori about his days there, but now his parents had brought up so many other things that night, Jason was beginning to feel like he had no secrets about himself to Lori anymore.

Jason had always told Lori that they were all partners in the Singles Register, but the way his father had described it, he made it sound like Jason was just working for them. Especially how his mother emphasized how "they" started the *Singles Register*, and almost made it sound like they rescued him from the wilderness of Las Vegas.

Jason thought that although his parents sometimes sounded like they were trying to build him up and be positive, they had a funny way of describing everything.

The four Coco-Loco's Jason had that night did seem to work, because they all made it through the next couple hours without an argument, and everyone acted happy when they left *The Islander*.

"See, that wasn't so bad, was it?" Lori smiled when they were back at Jason's apartment, "I thought your parents were great, and I don't know why you don't get along with them better."

"I thought it was a fun night, and I'm happy you finally introduced us," Lori added as she gave Jason an appreciative hug.

"Good," Jason said, still feeling uncomfortable, "I'm glad you all had a nice time."

Jason was relieved Lori didn't see the other side of his parents and was just glad that the night was over, but he felt even better after going into the bathroom and throwing up his entire dinner, mixed in with all the Coco Loco's he had guzzled down the past three hours.

He just hoped he wouldn't have to make Lori happy in that way again.

Chapter Nine

Gary Berwin was having a meeting with Jason and told him he had some bad news. He said that because of the *Yom Kippur War* that had recently started in the Middle East, and the oil embargo the Arab states had put on America for supporting Israel, everyone was getting concerned about an energy crisis. Gary said he was mainly worried about how that was going to affect his real estate business and other investments, and didn't think he would have time to concentrate on an *Artists and Models Ball* by New Year's Eve.

"There might be some major problems coming up in the next few months, and I don't think I should be worrying about a big party right now," said Gary, "I'm going to have to cancel the *Ball* for this year."

Jason was disappointed but had been following the news as well, and the oil embargo had even changed the conversation away from *Watergate* to the gasoline prices. Gas had jumped ten cents a gallon in just the past week and was now almost fifty cents a gallon.

"When do you think we can reschedule the *Artists and Models Ball* to then?" asked Jason, "I've been promoting it like crazy in the *Singles Register* and will have to write something to let the readers know."

"Well, if this thing doesn't get too bad, maybe we can have a big *Valentine's Ball* next February," said Gary, "Let's just play it by ear for the next month and see how things turn out."

Before he even left Gary's office, Jason was trying to figure out what to write in the newspaper to explain that the big *Singles Register* party he'd been promoting was postponed, but hopefully not canceled. His tie-in with the *Artists and Models Ball* had been getting the *Singles Register* a lot of good publicity, and he was worried about how it would affect the credibility of the newspaper.

Jason decided to sound optimistic and justify the cancelation by writing in his column, that because "Valentine's Day was a much more romantic date to have a Singles Register party," the producers were tentatively postponing their *Ball* at the *Beverly Hilton Hotel* until that date. But near Thanksgiving, Gary told Jason he was postponing the *Artists and Models Ball* indefinitely and said his other business interests were too important, and he may even discontinue the *Artists and Models Ball* altogether.

Jason was upset because not only had he been pushing an event heavily in the *Singles Register* that was now canceled, but because he let himself become involved in something that he had no decisions or control.

HIs father also did some yelling about how embarrassing it was going to be for himself, after having told all his newspaper distributers the *Singles Register* was the sponsor of that year's famous *Artists and Models Ball,* that it was now canceled. He was also upset because Jason had been depending so much on Gary to follow through on his end and produce the party, and said how bad it was going to look for the newspaper with nothing to show for all that work.

Besides trying to think of a way for himself and the *Singles Register* to save face for no longer being involved in a now canceled and possibly defunct *Artists and Models Ball,* Jason had been thinking of other ideas.

Gary Berwin did say he'd give Jason advice if he wanted to produce a separate Valentine's Day party for the *Singles Register* himself, but wouldn't be able to assist in any way financially, and didn't have time to help with any promotion.

Gary told Jason that he could still "make a lot of money" off his own party, and would give Jason his contacts at the *Beverly Hilton Hotel* if Jason decided to give it a try.

Jason knew without the name and reputation of *Artist and Models Ball,* the promotional benefits to the *Singles Register* were minimal. He also didn't like having to make his readers think that he wasn't going to follow through with something he'd promised them for months.

But he was also thinking about how Gary Berwin said he could still "make a lot of money."

Jason knew the additional benefits from all the trade outs and comps he generated for himself and, as a member of the press, made him appear to live like a millionaire, but two hundred and fifty dollars a week wasn't going to make him rich.

He never knew how much money his parents were making off the *Singles Register* because they never wanted to discuss what they considered "their part of the business," but he knew they had to be making a lot more than he was.

Since that one night at *The Islander,* Jason's relationship with his parents had gone back to being more businesslike, and there weren't any more personal stories they wanted to talk about together. But whenever Jason did try to talk about the "sharing in the profits" like they'd once promised, an argument would start, so he stopped talking about it whenever he saw them.

Jason had also been thinking about how his father always said the newspaper sales themselves were "just a *vehicle*" to make the *real money,* and how even Ricardo said Jason should find other ways to make money off of the newspaper.

He enjoyed his position as editor, but now was thinking about another *"vehicle"* for himself that might make at least a few extra bucks, and still be able to promote something to replace the *Artist and Models Ball* at the same time. Jason thought it was also something that he could do on his own without feeling that he was just working for his parents.

It was less than a week after Gary Berwin's news, when Jason was having dinner at *The Islander* with Lori and Stan Adams, talking about a new idea he had to start promoting his own version of the canceled *Artists and Models Ball.*

"I'm going to start a singles party club through the Singles Register," Jason explained to them, "Sort of like a Playboy Key Card but instead of my own Playboy Club, I'll have parties at different locations around town."

"Plus, it will give our readers and advertisers another way to meet other singles."

Jason explained that he could have his first party on the same date the *Artist and Models Ball* had been scheduled, and still advertise it as a big "Valentine's Ball," so he wouldn't have to cancel what he had been promoting.

"And then, if the first party goes over good, I can have some more singles parties at different nightclubs around town," Jason added with excitement, "Plus, more people would buy the Singles Register to see where the next parties will be."

Both Stan and Lori said they liked Jason's enthusiasm, but said the *Artist and Models Ball* had been a famous and established event for over ten years, and trying to fill the *International Ballroom* where the *Oscars, Golden Globe Awards,* and several other major events were produced, might be a "little too optimistic."

Stan mentioned that Jason should get some investors to help pay for the cost instead of trying to produce his own event by himself, but Jason continued explaining he'd learned some things about promoting the smaller parties at *The Comedy Store* and Hollywood Park, and said he wanted to try and produce his own *Valentine's Ball* without trying to ask anyone for money to invest.

Jason had seen so many so-called movie producers around town always trying to hustle money for some "independent movie" they said they were producing, and used to laugh to his friends that he never wanted to be in a situation like "those flakey old producers" when he was forty or fifty years old. He had never liked the idea of trying to get investors anyway and wasn't even sure if he knew how, but said he'd figured out how to make his Valentine's Ball, less of a gamble.

He told Lori and Stan he decided to rent the smaller *Grand Ballroom* at the *Beverly Hilton that* only held seven hundred and fifty people, and not even try to sell twenty-five hundred tickets as Gary did.

"It only costs a thousand bucks to rent the Grand Ballroom compared to thirty-five hundred for the International Ballroom," Jason explained, "And I figure it'll cost another two thousand for some promotion and entertainment."

"So, for less than what Gary would pay for just the rental, I can produce the entire Ball," Jason concluded confidently.

"I'm sure Gary spent a lot more money than that," said Stan, "But three thousand dollars is a still a lot of money, and do you even have that much to put out on trying something like this?"

"No, not yet," Jason smiled, "But hopefully I can sell at least three hundred tickets at ten dollars each through the Singles Register alone to cover the costs."

"And, I can probably still get quite a few celebrities from those two parties we've already had," said Jason. "They all like the publicity and seeing their pictures in the newspaper, so I'll just promise them a big photo layout from the party in the Singles Register."

Jason then told them the "great name" he came up with for his singles club that would make members feel like *celebrities* themselves when they came to his parties.

"I'm going to name the party membership club, *STARS!*" Jason excitedly said with flair as he spelled out the name "*S...T...A...R...S...*" and explained it was an acronym for the *"Singles Travel and Recreation Society."*

"The theme of my first party will be that *everybody is a star!*" Jason continued with a wave of his hand. "And I'll put a ten-dollar price tag on the membership card, but I'll give free memberships to everyone who buys a ticket to the first big *STARS* party at the Beverly Hilton."

Jason explained he thought of the name and the celebrity theme of his singles club, from title one of his favorite songs called *Everybody is a Star*, by Sly and the Family Stone.

"Leave it to you to think about something that comes from a song," laughed Lori, "But what's the deal with the *'travel'* part of the acronym?"

Jason said he needed a word to start with the letter *'T'* for his acronym, and he added *"Travel"* just in case he ever decided to have some junkets to places like Las Vegas or somewhere else, the way Ricardo Villasenor did with the *Las Vegas Star*.

"What the heck?" said Jason optimistically, "At least it may be something fun to try."

"Well, I'll try to help you any way I can," Stan Adams cautiously said, "But I hope you don't lose your ass on just *trying* something like this."

Jason knew more importantly than just *losing his ass*, he mainly wanted to follow through with what he had been promoting for the past several months and not lose any of the goodwill and credibility he'd been trying to build for the *Singles Register* and was confident that he'd found his *vehicle* for some extra money.

෨

In the over a year and a half, he'd been the editor of the *Singles Register*, Jason was able to have the newspaper's production run pretty much like clockwork every two weeks. He'd collect all the articles and columns from the different writers on the same deadline each issue, write his own column or copy while he was at the office, spend a day with Stan Adams or other photographers shooting that issues *Bachelorette of the Week*, and only have to spend the last four days before deadline overseeing and approving the layout and covers of each issue.

Jason figured he had all of his nights, and several days in between each issue, to work on promoting what he was now calling the *"Hearts and Flowers Ball."*

He knew that if he wanted to produce more parties in the future, it was important to fill the *Grand Ballroom* at the *Beverly Hilton Hotel* with as many people as possible, so it at least looked successful, and Jason decided a hundred or so comps would at least accomplish that goal.

Jason printed a hundred *"VIP"* membership cards for his *S.T.A.R.S* club to pass out free to friends and the attractive crowd he'd meet in his usual weekly routine of club-hopping and told everyone that those *"VIP Cards"* offered free admission to the *Hearts and Flowers Ball* for themselves and one guest.

His father was still upset that the *Singles Register* wouldn't be the co-sponsor of the *Artists and Models Ball*, and his mother thought Jason's idea for the *S.T.A.R.S Membership Club*, and trying to produce a party of his own, was what she kept telling him was a "stupid idea."

"Well, don't expect us to put any money into this and pay for it if it doesn't work out again," his mother bitterly said.

"I just wanted to follow through with a party to replace what we'd been promoting," Jason tried to calmly explain, "I'm just putting out a few bucks of my own money to try and keep our credibility intact, and it won't even cost that much."

Jason didn't want to let on that he'd taken just about everything out of his bank account to pay most of the expenses, and just wanted to sell enough tickets to get his money back, and hopefully make at least a small profit.

He had already tried to get some assistance from Gary Berwin but not as much as he had hoped. Gary had introduced Jason to a promoter named Michael O'Harro, who had promoted singles parties on the East Coast in the past, and Jason offered Michael half of his profits if Michael would be willing to help Jason with promotion.

Michael O'Harro also thought Jason "had a goldmine" with the *Singles Register* wished Jason luck, but could only offer some advice and not act as a co-producer with such short notice.

"You're a young guy, and I'm sure we'll figure out something to work on together in the future," Michael said, "But with less than two months to promote a big party like that, it sounds too tough this time around."

"Just make sure you invite a lot of *celebrities* to the party," said both Gary and Michael, "It adds legitimacy and gets you a lot of free press."

Jason decided to just produce his *Valentine's Ball* by himself and knew he only had about two months to get his *promoter chops* to work and also decided to follow the same promotional path as Gary and even have a *Queen of the Hearts* and *Flowers Ball Beauty Pageant*, where he would recruit contestants, have celebrity judges, and feature the contest at the *Ball* itself.

Most of the actresses and models he knew weren't interested in entering a beauty contest they'd never heard about, but Lori said she knew "a ton of pretty girls" from her job at *John Robert Powers* modeling school, and some at *Brooks Fashion College*, who she could have Jason talk to about entering the pageant.

Lori arranged a *celebrity* speaking engagement at both locations for Jason two weeks before Christmas and told her students that as "the editor and publisher of the largest singles newspaper in California," Jason was an expert on how to have both a relationship and career at the same time.

"*A little BS* never hurt anybody, right?" laughed Lori using Jason's occasional catchphrase, "And, it'll give you a chance to talk to a lot of girls about entering your beauty pageant.

Jason did prepare before speaking to the female students and actually surprised himself and Lori with how comfortable and knowledgeable he was and at least sounded like he knew what he was talking about. He also offered to put free personal ads in the *Singles Register* for the girls who didn't have boyfriends and told them it would build up their *self-esteem*, seeing how many men shared their interests and found them interesting.

"Not bad," teased Lori after his lecture, "You had me convinced you were a singles and relationship expert!"

"The world's a stage," joked Jason, "If I was able to convince audiences I was a rock star, then speaking in front of people as a *singles expert* is a piece of cake."

Jason was also satisfied he was able to recruit twelve students who agreed to enter his *Queen of the Hearts and Flowers Ball* beauty pageant.

He was glad he had Lori and other friends who at least were offering to help, and that's all Jason figured he needed.

By the end of 1973, Jason felt he was right on schedule, and spent New Year's Eve in Las Vegas with Lori at the new hotel that was built where the *Bonanza Hotel and Casino* once stood, the *MGM Grand*.

It was the grand opening week of the *MGM Grand*, and Jason and Lori celebrated the New Year in the *Ziegfeld Theatre* for an extravagant new production called *Hallelujah Hollywood*.

Jason was overwhelmed with the show and started realizing he could never hope to produce anything even a fraction as impressive as that show. He knew he probably couldn't even produce a party a fraction of what the *Artist and Models Ball* had done, but he was satisfied with what he had put together for his first production.

Jason's main focus was the entertainment that he would feature at his Ball to draw an audience.

He had occasionally stayed in contact with the booking agents he had worked with in *The Box Tops* but was unsuccessful in finding out whatever happened with Tommy and Alvin. But through those contacts, Jason negotiated with an agent named Steve Green and was able to book the famous 1950s band, *The Coasters*, for only five hundred dollars.

With *The Coasters* performing as the headliners, Jason also booked additional entertainment that would continue throughout the night including, a solo guitarist named Pete Wilcox he'd met at *The Troubadour* to perform early in the evening, an actress and *Bachelorette of the Week* named Cindy Daly, who would perform an exotic belly dancing act, and band named *Magic Grass* he met at the *Whiskey-a-Go-Go*, that would back up *The Coasters*, and play dance music throughout the entire party.

Jason knew his party wouldn't be as extravagant as the *Hallelujah Hollywood* show he saw that New Year's Eve at the *MGM*, or even previous *Artist and Model's Balls*, but he at least wanted it to be fun and with his entertainment now all set, Jason still had over six weeks to promote and sell tickets.

After the New Year's Eve celebration, when Jason and Lori were alone in their hotel room, she started singing the lyrics to a song she said was "stuck in her head" thanks to Jason's idea for his "S.T.A. R. S." singles club motto.

Lori softly sang a verse of *Everybody is a Star* as they were lying in bed and sharing a cigarette, after what Jason felt was his most romantic New Year's Eve ever.

That was another thing he loved about Lori, and what she said she also loved about him.

They even sang to each other in bed.

❧

Jason ended up keeping his entire budget close to the three thousand dollars he'd projected but didn't have anything left for advertising in other media except for the *Singles Register*.

He did send out press releases similar to the ones he received himself to at least get some free blurbs in the *LA Times*, *Herald Examiner*, and other local media, but Jason knew he'd mainly need to promote it heavily himself through word of mouth with his friends and contacts.

Jason had been optimistic he would sell out in advance, but by the week of the *Hearts and Flowers Ball*, he had only sold seventy tickets through the *Singles Register* and less than a hundred through his other contacts.

During the energy crisis for the past month, the long gas lines seemed to have everyone in a bad mood, and Jason was having a harder time getting people in the right mood for a party.

Stan and Lori were both telling Jason not to worry about it, and that most people just came "the night of the party" and paid at the door.

Jason appreciated that his friends encouraged him, but his mother saw the small amount of the tickets that came in the mail through the *Singles Register* and didn't hesitate to tell him that she always said, "what a stupid idea" Jason's S.T.A.R.S club was.

"Your Hearts and Flowers Ball is going to be a flop," his mother would say. "I told you not to blow your money on some stupid party."

She had never seemed to like any of his promotional ideas, even though she knew that the *Singles Register* was growing in circulation, subscriptions, and advertisers.

"It's been a real good promotion for the newspaper," Jason would argue, "And it's not going to be a flop!"

He was now even more motivated to prove her wrong.

Chapter Ten

"This party looks like a flop," said Sandi Shore, who was collecting admissions for the tickets outside the *Grand Ballroom*, "I've only taken in about four hundred dollars on the door so far."

"Don't worry," Jason tried to say with confidence, "It's only ten-thirty, and there should be some more people before *The Coasters* start at eleven o'clock."

"Well, if you hadn't let so many people in free, it would've been a lot better," Sandi lightly argued. "Most of the crowd in here are your friends or comps you gave out."

Even though he was only charging ten dollars at the door, compared to twenty-five as Gary Berwin usually did for the *Artist and Models Ball*, Jason had felt uncomfortable asking his friends to pay for tickets.

He was just glad that most of his friends did come to the party and brought guests that helped fill up the room, and saw the ballroom at least looked about seventy-five percent full.

Jason had already presented the *Queen of Hearts Beauty Pageant* earlier at the party and felt he'd arranged a good group of celebrity judges.

Dennis Cole, Alan Hale Jr., Edy Williams, Max Baer Jr, and Sammy Shore at least came early in the evening to be judges, and Jason had Bill Ballance act as the emcee.

Jason had decided to make his *Pageant* as simple as he remembered seeing Gary Berwin's *Queen of the Artist's* and *Models Ball* at Gazzarri's, and simply had the contestant's parade across the stage once in an evening gown while Bill Ballance read their name, astrological sign, and hobbies, and although Jason didn't think the beauty contest was that exciting, it had served his purpose.

Jason and Lori were mainly walking around and greeting the crowd, playing the party host and hostess, making sure that everyone received a current issue of the *Singles Register*. He decided that if he wasn't going to make money, he wanted to get whatever promotion he could for his newspaper.

Jason was happy that most of his friends and other acquaintances, Nicki Blair, Mark Marzouk, Ron Smith, Art Laboe, Hal Stone, Mike McInerney, Bill Gazzarri, and even Mario Maglieri from the *Rainbow Bar and Grill*, stopped by for an hour or so to at least show their support.

There were over a hundred people in the crowd Jason could tell came from the advertising in the *Singles Register*, because they were mainly well over forty years old and approaching the celebrities and asking for their autographs.

They seemed most excited to see Max Baer Jr, but Max hated being called *"Jethro"* after his *Beverly Hillbillies* character and would just respond to their questions about "How's Granny?" with a curt "She's *dead!*"

Stan Adams brought two guests, Alex Henig and Dave Curtin, and Jason reminded Alex they'd met a couple of times at *Nicky Blair's* restaurant and had once purchased tickets to a Rolling Stones concert from him.

Alex mentioned that he and Dave Curtain were opening a new private nightclub called *The Speakeasy* in West Hollywood, and suggested Jason should consider promoting singles parties at their new club, which "would cost a lot less" than the *Beverly Hilton*.

Jason figured he was at least making some good future contacts and was glad he had comp'd over a hundred people, because they brought some people who actually paid, and his party looked at least half impressive.

By the time *The Coasters* started their show at eleven o'clock, the dance floor was fairly full, and everyone was enjoying hearing the old classic hits like *Charley Brown*, *Poison Ivy*, and *Yakety-Yak*, but halfway through *The Coasters* concert set, Sandi Shore brought Jason the door receipts.

"Six Hundred and twenty dollars," Sandi said, "It looks like no one else is coming, so do you want me to keep working the front door?"

It was almost midnight, and Jason knew the party was almost over.

"No, it's okay," he said, "We'll just let anyone else who pops in for free, and it'll at least keep the party going a little longer."

The crowd started to thin out after *The Coasters* finished their show, and although he had contracted the dance band *Magic Grass* to play till one-thirty am, Jason told them they could just "call it a night" around twelve-thirty.

Jason and Lori stood by the front door thanking everyone as they exited and was happy to hear "great party" for the majority of those leaving.

"Let's get a drink," said Lori after most everyone had left, "It's not two am yet, and the bartenders are still here."

While they stood at the bar watching the band pack up their gear and exit themselves, the bartender also said it was a "great party."

"They drank good tonight," the bartender added, "We sold almost three thousand dollars on the bar, and the tips were pretty good."

Jason really didn't get satisfaction hearing "how great" the party was when he knew it was a financial loser for himself, but tried to sound enthused.

"Well, I'm glad at least somebody made money tonight," Jason half laughed, "It's too bad I wasn't selling booze instead of tickets."

It was after three am, and Jason was taking off his tuxedo in the complimentary suite the *Beverly Hilton* had given him that night and felt completely drained.

"Well, it wasn't the *party of the year*," Lori smiled as she took off Jason's bow tie,

"But I think everyone had a good time, and it at least looked successful."

"I think it was more fun doing the work leading up to it," said Jason, "Now that it's over, I'm not sure how I feel."

"You're not just a *publisher* anymore," laughed Lori. "Now, you can call yourself a *producer* too."

"Yeah, a big *producer*," Jason laughed sarcastically, "I was supposed to make at least a thousand, but I ended up losing about a thousand, and that's an expensive price to pay for another title."

"You put this whole thing together in less than three months," Lori tried to say with encouragement, "And you should be proud of yourself."

"It's hard to be proud of something that turns out losing money," said Jason, "I'm not even sure if it was worth the effort."

Jason then started to notice the song that was softly playing on the radio in their suite. It was the song that had been playing almost constantly on the radio for the past two months, *Goodbye Yellow Brick Road* by Elton John.

"Wow, listen to the song on the radio," Jason half laughed as he sang along with the lyrics about how he should have listened to *his old man* and *stayed on the farm*, which he actually associated more with his mother's attitude.

"How appropriate is that?" Jason smiled with sarcastic regret, "No *yellow brick road* for me tonight."

"You'll do better next time," said Lori giving him a hug," "At least you did what you said you were going to do and that's the important thing."

As Jason listened to the song as he looked at himself in the mirror, he suddenly told Lori he'd just made a major decision.

"I think I'm going to grow a beard and I think it'll make me look older," Jason said as he looked at his reflection in the mirror.

"Come on, that's so stereo-typical," laughed Lori, "People always seem to want to change their appearance when they've had some type of bad experience, so stop thinking that tonight was a flop!"

"No, it's not that and I just think I'm ready for a new look," Jason casually added, "After all, only the dead never change."

"Well, if you feel that's what you need, then I guess it's the right thing to do," Lori said trying to sound encouraging.

When they were lying in bed later, Lori started singing another verse from *Everybody is a Star* with the lyrics about loving someone for *who they were* and not about how someone felt they *needed to be*.

"There's something that's more important than having someone to share your success with," smiled Lori, "The most important thing is having someone to share your failures with."

Jason could tell Lori was in another one of her philosophical moods, but he was already thinking about another promotion that would help him recoup his losses.

He knew if he learned anything that night, it was that he didn't want to ever have to "share a failure" again.

§

Annie Gaybis had been performing on a USO tour overseas when Jason had his *Hearts and Flowers Ball* and wasn't able to attend, but she had become friends with Jason and Lori since they'd met at Hollywood Park the previous year.

Annie had even ended up moving into the same building as Jason, the *Park Sunset Plaza* and had become a part of Jason's regular circle of friends along with Lori, Stan Adams, Sandi Shore, Mark Marzouk, Bill Balance, Ron Smith, Art Laboe, Nicky Blair, Sammy Shore, Bill Gazzarri, and a few other photographers and members of the press.

Jason would usually always be with several of his friends at different times, and would also usually all have dinner at *The Islander, Nicki Blairs,* or some other restaurant where he had a trade-out at least once a week.

It was less than two weeks after the *Hearts and Flowers Ball* and Jason was celebrating what most thought was his twenty-sixth birthday with Lori, Annie, Stan Adams, Sandi Shore, and another actress named Mixie Thompson, who Annie had introduced Jason to as a possible *Bachelorette of the Week.*

Jason had already put Annie Gaybis on the cover as a *Bachelorette of the Week,* and Stan was arranging a good time to do a photo shoot with Mixie and Sandi Shore.

Besides always being a fun social gathering, they were also talking about ways to promote Jason's next possible party along with the *Singles Register.*

"I'm thinking of adding the word *'News'* to the title of the newspaper and calling it the *Singles News Register,*" said Jason, "I'm adding some more interesting topical stories that you'd see in a regular newspaper that might increase readership to a wider audience."

"We have to start getting some younger readers and advertisers," Jason continued, "The over forty crowd that came to the *Hearts and Flowers Ball* aren't going to be the type of crowd who are going to be coming to any *'Stars'* nightclub parties I'm planning on setting up at least once a month."

"Plus, we need to get away from that *'lonely hearts'* image and make the singles lifestyle more positive and fun," Jason also tried to emphasize.

They all agreed that it might be a good idea to even "give out half-priced, or even some free ads" to some of the younger crowd who came to any upcoming parties to have younger advertisers for dates in the newspaper.

"I can have forms for them to fill out at the front door," said Sandi Shore, "Plus, it'll give us more names for a mailing list for future parties."

"You should give out a free three-month subscription to the newspaper too", said Lori, "Then you can say everyone who comes to the parties get a door prize and people won't mind paying the cover charge if they get something for it."

"You've got to get your image as a producer and a publisher out there more," Annie suggested to Jason, "You're young and good looking, so keep pushing how great you personally think it is to advertise for dates."

"You should even tell them you met Lori through the paper," Stan then teased, "That'll get more people advertising!"

"Well, we did meet through the newspaper in a way," joked Lori, "Jason did try to pick me up by saying he was just looking for a bachelorette of the week."

"I was just thinking about using you as a bachelorette at the time," Jason lightly defended himself, "I thought you already had a boyfriend when we first met, remember?"

"Yeah, right," Lori added with a touch of sarcasm, "Like that was going to stop you."

"Well, as the editor and publisher of the upcoming *Singles News Register* always likes to say," joked Lori, raising her glass to make a toast, "A little BS never hurt anybody."

"I know Hugh Hefner has what he calls the *Playboy philosophy*," Annie Gaybis facetiously joked, "Is *a little bs* your new *singles* philosophy?"

"Okay, enough of the *BS* talk about business," Jason laughed along with their teasing, "Lori and I have something important to do, so let's all go over to the piano bar at *The Saloon* in Beverly Hills, and all sing some songs tonight."

Annie Gaybis also liked singing, and Jason and his friends would usually all end up at some piano bar during their nights they'd spend together.

Jason liked having a circle of friends that he could talk business and have fun with at the same time, knowing the circle could always keep growing with each new issue of his newspaper, and now, with each new party.

The new year may have started out rough for him, but Jason was confident that the rest of 1974 was going to be his best year yet.

Chapter Eleven

◇————————◇◇◇————————◇

The *Singles New Register*, as Jason had decided to slightly change the name of the newspaper, was now advertising on the cover as its catchphrase, "An Easy, Dignified Way to Meet Singles," and boldly highlighted the banner that read "Over *125,000* Singles Will See Your Ad" and everyone took it for granted that the newspaper was selling well over a hundred thousand issues every two weeks, which sounded very impressive.

After the newspapers were printed, they never came to the office but always to another distribution location that his father would load on trucks to deliver to the distributors. Jason never knew how many issues were actually printed, and would only receive a bundle of fifty copies for himself, to show his own business contacts.

Whenever Jason had tried to talk to his parents about the distribution, they always said it was something "that they handled" and to just concern himself with the "physical production and promotion" of the newspaper. Jason was still fine with that and always figured it was better not to have to spend more time with his parents talking business anyway.

He had run a two-page layout with photos in the newspaper about the *Hearts and Flowers Ball*, which made it appear like a huge success, and many people had become impressed that Jason and the *Singles News Register* had produced such a prestigious event.

Jason was at *McInerney's* handing out a few copies of the newspaper when he was also introduced to someone Mike McInerney said had been wanting to meet Jason.

His name was Steve Powers who explained he was an investor and was impressed with seeing how fast his newspaper had grown, and how it seemed to be in news racks everywhere.

Steve said he had been thinking about getting into publishing himself and was also best friends with Hugh Hefner, who had offered to assist him if he did find a newspaper to buy.

"Is the over hundred thousand circulation figures for your newspaper verified with the *ABC*?" asked Steve, "Because if it is, I could make you a very lucrative offer if you'd be interested in selling."

Jason wasn't familiar with what the *ABC* even was, but didn't want to sound clueless, and just said the "hundred thousand" number was accurate.

Steve seemed very impressed and said he'd like to invite Jason to the "Playboy Mansion" and talk business sometime.

They exchanged business cards, and Jason just told Steve he'd be in touch and would think about it.

A couple of days later, Jason decided to ask his father about what the *ABC* was and told him about his discussions with Steve Powers.

His father explained that the *ABC* was the *Audit Bureau of Circulation*, and was mainly needed to certify to national advertisers, that the claimed circulation of newspapers was accurate, and that the *ABC* audit mainly was needed for setting advertising rates for most publications. He told Jason that the newspaper wasn't "ABC audited yet" and that the figures mentioned on the cover were based on readership and not its actual circulation.

Jason's father also explained they could advertise over a hundred thousand readers because for a bi-weekly newspaper, they could claim that several people would read one issue when it was purchased, and then be passed around to their friends during those two weeks.

Jason knew the distribution was strategically spread around over a wide area, but he discovered the circulation appeared much larger than the actual number of the issues that were printed.

His father didn't volunteer the actual numbers that he printed each issue but did say the circulation was increasing each issue, with the number of news racks he was now selling and just said "not to be concerned" with anyone offering to buy the *Singles News Register*, and not to bother even mentioning to anyone that it wasn't *ABC* audited.

"Oh, and by the way," Jason's father added cheerfully changing the subject, "A couple of my distributors went to your party and said they had a good time."

"I know you didn't make as much money as you hoped," he added, "But I think it's great that you at least pulled it off, and I think you deserve something for that."

"So, I'm going to up your pay to three hundred dollars a week to help make up for some of your losses," his father casually concluded, "And keep up the good work, you're doing a great job."

Jason was disappointed the circulation wasn't as large as he thought, but also knew that information didn't need to be shared with anyone he knew or did business with.

Everyone was impressed thinking the newspaper sounded like it sold a hundred thousand copies each issue, and he just figured his motto of "A little *BS* never hurt anyone" should just be kept to himself.

He was going to just concentrate on constantly finding new ways of improving the newspaper readership, and eventually have a real *ABC* audit he could show, and not feel he had to BS anyone.

Jason called Steve Powers a couple of days later and explained that he wasn't interested in selling, but wished him luck in finding another publication to buy.

Steve wished Jason luck as well and said if he ever changed his mind, he'd be welcome at "The Mansion" any time to talk business.

Jason was a little disappointed he wasn't going to be invited to the Playboy Mansion and have the chance to meet Hugh Hefner, but he wasn't disappointed in the additional fifty dollars a week he'd now be earning.

He suddenly decided the *Hearts and Flowers Ball* had been somewhat successful after all.

❧

Jason was having breakfast with Bill Ballance at the *Old World* restaurant on Sunset Boulevard, talking about being a guest on Bill's radio show, *The Feminine Forum*.

"People are starting to know your name around town with all the running around you do," laughed Bill, "Radio exposure will be good for both you and your paper, plus anything to do with singles is a hot topic right now."

"I get some crazy women who call my show every day," Bill continued, "and we can talk about some funny things you've heard or seen, from some of the people who need to advertise for dates."

"I don't want to talk about anything that would make it sound like the people who advertise as being *hard up*," said Jason, "Let's just talk out how fun it is staying single and dating lots of different people until they find the perfect match."

Jason didn't want to say anything negative about the people who advertised but was still always trying to push for the younger and hip crowd, to get away from the *lonely-hearts* image of advertisers looking for dates.

"Well, we can probably talk about that in a humorous kind of way with innuendoes," laughed Bill, "But a lotta women who call my show just sound like they could use a *stiff dick* and want to how to get one."

"I definitely don't want it to come across like a swinging singles publication," Jason reminded Bill Ballance, "I just want the listeners that it can actually be positive in some ways, to spend time *volume dating* for a while before actually finding the right mate."

"It can also be *therapeutic* in some ways too," Jason continued trying to put a light but positive spin about advertising for dates.

"After a woman goes through a breakup or divorce, they're usually pretty dejected after feeling they've been dumped," Jason said, "If they put an ad in my newspaper, they can get dozens of letters from men who are interested in meeting them after seeing them describe themselves in the ad."

340

"And, when those women see that there's a lotta men who want to meet and go out with them," Jason added with slightly facetious certainty, "It makes them feel *hot and desirable* again, and helps builds up their self-confidence."

"Okay, *Mister Singles Expert*," laughed Bill, "But you know all they really want is the *stiff dick*!"

"We also need to talk about my next *'Stars'* party at the Speakeasy," added Jason changing the subject, "After all, you're going to be the emcee again in my new 'Bachelorette of the Month' contest."

Jason had first noticed how nightclubs were changing the last time he was in Las Vegas with Lori, when Victor Consuela had taken them to a nightclub called *Billy Jack's* and instead of hearing a live band performing that night, he saw that everyone was just dancing to records the DJ was spinning. He was surprised how packed *Billy Jack's* was without having musicians for entertainment, but since then, many of the nightclubs in Beverly Hills, including *The Speakeasy*, had also switched from featuring live bands to DJ's spinning what was becoming known as *Disco* music.

Jason had already met with Alex Henig and Dave Curtain, the owners of *The Speakeasy*, and arranged to have his next singles parties at their disco and felt having a *S.T.A.R.S.* party at an exclusive private membership nightclub in Hollywood, where singles could attend without having to pay for a membership, would be a great draw, not only for his *S.T.A.R.S.* members, but for others he could invite from his regular nights of club-hopping.

But this time, he wanted to make sure he made some profit off his promotional efforts.

In exchange for writing blurbs and including pictures from each party in his newspaper, Jason negotiated no rental fee, along with keeping the entire door charge for himself, as well as VIP memberships for both himself and Stan Adams, who Jason said was going to be the "*official* photographer" of all of Jason's *S.T.A.R.S.* parties.

Jason pitched Alex on the idea that the big draw at his party without having a band would be a "new and exciting beauty pageant" called *The Bachelorette of the Month Contest* with celebrity judges, and assured Alex that dozens of beautiful actresses and models would be entering the contest for the chance of being a cover girl on the next *Singles News Register*, as he had now titled his newspaper.

"That'll draw both guys and girls to the party," Jason had explained to both Alex and Dave Curtin, "And I'll have some other *singles mixers* to give it a *party feel* and not just another night at the disco."

Alex and Dave also agreed that if Jason's first-party went well and was profitable for both of them, it might turn into a regular monthly feature at *The Speakeasy*.

Jason's first parties wouldn't begin until May, which was still almost three months away, so he knew as much free publicity he could get like his upcoming appearance on the Bill Ballance radio show, would not only be good for the *Singles News Register* but his *S.T.A.R.S* parties as well.

After his thirty minutes of air time on Bill Balance's *Feminine Forum* radio show a few days after their meeting at the *Old World Restaurant*, Jason saw it was the best publicity he'd received yet. The girls in the newspaper office said they'd received over fifty phone calls and sold over two dozen subscriptions, and even some personal ads, from people who said they heard Jason on the radio.

And, some of Jason's friends who heard the radio show also said the familiar phrase he'd heard since he was very young.

They all said Jason was starting to get *famous* in Hollywood as well.

❧

"Jason, meet Rudy Vallee," said Sidney Skolsky as Jason was having his usual twice a month lunch with Sidney at *Schwab's Drug Store*.

"Rudy reads my column in each issue of the Singles News Register, and I mentioned to him that you're adding some more serious news columns in your paper," Sidney added, "So Rudy said that might be something he's interested."

"I'd like to write a political column called One Man's Opinion," said Rudy, "There's a lot of things about this *'Energy Crisis'* and all of this *'Watergate'* stuff that I'd like to write about in a regular column."

Jason was very familiar with who Rudy Vallee was but never thought of him as a political writer, and mainly remembered that although he wasn't as famous as Al Jolson, he was a big recording star back in the 1920s and '30s and was also said to have been considered the first teen idol in those days.

Even though Rudy Vallee was old enough to be Jason's grandfather now, he was still a legend that everyone knew from *old Hollywood*, and Jason knew it would look great to have another famous writer in the newspaper.

"Rudy was the first one to record that song that you said you and your girlfriend like to sing," Sidney added to Jason, "You did mention you both like to sing *As Time Goes By*, right?"

"I actually had a small hit with *As Time Goes By* ten years before it was even featured in *Casablanca*," Rudy smiled, "But after the song became so popular from being played so often in the movie, my record was re-released, and it went straight to number one in the country."

"There's probably a lot of other songs that you sing in the piano bars that Rudy originally recorded back in the 1920s," Sidney added.

"Sidney also explained to me about your policy of not paying any writers, and I'm fine with that," continued Rudy getting back to talking about his proposed column, "I have plenty of money and would be happy to write my column gratis."

Jason told him he'd be happy to look at something Rudy wrote and would "strongly consider" adding him as a regular columnist. Jason didn't want to come across like Rudy was *doing him a favor* and wanted to show his own serious "editor chops" by letting him know he needed to be convinced that Rudy was a good writer.

"I'll have something for you to review in two weeks," said Rudy before adding, "Oh, and by the way, Sidney tells me that you are a huge George Gershwin fan, is that right?"

Jason told him he loved Gershwin music and had since he was very young.

"I probably know almost every note and lyric to just about every Gershwin tune," Jason said, knowing it was probably true.

"Well, you know, I've been friends with Ira Gershwin for over fifty years," Rudy smiled, "And if you are interested, I could take you over to his house on Roxbury Drive sometime to meet him."

Jason immediately thought if Rudy was trying to bribe him with a reason to let him write a column, he had succeeded without having to say anything else. He knew the opportunity to meet the man who wrote the lyrics to his all-time favorite songs, and just the idea of meeting an actual *"Gershwin,"* would be one of the highlights of his life.

Rudy said he'd arrange a meeting sometime in the next two weeks, and Jason could "review his column" at the same time.

"By the way," smiled Sidney as Jason was leaving the meeting, "I like your new beard, and it gives you a more distinguished look."

Jason liked that he was getting compliments on his new beard that was growing out, but all he could think about were the dozens of Gershwin songs that were suddenly playing in his head.

Although he had always tried to act mature and not to act starstruck with all the celebrities he'd meet, Jason suddenly felt like a little kid inside.

It was less than two weeks later, and Rudy Vallee had kept his promise.

"It's nice to meet someone your age who still appreciates the old music", said Ira Gershwin as Jason shook his hand and sat down on the couch across from him.

Jason didn't want to come across like a *groupie* but just wanted to let Ira know how much the music had meant to him.

"Gershwin music old?" Jason tried to explain as a compliment, "The first time someone hears it, it's never out of their head."

"I first time I heard Gershwin music was when I was very young," said Jason, "I used to roller skate in competitions, and a couple of girls I knew did skating routines to *Rhapsody in Blue* and parts of *Porgy and Bess."*

"Then, after my mother started teaching me other Gershwin songs, with all of your great lyrics, I was hooked," Jason tried to compliment Ira.

"That's funny you mentioned you used to be in roller skating competitions," smiled Ira, "When we were kids, *Georgie* was known as the best roller skater in our neighborhood."

Jason continued to explain how he would spend hours in the listening booths at *Wallichs Music City*, and listen to almost every Gershwin album in the store until he learned the words to most of the songs.

"I probably know every lyric to *Porgy and Bess* as well," Jason added by trying to prove his point by lightly singing the opening lyrics to a minor song from *Porgy and Bess* called *A Red Headed Woman*. That song had slightly suggestive lyrics about how a red headed woman could make a *choo-choo train "jump its tracks,"* which made Ira laugh and joke that he *believed* Jason.

Ira then mentioned how some of his lyrics were considered "a little racy back in those days," and he and *Georgie* always had to worry about censors.

"You should have heard some of the lyrics I wrote that couldn't be published," Ira smiled.

Jason talked about at least a dozen songs that Ira had written with George and loved hearing every story that Ira was telling about who he kept calling *"Georgie."*

Rudy Vallee, who'd driven with Jason to Ira's house, would also include a story or two about George Gershwin, but mainly let Jason and Ira talk together.

After about a half-hour, Ira asked Jason more about himself.

"So, Rudy told me you're an editor of a newspaper for singles?" asked Ira, "Well, that would have been right up Georgie's alley, because he was the consummate bachelor and never talked about getting married."

"George loved women," Rudy smiled, "He was definitely considered a single playboy himself back then."

"You know, I know it's not proper to say," Ira lightly added, "But with Georgie passing away so young, I secretly hoped that because of all the women he was with, one of them would have come forward with a 'love child' that could have been his heir."

"My wife Leonore and I never had children of our own," Ira wistfully said, "and I would have loved to have seen a niece or nephew of Georgie's to carry on his name."

"There were rumors," Rudy Vallee joked, "But they were nothing more than the same rumors about *Anastasia* still being alive."

Jason loved talking *"Gershwin"* for over an hour but had one last question he wanted to ask Ira before he left the house that day.

"I've seen the movie *Rhapsody in Blue* on TV at least five times," said Jason, "And I always wondered about one thing in that movie."

"There's a dog that George has in the movie that's mentioned quite often," asked

Jason, "Did George really have a dog named *Tinker?*"

"Ah *Tinker*," laughed Ira, "Yup, that was a real dog. George had a few dogs, but Tinker was his favorite."

"Real sweet dog," Rudy also smiled, saying he remembered George's dog as well.

Jason was even more amazed thinking about the coincidences of George Gershwin being a roller-skater when he was young and having a dog named Tinker.

He loved that he had something in common with George Gershwin besides just loving his music.

Chapter Twelve

Lori had continued living with her father in Palos Verdes during the year they'd been together, and although Jason would occasionally pick her up there, she mainly would drive to Hollywood in her Toyota Celica for their dates.

They would continue frequenting most music clubs like the *Whiskey-A-Go-Go*, the *Roxy*, *Filthy McNasty's*, and *The Palomino* in North Hollywood, but they usually never missed the Tuesday night openings at *The Troubadour* and was always the highlight of their weekly entertainment.

Every week was a major recording act, and Jason and Lori had seen everyone from Jim Croce, Don Mclean, Bill Withers, Steve Martin, and Kris Kristofferson, to The Byrds, Billy Joel, Randy Newman, Harry Chapin, and Jimmy Buffett.

Jason and Lori were at *The Troubadour* for the opening night of *The Smothers Brothers*, less than a month after the *Hearts and Flowers Ball*, and noticed that only a couple tables from where they were sitting were Harry Nilsson and John Lennon.

Jason and Lori had already met Harry Nilsson just a week earlier, when they happened to end up having cocktails with Harry and Micky Dolez of The Monkees, at a bar called *Café Brasseri* on Sunset Boulevard.

Lori was dressed especially sexy that night at the *Café Brasseri*, and both Micky and Harry invited both Jason and Lori to join them in their booth.

On that night, after they all became acquainted, instead of talking about music, Micky Dolez seemed more interested in talking about everyone's latest obsession with astrology and other philosophies. But besides talking about the usual astrology beliefs that had everyone asking "What's your sign?' before even asking a person's name, Jason was amused listening to Micky semi-seriously explain why he and Jason's mutual astrological sign Pisces, was the most brilliant and important sign in the zodiac.

"We're the last sign of the zodiac and have already been here eleven times before," Micky tried to explain seriously, "So we need to use what we've learned in those previous lives and become enlightened in this life, or we need to start over again at Aries and go around twelve more times!"

They all also began talking about the current trendy and supposed meaningful philosophy called *E.S.T. Therapy*.

Jason had heard so many different and supposedly trendy philosophies in the past, from how the hippies he met in Hollywood would talk about *Nietzsche*, *Descartes*, or the *I Ching*, to the different philosophers Jason studied in college. But *EST Therapy* had been what Micky Dolez kept explaining was what everyone now claimed was the true answer to bring complete personal enlightenment.

The acronym *E.S.T.* stood for *Erhard Seminars Training*, and was created by a so called *"Guru"* named Werner Erhard, whom Jason had once talked with on the phone.

Jason thought that interviewing Erhard, while attending one of the group's *E.S.T.* sessions, would make a great story for the *Singles Register*. But both Jason and Lori had also heard what sounded like horror stories, from some people they knew who attended those sessions.

Those people had explained how they were all locked in a room together for fifteen hours a session, and besides not being allowed to use the bathroom, with many just urinating or defecating on themselves, they were screamed at for hours by the "Guru's," and were all encouraged to shout, scream, and even cry about their past lives.

Jason and Lori both laughed and agreed it sounded more like *brainwashing* sessions than anything *enlightening* after Jason told Micky he decided to pass on any interview or story and wasn't interested in that kind of therapy.

"A lot of people need that kind of stuff to find themselves," Micky said, "And I'm still considering taking that kind of therapy myself."

"We have to find the answers within ourselves without depending on someone else to give us the answers," Lori lightly argued back, wanting to give her own philosophical take, "There are a lot of other experts who say you only need to think for yourself and make your own decisions to find your true destiny."

Once again, Jason knew that he agreed with Lori completely, but they did both try to take what they called their own *"dime-store philosophies"* with a grain of salt, and not try and be *too deep*.

"Well, my destiny is to have another round of drinks right now," Harry Nilsson joined in that night, obviously not enjoying the discussions about different philosophies. But they did have a chance to talk about music at least briefly between those other deeper discussions.

Jason and Lori both told Harry how much they liked his latest album of song standards from the 1920s and 1930s, and joked about how they regularly sang some of those same songs *It Had to Be You*, *As Time Goes by* and *I Wonder Who's Kissing Her Now* in piano bars, and might record an album of those types of songs themselves someday.

It was also obvious that Harry Nilsson was pretty drunk, but he at least he had been a funny and entertaining drunk and kept everyone at their table laughing for the entire time they together that evening at the *Café Brasseri*. But that current night, when Jason and Lori were at *The Troubadour*, they both saw Harry Nilsson and John Lennon were obnoxiously drunk and had been heckling The Smothers Brothers continuously while they were trying to perform their act.

347

Jason thought it was funny, but at the same time surprising, how the audience was angrily booing Nilsson and Lennon, and then cheered with approval when they were both forcibly ejected from the bar.

"Wow, people cheering at John Lennon getting thrown out of the Troubadour," Jason sarcastically joked to Lori, "I guess he's definitely not *'more popular than Jesus'* these days."

"Imagine that!" Lori also joked about John Lennon's apparent fall from grace that night.

They were both a little disappointed that Harry Nilsson was too drunk for them to approach him that night because they both thought it would have been great meeting John Lennon.

The Troubadour was only one Jason and Lori's usual weekly stops, or as they often joked, "the usual *Chasin' with Jason* night out on the town."

There was also a new nightclub next to *The Rainbow* that recently opened called *The Roxy*, where Jason and Lori had seen Neil Young, as well as the band *Genesis*, perform in an intimate setting,

Jason called Lori a few days after that crazy night at *The Troubadour*, to tell her about the press invitation he'd received to attend another opening night show.

"The press release said it's a 1950's rock and roll science fiction musical", Jason told her, "It's called *The Rocky Horror Show*."

"I don't recognize any of the actor's names in the show," Jason added, "But Mario Maglieri from the Rainbow said it's something we shouldn't miss."

Jason and Lori were sitting in the front row at *The Roxy*, which was usually reserved for the press, and enjoying the complimentary cocktails that were always included.

Jason whispered to Lori, "How lame and dumb" *The Rocky Horror Show* seemed to be during the first ten or fifteen minutes, but then the show's main star appeared on stage, singing a song called *Sweet Transvestite*.

The actor, Tim Curry, then opened his cape and was even dressed as a transvestite himself as the entire audience began laughing hysterically. With Curry bumping and grinding only a few feet from where Jason and Lori were sitting, they both just looked at each other with shocked and surprised expressions.

"Oh my God!", laughed Lori to Jason, "You didn't tell me this show was X-Rated!"

They both realized that this *science fiction* musical was starting to get better.

Jason and Lori were both transfixed with the entire musical for the next ninety minutes and were exhausted from laughing and applauding by the time *The Rocky Horror Show* ended.

They were both still laughing as they walked down Sunset Boulevard after the show, and Lori was humming and singing some lyrics to one of the musical's closing songs.

"Don't dream it….be-eee it…," she kept singing lightly, *"Don't dream it….be-eee it…"*

"Those damn songs are still stuck in my head," Lori laughed.

"That had to be the craziest fucking thing I've ever seen," Jason was also laughing. "I can't believe something that *kinky* could play at the Roxy!"

"We've gotta come and see it again!" laughed Lori, "We'll bring Annie and Stan next time, because they won't believe something like this unless they see it themselves."

When Lori mentioned Stan Adams, it reminded Jason about a message he'd gotten earlier in the day.

"Stan said they're having a 'celebrity streaker' party over at the Speakeasy tonight," Jason lightly mentioned, "It's still early so let's just go there and tell him about this show."

"We may as well go see some more kinky stuff," laughed Lori, "I know streaking is the new fad, but what celebrity is supposed to streak tonight?"

"I don't know, Stan just said Alex Henig had someone famous coming," Jason said, "But there should be a big crowd so we can hand out some invitations to my party while we're there."

Jason's first *S.T.A.R.S.* party was still more than a month away, but he wanted to make sure it was a success and had already been passing out flyers and invitations everywhere he went.

The *Speakeasy* was packed to the limit when Jason and Lori walked in, and they immediately saw Stan Adams standing with his camera around his neck, apparently preparing to be ready to take pictures of the celebrity streaker.

"You won't believe this crazy and kinky show we just saw," Lori excitedly started explaining *The Rocky Horror Show* to Stan, "You've got to come see it with us sometime."

They all were standing alone together, laughing and talking about some of the sexy songs and scenes they had just witnessed when Alex Henig came over with a worried look on his face.

"I can't believe it!" Alex complained, "I had this TV star who was supposed to be here to streak, and he hasn't shown up yet."

"I have this place packed tonight," Alex added with a concerned tone, "My big *streaking party*, without a *streaker*, won't look too good for me."

"Well, Alex," teased Jason, "You'd better start getting ready to take off your clothes."

"That wouldn't be a pretty sight," Alex half laughed, "I even tried offering some people I know a hundred dollars just for a quick streak, but nobody has the guts."

"There you go, Jason!" joked Stan, "There's a quick way to make an easy hundred bucks."

Jason just laughed and said he'd have to be "a lot drunker" to do something that crazy as Alex just said he was going to keep looking for someone who would take him up on his offer as he walked away.

There was a back bar in a small area, and that was used as a banquet room that wasn't as packed as the main room of the nightclub, so Jason sat at that bar with Stan and Lori.

Both Jason and Lori still had a buzz from the comp'd cocktails at *The Roxy*, and because it wasn't a deadline week at the newspaper, he didn't need to be at the office the next day, so they decided to "keep the party going" and ordered some more drinks.

"That show tonight looked like it was so much fun to be part of performing," half laughed Lori, "It almost got me wanting to go onstage with them and join in singing."

Jason laughed as well and said he felt like that when he saw *Hair* for the first time in Las Vegas.

"But this show was a lot wilder than *Hair*," added Jason, "And I'm sure it got the entire audience in a pretty kinky mood tonight."

"Don't dream it," Lori lightly started singing one of the songs from the show again, *"Be-eee it…"*

"If you're both in a kinky mood," Stan joked, "Then you both should streak tonight."

"I know it sounds crazy, but I'd probably do it tonight if Jason would," Lori smiled half seriously, "I mean, everyone is streaking these days, and it's really not that big of a deal."

They were all laughing about it being a silly idea, but after another drink, they wondered "how much it would be worth" to Alex to have two streakers that night.

When they saw Alex still walking around and looking nervous, Jason joked to Stan and Lori that he was going to make a crazy offer he knew Alex wouldn't accept.

"How would you like to have two streakers tonight?" Jason half teased to Alex, "Besides the hundred bucks each, what else would it be worth to have both me and Lori streak?"

Alex's face lit up, and said it would "save my night" and how he'd "be indebted" to Jason if he was really serious.

"Okay, my parties are starting here in May, and besides the door money," said Jason trying not to sound drunk, "I also want twenty percent of how much you make on the booze those nights."

Jason remembered how much money the bartenders said they made the night of the *Hearts and Flowers Ball* and decided to see how desperate Alex really was to have streakers that night.

He was surprised when Alex took him seriously and said he had to go talk to Dave Curtin and see if he'd agree as well.

"We'll give you ten percent," said Alex when he came back to where they were sitting.

"Give me fifteen percent, and we'll do it!" Jason counter-offered.

Jason was only half-serious when he told Alex they would streak, but now that Alex had called his bluff and told Jason "He had a deal," he knew it was too late to back out.

It was only ten minutes later and Jason and Lori were both giggling like school kids while they were undressing in the private bathroom in Alex's office.

"I can't believe we're doing this," giggled Lori, "Here we are always trying to act mature and sophisticated in public, and here we are acting like kids."

Jason and Lori had both worn hats that night and decided to pull them as far down as they could over their heads, hoping their faces wouldn't be recognizable when they ran through the crowd naked.

"I'm worried about someone seeing this mole on my tit," said Lori as she took off her top, which Jason thought was funny because it was such a small mole, she was the only one who ever noticed it.

"They're not going to be looking at your mole," he smiled to Lori, "I can assure you of that."

Jason also gladly accepted Lori's offer to give him "a little head" while they were waiting in the bathroom so he wouldn't appear to be at "half-staff," as they both joked, while running naked through the packed crowd at *The Speakeasy*.

"The world's a stage so we may as well look our best," Jason teased Lori with the Shakespeare quote again as she was on her knees, helping prepare him to look "more impressive" while they streaked.

Alex Henig had arranged to let the audience know the "Streakers were coming" by having an employee who looked like he was at least seventy years old, run through the nightclub wearing only baggy boxer shorts, and blowing a loud whistle that would signal it was time for Jason and Lori to begin streaking.

Before Jason and Lori could even consider *chickening out*, the bathroom door opened, and the old man started running toward the main nightclub area, loudly blowing his whistle, and they both started running behind him.

Lori had a tight hold on Jason's hand as she led them both naked through the nightclub while the DJ had a song blasting called *Jungle Boogie* by Kool and the Gang, which Jason thought was a weird choice, but between the music and the old man's whistle, he didn't think about it for long.

The entire streak took less than a minute as they zig-zagged through the screaming and cheering crowd, and before they both knew it, they were back in the privacy of the bathroom, still hilariously giggling that they'd actually done it.

They heard Stan knocking on the bathroom door and halfway covered up before letting him in.

"That was OUTTA SIGHT!" Stan was laughing, "Let me get a quick picture of you two."

They both covered up their *vital areas* and let Stan take the picture.

"Did you get pictures of us running through the crowd?" laughed Lori, "I've love to have some photos to remember this by."

"It happened too quick," said Stan, "I tried, but you guys were running so fast, I didn't have a chance."

"Damn," laughed Jason, "It would have been fun to have a picture we could at least have for ourselves to remember this night."

Jason and Lori looked at each other and knew they were both thinking the same thing.

"Okay, Stan, get the old man and have him bring his whistle back here," said Jason, "And this time, get pictures cause we're going to do it again!"

Sometimes, when Jason forgot he wasn't really twenty-six years old and occasionally slipped and acted his real age, he'd always justify it to himself by remembering that he would only be young once.

Or, as the popular song by *Seals and Crofts* was titled, and the song Jason and Lori would often sing together, *We May Never Pass This Way Again.*

Chapter Thirteen

Jason and Lori were in Stan's darkroom at his Sylmar home before noon the next day, and even though they both said they had the worst hangovers they could ever remember, they wanted to make sure no one saw the photos before they did from the night before.

"Oh my God!" laughed Lori, "Look at your dick swinging sideways in that picture!"

They were watching the various photos develop in the water trays as they began to materialize, and Stan pulled them out to dry.

"Okay," laughed Jason, "I think we need to crop that photo."

"You're kidding!" said Lori, "Your dick looks great in that picture."

"Well, you did have a little something to do with it looking that way," Jason teased Lori without being descriptive enough for Stan to understand.

"If you ever want to advertise what you have," she laughed, "You should be happy to show that photo."

"I don't think so," Jason laughed back, "Crop that one, Stan."

He was still a little embarrassed about the night before and knew as little evidence as possible about the *more graphic* photos, the better.

"That was a once in a lifetime event last night," laughed Stan, "You should want to have something to remember it by."

Lori did talk him into keeping at least two *full-frontal* shots that she wanted for herself, but Jason made sure the others were cropped and also made sure Stan gave him the negatives after developing a few personal photos that he and Lori said they'd never show anyone else.

"I don't want these pictures floating around for anyone to see," laughed Jason. "We keep these in the vault."

"In the vault," said Lori, "These are for our eyes only."

A few days later, Jason and Lori were sitting in the Polo Lounge at the Beverly Hills Hotel, having lunch with Annie Gaybis and Jim Bacon, the Hollywood columnist for the *Herald Examiner*.

"I can't believe you two streaked," laughed Annie, "and at the Speakeasy no less!"

"We were drunk," Jason tried to joke, "and we'd just seen the Rocky Horror Show, and that must have got us in a crazy frame of mind."

"But Jason got Alex and Dave to pay him more money for his parties," Lori said, trying making it sound more positive, "So it actually worked out pretty good."

"Jason's going to start having singles parties every month at the Speakeasy, that new private nightclub," Annie said to Jim Bacon, "You should come to his first party, and there should be a lot of people that you can write about in your column."

"You know me," said Jim, "I always like a good party."

Jason had met Jim Bacon through Annie and had been a fan of his daily entertainment column in the *Herald Examiner* for as long as he could remember. He was happy that they had become friends and enjoyed the dozens of stories Jim would tell about *"old Hollywood"* and his adventures with Howard Hughes, Humphrey Bogart, Errol Flynn, Marilyn Monroe, and just about every other Hollywood legend.

"It'll be great to put some blurbs in your column about my *S.T.A.R.S* parties," said Jason, "I always like getting the name of the Singles News Register out there as much as I can."

"Plus, I'm actually thinking about discontinuing my *Chasin with Jason* column," added Jason, "I'm just going to write a more serious Message from the Publisher narrative in each issue dealing with *singles issues* and current topics."

"It doesn't look as good if I just write about *my parties* in *my column*," Jason smiled, "It'll look better to get some press from our events in other newspapers besides the *Singles News Register.*

"Well, I don't like putting the name of a competing newspaper in my columns," Jim lightly laughed, "But I'll just mention that the parties are hosted by Editor and Publisher Jason Mershon, without mentioning the name of the newspaper.

"I'll just include your name along with other celebrities who are there," Jim added.

"That would be good," Annie added to Jason, "Most people associate your name with the paper anyway, and the only other *Jason* I can think of is Jason Robards the actor."

"If you do want more outside publicity," said Jim, "There's this writer and publicist named Bud Testa who's been around Hollywood forever."

"Bud writes some columns in a few different newspapers," Jim explained, "and if you have him write a column in your newspaper, he can also get you some other publicity around town."

Jim said he'd get Jason a contact number for Bud Testa and then started talking about a new book he was writing.

"I'm going to call my new book *Hollywood is a Four-Letter Town*," explained Jim, "I've got so many juicy Hollywood stories from the past thirty years, that I couldn't have gotten away with writing just ten years ago, but I think the culture has changed enough these days where I won't get censored."

"Let's hear something good," Lori teased Jim, "Something that would shock us!"

"Well, right now, I'm writing about which celebrities have the biggest cocks in Hollywood," Jim started to tease back.

"Please!" Annie lightly responded with her half-serious prudish moan, "I'm trying to enjoy my lunch here."

"No, tell us!" laughed Lori, "Who are they?"

"Well, besides myself, who I won't write about," Jim boasted with a laugh, "It's Milton Berle and Forrest Tucker."

"Uncle Miltie?" laughed Annie with surprise, "You're kidding, I thought it would've been someone like Clark Gable or Errol Flynn!"

"They were both pretty good *swordsmen* themselves, but Milton almost seems to be deformed down there," laughed Jim, "Everyone in Hollywood pretty much knows about his monster cock."

"But I'm still trying to find out someone more current," Jim lightly added, "Who can *fill the shoes*, so to say, of some of the older stars."

"Do you have any stories, Annie?" he lightly teased Annie.

"I'm not talking!" Annie laughed, trying to again act prudish, "And can we please change the subject?"

"Well, from my personal experience," Lori smiled, joining in, "I'd say, David Cassidy. He has a long one, but it's skinny."

Jason just laughed along with everyone at the table.

Lori told him about some of her past boyfriends, and there wasn't any jealousy between them about anyone they *had been with* in the past.

"But I can show you the picture of when I streaked with Jason," Lori joked, trying to lightly embarrass Jason, "It was so funny seeing his dick flying sideways while we were running through the *Speakeasy*."

"Don't even think about it!" Jason joked back threateningly, "Remember, those are *in the vault.*"

"I'm the editor and publisher of a very straight and conservative newspaper," Jason facetiously added, "My readers don't need to hear or see anything about that."

"You're didn't sound so straight and conservative when you were on Bill Ballance's radio show last time," laughed Lori, "It sounded like you two guys were just talking about sex the entire time."

"Wait a minute," Jason lightly objected, "Bill and I were using some innuendoes, but we weren't blatantly talking about cocks or pussies."

"Okay, that's it!" Annie lightly feigned her embarrassment of the conversation, "I'm going to the bathroom, and hopefully, we can talk about something else when I get back."

"I'd like to put that information about David Cassidy in my book," Jim laughed to Lori as Annie left the table, "But *'skinny'* might be too derogatory of a word, and *'slender'* might sound less harsh."

Hearing the word *"slender"* immediately had Lori break out into a light parody of the famous song, *Love is a Many Splendored Thing.*

"Love is a long and slender thing…," Lori jokingly sang.

"That's funny," smiled Jim, "Maybe I'll use that too."

"But don't mention my name!" laughed Lori, "David would never speak with me again."

Jason didn't think Lori even still talked with David Cassidy but really wasn't that concerned. He'd stayed in touch with a few old girlfriends himself, but more in a friendly way and not romantic. He knew that he and Lori never had to be concerned about something as petty as jealousy and knew they were both too *mature* and *sophisticated* for anything like that.

He did think back to how he also tried not to be jealous of Gianni Russo when his old girlfriend Anne Sanderson used to talk about him, and always wanted to feel confident enough where he had nothing to be jealous of in his relationships.

His relationship with Lori was perfect and he wasn't going to let some funny story from her past even bother him.

☙

Jason was talking with Rudy Vallee on the phone from the office at the *Singles News* Register after starting to edit Rudy's latest column.

"Rudy, you can't write that kind of that stuff in your column," Jason tried to lightly and politely reason with Rudy into the phone.

"You can't call those Congressman and Senators, *'dirty bastards'* and *'sons of bitches'*, and I'm going to have to edit some of that language."

"Well, that's what they are!" argued Rudy, "The way they're trying to get Nixon impeached with this Watergate bullshit!"

"They've been trying to get him out of office since the day he was elected," Rudy continued arguing, "And it's just another witch hunt by the Democrats!"

Jason had learned that Rudy Vallee, besides being very grouchy, was a very opinioned Republican, and many of his columns had bordered pretty close to being libelous. Jason had even gotten another political and news reporter named Don Harris, from the local NBC station, *KNBC Channel 4*, to write a column that leaned toward a Democrat's view to help counter Rudy's column.

He wanted the newspaper to be more neutral and not alienate any readers, but usually had his work as an editor cut out for him, just trying to rewrite most of Rudy's columns.

"Well, my column is called *One Man's Opinion*," Rudy continued arguing, "The public needs to know how these damn Democrats are just trying to overturn the election and ruin our Democracy!"

Jason actually liked Nixon and thought he'd done some good things as President, but besides ending the Draft Lottery and the Vietnam War which had affected him personally, it did seem that the country had become a lot more civil in the past couple years with less violence and protests.

"Look Rudy, I agree with you on some things, and I even voted for Nixon myself, but everyone knows politics is a dirty business," said Jason, "And we know that politician's try to cover their asses all the time, but Nixon just got caught."

"It's the liberal media that exploited it," yelled Rudy, "They were trying to find anything they could for the past four years, and this was the only thing they finally found, and it's bullshit!"

"You can give your opinion and criticize to a certain point in your column," said Jason, "But watch the language and blatant name-calling."

"All right," Rudy finally added gruffly, "You're the editor!"

By the time he finished his call with Rudy, Jason's secretary said he had another call holding from Edy Williams.

"Jason," whispered Edy in her usual, breathy voice, "What are you doing tomorrow night?"

Jason knew she was talking about Tuesday night and told her it was his normal routine to be with Lori at *The Troubadour* on those nights.

"Well, as you know, tomorrow is also the night of the Oscars, so how would you like to be my date?" Edy invitingly whispered.

"It'll be great publicity for the *Singles News Register* having its editor and publisher walking the Red Carpet with a movie star at the Academy Awards," Edy added, "Hugh Hefner is going to be there with Barbi, and you can be there with me."

"What happened?" laughed Jason, "Did your date stand you up?"

"Of course not!" she defended, "It's just that I have two tickets, and I wanted to bring someone special who would look good with me when we walk down the Red Carpet."

"I want to bring a handsome young guy with me, and not some boring old man," Edy added in her breathy voice, "You should feel complimented that you're the first one I called."

Jason laughed at how Edy always tried to build him up when she wanted something.

"And the party afterward is at the Beverly Hilton where you had your party a couple of months ago," Edy continued pitching, "You'll feel right at home."

Jason had been offered press credentials for the Oscars, but it was only for one person, and he wasn't interested in going by himself and just being *just one of the reporters* in the press room.

Edy was making it sound fun, but with it being such short notice, he was trying to think if he had enough time to drop everything and prepare himself for something as big as the *Academy Awards*.

"It does sound tempting," said Jason, "Give me about a half-hour and I'll call you back."

"I've already got a limo coming to my house tomorrow at three pm," Edy added, "I'm paying for the limo and everything else, so all you need to do is show up here in your tuxedo."

"It'll be a blast!" Edy said before hanging up and convinced she'd gotten Jason to agree.

Jason knew he had to make some quick arrangements and decided to call Lori first to let he know he might have to postpone their date at *The Troubadour.*

"I don't think you should go," said Lori when Jason called her with the news, "I don't see how you going to the Oscars is going to be good for the newspaper."

"Well, Hefner is going, and he's representing *Playboy*," said Jason, "I think it might look good representing the newspaper as a guest at the Oscars and not just being there as a reporter.'

"It'll make the Singles News Register look more important," Jason justified.

"You mean, it'll make you look more important," objected Lori.

"As long as the other media mentions the name of the *Singles News Register* its publicity," argued Jason, "You know I'm always trying to get the name of the paper out there and seeing it mentioned in the mainstream press just adds more legitimacy to it being a major publication."

"Well, I don't know if I like it," said Lori, "And I thought we were going to celebrate our one-year anniversary tomorrow at the *Troubadour*."

"Look it, the Oscars start a five pm and will probably be over around eight," Jason reasoned, "So Edy and I will probably just stop by the after-party for an hour or so, and I'll probably be home by ten and we can go to the late show at the Troubadour."

"But if not, we can celebrate our anniversary later this week," Jason added, "But I think I want to go."

"Fine!" Lori said with irritation as she suddenly just hung up.

Jason didn't think Lori would be that bothered, especially because she'd met Edy before at different events and knew she and Jason were friends.

It was only about fifteen minutes after they first spoke when Lori called Jason back at the office.

"I just talked with your mother, and she doesn't think you should go to the Oscars with Edy either," said Lori, "She thinks it's a bad idea."

Jason's mood changed with not just surprise, but with a sudden feeling of betrayal.

"You talked with my mother?" said Jason.

"Jason, I talk to your mother at least once a week," said Lori nonchalantly, "We've been friendly since we met at *The Islander*."

Jason had no idea there were private conversations between Lori and his mother and neither one of them had mentioned anything to him about ever speaking with each other, but Jason suddenly began to get angry.

"You never told me anything about that," Jason said, "What exactly do the two of you talk about?"

"Just about stuff," said Lori, "It's no big deal, but we both agree you shouldn't go tomorrow night."

"So, you think I need my mother's permission?" Jason sarcastically said, "Well, that's perfect then!" and hung up on Lori himself.

Jason suddenly had a feeling of resentment that he'd ever introduced Lori to his parents. He always wanted to keep his life private and didn't like the fact that his mother had seemed to secretly be keeping tabs on him without his knowledge. Jason also began to get mad at Lori for what he thought was a betrayal of trust between them because she knew he didn't have a close family relationship with his parents and didn't like that she decided to become *"friendly"* with his mother.

He was still thinking about the whole situation and what to do when Lori called him again.

"Well, if you go to the Oscars with Edy Williams," Lori said this time with anger, "Then I think I'll call up David Cassidy and have him take me to the Oscars!"

Lori then hung up again, but this time Jason didn't hesitate to immediately call her back and give her his own message.

"Have fun with his skinny dick!" shouted Jason.

Jason was still angry after he slammed down the phone but then tried to sound calm when he picked it back up and dialed another number.

"Edy, tomorrow night sounds fun," Jason said in a calm voice, "I'll be at your house before three pm."

Chapter Fourteen

Jason pulled his car into Edy Williams driveway on Mulholland Drive and saw the limousine had already arrived and parked next to it. He also saw that the driver was standing next to the limo holding a large dog on a leash and started wondering what that was all about.

"Edy will be out in a few minutes," Edy's maid said as she led Jason into the living room to wait.

Jason hadn't spoken to Lori since the day before and still wasn't happy about their last conversation. He tried to call her earlier that morning, but her father said she'd gone to her classes at *Brooks College* and wouldn't be home until after four pm.

Jason knew he was mainly upset with Lori trying to get his mother involved with something he thought they should have just discussed themselves, but he didn't like that Lori added fire by trying to threaten him with personal retaliation if he went to the Oscars without her.

He felt Lori should have known that he would have taken her if he had two tickets for himself, but that not being the case, she shouldn't be upset about him just wanting to get some publicity for his newspaper by going with Edy.

Jason knew they'd work things out when they spoke and figured he'd just call her again later.

"How do I look?" said Edy as she walked into the living room.

Jason expected to see Edy wearing some extravagant gown as he'd seen the other actress wearing when he'd watched the Oscars on television, but she was only wearing a long fur cape that covered her entire body.

"There's more to this outfit," Edy said.

She then opened the cape, and Jason saw all she was wearing beneath it was a matching leopard-skin bikini.

"You're wearing that to the Oscars?" Jason laughed, "You aren't serious."

"I decided that this year," Edy proudly said, "I'm going to make a real *splash* on the Red Carpet tonight."

"It's not that easy getting press with all of the other famous stars that are there," Edy smiled as she did a turn for Jason, "But this outfit will definitely give the photographers something to focus on."

"And, it'll get you some attention for just being my date," she tried to lightly justify, "You want some press for your newspaper, right?"

"I'm not sure if walking the Red Carpet with someone who looks like a *flasher* is what I was thinking about," Jason sarcastically responded, "Are you sure that's the kind of press you want?"

"Any press is good press," Edy just smiled, "The public forgets about you quickly if they don't see your name in the newspapers often enough."

"And besides, I'm not streaking like *someone* I know," she added with a sarcastic grin.

"So, you're going to just sit at the Academy Awards in a bikini all night?" Jason asked with the same sarcasm, "While I'm next to you in my tuxedo?"

"This is just for the Red Carpet," Edy said more seriously, "I have another dress I can slip into once we get inside. And I'm not wearing this to the party afterward either, so don't worry, I'll be very presentable after our entrance."

Jason found out that wasn't the only surprise when Edy said she was also planning on walking the Red Carpet with the huge dog that was outside by the limo.

"Jesus, Edy!" Jason lightly complained, "I'm going to get dog hair all over my tux."

"Don't worry," Edy also casually said as they sat in the back of the limo, "The dog will sit in the front seat, and my driver will bring him back to the house while we're watching the ceremony."

"And stop complaining," she lightly scolded Jason, "You're going to have a memorable night tonight, and like I said, it's going to be a *blast.*"

It was less than thirty minutes later as they followed the caravan of limousines to the *Dorthey Chandler Pavilion* entrance where everyone was arriving, when Jason saw the huge crowds surrounding the roped off Red Carpet, and the bleachers filled hundreds of screaming fans, trying to get a glimpse of whichever celebrity was walking the Red Carpet.

"Okay," said Edy as they exited the limo, "Just stay close to me and let me know if my nipple slips out because they can't put a picture of that in the newspapers."

Jason and Edy would take only a few steps on the Red Carpet to stop with the other celebrities as they turned to acknowledge the screaming fans and allow the paparazzi to take their photos. Edy then gave Jason the leash to hold the dog and took off her cape, and the entire crowd and photographers started going wild and cheering, as Edy stood and turned in her bikini.

A few feet away from where they were standing, Jason saw Jack Nicholson was just looking at the scene in amusement as the photographers and the crowd were screaming, *"Edy! Edy! Edy!"*, trying to get her to face them. Jason was standing next to her and was also waving at the fans, even though he knew that no one in the bleachers knew who he was, but figured he'd at least look like he belonged there. He also looked behind back toward the screaming crowd and saw Linda Lovelace, who looked almost virginal in her white dress and hat, had arrived directly after they had, but in a horse-drawn carriage rather than a limo.

Jason saw that it was really like a circus.

Burt Reynolds and Dinah Shore were in front of them being interviewed from a podium by Army Archerd, the columnist for *Daily Variety*, and once their interview was finished, he then called Edy and Jason to the podium to be interviewed for the screaming crowd.

"That's quite an outfit!" Army Archerd half laughed to Edy before glancing at Jason, "And who is this gentleman with you tonight, Edy?"

"This is my dog I named after Muhammad Ali," whispered Edy in her usual, breathy voice, introducing the dog instead of Jason, "He's my escort and my bodyguard tonight."

Jason then quickly reached out his hand to Army and said clearly and loudly into the microphone, so everyone was sure to hear, "Hi Army, Jason Mershon with the Singles News Register."

Edy was showboating, so Jason didn't want to take the chance that she would forget to introduce him, and not just the dog.

After their interview, the limo driver took the dog back to the limousine, while Jason and Edy went inside the Pavilion lobby. Inside the lobby, several other members of the press and paparazzi were still talking to the stars and taking pictures, and one of the reporters came where Jason and Edy were standing.

"Okay, you guys win tonight," laughed the reporter. "Each year, the press gives an 'Oscar' for the '*Best Entrance on the Red Carpet*,' and you two just barely beat out Linda Lovelace."

The reporter handed Jason a toy replica of an Oscar, and he noticed it was inscribed, "*The Best Entrance by a Couple* at the *46th Annual Academy Awards.*"

"There's a nice souvenir for you," laughed Edy laughed to Jason, "I'll let you keep it, and I'll wait for my real one."

As they walked through the lobby and saying hello to everyone, Edy seemed a little irritated that Cher was getting more attention than she was for also wearing an outfit that showed most of her bare body.

"I think I look hotter than her tonight!" said Edy with slight jealousy.

"Don't worry," said Jason reassuringly, "The crowd outside was cheering the loudest for you."

But Jason was more interested in meeting all of the sexy women he'd only seen on the big screen at the theatres and was happy he grew his bread and could pass for older than twenty- three years old.

He also noticed that he wasn't the youngest one there that night.

"Jeez, she doesn't look anything like the little girl in the Exorcist." Jason sarcastically joked to Edy after they said hello to Linda Blair, "And I didn't see those tits in the movie."

Jason also saw who he thought was a *little boy* dressed in a tuxedo before seeing it was Tatum O'Neal.

After posing for several more photos with the paparazzi, it was almost five pm and time for everyone to take their seats, but Jason saw a payphone in the lobby and decided to try and call Lori again, while Edy changed into her dress.

Jason was a little irritated when there was no answer, but didn't want to it spoil his evening, and decided he'd just try again after the ceremonies.

He saw that Edy was right, and this night was turning into a blast.

The actual Oscars ceremony itself was long, and before even an hour had passed, Edy was bored because they were sitting near the rear of the theatre.

"I'm not going to be getting much camera time in these crappy seats," Edy complained from the minute they sat down.

During the awards ceremony itself, Jason only got up from his seat once to use the bathroom but was embarrassed when he heard a loud voice let out an *"EEY-OW!"* and realized he'd stepped on the foot of Peter Falk, who was sitting next to him.

Jason quickly apologized and made his way into the empty lobby, but after Jason went to the bathroom, he wasn't allowed back in the theatre right away and had to wait for a commercial break before he could go back in.

"You missed the streaker while you were gone," Edy whispered when Jason sat back down before teasing, "I thought it was you for a second."

The awards ceremony was long, but Jason still thought it was fun experiencing what he'd only seen on television for years. By the time they finally announced *The Sting* as *The Best Picture of the Year*, everyone looked anxious to depart the theatre, and Edy was probably the first one out of her seat.

"Let's go get the limo and get to the afterparty at the Hilton," said Edy, "I want to try and beat the long lines."

The limo lines were long, and they both could see it would be a while before their limo pulled up to the curb.

"I'm gonna go call Lori from one of the payphones and let her know I'll be home in a couple hours," Jason told Edy, "Don't leave without me."

When Lori's father answered the phone and said "Lori's not home yet, but I'll tell her you called," Jason was starting to get mad because it was almost nine pm, and he was starting to wonder where Lori was.

There had never been any jealousy or problems between them until the day before, and now it looked like she was playing games with him. He didn't even want to imagine Lori being with David Cassidy and remembered how sick he felt when Anne Sanderson told him she'd *"been with someone else"* and how he never wanted to feel that badly again. But even though he doubted something like that would happen, he decided to just put Lori out of his mind for the night and try to have a good time without letting any thoughts about her spoil this evening.

When Jason got back to the waiting line for limo's, he saw Edy was standing and talking with someone he didn't recognize.

"Jason, this is Paul Morrissey," introduced Edy, "He directs Andy Warhol's movies, and he's going to hitch a ride with us to the afterparty at the Beverly Hilton."

"If you don't mind," said Paul, "I've got to make a quick stop at the Beverly Wilshire Hotel and pick up Bianca to join us."

"Bianca?" asked Edy.

"Bianca Jagger," said Paul casually, "I told her I'd pick her up after the ceremony."

Jason was glad Edy asked Paul first, so he didn't sound like a groupie by asking the next question himself.

"Is Mick coming too?" asked Edy.

"No, unfortunately, my new movie *Frankenstein* was scheduled to open the same night as tonight's Oscars," explained Paul, "So Mick is with Andy Warhol for its premier right now."

Jason started feeling better as soon as they all got in the back seat of the limo and poured himself a double shot of Scotch on the rocks and suddenly, he wasn't even upset about not hearing anything from Lori.

It was over a half-hour drive to Beverly Hills from Downtown LA with the traffic, and Edy and Jason waited in the limo outside the Beverly Wilshire as Paul went inside to get Bianca Jagger. Jason was trying to act cool and not overly excited, but inside, he knew he couldn't wait to be sitting next to Mick Jagger's wife.

"Bianca, this is Edy and Jason," introduced Paul, as Bianca Jagger sat in the back seat across from them.

"Edy made quite an entrance at the Oscars tonight," Paul laughed. "Andy and Mick would have loved it."

"Tell Andy if he wants to paint me," joked Edy, "I'll recreate the scene for him anytime."

Jason tried to start a conversation with Bianca and casually mentioned that he was at the benefit concert *The Rolling Stones* performed the year earlier for the victims of the Nicaraguan Earthquake and fibbed that they may have met backstage that night.

He was at the concert, and it was the second time he'd seen *The Rolling Stones*, but he was nowhere close to being backstage and didn't want Bianca Jagger to think he was just some *schmuck* that was star stuck meeting her for the first time.

"Possibly," Bianca said, even though Jason knew she was just being polite. "There were a lot of people there that night, but it's nice seeing you again."

When Bianca asked Jason, "So what do you do?" he mentioned he was the editor and publisher of the *Singles News Register* and also produced events and parties around town.

Jason knew this was the night to say he was a *"producer"* and not just a member of the press. He also tried not to stare at Bianca, but he could immediately see why she was the one that Mick Jagger finally married. Bianca had a very erotic sexiness about her, not only how she looked, but just by the way she spoke.

The *Beverly Hilton* was less than ten minutes from the *Beverly Wilshire*, so Jason was a little disappointed they didn't spend that much time together in the limo, and when the limo pulled up to the entrance, Jason saw it was again roped off and packed with fans and some of the same members of the press he saw at the *Dorthey Chandler Pavilion.*

When the four of them were walking in together, Bianca handed Jason her fur wrap.

"Could you please carry this for me, darling," Bianca casually asked.

Jason didn't know if it was a mink, fox, or a chinchilla, but did notice that it had the small head of whatever animal it formerly was, still attached to the fur.

As Jason walked into the ballroom beside Bianca, he looked passed the ropes to some of the press members he knew and saw them gawking, and immediately had a quick flashback of the times he was a cab driver in Las Vegas.

He remembered the looks the other cabbies would give him when he sat in a private booth at *The Flame* restaurant with an attractive *working girl* instead of joining them for their free spaghetti dinners. Jason figured those press members were trying to figure out why he was *inside the ropes* and not *outside the ropes* like they were, and he just casually waved to the crowd as he walked past them.

The *International Ballroom* was already packed, and with everyone walking around and greeting each other, the four of them became separated amongst the crowd of famous faces in less than fifteen minutes.

Jason felt a little awkward still holding Bianca's fur, but knew it was probably very expensive and wanted to take care of it for her and decided to stand by the bar so he wouldn't look lost, and would just wait until Edy or Bianca found him. But after standing at the bar for about ten minutes, the crowd was even larger, and Jason decided to wander around the ballroom and find Edy or Bianca himself.

Jason recognized almost every face in the crowd and just gave a friendly nod to most of them, not wanting to look starstruck or act like he didn't belong there, but when he saw Paul and Linda McCartney sitting in one of the booths, he knew he had the perfect opening to talk to him.

"Hi Paul," Jason casually said as he stopped at McCartney's booth, "By any chance have you seen Bianca Jagger wandering around? I wanted to see if she needed her wrap."

"Is Mick here too?" Paul asked immediately.

"No," Jason also casually answered, wanting to sound like he was in their inner circle, "Mick had to go to a premier with Andy Warhol tonight for Andy's new movie, *Frankenstein.*"

Jason then introduced himself and shook Paul's hand, telling him that he thought Paul's song *Live and Let Die* should have won the Oscar that night.

"Thank you," said Paul, "But I think everyone knew *The Way We Were* would win tonight, but I did enjoy the way Connie Stevens performed my song."

Jason then lightly mentioned how he was at *The Troubadour* a few weeks earlier and told Paul he saw "Your old buddy John" getting ejected after heckling The Smothers Brothers.

"That's John," Paul just laughed, "He has been going through some strange times lately."

"*Imagine* that!" Jason answered back, deciding to use Lori's pun she had joked that night at *The Troubadour*.

Paul then politely introduced the other girl sitting at his table, whom Jason immediately recognized.

"Jason, I'm sure you know Twiggy?" introduced Paul.

"No, we haven't met yet," Jason said, shaking her hand, "But I was sitting next to Peter Falk tonight and saw you present an award with him."

"I accidentally stepped on Peter's foot pretty hard, and I hope he's okay." Jason tried to laugh lightly.

Jason was glad some things happened that night that allowed him to carry on a natural conversation. He also noticed Twiggy was sitting alone with Paul and Linda and decided to be a little bolder.

"But my foot's okay," Jason smiled to Twiggy, "If you'd like to dance?"

"Maybe a little later," she smiled back, "But It was a long night, and I just want to relax for a while."

Jason figured that was better than a "no" and said "maybe later" as well.

"When you find Bianca," said Paul before Jason left, "Do bring her by so I can say hello."

He couldn't believe everyone he was meeting that night and was mentally thinking about all the famous names he could "drop" in his next *Chasin' With Jason* column, in the same way all the other famous Hollywood columnists always did in the mainstream newspapers. Jason knew that letting his readers see that the "editor and publisher" of the *Singles News Register* was hobnobbing with the most famous celebrities in the world would also show how famous his newspaper was and definitely add credibility to its circulation claims.

He then decided to walk around some more, knowing that Bianca's fur was a great prop for introducing himself to everyone and finally saw Edy talking with a group that included Telly Savalas and Groucho Marx and joined them. But after about ten minutes of standing with that group, Edy told Jason that she was getting tired and wanted to go home.

"Jeez Edy!" said Jason, "It's not even eleven o'clock yet, and it's too early to leave."

"Well, if you want to stay, it's okay," Edy said, "But I'm taking the limo home."

Jason was starting to have fun at the party and wasn't ready to leave, so he just walked Edy outside and told her he'd get a ride back to her place for his car later.

While Jason was walking through the crowd looking for Bianca Jagger whose fur wrap he was still carrying around, he saw a very famous actress he recognized standing at the bar talking with Hugh Hefner and Barbi Benton, and decided to approach them in the same casual manner as he had Paul McCartney,

"Hi," Jason said as he joined them at the bar. "Have any of you seen Bianca Jagger wandering around? It seems we've become separated in the crowd tonight."

Hefner was the first one to ask if "Mick was also there," but Jason again explained how Mick was with Andy Warhol, and he had brought Bianca to the afterparty himself.

"Jason Mershon with the Singles News Register," Jason introduced himself as he shook Hefner's hand. "It's nice meeting you, Hugh, and we have a mutual acquaintance in Steve Powers."

Again, Jason was glad he had something in common he could mention with Hefner.

"It's *Hef*," Hefner just smiled, "It's nice to meet you, and yes, Steve is a dear friend of mine too."

After Hugh Hefner and Barbi Benton left to great some other celebrities in the crowd, Jason stayed standing at the bar and ordered another double Scotch for himself.

"He doesn't like being called *Hugh*," the actress smiled, "Everyone just calls him *Hef*."

"I'll remember that next time," Jason smiled, not trying to look embarrassed, "Can I order you a drink?"

"No thanks," the actress said, "This is my third glass of wine tonight, and I've already got a little buzz."

Jason had always thought that actress was one of the most beautiful women in Hollywood, and although he never had any fantasies about being with any one particular actress, because of a certain role she played in a movie several years earlier, he did think it was an amazing coincidence that he was actually standing next to her at the bar. He also liked that she appeared to be by herself, and knowing she was probably four or five years older than him, he decided he'd add a couple more years to his age if she asked.

"I'll just stay here at the bar for a while," Jason casually said, "And I'm sure Bianca will wander by eventually."

"So, you brought Bianca Jagger to the Oscars tonight?" asked the actress, "I didn't see her at the awards."

"Well actually," Jason smiled, "I went to the awards with Edy Williams, and just picked up Bianca afterward to bring her to the party."

"Ah, Edy Williams," she smiled back with amusement, "So you have two dates tonight, eh?"

"Nope. Edy already went home", said Jason, "And Bianca's not really a date, she just wanted to come to the party, so I picked her up at the Beverly Wilshire on the way here."

"Well, my date left too," said the actress, "He wasn't a real date anyway, but my boyfriend and I broke up a couple of months ago, so he was just more like an escort."

Jason liked that she volunteered that information and then suddenly saw Twiggy walking by, and decided to do a little more *name-dropping* in front of the actress. "Twiggy!" Jason called out to her, "Don't forget about that dance later." Twiggy smiled and just gave him the thumbs up as she walked by.

"Twiggy too?" smiled the actress, "You get around, don't you."

"Well, I am the publisher of a singles newspaper," Jason tried to tease, "And I do need to maintain a certain image."

"Just like *Hef*," he added with a smile.

Jason and the actress then began talking about the Oscar show and some of the highlights.

"I knew they weren't going to going to give Marlon Brando the Oscar again after he refused it last year," the actress said, "But it would have been funny to see who he sent up onstage to accept it if he did."

"But the streaker tonight was hilarious!" she added, "Everyone was wondering if it was a setup."

Jason told her how that was the one part of the show that he had missed when he had got up to use the restroom.

"David Niven came up with the classic line without missing a beat right afterward," she laughed, "He said the guy was brave, not for streaking, but for showing his shortcomings!"

"But it wasn't surprising," she added, "With all the streaking going on these days, it was bound to happen somewhere at a big event."

"Funny you should mention that," Jason half laughed, "Believe it or not, I somehow ended up streaking at the Speakeasy myself a couple of weeks ago."

The actress seemed amused and wanted to hear more details as Jason explained the circumstances.

"So, you weren't concerned about showing any *shortcomings*," she teased.

"Well actually," teased Jason back, "I'm not Milton Berle, but I saw the pictures that the photographer took that night, and it wasn't anything I should be embarrassed about."

Jason thought he'd impress the actress by showing her he knew some Hollywood gossip that she'd probably already heard about Milton Berle.

"Interesting," she laughed, "And pretty confident too, I see."

The actress continued laughing when Jason explained how he had to streak twice to make sure the photographer got pictures.

"Are you sure you're a *streaker* and not just an *exhibitionist*?" she continued teasing.

"Well, sometimes you do crazy things when you've had one drink too many," Jason just half laughed as he was starting to get comfortable joking with her.

"Then I think I will have another glass of wine," the actress said. "Got anymore crazy stories?"

"That is unless you have to go find Bianca?" she continued smiling.

Jason wasn't planning on going anywhere.

He was thrilled that he was having a fun conversation with his *fantasy* actress, and had almost completely forgotten about Bianca Jagger and was also hoping he wouldn't run into her anytime soon.

"Too bad I wasn't at the Speakeasy when you streaked," the actress continued her teasing tone, "Tonight was the first time I've seen a naked man in over two months, and I was starting to forget what they looked like."

Jason then decided to try and make a cute toast.

"A toast…," Jason hesitated before thinking of an appropriate rhyme, "To not forgetting those things we enjoy the most."

He liked how she kept her eyes on him and smiled as they toasted and was pretty sure he recognized the type of smile she was giving him, and as they continued to laugh and exchanged a few innuendoes, Jason was starting to realize that this huge movie star was actually flirting with him.

"You seem like you like to have fun," the actress smiled, "And pardon my pun, but you do seem pretty cocky for someone your age."

"You like dancing with British models, you like running around naked in public, and you like bringing half-naked actresses to the Academy Awards," the actress continued to tease, "So what else do you do for fun?"

Jason decided to make a corny pun that he'd used before, hoping to get another laugh.

"I like doing things on the *sperm*…," he said before quickly correcting himself with a smile, "I mean *spur* of the moment!"

"That's an intentional *Freudian Slip* if I ever heard one," she smiled before adding, "But it was a cute one."

The actress took the last sip from her glass and quietly smiled at Jason.

"So….?" she said.

When Jason realized what she had on her mind, he knew he wouldn't act starstruck and was ready to show her he was as *mature* and *sophisticated* as any other *celebrity* in the ballroom.

"So," Jason smiled back as he also took the last sip from his glass, "Shall we dance?"

It was less than an hour after they'd met, when the actress stood by the elevator doors in the lobby of the Beverly Hilton, while Jason was at the front desk paying for a hotel room. He was glad he had a personal check in his wallet because he didn't have enough cash on him to pay for the room.

Jason kissed her softly in the elevator, but they didn't speak until they were alone in the room.

"I want you to know something," the actress said, "We're going to do this, but we're not going to see each other, or talk to each other ever again after tonight."

But as he unzipped her gown, Jason wasn't even thinking about tomorrow.

Chapter Fifteen

Jason woke up around seven am and saw she was already gone.

He was still in a state of euphoria from who he had spent the night with and was disappointed they wouldn't be having a *morning encore,* but the first thing he noticed was the animal's face attached to Bianca Jagger's fur lying across the dresser, seemingly staring at him.

Everything seemed to happen so fast; he didn't even try to find Bianca before leaving the party with the actress.

Jason didn't want Bianca Jagger to think he'd stolen her fur and immediately called the *Beverly Wilshire Hotel,* and by her voice, Jason could tell that he'd woken her and apologized, saying he had to leave quickly the night before but told her he'd stop by her hotel later to bring her fur.

"Thank you," she said in a sleepy voice before hanging up the phone, "Just call me from the lobby when you get here."

Jason could tell she just wanted to go back to sleep and was relieved she didn't seem all that concerned. It also gave him time to take a taxi back to his apartment to shower and change into a suit and tie and didn't want her to see him wearing the tuxedo from the night before. He also needed to call his office and let them know he wouldn't be in until around noon.

By ten am, Jason was holding Bianca's fur when he called her room from the lobby of the Beverly Wilshire and was hoping the person who answered the phone was who he thought it was.

"Mick?" asked Jason when he heard the English accented male voice answer the phone.

"Yeah," answered the voice.

"Hi, this is Jason Mershon," he said, trying to sound as natural as he could, "I'm here to bring Bianca's fur she left at the Oscar party last night."

"Oh yeah," he said, "Bianca said you can just leave it at the front desk, and she'll come down for it later."

Jason was immediately disappointed he wasn't being invited to their room but didn't want to show it in his voice.

"Okay, no problem," said Jason, "And tell Bianca it was nice meeting her last night."

"Thank you, I will," Mick said and then hung up the phone.

Jason regretted not having the opportunity to meet Mick Jagger, but he was still walking around with a smile thinking about the night before.

He didn't want to believe that "he'd never see or talk to" that actress again, but even if that did happen, Jason knew it was something he'd never forget, especially because of the coincidence of who he had slept with, which seemed more amazing than just the sex.

Jason took another taxi to Edy Williams's house to get his car and saw she was excited when she answered the door.

"We're on the cover of *Variety!*" Edy said, holding a copy for Jason.

"Oh, and don't feel bad, but they spelled your name wrong and called you *'Joseph Mershon'* instead of *Jason,*" she laughed.

Jason looked and the article on the cover of *Variety* and saw it did mention *Joseph Mershon of the Singles News Register* and was briefly worried about the actress seeing the article and wondering if she'd think Jason had given her a phony name. But he was at least happy the name of his newspaper was spelled right.

"And this is just Variety," said Edy with more excitement, "There'll be pictures and stories in newspapers all over the world about our great entrance last night!"

"Hopefully, they'll spell your name right in the other articles," she added lightly.

"That's okay," smiled Jason, "It's the name of the newspaper I wanted publicity for and not myself. Plus, you're the celebrity, not me."

"Well, everyone should automatically think about the Singles News Register when they see your name in print," said Edy, "Like *Playboy* and Hugh Hefner!"

"I don't think I'm ready to be compared to *Hef* yet," Jason half laughed at her usual exaggerated comparison.

"At least you got what you wanted," he lightly added, "You didn't win an Oscar for acting, but at least you won the one for *best entrance.*"

"Like I said, baby," Edy answered, "Any press is good press."

It was almost noon, and Jason decided to drive straight to his office in Paramount after leaving Edy's house knowing it was also deadline week and he needed to start putting the new issue together as well as write his next *Chasin' With Jason* column. He knew it was going to feel strange getting back to *reality* and was still spent from the past twenty-four hours, but as he drove down the freeway, Jason also began thinking about his situation with Lori.

He was still trying to feel angry and blame her for anything that happened between them and decided that was probably the reason he wouldn't let himself feel any guilt about the night before. Jason decided that if Lori ended up saying she "had been with David Cassidy," Jason would tell her what happened the actress with his own retaliation and feel he'd *gotten even* with her. But the more he began to think about it, the more he hoped that wouldn't be the case.

Jason knew he wanted the night before to just be forgotten and looked at the fantasy it all had been, and just wanted his relationship with Lori to get back to normal somehow, but he still convinced himself he had nothing to apologize for and wasn't going to call her first, and was going to wait until Lori called him.

By the time Jason got to his office, at least a dozen messages were waiting for him from friends who evidently had read about the Oscars and wanted to hear the details and tell him how *famous* he was that day.

But Lori wasn't one of them.

For the rest of the day, any anger Jason had toward Lori was replaced with sadness and regret that he had even gone to the *Oscars*, but he still couldn't bring himself to call her first until he knew what she was going to say about the previous night.

It wasn't until the later that night before Lori did finally call him at his apartment.

"We need to talk about the stupid argument we had," said Lori trying to sound serious, but light enough to sound positive, "Do you want to go to the Islander on Saturday night and have some dinner?"

Lori's tone of voice seemed natural and not angry, so he wanted her to know he felt the same way and was suddenly excited that she had finally called to break the ice.

"Definitely and I was going to call you and suggest the same thing," Jason fibbed, "We shouldn't let one stupid argument ruin everything we've had together for the last year."

"I don't know how it escalated so bad," Lori said, "But we've got to make sure it doesn't happen again."

Everything about the previous night was over, and Jason knew he wanted, and needed, everything to get back to normal.

∾

There was a still slight chill between them when they first arrived at *The Islander*, and they were both trying to sound apologetic without putting the blame on each other.

"I know we've always tried to act like the *mature* and *sophisticated* couple in Hollywood," Lori tried to sarcastically joke, "But we did say some stupid things the other day that was a little childish."

Jason was at least glad they were looking at everything sarcastically instead of starting their conversation out with any anger.

"I'm sorry if talking to your mother was something you weren't comfortable with, and I didn't think it was that big of deal," Lori said, "But if you don't want me talking with her, I won't."

Jason knew getting upset at Lori over that issue was wrong, and he should never have blamed her for just trying to consider herself part of his family. He knew he was probably just concerned that his mother, without realizing it, would say something that might demean or embarrass him, as he felt she had done the year before at *The Islander*.

"I don't like sharing everything I do with my mother or parents," Jason tried to explain, "It was just a surprise that neither of you ever told me that you discussed things together."

"But I'm sorry I made a big deal out of it, and I don't mind you talking with her," Jason tried to apologize before lightly joking, "As long as you don't get too personal and tell her any stories about us streaking or some of the other crazy things we do."

Lori laughed, but still was trying to be serious.

"I also don't want you to think that I'm jealous whenever we aren't together," Lori continued, "and I don't want you ever to have to feel that way about me either."

Jason was slightly uncomfortable that the subject of jealously was even being mentioned after never having worried it about before, but he let Lori do most of the talking.

"I know that you and Edy Williams are just friends and it was mainly good press to be seen at the Oscars," Lori added, "and I didn't want you to think I didn't trust you enough to go there without me."

"Our relationship is strong enough to think about anything like that," Jason tried to add, hoping he wasn't showing guilt, "We're the perfect couple and shouldn't even worry about not trusting each other."

They both tried to be serious and convince each other of how much they *still loved* each other, but by the time they were on their second *Coco Loco*, they were both just laughing about the "stupid argument."

"Jeez, listen to us trying to sound so serious," Lori started joking, "Especially after we both promised each other we'd never talk to each other like this and make our relationship *gushy!*"

Jason was relieved that their conversation became lighter and after another Coco Loco, they both promised to put everything behind them and not even bring up anything about that week again. He wasn't sure if he was completely over some of the things Lori said earlier that week, and also noticed that she never asked anything about the Oscars, and also never mentioned what she was doing that night.

He knew how he would feel and probably change everything if Lori told him that she had *"been with someone else"* that night, and also knew he'd never tell her everything because he'd never want her to experience *that feeling* herself.

There were some secrets he knew were best to *keep in the vault*.

Jason also made a mental note to do some last-minute editing on his *Chasin' With Jason* column before it went to the printer. Although he naturally didn't write about *everything* that had happened at the *Oscars*, he decided he'd better to tone it down a bit and not appear he had *too much fun*, or remind Lori about that night again.

Later that same night, when they were back at his apartment, they were both lying in bed having their "after sex" cigarette and Jason agreed with Lori that "the make-up sex" almost made the argument they had worthwhile. As usual, Lori was softly singing along to one of her favorite Carly Simon songs, *Anticipation*, that was playing on Jason's stereo, which did make everything seem normal again.

As Jason held Lori close, he joined her in softly signing the closing chorus of *"These are the good old days,"* and thought about how appropriate the lyrics really were, but it mainly felt better knowing there were still some *good new days* ahead for both of them.

Chapter Sixteen

Jason's parents would still occasionally appear to be in the middle of some type of argument whenever he stopped by their townhouse, so the three of them would rarely see or talk to each other at the same time. But he was satisfied that they were happy about how well the *Singles News Register* had grown in the past two years.

His mother was the only one at the townhouse when Jason stopped by in early May to drop off the box of completed and pasted flats for the next issue of the newspaper that was ready to go to the printer. She also never brought up anything about the attractive girls he was putting on the cover ever again, since the "Bachelorette of the Week" had become a regular visual on each cover, and a "Brand" that everyone was familiar with, and had consistently been selling very well for the past year.

"Well, my first party at the Speakeasy is next week," Jason said after delivering the box to his mother, "And I'm hoping they turn into regular monthly singles parties."

"I hope it doesn't turn into another loser like your *Hearts and Flowers Ball*," his mother answered with slight sarcasm, "That was a waste of money just so you could have a fancy party."

"Look it, you know I mainly wanted to do that because we were pushing the Artist's and Models Ball for so long," Jason started to argue back, "Plus, so many of my *Stars* members were expecting a party, so I didn't want the paper to lose credibility."

"Besides, Dick always said the newspaper was just a *vehicle*, and I'm just trying to make a few extra bucks on the side," he added with slight irritation.

"Yeah, just like you were going to make so much money on your *big Beverly Hills party*," his mother chided. "How much did you lose, a thousand dollars?"

Jason knew that must have been something that Lori had shared with his mother, but he didn't want to start another argument and decided not to respond.

"We are a *singles* newspaper," said Jason, "And singles parties can be a natural attraction that should get the newspaper more readers and publicity."

"People are starting to go to nightclubs and dancing more than ever," he continued justifying, "and by having parties at exclusive private nightclubs where the celebrities hang out, adds a touch of prestige to the paper."

"Prestige doesn't bring in the money," she said, "It's the personal ads for dates and subscriptions."

"It's also a great place for our advertisers to meet for their first dates and have fun," Jason added, "It'll just open us to a bigger singles market to people who wouldn't ever think about advertising for dates and especially the younger singles."

"You and Dick still don't want to spend money on advertising," Jason continued justifying, "So the promotions are the only way to keep the name of the newspaper out there without spending money."

"Any press is good press," Jason decided to add.

"Whatever, but it just sounds like a bunch of bullshit and a waste of time," his mother continued to complain, "You should just be selling cash advertising for the newspaper, instead of those trade outs, if you want to make more money."

As usual, Jason left her house in a foul mood but wasn't going to let it keep him from staying motivated about his upcoming party.

Jason knew it was just a waste of time trying to get his mother excited about his ideas, or explaining he was doing promotions to replace not having an advertising budget.

He was sorry he even tried to share any of his ideas with her again, knowing that he didn't need her support to remain motivated, but was more motivated by not having to feel that his father's salary was his only source of income.

Jason knew his *S.T.A.R.S* club was something he started on his own.

Although Jason also hadn't been able to afford much money for an advertising budget for his first party at *The Speakeasy*, as he'd done with the *Hearts and Flowers Ball*, he only ran some print ads in the *Singles News Register*, but he did know that those ads alone could never attract the crowds he wanted to attend his party. He had already seen that his regular readers, who were mainly over forty and even fifty years old, weren't the type who would want to drive to a "disco party" in Hollywood.

His main advertising had been himself and his circle of friends, personally passing out flyers and invitations, pitching about "what a fantastic and exciting" party it would be, along with mentioning all of the "celebrities" and "beautiful single girls" who would be attending. Also, by recruiting contestants to be in his *Bachelorette of the Month* contest and letting them know half of the judging was by audience applause, he knew the contestants themselves would bring a group of their friends. Jason also received more free advertising when he appeared on Bill Ballance's radio show a second time the week before his party, and when he got a few blurbs from some other press contacts in other publications.

It took time and effort, but he knew that he had to put in the hours if he wanted to *make money* without *spending money*, and was more than satisfied with the crowd at *The Speakeasy* at his first *S.T.A.R.S.* disco party.

Jason only had about half the crowd he had at the *Hearts and Flowers Ball*, but because *The Speakeasy* was laid out differently from the *Grand Ballroom* at the *Beverly Hilton*, the almost three hundred people who were at his first *S.T.A.R.S* party made the disco looked packed.

Sandi Shore was again working the front door and was collecting the three-dollar door charge getting the names and addresses of everyone who entered, along with giving everyone a free three-month subscription to the *Singles News Register* just for attending the party.

Because there wouldn't be a live band playing at his first party, Jason wanted to have other things that would keep his crowd entertained throughout the night, and did come up with a fun party mixer idea and hoped it wouldn't seem like *kid stuff* to the Hollywood crowd.

Lori was at the front entrance with Sandi and helping giving out name tags to everyone who entered for a party mixer Jason decided to try, which seemed to fit in with his *Everybody is a Star* theme perfectly.

Jason called his new party mixer *"Famous Couples."*

He had two large jars filled with men's and women's names of historical, fictional, cartoon, and even biblical characters, along with dozens of famous Hollywood couples and everyone who entered the party would pick out a nametag at random from the jars based on their gender, and then go through the crowd trying to find who their *famous name* matched.

Because dancing had become so popular, besides the *Bachelorette of the Month* contest that Bill Ballance would emcee later in the evening, Jason also planned a "Famous Couples Dance Contest" where couples who found the match to their nametag would complete for a fifty-dollar cash first prize.

Jason definitely wanted it to feel like a special party rather than just another night at a bar, and the *Famous Couples* game was a perfect ice breaker.

What Jason liked about the *Speakeasy* was that besides the celebrities he would invite in keeping with his *S.T.A.R.S.* theme, on any given night, there would be other celebrities he hadn't been expecting who would often pop into the nightclub.

Jason didn't get that excited as many of the party-goers about meeting celebrities anymore because in his position, it seemed he was always running into someone famous in Hollywood and Beverly Hills. But during Jason's first *S.T.A.R.S.* party at The *Speakeasy*, Dave Curtin did introduce him to someone who Jason thought was a big deal and was excited to meet.

"Jason, meet Harold Robbins and his wife Grace," introduced Dave.

Besides being his favorite author when he was growing up, Jason knew that Harold Robbins was famous around the globe as someone who hosted the greatest parties in the world.

Everyone said the *Oscars*, or any other big parties in Hollywood or Beverly Hills, couldn't hold a candle to the parties Harold Robbins hosted himself, and just having Harold Robbins at his party that night, and having a chance to talk with him about parties and his books, especially *The Adventurers*, did make Jason's a little star-struck.

"*The Adventurers* is probably my favorite book of all time," Jason said to Robbins when they spent a few minutes talking, "It's a shame they didn't show the whole story in the movie version of your book."

"It was probably my favorite novel I wrote too," smiled Robbins, "Until I let Hollywood get hold of it and ruin the movie."

Robbins explained how he originally had written the screenplay for the movie, but because it was well over three hundred pages long, they hired other writers to rewrite and edit it, and the story was completely destroyed.

"And the asshole they cast to play Dax was a disaster," Robbins also half complained, "He wasn't even close to the Porfirio Rubiosa type whose life I patterned Dax's story after."

Jason mentally reminded himself to find out more about who Porfirio Rubiosa was so that he could read more about the *real-life* Dax.

"If you ever want to get things done correctly, never count on anyone else," Robbins added, "You're better off doing it all yourself."

Jason briefly thought about how he agreed with Harold Robbins after what happened with the *Artists and Models Ball* and having to depend on someone else. But besides having the opportunity to speak with Robbins himself, Jason also liked talking with his wife because he remembered *The Adventurers* had been dedicated *"To My Wife Grace"* and thought she very sexy, even though he guessed she was probably over ten years older than he was. He also started wondering if she was anything like the female characters Harold described in his novels.

Even though Jason knew they had probably just popped in for some drinks, and really weren't there specifically for his singles party, he hoped that when word got around town that Harold and Grace Robbins had been at one of his *S.T.A.R.S* parties, the publicity would be priceless.

Jim Bacon was also at the party that night, and Jason wanted to make sure Jim put a blurb in his *Herald Examiner* column about the celebrities who were there that night and also knew the pictures and write-ups about the party he'd include in the next *Singles News Register* should be good for at least twenty or thirty new *S.T.A.R.S.* memberships.

Although he had still given away a good number of comps that night to his friends and others just to make sure the disco was packed, Jason figured after all his costs, he still cleared almost four hundred dollars profit and considered the party a huge success.

But besides the money, he was also starting to think how amazing it was how he had met so many people that year, who had seemed to have always been in his thoughts since he was very young, that he could never have imagined meeting just a couple years earlier, or actually ever meeting at all.

Jason was beginning to believe that 1974 was actually turning into a *fantasy* year.

Chapter Seventeen

The singles market and lifestyle did seem to be the hottest subject in the mainstream media for the past year, and Jason wanted to try and focus more on his position as an editor and publisher and try to be taken more seriously than just an entertainment columnist. He had already replaced his *Chasin' with Jason* column, with a *Message from the Publisher* introduction in each issue, which dealt with more serious issues involving singles.

Having everything running smoothly editorially, gave him time to promote his upcoming parties and continue to think of other ways that would keep the name of the *Singles News Register* being mentioned in other media, which gave him his free advertising and publicity. Jason also decided to try and at least act like he was a serious *journalist* sometimes, and still tried to work on his *journalism chops* whenever the opportunity arose.

He'd get phone calls at his office regularly from someone who had a *"hot story"* they wanted to be interviewed about, like claiming to know things about the *real people* behind the JFK assassination or about some other *far-fetched* story that the *National Enquirer* had specialized. But most of those people turned out to be nut jobs, and Jason started ignoring people with their different conspiracy theories.

The one real news story Jason was interested in pursuing was to possibly get at least a telephone interview with kidnapped heiress Patty Hearst, who was now claiming to be a member of the radical *Symbionese Liberation Army*. Jason felt that would be a real *coup* for his newspaper but also knew there were hundreds of journalists who felt the same way, as well as the hundreds of law enforcement officers also looking for her.

Jason knew inside it was probably just a pipe dream, but it made him sound like a serious journalist when he told everyone he was at least trying to "use my inside contacts" to get the interview.

His friend Tom Casey had graduated college and was working as a police detective, but just laughed when Jason called to see if Tom, or his father in the FBI, had any tips Jason could pursue.

"If any of us had any tips," Tom laughed, "I think we'd pretty much keep them to ourselves."

Jason even tried a girl he knew from he'd worked with at *Johnny Reb's* named Mary Lou, who always said she knew some members the *Black Panthers* and another radical group, the *Weather Underground* back in 1969, and had stayed in touch with her even after she had moved back to Berkeley, to supposedly "join the fight" with her radical friends, around the same time Jason left Las Vegas in 1972.

"Yeah, I know some people," Mary Lou laughed, "But not any of the ones who have Patty Hearst."

"But even if I did," she added, "I'm sure they'd want a lot of money upfront before even allowing an interview."

Jason thought it was funny that even the so-called *radical groups* also were focused on making money like everyone else.

The one person who had been saying that "he knew how to contact Patty Hearst" was Mickey Cohen, who was once known as the main gangster in Los Angeles.

Edy Williams had been involved and occasionally dated Mickey Cohen since he had been released from prison, and Jason was able to set up a lunch meeting at the *Musso and Frank Grill* on Hollywood Boulevard through Edy.

Jason figured an interview with someone who had some inside information and may have talked to members of the *SLA* would show that he at least had tried to put some real effort into an investigative article about Patty Hearst. But after listening to Cohen talk for over an hour about his "old days" and what a "big shot" he used to be, Jason realized he was just probably a senile old gangster who was just looking a way to get his name back in the newspapers to act like a "big shot" again.

Jason gave up on his attempts to find Patty Hearst after witnessing the shootout between the *LAPD* and members of the *SLA* when he raced to the scene after hearing a tip that Patty Hearst was surrounded inside a house in Watts.

He could only get within about two blocks of where the house was and stood behind some barriers with the other members of the press, as they heard the shots going back and forth between the *SWAT* squad and the small house.

Jason saw Jim Bacon from *Herald Examiner* was already there, along with a couple of other reporters he'd met before, and they were all excited and laughing about how it looked like a scene from a movie. But when the house began to catch fire, and saw no one had surrendered, it was suddenly quiet as they all thought Patty Hearst was inside and burned to death.

When the charred bodies were later identified, and everyone learned Patty Hearst wasn't among the dead, the experience made Jason realize he really didn't like covering the serious stories and should stick with what he did best without fantasizing about trying to win a *Pulitzer Prize*.

He knew he wasn't a household name like Ben Bradee of the *Washington Post*, but he was still an editor and publisher of a newspaper that was starting to become famous for its own unique concept.

Jason figured that was good enough for now.

꙳

The *Singles News Register* was now being sold in news racks in almost every city from Santa Barbara to San Diego, and the banner on the front page now read, *"Over 150,000 Singles Will See Your Ad."*

Jason still knew that the newspaper's circulation wasn't nearly as big as it read on the cover, and didn't mind that most everyone believed it was.

Because of the high visibility of the newspaper, and the continued interest nationally about the *"singles market,"* Jason was also being contacted by many major national publications, including *U.S. News* and *World Report*, *Time Magazine*, and even another publication of Hugh Hefner's called *Qui Magazine*, to be interviewed about singles issues and the popularity and concept of advertising for serious relationships opposed to *swinger's ads*.

Jason knew he was being a little contradictory in the way he pushed meeting "that one special person" in the newspaper, and then pushing how great it was to "just date a lot of people" at his parties. But Jason would just explain whether or not he "brought singles together who were looking to get married', and then push how it was okay to "stay single and have fun" the main purpose was for his publication to become known as what he called "The *Spokes-Paper* for all singles."

Lori would usually just tease Jason when she heard him try to "sound so professional and businesslike" when being interviewed, and joke that his facetious motto of *"a little bs never hurt anyone"* was serving him well. He was definitely learning how to sound more professional and knowledgeable when he spoke to the national press, and even in his *Message from the Publisher* each issue, Jason was continuing to write about more serious topics.

Even though Jason was feeling good about what he'd accomplished so far, there were some things that made him realize he had a long way to go, especially when he finally visited the *Playboy Mansion* for the first time.

Jason had been invited to an afternoon party at the *Mansion* by a writer for *Qui Magazine*, Chris Hodenfield, who had interviewed Jason for a story about "The Singles and Classified Dating Craze" and had the opportunity to meet Hugh Hefner again.

After reminding Hefner they had met earlier that year at the Academy Awards party, Jason introduced his own beautiful *Bachelorette of the Month* he had brought to the party.

Although Jason was disappointed Lori wasn't able to come with him that day, he decided to bring another girl close to *Playboy* caliber, so it wouldn't look like he was just gawking at all the other sexy girls at Hefner's mansion.

"And this is the famous '*Playboy Grotto,*' said Hugh Hefner as he was giving Jason and a small group a quick tour of the *Playboy Mansion*.

As he continued with the Mansion tour, Hefner also talked a little about his roots, and Jason discovered they had something in common besides both being from Chicago. He learned that Hefner had attended the same school as his parents, *Steinmetz High*, although Hefner had graduated a few years earlier than Jason's parents, and they had probably never met.

Hefner also brought up that Jason's last name, *"Mershon,"* was similar to his own middle name, *"Marston,"* and joked that he and Jason might have had some common ancestor in the past.

Jason liked that he could at least talk about some trivial things they had in common, so it was more of a natural conversation, instead of feeling that Hefner was just acting as his tour guide.

"So, I've got pretty much everything I need right here at the *mansion* to keep me entertained," said Hefner with sarcastic modesty, "The magazine has been very good to me."

Although Jason knew he was a million miles away from being an editor and publisher of Hugh Hefner's status, as well as millions of dollars away, it did briefly make him fantasize about what he may be able to accomplish in the future.

Jason at least liked having something he could shoot for by the time he was as old as "Hef."

Chapter Eighteen

Between working as the editor and promoting his monthly singles party at the *Speakeasy*, Jason eventually arranged a schedule where he only needed to be at the newspaper office the last four days before each issue's deadline. Everything about the production of each issue now moved like clockwork, with his regular columnists always having their copy ready by the deadline, always having plenty of *Bachelorettes* for each cover, and being able to write any of his own copy and reviews from home, Jason had plenty of time to spend time promoting his parties in Hollywood.

One of Jason's celebrity judges in his *Bachelorette of the Month* contests, and someone he'd become friends, was John Bloom, a well-known entrepreneur from England, and who owned a popular medieval restaurant and theatre on La Cienega Boulevard called *1520 A.D.*

Jason had learned that John Bloom had been somewhat of a legendary businessman in England years earlier when he was involved with what was known as the *"Washing Machine Wars,"* which had made him a household name and millionaire before he was thirty years old.

John Bloom had given Jason a copy of his book to review in the *Singles News Register* called *It's No Sin to Make a Profit*, and Jason had learned that John was one of the pioneers to begin using direct advertising and mail order coupons to the general public, to compete with the major retailers in Great Britain. John had come up with the idea of selling washing machines, dishwashers, and refrigerators, which he was able to purchase directly from the manufacturers and sell them at half the cost than the retail markets in England.

Jason had joked with John Bloom how he had once tried to use the same idea to compete with *Mac's Ice Cream* truck by selling his ice cream bars at almost half price but was "just a kid back then" and was happy trying to make only about ten dollars a week, while John had been making millions.

"Any profit is a good profit," Jason remembered was what John Bloom had always emphasized.

Because John said he liked Jason's parties and saw how he had made them a side business to fit in with the *Singles News Register*, John decided to introduce Jason to a Middle Eastern businessman named Esau Ordines. John explained that Esau was his tenant who subleased a separate section of John's building attached to the *1520 AD* restaurant, that housed a nightclub called *The Cave*.

"Esau's nightclub had been doing poorly, and I'd hate to lose him as a tenant," John told Jason, "He might be able to use a good young promoter like you, and you might be able to pick up a few extra bucks for yourself."

During their first meeting, Esau Ordines mentioned to Jason that although *The Cave* was only open on weekends, the nightclub had lost its popularity, and he was thinking of changing the name of his nightclub to attract new business. Esau also sounded somewhat desperate to keep his business afloat and seemed very interested in having Jason promote singles parties to kick start the nightclub and said he'd be open to anything Jason could do to help.

Even before they finished their first meeting that day, Jason already had several ideas going through his head but told Esau he needed a few days to think about how he could help.

Jason saw that Esau's nightclub was attached prominently to the *1520 AD Restaurant* and the large entrance to *The Cave* had great visibility on the corner of La Cienega and San Vincente Boulevard, but most importantly, thousands of cars drove by there each day and the name *The Cave* could easily be seen by everyone driving by.

The monthly *S.T.A.R.S.* parties at *The Speakeasy* had always been scheduled for weeknights because Alex Henig and Dave Curtain didn't need any special promotions on weekends and Jason started thinking about how easier it might be to promote weekend *S.T.A.R.S* parties to his members on Friday's and Saturday nights.

He had also been thinking of producing multiple parties each month to make "a few extra bucks" and saw that this could be that opportunity.

When he met with Esau the next week, he had his pitch laid out with his plan that he knew besides making more money for both of them, was also a great opportunity for publicity and great advertising for the *Singles News Register*.

Especially with the new name for *The Cave* Jason wanted.

Because everyone was familiar with the popular bar in Beverly Hills called *The Saloon*, Jason told Esau he'd work a deal with him to allow the name change of *The Cave* to the *Singles Register Saloon* for as long as they worked together.

"People still remember the newspaper by that name, and calling in the *Singles News Register* just doesn't have the same ring as the Singles Register Saloon," Jason lightly joked, "It'll also differentiate it from the newspaper just a bit."

Jason also said he would not only give Esau a free full-page advertisement on the back cover of the *Singles News Register* each issue, but he would also produce his *S.T.A.R.S* parties exclusively at Esau's nightclub every Friday and Saturday night.

Jason was mainly picturing how great the signage of the *Singles Register Saloon* over the entrance would look to the thousands of cars passing by on La Cienega Boulevard each day, and how it would basically be like having a free billboard for his newspaper.

Jason had also suggested going with the trend of playing records instead of a live band, as *The Cave* hadn't switched over to disco yet, but Esau was completely against that idea.

"Discotheques are for the *queer* crowd," Esau said in his thick Middle Eastern accent, "I don't want those people in my bar and want to stick with live bands."

Jason saw that wasn't the case from his parties at *The Speakeasy*, but because Easu was showing great interest in everything he was pitching, Jason decided not to push that point.

There was another friend Jason had met at his parties at the *Speakeasy*, an attorney named Eliot Feldman, who offered to draw up a legal agreement that stated all the facts Esau had agreed upon. Eliot also came to the third meeting to make sure everything was legal and to work out the final agreements.

Jason and Esau eventually agreed on the name change to the *Singles Register Saloon*, but Jason was only able to negotiate fifty percent of the door money and ten percent of the bar receipts for both nights.

Jason figured with the volume of having at least eight parties a month instead of one, he should still be able to triple or quadruple the money he was making at the *Speakeasy*. He also joked to his friends about how having a nightclub named after the *Singles News Register*, could also look like his own version of Hugh Hefner's *Playboy Club*.

But mainly, he was satisfied he now had a full-time side business that he knew was going to be fun.

❦

Jason had a rare visit with both his parents at the same time when he stopped at their townhouse to drop off the box of flats for the next issue of the *Singles News Register*, and excitedly told them about the new promotions he was starting and especially the signage of the *Singles Register Saloon* on La Cienega.

"It's almost like having my own nightclub every weekend without paying for the overhead," Jason cheerfully explained, "And the name of the *Singles Register Saloon* will be seen by tens of thousands of people driving by every week."

"You should have got him to put your name on half the liquor license," his father said, "That's the only thing that's worth any cash if the guy does go out of business."

"Why would he give me his liquor license" Jason just half laughed, "I'm going to be making money off my parties, and I'm not interested in being in that part of his business."

"Well, if that Esau guy is that desperate to have you promote your parties at his place," said his father, "That liquor license is probably worth over ten thousand dollars, and you probably could have gotten half of it."

Jason thought they'd be happy at the deal he'd worked out, but saw they weren't as excited as he was.

"Richard always tries to get everything he can from his deals," his mother sarcastically added with a touch of resentment to his father, "Everyone he meets, he's just always figuring out how to get more money out of them and he's still just a salesman."

"Fuck you," his father snapped back at his mother, "I would've just gotten more money out of him.

As usual, Jason was sorry he'd brought anything up at all, and was just hoping there wouldn't be any traffic on his way back to Hollywood after deciding thirty minutes with his parents, was twice as long as he should have stayed.

જ

Jason began his new promotions in late summer, and the large name of the *Singles Register Saloon* above the entrance to the nightclub looked great from the street and gave him all the free advertising he had hoped for.

Even though Jason, Lori, and his other friends were constantly passing out flyers to the same crowds that had attended the parties at the *Speakeasy*, they saw that the Hollywood and Beverly Hills crowd weren't as interested in going to live music clubs as they were discos.

Jason was still making a fair profit off the door and bar money, and knew because it was Esau's nightclub, and he still was against changing the bar into a disco, he just needed to promote to a different crowd. He actually was drawing a few hundred people on weekends from the older crowd who still liked dancing and seeing live bands, including many who were readers of the *Singles News Register*. Unfortunately, that audience didn't drink or spend money nearly as much as the younger crowd had, but Esau did seem satisfied.

Jason was also still trying to continue his relationship with Lori as it always had been, but with her recently graduating from *Brooks College* and deciding to start working on her own career, they were only able to see each other on weekends and sometimes only at Jason's weekly parties at the *Singles Register Saloon*.

Lori was still trying to decide whether she wanted to be an actress, model or singer, and was usually busy during the week on interviews or investigating other opportunities for work. She also told Jason she also didn't mind if Jason took Anne Gaybis, Mixie Thompson, Sandi Shore, or others they both knew, to places like *The*

Troubadour, The Roxy, The Whiskey-a-Go-Go, or to attend other events he needed to write about in his newspaper when she wasn't available.

"I know you are getting an image as *'Mr. Singles Guy'* and people are going to talk when they see you with other women," Lori lightly laughed, "But I just want you to know I'm going to be secure enough about our relationship not to show any jealousy."

They had both come to an understanding after the one argument they had earlier that year that they never wanted jealousy to be a part of their relationship again, but Jason couldn't help but sometimes wonder if they had both been focusing too much on their careers, and very seldom even talked about their long-term plans together anymore. He also knew they had plenty of time to talk about anything that serious in the future and tried not to dwell on it very often.

Lori did attend an advance private movie screening in Beverly Hills of the Robert Redford movie that they both Lori and Jason were anxious to see, *The Great Gatsby.*

Both Jason and Lori had been fans of the book and they had even sometimes worn the matching nametags of Jay Gatsby and Daisy Buchanan, or even the author of *The Great Gatsby,* F. Scott Fitzgerald and his wife Zelda, at Jason's *S.T.A.R.S* parties for his *"Famous Couple's"* party match game. They both joked that wearing nametags that matched each other would keep everyone at the parties from trying to hit on either one of them, and let everyone know they had both "already found their matches" on those nights.

After *The Great Gatsby* movie screening, as they were walking up Doheny Boulevard towards Wilshire where Jason's car was parked, Lori was still singing the song that was *"stuck in her head"* that was the main theme song in *The Great Gatsby,* Irving Berlin's old standard *What'll I Do?*

"That movie was so romantic," Lori continued smiling, "We would have fit right in as a couple back in the days of *The Great Gatsby,* especially how we both love all those old songs that were in the movie."

"I liked the style of suits Robert Redford wore and the cars back then," Jason said, "I could have seen myself having fun back then."

"I could see you being like *The Great Gatsby* in a few more years and always having big parties at your big mansion someday," Lori smiled, "But I wouldn't want to be anything like Daisy Buchanan because she was the perfect example of someone who was never completely happy with herself, and gave up on her real dreams too early."

"That's why we both have to think about our career plans apart from each other sometimes," Lori again lightly brought up her mantra, "Remember, you can't make another person happy until you're completely happy with yourself."

Jason still basically agreed with Lori, and although he felt he was probably the happiest he'd ever been, he knew it still might take a couple more years until he was completely happy about everything.

The best thing about having live bands on the nights Jason and Lori would spend at the *Singles Register Saloon*, was that towards the end of the night, when the crowds got smaller, some of the bands would also let them sing more contemporary pop songs to each other, instead of the usual piano bar songs they had sung together multiple times.

Aside from having fun occasionally singing at the *Singles Register Saloon*, between promoting and hosting two parties a week instead of just one party a month, as well as putting together two issues for the *Singles News Register* every month, Jason and Lori had very little time for much else together.

Jason was a little disappointed, but actually somewhat relieved, when after a little over two months the *Singles Register Saloon* opened, it turned out that Esau Ordines had mainly been interested in having the club show an increase in business, so he could sell his lease on nightclub to someone else at a profit.

John Bloom told Jason he'd approved the lease transfer because Esau sold it to another Arab with "a ton of money," who was going completely remodel the nightclub and reopen it as a disco.

"This is what Esau was planning all along," Eliot Feldman lightly complained when he found out about the sale, "He was just trying to stay open long enough to sell his lease and the business to someone else."

"All the damn Arabs are moving to Beverly Hills now, buying and selling, buying and selling…," Eliot continued to lightly complain, "Pretty soon they'll be more *camel jockeys* in this town than *Jews* like me."

Jason's father was mainly bothered that Jason had never gotten his name on the liquor license so he could have squeezed some more money off of Esau when he sold the business.

"I was just promoting parties there and was never an owner," Jason argued back, "Why would he even think about giving me part of his liquor license?"

"Well, it had our newspaper name on it, and you should've gotten more from it," his father said with a touch of disgust, "You just don't know how business works yet."

 But Jason wasn't really that upset.

He'd at least netted over fifteen hundred dollars in the two months he promoted the *Singles Register Saloon* and knew he could always go back and start his monthly S.T.A.R.S parties again at the *Speakeasy*, which weren't nearly as much hard work.

Plus, during the time the new owners were remodeling the space for their new disco, the signage above the entrance still boldly read the *Singles Register Saloon* and remained visible for three more months to everyone driving past.

Jason had gotten want he wanted for at least a short time and kept reminding himself that *"Any profit was a good profit,"* no matter what his father would always argue.

Chapter Nineteen

Jason enjoyed getting the opportunity to meet Ronald Reagan again when he was invited to a private political event with Rudy Vallee and Stan Adams during Reagan's last term as California's Governor.

"You probably don't remember me, Governor," said Jason when he was shaking Reagan's hand at the reception, "But we met about ten years ago after you gave a speech for Barry Goldwater at Knott's Berry Farm."

"Of course, I do," said Reagan, "I never forget a face."

Jason smiled, knowing that Reagan had turned into a good politician and knew that there was no chance Reagan remembered some little kid from that long ago and already knew his *A little BS* never hurt anybody" applied even more to politicians.

Being a member of the press, Jason had already met several other local and statewide politicians socially at a few parties but really hadn't been involved with writing anything leaning in one political position or the other. Jason had never wanted to personally show partiality in the newspaper, and even though he had Rudy Vallee's column that leaned Republican, it was titled *One Man's Opinion,* and Jason always edited it enough not to sound so extreme. His other serious columnist, Don Harris, sometimes wrote about politics but generally covered both sides equally.

Jason still liked following politics personally and tried to keep up any with issues that he might be asked when he was being interviewed himself about the *Singles News Register.*

Stan Adams took photos of Rudy Vallee and Jason with Ronald and Nancy Reagan that night, insisting that "the photos would add gravitas," to Jason's newspaper.

When Eliot Feldman saw Jason's photo with Reagan in the next issue of the Singles News Register, he called Jason with an idea he had.

Eliot had placed personal ads in the *Singles News Register* for the past several issues and always told Jason about the nice women he'd meet and how he loved the newspaper's entire concept. He always said he was especially impressed seeing the banner of *"Over 150,000 Singles Will See Your Ad"* across the cover of each issue.

Eliot mentioned that he was heavily involved with Jerry Brown's campaign for Governor that year, and said "Jerry was also impressed" when Eliot had told him about Jason's large circulation and added to Jerry that he was "personal friends" with the owner of the newspaper.

"Have you ever considered a political endorsement for the election this year?" Eliot asked Jason, "Your newspaper represents a pretty good group of voters who fit Jerry's demographics."

Jason occasionally tried to show a serious side in his *Message from the Publisher* and had written about the unfairness of housing discrimination against single people because of their supposed wild images the past year, and also about how single people were taxed more than married couples, but he had never written about his views of any particular politician himself.

Because Jerry Brown was single, Eliot thought it would be great if Jason, as the "editor and publisher of the Singles News Register," would consider endorsing Brown for Governor.

"Some of the press has been making a big deal about Jerry still being single at thirty-six years old," Eliot said, "And his opponent, Houston Flournoy has been hitting him for not being a *typical family man* type of candidate."

"Maybe you can write about how by not having the distraction of a family will help a governor focus more on his job," Eliot continued to pitch lightly, "You can use your angle how you don't need to be married to accomplish great things, and how it may even be beneficial having a single governor."

"I'd be glad to do an interview with Jerry Brown," said Jason, "But I'd want to do an interview with Houston Flournoy as well, to at least show both sides to my readers before considering any endorsement."

Jason did think it was *cool* that Eliot and Jerry Brown felt the *Singles News Register* was important enough to want an endorsement, and it would be a good experience writing a serious interview. He had done dozens of interviews with celebrities, but they were usually all *fluff* pieces, so he knew he was going to need to brush up on some issues that year so the candidates would take him and his newspaper seriously.

"Well, I think it would look good for your newspaper to defend the *discriminatory* tactics against the only single candidate," Eliot facetiously half laughed, "But I just thought of something else I might be able to set up with Jerry's campaign for you."

Eliot said that if Jason wanted an even better story, he might be able to get Jason special access to Brown's campaign and spend a few days "hanging out with Jerry" for an "exclusive behind the scenes look" at him on the campaign trail. He also said that *Rolling Stone Magazine*, which Eliot said "had about the same circulation as the *Singles News Register*," was attempting to get similar access, and added that because he was friends with Jerry, he may be able to persuade him to choose Jason's newspaper.

"There's a party I'm setting up with some backers next week, and you can come and meet Jerry yourself," said Eliot, "I think you'll like him after you meet him."

"And, if I could say you were definitely going to endorse him, I can probably get you that extra access," Eliot smiled.

Except for Ronald Reagan, there weren't any politician's Jason liked, but what Eliot was offering sounded fun, and he wouldn't be bothered *selling out* with an endorsement for a little of the usual quid pro quo, as a favor, but he didn't want to make it sound like he was easy.

"Well, after I interview both Flournoy and Jerry," Jason smiled half-seriously, "I probably should make an endorsement in my Message from the Publisher for the governor who cares most about singles issues."

"I'll be glad to meet Jerry next week, and I'm sure we can work something out about an endorsement," Jason added positively to Eliot.

The following week, Jason was standing with Eliot Feldman and Jerry Brown having cocktails at the reception in Westwood before Jerry was to give a short speech to a group of supporters at a private home.

Jason thought Jerry Brown didn't have much of an outgoing personality for a politician and actually seemed kind of boring with his monotone and serious way that he carried on a conversation. Eliot had already told Jason that Jerry was just a deep thinker, after spending a couple of years studying in a Jesuit seminary to become a Catholic priest, before deciding to get into politics.

"Jerry is a very serious and thoughtful thinker," Eliot had said, "and he doesn't like really talking about trivial bullshit that much."

Jason wanted to appear serious and tried to keep their discussion on the upcoming interview.

"I actually want to play down the singles angle," Jerry Brown was telling Jason, "I'll be glad to sit down for an interview and talk about singles issues, but the other side has been slamming me with all the *family values* crap, and I don't need to keep reminding voters about that."

"That's fine," said Jason, "But as long as we talk about something that my readers can relate, so it geared to my market."

"No problem," said Jerry, "Just stay in touch with Eliot, and we'll set up a good day for the interview."

Jerry Brown only spent about ten minutes talking with Jason and Eliot before joining his other supporters at the reception, but Jason at least enjoyed having a *meet and greet* personally with him.

"Oh, and by the way," Jerry added before leaving, "I appreciate your endorsement."

Jason was slightly bothered that Eliot had already told him the newspaper was endorsing him before he had even done the interview and didn't want Jerry Brown to think that just an interview was all it took for his endorsement. He wondered if what Eliot told him about "special access" was just a little bs too, but he knew if he could actually spend time on the campaign trail hanging out with Brown, he'd still probably sell-out and give an endorsement just for the experience.

Jason knew having it appear that his newspaper had the *juice* to have that kind of personal access would add a lot of *gravitas* to the *Singles News Register*.

He also lightly thought back to eight years earlier when he facetiously joked to his friends that he *helped* Ronald Reagan defeat Jerry Brown's father, Pat Brown, by passing out bumper stickers and lawn signs and if Jerry Brown did win the election, he could again lightly joke that his endorsement had also *helped* Brown win that year,

But he was mainly thinking about how impressive it would sound to his friends telling them his newspaper had chosen over *Rolling Stone Magazine* to spend time with Jerry Brown on the campaign trail.

Then he'd really feel he had some *juice*.

꙾

Jason was having lunch at Schwab's with Rudy Vallee and Sidney Skolsky while looking over their columns for the next issue.

"Well, I don't like him at all," said Rudy, when Jason mentioned he'd be interviewing Jerry Brown in the *Singles News Register*, "The last thing we need is a god damned liberal like him running the state."

"Well, Nixon's resignation hasn't helped Republicans, especially here in California, and I don't think Flournoy has a chance," said Sidney, "I think it's going to be a big sweep for the Democrats this year."

"I've got my interview with Houston Flournoy next week before I interview Brown," said Jason, "So I'm at least going to see if I can get some *singles angle* that'll make it relevant to my readers."

"That's good," said Sidney, "They're both doing dozens of interviews, and you don't want to just write the same old garbage they always talk about."

"If you want my opinion," Rudy added in his usual gruff tone, "I think Jerry Brown a closet homo and don't be surprised if that news comes out before the election."

"Don't be silly," Jason laughed. "Everyone knows he's been fucking Linda Ronstadt."

"That's what I've heard too," said Sidney Skolsky, "plus I heard he had a thing with Natalie Wood for a while too."

"Well, that's another reason he shouldn't be governor!" countered Rudy, "Hanging out with those hippies and probably smoking dope all the time!"

"Well, that kind of stuff would make my interview a lot more interesting," joked Jason, "But I didn't see that side of him when I met him."

Jason couldn't picture someone as boring as Jerry Brown was actually a wild party guy but figured he might see another side of him when he got to know him better and spent more time with him.

"I've already talked with Don Harris about some questions I should ask, so it doesn't just look like a fluff piece," Jason lightly added. "I've got to show my *serious journalistic side* sometimes too, and don't want everyone to think that I'm just partying all the time myself either."

"Well, I still think he's a *homo*," Rudy said more sarcastically, "So just watch yourself when you are spending that 'special access' time with him."

"Oh, don't worry, Rudy, I will," Jason also sarcastically joked back, "I promise you that."

❧

During his first interview with Houston Flournoy, Jason saw that he was bringing up quite a few things about how *"family values"* was an important issue to consider in the election, just as Eliot had mentioned Flournoy had been doing.

But at least Flournoy seemed to be more personable than Jerry Brown and did give a cute quote that he said Jason could direct towards his readers to consider about his candidacy.

Jason even decided to split his cover story with his current *Bachelorette of the Month* with a photo of Flournoy and prominently featured the cute quote as the bold headline for that issue.

The *Singles News Register* with Jason's Houston Flournoy interview was in the news racks the same week as the second televised debate between Jerry Brown and Flournoy was being broadcast for a statewide audience.

Jason had a S.T.A.R.S party at the *Speakeasy* that night and missed the debate, but he did hear about it when an irritated Eliot Feldman called him at home early the next morning.

"Did you read the newspapers yet about the *little incident* that happened during the debate last night?" Eliot sarcastically asked Jason, "Here's what's written on the front page of the LA Times today."

Eliot then began reading the article and the *little incident* he was irritated about.

"Midge Flournoy, wife of the GOP candidate, sat in the front row during the debate and was holding a copy of the Singles Register newspaper under her arm," Eliot was reading with a touch of sarcasm, "When asked why she had the publication, Mrs. Flournoy stood and held it up to show a bold headline that read, Flournoy says, *Don't Hold It Against Me Because I'm Married!*"

"Hey, that's great publicity, and I knew that was a good headline!" Jason laughed, "I wish they would have said *Singles News Register*, but having the LA Times mentioning us in a front-page news story adds a lot of credibility for my newspaper."

396

"Well, Jerry didn't like that *your newspaper* came up during the debate last night for the entire state to hear about," said Eliot, "Plus the interview that you wrote, had so much stuff about family values, and how important they were to defining a person's character, it almost sounded like you were endorsing Flournoy."

"I was just quoting what Flournoy said during the interview," Jason lightly justified, "Hopefully, Jerry can give me a good front-page quote when I interview him for the next issue."

"And don't worry, Eliot," Jason added, "I'm still planning on endorsing Jerry in the issue that comes out right before the election."

"Jerry is still looking forward to your endorsement," Eliot said with slight resignation, "But we're not sure if an interview that reminds people that he's single again is good timing right now."

"But I've already wrote that my *exclusive interview* with Jerry will be in the next issue," Jason said with his own irritation, "It won't look good for me if he backs out now."

"I'll talk to him," said Eliot, "But it's on hold for right now."

Three days later, Eliot ended up apologizing that Jerry Brown's "schedule had just gotten too busy" to sit down for an interview, but "Jerry wished Jason well" and still hoped Jason would consider the endorsement.

"Oh, and Jerry has decided to give *Rolling Stone Magazine* exclusive access to the rest of his campaign," added Eliot, "It's nothing against you personally, but he just thinks it more of the market he wants to reach."

Jason wasn't happy about Jerry Brown backing out at the last minute, and guessing that all the talk about *special access* had also probably been bullshit. He also wasn't happy about having to write in his *Message from the Publisher,* an explanation and excuse to his readers for not having his exclusive interview he had promised.

Although he was going to keep it to himself, Jason knew that he really didn't like Jerry Brown and was now hoping that Houston Flournoy would pull off an upset and win the election.

Jason still thought it was fun that he managed to be a small part of the California governor's race that year, and the *Singles News Register* was at least discussed in the same breath as the *LA Times* and *Herald Examiner*.

His newspaper did have some *gravitas*, and Jason felt he had accomplished what he had wanted in his two and a half years as an editor regardless of a few bumps in the road.

Chapter Twenty

Jason and Lori were driving to spend another weekend in Las Vegas and talking about everything they were planning with their careers in 1975, and after laughing about how the *Singles News Register* was at least a minor story in that year's upcoming election, Jason was surprised about the career choice Lori said she was considering.

"I've been talking with a photographer I know who thinks I should pose nude," Lori carefully said.

Jason half laughed and thought she was joking.

"I am seriously thinking about it," she started explaining more, "The photos will be artfully shot and nothing sleazy, but it's a chance to make some good money for myself."

"You're not really thinking about posing nude, are you?" Jason smiled, "I hope that streaking we did once didn't give you that idea."

"I really need to get my career going and make some money," Lori said, "The photographer thinks he can get me in *Penthouse Magazine*."

Jason didn't want to act like he was that bothered by the idea but still lightly tried to discourage her.

"What about the mole on your left tit that you were so worried about when we did streak?" he joked, "Aren't you worried about everyone seeing that?"

"I can just cover it up with makeup or have him airbrush it," Lori joked back, "And Penthouse pays great money for their centerfolds."

Jason saw that if Lori had already thought about all of that, she was actually serious, but still thought he could dissuade her without being too obvious.

"Don't you at least think *Playboy* would be classier?" Jason asked, "The girls who pose in Playboy seem to get more respect."

"Well, I think Penthouse is classier," Lori disagreed with slight irritation, "I know you like Playboy because you've met Hugh Hefner, but I'm not a fan."

"Well, I don't really think it's a good idea," Jason finally decided to give his opinion, "I don't see how that can help your career."

"It didn't seem to bother you that Edy Williams posed nude!" Lori suddenly snapped back. "And besides, it's my body and my decision, so you shouldn't even worry about it."

Jason didn't want to start any type of argument but didn't like her defiant tone.

"I'm not worried about it, but I just don't like it.", Jason said with slight irritation before lightly adding, "And I hope you haven't been reading *Cosmopolitan* magazine too much lately and starting to turn into a feminist."

That last comment at least got Lori to laugh.

"I've also been thinking the past few months about my own future," Lori started speaking in a calmer voice, "And I've been spending so much time trying to support all of your different projects and goals this year, I've kind of gotten away from some of the things that I wanted to do."

"I know there's still a lot of things you want to accomplish, and there are some things I know I want to do as far as a career myself," Lori continued, "And I think you should support what I want to do."

The conversation made Jason wonder what Lori had been doing during the times they weren't together, and who she'd been even hanging out with who would ask her to pose nude.

"So, who is this guy that wants you to pose nude for him," Jason asked with a slight smirk, "Is it some photographer I know?"

"No, it's just the boyfriend of a girl I've been friends with for a long time," Lori said, starting to sound irritated again, "I wouldn't even have considered it unless it was someone that I felt comfortable with."

"I don't know why you think me posing nude should affect you," Lori added with her own smirk, "And it's nothing that you should even feel jealous about if that's what's bothering you."

"I'm not jealous," Jason tried to say more calmly, "There's just so many other things you talked about doing, and I'm just surprised you think posing nude will be good for you."

"Well, I've decided this is something I want to do," she added with finality, "And you should be happy that I'm even getting this opportunity."

"I still don't think it's a good idea but just do whatever you want," Jason said with enough irritation to let her know he still didn't like her idea. "Whatever makes you happy."

"Thank you," Lori said with a touch of sarcasm, "I'm glad you're supporting me as much as I always support you."

They continued driving silently for several minutes after Jason turned up the music louder on his stereo, not wanting to talk anymore about that subject, but when Lori finally turned down the music, she began talking in her philosophical tone.

"I know we're both planning on a lot of different things with our careers next year, but we should realize that we might have to work on our different goals separately sometimes without it affecting what we have together," Lori said less sarcastically but still serious, "But neither of us are ready to get married yet and we've always talked about not being able to make someone else happy until we're happy with ourselves."

Jason didn't like that that the conversation was still serious, but just let Lori talk.

"I know we're both in a city where there is constant temptation," Lori continued, "Especially in your line of work with all the girls you need to meet for your bachelorettes and the ones you try to get to come to your parties."

"But I told you that I'm secure about that," she added, "I don't want you to think I'm worried about what you're doing when we aren't together."

"Well, I'm not interested in being with anyone else," Jason tried to say without sounding irritated, "I'm happy just being with you, and I told you I'm not jealous."

"I just don't want you to be inhibited by what I'm trying to do either," she said, "Just like I don't want you to think I'm inhibited by all the girls that you're always with when we aren't together."

"As long as you don't fall in love with someone else," she tried to lightly break the seriousness, "Or screw around with anybody in public where everybody would know."

"Jeez, Lori, you know you don't have to worry about that," Jason tried to lightly joke back, "You know that I'm an open book with you and the other girls I go out with are just friends."

Jason really did feel his life had pretty much always been an open book, and he always shared everything with Lori that was doing. Except, for that night at the Oscars.

"I'm not saying it's okay to sleep around and wouldn't be happy if you did," Lori continued, "But we need to be mature and support each other without worrying about what we do when we aren't together."

"But if you do get too horny when I'm not around," she tried to joke again, "Just be discreet because I don't ever want to know."

Jason didn't know how the issue for fidelity came up or why she was joking so flippantly about the subject but was anxious to change the subject.

"You know I'll support you as much as you support me, baby," Jason decided to try and end that topic, "So if it's something you really want to do, you should do it then."

"Well, they're going to just be test shots anyway," Lori also said in a lighter mood, "They may not even want me, but I at least want to try."

"The photographer said I don't even have to use my real name in Penthouse," Lori also said more lightly, "It's just something I can do one time and make some good money to get me started with some of the other things I want to do."

"Well, I hope you do get it then," Jason tried to sound more positive.

Jason wasn't sure he completely felt that way but knew he didn't want to argue about it with Lori anymore and needed to act mature about it.

"Well, even if I don't get accepted by Penthouse, I'll at least have some sexy photos we can look at together," Lori started to tease as she sat close to Jason and started rubbing his leg, "Hopefully they'll get you horny, and our sex can get even wilder."

Jason knew that Lori had always been his *real-life* Sue Ann Daley from *The Adventurers*, and didn't need any naked pictures of her to enhance anything they had together, but he was just glad the conversation was over, and Lori was back to being her romantic self again.

But he still hoped she wasn't serious.

Chapter Twenty-One

Jason tried not to think that anything was changing in his relationship with Lori, but between everything he was doing with his newspaper and promoting his monthly *S.T.A.R.S* party, along with everything Lori was now doing with her own career, it did seem they were living separate lives even more since their last weekend in Las Vegas together.

Especially, after *Penthouse Magazine* accepted her test shots and decided to shoot more nude photos of Lori for an issue that would come out sometime in 1975.

Even though Jason had tried to act excited for her, he also didn't want to admit to Lori that the thought of her appearing naked in *Penthouse* seemed to be more of a *turn off* than a *turn on* to him, regardless of how Lori said it should make him *horny*.

Because Jason and Lori both agreed that their separate careers should be nothing to cause any jealousy or change their relationship, they seldom questioned each other about their time apart. There were still some other things that were said that weekend that did cross Jason's mind occasionally, but he didn't want to let it distract him from focusing on his own business.

Jason was still personally interviewing and writing the stories for all of his *Bachelorettes of the Week* and was at the apartment of an actress friend of Annie Gaybis he'd decided to use for his next cover.

Her name was Lilita Krisaan, and after she'd invited Jason to her Hollywood apartment for an early afternoon interview, they both said they thought they recognized each other and may have met before.

Lilita explained she'd only been in Hollywood for a little over a year after growing up in Boston and was originally from Latvia, but she added that since her country was now part of the Soviet Union, she hadn't been back to Latvia since she was a very little girl.

Jason and Lilita eventually figured out where they'd seen each other before when Lilita mentioned she regularly worked as a cocktail waitress at the *Café Brasseri*, and remembered seeing Jason there with Lori the night they were in the booth with Micky Dolez and Harry Nielson.

"You were all drinking a lot and keeping me busy," Lilita half laughed, "But you seemed like a pretty fun group that night."

"Well, I guess we were destined to meet eventually," Jason smiled, "I'm just surprised I didn't notice you enough that night to consider you for a bachelorette back then."

Although Jason guessed Lilita was only a few years older than him, he told her she had the glamorous look of the 1930s and 1940s blond actresses he used to see on The *Million Dollar Movie*.

"I used to have a thing for actresses like Lana Turner, Betty Grable, and Ginger Rogers when I was a little kid," Jason lightly complimented her, "And I like that you have that look and think you'll make an interesting bachelorette for my next issue."

"It's funny you should mention that," Lilita said, "I've got a small role in the movie *Day of the Locust* that takes place in the 1930s, and I'm playing the part of Marlene Dietrich in a couple of scenes this week."

"But this is the way I usually look, and it's not for just the part," she smiled, "So I guess that's why they cast me in the movie."

Jason saw that Lilita had a cute personality and liked that she laughed a lot and had a fun disposition, and felt like he was having more fun than usual talking with her during his interview that afternoon, and they'd often stray from his general bachelorette questions and talk more about each other.

They were both laughing more about personal stories rather than discussing the questions that Jason would normally ask during his other interviews, and he was starting to feel like their conversation was almost similar to a first date, along with noticing that Lilita was starting to feel the same way.

"This is a turning into a fun interview, and I hope this isn't out of line," Lita lightly laughed, "But would you like to smoke a joint with me?"

"It'll just relax me more," she half defended, "and maybe think of some more things to make your bachelorette story interesting."

"Well, I'm not really a pot smoker, but I don't mind if you have one," Jason said, not wanting to change the light atmosphere.

When Lilita left to roll herself a joint, Jason started thinking about how much fun he was having, and didn't feel guilty that they had also seemed to be lightly flirting with each other.

He hadn't seen Lori for over two weeks, and they had only spoken on the phone a few times during that time. Whenever he had been with Lori, everything seemed romantic as usual, but although he hadn't tried to feel different since she'd gotten involved with the *Penthouse* crowd, he found himself wondering if Lori was still *"The One"* at times.

When Lilita came back from rolling a joint and sat down, she also brought two glasses of wine, saying she didn't want to feel like she was relaxing all by herself.

"I didn't think I'd be having this much fun talking with you and being interviewed," Lilita smiled as she took a deep hit off the joint, "I'm glad Annie introduced us."

"Oh, and by the way," she added, "You can just call me Lita cause that's what all my friends usually just call me."

"Well, Lita, I'm having fun too," Jason smiled as he picked up his wine glass and held it towards her, "So I'd like to make a toast... to the interview I'm enjoying the most."

By the time they had finished the interview and were on their third glass of wine together, they were both surprised they'd spent four hours talking, and it was already after six pm.

"I wish I had some more stories to tell you," Lita smiled, "This was a fun day, and I'm sorry it's over."

Jason was sorry the interview was over as well and suddenly decided to extend it.

"Well, there's a restaurant I've been wanting to try called *Lawry's The Prime Rib*," Jason tried to say in only a half businesslike manner, "If you'd like to continue the fun we're having, how about having dinner with me tonight?"

Jason and Lori had never been to that restaurant, so he decided if she wanted him to be discreet, and not be seen by anybody they both knew, he would at least keep that end of the bargain with her.

He also had convinced himself that he wasn't going on a *romantic* date with Lita because he had been planning to review *Lawry's the Prime Rib* in his newspaper sometime that month anyway, and seeing he didn't know or ask what Lori was doing that night, he decided that a *little light flirting never hurt anybody*.

It was all just a part of his business.

❧

Jason had decided against giving any endorsement for Governor of California that year and even slightly slammed Jerry Brown for backing out of the promised interview in his *Message from the Publisher* a week before the election. He had explained to Eliot Feldman he felt he needed to write that for his *own credibility* as the editor and publisher, and although Eliot wasn't that happy about it, he said he wouldn't let it affect his personal friendship with Jason.

Jerry Brown easily won the election regardless, and even though Jason felt he didn't have as much influence as he hoped, he still looked forward to possibly having more in 1975.

It was only a couple weeks after Jerry Brown was elected, and Jason was having pizza at *The Rainbow Bar and Grill* with Lori, Annie Gaybis, Stan Adams, Mixie

Thompson, Sandi Shore, and Lita Krissan, who was now part of Jason's regular circle of friends.

"I've decided to have a contest for the *Bachelorette of the Year* at my *S.T.A.R.S* Christmas party next month," Jason announced to his friends, "I have twenty-four bachelorettes each year, and I think it's a good promotion to have all the cover girls end each year with a big contest."

"Sure, it's only natural having a contest like that," Annie Gaybis agreed, "Just like Hefner's *Playmate of the Year*."

"Or Bob Guccione's *Pet of the Year*," Lori lightly added with a little sarcasm as if to remind everyone *Penthouse* was as important as *Playboy*.

"Exactly," Jason quickly said, wanting to show Lori he agreed with her," "I mean, the Singles News Register isn't quite the caliber of those magazines yet, but it should get some good outside press for us to keep attracting new readers."

"We've got five beautiful bachelorettes sitting here tonight," Stan Adams smiled to the girls at the table, "I've enjoyed photographing all of you for your cover stories, and I'm glad I'm just the *official* photographer and wouldn't have to choose just one of you."

"Well, I'm keeping it out of my hands too," Jason continued, "I'm just going to have a page with the photos of all of this year's bachelorettes, and have my readers vote and decide.''

"Well, I can't win," Lori smiled to everyone at the table, "Everyone knows Jason's my boyfriend, and it wouldn't look too good."

"Besides Jason, I am under contract with Penthouse now, and I can't appear in any other publications," Lori added with light regret, "So legally, I don't think you're going to be able to use any photos of me in your newspaper for any contest."

"Lori's right, everyone knows we're a couple, and it wouldn't look good," Jason agreed without mentioning Lori's contract, "So I just won't run Lori's picture with the other bachelorettes in the next issue."

Jason was still a little disappointed that Lori had distanced herself as a bachelorette and seemed to insinuate that she had moved on to bigger pastures instead of being "just a *cover girl*" on the *Singles News Register*.

He knew they still had a romantic bond together and still tried to let Lori know he supported her.

"I also think that seeing we're going to have a bachelor governor in California next year," Jason decided to switch topics. "It's time we also started featuring a *Bachelor* of *the Week* in the Singles News Register."

"And by putting both an attractive young bachelor and bachelorette on each cover, might finally get the younger crowd to start advertising for dates," Jason added, "And, that's what our main purpose of the newspaper is anyway, so I've got to keep trying to get that across."

405

"I don't want to shoot any guys for the cover," laughed Stan Adams, "You can have Wally Eagler or James Mares shoot those pictures."

"Don't worry, Stan, they're not going to be posing like Burt Reynolds did in Cosmopolitan," Jason lightly teased him, "Just some headshots or dressed in suits and ties."

"Yeah, Stan, since *Cosmo* did it with Burt Reynolds, you won't have to worry about it looking that *gay* anymore," Mixie also teased.

"Sure, it's just equal rights for men," Lita added lightly, "You can be the *official photographer* of both the most eligible bachelorettes and bachelors of California now."

"And also, because you girls have finally got your *equal rights amendment* you all wanted," Jason lightly continued, "I think the guys should start being able to enter beauty contests, and I might even start some Bachelor of the Month contests at my parties."

"I like the idea of contests for men," Sandi Shore said with excitement, "You're always having us go around with you, hustling up girls to be in your contests, so it'll be fun to start hitting up all the hot looking guys in town too."

"And I'll be glad to judge those contests too!" Annie joined in the enthusiasm with the other girls.

"We've just been having dance contests and bachelorette contests and need something new to keep the parties fresh," Jason added, "Plus, it should attract even more girls to the parties."

"Well, seeing that equal rights is the big thing right now," said Lori, "Those guys should see what we have to go through being gawked at all the time."

"Oh brother, I can't believe how much things are changing these days and how crazy it's getting out there," Stan facetiously started to moan, "I think I'm starting to miss the good old days already.".

"Well anyway, that's just a couple new things I'm thinking about, but that's enough about business," smiled Jason, "Let's make a toast to the most important thing we all need to remember about whatever we do try and accomplish next year." Jason lifted his cocktail glass towards his friends to make a toast.

"Here's to always having *FUN!*" he cheerfully toasted.

"*To having FUN!*" everyone agreed as they clicked their glasses together.

Jason was again confident that 1975 was going to be his best year yet.

BOOK THREE PHOTO GALLERY

Chasin' With JASON

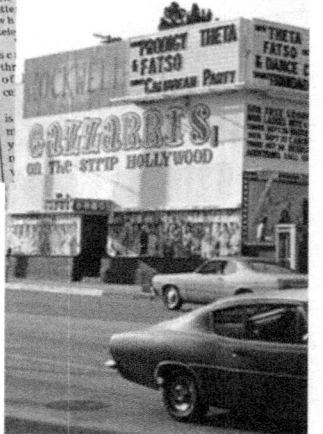

Top and Bottom: Some of the popular nightclubs on the Sunset Strip in the early 1970's. Center: Jason's new position as Editor of the Singles Register in 1972 and his new column called "Chasin' with Jason" about nightlife and the singles scene during that time.

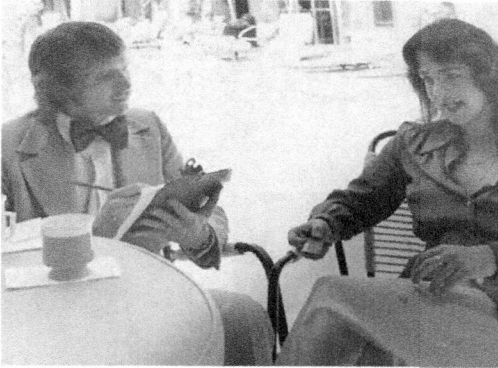

Two of Jason's early celebrity interviews for the *Singles Register* - Stockard Channing (left photo) and Minnesota Fats (right) with Mike McInerney (left).

Jason at Gazzarri's nightclub with actor Dennis Cole and contestants in the "Queen of the Artist's and Models Ball" in October, 1972.

Jason at Artist's and Model's Ball with his date Lynn, on his left arm, producer of the Ball, Gary Berwin, and actor George Montgomery.

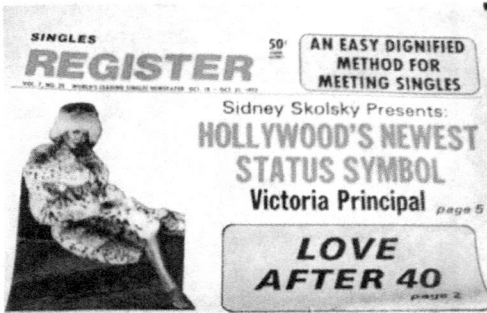

Top: Two copies of early issues of the *Singles Register* 1972-73 as Jason tried different styles as editor to make it a real newspaper as well as a dating service. Bottom left: Jason at one of his favorite spots on "Restaurant Row" on La Cienega Blvd in Hollywood, The Islander. Middle right: At Alan Hale's Lobster Barrel, where Jason's former taxi fare "Terri", was thrilled when Jason introduced her to "The Skipper" from Gilligan's Island. Bottom right: Jason and Lori Wagner at the Troubadour nightclub, backstage with Kris Kristofferson and Rita Coolidge.

The Islander in Hollywood (above), was Jason and Lori's favorite hangout, as well as where they could both sing along with the house bands in the Islander Lounge (below).

Jason and Edy Williams at The Comedy Store press party.

Sammy Shore and Redd Foxx at Jason's first press party at The Comedy Store.

Sandi Shore and Lori Wagner with a party-goer at the press party.

Lori, Jason, and Annie Gaybis at the second press party at Hollywood Park Racetrack, 1973.

Jason with actor/singer Rudy Vallee, one of his new celebrity columnists.

Dave Curtin, Grace Robbins, author Harold Robbins, and Jason.

Stan Adams, Jason, and Alex Henig at the Hearts and Flowers Ball at the Beverly Hilton Hotel, February, 1974.

One of the contestants in Jason's first beauty pageant, Queen of the Hearts and Flowers Ball.

Top: Jason and Lori "streaking" at The Speakeasy, March, 1974. Bottom: Jason and Edy Williams arrive at the 46th Annual Academy Awards (right) and pose with the "Toy Oscar" (left) they were facetiously awarded by the press for "Best Entrance on the Red Carpet" by a couple.

Jason, along with one of his Bachelorette's Of The Month, pose inside the infamous Grotto during his first visit to the Playboy Mansion.

The view from La Cienega and San Vicente Boulevard of the "Singles Register Saloon" (left of the 1520 AD restaurant).

Pico Post 8/ 1/ 74
74-19840
FICTITIOUS BUSINESS
NAME STATEMENT
The following persons are doing business as: Singles Register Saloon, 335 S La Cienega, Los Angeles, Ca. 90048.

Jason Mershon, 8440 Sunset, 1205 Hollywood, Ca 90069

Essau Ordenes, 331 S. Ardmore, Los Angeles, Ca. 90020.

This business is conducted by a general partnership

SIGNED
Essau Ordenes
Jason Mershon

This statement was filed with the County Clerk of Los Angeles County on July 25, 1974.

4T 8/ 1, 8/ 8, 8/ 15, 8/ 22/ 74

SINGLES NEWS REGISTER

Editor and Publisher
JASON MERSHON

Feature Editor   Advertising Manager
ROSEMARIE PERRONE   MARILYN ZURRIKI

Public Relations   Education Editor   Health Editor
GINI MIKS   ED LANE   DR. HENRY RICHMOND

Circulation Manager   Entertainment Editor   Sports, Adventure Ed.
JOHN MICHAELS   WOLFGANG CERDES-TESTA   BOB LeMAIRE

Legal Advisor   Art Director
ELIOT B. FELDMAN   ROBIN BLOMQUIST

The newspaper is an institution developed by modern civilization to pres the news of the day while fostering commerce and industry. It is also dedica to informing and leading public opinion and to furnish that check u government which no constitution has ever been able to provide.

SINGLES NEWS REGISTER is published every other week at P.O. Box Lakewood, California 90714. Subscription rate 13 issues - $6.00, 26 issues - $10 Outside U.S. 13 issues - $13.00, 26 issues - $26.00. Reproduction in whole or in p if any article (in any language) without permission is prohibited. Printed in United States of America. Unsolicited manuscripts cannot be returned un accompanied by a properly addressed envelope bearing sufficient postage. Sen remittances and correspondence about subscriptions, undelivered copies changes of address to Subscription Dept., Singles News Register, P.O. Box Lakewood, California 90714.

Dept., Singles Register, P.O. Box 40, Lakewood, California 90714. Opinions expressed in this paper are those of the author and not necessa those of the publisher, editor or staff.

Copyright 1975, printed in U.S.A.

(upper left) The newspaper DBA for the the Singles Register Saloon. (upper right) The masthead of the Singles News Register listing its staff

Jason pictured above with Governor and Mrs. Reagan in 1974.

With the "Singles News Register" having become considered a major publication by then, Jason also became more serious in his "Message From The Publisher" column.

MESSAGE FROM THE PUBLISHER

"Now is the time for all good men to come to the aid of their country."

This, in effect, is what President Gerald Ford is asking of his fellow Americans by urging us to save money and spend less on luxury items. The plain truth is that this country is in the economic throes of a recession. It seems highly unlikely that carrying out his suggestions is going to save us from sliding backward on the economic ladder into a depression.

His suggestions are not valid nor do they put the onus of responsibility where it should lie—on the government and not on the average American citizen.

If we save the dollars we earn in 1974, experts predict that by 1975, the dollar will be worth only eighty cents, a situation caused by the rising rate of inflation.

Secondly, with the increasing cost of gasoline, meat, milk, bread, sugar, etc., spending any money on luxury items is becoming a fantasy. We cannot afford luxury items anymore. The necessities cost too much.

Our country spends billions yearly in foreign aid, yet as a nation we are constantly being criticized because we live well, while millions of the world suffer in poverty.

As a people, we work hard for our money, yet we are being deprived of enjoying the economic results of our labor because of the bungling mismanagement of America's national affairs by our Washington leaders.

An example is the attempt by President Ford to increase the tax on a single person to an even greater degree than at present. He is proposing a five per cent surtax on single persons earning $7500 per year, but will allow married persons to earn $15,000 before they will be taxed.

This proposal is absurd and unjust. Ford chooses to ignore the fact that single individuals must pay the same price for gasoline, food, etc., as married persons. Why should the burden of greater taxation once again be placed on the single person.

Further, why should we, as average American citizens, be taxed more when big business, despite greater profits, escape heavier taxation.

We have come to the aid of our country by electing new leaders. Will they, in like manner come to the aid of its citizens by working out a program which will not take away from us, that which we work so hard to keep. JASON MERSHON

417

BROWN

A MESSAGE FROM THE PUBLISHER...

man didn't give anything to the schools" — a reference to Brown's father, a former governor.

Midge Flournoy, wife of the GOP candidate, sat in the front row, holding a copy of the Singles Register newspaper under her arm.

When asked why she had the publication, Mrs. Flournoy held it up to show a headline: "Flournoy Says: Don't Hold It Against Me Because I'm Married."

During the warm-up period, when the format for the debate was explained, university officials couldn't resist making an irrelevant announcement

seats were acoustics were echoing publ system didn't h

But in gener was at a low Brown's summ end had the laughing.

Taking cogni fact that the de educational iss a former semin said:

"We both ! good education

"Flournoy's of philosophy eight years of L

As this issue goes to press, the previously promised interview with Edmund G. Brown, Jr., Democratic candidate for Governor of California, has not materialized.

Despite assurances over the past several weeks by members of Mr. Brown's staff that an interview would take place, they informed us just this week that Mr. Brown's schedule would not enable him to go ahead with the interview.

His staff did supply us with a biography and campaign literature.

After holding a late editorial meeting with members of my staff, I felt that by printing Mr. Brown's campaign literature it would appear to be a commercial endorsement, rather than a non-partisan interview.

Therefore, we will be unable to furnish our readers with Mr. Brown's personal political views.

With the November elections almost upon us, we hope that all of our readers will exercise their right to choose the people that will govern us for the next few years.

So many of us fail to utilize our constitutional right to vote-but so many times after an election the non-voters do nothing but criticize the elected officials, even though by not voting they may have elected that particular individual to office!

Support your candidates in the polling booth and appreciate the fact that we in this country have the opportunity to do so.

JASON MERSHON

(above left) The article in the LA Times mentioning a moment in the televised 1974 gubernatorial debate betweeen Jerry Brown and Houston Flournoy, when Flournoy's wife held up Jason's newspaper, using the "family values" arguement against Brown because he was unmarried. Because of that moment in the debate, Brown cancelled an interview with Jason at the last minute, resulting in the above right Message From The Publisher.

418

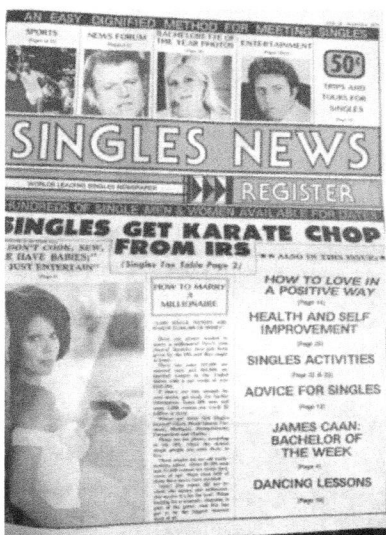

The 48-page edition of the *Singles News Register*.

Jason with his first "Bachelorette of the Year", Lita Krissan, December, 1974.

Jason toasting with three of his "Bachelorette of the Year" contestants to the conclusion of a successful 1974 - Denise, Jason, Mixie Thompson, and Lita Krissan.

PRELUDE TO THE LAST STAND
SUMMER, 2009

Jason was sitting alone at the poker table at Rio Hotel in Las Vegas with the entire stack of tournament chips in front of him, waiting to collect his winnings from his fourth single table satellite tournament he had won that weekend. His winner's share was only a little over two thousand dollars, but with the other poker satellites he had won in the past two days, going back to California with a nice addition to his bankroll was as good and easier than trying to win a bracelet in one of the main tournaments at that year's World Series of Poker.

It had been a profitable weekend since he had first hit his winning Keno ticket a couple of days before and had parlayed those winnings into a nice addition to his poker bankroll for the live cash games.

After collecting his winnings, Jason knew he only had about twenty minutes before he was meeting two other old friends, Amanda Miles and Hollie Vest, at the Orleans Hotel and rushed to the valet parking lot to get his car for the short drive. He had been friends with both Hollie and Amanda for well over twenty years, but it would be the first time either of them had met each other.

Jason had met Hollie Vest over twenty-five years earlier when she was performing as a lounge singer at a hotel in California, where he was producing a Miss Legs America beauty pageant in 1984. Since they had first met, Hollie had started performing a "Tribute to Tina Turner" concert act around the world, including working a gig in what had become the hottest show in Las Vegas since it premiered in the mid-1980s called "Legends in Concert." She had moved to Las Vegas from Los Angeles in the 1990s, where she was able to expand her music career as a tribute artist in different types of Legends in Concert shows, and also as a talent agent of other celebrity impersonators.

His other friend, Amanda Miles, had actually once been a contestant in one of Jason's Miss Legs pageants in the early 1980s and had lived in Las Vegas her entire life. Amanda was currently a photographer who specialized in shooting helicopter tours to the Grand Canyon or aerial tours above the Las Vegas Strip for newlyweds who came to Vegas to get married.

Jason hadn't seen either Hollie or Amanda for several years as was looking forward to seeing them both again.

Hollie was waiting for Jason at the restaurant entrance at The Orleans, and Jason saw Amanda already sitting at a booth inside as he led Hollie to the table and introduced them.

After introducing Hollie and Amanda, Jason saw a Keno girl collecting tickets for the next Keno game and quickly filled out a two spot with the numbers twenty-one and sixty-nine from the Keno rack on the table.

"Let's see if I'm still on a good winning rush," Jason smiled to his two friends as he handed the Keno runner a twenty-dollar bill with his Keno ticket.

"So, you had a good weekend gambling, eh?" asked Hollie.

"Betting on a football game and an occasional Keno bet is the only real gambling I do when I come up to Las Vegas these days," Jason added, "And those games are strictly for a little entertainment value when I'm at the poker tables."

"Jason always claims that poker isn't gambling," Amanda half laughed,

"Poker isn't gambling if you play the game right," Jason lightly tried to add, "Playing no-limit hold 'em is more strategy because there's no house advantage, plus you can't outplay a blackjack dealer or a pair of dice."

"But, there still is an element of luck in poker sometimes," he also smiled, "so I guess I have been a little lucky this weekend."

After ordering their meals, Jason looked up at the Keno board in the restaurant and saw that both twenty-one and sixty-nine had been drawn again.

"That's the way I like it," Jason smiled, "It always feels great winning a final bet before leaving Las Vegas."

The Keno girl collected Jason's ticket and paid him his winnings, and Jason decided to change the subject away from gambling.

"You have to see Hollie do her Tina Turner tribute show sometime," Jason said to Amanda after tipping the Keno runner twenty dollars, "She sounds just like Tina, and it almost a dead ringer when she darkens her skin with makeup."

"When Jason said you were coming today, I thought you'd be black," Amanda lightly laughed to Hollie, "But you do have a lot of Tina Turner's features for a white girl!"

"It's amazing what a little makeup can do," Hollie smiled back, "But performing as Tina has been a pretty good living for me for the past twenty-five years."

"And she can dance and has all of Tina's moves too along with sounding just like her," Jason added, making sure Amanda knew Hollie was more than a celebrity look-alike.

"I'm surprised that after all these years, I've been coming to Las Vegas, that you two haven't met each other yet," Jason said to them both, "I'm glad we had some time this weekend to get together and have you two finally meet."

"I can't even begin to count or remember all the different girls I've seen you with in Las Vegas since the 1980s," Amanda sarcastically joked, "So I guessed you were just introducing me to another one today."

"Join the club," Hollie joked back, "I feel the same way with all of the different girlfriends I've seen Jason with in LA and Palm Springs."

"Our famous playboy friend," teased Amanda as Jason just shook his head.

"Well, my businesses always did involve being around beautiful women in the old days if you both remember," sarcastically smiled, "But the girls always wanted to fool around as much as I did back then, so it was just a fringe benefit of my job."

"But that was the also the old days," Jason tried to add with a tease, "These days I'm just satisfied to play POKER and not POKE-HER."

"So, it's just lucky at cards and unlucky in love these days, eh?" Hollie joked with the old cliché.

"I spent over forty years being lucky at love, and now I'm just concerned with being lucky at cards," Jason tried to joke back, "Besides, I'll be sixty years old pretty soon and probably don't make the girls moan as much as I used to anyway."

"Have you ever actually tried to count all the girls you actually slept with?" Hollie continued to tease. "Sex, drugs and rock and roll did seem to be your lifestyle back then."

"Jason used to joke he could count the women he slept with on one hand," Amanda also teased as she made a fist and started opening her five fingers in a mock count, "Five, ten, fifteen, twenty, twenty-five, thirty....."

Hollie then joined in the joke as she made a fist and began counting with one finger at a time.

"No, it's probably more like one hundred, two hundred, three hundred, four hundred, five hundred....," Hollie continued teasing.

"Okay, okay, I get it!", Jason tried to lightly stop their counting, "I know you both think I was a slut back in those days, but I was just always very romantic."

"And, I was in love with a lot of them no matter what you might think, "he added wanting to try and justify,

Jason had stopped even trying to keep track of all the women he's slept with a long time ago, but was glad Hollie stopped at five hundred and didn't want to even try to think about how many he actually had been with. Especially, during what he now called his "crazy years" in the 1980s, when he spent almost every night in different nightclubs and different cities across America as the "Legs Hunter" meeting girls who were looking to have as much of a "good time" as he was back then."

"The ladies' legs been ver-dy, ver-dy good to Ja-son," Amanda joked in her bad impersonation of Garrett Morris character, Chico Escuela, from the old Saturday Night Live sketches that she'd been imitating for years.

Jason just shook his head and smiled, but definitely wanted to change the subject.

"You're both talking about someone even I don't remember anymore," Jason said with slight resignation before lightly adding, "My cat is the only girl I look forward to seeing to these days and my romantic days are pretty much over.

"So, if you've given up on romance's, does that mean you've given up on your music as well?" asked Hollie, "You always seemed happiest when you were up on stage with a microphone in your hand."

"The poker table is my only stage these days," Jason just sarcastically said, "There's really not any demand for someone my age to appear onstage anymore."

"You should go back on the road a play a rock star again," Amanda half-joked, "Mick Jagger and Paul McCartney are in their sixties, and they're still going strong."

"The so-called rock star was JJ Breeze when I decided to do a tour with the Box Tops again," Jason half smiled, "It was mainly for fun when I first did it in the early seventies but it wasn't as much fun when it did it again in the nineties."

"Besides, I always felt more like a celebrity impersonator myself because I wasn't the original singer who sang on the records," Jason added.

"Almost all those famous groups from the sixties and seventies who are still touring, hardly have any original members left in the band," said Hollie, "But they're still making the audiences happy hearing the old songs."

"Nope, my so-called rock star days are over," Jason said with finality about that subject as well, "But even though I never considered myself a great singer, my old voice just doesn't have enough to fake it anymore and I haven't even tried to sing in years."

"Well, I'm surprised you also stopped producing the musical-comedy that you wrote after those music and stage awards you won a few years ago," Hollie added, "I thought it was great and I don't know why you just stopped everything and never really capitalized on that show."

"It's a long story," is all Jason replied, "But I'm just a professional poker player these days, and all that stuff is in the past."

Jason was satisfied he'd ended the conversation about sex and music as he cheerfully changed the subject to how he managed to win his single table satellites with some great bluffs to go along with lucky poker hands.

"I didn't play in any bracelet or championship tournaments," Jason smiled, "But I won money at this year's World Series of Poker, and that's all that really matters."

"I'd really like to see you in the Main Event on TV one of these days," said Amanda, "You could win millions of dollars and become famous again."

"I don't want to be famous, and I've been making enough money playing poker to get by," Jason again explained with slight irritation, "Besides, what else could I do with millions of dollars that I haven't already done?"

Jason knew he was always a good bluffer and assured both Hollie and Amanda that he was completely satisfied with his current lifestyle.

"Well, as long as your happy," Hollie said with more of a question than a statement.

It was fun spending an hour with Amanda and Hollie again, but Jason knew three days in Las Vegas was long enough and told them he wanted to try and drive back to California before it was dark, after they finished their meal.

He'd had enough memories that weekend.

Jason also never liked leaving his cat Lucky alone for more than a few days at a time and knew she'd be going crazy without the usual amount of kitty treats and attention she'd become accustomed, and as soon as he got his car from the valet, he headed straight to Interstate 15 for his drive home.

He wasn't sure if it was the conversations he had with Amanda and Hollie, or if it was from the light and facetious song lyrics about poker players that had briefly crossed his mind that weekend, but during the drive home, Jason began to think again. He also remembered thinking about what he might try if he'd won some poker satellites, and if it was those thoughts about writing a stupid poker song was what may have subconsciously given him a more positive attitude to play poker better, and actually win enough money that weekend.

Jason still occasionally did think about his destiny, and for the first time in a long time, began to think about something else rather than certain ways to play his poker hands.

He tried to feel he'd been happy for the past year, but he knew he still wasn't completely satisfied. Besides feeling that he was getting too old to just use sex to make him happy as he always had in the "old days," there was something else that always managed to give him the most satisfaction. It was music that had always been his "second favorite hobby" and although he wasn't a "legs man" or a "playboy" anymore, he still had some songs in his head. Jason smiled to himself as he started to think about that.

BOOK FOUR

"CELEBRITY, MEDIA AND SEX"
1975

Chapter One

In 1975 Gerald Ford was President, and although a peace treaty had been agreed upon under Richard Nixon's administration a few years earlier, North Vietnam invaded South Vietnam in 1975, and the fall of Saigon occurred under President Ford's watch. Ford was also being mocked for how his only policy for fighting inflation seemed to be by distributing buttons for everyone in America to wear with only the word *"WIN"* printed on each button. *"WIN"* was the acronym for *"Whip Inflation Now!"* which he was trying to rally the country with what he thought was an optimistic message, but it wasn't working for most of America. The average yearly income was almost nine thousand dollars a year, but gasoline had also increased to over fifty cents a gallon, and the average price for a home was now over forty thousand dollars.

The top new television shows that year were *Stanford and Son, Welcome Back Kotter,* and a new sketch comedy weekly series called *Saturday Night Live,* while the top movies were *Jaws, One Flew Over the Cuckoo's Nest, Shampoo, Dog Day Afternoon,* and a movie version of the stage hit, with a slight title change, *The Rocky Horror Picture Show,* while the top songs of 1975 were, *Love Will Keep Us Together, Shining Star, Fame, Sister Golden Hair,* and *Feel Like Makin' Love.*

Time Magazine named for its 1975 Person of the Year simply *"American Women,"* with the trend of women remaining single longer to focus more on their own dreams and careers, without being as dependent on men to support them.

The new disco lifestyle was the biggest trend, with disco's becoming the center of the universe for those wanting to *just have fun,* instead of even considering marriage or a family. But away from the disco scene, everyone in America was also concerned with the rising inflation costs and ways to earn more money, including Jason Mershon who wanted 1975 to be a defining year before he turned twenty-five old the following year, and wanted something positive to show for his first quarter century.

With his lease having ended on his 1972 *Lincoln Mark IV,* his father leased some more luxury cars saying "having expensive cars parked at the office looked good" by showing how successful the newspaper was when he had meetings with new and current distributors. Besides getting a new Cadillac El Dorado for himself, his father leased a new a baby blue 1975 *Mercedes 450SL Convertible* for Jason, which he said would look good being driven around Hollywood and Beverly Hills when Jason was out promoting the newspaper as the editor and publisher.

Jason knew his trade outs, comps, weekly salary, and money from his monthly *S.T.A.R.S* party was allowing him to appear to be living comfortably, and that driving around in a new Mercedes was good *for show*, but with the rising costs of everything, he still wasn't where he felt any of it was ever going to make him wealthy.

Eliot Feldman had once asked Jason if the *Singles News Register* was a corporation and even offered his services for gratis if he ever did want to incorporate it, but Jason was just vague with Eliot, and explained he had a separate agreement with his *"partners"* and didn't want to mention that it was a family business with only verbal agreements. He decided it was time to try and have a somewhat serious discussion with his parents and exactly how his position as an owner of the business with them was going to eventually pan out.

He didn't actually know how much money his father made from selling distributors news racks but did see the hundreds of rolls of quarters the distributors would drop off at the office every two weeks to pay their share of the newspapers they sold. As far as profit from just the newspaper, Jason figured that almost half of the pages were paid personal ads that were coming in the mail each month with at least three hundred personal ads in each issue, and with the cost an average of fifteen dollars per ad, along with the paid subscriptions each month, he knew his parents had to be making a nice profit.

Jason understood his parents were paying the expenses for the newspaper printing and other weekly salaries for those who worked in the office, and although he didn't want to sound greedy or start any arguments, Jason felt he had been a big part of making the *Singles Register* a success. He still wanted to know if he was ever going to share in any profits as an owner the way his father had once talked about, but when Jason brought up how Eliot Feldman offered to set up a corporation to have a legal business arrangement between all of them with the newspaper, his father continued saying he didn't want to *"get screwed* in taxes" and didn't want to talk about how much the newspaper was really making.

"Isn't there any paperwork or contracts we need to work out about sharing our profits in the future?" Jason tried to ask seriously, "I am part of the business, right?"

"You're getting a weekly salary and a company car that we're paying for," snapped his mother, "Isn't that enough?"

"You've also got the extra money that you keep from your parties," his mother added with irritation, "and the money that comes into the newspaper is *our* money."

"I only make about an extra five hundred bucks a month off the party," Jason quickly added. "But you've always said I'm an owner of the paper with you, and I just want to know how that's going to work going forward."

"Of course, you're one of the owners," his father said, obviously playing the *good cop* that day, "It's just a family business with the three of us, and we don't need any paperwork to prove that point."

"But we don't want to make up any type of legal partnership agreement," his father added, "Because then we'd have to disclose everything that's coming in to the State and the IRS, which is something you shouldn't worry about right now."

"I just feel that I've built the paper to be what it is and think it's time we worked out some business agreement," Jason tried to reason, "I don't see how I'm ever going to get that much ahead with the money I'm currently making."

"Well, you would have had a lot more money saved up if you hadn't blown it on your stupid *Hearts and Flowers Ball* last year," his mother decided to remind Jason, "If you want more money, just spend your spare time selling more advertising instead of hanging out with your friends in Hollywood."

Jason felt it his "hanging out" was just another way he was always promoting the newspaper by keeping the Singles News Register's name mentioned with everything he was involved with and tried to ignore his mother's sarcastic comment.

"Well, I'd at least like to see something that shows I'll be sharing the profits eventually as the newspaper keeps growing," Jason just tried to say reasonably without starting an argument, "I think I've made the newspaper a lot more profitable than it was three years ago after I became editor and publisher,"

"The way you've set up the paper and the other publicity you've gotten has been great and even the distributors are talking about the stories they're reading everywhere about the Singles News Register," his father tried to compliment Jason, "But there are some bigger things I'm planning with distribution this year and once I get that all setup, we can figure out how we can work out some more money for you in the future."

"The newspaper is actually making very good money right now," he added, "and there is a nice chunk of money that's being put aside in different accounts because it's not good to show the money that's coming into one account mainly for tax reasons."

"You should be happy with the three hundred dollars we're paying you each week," his mother added with irritation, "That's a lot more money than a lot of people are making right now."

Jason could see that he was currently the *editor and publisher* in name only, and would need to find other ways to use the newspaper and his title as a vehicle to make more money on his own. But he did hope that in the next couple years, that the "nice chunk of money" his father had talked about putting aside, would at least be an annuity he could look forward to that they would all share in the future.

∽

Jason started 1975 by adding a couple of regular entertainment columns to the *Singles News Register* and had Annie Gaybis begin writing a regular column called *Dateline Hollywood*, which he knew would be a good replacement for his *Chasin' with Jason* column he had discontinued almost a year earlier. Because he took Annie as his

429

guest to several advance movie screenings and other opening night attractions, Jason figured she'd be able to write the reviews or put other blurbs in her new column that he had written about before. He also felt it would add some more gravitas having a well-known member of the *Hollywood Foreign Press* as a regular columnist, and added a column by Mark Marzouk, titled *Postmark Hollywood*. He knew there was always interest in entertainment news from Hollywood from whatever city in California his readers lived.

He decided until anything solid was worked out between his parents regarding the newspaper's ownership, and to start bringing in more income, to expand his singles *S.T.A.R.S* parties at the *Speakeasy* bi-weekly rather than once a month, and eventually alternate his bachelorette contest with a bachelor contest he was planning on starting.

Since he had started his singles parties a year earlier, Jason had met also dozens of new business contacts, many of which led to additional promotional benefits for the *Singles News Register* and occasionally a "few extra bucks" for himself.

One contact was Art Wilde, who along with Bob Goodfried, handled all the west coast promotion for upcoming movies at *Paramount Pictures*.

Jason had met Art Wilde the year before and because Art liked the idea of reaching the over a hundred and fifty thousand singles that regularly read the *Singles News Register* every two weeks, he invited Jason to his offices at the Paramount Studios on Melrose Avenue to talk about promotional ideas that could be beneficial for both of them.

Art Wilde suggested that in return for doing a little *quid pro quo* with Jason for some extra publicity and press for certain movies that they needed assistance in promoting, Art would arrange private advance movie screenings inside the Paramount Studio lot, which enabled Jason to sometimes host a third party each month for his *S.T.A.R.S* members where they could also meet some of the stars, directors, and producers of the films.

Jason mainly liked that another occasional celebrity themed party outside of the discos would keep his promotions new and fresh, and the first promotion he had worked on with Art and Bob, was for the *Paramount Pictures* movie *The Conversation* with Gene Hackman.

Because of all of the scandals that had come out about *Watergate* in the past year, and because *The Conversation* was about wiretapping and illegal surveillance similar to what the Nixon administration had been accused of doing, Art and Bob wanted to capitalize and give some type of an award from the press to Francis Ford Coppola for directing a movie that dealt with the important subject of personal privacy.

"People always go see movies that are advertised for having won awards, Goodfried smiled, "and it'll look good having an award from a newspaper which always makes it sound more legitimate."

They wanted to see if Jason would be their "press guy" and figure out a good sounding *media award* to present to Coppola. After a couple of days of brainstorming and research, they came up with the *Singles News Register's* first annual *George Mason Award* that Jason would award to Coppola for what they announced in the press releases was for *"Outstanding Service in Protection of the Right of Personal Privacy."*

"Well, it should be something that'll get us some extra press," smiled Art, "and at least it sounds like an authentic award."

"Of course, it's authentic!" Bob Goodfried added with a sarcastic expression Jason had heard him use often, *"Would I lie to you, baby!"*

Jason thought it was funny that Bob used a similar facetious expression to his own *"a little bs never hurt anybody"* about how authentic the award actually sounded. But he had already learned by then that promotion, advertising, and public relations all needed a certain amount of *bullshit* attached in order to be successful.

Francis Ford Coppola was in Europe, so accepting with the award on his behalf, was Cindy Williams, the lead actress from *The Conversation*, who was also preparing to star in a new spin-off of the hit TV show *Happy Days* called *Laverne and Shirley*.

Paramount Pictures arranged the press conference at the *Century Plaza Hotel* for the presentation of the award, and as Jason and Cindy Williams posed holding the large plaque for the over dozen press photographers present that day, Jason knew that all major media would have to mention the *Singles News Register* along with the award. Also as usual, he knew that would again show that his newspaper was a legitimate media publication which he was satisfied had been his best accomplishment so far.

Art Wilde also occasionally would ask Jason to give him a quote he could use from any reviews Jason would writing about some of *Paramount Pictures* films that were being released that year.

"We've got this movie coming out called 'Sheila Levine is Dead and Living in New York,'" said Art the first time he asked Jason to contrive a press quote, "It hasn't had any good reviews yet, and we need to get at least one positive quote from a reviewer we can use in our print advertising."

"But the movie is actually about a single girl and her relationships," Bob Goodfied added, "So I think it would look great having a positive review coming from the editor of the Singles News Register and hoped you'd be able to give us one."

As Jason sat in Art and Bob's office, they started throwing around quotes that might look good in their print ads for the movie.

"How about something simple like; *"Every person who is single should see Sheila Levine is Dead and Living in New York,"* said Jason, "I can get that phrase in the review somehow."

"It's a little long," said Art, "But it should still hit the singles audience and will work okay."

"Yeah, the movie is a bomb," laughed Bob who liked the quote, "I'll be happy with any positive quote."

Just having to give Art and Bob movie quotes was easy, and Jason would just include the quotes in the reviews he would write himself., but he did it was fun seeing his name listed in reviews with more well-known reviewers like Rex Reed, Vincent Canby, Roger Ebert, and Gene Shalit. He learned that all publicists always tried to use a little *quid pro quo* with the press, and he didn't mind obliging for what he usually got in return.

Jason had also decided in early 1975 to hire the writer and publicist Bud Testa who Jim Bacon had recommended the year before and paid him fifty dollars a week for additional publicity and press. Bud began arranging promotional appearances for Jason to attend that allowed him to publicize Jason's appearances as the editor and publisher of the *Singles News Register*, not only in the daily newspapers, but also in the showbiz trade papers *Variety* and *The Hollywood Reporter*.

Bud was constantly finding events he knew he could publicize, whether it was Jason appearing at some charitable event or benefit, being a celebrity guest on a radio talk show to talk about singles issues and dating, or even being a celebrity judge in different beauty pageants from *Miss Apple Valley*, *Miss Marna Del Rey* or *Miss Gardenia* around Southern California. Whatever was written or said about Jason in the different media, it always included that he was editor and publisher of California's largest singles publication, the *Singles News Register*, and Jason figured he at least was earning his three hundred dollars a week salary his parents paid him by continuing to make his newspaper's name *famous*.

Along with the extra money he was making from his promotions, Jason also moved from his apartment on Sunset Boulevard to a larger apartment on South Rexford Drive in Beverly Hills, feeling the sixty dollars a month rent increase to three hundred and ten dollars a month was worth it to have a Beverly Hills address and would sound good for business. Everyone he was meeting still thought he was twenty-seven years old and already wealthy, so he at least wanted them to see he was on his way to "being a millionaire before he was thirty," which is what everyone had always said was their goal.

But he was also confident that eventually, he really would be someday.

Chapter Two

Since Jason had been at *The Oscars*, it started almost to feel natural hanging out and talking with people he would have never imagined just a couple of years earlier. But he also knew because everyone thought he was older than he was, he always tried to act more sophisticated and someone who wasn't starstruck or intimidated with the celebrities he was meeting. He had also mentally convinced himself that he was basically on their same level being an editor and publisher of a very well-known newspaper and tried his best to always act *cool* no matter who he met.

But sometimes it wasn't always easy.

Ron Smith had always mentioned that he was friends with Elvis Presley, so when Ron invited Jason to a party at Elvis's house in Beverly Hills, Jason jumped at the chance and tried not to act like it was a big deal even though he knew inside he was thrilled. But Ron also said there were "some rules" at those parties and Jason needed to act "even more cool" when he met Elvis.

"Listen, Jason, there's going to be a lot of hot girls up there, but just be cool and don't piss Elvis off," said Ron. "You can't hit on them about being bachelorettes for your newspaper or even talk to them until Elvis picks out the ones he wants."

Jason was also disappointed that even though he and Ron's mutual friend and photographer, James Mares, was also going with them to the party, photographs weren't allowed which he knew would have been great for the cover of the *Singles News Register*.

Besides not being able to talk to the girls at the party, Jason became bored quickly as it seemed everyone there was part of Elvis's inner circle and mainly sat around talking amongst themselves. Elvis himself didn't even join the party till after eleven pm and looked like he had just woken up, but Jason was still anxious to introduce himself. The only subject he thought he could mention to Elvis that they might have in common when Ron Smith did introduce them, was when he told Elvis that he was "acquainted" with Harold Robbins, who had written the book *A Stone for Danny Fisher*, which Elvis' movie *King Creole* was based and added was his favorite Elvis movie.

One of the guys near the stereo also began playing what he said was Elvis' newest upcoming single, titled *T-R-O-U-B-L-E* which was also coincidentally the same title of his earlier, but different song from the movie *King Creole*, as the crowd all enthusiastically assured Elvis that it was "sure to be" another number one hit.

433

But Elvis told them to stop playing that record and sat down at his piano and started half humming and half singing a gospel song as everyone became quiet and attentively listened.

Even though Jason did think it was incredible actually to be sitting that close to "The King" watching him at the piano, and was thrilled being at one of his "private parties and meeting him in person, it was Elvis' appearance that was a disappointment and looked nothing like he remembered seeing him in Las Vegas.

Along with being overweight, his face was puffy, he was sloppily dressed while he sat at the piano, and still acted if he was half asleep for most of the night. But the main thing he noticed the rest of the party, was how everyone was constantly praising Elvis, which reminded Jason of the *Twilight Zone* episode about the little boy who needed to be patronized with happy and complimentary phrases constantly, or the little boy had the power to make them disappear and *"send them to the cornfield."*

Jason was a little disappointed that attending a party at Elvis' house wasn't as exciting as he thought it would be, and he didn't really feel like he'd met the *real Elvis* that night.

He found it was more fun to attend the many Black-Tie dinners and parties at the *Beverly Hilton* or the *Century Plaza* that he was now regularly invited, and it seemed there was something big going on at least once a week.

Lori tried to be available for all the big events like *The Grammy's, The Golden Globe Awards*, or *The American Music Awards*, and by being seen together at so many events, they were becoming known as one of the most attractive couples in Hollywood, and sometimes the paparazzi would even start snapping photos of them arriving somewhere or inside some of the parties.

"I know you both aren't really all that famous," one of the photographers had half-laughed, "But I see you both everywhere and just want to have pictures when you are."

The socializing before many of the different functions began was always more enjoyable than the events or awards ceremonies themselves, and at one of the parties he had attend with Lori at the *Beverly Hilton Hotel*, Jason was talking with Carroll Rosenbloom, the Los Angeles Rams owner, and Lori was talking with his wife Georgia.

Both Jason and Lori were Rams fans and attended many football games at the LA Coliseum, which gave them something in common they could talk about with some knowledge with the Rams owners. While Jason talked with Rosenbloom about how he thought the Rams coach, Chuck Knox, should give their second-string quarterback Ron Jaworski a shot at being the starter, Carroll said it was up to Chuck Knox, but he also mentioned how proud he was of being the owner of a team whose current starter, James Harris, was the first *black quarterback* to ever win a playoff game in the NFL.

434

"Well, I've been waiting for the Rams to be in the Super Bowl for a long time," smiled Jason, "But the darn Rams always seem to fall short each year, and I just thought a change at quarterback might finally get them there."

"I promise you," said Carroll, "We'll win a Super Bowl with James Harris in the next couple years."

While Jason was talking football with Carroll, Lori was telling Georgia about her favorite Ram players, including Jack Youngblood and Fred Dryer.

"Well, Jack is my favorite too," smiled Georgia, "And he's not too bad to look at when he's off the field either."

"He's the one that my binoculars are usually focused on!" laughed Lori.

Carroll also introduced Jason and Lori to a couple of other guests attending the party, whom Jason also didn't want to act starstruck meeting, U.S. Senator's John Tunney and Ted Kennedy.

"Jason is the publisher of a very successful singles newspaper here in Los Angeles," said Carroll Rosenbloom as he introduced them.

Even though Jason wasn't a fan of his politics, he still thought it was great talking with a *Kennedy* and always remembered exactly what he was doing when both of Ted Kennedy's brothers were shot. Although Chappaquiddick was in the back of his mind when they were talking, he thought Kennedy was very personable and gladly said he'd pose for some photos for Jason's newspaper after a couple photographers asked for a group shot.

While Jason and Lori were posing for the press photographers, Kennedy complimented Jason on having such a beautiful girlfriend, and Jason casually mentioned that Lori would be soon appearing in an upcoming *Penthouse Magazine*. Something about that comment made Kennedy a little apprehensive about standing next to Lori in the photos, and he made sure he wouldn't be standing directly next to her as the photographers took their pictures.

Jason had heard all the rumors about Kennedy's womanizing and wasn't surprised he didn't want to take a chance on being seen in a photo that someone might try to exploit in a scandal tabloid.

When Jason and Lori were back at his apartment after that party, he was still joking about how nervous Kennedy seemed about being photographed standing next to Lori.

"I guess he was afraid I'd put 'TED KENNEDY SEEN WITH PENTHOUSE PET' on my next cover," laughed Jason, "But I did notice he couldn't keep his lustful eyes off you."

"That's not bad for my ego," Lori also laughed, "But I still think George Harrison trying to pick me up when he saw me walking in Beverly Hills was more impressive."

Lori had already told Jason about the former Beatle George Harrison pulling his limo over when he saw Lori walking alone on Rodeo Drive, and how she spent some time talking with him after accepting a ride in his limo a few weeks earlier.

They both usually volunteered some funny stories about what each of them was doing when they weren't together, but still never really questioned each other about too many details. Neither of them wanted ever to feel that they were giving each other what they joked was the *'third degree"* like some police detective.

Jason would still usually tell Lori who he took someone else to an event when she wasn't available like Anne Gaybis or some other mutual friend, and he'd even tell her when he occasionally had a new bachelorette accompany him to some press function or party, which he always explained was "just business."

But both of their "business" lives had seemed to be going in different directions that year.

Jason and Lori were still trying to act as nothing had changed between them, but having stopped talking any long-range plans together, Jason's priorities had changed and he figured they both knew that their relationship wouldn't last forever.

"We have no secrets, we tell each other ALMOST everything," Jason would now tease Lori by singing different words to the Carly Simon song *No Secrets*, which always gave Lori a good-natured laugh. If there was ever something that did bother them about their separate careers, neither wanted to be the first to admit it to each other and they both still wanted to be a couple.

But the song and lyrics Jason associated with their relationship even more in the past several months was Lynyrd Skynyrd's *Don't Ask Me No Questions* so Jason wouldn't have to *tell no lies*, as the song described.

He knew he didn't want to tell Lori everything.

Chapter Three

Besides having hosted his *S.T.A.R.S* parties at private studio screenings for the movies *Once is Not Enough*, *Nashville*, *Day of the Locust* and others, the movie studios would also sometimes hold wrap parties after the screenings that Jason would host at the *Speakeasy*. Alex Henig and Dave Curtain also didn't mind paying Jason a "few extra bucks" for the additional promotions he would arrange at their disco.

Lori didn't attend every promotion Jason hosted, so when he did find himself stag at one of his own parties, he had already decided that *a little flirting never hurt anybody*.

At the wrap party for the movie *Shampoo*, Jason saw over a dozen beautiful girls who were anxiously waiting for the star of *Shampoo*, Warren Beatty, to arrive at *The Speakeasy* that night. Jason figured any one of them would be perfect *Bachelorettes of the Week*, but saw the only interest any of them had, was to hopefully be the one that Beatty, known as the "biggest stud and playboy in Hollywood," would choose to be his *conquest* that night.

Jason was more interested in talking with another star of *Shampoo*, Goldie Hawn, who was already at the wrap party. Although Goldie seemed to have intentionally *dressed down* that night, by just wearing overalls, which made her look more like a house painter than a sexy actress, Jason still thought she was one of Hollywood's most adorable actresses.

Goldie had already been a *cover girl* on the *Singles News Register*, but although Jason would have liked her to have been one of his *Bachelorettes of the Week* and personally interviewed her, Jason had only used a publicity photo of Goldie from a film that another studio publicist wanted to be promoted.

He was a little disappointed that Goldie was with her boyfriend that night, and he couldn't do a *little flirting*, as he had done with the actress he met at the Oscars the year before, but did make a point in telling Goldie that the issue with her on the cover had been a great seller in the news racks.

Between the different parties he was promoting, Jason still needs to play both sides of the aisle when it came to differentiating his disco parties from those advertised for dates in the *Singles News Register,* especially the way some of his parties were written about in various other Los Angeles newspapers and magazines.

Jason thought one column in the *Herald Examiner* about his parties was geared too much to the current disco culture and was glad they didn't mention the *Singles News Register* by name.

The blurb in the entertainment column read, *"Besides always having the most beautiful women in town hoping to be named the next Bachelorette of the Week by editor/publisher Jason Mershon, many of the top Hollywood celebrities often pop into the S.T.A.R.S parties hoping to either find the next love of their life. Or at the worst, at least their next love that evening, which with Women's Lib has become more of the norm lately with women enjoying more romantic variety in their lives as well."*

With one-night stands having become the *norm* in disco's more than ever before, Jason still wanted to emphasize that the *Singles News Register* was the perfect alternative to the singles who didn't like the bar scene and were more interested in *getting married* instead of the current trend of volume fucking it seemed everyone was now partaking. He did feel he was still able to separate his Hollywood *S.T.A.R.S* parties from the *Singles News Register's* main concept without feeling contradictory because most of his *S.T.A.R.S* members from the newspaper preferred coming to his movie screening parties rather than the disco parties.

Jason felt he had enough variety to keep his readers happy regardless of how they felt about relationships, and he was also starting to make more from his parties than he was making from his salary at the newspaper. But he also knew his title as an editor and publisher was what was giving him the "juice" instead of just being a Hollywood party promoter, and as it had always been, with all the press Jason had been getting that year with Bud Testa's job as his publicist, some of his friends would still tease him out *how famous* he was becoming himself.

"I'm feeling like I'm hanging out with a celebrity these days and it seems there's something about you in the newspapers every week," Stan half joked, "You're either judging a beauty contest, appearing on a radio show, having private movie screenings, presenting some award, or being seen at some big celebrity event."

"I don't know how you're doing all these things along with putting together a newspaper and promoting singles parties twice a month," Stan teased, "Are you sure there's only one Jason Mershon?"

Jason just laughed and told Stan it wasn't all that difficult.

"The newspaper is pretty much a piece of cake to put together these days and it just needs to be typeset, pasted up, and proofread before someone else takes it to the printers," Jason casually explained, "We've got all our regular writers and columnists with more than enough copy for each issue, and I just need to put together the covers with the bachelorettes and write my message from the publisher which gives me plenty of time for the other promotions that Bud Testa sets up."

"Plus, the Speakeasy is always packed every weekend with people who love to party," Jason added, "So I get plenty of in-house promotion for my S.T.A.R.S parties every other week."

"Well, you're definitely keeping busy and seem to be having fun," Stan lightly laughed, "But you sure have changed a lot since I met you three years ago."

"Only the dead never change," Jason smiled, "But I'm just showing everyone how fun it is being single plus when the other media outlets write about what I'm doing, they usually always mention the Singles News Register."

"It's all just publicity, and you know what I like to say," Jason smiled with his other new catchphrase, *"A little press never hurt anybody!"*

❧

Lori was excited when she popped into Jason's apartment in Beverly Hills.

"Here it is!" she said, handing him a wrapped package.

Jason opened the package and saw it was an advance copy of the May issue of *Penthouse Magazine.*

"I decided to use a pseudonym in the story," explained Lori as she excitedly turned to the page that began the story and photo layout, "I thought the name *Octavia Corriell* sounded classy."

"Plus, I didn't want guys who might remember me from high school to jerk off on my picture if they see my real name," she sarcastically added.

Jason didn't say anything to Lori, but even though she looked beautiful in the photos, he thought they were far from classy or in good taste and looked more like pornography than art. The photos were of her lying on a bed and mainly showing different angles of her touching herself.

"Ah, I can still see the mole on your left tit," Jason tried to joke lightly without showing that he wasn't impressed with the photos.

"Only in one photo," she laughed, "I covered it up with my hand it those other shots."

Jason didn't want to mention how busy her *other hand* looked in the photos that most people would be looking at more than her tits and the only good aspect Jason noticed was that her blond pubic hair wasn't as dominant in the photos as other centerfolds he'd seen, or even like most other girls he'd known, who looked like they had big black steel wool pads between their legs.

"Oh, by the way," Lori added, "Don't be upset with that story they wrote, it's just some stuff to make me sound *sexier*."

The story was the worst part of the layout, and Jason didn't like it and no matter how mature he tried to act, and there was no way that Lori didn't know it would embarrass Jason when people who knew them both read what was supposedly her quotes. In the story, *"Octavia"* emphasized her sexual powers and techniques she used with *"all of her men"* and was supposedly quoted saying, "Most men are only concerned with themselves, and I find that older men take a great deal of interest in

439

my pleasure," the story read, "*When I'm with them I know they're fucking me*, and that my pleasure is paramount."

"That story is so funny," Lori casually laughed, "But I will feel a little funny having my mom and dad read that about me."

Jason tried to laugh with Lori, but was only able to give her a smile and just said "Well, it's interesting,"

"You're the one that always says *a little bs* never hurt anybody," Lori tried to add as Jason often joked, "I think that story is hilarious, and all of our friends will probably just laugh about it too."

Most of their friends had already told Jason they thought Lori was "too classy" to be in *Penthouse*, but they never mentioned it to her personally and tried to act supportive. Jason still felt it wouldn't have been as embarrassing if she had appeared in *Playboy* rather than *Penthouse*, and the story wouldn't have been nearly as exploitive and sleazy.

But he also knew that had been Lori's choice.

Although Jason had never liked the idea of her posing in the first place, he wanted to continue being mature and not make a big deal over it and just told her she did look beautiful in the photos, and was glad it turned out the ways she had hoped, but he was still wondering how his other friends would react when they saw the story.

When Jason was at Annie Gaybis' apartment the next day, the way Annie rolled her eyes and shook her head as she read the story in *Penthouse* let Jason know she felt the same way as he did.

"So, who are the older men she's talking about in the story?" Annie laughed with more shock than humor, "I can't believe that Lori would talk like that!"

"I'm sure someone at the magazine just made up the story the way they make up the *Penthouse Forum*," Annie tried to lightly justify.

Jason tried to act like it was no big deal and laugh it off and told Annie it was written "just to make Lori sound *sexier*," the same way Lori had told him.

"Well, this is nothing that I would have imagined Lori doing and especially those pictures!", Annie said still shaking her head, "I sure hope she made a lot of money off of this."

Jason never did talk to Lori about how much money she was being paid, but he had heard that *Playboy* paid centerfolds ten thousand dollars, and figured if Lori got anything close to that amount, she might have made almost as much money for that one photoshoot as he made in a year. But he also thought if he could have afforded to pay Lori the same amount not to pose nude, he may have paid it.

The whole thing was embarrassing to him, but he promised himself he was going to act sophisticated enough never to show it.

Chapter Four

Because of the success and all of the publicity the *Singles News Register* had received in the past year, a couple of new publications started trying to use the same format of classified advertising for dates and had some title that included *"Singles"* in its name.

Although none of them were considered serious competition, a couple were now being sold in the news racks alongside the *Singles News Register.*

Jason and his parents decided that adding a full four-color cover instead of the basic two colors they had been using for years, would make the other singles newspapers that were beginning to appear in the news racks look cheap and insignificant.

When Jason's father mentioned he was planning on selling news racks in Las Vegas and talked about possibly expanding distribution into Arizona and Texas, Jason and his parents had also been discussing changing the newspaper's name to the *National Singles Register.*

The name change did seem to make sense because there were also now many subscribers and personal ads in the *Singles News Register* from several other states, thanks to having news racks at all of the California airports, that single people would buy before flying and take back to their own states.

Jason had previously tried to suggest easier ways to add more circulation by selling the newspaper inside stores like *7-11's* or supermarkets and even printing a quarter-fold edition for inside the stores to give it more of a magazine look, and again brought it up.

"Why not just work with larger distribution companies that get newspapers like the National Enquirer and those other tabloids inside stores?" Jason again asked, "Think about how many more newspapers we could sell each issue if the newspaper was available in other places besides the news racks."

"The money from the percentage of sales of the newspaper is minor compared to what I can sell the news racks and different distribution routes to independent buyers," his father said with a dismissive tone, "The way I've been selling news racks for distribution has been working out fine for right now."

He had learned that his father usually bought used news racks for around twenty-five dollars each and, after refurbishing them, sold hundreds of them at a much higher price, as a business opportunity to buyers who wanted to invest in vending distribution routes for the *National Singles Register* as a full or part-time business.

"Richard is still just a salesman," his mother sarcastically added, "The newspaper is still just a vehicle for him to sell his stupid news racks."

"Well, I don't hear you complaining about the fucking money I'm bringing in!" his father snapped back at her before trying to speak calmly to Jason, "It's just too complicated to get involved with right now, but maybe in a year or so we can talk about it."

They all finally decided that if Jason's father eventually got the newspaper in some other major cities out of state, they would need to replace the four-page centerfold with an insert with a local calendar of events and a few local stories for that market.

Most of the current articles and stories in each issue dealing with relationships and dating, movie and record reviews, as well as the Hollywood columns and celebrity stories were generic enough to be considered national stories that would fit in with any market. The singles calendar sections in the centerfolds of each issue were mainly all Southern California activities and photos from Jason's local S.T.A.R.S promotions and would need to be replaced for any out of state editions.

His father also wanted Jason to highlight that the National Singles Register was now America's Leading Singles Publication instead of just California's, and also add, *"Over 200,000 Singles Will See Your Ad!"* on each cover.

"You've got the newspaper pretty well set up on autopilot each issue," said his father, "I know you're busy doing your promotions, so when I do add some more distribution, I'll just bring in someone else to work on the out of state calendar inserts for those cities."

Jason also liked changing the name to the *National Singles Register*, which would enhance his own position as the editor and publisher and let everyone see he was moving forward.

1975 was turning into his best year ever.

&

The *Speakeasy* was also going through a major change, but it wasn't as positive.

The disco was about two blocks off of Santa Monica Boulevard and located across the street from a residential neighborhood whose residents complained about the loud music and crowds that had been keeping them awake for months.

Alex Henig and Dave Curtain had been having a problem with city ordinances regarding too much noise at night, and the city threatened to suspend Alex and Dave's liquor license until they either soundproofed the disco better or agreed to close the *Speakeasy* at midnight.

Alex told Jason that they were closing for at least a month before deciding how they should restructure their business.

"We aren't planning on closing down until June, so it won't affect the next couple parties you have scheduled here," Alex explained to Jason, "But after that, we're putting everything on hold until Dave and I decide what we're going to do."

It had been almost exactly a year since his first *S.T.A.R.S* party with Alex and Dave, and besides noticing that *The Speakeasy* was losing some of its popularity to other disco's that had recently opened, Jason had been thinking of changing the location of his parties himself for something new and fresh.

With Jason not knowing how long the *Speakeasy* would be closed down and not wanting to lose any of his extra monthly income, it took Jason only a few days to find a new location to continue his bi-weekly *S.T.A.R.S* parties.

Mike McInerney's nightclub had also closed down, and had sat empty until a Middle Eastern businessman named Sia Amiri purchased the same space, and recently reopened as a disco called *My Place*.

Jason had always liked the location of that disco in Beverly Hills, which was located on Canon Drive right of Wilshire Boulevard, and was only a few blocks from his own apartment on Rexford Drive.

Plus, it had the same seating capacity as the *Speakeasy* of around two hundred and fifty, which was the average size crowd Jason usually drew to his parties.

Sia Amir agreed to the same terms Jason had with the *Speakeasy* at *My Place*, and Jason set up his parties for every other Sunday beginning the Sunday before Memorial Day, which would keep the continuity of his parties intact.

It was about a week before Jason's final *S.T.A.R.S* party at *The Speakeasy* when he got another phone call from Alex Henig.

"Jason, I know you've got your last party scheduled here next Tuesday," said Alex, "But Berry Gordy from Motown just called me up, and they want to use the Speakeasy for a surprise twenty-fifth birthday party for Stevie Wonder on the same night as your party and want to see if we can work something out."

"Berry Gordy said he only needs the club between nine and eleven pm," Alex continued, "But I'm sure a lot of them will want to stay at the party after that."

"Well, I've already got most of my regulars coming," said Jason, "But it's no problem if they don't mind just sharing the club."

"Besides," Jason half-joked, "Stevie Wonder won't know the difference and just think everyone is there for him."

"I was kind of thinking the same thing," Alex lightly laughed, "But there are a couple of things we need to work out if we do have both parties on the same night."

"First, you can't let anyone know that Stevie Wonder is coming or publicize it," said Alex, "And second, I don't want to have a cover charge or any other contests that night."

"I'd like you to just let your crowd in free and let them party and dance, so it doesn't look like I'm capitalizing on Motown's party," Alex said, "It'll still look like a big celebrity S.T.A.R.S party, and it will be a nice swan song for your parties here."

Although Jason didn't like losing the around the five hundred dollars profit, he was making from each party, he figured it would be a fun party to end his promotions *The Speakeasy*, and told Alex that arrangement would be fine.

Alex had become a good friend and had been supportive of everything Jason had promoted the past year, so he wanted to be fair with Alex.

Besides knowing that his regular crowd would have fun partying and meeting all the Motown music stars, Jason knew it could be something big to feature in the first issue of the newly named *National Singles Register* that would encourage more people to come to his new location at *My Place* in Beverly Hills two weeks later.

Jason knew Stan Adams would be there, as usual, taking photos, and including pictures of that party with all the Motown stars in attendance, would look like just another typical celebrity S.T.A.R.S party and be more great publicity.

Jason was disappointed he wouldn't be able to promote his party by mentioning that Stevie Wonder would be celebrating his birthday there the same night, but it was a surprise party, and knew he needed to keep it a secret.

He also knew that wouldn't be a problem because he had been good at keeping secrets lately.

Chapter Five

On the same day of his final *S.T.A.R.S* party at the *Speakeasy* that week, Jason had also been invited to a press party at the *Playboy Club* in Century City for Hugh Hefner's afternoon announcement of the 1975 Playmate of the Year.

Lori was in New York that day meeting with Bob Guccione about doing some promotion for her photo layout, and although Jason had wanted to bring his own current Bachelorette of the Year Lita Krisaan, she had an audition for a movie role that afternoon and couldn't attend. Jason had also told Lita that with Lori in New York, it was a good night to see her, and he'd pick her up after he left the *Playboy Club* to attend his party at *The Speakeasy* together.

Jason decided to attend the first party that day stag and when he arrived at the *Playboy Club* around 2 pm, it was already packed with the press members, probably over two dozen photographers, and as usual, dozens of beautiful Playboy Bunnies and Playmates.

Playboy Magazine and Hugh Hefner in particular, had been getting very bad press for the past few months for a scandal that started with the apparent suicide of Hefner's closest personal assistant Bobbie Arnstein, who had been involved in a major drug operation involving cocaine and Quaaludes which federal agents and the FBI were trying to link directly to Hefner. There were even rumors that Hefner himself was involved in Arntein's death, and the rumors had caused revenue and Playboy stock to plummet in the past three months.

Penthouse Magazine had been increasing in popularity at the same time and was being looked at as a sexier alternative to *Playboy*.

Jason saw Hefner was wanting to show that *Playboy* was still carrying on successfully despite the scandal and competition from *Penthouse*, and was appearing in public much more than he had in the past. Jason had also been to a few other parties at the Playboy Mansion since the first time he'd been there, and although he usually only had brief conversations with Hefner and couldn't consider him as a personal friend, it was still always fun knowing they were on a first-name basis.

"It's good seeing you again, Hef," said Jason as he greeted Hefner, "Hopefully, someday I'll be able to attract a crowd like this by the time announce my next Bachelorette of the Year winner.

"You're young," said Hefner encouragingly, "You'll do it someday."

445

Jason did briefly think it was ironic that he was talking with Hugh Hefner around the same time Lori was meeting with Bob Guccione in New York and what a funny coincidence it actually was.

He did have fun being stag at the party socializing and didn't leave the Playboy Club until almost seven pm before realizing he hadn't called Sandi Shore to tell her she wouldn't be needed to work the door at The Speakeasy that night. Jason had kept Stevie Wonder's surprise birthday party a secret even from his friends as he'd promised Alex Henig.

Sandi's place was on the way to Lita's apartment, so instead of stopping at a payphone to call her, he just drove to her house. When he arrived, Sandi's bratty seven-year-old kid brother Pauly answered the door and, as usual, was being a pest while Sandi was trying to do her Buddhist chants of *"Namu Myoho Renge Kyo"* while she rang a chime over a lit candle.

Sandi had often described her Buddhist philosophy to Jason about how everyone was constantly being reborn and continually discovering everything about life "until you get it right" and discover Nirvana. Jason found some aspects of Buddhism interesting and also similar to what Micky Dolez had once described about astrology, but after hearing so many people try and convince him their philosophy was the one that he should follow, Jason would just sarcastically joke he was waiting until he heard from a few dozen more "expert philosophers" before he picked out his favorite.

He usually would wait until Sandi finished her chants before bothering her, but because Jason felt he was running late, he quickly interrupted her and told her she could take the night off. Sandi seemed unfazed as she stayed in her trace and continued chanting, so he figured he'd call her later and tell her Stevie Wonder was coming to his party.

When Jason finally arrived at Lita's apartment, he could smell the aroma of marijuana as soon she opened the door and saw she decided to get in a party mood as early as he had.

"Man, I knew it was going to be a long day," Jason was telling Lita as she was rolling another joint before they left for *The Speakeasy*, "I drank three or four Bailey's and Coffee at the Playboy Club, so I wouldn't get tired tonight, and now I feel completely wired."

"You should just take a couple of hits of this," Lita offered, "It'll relax you a little."

Jason still didn't like pot but thought it might relax him a bit, so he took a couple of hits, but by the time they were sitting in a booth at *The Speakeasy* an hour later, he was still feeling the effects.

Stan Adams was already there and planning on getting some good pictures for the *National Singles Register's* first issue and joined Jason and Lita in their booth.

"I'll make sure I get some good pictures of you and Stevie Wonder," said Stan before adding, "You look a little off tonight, are you okay?"

"Damn, I'm such a lightweight," Jason just laughed, "A few hits off Lita's shit, and I feel loaded, but I should be okay by the time Stevie gets here."

It was after nine pm, and the DJ was blasting Stevie Wonder's current hit single, *Boogie on Reggae Woman* when Jason saw him walking with a group through the front door and decided to take some action and surprise all of his regular party crowd.

Jason rushed up to him and slowly guided him to the center off the dance floor, letting him use his cane for balance.

"Okay, everyone!" shouted Jason as he signaled the DJ to cut the music, "Let's all join in and wish Stevie Wonder a happy birthday!"

As Jason started singing Happy *Birthday to You*, someone from Motown came up to Jason on the dance floor and quietly interrupted him.

"Jason," he said politely, "That's not Stevie."

Jason looked at the man next to him and suddenly realized it wasn't Stevie Wonder, but amazingly another blind black man, who had coincidentally walked in with some other Motown guests.

"Oops, sorry," Jason sheepishly tried to say, "It's dark in here and my mistake."

As he quietly tried to back up from the dance floor and sit back down with Lita feeling completely embarrassed, Jason also realized what he'd just said about it "being dark in here" also probably didn't sound that good to the large Motown crowd at the party and decided it would be best to just sit quietly in his booth to try and stay inconspicuous at the party for the time being.

It wasn't until later when most of the effects of the marijuana had worn off, and someone brought over the real Stevie Wonder to Jason and Lita's booth before Jason began to feel better.

"Hi, are you Jason?" asked Stevie Wonder as he stood at Jason's booth. "Someone said you tried to meet me earlier, and I just wanted to say hello."

"Stevie, I'm so sorry," Jason tried to apologize, "I think I just had one drink too many and got confused for a minute."

"You don't have to apologize for anything," Stevie lightly joked, "All people look the same to me too."

Jason was just relieved that Stevie Wonder was able to laugh it off, and even joined Lita and him in their booth to pose for some photos that Stan Adams was taking.

"I just wanted to thank you for helping with this party tonight, and I'll see you again sometime," Stevie joked again before he left.

The rest of the party went fine, but Jason was still feeling a little buzzed by the time they left the Speakeasy that night and knew he'd better let Lita do the driving.

"That was so embarrassing," Jason tried to laugh as Lita drove from the parking lot, "What were the odds of two black blind guys being there at the same time tonight?!"

"That was funny," giggled Lita, "But at least Stevie thought it was funny and was able to laugh about it."

"Man, this has been a long day," Jason said as he casually snuggled next to Lita while she drove, "First spending all day with Hefner and all those Playmates, and then this party tonight has really knocked me out."

"Oh, you have such a tough job," Lita sarcastically teased.

"Let's just stay at your place again tonight," Jason smiled as he lightly kissed Lita's cheek, "I want to sleep in, and Lori might call me too early in the morning if we stay at my place."

"Are you sure you're not too drunk tonight" Lita smiled, "Or still stoned from the pot?"

Jason took her hand and gave it a kiss and tried to say without slurring his words, "You know I'm never too drunk for you, baby."

"You are such a sex fiend," Lita lightly teased with what seemed like her favorite expression since he'd known her.

"You know that's why you like me so much," Jason teased back. "I never let myself get too drunk for that!"

Jason had decided that it wasn't even worth feeling guilty about anything that was making him happy, but was still trying to be at least halfway discreet as Lori had asked him to do.

If their relationship did ever end, he didn't want to feel heartbroken and alone ever again.

Chapter Six

The next week, Jason was at his desk, waiting for the *National Singles Register's* new issue to be delivered, and to meet someone his father told him he wanted him to meet.

Although Jason had included pictures from the previous Stevie Wonder and Hugh Hefner parties, he didn't include any of himself with Stevie or Hefner.

Jason didn't like the way his beard looked in the photos and started thinking the beard was beginning to make him look too grubby. Although it took him over a half hour to shave that morning, he decided he looked better and was satisfied when his beard was completely gone.

"You look a lot better," said his father as he came into Jason's office with the new girl he wanted Jason to meet.

"Thanks," said Jason, "I was ready for a new look anyway."

"This is Joy," introduced his father, "She recently graduated college with a degree in journalism, and I think she'll be good for what we talked about doing before with the national editions."

"You don't really need to spend time being in the office as much as you did a year ago," explained his father, "So Joy can be here every day as kind of an of assistant editor, and can also help you out with the other minor stuff you need to have done with the newspaper."

"Joy is mainly going to start by putting together the calendar inserts we're going to need up in Las Vegas," his father added.

Jason thought Joy looked professional and sounded qualified, but he wondered why someone with a journalism degree would want to work on just putting a calendar together for a singles newspaper.

Jason also knew he had been able to put each issue of the newspaper together every two weeks with no problem with the staff he already had and didn't know why his father thought he needed an assistant editor.

"Well, I'm also thinking of starting another publication," said his father, "We haven't got too many more areas in California to sell news racks, and the distributors said they'd buy more racks if I give them another newspaper to distribute."

Jason was surprised, because it was the first time he'd heard anything about another newspaper but knew how much his father loved selling news racks, and figured another publication would probably be another vehicle for him to make more money.

"What kind of newspaper?" asked Jason, "Not another singles paper, I hope."

"No, nothing like the *NSR* at all," said his father deciding to use the new shorted acronym for the *National Singles Register* as Jason did with his *S.T.A.R.S* party club, "It'll be more of an investigative newspaper and not have anything to do with singles."

"We're thinking of calling it *The Explorer*," Joy joined the conversation, "It's going to be more about unusual news stories with a lot of great eye-catching photos on the covers to draw attention in the news racks.

"I hope it's not something that I'm going to need to spend some extra time on," Jason said, "I've got a lot of promotional things that are taking up most of my time when I'm not at the office."

"No, it's going to be completely separate from the *NSR*, and you won't have to worry about spending any time putting it together," his father quickly said, "That's something that Joy is going to work on along with the calendar section."

"But like I mentioned," his father continued, "Until we're ready to publish *The Explorer*, Joy can also save you some time by helping out with the *NSR*, so it would be great if you could show her how you put everything together."

Jason wasn't even interested in being involved with his father's idea about a new publication. Still, he did mention that if Joy could become a part-time assistant to him, it might free up enough time to add another weekly *S.T.A.R.S* party during the month.

He knew he was getting over twice as much money from his singles parties as his monthly salary with the *National Singles Register*, and it would be nice to add another five hundred or so to his income each month.

"What you also might want to consider to make more money in the next month or two," suggested his father, "Would be to think about producing a singles party or two in Las Vegas so I can show the distributers there's some local promotion we're doing up there."

Jason told his father he'd be glad to help train Joy, and "show her the ropes," and how he was currently putting the *NSR* together. He also agreed that a singles party in Las Vegas might be a good idea he'd consider.

"Lori and I are planning on spending a weekend in Las Vegas in a couple of weeks anyway," said Jason, "So I'll check out some nightclubs and some other ways to get some publicity for the *NSR* while I'm up there."

Jason also started thinking having a *S.T.A.R.S* party in Las Vegas would be a great way to let everyone he knew from his first time he lived there to see he had come a long way from being a cook, casino shill, and taxi driver. He also thought it might be something that could finally add the *"Travel"* part of his *S.T.A.R S* acronym.

Jason felt everything was starting to fall into place, almost like magic.

ॐ

It was only a few days after Lori returned from her latest trip to New York when Jason and Lori drove to Las Vegas for a weekend of both pleasure and business.

450

This time besides just having fun, Jason and Lori were both appearing on a very popular late-night television show to talk about the *National Singles Register* now beginning to being distributed in Las Vegas, as well as the possibility there may be some upcoming singles parties Jason would be producing around town.

Jim Parker, who had been Jason's regular Las Vegas columnist since the beginning in 1972, was actually more famous for his alter ego, *The Vegas Vampire*, and hosted a weekly live show on Friday nights called *Shock Theatre* that featured low budget science fiction and horror movies.

Jim Parker was also excited that the *National Singles Register* was now being distributed throughout Las Vegas, where his column could be read by even more people than *The Panorama* and was happy to give Jason some free publicity on his *Vegas Vampire* television show.

Jason and Lori arrived at the *Channel Five* television studio in Henderson around ten pm for what would be two live segments between the commercial breaks of the horror movie Jim Parker was hosting as the *Vegas Vampire* that night.

Jason tried to add some humor to fit with Jim Parker's format, but still he was also able to push the main concept of how popular classified dating had become, and teased how a "*close friend* of the Vegas Vampire" Jim Parker, also had a regular column in each issue.

The *Vegas Vampire* also couldn't resist telling his television audience about Lori's photo layout in *Penthouse Magazine* and spent the entire second segment mainly talking with her about her sexy layout and story.

"The *Vegas Vampire* takes that issue of *Penthouse Magazine* into his coffin every night to enjoy before he goes to sleep," Jim's alter ego teased with his usual light innuendoes before adding another light comment about Jason's newspaper.

"And now with the *National Singles Register* in Las Vegas," Jim added, "The *Vegas Vampire* can meet some new victims with tasty blood to quench his hunger."

Jason wasn't too crazy about having the *National Singles Register* being mentioned along with *Penthouse Magazine*, but he knew the television show was just being seen in Las Vegas and wouldn't hurt the reputation of his newspaper that much. But he also knew it would make Lori feel like she could say something about herself, and not make her feel like she was just a *shill* for Jason that night.

Jason and Lori ended up leaving the television studio by one am, which was still early in Las Vegas, and they had arranged to meet Victor Consuela, who told Jason he knew the perfect disco to host a singles party.

Victor had attended some of Jason's *S.T.A.R.S* parties in California and was excited to see him expanding them in Las Vegas and offered to help Jason with any promotion he needed.

He always joked he liked trying to find "his next ex-wife" at Jason's parties and had already sarcastically told Jason about his first marriage and divorce a few years earlier.

Victor had lightly explained that one of his girlfriend's back then wouldn't have sex with him unless he married her, so Victor claimed he did marry her just for the sex and then decided to "dump her" and get a divorce only three months of marriage.

"It was no big deal," Victor always flippantly added, "Marriage is just a stupid piece of paper anyway."

Jason didn't know if he completely believed that was the entire story because he learned that Victor also had to close his clothing store after the divorce, but because Victor always liked describing his first marriage that way, Jason never questioned him further.

Both Jason and Victor kept their usual light, and sarcastic *sex talk* to a minimum around Lori when they met at the *Sahara Hotel and Casino* so Jason could say hello to Frank Reich while he was in Las Vegas.

Frank still worked the graveyard shift as a craps dealer, and Jason could only speak with him for a few minutes during one of his breaks, and was surprised learning that he had been through a bitter divorce in the past year and had to close *Johnny Reb's* after paying so much money in his divorce settlement.

"I'm still planning on getting back into the restaurant business someday, but I need to keep working here at the Sahara till I get my bankroll built back up," Frank said with optimism, "But it actually feels great to be starting from scratch again because of how good I feel after finally dumping that bitch that I was stuck with for over ten years."

Jason had always thought Frank and his ex-wife had a great marriage back when he worked at *Johnny Reb's*, but had also heard about Frank's brother Johnny's bitter divorce with Kay Adams a couple years earlier, and knew that the expression "nothing lasts forever" applied very appropriately most of the time.

After Frank also spent time complimenting Lori on her photo layout, when his break was over, Victor drove with Lori and Jason to where he said the crowds were just beginning to arrive at two am.

"No one goes to *Billy Jacks* anymore," said Victor. "The hottest disco in town now is *Dirty Sally's*, and that's the place you'll get big crowds for your parties."

Jason thought it was ironic that *Dirty Sally's* was also the former location of the *Pussy-Cat-a-Go-Go*, which had closed down a couple of years earlier.

The nightclub had been transformed into an extravagant disco, and although Jason recognized a few remnants of the former rock and roll bar, the lit dance floor and flashing disco lights had left very few familiar features.

"This is where the *'beautiful people'* of Las Vegas come every night," Victor said as they all sat in a booth at *Dirty Sally's* and observed the wall-to-wall crowd, "I can pass out your invitation's and flyers for the next month every weekend here, and this place will be packed with crowds for your party."

Jason saw that *Dirty Sally's* did still attract the trendy crowds as the *Pussycat* once had, and decided that was where he wanted to promote his first *S.T.A.R.S* party in Las Vegas.

"I actually sang here with a band once when they had live music," Jason smiled to Lori, "So it'll be fun actually hosting a party here again for *sentimental reasons.*"

It was too busy to talk about any business that night, but Jason did arrange a meeting with the management for late the next afternoon.

Before meeting with the manager at *Dirty Sally's* the next day, Jason and Lori also had lunch with Tom Casey, who was off work that Saturday afternoon.

Tom Casey was now a full-time detective with the vice department in Las Vegas, and Jason used to teasingly call him *"Serpico"* with his new unshaven look similar to the undercover cop Al Pacino portrayed in the movie.

Tom never fully explained why he wasn't able to get hired into the FBI like his father had been, but he vaguely explained it had something do with a guy his sister was involved who may have had some "connections to the mob" and might have also even been the reason Tom's father retired from the FBI earlier than he had planned.

Tom said the FBI was very thorough with background investigations with potential agents, and his sister's questionable connection wasn't helpful to him or his father.

"So, when are you two getting married," Tom lightly joked to Jason and Lori over lunch, "You guys have been together a long time now."

Jason and Lori just laughed about "Why ruin a good thing?" knowing they had the same opinion about marriage's never working out by marrying too young.

Tom had already been through several relationships, and said although he didn't rule out getting married completely, he hadn't even thought about marriage since he was "young and dumb," when he and Shannon King had discussed getting married as soon as they graduated high school.

"Can you imagine what a mistake that would have been?" Tom sarcastically said, "We probably would have had two kids by now, and my life would have been pretty much over with nothing to look forward to except working to keep supporting a family."

"Well, as soon as both Lori and I are independent millionaire's," Jason added facetiously, "It might be something to consider, but we're years away from even thinking about marriage anymore."

"That was something we only talked about when we were *young and dumb* too," Lori added, "We need to make ourselves happy first."

Jason enjoyed seeing all his old friends that weekend and was even happier later that day when the manager at *Dirty Sally's* liked Jason's pitch and agreed to be the location of Jason's first *S.T.A.R.S* party, which he booked for early August.

By the time they were driving back to California the next day, both Jason and Lori agreed their current lifestyle of mixing business and pleasure fit in perfectly with the time they were now spending together.

They both often joked about how their relationship was almost like a movie musical, the way they'd always just break into singing a song when they were in bed or even driving together.

Lori smiled at Jason as she sang Captain and Tennille's current number one song *Love Will Keep Us Together* playing on the radio during their drive home, and as usual, changed a couple of lyrics to make the song sexier.

Then, Jason heard the other current hit by the band America he liked to sing to Lori, *Sister Golden Hair*, and also lightly changed a lyric from about how Lori should see how he felt "in his thighs rather than in his eyes," just as they always had since they'd first known each other.

Besides still not wanting to ever sound too *gushy* with each other, they both knew that sometimes it was fun just acting like kids again.

"This was a great weekend," Lori smiled, "It's too bad it couldn't have been longer."

"We were just lucky we both had time off this weekend to get away from everything for at least two days," Jason agreed, "We should definitely try to spend a few days like this again sometime."

But, although they both agreed it was the best weekend they'd had together in a long time, they also knew it was time for each of them to get back to work on their own careers.

And, back to reality.

Chapter Seven

Jason was still asleep in bed when his phone rang around seven am.

He knew Lori never called him that early, plus she was back in New York City again that week and had mentioned that she never woke up before noon herself when she was back east.

Jason was still pretty groggy, but he decided to answer the phone anyway.

"What's the deal with Rudy Vallee's column?" Jason heard Joy's voice through the phone, "You aren't allowing him to say all of this stuff in his column, are you?"

"Wow, you have an early start today," Jason tried to laugh, "Are you at the office already?"

"Yeah, I woke up early and decided to come in," she said in her usual businesslike voice, "I was just looking over some of the copy for the next issue of the *NSR*."

Jason liked that Joy only lived a couple of miles from the Paramount office and was able to be there in his place most of the time.

Since Jason had shown Joy the basics of how he laid out each issue of the *NSR*, he only needed to be at the office a few days every two weeks and mainly just needed to oversee each completed issue and do a few minor edits. He had also begun to dread the drive between his apartment and the office, which was now usually taking over an hour each way with how bad the traffic had become.

Joy had been working out well with his other staff in having everything ready when he went to the office, and even delivered the completed flats to his mother in Los Alamitos, which was something else Jason didn't miss along with the traffic.

Jason didn't have any problem staying in Beverly Hills and Hollywood, handling any business that needed to be done with the newspaper, and besides only supplying the photos and story for his *Bachelorette of the Week*, Jason also only needed to write his *Message from the Publisher* each issue.

Jason would occasionally include something about national issues related to single people, but he mainly was writing the same generic message about how positive advertising for dates through classified ads had become and wrote about the hundreds of marriages reported by those who met through the *NSR*.

Just by the number of other magazines Jason had seen appearing in the news racks that included personal ads, it was now obvious that classified dating had gone mainstream and was no longer looked as a *"lonely hearts"* concept, or for people who were *"hard up"* for dates.

"Well, don't worry about Rudy Vallee's column," Jason said to Joy after she gave him a quick overview of the other articles for the current issue, "I'm coming down around noon today, and I'll do my usual edit on it."

"Okay, Joy said, "I was just trying to help."

"Just start getting the other articles typeset, and I'll see you then," Jason added in his own businesslike voice before he hung up the phone.

Jason liked Joy's enthusiasm and liked having what he considered an *assistant editor*, but he also thought he'd remind her not to call him so early when he saw her later that day.

He then looked over and saw Sheri Varran was still asleep next to him.

Jason always did have a thing for female figure skaters, and Sheri was a professional ice skater in the *Ice Follies* who Jason had made *Bachelorette of the Week* in one of his previous issues.

Along with how he'd had an immediate attraction with Lita Krisaan, who Jason had been still seeing at least once a week, he'd also started seeing Sheri when he wasn't spending time with Lita or Lori. But unlike the time he spent with Lori, there had never been any mention of the "love word" with either Lita or Sheri, and they just enjoyed the passionate romance they had together in bed.

Jason decided to wake Sheri with a parody of Rod Stewart's song *Maggie Mae*. He liked to sing in the mornings, which always got a light groan and laugh from his other girlfriends.

"Wake up, Sheri, I think I've got something to *put in' you...*," he teasingly sang the parody as he began to kiss Sheri on the shoulder to wake her.

Jason liked that his bed was just at least another stage where he could always perform his funny songs to someone and also liked that the "other" girls seemed to enjoy it as well.

❧

Jason was at Ron Smith and Stan Adams's office on Sunset by eleven am that same morning, picking up the photos of his next *Bachelorette of the Week*.

"You look pretty hungover," said Stan, as Jason was looking at the photos.

"No, not really. I didn't get to sleep till after three am and just woke up early," said Jason, "I was out at different clubs last night promoting and partied late."

"You've been partying a lot lately," said Stan, "You should slow down a little."

"Well, that's how I make my money," Jason just smiled, "It's all just part of my business."

"Yeah, monkey business," Stan sarcastically half laughed, "You've been getting a little wild lately with all these other girls you've been seeing."

456

"Well, I don't see Lori that often anymore, and she's been busy going on auditions and spending time in New York City at least once a month," Jason just smiled, "and I don't like to go out alone."

"I mean, here you've got the greatest girlfriend in Lori, but you can't seem to keep your dick in your pants when she's not around," Stan said with more sarcasm than disappointment, "You know, you can't make a living out of screwing every girl you meet in town."

Jason didn't feel that he was *volume fucking*, but although he did have a couple other "one-night flings" besides Lita and Sheri, evidently, he wasn't being as discreet as he thought.

"Lori and I are getting along fine together, but we're both single and have our own careers right now," Jason tried to casually justify. "Besides, Lori is the one that suggested we shouldn't be inhibited from having fun when we aren't together,"

"I mean, she didn't really encourage me to fool around, but did say if anything happened to at least be discreet," Jason added, "Plus I don't know what Lori is doing when we're not together either.".

"I just don't get it," sighed Stan, "You and Lori seemed like the perfect couple, but obviously you're not in love anymore, so I don't know why you both bother even trying to stay together."

"Lori always says there's a thin line between love and hate," Jason tried to smile without showing regret, "And sometimes I do hate how she got involved with *Penthouse*, but at the same time, I know how sweet she really is, and it's hard not to stay in love with her."

"I know that there are some other things that probably bug us about each other," Jason added, "But when we do see each other, we still have fun, and neither of us has ever talked about breaking up."

"Pretty weird, huh?" Jason shrugged to Stan.

"It's weird alright!", Stan agreed.

"I just have too many things on my plate businesswise to worry about our relationship right now," Jason said, hoping to end the subject, "But Lori and I are still doing great together, so everything's fine."

"Well, I guess I was wrong about Lori being *'The One'* you were finally going to settle down with,' Stan said with light resignation.

"Well, I have been meeting a lot of girls who may actually be *The Next One*," Jason facetiously joked, trying to lighten the mood, "Besides, being seen with a variety of beautiful women isn't bad for my *singles and party guy* image and is good for business."

"And the other girls don't mind that you're still with Lori?", asked Stan.

"All of the girls I know or meet have the same philosophy that I've been feeling lately," said Jason, "They aren't even remotely interested in getting married or having families right now and just want to have fun."

"Plus, they all understand Lori is my main girlfriend and know to be discreet when they see me with her," Jason added, "and I'm just as discreet if I see any of them with any other guys or their own boyfriends."

"I'm not saying there aren't some strong romantic feelings with a couple of them," Jason kept justifying, "But, they're not looking for anything permanent and know our flings are mainly for fun."

"Well, I guess if you think that's what it takes to have fun," Stan said, shaking his head, "I don't understand it and was just was raised in a different world, I guess."

After Jason got the photo he needed from Stan Adams for the next cover of the *National Singles Register,* and started his drive to his office in Paramount, he decided he wouldn't be concerned by his conversation with Stan.

He also thought how contradictory it was for Stan even to act disappointed in the way Jason was currently living his life after what Stan had gone through himself the past year during his bitter divorce and how much money it had cost him.

Seeing the toll marriage took on many of his other friends like Sammy Shore, who lost *The Comedy Store* to his wife Mitzie in his divorce, or his high school friend Dan who was devastated when his wife left him, as well as the others he knew who all also once felt they were married to *"The One,"* Jason didn't even have to consider his parents apparent unhappy and argumentative lifelong relationship.

Plus, Jason enjoyed the freshness of new relationships and was able to send flowers or exchange romantic greeting cards, which he seldom did with Lori anymore.

Jason had seen enough other problems with long-term relationships and currently wasn't interested in having just *one girlfriend* or even trying to look for *"The One"* that Stan had always talked about.

He also knew he wasn't going to be the first one to admit it to Lori.

Chapter Eight

The DJ at *My Place* in Beverly Hills had the dance hit *Get Down Tonight* by *KC and the Sunshine Band* blasting through the disco as Jason and Lori were walking into his bi-weekly Sunday night *S.T.A.R.S* party.

Sandi Shore was again collecting the three-dollar door charge and gave Jason a thumbs up, letting him know the door money that night was great as Jason saw the disco was almost already filled to capacity.

Mixie Thompson was also at the door helping pass out the famous couple nametags, and Annie Gaybis was also already there talking with Nicki Blair, Ron Smith, and Mark Marzouk.

Jason saw Stan Adams, Wally Eagler, and James Mares were all at his party that night and hoping their photos would be chosen for the *National Singles Register's* next issue. All three of them were already taking photos of couples on the dance floor, including the former heavyweight champion Joe Frazier, who Jason had met earlier that week in Beverly Hills and invited to be a judge in his *Bachelorette of the Week* contest. One of Jason's other celebrity judges there that night, was former pop music star Jan Berry from the group *Jan and Dean*.

Jan and Dean were mostly famous for being The Beach Boys main competition in the early 1960s with hits like *Little Old Lady from Pasadena, Honolulu Lulu*, and *Surf City*. Jason had also been a fan of many Jan and Dean hit songs since he'd been a little kid, and even remembered singing a couple of their early hits *Heart and Soul* and *Baby Talk* along with his babysitters.

Most of those who met Jan Berry at Jason's parties always thought he was just "some stoned guy" when they first met him, and were also seemingly unaware of the brain damage Jan had suffered in a near-fatal car accident almost ten years earlier.

Jason and Jan Berry had been friends since they'd met at a *7-11* store on Sunset Boulevard several months earlier when Jan needed help after his Corvette was stolen from the parking lot that day.

Jan had explained to Jason that he had left his Corvette running when he went into the *7-11* store to buy a *Slurpee*, and someone just jumped into his car and drove off.

Jason seemed to be the only one at the *7-11* who was taking Jan seriously or paying attention to his almost childlike whimpering, so after the police came and finally took a stolen vehicle report, Jason did drive him back to his Bel-Aire estate where Jan lived with his parents.

Jan Berry was immediately impressed learning that Jason knew the opening doo-wop lyrics of *"Bom ba, ba bom bab, um dab um wah wah wah,"* to Jan and Dean's late 1950's hit song *Baby Talk* when Jason lightly began singing the lyrics during their drive.

"The r-r-radio stations don't play those songs anymore," Jan half sighed, "I can't believe you even know that song."

"Hey, it was a fun song to sing," Jason smiled.

Since then, Jan had been a celebrity judge in a few of Jason's previous bachelorette contests, but having to constantly remind everyone what a huge music star Jan had been in the late 1950s and early 1960s was always irritating to Jason with those who didn't appreciate the progress he'd made since his accident.

It made Jason remember Edy Williams' remark about how fast people forget about celebrities if they aren't mentioned in the media regularly.

Jan Berry had brought the drummer from The Beach Boys' Dennis Wilson to also be a celebrity judge in one of Jason's earlier bachelorette contests, and it was Dennis Wilson who first suggested to Jason he should have the girls be judged in swimsuits or bikinis to spice up his contests and make them sexier. Jason was also feeling his contests had been getting a little monotonous with the contestants just parading around the dance floor once in their dresses, and agreed that it was time to liven up his parties.

Even though the club owner Sia Amiri at first thought it seemed a little racy and strange to have girls wearing bikinis inside a Beverly Hills disco, he quickly warmed up to the idea.

Since he had begun his parties at *My Place*, Jason had his contestants dance individually to a popular song of their choice in their swimsuits, and his Bachelorette of the Week contests had become even more popular.

Jason had also added a one-hundred-dollar cash first prize, which along with being on the cover of the *National Singles Register* was an added enticement to the contestants.

For his party that night, Jason decided to combine his bachelorette and bachelor contest on the same night to premiere his new idea for his bachelor contests that he thought would be funny. He decided to have his *Bachelor of the Week* contestants also begin to be judged in swimsuits that night, which he facetiously joked was showing that he was just giving the men their equal rights to be judged in the same way as the girls were.

Jason saw several of his former bachelorettes who were going to be judges in the bachelor contest that night, including Lita Krissan and Sheri Varran, but wasn't concerned because they knew to act like they were all just friends when they saw him with Lori.

Tom Casey and Victor Consuela had both driven in for that night's party as well, and Jason had already given them hundreds of invitations and flyers for his upcoming party at *Dirty Sally's* in Las Vegas, that they could begin distributing the next week.

Tom and Victor both said they were looking forward to hopefully meeting a new girlfriend, "at least for the night," which by then was just the normal custom after a night at the discos.

Jason had introduced Mixie Thompson to Tom Casey that night after she told Jason she thought Tom was sexy, but after also meeting Victor, she had been having fun alternating dancing with both of them most of the night.

Most of the early part of the party was just disco dancing as most of the partygoers were approaching everyone looking for their famous couple's match, which had continued to be the best party mixer Jason had tried.

After several dances with Lori and a couple of other former bachelorettes, Jason spent most of his other time at the party greeting the partygoers and making sure they were having fun, before planning to start his contest with the bachelorettes around eleven pm.

While Lori was mingling and talking with several other of their mutual friends at the disco, Jason talked with Jan Berry and Joe Frazier about the party and the upcoming contests.

"Don't you think it's going to look a little *queer* or *gay* having guys parading around in swimsuits," Joe Frazier joked with light apprehension, "And to be honest, I ain't interested in judging no dudes tonight."

"M-m-me either," Jan Berry half stuttered and half-laughed, "I j-j-just wanna j-j-judge the chicks."

"Don't worry, you'll both just be judging the bachelorettes tonight," Jason half laughed as well, "I've got plenty of girls here tonight who are more than happy to judge the bachelors."

Jason also liked talking with Joe Frazier about his boxing career especially about his competition with Muhammad Ali. Since Frazier had lost his title to George Foreman a couple of years earlier, and then Mohammad Ali had defeated Foreman to regain his boxing title, Frazier had worked his way back to be the number one contender to fight Ali again for the world heavyweight championship.

Joe Frazier lightly complained that Ali had just been "boxing *stiffs* like Wepner and Lyle" because Ali knew that Frazier wouldn't fall for the "rope-a-dope crap" and would "kick Ali's ass" if they fought again.

Frazier also added that he was confident a third fight between him and Ali would be set sometime that year because that was what the public wanted to see.

"But I still don't know if the public is ready to see those dude's showin' their bulges on the dance floor tonight," Frazier joked again before Jason went to round up all of the girls for his bachelorette contest, he was presenting first that night.

"Well, I hope it doesn't look too gay either," Jason lightly added, "I just thought it might be fun to try once to see if the girls like it."

Jason knew not to take too much time running his contests as to not have too long of a break in the disco dancing, and limited his contestants to eight for each contest that night, knowing they wouldn't take more than ten or fifteen minutes each to complete.

Bill Ballance's *Feminine Forum* radio show had gone off the air, and although he still occasionally would attend some *S.T.A.R.S* parties, he hadn't emceed any of Jason's beauty contests since the parties at The Speakeasy.

Jason had the DJ at *My Place*, introduce each contestant by their name, astrological sign, and occupation, and then have them circle the dance floor in front of the judges and then dance for the audience for about a minute before the DJ introduced the next contestant.

The response for his Bachelorette contest that night was filled with the usual hoots and cheers from the men in the audience as the girls danced in their bikinis to the sexually suggestive song *Lady Marmalade*, but Jason couldn't believe the response from the women at the party when he started the bachelor contest at midnight.

Jason and the DJ had chosen a slower song called *I'm a Bachelor* by The Temptations, and while the guys were trying to slowly dance suggestively in their swimsuits, which Jason thought would just be funny, it turned into something entirely different.

It almost started sounding liked early Beatlemania or the response Elvis Presley used to get with the ear-piercing screaming and attempts by some of the girls in the audience to run on the dance floor to grab the bachelor contestants.

It was also obvious that one of the male contestants did have a bulge that all the female judges couldn't miss as he paraded in front of them and bought more screams of approval from almost every girl in the audience.

Jason lightly wondered if that bachelor contestant had a girlfriend who prepared him for the contest the way Lori had with Jason the night they streaked.

Sia Amiri stood with Jason near the DJ booth while they both watched in amusement at the reaction from almost every girl in the audience.

"I think you're on to something here, Jason," Sia laughed, trying to talk over the screaming women, "If the word gets out that all your bachelor contests are going to be like this, we'll have a thousand girls waiting in line to get in the door."

"I guess it doesn't look '*too queer*' after all," Joe Frazier joked to Jason when he approached him after the contest, "It looks like it was just making a lot of women horny."

Most of the guys at the disco that night said it was something they weren't excited about seeing again, but every girl that Jason talked to that night was almost begging to be judges in his next *Bachelor of the Week* contest.

Jason knew the guys would still be coming on the nights of his bachelor contests, knowing that there would just be more horny girls to meet after the contest and knew that attracting more women meant more guys at his parties.

He also knew that would mean more money for him, and that's what mattered most.

Jason usually took circle of his friends to *Ollie Hammonds Restaurant* on La Cienega after his parties for a late breakfast, and ten of them were still eating at three am after that night's party at *My Place*.

Mixie Thompson was sitting with Victor Consuela after Tom Casey had met another girl he wanted to bring to breakfast, and Annie Gaybis, Sandi Shore, Lita Krissan, and Jan Berry had also joined Jason and Lori at *Ollie Hammonds*.

After laughing about everything that happened at the party as well as the girls discussing whether the guy who won the bachelor contest "really had a boner or was just well hung," the conversation got around to their own career activities.

Lori was telling everyone about a new stage musical she was planning to audition for in the next few weeks called *Let My People Come*.

"I heard about that musical," said Annie, "It's written by Earl Wilson Jr., the son of the famous columnist, and I heard it's supposed to be pretty wild show."

"Well, the director did say it involves a *little nudity*," Lori lightly laughed, "So I'll probably have to show him my tits during the interview."

"That seems to be the usual requirement for all my auditions lately," Mixie sarcastically agreed, "Especially all the low budget indie movies."

Annie joked about an independent movie she had just finished called *Wham-Bam Thank You Spaceman* that she was originally told involved "*just a little* nudity" but was a bit more once filming had started.

"It wasn't anything pornographic, but I definitely ended up showing more than my boobs," Annie joked, "Hopefully, that movie never gets released nationally, and it's definitely not one of my movies I'm going to tell my father about."

Lori continued explaining she was mainly excited about her upcoming audition because *Let My People Come* was going to be performed at the *Whiskey-a Go-Go* for an opening sometime that fall.

"It might run for a couple of months the way *The Rocky Horror Show* did at the *Roxy*," Lori excitedly continued, "But just getting to perform live at the Whiskey would be like a dream come true for me."

"That would be great," Jason said encouragingly, "I once hoped that I'd sing there a long time ago, so at least one of us might get a chance to perform there."

Jason was glad to see Lori so happy but noticed something else Lori was doing again that night that his friends had also noticed in the past couple of months.

Every time Lori was excitedly telling a story, one minute she'd be laughing and then suddenly start crying before going back to laughing as nothing had happened.

Jason's friends would usually just joke that Lori was so excited it sometimes brought her to "happy tears," but it did occasionally make Jason wonder. But he would usually decide that his friends were right because Lori was accomplishing everything she had once only fantasized about, and probably was just excited.

Jason didn't need to shed "happy tears" but knew he was as happy himself as Lori was about where own career was heading.

It just felt good to be happy, successful, and be able to have fun at the same time.

Chapter Nine

Jason was getting ready to leave for Las Vegas, his *S.T.A.R.S* party at *Dirty Sally's* when he got a call from Terri Larson from San Francisco. He had always tried to stay in touch with Terri by phone occasionally, and always thought it was funny that she was still driving a taxi, but she had also mentioned she was going to interior design school and still had plans for bigger things eventually.

"You should get my brother Mark to judge your dance contest in Las Vegas," Terri said after Jason told her about his party at *Dirty Sally's*, "He's a regular dancer on American Bandstand and is staying at the *Thunderbird Hotel* and rehearsing for some live shows that Dick Clark is producing in Vegas."

Jason had only met her brother once, but figured a regular dancer from *American Bandstand* would be another good celebrity judge for his dance contest. For his first *S.T.A.R.S* party, Jason had just scheduled a dance contest at *Dirty Sally's* with a two-hundred-dollar first prize and was saving his other contests for any other parties he might continue in Las Vegas.

Jason already had Sammy Shore, who was appearing at *The Flamingo* with Connie Stevens that week in Las Vegas as one judge, and Sammy was bringing another comedian, David Brenner, so along with local personality Jim Parker, Jason figured adding a professional dancer like Mark as another judge, would be impressive for his first party at *Dirty Sally's*.

Jason told Terri he'd definitely get a hold of her brother Mark when he was in Las Vegas that week.

Lori was busy planning for her audition for *Let My People Come* and had other business that week, so Jason drove to Las Vegas with his current *Bachelorette of the Week* he had become friends, Paula Summers. Besides being a part-time actress and model, Paula was also a hairdresser and had talked Jason into letting her give him a new hairstyle.

Paula decided to give Jason a *permanent* to his hair, saying it would give him more of a "hip disco look" that was very popular at that time.

Jason thought at first that the hairstyle made him look like what he joked was a "white Jimi Hendrix" the way his now curly blond hair stood out like an *Afro*, but after he'd gotten used to it, he decided he liked his *new look*.

Jason again stayed at the *MGM Grand* and decided to take Paula to see what had become his favorite show *Hallelujah Hollywood,* just as he had his other "friends" he brought to Las Vegas when Lori wasn't available.

One of the featured performers in the production was a magic act named *Siegfried and Roy* and Jason had tried sitting in different locations in the showroom in the half dozen times he'd already seen them, but could never figure out how they were making the lions and tigers disappear or their other magic. But he decided he was going to keep coming to see the *Hallelujah Hollywood* until he could figure out their secrets.

After the show at the *MGM,* Jason and Paula took a taxi to the *Thunderbird Hotel* to have a late breakfast and get re-acquainted with Terri's brother Mark.

Mark had told Jason and Paula to meet him inside the casino at the entrance of the *Continental Theatre,* and as soon as they were approaching the entrance, Jason started hearing Elvis Presley's voice coming from inside of the showroom singing one of his favorite Elvis songs, *A Fool Such as I.*

After Mark walked them inside the showroom to take a quick look, Jason couldn't believe what he saw at first.

There he was onstage in his gold lame jacket looking young, thin, and sounding almost exactly as he sounded on the record.

But it wasn't Elvis Presley.

"He just goes by the name *Alan,*" explained Mark, "Doesn't he do a great Elvis imitation?"

"The women even scream for Alan the way they used to for Elvis," Mark added with a laugh.

Jason thought Alan looked so much better than the way he remembered seeing Elvis Presley the night he had met him, but was more surprised how the audience was responding.

"It's amazing," Jason said as they watched Alan sang another Elvis Presley hit song. "But why would somebody come and see some guy imitating Elvis Presley when they can see the *real Elvis* over at the Hilton?"

"Well, it's cheaper for one thing," said Mark, "But audiences can also see what Elvis was like when he was in his prime and not just a fat parody of himself which he seems to be lately."

"Alan also sings of all of Elvis's hit songs," added Mark, "The real Elvis only sings a few of the old songs these days, and the audiences here seem to like just seeing a recreation and hearing all the big hits."

Jason remembered the cover of *People Magazine* earlier that year that had the headline *"ELVIS IS 40!"* and had also read that his live shows weren't very good anymore and did seem more like a comedy show at times.

He would have liked to have seen more of the "Alan" show that night, but Jason decided he'd come back again when he had more time and mainly came by to get reacquainted with Mark before he judged his dance contest at *Dirty Sally's* the next night.

After deciding to all have breakfast together in the coffee shop at *The Thunderbird*, Jason was also listening to Mark explain the show he was rehearsing and the deal Dick Clark had with the hotel producing his shows in the *Continental Theatre*.

"The show is almost like a live version of American Bandstand and called Dick Clark's Good Ole Rock and Roll," explained Mark, "He's got acts like Chuck Berry, Jackie Wilson, Dion, Bobby Vee, The Flamingo's and a lot of other oldie acts alternating so he can always offer different shows every month here in Las Vegas."

"Plus, that Elvis imitator you saw is one of Dick Clark's show's too," Mark added, "So he's pretty much always got a production going on here at The Thunderbird."

"The deal for the showroom here is different than the other Strip hotels," Mark continued explaining, "It's strictly a 'four-wall deal' so he can basically do shows here in Las Vegas anytime he wants."

"Dick just pays a rental fee to the Thunderbird and keeps all the ticket sales," Mark added, "It's great to have a venue that's available all the time."

Jason knew what a *"four-wall deal"* was, and that's pretty much the way he had all of his singles parties set up with the nightclubs. He did the promotion, advertising, and supplied the entertainment, and kept the door money, but the big difference was that he didn't pay a rental, and usually got a piece of the bar receipts. Plus, having his shows in the popular nightclubs gave him great in-house advertising that didn't cost him anything, and Jason considered his deals more of a *"two-wall"* arrangement.

But Jason was surprised that there was a Las Vegas Strip Hotel that rented their showroom the same way he had paid the Beverly Hilton, and anyone could produce their own show on the Las Vegas Strip.

"Do you know how much Dick Clark pays to rent the room?" asked Jason.

"I don't think it's that much," said Mark, "The hotel is happy not having to pay for entertainment, and just like all the other casinos, they're mainly interested in attracting crowds for the money they spend gambling."

Jason wasn't considering anything that he could actually produce in a Las Vegas showroom and was satisfied with how he had set up his deals with the nightclubs without ever having to put out any rental costs.

But he thought it was interesting to know just in case he ever did.

❧

The next night at *Dirty Sally's*, Jason had Victor work the front door collecting the three-dollar cover charge and agreed to pay Victor twenty percent of what he collected for helping him with his party promotion in Las Vegas.

Jason knew it didn't hurt that there was a row of news racks almost directly in front of *Dirty Sally's* as well as almost every hotel and casino on the Strip and liked seeing the *National Singles Register* displayed in the rack right in between the *Las Vegas Sun* and *Review Journal*.

While both of those newspapers had basically the same headline all week about the disappearance of Jimmy Hoffa, and speculating whether the Las Vegas unions or the local mob was involved with kidnapping him, Jason had prominently listed as one of his secondary headlines on the cover of the *NSR*, that the first *S.T.A.R.S* party in Las Vegas was being presented that week at *Dirty Sally's*.

Jason also decided to have Paula Summers be a celebrity judge that night to remind the audience at *Dirty Sally's*; they could pick up a current issue of the *NSR* almost anywhere on the Strip and read all about her.

Victor didn't start collecting the door money until eleven pm that night because just as it had been at the *Pussycat-a-Go-Go*, very few partygoers went out before then in Las Vegas. Although Mark and Jim Parker had arrived early, Sammy Shore and David Brenner had show's that night and couldn't arrive until after 1 am.

It definitely felt different to Jason not starting his *Famous Couples Dance Contest* until three am, but it wasn't until two am before *Dirty Sally's* really began to get busy enough for crowds to look for their matches for the dance contest.

Jason had met a local photographer to shoot photos of the party and was confident the photos of the very attractive, trendy crowd of what Jason guessed was close to three hundred, would look great for the Las Vegas insert of the *National Singles Register*.

Even though his *S.T.A R.S.* party was officially over at four am and was the time management at *Dirty Sally's* said he needed to cut his door charge, Jason, Paula Victor, Mark, Sammy Shore, and David Brenner ended up partying there till almost six am before having a late breakfast nearby at the *Sands Hotel*.

Jason was a little disappointed that after paying out two hundred dollars cash to the winners of his dance contest, forty dollars to the photographer, and another hundred and twenty-five dollars to Victor, he netted less than two hundred dollars for himself when he figured in how much he spent that weekend.

As he always did with Sandi Shore, Jason had told Victor that he could comp some of his friends and not lose any customers over the three-dollar door charge. He wanted to make sure his parties always had great crowds and left it at their discretion to decide on how many people to comp for each party.

Jason was surprised when Victor said he had to let close to a hundred people in free that night who refused to pay a cover charge and started to leave unless they were comp'd.

Although he was planning on making a lot more money from his party at *Dirty Sally's*, Jason figured the promotion would at least look great in the next issue and be something for the local distributors in Las Vegas to see as his father had wanted.

"Well, at least it was fun and actually like a free weekend vacation," Jason lightly joked to Paula after they were back in their room alone, "But before I do any more contest's up here, I've got to figure a way to make it more profitable."

Jason never had a chance to sing his Rod Stewart parody of *Maggie Mae* to wake up any girls when he was in Las Vegas because they rarely went to bed until sometimes after seven am, and were usually still awake in the early morning. But during the drives back to California, Jason would usually sing *It Had to Be You* at least once a cappella, to let whoever he was with know he enjoyed the weekend with them.

Singing was still his second favorite thing to do whenever he got the chance.

Chapter Ten

After Lori had gotten the role in the musical *Let My People Come*, and the rehearsals began, she had decided to get her own small studio apartment in Hollywood that October, but Jason was still only seeing her a few times a month by then.

They both had so many things going on with their careers that only saw each other for special dates, including a night at *The Roxy* when they saw the new musician the record company and media was pushing heavily named Bruce Springsteen.

Another special date was when they had gone to see *The Rolling Stones* together at the *Los Angeles Forum* after Jason found out Lori had never seen them live before.

Jason thought *The Rolling Stones* were even better than the last time he'd seen them, and Lori especially liked one of the songs from their album *Goats Head Soup* called *Star Star*.

Star Star was a song that couldn't be listed by its actual title on the album or even played on the radio because of its X-rated lyrics, but it was definitely the highlight of the Rolling Stones concert that night.

While Mick Jagger was onstage singing the racy lyrics, along with the chorus of the actual title of the song, *Starfucker*, a giant inflated penis rose from the stage, and Jagger straddled it as confetti blew out of the tip, simulating an orgasm. Jason also thought it was funny that instead of being the typical song about groupies, *Star Star* was more appropriate to so many of the actresses and models Jason personally knew in Hollywood since he had first heard the expression "Starfucker" from Dennis Cole years earlier,

"I always liked the Rolling Stones," Lori laughed after the concert, "But seeing how sexy and nasty Mick Jagger was live on stage, I love them now!"

Jason wasn't surprised by Lori's comment because he'd already figured out when it came to sexual attraction, most girls always seemed to like the bad boys the best. He had also taken both Lori and Annie Gaybis to the *Los Angeles Forum* to see the *Thrilla in Manilla* championship fight between Joe Frazier and Muhammad Ali on closed-circuit TV.

Jason had come to consider Annie one of his best friends and was glad they had both never even considered having a fling together, and their friendship was almost like a brother and sister. He'd often invite Annie to be with him on other dates with bachelorettes knowing that she would always be discreet and be a good *buffer* to make it appear he was "just out with friends" whenever he told Lori about some of the places that he went without her.

470

Jason would also lightly joke to Annie that it wasn't bad for his image to always be seen with at least two beautiful women whenever he was out.

The *Thrilla in Manilla* was a brutal fight for fourteen rounds, and although Jason had been cheering for Joe Frazier, it looked like the fight wouldn't be decided until the fifteenth and final round, but Jason and the entire crowd at *The Forum* started booing loudly, and couldn't believe it when Joe Frazier's trainer threw in the towel before the last round giving the fight to Ali.

"Damn, I can't believe Joe Frazier just quit like that," Jason complained after the fight.

Jason also decided not to let Lori or Annie know that he had bet two hundred dollars on Joe Frazier the last time he'd been to Las Vegas, and felt worse for himself than for Joe, after losing that much money on just one bet.

Although Jason and Lori still were having fun together, because he was only sleeping with Lori three or four times a month, it did seem like she had become more of a parttime girlfriend than a couple of other girls he saw regularly. But neither of them had ever said anything should be different or needed to change between them, so Jason guessed it was best to follow the old saying, "Why change a good thing?"

There was a big change in Jason's living arrangements after he decided to adopt a stray cat who had been hanging out on his porch and meowing for food and milk every day for several weeks, and decided to call the cat "Old Lady," when less than a month after adopting her off the street in Beverly Hills, she had a litter of kittens.

Having six cats in his apartment was a mess for two months that fall, but he was eventually able to find homes for all the kittens, and soon after, took *Old Lady* to the vet to be fixed.

Jason decided having a cat for a pet did seem fairly low maintenance, and although *Old Lady* was very independent and he didn't feel that much of a bond with her, he didn't want to just throw her back on the street after she had gotten used to having a home to live.

He at least enjoyed her as a part-time pet on the rare times his cat did like to be affectionate and didn't mind sharing his apartment with her and also liked knowing that he would never have to have to wake up alone in the mornings one way or another.

The new *National Explorer* tabloid also premiered that fall and was published on the alternate weeks of the *National Singles Register*, and Jason's only contribution was occasional ideas for the covers.

The content of the *National Explorer* was an investigative theme on one main topic for each issue, and Jason agreed with Joy because there weren't attractive girls on the cover to attract attention, the paper needed to be sensationalized with a wild cover photo and headline to draw attention in the news racks.

The premier issue's headline was *"MOBSTERS!"* and the cover featured the famous death photo of Bugsy Siegel riddled with bullets as he lay dead sprawled across s sofa. For another issue that was headlined *"FREAKS!"* Joy found the most outrageous photos of deformed people and circus sideshow freaks and splattered them on the cover.

Jason's father said the distributers said those issues sold great, so Joy agreed that "exploitation" and "outrageous photos" are what she'd focus all future covers.

Jason rarely saw his parents in person anymore and was only speaking with them separately on the phone a few times a month, which was fine with him because they both had seemed in foul moods whenever they spoke. His parents had also sounded like they had been arguing more than usual recently, and his father had also casually mentioned that he may be leaving town for an extended time and wouldn't staying at the townhouse in Los Alamitos regularly.

"You know how crazy Vi gets sometimes and it's probably best if I just get away from her for a while to see if things calm down," his father said, "I just can't let myself go crazy with all of her rants."

Jason knew how crazy *both* his parents got at times and didn't really want to hear anything about their personal problems, but also thought if they were getting ready to separate, it was no big deal and something that should have happened years earlier.

"But there's nothing for you to worry about as far as the business", his father added, "I'm just going to be spending the next few months in Dallas to work on selling news racks for more distribution, so we'll see what happens after that."

Jason just said whatever worked was fine with him. His parent's private life was something he had never wanted to think about, and just wanted to stay in a positive mood himself without having any of their negativity to ever rub off on him.

But it was shortly after his father traveled to Dallas, when Jason walked into the newspaper office to drop off photos and his *Message from the Publisher*, when besides seeing Joy sitting at her usual desk, he suddenly became very uncomfortable seeing his mother sitting at his desk.

"I'm going to start working here at the office," said his mother, "You're not here every day anyway, and it's about time I see how things are run down here."

"Well, there's not too much you can do in the office," said Jason, "The regular writer's just mail in their columns by the deadline without any problems."

"Plus, Joy seems to have everything working the same way with *The Explorer*," Jason added, trying to convince his mother she wasn't really needed at the office. "It's mainly just some proofreading, typesetting, and paste-up that everyone here pretty much handles like clockwork."

"Well, I can help with all of that for both newspapers," said his mother, "The mail only takes me a few hours in the morning, so I've got plenty of free time to act as an editor too."

Jason noticed that Joy was sitting silently at her desk and just reading some copy without saying anything.

"Plus, you're not even in the office every day, so I don't even know why I'm paying you a salary anymore," his mother decided to add with some sarcasm.

Jason didn't like the way she said that "she was paying his salary" as if he was one of her employees or was paying him an allowance like he was a teenager.

"That's because I've worked like shit the last three years turning it into a real newspaper and making it easy to put together every two weeks," Jason snapped back, "Everything I do away from the office always has something to do with the NSR, and I know you're making plenty of money from what I've done!"

"That's my money!" his mother yelled back, "And if you think your promotion is so good for the paper, then you can just make your salary off your stupid parties."

Jason didn't want to argue in the office and just said, "Fine!" after throwing the photos and news copy on the desk, and immediately left for the day.

He had always been able to keep a good distance between himself and his parents and feel independent, but it started to feel like things were starting to become different. Jason felt that even though his work helped the newspaper become the *National Singles Register*; he knew his position as one of the owners was basically in name only and had accepted that his parents would never actually share in any of the other income that was coming in each week.

As his mother had said, that was all "*their* money" and not Jason's.

The next day, Jason called his father in Dallas to find out what the deal was with his mother starting to work in the office.

"Like I said before, she's just being a pain in the ass right now," said his father, "Vi said because I'm setting up an operation here in Dallas, she wants to start working in the office as some type of manager to keep an eye on things."

"But there's really nothing for her to do," said Jason, "I've got everything organized, and I don't see why she needs to be involved."

"I think it's just an ego thing with her right now," said his father, "Joy doesn't like it either but just try to go along with it for right now."

Jason also had felt for several months that his position was strictly a three hundred dollar a week job, which although was around three times the minimum wage of two dollars and fifty cents an hour and paid most of his monthly expenses, that money wasn't enough to let him live his current lifestyle without the additional cash he made from his parties each month.

"Well, I've been thinking a lot about it, and I think I'm mainly going to focus on my own *S.T.A.R.S* parties, which bring in most of my money now," Jason decided to tell his father, "If Vi is going to be at the office every day, and with Joy also working on both newspapers, I don't even need to be at the office anymore as the editor."

"Everyone knows that you're the editor, and don't worry, I'll make sure you still get your regular salary," his father said, "You've been a great face for the NSR, and it's fine to concentrate on your promotions for on right now."

"But just try to get along with Vi for the next couple months to keep things running smoothly," his father added, "There's going to be some good things going on with both newspapers next year, and there will still some things you can do as the editor that will make you some more money."

Jason had heard that before and pretty much decided that although he wanted to keep his editor and publisher's title, he still didn't want to have to work with his mother on a regular basis.

"Well, I can still call in or answer any questions they might have," Jason said, "But I do want to spend more time just working on the promotions for the *NSR* and maybe start doing some bigger things."

"That's fine, but just don't rock the boat right now with business," his father said, "The *NSR* does work like clockwork now, so let's not change anything that will cause any problems."

With Jason not having to be concerned with any content in the *National Explorer*, and with the *National Singles Register* editorial formula established and enough of a backlog of bachelorettes to cover the next few months, Jason's only challenge was to keep promoting events for the newspaper and to figure out ways to make more money.

Jason knew that things always changed, but changes were happening too quickly that he wasn't feeling good about, but also knew he needed to keep making some extra money away from the newspaper,

Just in case.

Chapter Eleven

Jason hadn't had another promotion in Las Vegas since his party at *Dirty Sally's*, but started thinking again about what Terri's brother Mark told him about how *The Thunderbird Hotel* rented out *Continental Theatre* showroom to independent producers.

Jason had long been thinking of a larger event that could make thousands of dollars rather than just a few hundred, and also, if there was a *"Travel"* angle, he could finally promote to go with his *S.T.A.R.S.* acronym.

Let My People Come was set to open at the *Whiskey-a-Go-Go* beginning in November, so Jason started thinking about a big show he could also produce himself before the end of the year.

Through Mark in Las Vegas, Jason was able to contact the entertainment and public relations director Jim Seagrave at the *Thunderbird Hotel* to at least find out what the deal was with the *Continental Theatre*. Seagrave explained the showroom was booked till the end of the year, except for the two weeks before Christmas, when the showroom was closed and considered a dead time in Las Vegas.

Jason thought it was amazing that the timing was perfect for what he was actually thinking about doing that Christmas.

The year before, Jason had announced the *Bachelorette of the Year* in a fairly lowkey manner at his Christmas *S.T.A.R.S* party in Hollywood when he named Lita Krissan the winner of his readers mail-in voting contest. That announcement didn't receive much publicity outside of what he included in the *National Singles Register*, but this year, he was hoping for a bigger media event along the lines of the *Playmate of the Year*.

Jason figured that by announcing his *Bachelorette of the Year* at a Las Vegas Strip hotel instead of just a nightclub, and making it an actual big national beauty pageant, it would add some national flair to the title and attract more press coverage. At the same time, he could have a junket type of *S.T.A.R.S* party for his members, which would finally be complete his "Singles Travel and Recreation Society" acronym.

Jason also didn't want to risk spending any large amount of money upfront as he did for the *Hearts and Flowers Ball*, and still knew even when one of his bi-weekly *S.T.A.R.S* parties didn't draw as many people on a particular night, he never really lost anything, and would just make a smaller *profit* than usual. He also knew it would be tougher to promote a big party without his usual in-house promotion he always received by having his parties at popular discos, and would need to mainly draw from his group friends and regulars, which he figured was at least a few hundred.

Besides making money, he knew a big party in Las Vegas would be a fun way to celebrate Christmas with his friends that year.

Jason decided to pitch Jim Seagrave his idea of how the *Thunderbird Hotel* could benefit by having "America's largest singles newspaper" host their annual Christmas party at the hotel in return for the free use of the showroom for its party, and where they would produce their annual Bachelorette of the Year Pageant with well-known celebrity judges.

"The showroom will be dark that weekend anyway," Jason pitched Seagrave, "But seeing it's also a dead period in Las Vegas, I can also make it a singles weekend junket if you give me a great deal on a weekend hotel room package."

"I'll advertise it heavily in *National Singles Register* for the next couple months," Jason continued. "So, you'll have a huge group of singles the weekend before Christmas that will not only make you money on the bar in the showroom but who will probably will gamble a lot that weekend."

Jim Seagrave was also impressed that the *National Singles Register* had such a "huge circulation" and also liked the free advertising, so he gave Jason a three-day, two-night hotel package deal for less than twenty-five dollars a person, which included a couple of buffets and some other spiffs, and also was able to get the hotel to waive any rental fee for the *Continental Theatre*.

Seagrave said he would still need a "two-thousand-dollar bar guarantee" to cover the cost of a fully staffed showroom the Saturday night of his party. Jason figured most of his party crowd would only need to buy a couple of drinks each that night to cover the bar guarantee and wouldn't be a problem. He was mainly satisfied to have gotten everything he wanted without having to risk any of his own money upfront, but was mainly excited he'd be producing a show in a major hotel showroom on the Las Vegas Strip.

Jason started to figure out the price that he would need to charge his *S.T.A.R.S* members to come for his Las Vegas weekend party to cover all costs and came up with a price of fifty dollars, which would leave him a profit of about twenty-five dollars a person for himself.

He hoped with about two months of advertising in the *National Singles Register*, he could attract close to a hundred readers to buy the weekend package and then hopefully draw close to a couple hundred more of the locals in Las Vegas just to attend his Saturday night party.

He decided to charge the Las Vegas locals who just wanted to see the *Bachelorette of the Year* pageant and party with celebrities all night, ten dollars a person.

Jason knew he could also charge at least forty or fifty of his regular friends just the hotel rooms' cost, mainly wanting it to be a fun way for them all to conclude the year together at his last party of 1975. He knew could still make a nice profit of several thousand dollars even if he only sold a total of hundred package deals to his readers, regulars, and friends to travel to Las Vegas that weekend.

Besides just the beauty pageant, Jason was also feeling the party needed to have more of a draw that would look great on the large marquee in front of *The Thunderbird* and could be more memorable for his first Las Vegas Strip production.

He knew he had over two months to plan something special and would easily figure out something well before then.

❧

Jason decided to put a temporary pause on all of his other *S.T.A.R.S* parties in November and December so he could put all of his promotional efforts into producing his biggest show ever for his last party of 1975.

He had decided to just hire a DJ that fit into his budget to spin records for the party after Jim Seagrave said the house PA system would be fine to use without any additional expense for dancing on the stage, and for emceeing Jason's *Bachelorette of the Year Pageant.*

Jason knew he needed to make his beauty pageant have more flair than how he presented the contest in the nightclubs and needed to find out how many of his bachelorettes were available that weekend to compete in the contest. He quickly learned that over half of them were unavailable the weekend right before Christmas and decided to just call the ones who could come to Las Vegas as his "top finalists" and offered them complimentary hotel rooms and meals for the weekend. He was also able to find a great "Grand Prize" for the winner through a company called *Windjammer Barefoot Cruises* that he worked a trade out for a "Caribbean Cruise for Two" in return for a full-page ad in the *National Singles Register*.

Jason had already gotten a couple of his friends Jan Berry and the *Vegas Vampire* Jim Parker, as two of his judges, but still wanted a couple of bigger names he'd be able to advertise who be judges and be at the party to attract a crowd. He decided that a famous comedian emcee for his pageant might also be able to perform at least a short comedy monologue for additional entertainment that evening.

Jason was trying to get some friends he knew that wouldn't charge him their regular Vegas rates that he hoped could emcee or at least attend the party for just a comp'd weekend in Las Vegas.

"I'd love to do it," said Sammy Shore, "But Christmas week is a really tough time, and I've already got plans for that week anyway."

Most of the other comedians he knew already had contracts in other Las Vegas hotels had to decline.

"Just going to a party at a disco is one thing," most of them said, "But being advertised as performing or even appearing in advance is something that my agents wouldn't be too happy with me doing for just a favor."

Most of the other celebrities he invited to attend the party all said the weekend before Christmas was a time they spent with their families or had other plans and wouldn't be available.

He had hoped to have some decent named celebrities to include in his *S.T.A.R.S* party advertisement in the next several issues of the *National Singles Register* but decided to just advertise "Surprise Celebrity Guests" along with pushing his "Bachelorette of the Year Pageant and Christmas Party" along with the great low price of the weekend hotel package.

Jason figured "surprise guests" always sounded better than nothing at all and would buy him some time until he actually found someone.

Chapter Twelve

Jason had decided to invite a group of his bachelorettes he'd featured on the cover that year to have lunch at the *Old World* restaurant on Sunset Boulevard, not only to make sure they'd be able to be contestants in the bachelorette pageant, but also to see if they knew any other celebrities who may be available to come to Las Vegas that weekend. He'd become good enough friends with a few of his bachelorettes to be able to sometimes facetiously tease them as being "Starfuckers" after stories they had told him about all of the famous celebrities they'd been *intimately* involved with in Hollywood.

He had heard so many stories from those bachelorettes about the famous supposedly *happily married* celebrities they had already had sex with, or were also discreetly "seeing on the side" away from their regular boyfriends, Jason realized his feelings about monogamy weren't anything out of the ordinary. He also lightly joked to several of them that if he ever did decide to start a scandal tabloid, or expose some of their secrets, he'd have some juicy stories to write about.

But Jason really didn't consider them "Starfuckers" and had always known, and seen, that women wanted and needed sex just as much as men, and if they didn't get it regularly from their boyfriends, they still wanted regular orgasms."

"One way or the other," he'd always hear them joke, "Men aren't the only ones who jerk off every day if they don't get laid."

One of the bachelorettes liked telling the story of the night she spent with baseball legend Joe DiMaggio and joked about how she "couldn't even hold his dick in both her hands" because it was so big, and always described it like trying to fit a "telephone handle" inside of her when they had sex.

"I guess that's why Marilyn Monroe didn't stay married to him that long," she also joked about DiMaggio, "It was way too much take in."

There was another bachelorette who was involved in a long-term affair with Bob Hope, whom Jason had personally met several times when he'd go with her to tapings of the Johnny Carson Show or one of Bob's television specials.

Jason had already heard stories about Bob Hope from his friends at Paramount Studios who said Bob Hope was comparable to Warren Beatty back in the 1950s, and was still known for having "a lot of young girlfriends" currently.

"Even Hugh Hefner has nothing on Bob Hope," Art Wilde had once told Jason, "And I hear that he's still going strong today even at his age."

479

After learning that information, Jason used to joke that "Bob Hope was his idol" for being over seventy years old and still having a stable of young girlfriends, and joked that he hoped he'd "be able to do the same thing" when he was Hope's age.

But Jason did personally have an embarrassing incident with Bob Hope one time himself.

The bachelorette he knew, who was "discreetly" seeing Hope *on the side,* had once called Jason well after midnight and said she had gotten pulled over by the police for making an illegal U-Turn.

She said the police discovered she had several unpaid traffic tickets, and after they arrested her, she called Jason, saying she needed a thousand dollars in cash to be bailed out of jail that night.

Jason was still only making two hundred and fifty dollars a week during that time, so he didn't even have that much cash available to himself, but the bachelorette gave him Bob Hope's private number at his house in Toluca Lake to see if he could get the cash from him. Jason was also surprised that Bob seemed wide awake when he called after one am and casually said he was getting ready to take a walk and told Jason he could come right over.

It was after two am when Jason pulled into Bob Hope's driveway on Moorpark Street, and Hope walked Jason to a guest house where he also had a small office. As Bob was counting out a thousand dollars in cash from a metal box he pulled from his desk, Jason was surprised when he asked, "You're going to give me a check for this, right?"

Jason didn't expect that, but he also didn't want to look like a mooch to Bob Hope, either. He did have a personal check in his wallet and knew the bachelorette would reimburse him in the morning.

After he had bailed out the bachelorette, she laughed when Jason told her he had to write Hope a check for the thousand dollars.

"Oh brother!" she laughed, "He's the richest man in Hollywood, but he's also the cheapest."

The bachelorette joked to Jason that Bob Hope shouldn't even have worried about a thousand dollars, but that Bob sometimes joked that he "watched every penny" and was the reason he was able to become so wealthy.

"Don't worry about it," she added, "I'll just give him the cash back myself and tell him not to cash your check."

Even though the bachelorette said she did reimburse Bob Hope the money, Jason's check still somehow ended up being deposited in Hope's bank account and had bounced for insufficient funds.

It was strange hearing Bob Hope try to explain his mistake for depositing the check over the phone, but Jason was more embarrassed having him discover that the editor and publisher of such a *famous* newspaper didn't even have a thousand dollars in his bank account.

There were some other bachelorettes at the *Old World Restaurant* that day. Jason knew also had some celebrity boyfriends on the side, and was hoping some of them could help with his promotion at *The Thunderbird* for his party in Las Vegas.

"I know you never could get *'Roberto'* to come to Vegas," Jason smiled at the bachelorette with the code name they sometimes used for Bob Hope when they were in public, "But I've been advertising that surprise celebrity guests will be coming to my party."

"So, it would be great if any of you could invite any of your *special* friends to at least come up to Las Vegas that weekend," Jason added, "They don't need to perform or anything, but I'd at least like to have another big name for a celebrity judge."

"Ah can probably get Telly to come and be a judge," a bachelorette named Denise said in her strong southern drawl, "It'll be a good excuse for him to get away from his live-in girlfriend and spend the weekend with me."

He knew that she was talking about Telly Savalas, who was currently one of the hottest celebrities in America since his hit television series *Kojak* had premiered a couple of years earlier. Jason also had a brief fling with Denise earlier that summer and felt somewhat responsible for getting Telly and Denise together. They were on a date together at Del Mar Racetrack when they ran into Telly Savalas and movie producer Howard Koch who was partners in the racehorse *Telly's Pop* who was racing that day. Jason had met Howard Koch earlier that year at his *S.T.A.R.S* movie screening party for Howard's film *Once is Not Enough,* and Jason also reminded Telly that they had already met briefly at the Oscars the year before.

After Jason and Denise joined Telly Savalas and Howard Koch in their box seats to watch *Telly's Pop* win the *Del Mar Futurity* that afternoon, they all talked about the usual showbiz stories and different movies they had been involved.

Jason facetiously joked that it was a shame Telly didn't reprise his role as the James Bond villain Blofeld in *Diamonds Are Forever*, after portraying him in *On Her Majesty's Secret Service,* because then they could have had "the common bond" of having appeared in the same movie together.

Telly did get a laugh when Jason sarcastically described his own "big role" as an unpaid extra in *Diamonds Are Forever* when he stood in the crowd on Fremont Street watching the chase scene being filmed.

"Yeah, I would have preferred playing Blofeld in one of the movies Sean Connery played Bond," said Telly, "The last couple movies with Roger Moore have seemed to turn into comedies and aren't quite as good."

Telly Savalas had become as well-known in Hollywood as Warren Beatty, Jack Nicholson, and Hugh Hefner as someone who loved engaging in *volume fucking,* and Jason even knew a couple of former bachelorettes that already had a fling or two with

Telly, and it was also obvious that he was also interested in Denise that day. After he kept telling Denise how sexy her southern drawl sounded to him, Telly ended up giving her his business card, saying he may have a small part for her on *Kojak*.

Since that day, Denise told Jason she'd also been seeing Telly "on the side" for the past several months not concerned about him already having a girlfriend and just "enjoyed the sex" with him.

"Ah'll tell Telly you're gonna call him," Denise smiled after giving Jason Telly's personal phone number during lunch," "Just remind him I'll be in Las Vegas the whole weekend, and I'm sure he'll be glad to *come*."

"If y'all know what I mean," Denise added with a wink.

"Well, Telly will be a great name to have for a judge," Jason said, "But I'd still like to get a fairly well-known comedian to be the emcee for the bachelorette contest."

"Damn, a couple of years ago I coulda got Gabe Kaplan for probably a hundred bucks," Jason facetiously joked, "He used to come to my parties, but now that he's such a big star on *Welcome Back Kotter*, I can't even get him to return my phone calls."

"Plus, I hear he's too busy screwing half of the girls in town since he became famous," Jason continued joking, "I guess he's trying to prove he's a big stud like Telly Savalas or Warren Beatty too."

Jason suddenly felt one of the bachelorettes kick him from underneath the table.

"Ouch, what's that for?!", Jason lightly teased her, "What's wrong, are you screwing *Gabe Kaplan* too?"

The bachelorette just rolled her eyes and motioned Jason to look at the table behind them.

"Oh, Hi Gabe," Jason tried to laugh when he saw Gabe Kaplan at the table directly behind them. "And congratulations on *Kotter.*"

"A hundred bucks, eh?" Gabe sarcastically laughed, "We must be sitting in a time machine here today because I haven't heard an offer that good since 1972."

"Well, I was just kidding," Jason joked, "But if you'd like to *slum it* for a night and have some fun, I'll even double it to two hundred bucks if you want to do a short monologue and emcee my beauty pageant in Vegas."

"Thanks, but I don't think my agent would be too happy," laughed Gabe, "But good luck and nice seeing you again."

"Oh, and if you're still interested in being a bachelor of the month sometime, just give me a call," Jason added, trying not to show any embarrassment.

After Gabe finished his meal and left, the bachelorettes laughed at Jason's *faux pas.*

"That's the thing about Hollywood," said one of the bachelorettes, "You never know who you're going to be sitting next to in some restaurant and you gotta watch what you say."

"I'm sure Gabe just thought it was funny," Jason said unconcerned, "And he probably knew I was right, and he probably would have paid me a hundred bucks to perform in a big Vegas showroom back in those days."

"But you girls in the bachelorette contest will be the main draw to the show anyway," Jason continued, "I'll just need some of you to come to Vegas with me sometime over the next eight weeks to do some advance promotion."

"I've got a couple of appearances on Jim Parker's Vegas Vampire TV show already set, and I've also got some radio interviews with Sig Sakowicz and Forrest Duke up there around the same time," Jason added, "We want to make sure we attract the locals too."

Jason knew the bachelorettes would be more than willing to help with promotion if they would have the chance to appear on any television or radio show, just as they had wanted to appear on the cover of the *National Singles Register.*

He knew everyone he met still wanted their *"fifteen minutes of fame"* to last as long as it could.

After getting commitments from at least ten bachelorettes to be in the *Bachelorette of the Year Pageant* over the next week, and a few others to travel with him to Las Vegas to help with promotion, Jason felt everything was on schedule and he was ready to start promoting. He also did call Telly Savalas, who said he'd "love to come to Las Vegas and judge sexy bachelorettes," and also didn't mind having his name used in the advertising as being a celebrity judge.

Jason knew having a star as famous as Telly as a judge would be enough of a draw to make his *Bachelorette of the Year* sound nationally famous, and would attract a large audience and press coverage at his party. He knew all he needed to do was get close to his usual crowd size, and having almost two months to promote just one party would be a very profitable way to end the year.

And, he knew it would also be the start for even bigger shows in 1976 and a great way to end the year.

Chapter Thirteen

Jason was at the *LA Coliseum* watching the Rams playing the Chicago Bears with Stan Adams while Lori was performing a matinee at the *Whiskey-A-Go-Go* completing her first week of previews for *Let My People Come.*

Lori asked Jason not to come and see her show at *The Whiskey* till at least a week into its run, so she and the cast would be able to work out "all the kinks," and she'd feel much more relaxed.

Jason missed not having Lori with him at the football game for the first time, but still enjoyed watching the Rams completely dominate the game and completely shut down the Bears rookie running back they had been hyping all week, Walter Peyton.

Plus, Jason had bet fifty dollars on the Rams when he had been in Las Vegas earlier that week signing contracts with the *Thunderbird Hotel.*

"That was an easy win and an easy fifty bucks," Jason told Stan as they drove back to Hollywood, "We'll just have something to eat at the Rainbow and walk to the Whiskey afterward."

Lori had decided that Sunday night's performance of *Let My People Come* would be the best time for Jason to finally come and see the show.

"Lori doesn't want any of our other friends to see it yet," said Jason, "But she said it's okay if I bring you tonight."

"Well, if you remember," Stan laughed, "I've seen her naked before, so that's probably why."

"I think everybody has pretty much seen her naked since *Penthouse*, so I'm sure that's not the only reason," said Jason. 'She said it has some pretty X-rated stuff and probably wants to see our reaction first."

Jason had seen the posters and advertisements for *Let My People Come*, which was sub-titled "*A Sexual Musical*," and Lori had said that he might be "a little shocked" when he saw the show.

Lori said besides the nudity, it was "pretty risqué" and featured some things no one had seen live at the *Whiskey-a-Go-Go* before, but Jason just told her he was excited for her and couldn't wait to see her stage debut and hearing her sing live on the Sunset Strip.

Lori had gotten Jason and Stan a front-row table for the show, and Jason thought of something funny he and Stan could do when there were some nude scenes during the performance.

"Let's bring in our binoculars we took to the football game," Jason joked, "And when there's some naked stuff, let's both look through them and aim at the cast."

"They'll think we're crazy or some kind of perverts," Stan laughed, "But it would be funny."

They both discreetly carried the binoculars into the *Whisky-a-Go-Go* and kept them under the table until the lights were dimmed and the musical began. Jason and Stan also didn't have to wait long for the nudity and were impressed when the cast showed no reaction to their *binocular joke,* as they aimed their focus at various cast members during the first nude scene. But they both decided that one time was enough to give them at least a laugh between themselves and just focused with their eyes for the rest of the musical.

Jason noticed that Lori stood out as the most attractive girl in the cast, because also again, most of the other girls appeared to have the big black *steel wool* pads between their legs, while Lori's pubic hair was barely visible. It was obvious to him that Lori was the only natural blond in the cast.

Let My People Come didn't have a storyline like *Hair* or *The Rocky Horror Show* and just seemed like different skits about almost every type of sexual acts.

Jason soon realized that Lori was right, and the nudity was the least X-Rated aspect of the show. It wasn't just the sexual choreography of the naked bodies inter-twining, but it was mainly the lyrics to the songs.

With titles like *Cum in My Mouth, Everybody Loves to Screw, The Cunnilingus Champion of Company C,* and the others, Stan whispered to Jason that he felt like he was at an *X-Rated Pussycat Theatre* on Santa Monica Boulevard.

Jason was surprised how much kinkier *Let My People Come* was than even *The Rocky Horror Show,* and couldn't believe something that was almost pornographic could play live on stage at the *Whiskey-a-Go-Go.* He also briefly thought back to how the band leader Bobby Douglas once thought Jason was too dirty when he sang, *"You can cream all over me,"* in a talent contest in Las Vegas, and smiled to himself about how much things had changed in just five years.

Although Lori looked beautiful and sang and danced well, Jason wasn't as comfortable as he thought he'd be seeing Lori dancing around the stage naked and singing the suggestive lyrics so naturally to a live audience.

He didn't want to show any negativity, but it did again remind him how much they had also both changed since they first saw the *Rocky Horror Show* at the *Roxy* almost two years earlier, and ended up streaking that same night.

As Lori had always said, she was achieving her dream and doing what she wanted to do to make her happy, so Jason wanted to show he was supportive.

Jason and Stan greeted Lori and the rest of the cast backstage at the end of the show, and everyone was laughing about the *binocular joke.*

"After the first scene, everyone was asking me if I saw those two nuts in the front row with binoculars," laughed Lori, "And I had to say, 'that's just my boyfriend' and he's always doing something crazy!"

"Well, the show definitely was interesting," Jason tried to laugh with her, "You did a great job, and I'm sure Annie, Mixie, Lita, and everyone else are going to love it."

"I'm glad you liked it, baby," Lori added, still excited, "I think this show is going to be a big hit."

Jason saw how happy Lori was to just be performing at the *Whiskey-a-Go-Go*, and was also thinking how lucky Lori was to at least be performing on a major stage as she had always wanted.

And that's when he started thinking about a crazy idea.

With Lori singing on the Sunset Strip, and with Jason having his big party in a major showroom on the Las Vegas Strip, he decided that maybe it was time for someone else to make a surprise comeback and make one unfinished dream of his own come true.

At least for one night.

∾

It was less than a week after seeing Lori's show at the *Whiskey-a-Go-Go* when Jason was at Annie Gaybis' apartment, letting her be the first to know about his crazy idea.

"Who is *JJ Breeze*?" Annie asked with surprise, "I've never heard of him."

"It's just a stage name I used a long time ago," Jason lightly explained, "I'll just be one of the *surprise guests* that I've been advertising, and it might add some light comedy to the party."

"If you want some comedy," Annie added with a laugh, "Just let Telly Savalas sing because he thinks he's a singer too."

Telly Savalas had recorded some record albums that most of those in Hollywood joked he *shouldn't* have recorded and considered his singing more of a joke or novelty to capitalize on his fame. But because of his huge worldwide popularity as *Kojak*, Telly did have a recent hit song that got considerable airplay on the radio and in the discos called *If*, which was more of a spoken version of the same song the pop group *Bread* had a huge hit with five years earlier.

"I know you like to sing," Annie lightly laughed at his idea "But a big Las Vegas showroom is a lot different than just the piano bars."

"I used to be a professional," Jason sarcastically teased back, "And besides, how many people can say they sang live on the Las Vegas Strip in a major showroom?"

"Lori is performing and singing on the Sunset Strip in Hollywood," smiled Jason, "So I thought it would be fun to surprise her at my Christmas party and perform and sing on the Las Vegas Strip."

"Well, it should be a surprise all right," Annie sarcastically laughed, "Seeing the editor, publisher, and producer of the show singing will probably the last thing they're expecting."

"The audience probably won't even notice it's me singing anyway," Jason lightly continued, "They'll just think it's just some crazy guy named *JJ Breeze*."

"Most of my *S.T.A.R.S* club members from the *National Singles Register* haven't seen me since my last party at *My Place* and probably won't even recognize me with my new curly hairstyle," Jason continued explaining, "Especially if I use a pick to really make my hair look wild that night."

"I mean everyone will see me in my tuxedo running around and on stage during the bachelorette contest," Jason continued explaining his plan, "So right after I finish the contest, I'll change into some wild costume, sing some songs with a band I'll just hire for the night, and then change back into my tuxedo to announce the winner."

"So, how are you going put together an act in less than a month?" Annie asked with light skepticism, "Are you sure that's something you're going to be able to do?"

"Look it, over half the crowd will probably just be my regulars and friends anyway," Jason continued, "So it's just something that'll be light and fun to keep the party atmosphere going that night."

"Oy Vey, this should be interesting," laughed Annie with her mock Yiddish groan, "Well, if it's something you want to do, then I guess you're going to do it."

"Yes, it's something I want to do," Jason smiled, "Who knows if I'll ever get this chance again."

Chapter Fourteen

Jason did want to keep it a surprise that he'd be singing during his show in Las Vegas and told very few of his friends what he was planning. He had already sold over eighty weekend packages for his Christmas party at fifty dollars each and still had one more big advertisement in the issue of the *National Singles Register* coming out two weeks before Christmas.

He hoped to sell twenty or thirty more packages from that issue to go along with the couple hundred people he was expecting from Las Vegas locals who would only be paying ten dollars.

Jason figured even with the additional expense of hiring a band and a few other costs he needed to include, he was still going to end up with a big profit for his Las Vegas show.

Bill Gazzarri tried to convince Jason to hire a local band he'd been pushing for over a year and had made a house band at *Gazzarri's* called *Van Halen*. But besides the band members wanting three hundred dollars each plus expenses in Las Vegas, they also wanted to be paid for their time if they had to rehearse any songs for Jason to sing. Plus, Jason and most of his friends had seen *Van Halen* so many times at Gazzarri's, he'd didn't think they'd be a big enough draw for that kind of money.

Jason ended up finding a five-piece band who would rehearse with him and travel to Las Vegas for a flat seven hundred and fifty dollars, plus rooms, that was within his budget.

Between his regular work and promotion, he did spend several days a week with the band to rehearse the show he wanted. Jason remembered how he had rehearsed with Tommy and Alvin years earlier for his audition at the *Pussycat-a-Go-Go*. He decided four weeks would be plenty of time for the band to learn eight special songs that he could sing well, and also be funny and a little sarcastic to many of his friends in the audience.

He also decided to have three of his bachelorette contestants who said they could sing rehearse with him as back-up singers and hired two sexy dancers who occasionally performed in a disco trope at *My Place* called *Jeff Kutash and The Dancing Machine*, to add a little choreography and movement on the stage.

Another bachelorette mentioned she was a "fire dancer," which Jason figured would also fit in well with one of the songs he had chosen to sing.

488

Jason liked the way Elvis used three back-up singers in his show and figured the additional dancers it would help fill the large stage, so it wouldn't look like he was just up there alone singing during his short set. He knew to make his show look close to a real Las Vegas production; he'd need some special effects and some props onstage for a few of the songs he was planning that night.

During one of his trips to Las Vegas after Thanksgiving, Jason had another meeting with Jim Seagrave to go over some of his ideas.

"I don't have too big of a budget and don't really need anything that is all that elaborate," Jason was explaining to Seagrave and several others in the conference room., "I'll just need a fog machine, a portable type of bar with bar stools we can roll out on and off the stage, and some special effects lighting for some of the songs the band will be performing."

Jim Seagrave was taking notes with his staff members as they figured out the additional cost needed to fit Jason's needs.

"The one big prop I would like," Jason added, "Is a big flashing neon sign to be lowered from above the stage that spells out one song's title."

"What do you want the letters to spell out," asked Seagrave as he continued taking notes.

Jason knew there were some ladies in the meeting and tried not to be too graphic or obvious with the lettering he wanted.

"S-T-A-R-B-U-C-K-E-R," Jason tried to spell out with a straight face.

Jason figured he could have a stagehand unscrew a couple of the lights to make the "B" look like an "F" on the night of the show.

Jason decided to take away the four or five hundred dollars more from his profits, which is what Seagrave said the cost would probably be, was well worth it for the opportunity to put on a wild and fun show in Las Vegas. Seagrave also gave Jason a dozen complimentary three-day, two-night packages at *The Thunderbird* to give away as door prizes at his party, that the winners could use anytime in 1976.

Jason had also met someone else who said he could make the party memorable and appear to be a huge Las Vegas production.

Mixie Thompson had introduced Jason to her current boyfriend, Michael Ritz, who had become part of their circle of friends during the past month.

Michael was the son of the comedian Harry Ritz from the 1930s and 1940's comedy team *The Ritz Brothers*, who were often called "The poor man's *Marx Brother's*" during that era. Although they never achieved the same success the *Marx Brothers*, they were considered by many of their peers in show business to be a funnier comedy team.

Jason also remembered that *The Ritz Brothers* had starred in the 1938 movie *The Goldwyn Follies*, the last film George and Ira Gershwin had written the music for before George suddenly died of a brain tumor filming of that movie.

Coming from a show business family, Michael Ritz had also planned a career in show business, but because the draft lottery wasn't in effect when he became eligible to be drafted during the Vietnam War, he joined the Air National Guard.

In between building up his show business contacts, Michael was still an active reservist in the Air National Guard, which gave him additional income and said it was "better than waiting tables at a restaurant" while waiting for his "big break" in the movie business.

Michael told Jason he had access to a new type of camera at the Air Force base, where he worked as a public affairs officer and explained it was a reel-to-reel recorder that was on videotape instead of film.

"This new videotape looks like a live broadcast," Michael explained, "I want to get into movie production or cinematography myself, so I can record your party just for expenses for me and a second cameraman to help shoot the video and set everything up."

"Plus, it'll look impressive for your audience to see television cameras in the showroom," Michael added, "It'll make it look like a live television show is being shot of your party and beauty contest that night."

Jason had already tried to get national television coverage by contacting producers of a new live television show on ABC called *Saturday Night Live with Howard Cosell*, which was a variety show that used remote cameras from different cities worldwide to live stream different major musical stars, acts, and events from different time zones.

The ABC show was being broadcast in prime time, and earlier than another new show on NBC just called *Saturday Night*, which was more of a sketch comedy show that wasn't broadcast live until eleven-thirty pm on the East Coast.

Jason had pitched the idea of a brief segment on Howard Cosell's show to have his *Bachelorette of the Year* announced by Telly Savalas in Las Vegas, but after realizing how complicated it would be to arrange, and that he would have to have his pageant and announce a winner before seven pm to fit in with the three-hour time difference from New York, it just didn't work out.

After Michael Ritz said he could keep the expense of videotaping the *S.T.A.R.S* party to not more than three hundred dollars, Jason decided besides looking impressive for the audience to see the showroom set up with television cameras, he also thought it would be great to have a recording of his big party with almost every one of his personal friends from the past six years.

Almost all of his friends from California would be coming, including Terri from San Francisco, as well as those from Las Vegas, and even though he was comp'ing many of his friends and paying for over a dozen weekend packages himself, he knew he could afford it with the profits he had already collected.

Even with the additional costs, Jason's ticket sales had already been more than enough to pay for everything, and he knew any other money that came in during the next three weeks would be all profit. Jason felt he had everything well organized and would also be collecting a good amount of money on the door from locals that night.

Sandi Shore couldn't get away and had to babysit her little brother Pauly the weekend before Christmas, but said she would stop by Jason's apartment the week he was gone to take feed and clean the cat box for *Old Lady*. He also asked Victor if he'd be able to work the door, but Victor said he "just wanted to party with his girlfriends" that night and have fun.

Jason was surprised when he found out that Victor was living with two college girls who worked as hookers part-time to pay their living expenses.

"So, you're a pimp now?" laughed Jason, "That sounds really classy!"

"No, they're just a couple girlfriends who I share my apartment with," Victor causally explained, "I just have them go to the hotels on weekends to make us some extra cash while I'm going to dealer school."

"But I am fucking one of them, and they're both cool with the arrangement," Victor smiled, "So at the worst, I'm just a casual and part-time pimp until I get a job at a casino."

Luckily, Tom Casey agreed to work the door that night, so Jason knew he had somebody he could trust collecting the ten dollars per person.

He felt he had planned a full night of dancing, prizes, and entertainment to make it a great party and everything was working just as he'd planned.

Chapter Fifteen

Jason had just gotten back to his apartment from a rehearsal with the band he had hired when he got a phone call from his father in Dallas.

"Listen, Jason, is there any way for you to fly to Dallas for just a day?" he asked. "I've been telling some of the guys who want to buy a lot of news racks all about you and the different celebrity parties you produce to promote the newspaper."

"I thought it would look good if they could meet you for an hour or so and maybe let them know you're thinking about doing some parties with celebrities in Dallas," Jason's father added, "I've already shown them the issues of with the photos the celebrities at your parties."

Jason half smiled to himself, thinking how even his father was dropping celebrity's names to help tie it to his distribution business.

"Maybe after Christmas," Jason said, "I'm just too busy now getting this Vegas show ready, and it's less than three weeks away."

"Well, the deal is," his father added, "Is that I've built you up a lot as the editor and publisher of the National Singles Register, and it would help me out for them to at least meet you to let them know we're serious about doing business here in Dallas."

Jason thought it was weird why the distributors would want to meet him. He had promoted his party at *Dirty Sally's* in Las Vegas without ever having to meet distributors before, and wondered why his father needed to "build him up" in order to just sell news racks.

"Well, I'm sure I can set up a party or two next year in Dallas, but why do you need me to come up there now?" asked Jason, "Can't it wait a few weeks?"

"It's just that I'm trying to close a deal with these guys before Christmas," his father said, "And they're ready to buy a shitload of news racks this week."

"I'll tell you what," his father finally said, "If you can come up tomorrow, I'll pay for a round trip plane ticket and give you two hundred dollars just for coming up and meeting them."

"It's only about a three-hour flight for LA, and you can be up and back in one day," he kept insisting, "So how about if you just come up tomorrow for a few hours?"

Jason still thought it sounded strange, but he didn't need to be back in Las Vegas for five more days, and a quick trip to Dallas for two hundred dollars didn't seem like too bad of a deal.

He knew another two hundred dollars would cover a nice portion of the extra cost he was paying for the weekend hotel packages for some of his bachelorettes.

"Tomorrow is too soon," said Jason, "But the day after tomorrow should be okay as long as I'm back in town that night."

"Great," said his father, "I'll make the reservations and call you back with the details."

It wasn't more than ten minutes after Jason spoke with his father before Lori also called.

"Have I got some crazy news for you!" Lori said excitedly, "I didn't want to say anything till I knew it was official, but *Let My People Come* is going to New York in January, and I'm going to be part of the cast."

"I'm might be performing on Broadway next year!" Lori shouted her excitement.

That was something Jason hadn't expected, and was completely surprised.

Besides thinking that *Let My People Come* wasn't the type of show that could ever play on Broadway, Jason was mainly surprised that Lori would be leaving California so quickly without giving it a second thought.

"Let's meet at the Rainbow in about a half an hour so I can tell you all about it," she quickly added.

"That is incredible!" Jason tried to say with enthusiasm," "I'll head down to the Rainbow in a few minutes."

Even though their relationship had become somewhat distant that year, they had still been seeing each other regularly for almost three years, and now it appeared that they would be separating and become even more distant, but neither of them said anything about that being a concern when they were together at *The Rainbow* sharing a pizza an hour later.

Instead, they were both congratulating each other on both Lori's future with *Let My People Come*, and Jason's upcoming big production at *The Thunderbird*, and how 1976 would definitely be a "breakout and positive year" for both of their careers.

Lori also mentioned she had some disappointing news, when she told Jason her show at the *Whiskey-a-Go-Go* had been extended until Christmas, and she would need to perform her show the same night as Jason's show at *The Thunderbird* and wouldn't be able to see him that weekend in Las Vegas.

Jason was disappointed because he not only wanting to surprise Lori with his performance in the *Continental Theatre*; he had also chosen a couple of songs that he knew she'd probably get a good laugh hearing him sing. But he was now more satisfied that he had Michael Ritz there to record his performance that night, knowing that he'd still be able to show Lori the performance when he got back from Las Vegas.

He still had all of his other friends coming who would see him perform live and wasn't going to let one little change of plans lower his optimism about how much fun his party would be even without Lori there. He also knew he had a lot of other bachelorettes coming that weekend, who would also get some laughs at a couple of songs he was performing, and it actually might even turn into more fun than he thought by not having to be discreet.

But Jason was also feeling that besides 1975 coming to an end, there were some other things that were ending as well.

It was after one pm Dallas time two days later when the taxi took Jason to where his father said he had an office on Mockingbird Lane directly across from Love Field Airport.

Jason had been to Dallas once in 1968 when he was on a trip with one of his high school friends and visited the downtown location of the JFK assassination, and also remembered Love Field was the airport Kennedy had landed in Dallas the day he was shot.

His father only had a small one-room office with a desk, and Jason was immediately surprised when he walked in and saw that Joy was also there that day.

"Joy just came up for a couple of days to help out with some things here in Dallas," said his father. "She'll be actually flying back on the same flight as you later today."

"I'll be back at the office in Paramount for the *NSR* deadline this weekend," said Joy, "Everything is under control for the next issue."

Jason briefly wondered if there might be something going on between his father and Joy, but tried to keep it to himself and just wanted to talk business.

"So, who are these guys you wanted me to meet?" asked Jason, "I'm only here till six pm."

"We're meeting them for drinks in about an hour," said his father, "They've already met Joy, and I just wanted you to talk to them about some promotions you might do here in Dallas."

When they were driving alone together to the meeting, there was some small talk about Jason's promotions and how his Las Vegas show was going before his father explained more details about why he was in Dallas.

"The *NSR* can be a goldmine here, and I've got a lot of deals cooking," said his father, "There's a lot of money involved, and in case anything happens in California, it's good to have a second operation here in Dallas."

Jason said everything in California was running smooth and wondered what could go wrong.

"Your mother is causing a lot of problems with the business right now," his father said, "And you know how hard she is to talk to and just doesn't understand business sometimes."

"Everything is under control right now and I'm sure things will calm down in a month or so," he continued, "But I would like to build up Texas as big as we did in California and maybe even have an entire Texas edition."

"It would be great if you just did the same things here you've already done there just to get things rolling," his father added, "You may even want to move up here for a few months and can make a lot of money yourself in a short time."

Jason just told him he had too many other things going on even to consider anything like that currently.

When Jason and his father arrived for the meeting, three men in suits and cowboy hats were already waiting for them at an upscale cocktail lounge, and his father just introduced everyone by their first names.

"Jason, this is Mark, Ed, and Dave," said his father, "They all have successful businesses here in Dallas already and want to handle all the exclusive distribution for the *National Singles Register* and *Explorer* in Texas."

"You're a lot younger than we thought you'd be," smiled Mark with his Texas drawl as they shook hands.

"I guess it's from leading a *clean and pure life*," Jason facetiously joked as he did to others whenever they mentioned his youthful appearance.

They all spent about forty-five minutes talking about the *National Singles Register's* success, how advertising for dates was now acceptable, all of the couples who's gotten married through the paper, the growing singles market, and how his celebrity singles parties always attracted new readers.

Mark and Dave seemed to like hearing the celebrity stories and were impressed that Telly Savalas would be at Jason's next party in Las Vegas.

"Sort of like the parties we read about in Playboy every month, eh?" Mark continued smiling, "Being single is making everybody a playboy these days."

"Well, the parties are just another way for our readers and advertisers to meet," Jason said, "We are a dating publication, so the parties are just another fun option for dates."

Jason figured his father wanted him to keep the focus on the *National Singles Register*, but his father also started talking about his parties.

"Jason did say he might come up here once we start our distribution to produce a couple of his big parties," his father said, "They always attract new readers and keep the name of the newspaper out there to the singles crowd at the popular nightclubs.

Nothing about any actual business deals or money was even discussed, and by the time the meeting was over, it just seemed to Jason like a friendly talk over drinks.

Jason had no idea why he needed to be there for that meeting, but he thought it was an easy way to make two hundred bucks, which his father gave him in cash as they drove back to the office.

"Oh, and one more thing," his father added during the drive, "If you do talk to Vi and she mentions anything about when you were here with me, just tell her that you brought Joy with you to Dallas, okay?"

"I don't need any other problems with her right now," he added, "And I already mentioned that you were both coming up here for this meeting."

Jason didn't want to discuss anything else personal with his father but hoped the reason he'd come to Dallas wasn't for the reason he was thinking.

Later, seeing Joy sitting the row behind him on the jet, made Jason start wondering if his father had really needed him to meet with those three guys at all.

Jason decided to act like he was sleeping during the flight, so he wouldn't need to talk to Joy about business or find anything that would make his suspicions worse.

Jason had heard the expression of calling someone *"a beard"* one time before, when his bachelorette friend who was seeing Bob Hope, asked Jason to join them once for dinner so when people saw them all together, they would think that Jason was with the bachelorette and not Bob. But that one time was enough, and Jason knew there was no way he was ever going to be anything like "a beard" again.

Especially for his father.

Chapter Sixteen

Jason traveled to Las Vegas twice a week during December, trying to do local promotion and get advance press for his party and started preferring to fly rather than drive.

It only took him fifteen or twenty minutes to get to the airport from his apartment in Beverly Hills if he left in the evening, and he'd usually find a flight he could hop on within fifteen minutes after arriving. *Western Airlines* had flights leaving for Las Vegas every hour almost twenty-four hours a day, and after midnight, he was able to get airfares as low as fifteen dollars each way. *Western Airlines* always offered complimentary Champagne during the short flight, so he and anyone else he brought with him could always have a nice buzz before they arrived.

The Thunderbird was comp'ing Jason's hotel rooms each time he came to promote, so the cost was minimal, and it was also fun.

Jason had Annie Gaybis and his current bachelorette, Melissa, who he was going to feature in an upcoming edition, come to Las Vegas for a photoshoot for the *Las Vegas Visitor Magazine*, which was distributed in every hotel room throughout Las Vegas. He had arranged a cover story that would be featured the week of his show that would feature Annie and Melissa in bikini's promoting the *Bachelorette of the Year Pageant*, and prominently mention that Telly Savalas would be heading the celebrity judging panel.

It was the morning after they'd arrived, and Melissa was still sleeping, so Jason decided not to wake her. He knew she was still tired from the party the night before and met Annie alone for breakfast in the Thunderbird's coffee shop.

"I can't believe you just lifted up Sammy Davis Jr. and carried him over to me.", laughed Annie over breakfast, "That was so embarrassing!"

"Well, you said you were his biggest fan, and I thought I was doing you a favor," Jason just smiled, "You got to meet him, right?"

Jason had been out with Melissa the night before, hitting different showrooms and lounges talking to many of the headliners backstage before and after their shows. He was making a last-ditch effort to invite more celebrities to at least attend his party, who were still going to be in Las Vegas in two weeks.

Jason usually just needed to flash his press card to anyone working the backstage entrance, which always got him access to visit most of the headliners or lounge acts in their dressing rooms who never seemed to mind meeting someone from the press.

Jason also mentioned to the entertainers that he was also the producer of a big show and party at *The Thunderbird*, and just stopped backstage to invite them and come and mingle with other well-known celebrities who were already coming that night.

When Jason and Melissa were backstage at *The Riviera* talking with Don Rickles after his show and inviting him to his party at the Thunderbird, Don mentioned he was on his way to Sammy Davis's fiftieth birthday party at *Caesars Palace*, which wasn't starting until two am.

Annie had gone to sleep in her room at the hotel around midnight, but Jason knew she wouldn't mind being woken up to come to that party.

When Annie met Jason and Melissa at Caesars Palace around three am, the private ballroom was already packed with almost every major entertainer in Las Vegas, and Jason again had no problem getting the three of them all admitted inside the party.

Besides enjoying the incredible layout of gourmet food at the party, the party-goers were all having their champagne glasses of Dom Perignon constantly being refilled by the waiters, and everyone seemed to have a good buzz still going at that hour.

Jason was surprised when he again ran into Gabe Kaplan at the party so soon after his *faux pas* at the *Old World* restaurant, and jokingly said he'd up his price to three hundred dollars for Gabe to perform at his party at *The Thunderbird*.

"I should do it to just keep me away from the craps tables for a few hours," Gabe joked, "I think I forgot what it's like to walk out of a casino even a measly three hundred dollars ahead lately."

Jason decided to just enjoy that party without trying to pitch his party or sound like he was there for business and mainly socialized.

When Annie saw Sammy Davis Jr talking with another group of entertainers, she told Jason that "he was her *idol*," and she'd love to meet him.

Jason had a good buzz going himself by four in the morning and just flashed back to when he saw the TV image of Sammy hugging and picking up Richard Nixon at the Republican Convention in 1972 as a way of showing his support.

Jason suddenly thought something similar to that moment would be a funny way to introduce Sammy to Annie and just boldly walked up to him, saying he wanted him to "meet his biggest fan" and proceeded to lift Sammy up and carry him the short distance to where Annie was standing, plopping him right in front of her.

"That was so embarrassing," Annie lightly laughed to Jason as they continued with their breakfast that next morning, "Sammy didn't know what to say, and neither did I."

"Sammy didn't seem to mind, and everyone else got a laugh out of it too," Jason half laughed at his own actions, "It was a party, and we were all just having fun, and you did get to talk with him for a while."

"Well, it was fun," Annie smiled as she shook her head, "But I just can't believe some of the things you do sometimes."

"Wait till you see the show I'll be performing," smiled Jason, "I think you'll get a good laugh out of that too."

Jason and Annie were suddenly interrupted by two men in suits who walked up to their table in the coffee shop.

"Hi, Jason Mershon?" one of them asked, "Jim Seagrave said we could talk to you about your show in the Continental Theatre."

"We're with the Stagehands Union and just needed to go over some details about what you have planned in the showroom."

"Sure," said Jason, "Just let me finish my breakfast, and we can talk in about fifteen minutes."

The two men went to another booth and said they'd wait.

"What's that all about," asked Annie, "They don't look too friendly."

"Probably just something about the props I need for the show," said Jason, "I'm sure it's no big deal."

But when Jason was talking with them privately later, it did seem like there were a few problems.

The *Thunderbird Hotel* was under contract with all of the different unions in Las Vegas, and although Jason wasn't responsible for any *Culinary* or *Bartenders Union* workers who were contracted by the hotel, Jason was personally responsible for making sure everything dealing with entertainment or anything that happened on a live stage in the showroom abided by the Union contracts.

"I mean, who's going to open the curtain or bring props onstage?" said one of the men, "You're responsible to have union workers overseeing everything that goes on in that room."

Jason thought everything had already been worked out with the hotel, and he had hired some of his friends to assist with anything he might need that night.

"You can still use those people," said the union rep, "But you'll still have to pay union members to be there overseeing anything that goes on."

"Plus, you may also be getting a call from the Musician's Union about any musician's and soundman you've hired," said the other one, "If they're not union, it's the same deal, and you'll need union musician's present and pay them their standard salary even if they don't work."

"Or, you can just pay a waiver, which is actually a lot more expensive," he just smiled.

The whole thing sounded crazy to Jason, and he didn't want to sound completely clueless, so he got their business cards and said he'd work it out after he talked with Jim Seagrave.

Although Jason still had a slight headache and hangover from the party the night before, he immediately went to Jim's office in the hotel.

"Well, I didn't think it would be a problem when we first talked about it just being a party," said Jim Seagrave, "But once you added a live band and all those stage props for additional entertainment, it gets into union stuff."

"I guess I forgot to mention that to you," Seagrave tried to say with a laugh.

"I mean the party is less than two weeks away," argued Jason, "How much is all this union crap going to cost?"

"It shouldn't be too bad," said Jim, "They're pretty easy to work with, so just sit down with them and I'm sure you'll be able to work something out."

But it wasn't too easy.

By the time Jason figured the cost of paying union salaries to all the "guys who would just be standing around" his budget for the show had more than doubled, but he also saw he had very little options.

He could either cancel the whole thing and tell them to *"fuck themselves"* or just pay them.

Jason had already paid the hotel for the rooms he had sold to his *S.T.A.R.S.* members and had also already paid the band, DJ, and quite a few other expenses. He also worried about his credibility and how much he'd lose if he stopped everything now.

Almost all the money he had brought in for the show so far, which included money he thought was all profit, would need to be paid to the unions upfront before he would be allowed even to open the doors to the showroom.

After thinking long and hard, he decided to bite the bullet and pay them and just hope he could still make a profit off the door money the night of the party.

Although he was having a hard time feeling it, he was still trying to convince himself that he was going to have fun.

No matter what.

Chapter Seventeen

Dick Clark's *Good Ole Rock and Roll Show* concluded its run at *The Thunderbird* the weekend before his *S.T.A.R.S.* party, and Jason decided to spend the entire week prior in the hotel suite Jim Seagrave had comp'd him.

The band he hired was all set to come in on Friday and would set up Saturday afternoon for sound checks, along with a final rehearsal with the dancers, backup singers, and try out all the props. He also had one more radio interview with Forrest Duke set up that week and one more appearance on Jim Parker's *Vegas Vampire* TV show to make one last push for ticket sales form the locals.

Jason was sitting in the hotel coffee shop, having breakfast with Dion DiMucci, Dick Clark's show's main headliner, and Terri's brother Mark, the morning after their final show in the *Continental Theatre*.

Jason was only a ten-year-old roller skater when Dion had most of his biggest hit records like *Runaround Sue* and *The Wanderer*, and remembered dancing to those songs at the sock hops at *The Rollertorium* with Joyce Paxton.

"It's too bad neither of you are going to be in town for my party next week," Jason said to Dion and Mark, "I could have made you both judges in my Bachelorette of the Year pageant.

"Well, my sister Terri is coming," Mark suggested, "You can always use her in a pinch if you need a female judge to even out the judging panel."

"I've already got one female judge, so I think I'm okay for now," smiled Jason, "But I will be singing a song that I think will give Terri a laugh."

Jason did always have to smile at the songs picked out to perform at the party and figured whatever happened, he at least be entertaining to his friends who attended.

Dion then noticed a necklace pendant that Jason had hanging from his neck. "That's an interesting necklace you're wearing," Dion said to Jason, "Do you know what it represents?"

Annie Gaybis had given Jason an early Christmas present to wear for what she said was a "good luck charm for his big Vegas show," a gold razor blade pendant and chain which he began wearing just that week.

"A friend of mine gave it to me for Christmas and said she just liked to way it looked," said Jason, "I just thought it was kind of different too."

"It means you like cocaine," Dion smiled, "Razor blades are what they use to chop up the coke before they snort it."

Jason was surprised but did feel a little embarrassed that he didn't know what the pendent represented.

"I've never done any cocaine, and my friend who gave it to me probably didn't know what it meant either," Jason just laughed, "She'll probably be surprised as me when I tell her."

Jason tried to make a joke out of it to Dion and jokingly sang a parody verse of Dion's hit song *Abraham, Martin and John*.

"Anybody here, seen my gold raz-or neck-lace?" Jason teased, singing a parody line, *"Can you tell me what it means..."*

"If I'm good for anything," Jason joked to Dion, "I can always think up an appropriate parody on the spot, and that song has been stuck in my head since I heard you sing it last night in the show."

"Well, that necklace makes you look like part of the hip crowd now," joked Mark, "Or at least it'll make the girls think you're rich enough to afford coke."

"I just like my scotch and an occasional liqueur," Jason smiled to Dion as he let him look closer at his pendent, "But I don't even like pot and have no interest in cocaine."

"Coke has always been around, but now it has the chic accessories," Dion smiled, "I went through all that in the 1960s, but finally figured out that drugs were either God or Satan's way of telling me I was making too much money."

"I may not have had a hit record in a long time," Dion said more seriously, "But it feels great being clean and sober and to have found Jesus."

"You can learn a lot about yourself once you accept Jesus into your heart," Dion started explaining.

Mark had already told Jason about how Dion was a born again Christian and would sometimes start preaching his beliefs. But Jason didn't want to get into any discussions with Dion about his religious philosophy and politely tried to change the subject.

"Well, what I've learned in the last few weeks is to not to try and produce any big shows so close to *Jesus' birthday* from now on," Jason tried to say with humor. "I probably could have had twice as many people coming, but Christmas was just a tough time for most people to come to a party in Las Vegas."

"And of course, I've also learned to make sure I know the deal about any union requirements next time, too," Jason added with light regret.

"I heard that Dick Clark ran into the same problem the first time he did a show here at the Thunderbird too," Mark said, "It does sound like a great deal to get the showroom so cheap until you find out what else is involved."

"And you don't want to screw around with the unions in this town," Dion added, "They pretty much have all the hotels and showrooms locked up."

"Well, I just wish I would've known a little sooner," Jason said, "But it's too late to worry about now."

"At least you'll know next time," said Dion, "As they say, *live and learn*."

"Yup, *live and learn*," Jason wholeheartedly agreed.

❧

The big lettering on the *Thunderbird Hotel* marquee would be displayed the entire week before his show. Jason also figured those additional five days of advertising would also help sell tickets to the locals.

Unfortunately, Telly Savalas had also mentioned at the last minute that because he was appearing for free as a judge as a favor to Jason and Denise, he might also run into union problems with his *SAG* or *AFTRA* unions if his name appeared on the marquee and they found out he wasn't getting paid anything to appear that night.

"But if you do want me to sing a song or two," Telly lightly mentioned, "I'll consider doing it for the minimum union wages if you're interested."

Jason just politely told Telly he didn't have any more money in his budget and would just keep his name off the marquee that week. Jason was also disappointed that Jan Berry's father had decided not to let Jan travel to Las Vegas alone that weekend to be a celebrity judge, but Jason had found a last-minute replacement with a famous photographer from *Penthouse Magazine* Lori had recommended named Earl Miller. He still had Telly, Jim Parker, and last year's Bachelorette of the Year Lita Krissan to be judges, after deciding to make her what he joked was his "token" female judge on the panel as well.

Jason just had Jim Seagrave advertise in huge lettering "Super Stars Singles Party," along with "Bachelorette of the Year Pageant," "Surprise Celebrity Guest's and "Live Music and Dancing." Also listed in small print at the bottom of the marquee was *"Produced by Jason Mershon,"* and Jason briefly wondered if Anne Sanderson would see his name.

He thought back again to what Anne Sanderson had said on New Year's Eve in 1970 when she asked him, "What he'd be doing in five years?" and Jason wondered if she'd be impressed if she happened to see the marquee. But he didn't really dwell on it because he had never seen or spoken to Anne since they broke up, and had by then pretty much compared their old relationship as just another girl he knew when he was young.

Jason mainly liked having the marquee up for a week because he knew he needed good local support to make a profit that night. The expenses for the party had pretty much cleaned out his bank account, and he not only wanted to get that money back but hopefully make this big gamble in Las Vegas a winner.

He was banking on it.

Most of Jason's friends, bachelorettes, and *S.T.A.R.S.* members began arriving by two pm that following Friday to check in to their hotel rooms.

The phone in his room was constantly ringing from arriving guests, and even when Jason was in the coffee shop, he heard his name being paged over the PA system every few minutes. Luckily, there were paging phones in the booths so he could just answer all the calls from the coffee shop without standing in the lobby all day.

Jason had greeted almost everyone who had arrived by eight pm that night before he then had to drive to the television station in Henderson to appear one last time on the *Vegas Vampire Show*.

When he finally got back to his room after two am, he was glad Lita Krisaan was still awake to have a quiet nightcap and relax for a while.

Jason had been close with Lita for over a year and wanted her to stay in his hotel suite that weekend, but also wanted her to keep it low profile and discreet. There were a few other bachelorettes, backup singers, and dancers whom Jason had casual relationships that year, and he wanted to come across that he was "too busy" to be involved with any of the others that weekend.

It was a long first day, but Jason knew he had an even longer day ahead and hoped to sleep till at least nine am. Unfortunately, the phone in his room started ringing at seven am the next morning from many of his *S.T.A.R.S* members asking what they were supposed to do all day until the party started at eight pm that evening.

Jason found it hard to believe that they couldn't figure that out for themselves and tried to politely explain that Saturday afternoon was their 'free time" to spend enjoying Las Vegas and said he'd just see them all when the party started.

The bachelorette contestants, dancers, and band members were also calling early about rehearsals, and Jason kept explaining it was scheduled for noon like he'd told them the day before. He had printed up a schedule that he gave all of them when they arrived and was also getting slightly irritated that everyone was calling him that early in Las Vegas.

Jason could see he wasn't going to get much sleep, so he went with Lita to meet Annie Gaybis, Mixie Thompson, Michael Ritz, and Stan Adams in the coffee shop by nine am for breakfast.

"Jeez, I can't believe that with everything there is to do in Las Vegas," Jason tried to laugh, "That so many people are calling me up asking how to spend their day."

"Well, they know you're the one in charge of everything," said Annie, "You're the only one they can call."

They weren't in the coffee shop more than twenty minutes before Jason again heard his name over the paging system and answered the phone next to their booth.

"It's deadline today, and Joy's not at the office yet!" Jason heard his mother's voice yelling into the phone. "Do you know where the fuck she is?!"

"She'll probably be there soon," said Jason, "It's not even nine-thirty yet, and everyone else in the office knows what to do, so it's no big deal."

"Well, she'd better be in the office soon!" his mother yelled again before hanging up the phone.

Jason couldn't believe what his mother was freaked out about.

The NSR was a cinch to put together every two weeks, and everyone else in the office knew what to do, so Joy didn't really even need to be there.

Jason called the office back to make sure everything under control and was relieved when they said everything was going "smooth as usual," and it would be "no problem" making the deadline. But within the hour, his mother had him paged again, still freaking out.

"Is Joy up there with you in Las Vegas?!" his mother yelled again. "I know she went with you to Dallas, so don't lie to me!"

This time Jason started getting irritated.

"No, she isn't!" Jason said, "I've got a lot of things going on right now and can't talk, but everything is under control with the newspaper, so don't worry about it!"

Jason just hung up the phone before she did, hoping his mother would get the message not to call him back. He also decided not to answer any more pages until he was at least finished with his rehearsals that day.

The band had all their equipment set up by eleven am and everyone was in the showroom by noon for the sound checks and rehearsals. Jason also made sure he had the doors locked during rehearsal and was still trying to keep his appearance secret from a lot of his friends and didn't want to ruin the surprise.

Twice during the rehearsal, he was interrupted by someone from the front desk with a note saying he had "an emergency phone message to call Vi" but just ignored it and tried to finish the rehearsal without being distracted.

Jason also went over the different props and lighting with his assistants for that night's show and didn't get back to his room until almost five pm. He had hoped to get a couple of hours of sleep but realized that wasn't going to happen with the phone ringing every ten minutes, including another call from his mother.

"Well, the bitch finally called in sick around eleven am," she said with anger, "So I had to go down to the office early and take care of everything myself without Joy there."

"Whatever, but there was really nothing that needed to be done by you," Jason said with irritation, "Everything was taken care of already."

That comment, for some reason, made his mother angrier.

"Your father is in Dallas, you're in Las Vegas, and no one is here to take care of anything but ME!" she yelled, "Have fun with your fucking party tonight!"

Then, as usual, he heard the loud sound of her hanging up on him.

Jason stayed in the shower for at least thirty minutes as he got ready for his big party and kept telling himself, "I'm going to have fun tonight, I'm going to have fun."

He'd gotten used to ignoring all of his mother's negativity and he wasn't going to let it bother him that night especially.

Chapter Eighteen

Jason was happy when he saw most of his friends were already there and dancing on the stage when he walked into the *Continental Theatre* at nine pm.

The one friend Jason did miss not being there that night was Frank Reich, who explained Saturday night was his best night for tips at *The Sahara* and needed to work his graveyard shift.

Tom Casey was still selling tickets at the front door, and Jason had already told the maître d' how to strategically seat the showroom's crowd. The showroom had seating for about five hundred, and besides his friends, Jason had reserved tables near the front of the stage; he wanted to completely fill the lower area before letting anyone sit in the upper booths to make sure the room looked full.

Jason guessed that by ten pm, there were over two hundred and fifty seats occupied, and although the crowd looked decent, there were still many empty booths toward the back of the showroom.

"This is a great crowd for the Saturday before Christmas," said Jim Seagrave when he stopped in to look at the crowd.

Jason didn't want to let Seagrave know it wasn't as big as he personally hoped, but figured it at least looked more successful than it was.

When Telly Savalas entered the showroom with Denise and went to the judges' table in front of the stage, Jason was glad to see how personable he was with the crowd.

Instead of just saying *"Granny's dead!"* the way Max Baer Jr had at his *Hearts and Flowers Ball*, Telly greeted everyone with his smiling catchphrase, *"Who loves ya, baby!"*

Stan Adams was flashing dozens of pictures at different tables, and booths and Jason tried to greet and talk with everyone as he strolled around the showroom and would occasionally go onstage to award door prizes or dance with many of his friends at the party.

The DJ was mixing current disco hits with an occasional Christmas song like *Jingle Bell Rock*, *White Christmas*, or *Blue Christmas* in keeping with the Christmas Party theme. Besides just dancing with Lita, Jason also danced with some other bachelorettes, as well as Annie, Mixie, and Terri, who did joke about how amazing it was how much they had both changed in five years.

"Who would have ever believed we'd be both be here tonight back in Las Vegas again after what we both we were doing back then", Terri smiled.

507

"Well, I think you'll get a smile from one of the songs the band will be performing tonight that might bring back a few memories," Jason joked without letting her know he'd be singing in that band.

Victor Consuela introduced Jason to his *two roommates*, Amber and Carol, and assured Jason they were both there strictly to party and wouldn't be "working" or looking for customers that night.

For the last song, before he started his *Bachelorette of the Year Pageant*, Jason had the DJ spin the big hit song that had been the craze that year, Van Morrison's *The Hustle*.

Amber and Carol were on both sides of Jason expertly doing *The Hustle* and even Telly Savalas joined the over thirty dancers on stage, which made the entire group dance look like a part of the show in itself.

After a big group dance with all of his friends and party-goers, Jason figured it was a good time to have his first break and begin the beauty pageant. But he also didn't want to have the contest take too long of a break in the party and only had one segment that wouldn't last longer than twenty minutes.

Jason decided to emcee the pageant himself but had also arranged for the judges in the front row to have microphones to ask the contestants a question as part of the judging on *poise and personality* as they did in other national beauty pageants. As Jason called out each contestant individually and had them parade on stage in their evening gowns, the judges would alternate, asking them each a question about what qualified them to be Bachelorette of the Year.

Lita was mainly asking the standard questions about the bachelorettes' ambitions and hobbies, but Telly Savalas, Earl Miller, and Jim Parker decided to ask more personal light and teasing questions with innuendoes that got the audience laughing like "Tell us the truth, why do you *really enjoy being single*"? "Do you like being with a lot of *different men?*", "What really *turns you on* in a man?", or "What would it take to *satisfy you enough* to get married?"

The questions weren't overly sexual, but Jason noticed that when the bachelorettes gave their own teasing innuendoes back to the judges, or how one even teased Telly about what she would like to do with *"his bald head,"* the audience laughed even more and cheered at their answers.

Jason liked the audience's reactions and made a mental note to possibly try more suggestive questions in any future contests.

After all the contestants had been questioned and left the stage, Jason told the audience he'd announce the winner after a "special live show band" that would begin the next part of the evening's entertainment.

Jason had scheduled his surprise appearance and to be introduced about halfway through the band's upcoming set.

While the DJ spun some more dance music before the band was introduced., Jason checked with Michael Ritz, who had two cameras set up on tripods in the back of the room, and check on how the video-taping was going.

Jason's upbeat mood changed when Michael said "one of the *union guys*" had told him they weren't permitted to record anything with cameras in the showroom because there wasn't the appropriate union rep there that night.

"We've at least been acting like we're recording something, so it looks good to the audience," said Michael, "But the union guy said we can't turn on the cameras, so we haven't really recorded anything tonight."

Jason was getting pissed and found the *union guy* who was in charge and started trying to find out what it would take to at least allow the next band set and the announcement of the bachelorette winner to be recorded.

"Well, I could kind of look away and not notice that they have the cameras on for a while," said the union guy, "But I'd need something to keep me pre-occupied during that time."

"Fifty dollars in cash might work," the union guy casually smiled.

Jason wasn't happy about it but talked him into accepting forty dollars as he handed him two twenty-dollar bills.

He also saw the band was starting to begin their set, and after telling Michael Ritz what the deal with the union guy was, hurried backstage to change into his costume.

Jason suddenly was feeling some apprehension and wasn't as excited as he knew he should be, and briefly thought about scraping the whole music set. But he decided to try to forget about anything else for the next hour and at least go through with he planned.

This was going to be his musical trip down memory lane with all his friends he had known since he moved to Las Vegas in 1969, and had chosen songs that represented certain times since then. He also knew it was going to be his last big party before he turned twenty- five years old and wanted this night to almost a compilation of his first quarter-century.

Jason had rented a wild blue sequenced jumpsuit and cape that he thought would look hilarious to his friends seeing him perform a funny parody of the *glam rock* performers like David Bowie and Mick Jagger.

Several of the back-up singers and dancers who would be onstage with Jason hurriedly helped him change from his tuxedo into his costume, knowing they needed to be onstage in less than ten minutes.

Toward the end of the last song the band was playing before introducing him, the back-up singers took their places onstage, and before Jason knew it, he heard the guitar player announce, "Ladies and Gentlemen, please welcome our surprise guest tonight, *JJ BREEZE!*" as the drummer's downbeat to the opening song, *The Letter*, immediately began.

Jason chose a couple of easy opening songs he knew well, *The Letter* which he'd sung with *The Box Tops* a few dozen times, followed by Johnny Rivers old hit song *The Seventh Son* which he had sung a few times in talent contests, to get himself warmed up and comfortable with performing onstage again with a full band again.

The stage was huge, and with the band off towards the rear and the back-up singers to the side, Jason was the main focus and needed to constantly move around with his hand-held microphone and sing to different areas in the showroom.

He did change a couple of words in the song *The Seventh Son* to give it a funny sexual meaning wanting the audience to take his show lightly and not too seriously and cockily sang; *"I can heal the sick, raise the dead and make all you women cum out of your head... cause I'm the one, I'm the one, the one they call the seventh son..."*

During his first two songs, he saw the surprised looks on the faces of the dozens he knew in the audience once they recognized him, but felt more comfortable when he saw them applauding and laughing.

Jason wanted to sing a current hit for his third song and chose Elton John's *Island Girl* mainly because it was about a hooker in Jamaica and had a line about "turning *tricks to the dudes in the big city"* that he knew would at least make a few in the audience smile.

Island Girl was also the first song that had some production effects and props.

The stage darkened during the instrumental break while one of the girls did a dance routine with fire bolos, but when Jason was singing the last chorus of the song, his microphone suddenly went dead and cut off his vocals before the song ended. One of the soundmen came on stage to adjust the microphone, and although Jason was irritated, he continued as though nothing had happened.

After three upbeat songs, Jason sang a slower blues song, The Rolling Stones minor hit *The Spider and The Fly*, which lightly described a rock singer who had problems with staying faithful to his girlfriend who always warned him about *"keeping fidelity in his head"*, when they were apart. Jason sarcastically thought besides being a song that many girls in the audience would lightly associate with him, he also personally felt the song described his own relationship with Lori at times.

He then decided for his own sentimental reasons, to sing a song he knew he always nailed vocally and hoped would give his old friends from Las Vegas who were in the crowd that night, a smile remembering when he first sang it. He confidently sang the song *It's All Over Now*, as he strutted off the stage into the audience and sang to several girls he knew well.

For his last two songs before his planned *encore*, Jason chose the two songs he knew a few of the girls in the audience would lightly relate as songs he was singing to them personally. As the room darkened, the stage was flooded with red lights as the fog machine filled the stage with smoke, and the prop cocktail bar and bar stools were rolled centerstage.

510

The piano player and saxophonist slowly began the ballad while many in the audience gave appreciative whistles and catcalls as two scantily dressed dancers suggestively moved past Jason towards the prop bar onstage and sat at the barstools.

Jason stood by one of the girls at the bar and began singing the opening verse to Elton John's *Sweet Painted Lady*, which was his homage to hookers and the services they provided.

Having a somewhat choreographed storyline during that song was what Jason had wanted to be a personal and light joke for *old time's sake* to least Terri that night. But with Carol and Amber also in the audience, Jason made sure he lightly made occasional eye contact with them as well and smiled towards them both during the song. He had always loved the melody and message of the song *Sweet Painted Lady* and felt Elton's John's sentimental and romanticized lyrics about prostitutes simply *being paid for getting laid* would be a complimentary and funny song to sing that night.

Before the song concluded, Jason's microphone again went out during his last chorus, which Jason felt ruined the end of the song's sentimental feel.

Jason was suddenly just anxious for his set to end and at least hoped his next song would get the audience lively again and lead to his big finish.

His *biggest production* number was the last song he decided to sing before his *encore* and knew that many of the bachelorettes in the audience from Hollywood and Beverly Hills would get a chuckle and know it was just his way of sarcastically teasing them as he always had. Jason had also originally planned on singing that song as a light joke for Lori, knowing how much she enjoyed seeing Mick Jagger perform it, and was disappointed that she wasn't there to hear it.

Star Star was definitely as *dirty*, and probably even *dirtier*, than any songs Lori sang in *Let My People Come*, and Jason also realized as he began singing the upbeat rock song that the lyrics were now even more appropriate after learning Lori was moving to New York in a few weeks.

With Jagger's opening lyrics about a girl who had moved back to New York City and about how he was going to make her *scream and jump with pleasure* if they ever met again, it also was coincidentally appropriate when he learned it was rumored that Mick Jagger had written the song about one of his ex-girlfriends, and Lori's idol, Carly Simon.

Jason had a hard time at first understanding every lyric that Mick Jagger delivered on the recorded version of the song, but was surprised how dirty the song actually was when he had been able to find all of the song's lyrics during his rehearsals with the band.

As the sexy dancers joined Jason onstage for the dance routines they had rehearsed, Jason figured the dirty lyrics with lines about how the girl in the song *kept her pussy clean by using fruit*, and how he missed feeling *her legs wrapped around him*,

511

would get the same shocked but humorous response as Mick Jagger did when Jason saw him perform at *The Forum*.

While Jason and the back-up singer began the chorus that kept repeating the title about the girl in the song being a *"Starfucker"*, and the two sexy dancers on either side of him began giving suggestive pelvic thrusts, the large flashing neon sign was lowered centerstage spelling out *S.T.A.R.B.U.C.K.E.R.*

Jason was irritated that he was too pre-occupied that day to remind the stagehands about unscrewing a couple of bulbs to make the *"B"* look like an *"F"* as he had planned. He was also irritated that during the second chorus while he was singing with the *pelvic thrusting* dancers, some guy started walking onstage as if he was waving his hands in objection to the song, but Jason ignored him as the big finish was coming up.

One of the dancers laid flat on her back away from the audience, with her legs propped wide apart holding the microphone while the back-up singers and other dancers lowered Jason above her holding his arms and legs.

The girls then began moving Jason's lower body up and down between her legs, as he sang the last verse towards the audience while flashing strobe lights and other lighting effects filled the showroom.

With more dirty lyrics mentioning how *Ali MacGraw got mad* learning how the girl in the song had given head to her husband Steve McQueen, and how he was making bets that the girl would also probably *fuck John Wayne* before he died, Jason just hoped his friends would get a good laugh at his outrageousness of the song's lyrics and join in all singing along with the last chorus repeating *"You're a starfucker, starfucker starfucker, star..."*

Jason saw as he was concluding the song that only a small portion of the audience was singing along and that many others were just sitting with shocked looks and their mouths half-open. The applause was mixed at the end of that song, and Jason was fairly certain if he left the stage, he wouldn't be called back for an encore. He decided to change the plan and asked all the bachelorette contestants to come onstage and said he was going to announce the winner "after his last song," which also got a cheer from some in the audience.

The last song he planned to sing was the upbeat live version of Joe Cockers *Delta Lady*, but because he was now singing to the dancing bachelorettes onstage, he changed the lyric from *"Delta"* Lady to *"Single"* Lady.

"Cause you're mine, yes you're mine, Single Lady," Jason sang to the bachelorette contestants as they danced around him on stage.

During the song, Jason was a little surprised when Lita Krisaan just casually walked onstage while he was still singing, and handed him the judges results, seemingly oblivious that he was still performing his concert.

He figured that Lita had probably gone back to the room and smoked some of her stuff and wasn't completely aware of what she was doing, but he tried to continue singing and ignore Lita's distraction. But Jason was also more embarrassed than irritated that his show wasn't going perfectly as he planned.

While he was singing the final verse of *Delta Lady* before the last chorus, Jason decided to change the last line with lyrics that just suddenly popped into his head and sang, *"But yet it seems, the singles scene is lackin' you, I'm so glad you're waiting for me at The Whiskey…"*

He was surprised that those lyrics even popped into his head, but because Lori was the only one he was close with who wasn't there that night, he realized he probably subconsciously wanted to have Lori see he was still thinking about her, just in case she ever did see a video of the show.

Jason felt completely spent as he lined up the bachelorettes and announced the winner, before taking a light and sarcastic bow to the audience without showing any embarrassment and exiting the stage. He did shake a few hands of those who were applauding in the front rows and even got a cheerful "Who loves ya, baby!" from Telly Savalas after he shook his hand, but it still hadn't turned out like he had hoped.

As Jason walked backstage, one of the union guys he was paying to "just stand around" made a sarcastic remark that he tried to ignore.

"Too bad about those problems with your microphone," he seemed to sarcastically say, "If you'd had had a professional union guy working the sound system, that never would have happened."

Jason just ignored him and joined the back-up singers and dancers who all seemed happy, saying how well the show went and was thrilled for just having the experience to perform live in Las Vegas.

As Jason slowly changed back into his tuxedo, he didn't know what kind of emotions he was feeling and just said to himself, but loud enough for the other girls to hear, "Well, *that's that*."

❧

It was the next day, and Jason looked next to the bed and saw his crumpled tuxedo on the floor, and started to remember how he ended up with Amber at Victor's apartment.

His "JJ Breeze" show had been over for about thirty minutes, and although there was still a good crowd dancing to the DJ, some of his friends were leaving, and Tom Casey wanted to know if he should continue charging the ten-dollar cover charge at the door.

"How did we do on the door money," Jason asked him.

"Well, not as good as you hoped," said Tom, "A lot of the people said they were your friends, and I probably let about thirty of them in free."

Jason knew he only had about a dozen people on his guest list and hoped all of his other friends would support his production and not worry about paying a ten-dollar door charge after having given many of them hotel rooms at only his cost.

"Oh, and there were a few people who asked for their money back," Tom half laughed, "They said they could've gone next door to the Riviera and saw Don Rickles and Jose Feliciano for almost the same price they paid to see you."

"Jeez, the ten bucks was for the party, dancing, and beauty pageant!" Jason said with more irritation, "That thing I did onstage was just a crazy surprise I did for some of my friends."

"Well, some of the older people in the crowd who didn't know you said it was disgusting," Tom continued trying to laugh, "Especially that last *starfucker* song and I think I gave around a hundred and fifty bucks in refunds."

"What the fuck, nobody was supposed to take it that serious!" complained Jason, "Haven't they got a sense of humor or see it was supposed to be something just for fun?"

He was disappointed learning the door money wasn't a much as he'd hoped and told Tom he could just charge five dollars to anyone else who wanted to come into the party, which was still scheduled to continue until four am. Jason just took a hundred dollars from the cash register to tip the maître d' and bartenders. He also found out from the maître d' that even though they easily made the bar guarantee of two thousand dollars that night, Jason still owed over three hundred dollars from his personal tab from some friends who had charged all their drinks to him.

Learning that some of his friends he had already paid for hotel rooms that weekend as a Christmas present, had also thought Jason was paying for everything else and charged all of their drinks to him, was getting Jason even more irritated.

Jason was suddenly feeling some resentment but didn't want to start any arguments with his friends that night, and just told the maître d' he'd settle everything with Jim Seagrave the next day and signed all the tabs. He was still embarrassed that his show didn't go over as he hoped with the crowd, but after joining Victor, Carol, and Amber at the bar, he saw that at least they said they loved his act.

"Well, I glad some of you liked it," Jason half laughed, "Tom said he had to refund money to some people who didn't."

"Fuck 'em!" said Victor, "We thought it was hilarious, and I just wish you would've sung, *Let it Bleed* like back in the old days."

"Yeah, fuck 'em, I thought it was great," added Amber, "Let's just get drunk and keep the party going!"

That sounded like the most positive thing Jason heard since he woke up that morning, but wasn't in the right frame of mind to continue trying to party with his other friends for the rest of the night. He figured he had finished all of his duties as the host of the party and just wanted to get away from the *Continental Showroom* to try and get the irritation and disappointment out of his head.

Jason ended up telling Tom Casey just to cut off the door charge and decided to party the rest of the night somewhere else with just Victor, Amber, and Carol., and after deciding to go to *Dirty Sally's* get drunk as Amber suggested, by six am, Jason ended up back to Victor's apartment which sounded as good as place as any to finish off the night.

As he saw Amber's panties and bra also lying next to his crumpled Tuxedo on the floor that morning, he also remembered how he had spent the rest of the night before.

"Amber, what time is it?" Jason asked as he saw that she was also just waking up.

"It's only about two pm," she said as she looked at the clock next to her, "Victor and Carol never wake up till after four pm, so they're still sleeping in their room."

"So, let's just stay in bed for a couple more hours," Amber smiled, rolling closer next to him, "You said you didn't need to be anywhere today, right?"

"No, not really, but I think I want to head back to California before it gets too late," said Jason as he sat up from bed, "The party's over, and I just want to get back home."

Jason knew check-out time for all of his guests at The Thunderbird was noon, and almost everyone had probably already left town. But although he really still wasn't that anxious to see anyone still there from his party the night before, he still had some things in his hotel room he needed to pack up himself.

"Well, it was nice meeting you and I had fun last night," Jason kissed Amber goodbye after he quickly got dressed and prepared to leave, "Maybe I'll see you again sometime."

"I hope so," Amber smiled, "And Merry Christmas!"

Jason sarcastically thought how crazy it was that he was getting his final Merry Christmas wish that weekend from a part-time Las Vegas hooker, but at least it didn't cost him anything, unlike anything else had that weekend. He just decided to remember Amber more as a "psychology major at UNLV," as she also had described herself, so he wouldn't feel he ended up being with anyone too sleazy that night.

When he finally got back to the Thunderbird, Jason felt completely drained but somewhat relieved after the front desk clerk said everyone had already checked out and left hours earlier. He figured Lita must have driven back to Los Angeles with Annie Gaybis or his other friends and knew everyone needed to get back to work or their regular lives the following day.

After Jason packed his bags and paid the bar tab his friends had charged to him, along with paying another two hundred for his own personal expenses that week, it took over half the cash he had left from the door money, and Jason left *The Thunderbird* with less than five hundred dollars in his pocket. He tried to optimistically think that "any profit was a good profit' but knew that "any" hadn't been good enough that weekend.

He did take one last look inside the *Continental Theatre* and suddenly began to feel strangely alone seeing how cold and empty the room felt seeing it without his partygoers from the night before. Jason also suddenly wished that a few of his friends would have stuck around to talk with, and was still surprised he had no messages from anyone else without at least a goodbye or thank you note. He also saw his big *Starbucker* sign lying on the side of the stage and wondered that if seeing he already had paid for it, he should take it with him for a souvenir, but decided he didn't need anything else to remind him about the night before.

His big party was over

On his drive home from Las Vegas, Jason had so many different thoughts going through his head but was mainly trying to fight off any type of disappointment he was feeling and was having a hard time trying to think of anything positive that resulted from his big party.

The party had felt as if it had been a compilation of many different aspects and friends he was involved since 1969 but lightly thought that perhaps he shouldn't have included his brief "musical career" as part of his memories.

Jason knew he probably would have made at least a two or three-thousand-dollar profit if he hadn't decided to perform a live show, which lead to all the extra expenses and union problems. But he also knew that was his decision and didn't have anyone to blame except himself for choosing to add the additional cost to make his party more memorable.

The only thing positive he could think about from the entire experience, was that what he had pictured doing as "just an idea" months earlier, had actually happened and turned into a reality. It may not have gone exactly as he hoped, but at least he had done it. Jason figured that was at least worth something.

Chapter Nineteen

Lori almost fell out of her chair laughing, and Jason was trying to laugh as well, as Stan Adams was describing to her how outrageous Jason's show had been at *The Thunderbird*.

Jason was back at *My Place Disco* in Beverly Hills three days after returning from Las Vegas celebrating Christmas Eve with a small group of friends, which was also serving as a going-away party for Lori, who would be leaving for New York right after the first of the year.

"I mean, I look up on the stage and here's this strange looking guy, dressed in what looks like a spacesuit", Stan Adams laughed, "And then I realize it's JASON!"

"Lori, you wouldn't believe the way he looked," Mixie was also laughing, "And then he just starts singing like he's a famous Las Vegas entertainer or something."

"And some of the songs he sang!" Annie added lightly, shaking her head, "I mean, the whole audience was sitting with their mouths open, wondering who they were seeing."

"They're exaggerating it a bit," Jason tried to laugh with them, "But I was hoping that no one would know it was actually me up there and just wanted to do something crazy for a night."

"I know a lot of people didn't expect you to be the surprise guest," Stan joked to Jason, "But you surprised us to when you just disappeared after that and didn't even come back to the party."

"I was just wanted to lay low afterward," smiled Jason, "There wasn't much else for me to do there that night anyway, and I was exhausted."

"Well, I wish I could've been there," said Lori, "But who would've thought our last weekend of *Let My People Come* would end up being the same one as your party."

"Well, Michael said he recorded at least that part of the show on the camera," said Mixie, "But he has to wait until he can borrow a special playback machine, he needs to show it to us on."

"I wanna see it too!" said Sandi Shore, "I would've there if it wasn't for damn Pauly."

Jason wasn't in that much of a hurry to see the footage either and just lightly joked that he wasn't quite ready to relive the experience.

"I think the old saying *'too soon'* is the way I feel about any watching any repeat of that night right now" Jason just smiled, "I think that camera footage should probably stay in the vault for a while until I'm ready to look at it and just be able to laugh."

After they decided they ribbed Jason enough about his party in Las Vegas, some of them began exchanging Christmas presents and "going away gifts" to Lori as Stan started taking photos of everyone.

Jason had already discreetly given small heart-shaped rings with a small ruby that wasn't too expensive to a few of his other girlfriends as Christmas presents, but gave Lori a gold watch with diamonds that had cost him almost five hundred dollars.

He didn't know if it might be the last present he would ever buy for Lori, so Jason wanted to give her something he hoped she would keep for a long time.

Lori had given Jason a gold ring with star sapphire stone for Christmas, and like Jason, they both wanted to give each something that would always remind them of each other even though they would soon be living three thousand miles apart.

"Okay, for this one picture, just Jason and Lori," said Stan, aiming his camera, "I think I took the first pictures of you two together almost three years ago, and this might be the last one I'll be able to take for a while."

Jason and Lori squeezed together tight, and Jason decided to pose, giving Lori a big kiss on the cheek as a wish for good luck in New York.

As everyone raised their glasses to toast to Lori's future success in New York, they also made toasts to the upcoming "New Year and a new beginning" for all of them, along with their usual toast to continuing to have "fun" in the coming year.

Jason joined in on the toast but was still trying to figure out what his own "new beginning" would be in 1976.

He also wasn't even sure what sounded fun anymore and knew he had some things to think about.

෴

Stan Adams had developed the photos from Christmas Eve at *My Place* and gave Jason a couple of copies of the photo he took of him with Lori kissing her cheek.

"That's a great photo of you two," said Stan, "Make sure you give a copy to Lori before she leaves."

Jason planned to give Lori a copy of the photo after they decided to have New Year's Eve dinner alone together at *The Islander*, which was only two days before she was leaving for New York City.

While they both agreed that the photo was probably the cutest one that they'd seen of them together in a long time, they were also sarcastically joking about how ironic it was that the biggest hit song in America that week was *50 Ways to Leave Your Lover* by Paul Simon.

"I must have heard that damn song twenty times this week," Lori half laughed, "I'll probably take this photo with me to New York, but I hope I don't associate it with that Paul Simon song whenever I look at it."

After their dinner at *The Islander*, Jason and Lori decided to make one last visit to their favorite piano bar, where the piano player knew most of the George Gershwin and Irving Berlin song's they liked singing to each other. They also both joked they wanted to sing a better going-away song than *50 Ways to Leave Your Lover* to remember that particular New Year's Eve.

Jason decided Gershwin's *They Can't Take That Away from Me* was the perfect romantic song to sing to her at the piano bar, while Lori decided to lightly sing Irving Berlin's *What'll I Do*, while facetiously acting like she was singing the song to the photo Jason gave her that night.

Even though their relationship had changed to more of a romantic friendship that year, Jason and Lori had still never discussed the words break-up or ever talked about ending it permanently. When they kissed and cheerfully sang *Auld Lang Syne* at midnight, Jason guessed they both knew that their relationship would never return to what it once was and that 1976 was going to actually be their goodbye this time.

Jason had also decided years ago that it was always more positive to keep any goodbyes silent without ever saying the words out loud.

❧

It was only two weeks after the New Year when Jason got another phone call that really didn't surprise him.

"Your mother is being a real bitch down here," Joy complained over the phone, "It's her whole attitude the way she talks to people and is trying to boss everyone around."

"She's been like that her whole life," Jason tried to joke, "That's just her personality, and you'll get used to it."

"She's even trying to tell me how to put together the Explorer now too," Joy complained, "We have everything running smoothly already, and I just don't know why she thinks she needs to be here."

"I'll try to talk to her," Jason said, "So just try to ignore it for now until I see how we can work things out."

Jason didn't enjoy talking to his mother at the office either and was trying to just ignore her complaining without letting it irritate him. But he did feel the whole situation at the office was getting too weird lately, especially with his mother now wanting to work there every day, and his father seemingly putting his full-time efforts into Dallas.

When Jason talked to his mother again and explained that "some people in the office" felt it was becoming more difficult to do their work with her being there every day, it turned into another argument.

"This is my business, and I don't care what they think!" she started yelling, "You don't even work in the office anymore, and I don't think you even deserve a salary anymore either."

"This is my business too, and that money is for how I've organized the newspaper as the editor," Jason yelled back, "I was supposed to be one of the owners but seeing that was all bullshit, I still expect my salary for what I'm doing."

"Well, if you expect a check each week, get it from your father in Dallas because you're not getting it from me anymore!" she yelled again before slamming down the phone.

That was the last thing Jason wanted to hear and wasn't the way he expected to start out his New Year.

"What the fuck!" Jason argued over the phone to his father when he called him in Dallas, "Does Vi think she's paying me an allowance like a little kid by threatening not to pay my salary anymore?"

"It's just been very complicated for the last few months," said his father, "There's some issues I'm still trying to work out and just want to finish my business here in Dallas without having any problems with Vi right now."

"Well, since I've been back from Las Vegas," Jason continued arguing, "I haven't set up any new parties yet and need that three hundred dollars a week to pay my bills."

"If there's not anything tying you to California or Vegas right now," his father suggested, "It might be a good time to come here to Dallas for a couple of months and work on some promotions for the Texas edition."

"I did tell those distributors you'd be promoting some singles parties for the newspaper here," he added, "So I'll just pay your salary as the editor while you're up here."

"I don't know even know anyone in Dallas or even anything about the nightclubs there," said Jason, "It would take a while to set something up, and I'd have to drop everything I'm doing here now."

"Well, everything does seem pretty much under control with the NSR in California," his father said, "Joy already knows how you lay out all the cover stories, and with Vi wanting to work in the office every day, you can just oversee everything by phone the way you are now."

"Dallas is a big city, and there's plenty of nightclubs where you can set up singles parties," his father added, "So you can still make some extra money."

That wasn't exactly what he was hoping to hear, and didn't like the idea of working with his father any more than he did with his mother, but also knew he'd be in a tough place financially unless he continued to make his weekly salary.

Jason had also been having a hard time feeling motivated again since his show at *The Thunderbird* and wasn't that excited about just going back to his old schedule of parties and promotions with his usual crowd. With Lori in New York and his lease on his Beverly Hills apartment expiring in February, he began wondering what was really keeping him from going to Dallas. He figured he could always store his furniture and find somewhere else to live when he came back, and the only responsibly Jason could think of that would keep him from leaving for a few months was his cat.

He had already gotten his mother to adopt one of *Old Lady's* kittens, which he simply named *"Little Boy,"* and even though they currently had a strained relationship, he knew she wouldn't mind having another cat for a pet if he left town for a while.

Jason or his parents could never bring themselves to have another dog for a pet after the pain they all felt after Tinker died. Although they never planned on having other pets, there was always a stray cat in the neighborhood who would hang around long enough looking for a home that they would end up adopting.

The one thing Jason felt he had in common with his parents was that they had both come to like cats.

Jason suddenly felt that taking a break from everything in California for at least a few months might be just what he needed, and would be a good thing for his own psyche to see if there was something better in his future.

He did have some new ideas and figured a new city would be a good place to try them out, and it wasn't long after his last phone call with his father, when Jason made his decision. He had already analyzed everything he'd been through and accomplished in the past five years, and started wondering were he'd actually be in the next five years.

Jason decided that getting away for a somewhat *"new beginning"* in a *"new city"* like Dallas, might give his some of those answers.

Jason and Lori at American Country Music Awards with Doug Kershaw, 1975.

Jason, actress Lynda Carter (television's first Wonder Woman), and country music legend Roy Clark.

Annie Gaybis, Jason and Buddy Hackett, 1975.

Paparazzi photo of Jason and Annie Gaybis arriving at Friar's Club Roast at Century Plaza Hotel, 1975.

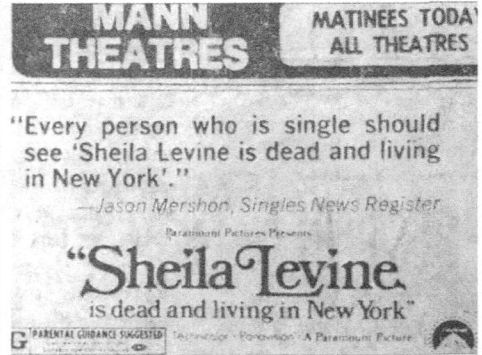

Jason presenting an an award to Actress Cindy Williams accepting on behalf of Francis Ford Coppola for the film *The Conversation*. Jason worked with the Publicity Department at Paramount Pictures on promotional benefits for both the studio and the *Singles News Register*, including providing reviews for films.

Jason with Hugh Hefner for the announcement of the 1975 "Playmate of the Year" at the Playboy Club in Century City. Jason later that same night, with Stevie Wonder at Stevie's surprise twenty-fifth birthday at The Speakeasy.

Pictured at the Esperanza Ball in Beverly Hills are Lori Wagner, Claude E. Hooton, Jr., Sen. Edward Kennedy and Jason Mershon. Hooton received "Man of Hope" Award and Kennedy was a guest speaker.

Newspaper clipping of Lori Wagner and Jason at a party with Senator Edward Kennedy.

Jason, Teddy Kennedy, Jr. (Ted Kennedy's 13-year old son), and Lori Wagner.

Jason with "Bachelorette of the Month" Sheri Verran.

Jason with "Bachelorette of the Month" Barbara Piotrowski.

One Night of a S.T.A.R.S party at My Place Disco in Beverly Hills

Tom Casey (left) and Jason in the middle of two bachelorettes, Paula and Denise.

Nicky Blair (left) with disco owner Sia Amiri (right) and a guest at his "Famous Couples" game match.

Jason and Heavyweight champ Joe Frazier.

Jason and Edy Williams, with what became her "normal" way to be introduced at events, since the Oscar's the year before.

Jason pictured in front of his Mercedes 450SL with his new disco hair style.

Jason began "Bachelor of the Month" contests with men being judged in swimsuits in 1975.

Jason expanded his S.T.A.R.S. parties to Las Vegas at Dirty Sally's in 1975.

Lori (far right center) appeared in "Let My People Come" at Whiskey-a-Go-Go in 1975.

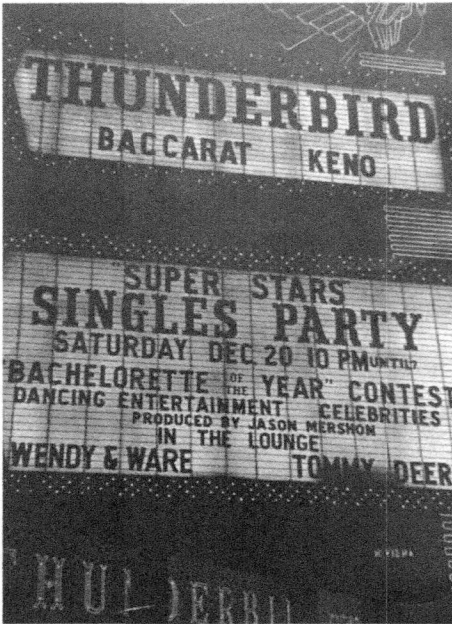

Jason closed out 1975 with his "Bachelorette of the Year" Singles Party in Las Vegas.

"Bachelorette of the Year" finalist Sheri Lynn (left) walks to the microphone to be questioned by the judge

Actor Telly Savalas questions the contestants. Also pictured and judging, Lita Krissan (far left) and Penthouse photographer Earl Miller (far right).

Most of the audience was surprised when Jason (aka JJ Breeze) was a surprise celebrity guest performer at year-end party.

Jason and Lori with Jonathan Winters at another Black Tie Party earlier in 1975.

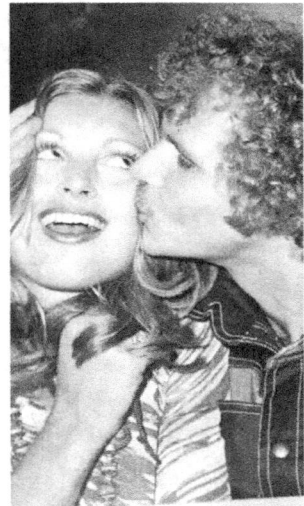

Christmas Eve 1975 photo of Jason and Lori.

PRELUDE TO THE LAST STAND
FALL, 2009

Lake Elsinore Casino was only a fraction of the size of the major poker rooms in Southern California but Jason had been friendly with Ted Kingston the owner of the casino for years, and was one of the casinos included in Jason's usual weekly rounds of playing poker.

Ted had allowed Jason full access to his casino that day to tape a music video for the new poker song he had written, plus, Jason felt he owed Ted a favor and hoped taping a music video at his casino would at least give Ted some free publicity and advertising.

Jason was standing on top of the poker table as if it were a stage inside the casino, as the video cameras were rolling, holding a prop guitar and lip-syncing lyrics to the music tracks were playing loudly from a boombox nearby.

Two sexy female poker dealers from the casino he was friends with, were also enthusiastically dancing beside Jason while a couple dozen of his poker buddies sat around the poker table below him jubilantly singing along with the chorus to the recorded tracks of his song.

He did use the opening lyrics he had remembered about how he was "Drinkin' pissin' somkin' and gamblin' for his opening lyrics, and added that he was also "holdin' foldin' muckin' and a bluffin' to add some other rhyming poker terms that that poker players could associate with as the "hook" before the first verse of his song began.

"Well, I make my livin' playing Texas Hold Em every day
but I've been playin' for eight hours and have yet to make my pay
I always try to play good win most every other time
but then there's times I just leave with a dollar and a dime
The dealers want their tips and the house just wants their rake
but all I want are decent cards and donkey's I can break
Oh Yeah-ah… Oh, Yeah-ah"

Jason didn't think it was the greatest song or lyrics he had ever written, but he had been having fun again with something he realized he missed.

In between playing poker the past two months, Jason had written his new poker song called Playin' Poker for a Livin' and hired local musicians to record the music tracks at a local recording studio. He had also decided, as he had done many times in the past thirty years or so, to revive his music pseudonym JJ Breeze as the music artist rather than using the name Jason Mershon. He knew he couldn't deliver the best vocals by himself any longer, and decided to have his friend Bill Richardson who was a better vocalist, sing the lead verses on the music tracks when he had recorded the song a few weeks earlier.

Bill had been in the San Diego version the rock musical that Jason wrote, produced and directed called "Heaven Rocks" before he decided to change the name to "Rock and Roll Heaven: The Musical Comedy" when he revived it in Hollywood a few years earlier. Bill had been a standout in both productions with his portrayals as both John Lennon and Freddie Mercury and also used a music pseudonym himself, using the name Jose Sinatra, so the recording artists named on the song were Jose Sinatra and JJ Breeze, with Jason only singing back up on a few verses and the chorus when they had both been in the recording studio.

Amanda Miles had driven in from Las Vegas to shoot video and still photos at the casino that day, along with another longtime friend who had become a well-known Hollywood photographer and videographer, Sheri Determan, who had also been one of Jason's Bachelorettes of the Week in the 1970s under a different last name.

After over thirty years, Jason had reconnected with Sheri when she happened to be at the Hollywood opening night of the revival of his musical-comedy in 2006, and she had also been Jason's date when he accepted a couple "Los Angeles Music Awards" for his production later that same year. Since then, they hadn't lost touch again and Sheri had been on of the few that Jason had wanted to stay close with from that period of his life, and also who were still alive.

Amanda had already videotaped some B-roll footage a couple weeks earlier of Jason lip-syncing some of the verses and the chorus to the song, as he drove down the Las Vegas Strip in front of several Las Vegas casinos and landmarks. Sheri said the footage that Amanda shot could be edited in with the footage they were shooting that day showing Jason playing in a poker game that followed the song's lyrics and storyline.

Bill "Jose Sinatra" Richardson was also at the casino that day to appear in the music video as the "Donkey" that cracks Jason's pocket aces with three deuces, and Jason did think it was a bit ironic that he ended up writing a song about a poker player getting beat by a "Donkey" who ended up cracking a pair of aces in a big poker hand with three deuces. He realized how similar it was to a poker hand he had actually once been involved in himself and probably had subconsciously remembered it when he was writing his song.

Jason briefly considered that his song was an example of "art imitating life" which was the opposite of what he'd come to mostly believe that "life imitated art" more often. He had sometimes tried to recall when it was that he had first begun to associate everything with a certain song that was popular, but knew it had been fairly constant for most of his life.

That at least made him realize it wasn't just all the cocaine he did in the 1980s that did make him think back to what he called his "crazy years" which was how he often sarcastically described the life he was leading back then. But there had been so many songs that seemed to be popular at appropriate times in his life, he knew if he ever tried to explain to anyone about what he had started to believe back then, they would never understand why he believed so strongly about destiny and fate rather than simple psychology.

Even though it had been almost thirty years since he had done cocaine, he still tried to believe that it had "opened his mind" to an extent, and just like the songs that had always stayed in his head, he decided those "crazy years" were just something he needed to go through to keep moving forward. He also already figured out that it was probably "just the cocaine" that was what had made him and those he met so "promiscuous" back then, and that things did seem to "Go better with Coke" like the old catchphrase Coca-Cola had used in its advertising back then.

Jason also figured no one would take the time to analyze his lyrics or realize that the poker song was just basically a metaphor of how everyone monotonously spends their lives winning, losing, paying their dues, and trying to get ahead, while hoping that all their work will eventually let them achieve their true goal or destiny. He figured that his song also told a sarcastic story about how monotonous it was trying to make a living as a professional poker player that probably only those who had played poker for years would completely understand.

He was also thinking about where his destiny had brought him that day, as Jason continued to use the poker table as a stage while lip-synching the lyrics, as Amanda and Sheri were taping and photographing the different shots for the music video.

As his friends were circled around the poker table, they were all excitedly raising their arms in the air as they all sang along with the final "out chorus" to the song in unison.

"PLAYIN' POKER FOR A LIVING, YEAH, YEAH!!

"PLAYIN' POKER FOR A LIVING, YEAH, YEAH!!

PLAYIN' POKER FOR A LIVIN' AND JUST TRYIN'

TO WIN SOME MONEY TONIGHT!!"

After the video-taping had ended, everyone had agreed that the entire day and video shoot had been fun, and at least for the time being, that was really all that mattered to Jason. He had stopped trying to even consider any "long range plans" a long time ago, but he was "thinking" about what he was going to do with his song next.

"Once you get the music video on YouTube, it might go viral," Sheri Determan told Jason, "Or you can try selling in on a website or iTunes with the promotional gimmick you're thinking about trying."

Jason didn't completely understand all the current "twenty-first century technology" for promoting and was just playing it by ear as he went along. He mainly figured the song could be used as a "vehicle" for what he was actually trying to accomplish with a "crazy idea" he had thought about during his drive back from Las Vegas months earlier.

He had always been known as a "great promoter" in the past, but now, he just needed to find out if he could find a future from that past and see if his new song might lead him to his next destiny.

Jason knew he had promoted a lot of crazier things than a poker song.

BOOK FIVE

"MEDIA, DISCO AND COCAINE"
1976-1977

Chapter One

In 1976, Gerald Ford was still president, but with his controversial pardon of Richard Nixon, the compete fall of Vietnam, and the terrible economy all happening under his administrations he was a very unpopular. The Republicans did re-nominate him for President after he barely defeated a challenge from Ronald Reagan, while Jimmy Carter, a self-described "born again Christian," had won the Democrat nomination for president that year. Carter's victory was almost a foregone conclusion because of Ford's unpopularity, until he generated controversy in an interview with *Playboy Magazine* by using the word *"screw"* and admitting that he *"lusted in his heart"* for women other than his wife. That *Playboy* interview did hurt his support from Christian evangelists and women, but regardless, Carter still was able to narrowly defeat Ford in the Presidential election later that year.

Happy Days, M.A.S.H, Charley's Angels, Baretta and *Three's Company* were the popular television shows, and there was also a new concept that premiered known as a mini-series and subtitled "A Novel for Television" called *Rich Man, Poor Man*.

Rocky, Taxi Driver, Network, All the Presidents Men, One Flew Over the Cuckoo's Nest and the third remake of *A Star is Born* were popular in the movie theatres, and the hit songs were *Disco Lady, Love Machine, Play That Funky Music (white boy), Fooled Around and Fell in Love, Bohemian Rhapsody* and the top song of the year, *Tonight's the Night* by Rod Stewart.

Also in 1976, Uganda's flamboyant dictator Idi Amin became a major player on the world stage when he supported Palestinian terrorists after they hijacked an airliner and held hostages at Uganda's Entebbe airport. Although Amin displayed himself as the *"one in charge"* and the main negotiator for the hostage's release, he suffered a major embarrassment when Israeli commandos stormed the airport freeing the hostages and killing dozens of Ugandan soldiers.

Along with other major events such as Howard Hughes dying and Isabel Peron being overthrown as President in Argentina, 1976 was also the year a new company was formed by Steve Jobs and Steve Wozniak called *Apple*. Some so-called "biblical scholars" stated because it was reported that Job's and Woziank's first computer sold for six hundred and sixty-six dollars, they claimed just as "the Apple" had been linked to Satan in the book of *Genesis*, computers were the "sign of the beast" because of the cost being the same *666* number that was described in the book of *Revelation*.

But inflation was still everyone's main concern in 1976, because although there was a slight increase in yearly income to almost ten thousand dollars a year, gasoline jumped to sixty cents a gallon, and the average housing price increased to forty-four thousand dollars.

Regardless of world events, the new generation of who had been recently labeled as *baby boomer's,* were controlling the culture in America with what was being looked at by many as hedonistic and self-serving lifestyles and caused Tom Wolfe to declare the 1970s as the *"Me Decade.""*

With the beginning of a new year in 1976, as many had always done in the past, it was also looked at as a new beginning and in some ways, a time to start over again.

Jason Mershon also felt he had brought closure to his first twenty-five years and would begin his next quarter-century in a strange city where he never pictured himself just a few months earlier.

The morning after he arrived in Dallas, Jason was having breakfast with his father in the *Holiday Inn* coffee shop, not far from the office on Mockingbird Lane.

His father had just been renting hotel rooms by the week during his time in Dallas, and he'd arranged another room for Jason to stay until he decided if he was going to stay longer and rent an apartment.

In the past two months since his Las Vegas party, Jason had pretty much felt inactive and isolated and even spent this twenty-fifth birthday alone at a *Denny's* in El Paso on his drive to Dallas. He had told less than a dozen friends that he was even leaving California and was surprised how eager he felt himself about leaving everything behind so quickly. Jason didn't even know how long he was planning on staying in Dallas but knew he needed something new and fresh to feel motivated again after the way everything turned out at *The Thunderbird* in Las Vegas.

"I've already got over three hundred news racks ready to be spread around the city with the National Singles Register," his father began explaining, "And I'm planning on having five hundred more in a couple of months between Dallas and Fort Worth."

"I'm telling you, there's a lot of money here in Texas," he added, "And I think a Texas edition can be as big here as it is in California."

Jason had tried to calculate a long time ago about the amount of money his father made off each news rack, but his father was always vague whenever Jason brought it up, and it was almost like a taboo to discuss.

"I'll need some time before I can get some current copy for the Dallas inserts," said Jason, "I'll have to spend the next couple weeks checking out the town and try and find the best spots to start setting up some parties."

"But I've also been thinking about what else there is for me to do with the newspaper going forward," Jason continued, "You and Vi are making money from the advertising, subscriptions, sales, and distribution, and the NSR has mainly been my vehicle for making money off my parties."

"I think I've done everything there is to do editorially with the newspaper, and its format is pretty much the same each issue now," Jason added, "But I don't feel I'm really part of the business anymore and the older singles who advertise for dates and want to get married, aren't really the market that makes me any money."

"I know that you've figured out that there's been some serious problems going on with Vi right now, but it should be temporary," his father said, "I'm still flying back to California a few times a month trying to get things worked out with her, so don't worry about it interfering with what you usually do."

"But once I get things organized here, I'll see what we can all work out together to get you more involved with the money," he added, "You've been a great promoter, and a well-known face for the newspaper, and Vi knows that you're still going to stay the editor and publisher."

Jason had heard all that before and was mainly focused on his future plans without being involved with his parents.

"Well, what I'd like to start doing is to add a bigger insert in each issue that will just focus on the singles who party at the nightclubs and discos," Jason continued, "It can almost be like a separate small newspaper inside each issue."

"But what I'd like to do is eventually do is turn that into a completely different publication that will cater to that party crowd," Jason added, "The disco singles scene is turning into the biggest thing in America right now, and I'd rather be an editor and publisher with my own magazine or newspaper that I'll actually own and fit with my singles market."

"Of course, I won't mind if you want to sell news racks to distribute it," Jason lightly smiled to his father, "That's your expertise, but I've decided that being a nightclub promoter is what I enjoy most and mainly going to focus on from now on."

"I understand why you want to branch out on your own, and that might be something we can talk about after Dallas," his father said, "But let me get things worked out with Vi first with some of the personal issues we have right now."

"That's fine," said Jason, "but I'll need to find some gimmick that can draw people right away seeing the paper isn't very well known here yet."

Jason still wasn't interested in knowing about his parent's personal problems and was just anxious to start working again. But he was still currently the editor and publisher of the *National Singles Register* and wanted to do what he needed to do to promote the newspaper until then.

After Jason went back to his hotel room alone, he started going through his yellow legal pads he had written down his notes and thoughts on how he could start fresh again.

Jason had decided that his *S.T.A.R.S.* party theme had been appropriate in Hollywood, Beverly Hills, and Las Vegas, but he wanted to think of a new name for a singles club that would have more of a universal flair.

The new name he decided on was the *World Entertainment Club*.

Jason knew he could always start local bachelorette and bachelor contests, dance contests, and his usual party mixers as another attraction tied to the newspaper as a starting point. But he also knew that having a celebrity name attached to any promotion always got him in the front door with nightclub owners.

Besides the *National Singles Register* not being that well known yet, no one in Dallas knew who Jason Mershon was either.

It was never a problem getting celebrities to either act as judges or just come to his parties in LA or Las Vegas because they were so common to the area, but Dallas was going to be tougher. Jason needed to find out when there were touring shows with some celebrities he had contacts, that would be passing through Dallas or Fort Worth, and then just invite them to what he was going to tell them were "local press parties" in their honor.

As he'd done in California and Las Vegas, he'd promise any celebrities publicity and press in the *National Singles Register* and possibly other local media by just attending his parties.

Jason had never met any celebrity or contest winner that didn't like seeing their names in the newspaper.

He had his notes and ideas, and now he just needed to get back to work.

❧

After the first week, Jason learned one of the most popular and trendy discos in Dallas was the *Number 3 Lift* on Northwest Highway and had spent a couple of nights at that disco just introducing himself to the club manager and employees trying to set up a meeting with the owners.

He had already learned that the owners and managers of the discos never minded giving up their door money or a percentage of the bar on weeknights if the promotions turned out to be a good deal for them as well.

Jason made sure the disco owners understood that he wouldn't make any money himself, unless it turned into a good promotion for the discos, and they made a good amount of money from all his promotion before he did.

He liked what he saw at that disco and that it was very busy both nights he attended and knew that advance in-house promotion was essential in helping him promote his own parties.

Jason also liked the people he met at the *Number 3 Lift* and saw they looked as attractive and dressed as well as any of the crowds he'd had in Beverly Hills or Las Vegas.

The popularity of disco's had seemingly started to "class-up" nightclubs everywhere and both the guys and girls were always groomed and dressed up to the max. The liquor laws were different in Texas and had something called the *Blue Law*, and the legal drinking age was only eighteen years old, which opened up even a larger audience for him. He also found in some ways, the Dallas girls seemed sexier and more attractive with their flirtatious Texas drawl. Plus, they also seemed to have matured faster, being able to start drinking legally at an earlier age.

Jason was standing at the bar at the *Number 3 Lift* watching the crowd on the dance floor when a cute blond he'd seen dancing earlier came to stand next to him.

"Hi there, I haven't seen you here before," she said in her Texas drawl, "Y'all from around here?"

After Jason introduced himself and found out her name was Candy Bradley, he figured now was as good as time as any to start recruiting some bachelorette contestants.

While he was having a drink with Candy at the bar, she called out to another very pretty brunette that was walking by.

"Hey, Melanie!" Candy called out, "Come on over here and meet Jason, he's from California!"

"Jason, this is Melanie Boston," Candy introduced them.

"Hi y'all," said Melanie with the same sexy and flirtatious twang.

Jason was starting to enjoy this and decided to start using his old charm by kissing her hand before inviting her to join them for a drink.

They were all on their second drinks together when Candy decided she wanted to dance.

"C'mon Jason," said Candy, "This is my favorite song; let's dance."

"Then I get the next dance," said Melanie.

The song was a current hit by The Who called *Squeeze Box*, and Candy suggestively sang along while they danced and gave slight pelvic thrusts while she sang the *"In and out"* parts of the chorus to the song.

Jason liked that she wasn't subtle about her intentions, and after dancing Melanie to her current favorite song, *Golden Years*, by David Bowie, Jason danced with them both to the song that everyone at the disco's loved advertising their intent, *Love to Love You Baby*, by Donna Summer.

It didn't take Jason long to realize that he was going to enjoy his time in Dallas and that nothing was better than disco music to get the fire started.

Jason knew he had nothing to feel guilty about and also didn't mind that he wouldn't even have to try and be discreet any longer, knowing he could have as much *fun* in Dallas as he wanted.

Chapter Two

Jason had discovered that Dallas was like a virgin city where having special parties or contests at nightclubs was a brand-new concept, and he was the only promoter in town.

When he had met with the owner of the *Number 3 Lift* a couple of months earlier and told him that the *National Singles Register*, the largest singles publication in America, was having a *"press party"* for the rock group *Blood Sweat and Tears*, and was looking for the right location to host that and future parties, the owner almost begged Jason to choose his nightclub.

Jason was able to set up his agreements for the entire door charge and fifteen percent of the gross bar receipts the night of his parties with no problem.

He had already learned that *Blood, Sweat, and Tears* would be performing at the *Fairmont Hotel* for a weekend and contacted David Clayton-Thomas about attending a *"press party"* in their honor.

Jason had met the lead singer David Clayton Thomas when he performed at *The Troubadour* a year earlier when David was trying to start a short-lived solo career before rejoining the band.

David Clayton-Thomas had always been one of Jason's favorite vocalists and always figured if he himself had a voice like David's, he'd been spending seven nights a week on stage doing nothing but singing full time.

When Jason met with him in the bar for cocktails at the *Fairmont Hotel* after the opening night concert in Dallas, they talked for about an hour about music and their previous connection.'

"I don't think anyone will sing a better version of *God Bless the Child* as you did on your first album," said Jason, "I was glad to hear you sing that song again tonight now that you're back with the band."

Jason then reminded him of the time they met at *The Troubadour*.

On that opening press night, David was the headliner, but Motown had filled the club with an audience that only came to support the opening act, a new singer named Minnie Ripperton that Motown was promoting heavy.

When Minnie Ripperton finished her set, almost everyone in the audience exited *The Troubadour*, and there were only about twenty people who stayed to watch David perform his big solo debut.

"You must have been pissed with it being opening press night and having no audience," Jason reminded him, "That was actually kind of rude for the Motown crowd not to even stay for your set."

"Nah, it didn't bother me," David said at first, but after thinking about it for a minute, lightly laughed, "Well, actually, it did really *piss me off!*"

"The problem was they didn't advertise me as David Clayton-Thomas, lead singer of Blood, Sweat, and Tears, who sang *Spinning Wheel, You Made Me So Very Happy* and the other hits," said David, "A lot of people just seem to know the name of the groups and not the band members, so my name just wasn't as well known by the general public then."

"That's why when I rejoined the band," he smiled, "It's now billed as David Clayton-Thomas and Blood, Sweat and Tears."

Jason told him of his own brief experience as the lead singer of *The Box Tops* and how no one even thought of asking about Alex Chilton.

"That's a perfect example," said David, "Just sing the hits they know, and the audience is happy."

Having a friendly conversation with David Clayton-Thomas was all it took to get him and the band to agree to attend a "press party in their honor" at the *Number 3 Lift* after one of their shows at the Fairmont.

It was also easier after he offered to make David the celebrity judge in the Dallas *Bachelorette of the Month* contest, and reminded the other band members of all the beautiful girls who would be at the party.

As he had always done, Jason handed out a few hundred free passes to his party, to every attractive girl he'd see while he was out promoting, and knew that always having a disco filled with beautiful women was the biggest draw to his parties.

Jason had used the same technique when he spoke with other celebrities, who were passing through Dallas with a touring show, and he had also worked a trade out for a limousine service to arrange limos to drive celebrities to and from his parties.

Limousines parked in front of the discos always made his press parties seem more official and glamourous, and Jason would also alternate between limos and his *450 SL Mercedes* himself.

Jason never mentioned to any celebrities that he was making a nice amount of money from the nightclub for being able to advertise that a famous personality would be attending the parties, but he always made sure they had fun and got the press in the *National Singles Register* he promised.

The Dallas crowd wasn't used to seeing famous celebrities socializing in discos, and they were much more excited about meeting a famous star in person than his crowds in LA or Vegas.

By early April, *World Entertainment Club* parties, the *National Singles Register*, and even his name quickly became the talk of Dallas, and Jason realized he was back in business better than ever.

&

The television reporter from *KDFW-TV* was standing by the *Number 3 Lift* front door while the cameraman was filming the reporter's news story.

"This is Van Dunn reporting from Dallas Texas, and tonight Jason Mershon, the editor and publisher of the *National Singles Register* as well as president of the *World Entertainment Club,* is hosting another one of his celebrity singles parties here at the *Number Three Lift*," the reporter was speaking into the camera, "Jason Mershon, who has been in Dallas only two months since moving his operations here from Beverly Hills California, has already hosted parties for such well-known celebrities as David Clayton Thomas and *Blood Sweat and Tears,* the legendary rock group *Chicago*, Breck Wall producer of the smash musical revue, *Bottom's Up,* and James Drury, star of TV show *The Virginian*."

Van Dunn then told the cameraman to "Cut" after he decided to continue his next voiceover inside the *Number 3 Lift* filming the crowd dancing.

"Tonight, Jason is hosting a party for rock music superstar Joe Cocker, and Joe will be joining us a little bit later, but first, we're going to be talking with Jason about the *National Singles Register* and his parties……"

During one of the breaks in filming with his cameraman, Van Dunn, the reporter at his Joe Cocker press party that night, explained to Jason that he was shooting four rolls of 16-millimeter magnetic film, which were five minutes long each.

"We're only usually to shoot about twenty minutes of film of an event like this," explained Van Dunn, "But that's usually enough to edit down for a good one-minute segment on the news station."

"You know, I heard the news stations in Los Angeles are starting to use something called *videotape* now," said Jason, "Video is supposed to be easier to edit than film and also gets a lot more footage to use."

"Well, we're not LA," laughed Van, "Maybe in five years we might catch up."

While he waited for Joe Cocker to arrive, Van Dunn wanted to include an interview with Jason for all the *who, what, where, when, and why's* about Jason's future plans.

Jason was sitting a booth inside the disco with both Candy and Melanie after Van Dunn said it made for a more colorful shot for filming having two sexy girls in the frame.

During the interview, Jason tried to include as many selling points as possible about the *National Singles Register* and how everyone could learn about the parties and get a free membership in the *World Entertainment Club* by just buying a current copy from the hundreds of news racks throughout Dallas.

Jason also wanted to come across like the main spokesperson for singles by reminding any politicians who may see that night's news story, that as it was a presidential election year, not to forget about how important the singles market was, and how much they contributed to the economy.

Jason ended up talking through over two rolls of the film and didn't know how much would end up being edited on the news, but he wanted to at least sound like he was more than just a *party guy*.

"Jeez, I never thought you were going to stop talking!" Van Dunn sarcastically laughed after the interview, "I hope I have enough film left to talk to Joe Cocker."

As soon as the interview was completed, Jason headed out to his limousine to go pick up Joe Cocker at the main concert venue in Dallas, *Memorial Auditorium*.

Jason already knew about what time Joe's concert would end and wanted to make sure he got him in the limo to take him directly back to his party at the *Number 3 Lift*.

By 1976, Joe Cocker had become notorious for his drunken antics onstage, and it was often advised "not to sit in the front row" at a Joe Cocker concert, because he was known to vomit into the audience. Because Jason had an overflow crowd at the disco that night and was also getting his first Dallas television news coverage, he wanted to make sure there were no distractions that would keep Joe Cocker from making his appearance as he had advertised.

Jason's limo pulled almost directly backstage through the underground garage and arrived right about the time Joe was singing his last song *With a Little Help from My Friends*.

When he walked off stage, Jason could see Joe Cocker could barely walk straight, and some of the band members had the same looks on their faces as Jason remembered the other members of *The Doors* had when Jim Morrison was also obviously wasted and drunk.

Jason just led Joe and his road manager into the limo and hoped he'd make it back the disco before Joe passed out and who was still guzzling from a bottle of whiskey from the limo's bar supply when they pulled up to the *Number 3 Lift* entrance.

He could see Van Dunn and the TV cameraman aiming the camera at the limo to get shots of Joe Cocker entering as a wall-to-wall crowd of party-goers were also anxious to see the arrival.

As Joe stumbled out of the limo, Jason had to almost carry him through the front door, hoping he wouldn't vomit as the crowd was cheering, and the camera was rolling.

Jason was relieved when he finally was able to sit Joe at a table inside where he wouldn't fall down, but even though Joe was a mess, Jason at least got him to the party as he'd advertised to keep his own reputation intact.

"I don't think you're going to be able to get a comprehensible interview with Joe Cocker tonight," Jason laughed when he saw Van Dunn, "Hopefully, you've got some good footage earlier."

"Hey, this looks even cooler," laughed Van, "It shows a slice of real-life that no one usually gets to see up close… a drunk and wasted superstar!"

With the TV cameras there, Jason knew he was probably getting as much publicity for the newspaper and his parties in that one night as it took him months to get in California.

Instead of a small fish is in a big pond like Los Angeles or Las Vegas, suddenly Jason felt like Dallas might be a good place to spend at least a few more months.

Chapter Three

Ever since the Joe Cocker party had gotten so much media coverage, nightclubs all over Dallas were giving Jason great offers to host parties at their nightclubs.

KDFW-TV regularly had TV cameras with either Van Dunn or another reporter named Bob Phillips, covering his Sunday night celebrity parties, and Jason was always trying to find new ways to keep each party different and newsworthy and something fun them to report.

He had also talked with Art Wilde at *Paramount Pictures* about arranging some advance movie screenings in Dallas for his *World Entertainment Club* members and possibly planning some premiers with some of the films' stars.

Being a newspaper editor as well, the producer of entertainment events in Dallas allowed Jason to have enough juice even to have local politicians running for office attend his parties looking for press and endorsements for their campaigns.

He had some judges, city councilmen, and two candidates for mayor, Gerry Weber, and the eventual winner, Robert Folsom, who would always say something good on the TV cameras about the *National Singles Register* or Jason's parties.

If he didn't have a major celebrity one week, Jason had become good friends with a popular Dallas radio DJ named Gary Fox and would have him as at least act as a celebrity emcee for his beauty contests as he had with Bill Ballance.

Although he'd only been away from California for less than three months and he missed some of his friends, he was feeling more comfortable where he was, and even started feeling that Dallas might turn out to be his permanent home.

Jason had rented a luxury two-bedroom townhouse in Dallas for the same price he had been paying for his smaller one-bedroom apartment in Beverly Hills and even had a new circle of friends to help him promote his parties and would spend time with them almost every day.

Jason was overseeing the production of the *National Singles Register* by phone and always hoped someone besides his mother would answer the phone when he called the office because she was always complaining about some employee or writer, just so she would sound like she was in charge. Both newspapers were being published every two weeks as they had always been with no problem, and it was irritating to always listen to her complaining.

Jason regularly mailed his *Message from the Publisher*, along with enough copy and photos for an eight-page Dallas insert featuring *World Entertainment Club* parties, and had also already included four Texas *Bachelorettes of the Week* as cover girls to go with his backlog of bachelorettes in California.

His father was only in Dallas about ten days out the month, but Jason rarely saw him at all anymore. But he did tell Jason he was still considering opening up a full-time production office in Dallas for a statewide edition of the *National Singles Register* and *The Explorer*.

Jason tried to call his friends in California regularly, but his phone calls were becoming less frequent than when he first came to Dallas.

Annie Gaybis, Mixie Ritz, and some other friends would tell Jason about some movie roles they were filming, and Lita Krissan's big news was that she'd moved to Malibu into a converted oceanfront apartment from a house that once belonged to Otto Preminger.

While Jason occasionally talked to Lori in New York, she said *Let My People Come* was still playing Off-Broadway at a theatre in Greenwich Village, but was scheduled to open at the Morosco Theatre on Broadway that summer. Although they continued acting as if nothing had changed between them, neither of them really talked about when they might see each other again.

Jason was surprised how quickly he was forgetting about his previous life and did sometimes feel like he was now living in a completely different world, which seemed much more relaxed and, surprisingly, much more gratifying.

The press and publicity were great, the money was great, and he also had nothing to complain about with his love life.

There was just something about the Texas girls that seemed more real and attractive than all the "actresses and models" he'd become accustomed for the past five years.

Dallas was like a constant thunderstorm, and he was being hit with some form of "The Thunderbolt" by someone different at least once a week.

Everyone seemed to be going to the discos every night to "just to get laid" and no one seemed interested in finding a steady girlfriend or boyfriend. Some of Jason's new friends in Dallas would facetiously joke about the current culture, "The only good thing about having a wife or a girlfriend is that you've always got someone to cheat on," and Jason saw how the girls in the discos seemed to feel the same way.

The disco culture was centered around casual sex as much as it was in LA and Las Vegas, and that segment of the singles lifestyle was definitely in full swing.

While the *National Singles Register* still was dominated with personal ads for those who were seriously looking for a *"that one special person"* and marriage, Jason's eight-page *World Entertainment Club* insert in Dallas was all about his parties and the disco scene, and he felt he at least had a somewhat separate newspaper he could eventually expand upon.

Although Jason did have some casual flings, he never really considered himself to be *"volume fucking"* and still liked having at least one he considered a part-time girlfriend.

Martha Bland was someone Jason had met away from the disco scene he had been seeing at least once a week for over two months. When he first began seeing her regularly, Jason teased Martha and said that he should *"marry her just for a week"* to allow her to change her last name because the name *"Bland"* didn't fit her at all.

Although she didn't have the outward sexiness as the girls who were always made up and dressed to the max in the discos, Martha had a certain sensual look and attitude about her that immediately attracted Jason.

Martha had recently graduated college and was more interested in a regular business career than partying in the discos every night, but she also had a cocky Texas girl attitude that Jason liked. She also had a regular day job, and although Jason did bring Martha along to a couple of his parties, she didn't even seem that impressed with the celebrity and glamourous aspects of what Jason was doing with the *World Entertainment Club*, and most of their dates were away from discos.

Most of the time they spent together was having dinner or going to a movie, which Jason always joked was something the *"ordinary singles"* who read the *National Singles Register* liked to spend their time doing.

"I need to associate with all my readers, and it's fun to just go on normal *'bland'* dates sometimes," Jason would joke to Martha.

Although Jason didn't want to be as flippant as his friends and joke that he at least had *"someone to cheat on"* by having a girlfriend in Dallas, he also wasn't seeing Martha every night and knew he wasn't a Monk.

He was still the *Singles Guy* and had an image to maintain.

Chapter Four

Bob Phillips, another *KDFW-TV* news reporter, was with the cameraman filming the final segment of one of Jason's parties and was outside filming Jason and over a half-dozen bachelorettes who had been in his contest that night, leaning on his *450 SL Mercedes* for his closing report as he was walking past them.

"A lot's been said about what goes on at Jason's parties." Bob said into the camera as he glanced at Jason and the bachelorettes, "But one thing is certain… Jason's parties never end, do they, girls?"

The bachelorettes surrounding Jason then gave a sexy and inviting response, *"Noooo, the parties never end,"* to the television viewers watching that news segment, which Jason knew was better advertising for his parties than any print or radio ads.

At another party, at a nightclub called After the *Gold Rush*, Bob Phillips was already inside, waiting for Jason to arrive and started filming Jason's entrance with his circle of friends, as he started his narrative as the group walked by the cameraman.

"Here comes Jason Mershon and his *entourage* now," said Bob Phillips, "Maybe we can get a chance to talk to him about his upcoming parties."

Bob then tried to get Jason to announce on camera the name and location of the *"secret* private party" he would be hosting for a rock music superstar.

Jason said he "couldn't reveal the name" of the superstar, but coyly sang the word, *"Yester-day"* and teased it was a secret and he couldn't say.

"He does have '*Wings,*' I understand," Bob lightly teased back, as if they weren't talking about Paul McCartney.

Jason figured if those types of teasers didn't want to make people buy the *National Singles Register* and come to the parties, then nothing would.

Paul McCartney had been spending several weeks in Dallas rehearing with his band *Wings* for his first American concert since The Beatles in 1966, which would premiere at the Tarrant County Convention Center in Fort Worth.

Jason knew it would be a real coup and could probably double his door charge and get an extra ten percent of the bar receipts if he could arrange a press party for McCartney and *Wings*.

He also knew he always needed something bigger and better to solidify his reputation as "throwing the best parties" in Dallas.

Jason was able to contact Trevor Jones, the tour manager for *Wings* at the *Le Baron Hotel* in Dallas. Jason explained Paul would know him from the Oscars a couple of years earlier when he was with Bianca Jagger at the afterparty.

Evidently, Paul did remember, because Trevor called Jason back and said he could come to one of the "*secret locations*" in Fort Worth where Paul and the band were rehearsing.

Trevor drove Jason to an out of the way auditorium where a small group was watching *Wings* going through a rehearsal on a small stage.

Trevor told Jason to "just sit with the others," and he'd have a chance to talk about a "press party" after rehearsals.

Jason was barely thinking about the press party as he sat in awe, watching what was almost like a private concert sitting next to the stage.

Although Jason always tried to act cool and not star stuck around the big celebrities he met, this was '*Paul McCartney*' on stage singing *Yesterday*, *Lady Madonna*, and *Maybe I'm Amazed* just a few feet from him.

It was much different than when he'd briefly talked to Paul at the Oscars, and it was as big of a deal, if not bigger, than when he had the chance to meet Elvis.

Jason watched over an hour of rehearsal before the band took a break, and Jason was able to talk to Paul and some band members briefly.

"Of course, I remember meeting you," said Paul after Jason reintroduced himself, "What are you doing in Texas?"

Jason recalled how Ronald Reagan was more than likely fibbing a bit when he claimed to remember meeting Jason when he was young, and even though Paul claimed to remember him as well, if Paul was fibbing as he felt Reagan had, either way, was fine with Jason.

That brief meeting at *The Oscars* was somehow paying off two years later.

Jason then mentioned the "press parties" he was hosting, and even though Paul said he and Linda probably couldn't attend, Trevor and several band members said they would stop in at his next party.

Jason was disappointed that Paul McCartney wouldn't commit to attending, but the commitment from the other band members, including Denny Laine, who had once been a member of *The Moody Blues*, was enough to at least let Jason tease Bob Phillips during the interview about it being a "secret party" for Paul McCartney and Wings.

He never had to mention that Paul McCartney himself might not be attending and decided it wasn't *BS*, but just good old-fashioned *promotion*.

Jason had come to know that advertising and promotion were all basically *a little BS* in almost every business. Everything always had to sound *bigger and better*, or no one would even care.

Jason's party crowd still thought it was impressive when Trevor and most of the *Wings* band members, along with about a dozen groupies, did come to his next party and ended up judging his bachelorette contest.

He at least come through with what he *teased*, and his parties continued to grow in size each week.

～

Jason's parties were making him almost twice as much as his parties in California ever had, and besides the publicity for both the *National Singles Register* and the *World Entertainment Club*, the local media was making Jason a type of personality himself.

He had parties every Sunday night, and they had turned into almost a regular weekly feature on the Sunday night news broadcasts with the television cameras always there.

The other reporter from KDFW-TV, Van Dunn, covered the majority of Jason's parties, and he began referring to Jason as "getting a reputation as a modern-day *Gatsby*," or he'd ask Jason, "How he managed to always be surrounded by beautiful women?" or, "If he considered himself the Hugh Hefner of the South?" because Jason was also a famous editor and publisher.

Jason was getting himself out there to the media even more than he had in California, wanting to project whatever he was promoting confidently. But he did notice when he saw the news footage, he was starting to come across as a little *cocky and overblown* and knew he needed to tone down his *confidence* level a bit.

"Damn, that guy talking on TV sounds like a real dick!" Jason laughed to Martha Bland about himself as they watched the latest news segment of him being interviewed by Van Dunn.

"Yeah, everything is *Jason Mershon* is doing this or *Jason Mershon* is doing that," teased Martha, "They're making you and your parties sound like the greatest thing since *Texas barbeque*, and you look like you're eating it up."

"It's just a little showbiz," Jason smiled with a little embarrassment, "I've only got a few seconds on camera each week, and I want to any future business contacts to see how successful everything is going and how fun everything is as well."

"All advertising and promotion are exaggerated a bit," Jason tried to justify, "It's just bringing the Hollywood attitude to Dallas."

"Yeah, I get it, but Texas isn't Hollywood," said Martha, "Maybe you shouldn't make it look like you're boasting about it so much."

"There's a thin line between confidence and arrogance," Martha added more seriously, "So if you're trying to get people to like you, remember that envy can quickly turn into resentment."

But Jason couldn't help but feeling a little *cocky*. Just five months earlier, after his Las Vegas party, he felt like he'd lost his motivation, and now he felt he was more motivated than ever before.

1976 was definitely turning into his best year ever and he felt great.

Chapter Five

The week after Memorial Day, the owner of a new disco called *Bogie's* had paid Jason an additional fee to promote his grand opening with a *World Entertainment Club* party that also attracted the usual TV cameras and a big crowd.

Jason decided to host his first *Bachelor of the Month* to see if it went over as good in Dallas as it had in California. However, the owner of *Bogie's* and most of the men Jason talked with felt it would look "too homo" to have the men in swimsuits, so Jason just had them dressed in suits the way he had originally in California.

Van Dunn did come to *Bogie's* to cover his new concept of beauty contests for men, but Van also had something else he wanted to talk to Jason about.

"I ran into a guy at a restaurant who recognized me from covering your parties," said Van, "He was asking me if everything is on the up and up with the *National Singles Register* and said he invested some money in the newspaper."

"I told him I'd be here tonight covering this party," Van continued, "So I just wanted to let you know he might be coming down tonight to talk to you."

Jason had no idea what Van was talking about.

Although his father had talked about setting up a separate operation in Dallas, nothing had been discussed about it recently. Jason hadn't even seen his father in over three weeks and never had a reason to go to the small office on Mockingbird Lane. He preferred just working out of his townhouse and was sending in the news copy for the Dallas inserts to California without even needing to see his father.

"I haven't talked to any investors about anything," Jason told Van, "So I don't know anything about that, but let me know if you see him, and I'll talk to him and find out."

There was a crowd of over five hundred at *Bogie's* that night. The majority were women who ended up having an even wilder reaction to seeing the men compete than the women in California had, even though they weren't even in swimsuits.

"It was just another fantastic *Jason Mershon* and *World Entertainment Club* party here in Dallas tonight," Jason saw Van Dunn speaking into the news camera as he finished his filming for the night.

Jason smiled at the usual hyperbole Van Dunn always added to his news coverage, and almost felt like he had a free full-time press agent working for him.

It wasn't until after midnight when Jason saw someone trying to make his way through the crowd and approaching him who he thought he recognized, but couldn't quite place.

"Hi Jason, it's Mark," he said, "We met late last year when you flew into Dallas from LA, remember?"

"Do you have a few minutes to talk outside?" Mark added in his friendly Texas drawl.

Jason then remembered him as one of the three guys his father had once wanted him to meet and walked outside, figuring Mark was the one that Van Dunn was talking about.

Mark was friendly and commented how great he thought that night's party was, and had been enjoying seeing the coverage of the parties on television, but said he also had a couple of concerns.

"I just wanted to know how long it would be before you move the entire business operation here to Dallas," he asked, "Your brother said it would be set up by summer, but we haven't heard from Dick in almost a month."

Jason was immediately irritated that his father was saying he was his brother again but also wondered why Mark would have thought the entire *operation* was moving.

"Well, Dick talked to me about setting up an office here for distribution and a separate Texas edition," Jason said, "But nothing was discussed about moving the entire operation here."

"Well, you know I did pay Dick twenty-five thousand dollars for a piece of the *National Singles Register* and *The Explorer*," Mark added, "And I know that Ed and Dave also invested some money with him."

"You're the owner, so I thought I'd check with you to see what's going on," Mark said, still smiling, "We just need to know that everything is still on schedule."

Jason didn't want to sound completely clueless and didn't feel like talking about something he knew nothing about, and just tried to put off the conversation until the next day.

"Well, let me talk to Dick tomorrow and find out for you," Jason tried to say in a natural and friendly tone, "I've been busy promoting these parties and have been preoccupied, but I'll call you by tomorrow afternoon."

Jason got Mark's business card and immediately knew he was going to have to get up early the next day and start investigating what was going on.

He was suddenly pissed not only because his great mood had dissipated, but also because he knew it wasn't a good night to take someone home and get laid.

His *"fantastic World Entertainment Club party"* wasn't going to have its usual fantastic ending that night.

❧

Jason tried calling the *Holiday Inn* his father usually stayed by eight am the next morning, but when the desk clerk said he hadn't checked in recently, Jason drove to the office on Mockingbird Lane.

His father only used the office a few days a month and said he mainly set it up for meetings so it "would look better" than meeting in a hotel coffee shop.

Jason started getting concerned when he found the office was locked and noticed that some items that were usually inside looked like they'd been removed and immediately knew that something didn't feel right.

He knew it was too early to call the office in California and didn't want to call his mother at home, so he waited till eleven am before he called her at work.

"I haven't talked to Dick in over a week, and I thought he was with you in Dallas," his mother said over the phone, "But there's been nothing discussed about moving the offices up there, so I don't know in the fuck you're talking about."

Jason tried to explain that he didn't know what was going on either, but she didn't seem to believe him.

"Is Joy up there with you?" his mother suddenly asked accusingly, "She quit last week, and I know you've been fucking her, so don't lie to me!"

"I don't know what you're talking about!" Jason argued back, "I don't have anything going on with her."

"I know all about you and Joy," his mother yelled back, "Dick told me everything!"

From what he could understand from what his mother was yelling, she had seen Dick and Joy together at a coffee shop near the office a couple of months earlier.

"Dick said Joy was upset because you had broken up with her to go back to Lori," his mother continued, "He said he was trying to console her and not have her quit the newspapers."

That sounded like the most ridiculous story Jason had ever heard but listened silently as she continued her rant.

"He even made me promise not to ever mention anything to Lori about it so I wouldn't get you into trouble," his mother sarcastically added, "So was that all just a bunch of bullshit!?"

Jason was becoming angry as he started to realize what had been going on.

Not only did his father probably have the relationship with Joy he'd always suspected, but he had been using Jason as a cover story to his mother.

"Well, I'm gonna find out what's going on!" is all Jason said when his mother finished her rant.

"I'm going to find out too!" she yelled again. "I knew you'd find some way to fuck things up just like you always have!"

After he heard his mother slam down the phone, Jason had no idea why she had added that last remark but was too pissed to worry about it.

He was more concerned about the entire situation and knew he needed to find out where his father was.

Jason called the home phone number he had for Joy in California and became even more concerned when it was disconnected, but he didn't know anyone else he could call and just decided to sit by the phone for the next few hours and hoped it would eventually ring with some answers.

Jason did get a half dozen phone calls but was only from his friends wanting to talk about "the next party" and "getting together later," and he tried not to sound like anything was wrong. He knew that regardless of any current problems, he still had responsibilities and needed to take care of his *World Entertainment Club* business in Dallas.

He also knew he needed to call Mark as he'd promised and try to find a way to stall him until he knew the situation.

"Hi Mark, it's Jason Mershon," he tried to into the phone with his friendly tone, "Dick is still in California trying to tie up some loose ends, and it's going to be a few weeks before I can get any firm dates about anything that's going to happen here."

"But I'm sure it won't be until after the Fourth of July," Jason said, "So we'll talk in a few weeks, and I should have a definite answer for you then, okay?"

Jason was relieved when Mark said, "That sounds good," and after hanging up the phone, he just hoped he would have some answers by then himself.

It was around five pm before he got a call back from his mother.

"All right, you son of a bitch!" she yelled into the phone, "Where's the money?!"

"What are you talking about!?" Jason yelled back.

"One of the bank accounts has been cleaned out!" she yelled, "What the fuck have you two been doing up there and what's going on!?"

"Well, it's not me!" Jason yelled back, "I don't even know what bank accounts you guys have, so don't start trying to accuse me of anything!"

"You lying bastard!" she yelled before again, hanging up on him.

Jason called right back, but she just picked up the phone and said, "Fuck You!" before hanging up again.

When he tried again ten minutes later, another girl who worked in the office picked up the phone and just said, "Vi doesn't want to talk to you," before also hanging up on him.

Jason only had one thought as he sat alone for the next hour and again found himself talking aloud.

"This is going to be a problem," he said to himself.

Chapter Six

For the next several days, Jason tried to carry on, hoping something would miraculously happen that would clear everything up and become normal again, but it wasn't looking good. His mother would call him and yell something into his phone at least twice a day and hang up before he could say anything, and she wouldn't respond to any of his calls.

Some of the things besides the obscenities he heard his mother yell into the phone, was "Don't send me anything from Dallas!", "The paper is done in Dallas!" and finally, "You're done here too, so just stay in Dallas!"

But even worse was that he heard nothing from his father.

Jason didn't know anyone in California or Las Vegas that his father ever associated with, so he didn't have any idea how to reach him.

He knew he still had to appear completely normal to everyone he knew in Dallas and couldn't let on that there were any problems.

Jason did have some parties that he was committed to producing the next two Sundays, but decided to be on the safe side, not to have any *Bachelor* or *Bachelorette* contests, or even mention the *National Singles Register* in his next two promotions.

He still needed to make money and began wondering if there was a way to make a clean break for being an editor and publisher for a while, and strictly make the *World Entertainment Club* his only business in Dallas.

Jason was still concerned about straightening things out with Mark before he made any more long-range plans and called Mark to see if he heard from his father, but when Mark said he hadn't heard anything, Jason decided it was time to try and deflect any responsibility away from himself.

"Listen, Mark," Jason calmly tried to explain, "Dick was the one in charge of the distribution and news racks only, which is completely separate from the newspaper itself."

"So, any side deals you made with him," Jason also calmly added, "You'll really just need to talk with him about."

"Listen, Jason, Dick has always said that you're the owner, and he just worked for you," "Mark began speaking in a less friendly tone, "Now one of you guys must be lying, or something here is starting to stink."

"We just want to either get our piece of the business or better yet," Mark continued in a more threatening voice, "Just give us our god damned money back!"

"I think between the three of us, Dick got sixty-grand," Mark added with a bit of disgust.

Jason couldn't believe that his father had gotten that much money, but knew the last thing he wanted to do was argue with Mark and sound panicked.

He also knew he needed to buy some time.

"Okay," Jason tried to calmly say, "I just know that I won't be seeing Dick till after the Fourth of July, so I'll just tell him whatever deal he had with you is off."

"And I'll get the checks back to all of you after that," Jason tried to add with confidence.

"At his point, that sounds like the most-friendly way to handle this," said Mark in a friendlier but sarcastic tone, "Just give us our money back, and there's no hard feelings."

"Sounds good to me," Jason tried to say with a friendly tone, "And sorry about the misunderstanding."

As soon as Jason hung up the phone, he felt his hands shaking and his chest pounding.

Hearing that his father had left town with *sixty thousand dollars* was shocking enough, but having Mark think that Jason could return that large amount of money so easily was making him panic even more. He was also thinking about how much money his father, and even his mother, had been probably making all this time off the *National Singles Register* and the distribution.

Jason knew he needed to tell them to get that money back immediately or at least convince Mark that he wasn't involved with that part of the business.

He tried to call his mother again at her house, but when she heard his voice, she just said, *"Fuck you!"* and again hung up the phone.

Jason knew if he called back, he'd get a busy tone from her taking the phone off the hook as she always did, so he didn't even bother and just sat alone for several hours thinking about what he was going to do.

He couldn't believe that his father would just take off and basically *throw him under the bus without* a word. But the more he thought about it, the less it surprised him.

They had never been close as a family and it was the same with his mother. The only difference now was, instead of having an emotionless relationship, the emotion of hate was quickly taking over the way Jason felt towards both of them.

He also hated that everything he had set up in Dallas was in jeopardy and hated the thought of having to suddenly leave town until things with Mark were straightened out.

It also appeared he had nothing to go back to in either California or Las Vegas and finally realized what he needed to do first.

He needed some *getaway money.*

On June 27th, the week before the Bicentennial, Jason was at *Bogies Disco*, promoting a press preview of what he billed as the "Biggest and Most Extravagant Beauty Contest Ever Conceived in Dallas!" on his posters and flyers.

He called it *The Sexiest Girl in Dallas Contest*.

Jason had tried to make his previous two parties without the National Singles Register's name attached, seem wilder to separate himself from the normal singles theme and try something new that would attract a big crowd and make some quick money.

Since those parties had seemed to go over so well, Jason had set up a marathon of beauty pageants to be presented over eight consecutive nights at eight different nightclubs in Dallas, including the *Number 3 Lift, Bogie's, Carlo's and Pepe's, Bob Lilly's Other Place* and *Oz Disco* which would begin in two weeks, July 11th through July 18th.

To attract contestants, Jason arranged through a girl he knew at a travel agency to buy a trip for two to Paris for around five hundred dollars and would also give the winner two hundred and fifty dollars in cash.

By far, it was the biggest prize Jason ever offered in one of his contests and knew it would be impressive and draw attention. He then offered each nightclub manager the opportunity to host one of the preliminaries for what he pitched as a "low cost of only five hundred dollars", and got the manager at the trendy *OZ Disco* to pay him seven hundred and fifty dollars to host the city finals.

Jason would choose three finalists at each nightclub preliminary, and so he'd have twenty-one contestants for his finals at *OZ*, which he knew would be the draw the biggest audience.

He figured after expenses, and with the money he already had in the bank, he should have over five thousand dollars to take back to California and regroup. He had also decided to tell everyone he needed to go back to California for a few weeks and wanted to produce something big and extravagant before he *temporarily* had to attend to other business, and planned on leaving town the Monday after his finals of the *Sexiest Girl in Dallas Contest* on July 19.

Jason had arranged for over thirty contestants to be at his press preview to receive some outside press over the next two weeks, knowing that nothing would be mentioned about his contest in the *National Singles Register*.

Van Dunn did come down to *Bogies Disco* that night for the press preview, but told Jason he wasn't there for a "fluff piece" as he'd always done, but wanted to talk about the "Sexiest Girl Contest" as being controversial.

Jason just said "whatever works" as he sat down in front of the camera for his interview and didn't really care about how Van wanted to cover his contest for the news and just wanted everything to go smooth for the next couple weeks and appear that everything was continuing as it normally had.

"Jason, you've had the Most Kissable Lips Contest, the Miss Flimsy Negligee Contest, and now you have the Sexiest Girl in Dallas Contest," said Van as he began filming the interview, "What are you trying to do, destroy the Bible Belt?"

Jason couldn't believe that Van Dunn opened up the interview with that question and wondered why he wanted to make a big deal out of a sexy girl contest.

"The words *sex* or *sexiest* gives the connotation of something immoral," Van continued seriously, "Do you think a contest like this is something Dallas is ready for?"

"Sexy is just an adjective like pretty or cute," Jason tried to say lightly into the camera, "I don't see anything wrong with it, and as you can see, we have plenty of contestants here tonight who don't mind it either."

Van Dunn continued asking questions about possible protesters from Women's Lib groups and whether Jason's new sexy contests meant his so-called *straight and clean* newspaper was turning into a *"swinging singles"* publication.

Jason tried not to sound flustered and gave what he thought were logical answers to other questions he didn't expect. But then when Van asked him if he had a personal interest in learning who the sexiest girl in Dallas was, Jason briefly got cocky and said, "Yeah, I'd like to find the sexiest girl myself and spend some time with her."

Van then interviewed some of the contestants who would be entering the contest, asking them "what the word sex meant to them" and seemed to take pleasure in asking them to bend over a little and "give us a butt shot" for the camera.

When Van was through filming, Jason went over to talk to him.

"Jeez Van, what was that all about?" Jason tried to lightly laugh, "You trying to make the contest sound scandalous?"

"I can't just do fluff stories on you all the time, and those last couple contests you promoted, weren't your typical World Entertainment Club parties," Van tried to justify, "A little controversy is good for the news, especially if you're starting to change your party formats into something more risque."

"This is still the Bible Belt, and it might be good to make you out as a bad boy," Van added, trying to lighten his seriousness, "I don't think it'll hurt your image cause the girls love that kind of stuff."

While they were talking, one of the girls who was planning on entering the contest walked over to Jason and Van.

"Jason, my boyfriend, said the way they were just filming us and talking about your contest sounds too nasty," she said with disappointment, "He doesn't want me to be involved with it anymore."

"Just tell him that stuff was just hype, and the contest won't be anything dirty," Jason tried to joke.

"I'm sorry, but he said he'd shoot you and me both if I enter the sexiest girl contest," she joked with regret, "So I'm not going to be a contestant."

When she left, Jason just shook his head at Van.

"Brother, can you believe that and see what you started?" Jason lightly scolded Van.

"Hey, death threats!" Van lightly teased, "There's a good hook to add some controversy."

"Don't even go there and try and exaggerate anything like that," Jason half laughed, "I want to have my reputation intact when I come back from California, so don't try to make this contest sound so bad."

Even though Jason hoped the sexiest girl contest wouldn't be his last promotion in Dallas, and he'd eventually be able to come back, he wanted to make sure that his swan song was successful just in case it was.

કે

It was the week before his marathon of contests was to begin, and Jason was promoting and passing out flyers with some friends at the *Oz Disco*.

"Damn, it's supposed to rain all day in Dallas tomorrow," said one of his friends, "That's going to ruin a lot of the big celebrations that have been planned all year."

The following day was the Bicentennial, and extravagant celebrations had been planned across America for months.

"That's too bad," Jason said unconcerned, "I was looking forward to seeing a great firework's show."

As they were all drinking at the bar, Jason felt like he had a million thoughts going through his head about everything else that had been happening for the past month.

He hadn't told anyone about the problems he was going through and had been acting like everything was great as usual with his friends. But inside, his mind had been so preoccupied with what he was going to do when he left Dallas in two weeks, now that it was obvious that his father wasn't coming back to give Mark back his money. Jason knew besides being done with the *National Singles Register* he was also done with both his parents for good this time.

The DJ at *Oz* was spinning the older disco song Jason had always liked *Get Down Tonight*, and suddenly he began picturing himself back where he was a year earlier when that song was first popular, along with what he was doing the last Fourth of July.

"I'll be right back," he told his friends at the bar when the song was over.

Jason went to the payphone and decided to called *American Airlines*.

562

"What's the last flight going out of Dallas tonight that can get me to New York City by tomorrow morning?" he asked the reservation clerk, "and then get a flight back to Dallas on July fifth."

He knew it was a crazy idea, but there wasn't anything he was scheduled to do the next day in Dallas, and just had a sudden urge to want to see Lori Wagner.

It wasn't because of any strong romantic feelings, because they both knew those days were probably over, but Jason just needed to be with someone he felt he still had a close enough bond that he could talk to about everything, even if it was only for a day.

Most importantly, he needed someone to share his feelings.

Chapter Seven

"Do you want me to drive you by the 'Tall Ships Parade' on the Hudson?" asked the cabbie as he pulled the flag down on his meter and drove away from La Guardia Airport, "It's the biggest thing going on for the Bicentennial in the city today, and you really should see it."

Jason had been flying all night and was exhausted and wanted to get five or six hours of sleep before he did anything.

"No thanks, just take me to the *Plaza Hotel*," he told the cabbie.

Jason figured as this was his first big trip as an adult to New York City, he'd stay somewhere with style. He'd read about *The Plaza* in so many novels and heard it often mentioned in movies, so he decided to experience it for himself.

Plus, Lori had told Jason after she moved to New York that she was going to be living at Bob Guccione's Penthouse mansion on East 67th Street, so he knew he wouldn't be able to stay there.

He also wanted to be refreshed when he popped into the *Village Gate Theatre* later that evening, after deciding not to tell Lori he was even coming to New York, and to surprise her during her performance of *Let My People Come.*

As Jason glanced out the window of the taxi as they drove past Central Park, and then pulled in the driveway at *The Plaza*, he convinced himself he'd made the right decision about coming to New York.

He had been barely able to sleep at all in Dallas with everything he had on his mind, and five or six hours in complete solitude would feel like the most sleep he'd had in a month. Hopefully, getting away from everything for at least twenty-four hours would clear his head.

After he did sleep for several hours, Jason arrived in Greenwich Village only a few minutes before the musical was scheduled to begin and gave the hostess at the *Village Gate* five dollars to be seated as close to the stage as possible.

It wasn't until almost ten minutes into the performance before Lori made eye contact with Jason, almost losing her place in the song with a shocked expression, but she quickly recovered and continued to smile and make eye contact with Jason several more times during the rest of the performance.

Let My People Come only varied slightly from when he saw it at the *Whiskey-a-GoGo*, and Jason was already familiar with most of the *dirty songs*, but he was mainly impressed with how professional and talented Lori had become on stage since he last saw her.

After the curtain calls, Jason remained at his table to wait for Lori, and it took less than two minutes before she rushed to his table with a few other cast members and hugged him.

"You are such a crazy guy, and I can't believe you are actually here!" Lori excitedly laughed, "Why didn't you tell me you were coming?"

"Surprise, surprise!" Jason smiled as he gave Lori another hug and shook hands with the other cast members.

"This is Jason, my boyfriend from LA," smiled Lori as she introduced him, "Jason is always full of surprises."

"You won't believe what he did the first time he came to see me at the Whiskey," she laughed to the others, "He sat in the front row with binoculars and aimed it at the entire cast during the nude scenes!"

"Damn, you should have waited until next week to surprise me," Lori continued, "These are our last two nights here at the Village Gate, and we open on Broadway next week."

"I can't wait to have you see me perform at a real Broadway theatre!" she excitedly added.

"Unfortunately, I need to be in Dallas next week for my own show," said Jason, "But I'm sure I'll be able to come back and see you again."

"I'm actually only in New York until tomorrow," Jason added, "I just had an urge to come up here for a day."

Lori seemed surprised as well as disappointed.

"Well, we still have another late show we need to perform at eleven pm, but let me get changed and we can spend at least a couple of hours together," Lori suggested more cheerfully, "Macy's is sponsoring a great firework's show tonight, so we can go down to the harbor and see the big Bicentennial celebration before I have to get back."

While Jason sat at the table and waited for Lori to change clothes, he wished Let My People Come had gone on for two more hours because it had gotten his mind off everything for at least a short time. He was back in a daze again as the reality of everything came back to him, knowing that in less than twenty-four hours, he'd be back in Dallas and suddenly realized how crazy he was for thinking a quick trip to New York would magically make everything go away.

But he still needed to talk out loud to someone he trusted.

It was less than thirty minutes later, and they were sitting on the grass near the harbor waiting for the fireworks to begin, and Lori was listening quietly and shaking her head with disbelief as Jason was telling her about what was happening in Dallas and his situation with his parents.

"I haven't talked to your mother since I was in *Penthouse*," Lori said, "You know what a prude she is and didn't want anything to do with me after that."

"And to be honest with you," she added, "There was always something about your father I didn't trust."

"Well, I never really have either," Jason smiled bitterly, "Now these guys who gave Dick sixty grand, think he's my brother who just works for me, and I'm the only one they're coming after for the money."

"Can't you tell them that you're just one of the owners and aren't responsible for anything Dick has done?" asked Lori.

"I tried to, but that's the main problem," Jason continued explaining bitterly, "Dick has taken off with all the money and evidently disappeared with his new girlfriend."

"Vi won't even communicate with me anymore and just thinks everything is my fault," he added with disdain, "I'm sure she just cares about her own money."

Lori just shook her head in continued disbelief.

"I always wondered why neither of them, especially Dick, never wanted to have their names listed in the masthead of the newspaper or let it be known that they were owners," Jason continued with more bitterness, "It's almost like Dick has had this planned for a long time."

"Well, something really bad must have happened for all that to happen at once," Lori quietly sighed, "I just find it hard to believe that they would intentionally just cut you off and leave you holding the bag."

"I don't know what to think about anything anymore," Jason added with disgust, "I do know that they're dead to me now, so as far as I'm concerned, fuck 'em, and I do wish they were both dead."

Both Jason and Lori were silent for a minute before the fireworks were starting to begin, which gave Jason at least something else to focus on for the next half hour to keep from showing any more anger.

They both kept their attention on the extravagant fireworks show and only commented on the excitement during the celebration and didn't discuss anything else about Jason's parents.

"I'm sorry, Lori," Jason tried to lightly apologize after the fireworks ended, "I didn't mean to come all the way here to just complain to you about my problems."

"But I did want to see how you were doing," he added more cheerfully, "And I'm glad everything is working out great for you."

"It's great to see you too, but I am worried about you," Lori said with concern, "Do you have enough money to get set up with something else?"

"Well, after my contests in Dallas next week, I should have enough money to last me until the end of the year," Jason tried to sound more optimistic, "So I should have enough time to figure something out eventually."

"But I can't stay in Dallas, and I gave up my apartment in Beverly Hills when I moved there," Jason added, "So I don't even know where I'm going to live right now."

"Well, I was thinking about something that might work for you at least temporarily," Lori began explaining, "I've been keeping my apartment in Hollywood and still paying on the lease, but I'm not sure when I'll even be in California again."

"My lease isn't up until January, so if you need a place to stay, you could stay at my apartment for a couple of months," she continued, "At least until you figure out what you're going to do."

"I appreciate the offer," Jason smiled, "But I won't know what city I'll even end up in until I take care of these problems."

"If you do, you do, and if you don't, don't worry about it," she half-laughed, "I've been paying on it anyway, so I thought it might at least be a good hideout for you until you get things straightened out."

"I might even be going over to Rome later this year to be in a movie that Bob Guccione is producing," Lori continued, "So you might even be able to stay there until the end of the year."

"Wow, a movie in Rome sounds exciting!" Jason congratulated her, "You are doing great here, and I'm really happy for you."

"Hopefully, next time we talk," Jason smiled, "I'll sound a little more positive myself."

"I'm sorry I can't spend more time with you tonight," Lori smiled as she stood up, "But I have to get back to the *Village Gate* for the second show."

"I will call you and let you know how this all turns out," Jason smiled as he gave her a last hug, "And I appreciate your apartment offer more than you know."

"You're the only person I feel I can really trust right now, and I wanted you to know that," he added with sincerity.

"Please take care, Jason, and I know you'll figure something out," Lori smiled sadly but with some optimism, "You always do."

Jason kissed her on her cheek as she turned to flag a taxi and suddenly wished he'd come to see Lori a couple of months earlier when he wouldn't have sounded so negative. He also wished he didn't have to leave so soon and could have stayed with her longer.

His flight back to Dallas was leaving early in the morning, and knew he had to get up early, but Jason wanted to walk a few blocks alone in the city before hailing a taxi to take him back to *The Plaza Hotel*.

As he passed by a newsstand, a tabloid newspaper immediately caught his attention, and he stopped to buy a copy.

It was called *Singles News*, and the cover almost looked identical to the *National Singles Register* from the way the copy and wording were displayed. Even the sub-headline, *"Real People, Real Ads and Real Results"* Was the exact words Jason had come up with for his own cover and had used a few times.

Inside, the copy and types of articles were exactly the same type of stories that Jason had decided to feature years earlier, and even the personal ads and clip art were identical to the way he had displayed his pages.

Jason's immediate first thought was that he had to tell his parents that someone in New York had completely ripped off his entire concept of the *National Singles Register* and if there was anything that they could do about it, but then, he came back to reality and remembered he couldn't. He also saw that newspaper was advertising its "One-Year Anniversary" and could never have been something his father or Joy could have been involved with and had have different names in its masthead.

He crumpled the *Singles News* copy and threw it in a trash can before hailing a taxi.

Jason knew that it was nothing that concerned him anymore.

Chapter Eight

It seemed like a year since Jason flew back from New York City, but it was only two weeks. The final night of his *Sexiest Girl in Dallas Pageant* would be starting in about five hours at *OZ Disco*, and after seven consecutive nights of preliminary contests at different nightclubs, Jason was anxious to announce the finals' winner that night and get out of town the next day.

With everything happening in Dallas since he'd been back, he was glad that he at least remembered to send Lori a dozen roses backstage for her opening night at the *Morosco Theatre* on Broadway.

Jason was at his townhouse, loading his Mercedes with most of his clothes and personal items so he wouldn't have to worry about packing anything else and hopefully be able to leave by ten am the next morning.

He was planning on spending his last night in Dallas with Martha Bland, and although he hadn't told her everything about his situation, he had become close enough with her to let her know some details. He'd also assured her that even if he didn't come back to Dallas right away, it didn't mean their relationship was over and that they'd definitely be seeing each other again regardless of what happened.

Jason had almost come to feel that Martha had become his Dallas version of Lori, and although they never exchanged any *"I love you"* words together, he still felt a certain strong bond with her and didn't want his leaving to be a goodbye.

He had also wanted something else from all of his efforts in Dallas to take back to California that he could use for promotion.

Jason knew he wouldn't have the *National Singles Register* to show press clippings of his parties to help him sell any future promotions, so he had talked to Van Dunn earlier that week to see if there was any way to get any copies of the news footage and film Van had shot at his parties.

"Well, I can't give you the exact clips we used on the news," Van explained, "But I still have some of the unedited rolls of film I might be able to get you."

"But you'll need a sixteen-millimeter film projector to view it, and it might not be easy to drag one around if you want to use it for promotion," he added.

"Well, I'm sure I'll find some way to use them," said Jason, "And if not, they might be fun to have for some memories or a few laughs."

"Well, your memories will cost you twenty-five dollars for each can of film," smiled Van, "I'm sure they won't miss them, but I will have to sneak them out of the television station."

"I guess it'll be worth it," Jason tried to lightly joke, "I've always thought without memories you've got no past, so I'll at least have that."

Jason found out there were about thirty cans of film, which were five minutes each, and got Van to agree to sell them all for only five hundred dollars in cash.

Van said he was coming to cover the sexiest girl contest at *OZ Disco* for the news station, so he'd bring the copies of film on the night of his finals.

Jason was again getting a little sentimental after he'd packed everything he could fit into his Mercedes before he left for OZ that night, and was still hoping that he would find a way to return to Dallas.

But he wasn't really that optimistic.

ૐ

Jason drove into the parking lot of *OZ Disco* around seven pm and knew he'd have time before he started the contest's finals around ten pm.

After he parked, he saw Van Dunn was already there with his camera crew outside the disco.

"You're here early," said Jason, "The contest isn't starting for a few more hours."

"I wanted to be here early to get some set up some B-roll footage," Van smiled before sarcastically joking, "And to see if there were any protestors or if you get shot at."

"Well, no matter how hard you press guys tried to make the *sexiest girl* thing a big deal," Jason joked back, "Everything went fine this week with no controversy."

Although some other freelance news reporters had covered his preliminary contests during the week and tried to start a scandal, nothing came out of it, and there were no protests or controversy as the reporters hoped.

Van had the all the rolls of film from his previous *World Entertainment Club* parties packed into a large box and helped Jason fit them into the trunk of his Mercedes after Jason paid him the five hundred dollars in cash.

"Wow, you've got your car pretty well packed up with everything there," Van started to tease with mock suspicion, "Are you sure you're only leaving for a few weeks?"

"It just looks like a lot because the Mercedes is so small," Jason teased back, "So don't worry, I'll be coming back."

"You know, we've been covering your parties every week for the past three months," said Van, "And seeing this is your last party for a while, can I just get a shot of you waving goodbye and driving off in your car?"

"It might add a little dramatic angle at the end of my news clip," he added with a smile.

"Jeez Van, it's just another party," Jason half laughed at the suggestion, "Are you trying to be a serious newsman all of a sudden?"

"I've got four more rolls of film with me, so I need something to shoot leading into the contest," said Van, "It's just an idea I have to make tonight's last party a more interesting story."

Even though Jason thought it sounded overblown, he went along with him and staged some exit shots, and watched Van film the usual pre-contest interviews.

Jason had invited just about every person he knew in Dallas to show up that night and was happy to see almost everyone he invited was there and had been buying most of them drinks all night as a type of "till we meet again" celebration.

He was trying to act like everything was fun as usual and how he was looking forward to coming back to Dallas, but he also wanted to make sure he'd see them all one more time, just in case.

Besides interviewing a couple of contestants, Van wanted to talk to some people who were regulars at Jason's parties and chose Martha Bland, Candy Bradley, and another contestant Jason had briefly been involved with named Sherry Wall to see "how they felt about a pause" in all of Jason's weekly parties.

He then saw Van standing alone under the *OZ* marquee and being filmed giving a report, and briefly overhead the words *"death threats"* and started to wonder how overblown Van was actually trying to make his contest sound.

"Okay, what's that all about?" Jason lightly tried to joke, "Don't you think you're overdoing it a bit?"

"Don't worry," Van lightly chuckled, "It'll probably all be edited out for the news, but you're paying me for these rolls of film, so I at least want to give you your money's worth and use all the film."

"But those girls I interviewed were great," said Van, "Candy and Martha sounded good, and that other girl Sherry almost started crying when I told her you were leaving town and that should make some good dramatic effect for your memories."

"That's funny," smiled Jason, "I only went out with Sherry a couple of times."

"Well, you know how these girls are," Van said with light facetiousness, "A couple of good fucks and they're in love."

Jason was glad that Van was still in a light mood and was just shooting footage to fill up the rolls that probably couldn't be used in a one-minute edited news segment, and it had turned into a great party and a huge crowd over the next few hours.

Jason had already completed all contest segments and told the audience he'd be announcing the winner of *The Sexiest Girl* in Dallas and present the trip to Paris and two hundred dollars in cash at midnight.

He had already collected the seven hundred and fifty dollars from the manager at *Oz*, and with the other money he'd collected for the preliminaries that week, after his costs, he did have almost five thousand dollars in cash to take back to California the next day.

It was around eleven-thirty pm when he saw the three men in cowboy hats approaching him. Jason immediately saw it was Mark, Ed, and Dave, and they didn't look happy.

"A little birdie told us that you were getting ready to leave town," said Mark, "So the three of us decided to come by and say hello before you left."

Jason immediately thought about Van Dunn and wondered if he was the "little birdie" that Mark mentioned.

"I just need to take care of some other business in California for a few weeks and was going to get the checks from Dick while I was there," Jason tried to say in a natural and relaxed voice, "I was going to call you tomorrow and give you some money before I left and give you the rest when I come back."

"Well, we talked to some lady at the office in California yesterday," said Mark, "She didn't give us her name, but she said Dick is gone and also claimed that you're not even involved with the National Singles Register anymore."

Jason took them aside privately and knew he had to give them the whole story or at least something that would buy him time.

"Look it," Jason said, "That lady you talked to is my mother, and Dick is my father, not my brother, and I have no idea why he ever told you that."

"The deal is," said Jason, "Is that they're having some marital problems right now, and it's been kind of a mess for the past couple months."

"That's why I'm going to California for a few weeks to get things straightened out and get you back your money," Jason tried to say convincingly.

"Well, I just think we need to have a talk tonight when you're finished here," said Mark, "So if you don't mind, we're just going to wait around till then."

"No problem," Jason tried to say in a cheerful voice, "I'm getting ready to announce the winner of the sexiest girl contest, so stick around and we can go out have breakfast afterward."

Jason was temporarily relieved when they sat at a table near the dance floor and said they'd wait, but his heart was pounding, and he tried not to panic, thinking about what he was going to do.

He did briefly think about just running out to his car and taking off, but he knew he had to try and act normal until he thought of something else that wouldn't make him appear guilty or ruin any chance of him coming back to Dallas.

He didn't know if Van Dunn had even talked to Mark and was hoping to film some confrontation like some ambush journalist on *Sixty Minutes*, but didn't want it to look like he was running away from anything just in case he was.

Although Jason doubted that Van Dunn would even think about something crazy like that and overdramatize his situation, he was actually starting to feel very scared.

He went into the bathroom and ran cold water over his face as an idea did come to him. He had no idea if it would work, but it was the only thing he could think of in the short time he had that wouldn't look suspicious, and he'd be able to make some stupid excuse for later.

Jason then went to the DJ booth to ask what the longest and upbeat disco song he could play right after the contest that Jason could cue him to spin.

"Well, I just played *Love to Love You Baby*," said the DJ, "But I've got an extended disco mix of *Love Hangover* that run almost eight minutes."

Jason didn't think that song sounded lively enough, but then the DJ made another suggestion.

"Hey, I got a new promo twelve-inch dance song by Elton John," said the DJ, "It hasn't been released yet, but the record companies like me to try them out for the disco crowd."

"It's called *Bite Your Lip, Get Up and Dance*," added the DJ, "And it's actually pretty lively and danceable, and it runs over seven minutes."

Jason was hoping for at least a ten-minute song but figured seven minutes should work.

Even though he was panicked, Jason half smiled to himself, thinking a seven-minute version of *Gimmee Three Steps* by Lynyrd Skynyrd would have been perfect for a getaway song.

"Okay, have that Elton John song ready to start as soon as I give you a cue," Jason told the DJ.

He was due to announce the winner in ten minutes but first went to find some other girls besides Martha he'd stayed close since he'd been in Dallas.

Jason saw Candy Bradley, Melanie Boston, and Sheri Wall standing at the bar and gathered them together.

"You see those guys sitting over there in the suits and cowboy hats," Jason pointed to the girls, "They're friends of mine, and they don't seem to be having fun tonight, so after I announce the winner, I'm going to have a type of group dance."

"If the three of you could all just get them to dance with you for one song, it would be great and be a big favor to me."

"No problem," laughed Candy, "We never have a problem getting guys to dance with us."

Jason decided he'd announce the winner and have the prize ceremony, and then just have a distraction where no one would miss him long enough for him to leave discreetly without having to worry about Mark and the other two guys that night.

He figured so it wouldn't look like he had run away to them, or any of his friends if they heard anything negative about him, he'd just call everyone later and tell them he got drunk and left with one of the sexiest girl contestants right after the contest.

Jason then waited for the current song to end, took the cordless microphone, and called all twenty-one contestants in their bikinis to the dance floor to announce the winner.

The audience was packed around the dance floor, cheering loudly for each of the two runner ups Jason announced, and by the time he shouted "Deanna is your Sexiest Girl in Dallas!" the crowd continued to cheer wildly. As he presented Deanna with her prizes, Jason did think she was the sexiest girl he'd seen in Dallas lately and was briefly disappointed he wouldn't have a chance to get to know her better, but he knew what else he needed to do at that minute.

"Alright, don't any of you sexy girls leave the dance floor just yet," Jason announced through the microphone, "I've got a treat for all you guys!"

"You know, these girls have been working hard in this contest all week," Jason continued speaking, "And I think they'd like to have a little fun right now."

"Are there any guys out there that would like to dance with the sexiest girls in Dallas?" he teased.

The men in the crowd immediately began cheering and rushing to the dance floor to choose a contestant for their dance partner.

"The DJ said he has a new disco hit by Elton John he's premiering tonight, and the title sounds very appropriate," Jason said before shouting out, "So, let's get everyone on the floor and Get Up and DANCE!"

Jason then cued the DJ, and the song began as the dance floor was completely becoming full.

As Jason walked off the dance floor, he saw Van Dunn was pre-occupied with his cameraman filming the dancers and tried to look and see if the girls were able to get Mark and the others to dance.

He became concerned when he saw them first refusing but then finally give in when Candy, Melanie, and Sherry continued pulling their arms and led them to the dance floor.

Jason didn't waste any time and started to walk away calmly towards the front door, but then he saw Martha Bland in the crowd and quickly pulled her aside.

"Martha, there's some problems going on, and I have to leave right now," he quickly said, "But please don't tell anyone you saw me leave, and I promise I'll call you in a few days and tell you everything."

574

The one big thing Jason hadn't told Martha about was the sixty thousand dollars and how serious his situation really was and had only told her about his departure from the *National Singles Register* and his parents' problems.

"A broken date on your last night?" Martha half laughed, "I just can't believe y'all sometimes."

"But okay," she smiled, "I'll let it slide again this time, but don't forget to call me."

Jason was just glad she didn't see the panic in his face and just gave her a strong hug and kiss before he headed out the front door.

As Jason drove onto the LBJ Expressway with the catchy chorus of *"Bite Your Lip, Get Up and Dance"* still ringing in his head, he remembered it took him almost nine hours to drive from El Paso to Dallas when he first made the trip.

Tonight, he was going to try and make back to El Paso in seven.

Chapter Nine

It was midnight and over twenty-four hours since he left Dallas when Jason turned left on to Highland Boulevard off the Hollywood freeway and headed toward Sunset Boulevard.

Jason had driven straight through and had only stopped once after he crossed the Texas border into New Mexico when he pulled off Interstate 10 and tried to sleep for a couple of hours in his car.

As he made a right turn on Sunset, he finally turned on his radio after driving almost the entire distance in silence and needed to hear something in his head other than everything he'd been thinking about.

When the first song Jason heard playing on the radio was the Beach Boys version of Chuck Berry's *Rock and Roll Music*, everything briefly seemed normal again.

Jason was back in Hollywood, and Dallas seemed like a bad dream, like in the movie *The Wizard of Oz*, but although he tried to imagine that was true, he knew it wasn't. He was at least satisfied he'd stayed at *OZ Disco* long enough to complete his *Sexiest Girl in Dallas* contest without it seem like he had just run away before his party ended, and hoped his "I got drunk and forget about you guys" excuse would work when he did call anyone in Dallas to see what happened after he left.

He didn't want to talk to anyone yet until he thought about everything else and just wanted to be completely alone and sleep for as long as he could.

Jason checked into a motel next to the *Seventh Veil Restaurant* on Sunset Boulevard and was asleep within five minutes of taking off the same suit and tie he had been wearing at *OZ* the night before.

But unlike Dorothy in the movie, he knew he didn't want to wake up back in *OZ*.

It was two days later when Annie Gaybis opened the front door to her apartment, and Jason saw her surprised but happy look as she motioned for him to come inside while she was finishing a phone call.

"Guess who's back from Dallas!?" Annie excitedly talked into the phone as Jason walked into her apartment.

"No, it's not Jack Kennedy," she laughed to the person she was speaking, "It's Jason!"

She let Jason know she was talking to Nicky Blair and would be off the phone in a minute.

Annie was the first friend Jason trusted enough to tell he was back in town after spending the last two nights alone at the motel, thinking about what happened, and what he was going to do. But hearing Annie mention President Kennedy to Nicky Blair made Jason wonder what may have happened if he would have gone with Mark and the others that night in Dallas if he hadn't had taken off.

Jason was still worried that they might come to California looking for him and was furious that his mother had basically thrown him under the bus, in the same way his father had done, by telling Mark that Jason had nothing to do with the *National Singles Register* any longer, and that what he and his father did in Dallas had been separate from the newspaper.

He knew that Annie Gaybis was still writing her *Dateline: Hollywood* column in the *National Singles Register* and needed to find out if she'd heard anything at all about what was going on for the past month.

"I've never even met Vi," said Annie, "I think I may have only talked to her on the phone once, but I just mail in my column to the office every two weeks."

"As far as your father," she added, "I only met him that one time at the racetrack when he said he was your brother."

Jason told Annie the entire situation about what was happening, and she looked even more shocked than Lori had as she listened to the details.

"What are you going to do?" she said, "Do you want me to call Vi and ask her what's happening?"

"No, I don't want her to know I'm back in town or that you've even talked to me," said Jason, "Lori said I might be able to use her apartment here in town, so I'm just going to lay low until I find out a few things myself."

Jason then used Annie's phone to call the only other person he needed to get immediate information, Martha Bland.

"Everything seemed normal after you left," Martha said, "Except a lot of your friends were disappointed you didn't say good-bye to them."

"I didn't see or hear anything on the news this week either," she added, "So I guess Van Dunn didn't get the station to run anything about your contest."

Jason then told Martha the rest of the story about what happened and gave her Annie's phone number if she did hear anything.

He realized that he had probably just been paranoid about Van Dunn's involvement that night as well, and was glad for the first time that he didn't receive any media coverage. and was mainly relieved that no one he knew in Dallas thought he was an escaped fugitive, and that his *escape plan* had seemed to work.

At least for now.

❧

A week later, Jason had been still staying at different motels and still racking his brain with possible options.

Jason had called some other of his friends in Dallas to at least let them know he may not be coming back soon, and after a few days, he decided to call Mark and try one more time to get things straightened out.

As Jason was trying to explain his excuse for leaving OZ so quickly, Mark just coldly cut him off.

"At his point," said Mark over the phone, "I don't believe anything from any of you people out there anymore."

"I just know you owe us a lot of money, and we want it back now, or there's going to be a lot of problems!" he threatened loudly.

"Listen, Mark, you gave that money to Dick, and I had nothing to do with it," Jason tried to reason, "If I knew where he was, I'd tell you, but I don't have anything near that type of money."

"I don't believe that either," Mark laughed bitterly, "I saw you on television all the time livin' the high life, and drivin' around in limos and your fancy Mercedes."

"You don't look too poor to me," he added more threateningly, "And it's just your name in the newspaper listed as the publisher, so if I don't hear something by next week, you'll be hearing' from us sooner than you think!"
Mark then hung up the phone.

Jason decided to pick up a copy of the *National Singles Register* from a news rack to see if anything had changed in the last month, but besides seeing it looked as it always had, he also saw his name was still listed as *Editor and Publisher* in the masthead.

He still felt nothing but anger and hate toward his parents and just wanted to bring some type of closure to everything and try to start fresh somehow. But Jason also knew he couldn't do anything until he had at least some sort of civil conversation with his mother to try find out anything she knew, and at the worst, he'd tell her to "Get his name off the fucking masthead!" He finally called her at the office rather than her home, hoping they could at least have a business conversation without making it personal.

"Your mother's not here yet, Jason," said the girl who answered at the office.

"Good, I need to talk to you," Jason quickly said.

He had worked with the girl who answered for over two years and was relieved that he might be able to have a normal conversation with someone at the office.

"Vi told me to just hang up if you called," she said, "But I'd like to know what's going on myself."

"I have no idea what happened," said Jason, "Vi won't even talk to me, and all I know is that suddenly everything got fucked up somehow."

"The only thing I heard is that Dick took off with Joy and they took a lot of money," she said, "And Vi said it's all your fault because she was your girlfriend and Dick wouldn't have met her if it wasn't for you."

"That's a bunch of bullshit!" said Jason, "I didn't have anything to do with Joy."

"Well, all Vi says almost every day is that she hopes you both rot in hell and die," she tried to half-laugh.

"Have you gotten any phone calls from Dallas about anything?" asked Jason, "Or heard anything about Dallas mentioned?"

"Nothing," she said, "Vi gets phone calls, but I don't know who they're from and there's still a few calls for you coming in who don't leave messages."

"I'm done with the newspaper, so I probably won't be seeing you again," said Jason, "So if anyone else calls, just tell them I've resigned and started another business out of town."

"We're going to miss you down here, Jason," she said, "But good luck with everything."

"Oh, there's one more thing," she added, "Vi said if you did call in, to tell you to bring the Mercedes back that you're driving or she's going to report it stolen to the police."

"Okay, and you can give her a message from me," Jason said, "Tell the bitch to fuck off and take my name off the *fucking masthead!*"

a⤳

Eliot Feldman was also giving looks of disbelief as he sat behind his desk in Beverly Hills as he was listening to the story Jason was telling him.

"Wow, that sounds absolutely crazy!" Eliot half laughed, "You're lucky you got out of Dallas alive."

"I just need to know my legal situation," said Jason, "I don't want anything to do with the newspaper anymore and just want to get this whole thing over with."

"It sounds like it's something for civil court," said Eliot, "But I'd have to see any paperwork your father signed with them to see if there's any fraud involved."

"I don't think there's a chance in hell of seeing any paperwork," said Jason, "I don't even know why they gave him that much money, and always thought he just sold news racks."

"Well, I don't think you have any liability at all," said Eliot, "You never signed any ownership papers, and you were always just a salaried employee with a title."

"I think everything is just on your father," he added confidently, "And even your mother if she's involved in any way."

"Well, I could care less about them, and I'm just worried that I looked guilty for leaving Dallas the way I did," said Jason, "But as long as I don't have to worry about those guys in Texas, I can at least breathe easier."

"You never signed anything with your parents or the guys from Dallas, so I wouldn't worry," Eliot added, "You were just the editor who resigned because of your parent's bad business dealings, and I don't see anything you need to hide from."

"Of course, those Dallas guys could always just shoot you, and I hear that's not too difficult to have arranged in Dallas," Eliot tried to sarcastically joke, "But as far as coming after you for any money or suing you, I don't think there's anything there."

"Just watch your back and don't go back to Dallas," Eliot concluded with another chuckle.

Jason felt a little better after talking with Eliot and was satisfied that any problems with Dallas didn't involve him, but still felt lost about what he was now going do with his life now that everything he had been doing for almost five years seemed to be over. Because he hadn't really promoted anything in California for almost a year, had nowhere permanent to live, he also knew he soon wouldn't even have a car.

Because he was basically now unemployed, Eliot Feldman also assisted through a contact he had, with a deal that allowed Jason to rent a new Oldsmobile Cutlass by the month until he could get himself re-established. Eliot also suggested going with Jason as a witness, in case there was any confrontation when they went to drop off the Mercedes at his mother's townhouse in Los Alamitos.

Luckily no one was at home when Jason and Eliot dropped off the car, and although he still had many of his belongings stored at his mother's townhouse, Jason decided just to leave them all behind and didn't even feel bad about not seeing his cat *Old Lady*.

Jason knew after spending the year with his mother, the cat had also probably turned into a miserable bitch and was just going to try and forget about her as well.

Chapter Ten

Jason still didn't feel completely safe and knew he wanted to lay low for at least another month without contacting too many of his former friends or letting them know that that he was back in California.

Knowing he was no longer an editor and publisher or promoting parties locally, he wasn't sure how much he had in common with most of them anymore.

Jason did reconnect with Stan Adams, who had finally recovered from his bitter divorce and now had his own private photography studio in the basement of an office building on Canon Drive in Beverly Hills.

Stan had decided to focus more on commercial photography rather than covering celebrity and media events and had pretty much been out of contact with most of their old group of friends since Jason had left town.

Since he hadn't had any promotions in Hollywood or Beverly Hills since the end of 1975, most of his former circle of friends had also moved on to different projects of their own since he'd moved to Dallas.

Jason was also surprised to learn that Mixie Thompson and Michael Ritz were moving on even more dramatically and had become engaged to get married.

Everyone in his circle of friends had always seemed as committed as he had been, about remaining single until they reached their personal goals, and couldn't picture either of them becoming an *"old married couple."*

So much had changed in the past year, Jason was almost beginning to feel like a stranger in town, and he was also starting to feel that the good old days of "just having fun" seemed to be over with at least part of his circle.

Jason also spent a lot of time driving alone, listening to music, and thinking.

He knew that he wouldn't forget about Dallas for a long time, and it seemed there was always something on the radio that would remind him.

There was a current hit song called *Take the Money and Run* by the Steve Miller Band about a couple from Texas who were on the run after absconding with stolen money and that song would always get Jason in a foul mood, being so appropriate to what his father and Joy had done.

Another current hit song was constantly blasting on Jason's radio called *Right Back Where We Started From* by Maxine Nightingale that also seemed to be very appropriate that month to the way he currently felt.

He was grateful he still had a few other friends that kept him from feeling completely alone during the major change in his life he was facing.

Jason could at least *get back where he started from*, with some of those he hadn't seen since he moved to Dallas and reconnected with Lita Krisaan and spent several nights at her Malibu apartment the first few weeks he was back in California, wanting to stay away from his old haunts in Hollywood and Beverly Hills.

The only other former bachelorettes and old girlfriend he was discreetly spending time his first month back was Barbara Piotrowski, who had both been in his first *Bachelorette of the Year* contest in 1974 that Lita had won.

Jason thought Barbara probably had the sexiest looking legs that Jason had seen in Hollywood since he'd known her, but he also liked that she had started a normal career as a full-time nurse and wasn't just hoping to be a model or an actress any longer.

When Jason wasn't staying with Lita, he'd rent hotel rooms and saw Barbara on those other nights, with Barbara still living at home with her parents.

Seeing both Lita and Barbara during his first month back in California at least reminded him he was still alive when he was with them.

Barbara Piotrowski also convinced Jason to try the newest craze for energy boosts in Hollywood and Beverly Hills, offering him free Vitamin B-12 shots she would administer herself when they were in Jason's hotel room.

She said most of the celebrities in Hollywood were paying over fifty dollars for each Vitamin B-12 shot, and it was just a healthy benefit she said would keep Jason's mind sharp and keep his attitude positive.

Jason reluctantly agreed to give it a try but had Barbara give him the shots in his butt because he had never liked the sight of needles when doctors gave him a shot in the arm when he was young.

Lori did let Jason know she was definitely going to Rome when *Let My People Come* concluded its run on Broadway, and had gotten an acting role in a movie called *Caligula*, and said she probably wouldn't be coming back to California for the rest of the year.

"I've paid my lease on my apartment in Hollywood till the end of the year anyway," Lori told Jason by phone, "So I can arrange to get you a key, and you can stay there for as long as you need to till then."

Although he appreciated the positive encouragement from some of his friends, he really felt he was *"right back where he had started from"* over four years earlier when he had first moved back to California from Las Vegas. But he knew he still needed to think about moving forward and not dwell on it too long, and was at least glad he did have a temporary *hideout,* where he could be alone to think for a while.

Because he had spent so many years writing columns and articles for the *National Singles Register*, writing had just become a habit Jason couldn't break and still found himself always writing out his thoughts and ideas on yellow legal pads keep his mind occupied with positive thoughts.

He was mainly just trying to clear his mind and keep himself entertained when he was alone trying to think of anything new and fresh.

Jason briefly had a crazy idea when he first moved into Lori's apartment, which he knew was mainly something to give him his writing fix, but briefly thought about an idea for a disco musical revue along the same line as *Let My People Come.*

He figured if a show that just had dirty songs could make it to Broadway, he could write dirty songs with the best of them and at least have some fun to kill some time while he was thinking of other ideas.

Jason had always included short risqué poems or limericks on the romantic greeting cards he gave to Lori and other girlfriends, as not to make them sound so *gushy*, and figured he'd just expand on his cute, funny poems, and try and turn them into songs.

He spent a few weeks writing out stanzas in the standard three verses and two chorus structure, along with a connecting storyline about a typical night in the discos and how it seemed everyone considered the night a total loss unless they took someone different home to get laid each night.

Jason did surprise himself how easily a melody would come to him with each set of lyrics he scribbled out to the sexually themed songs but knew he was mainly amusing himself and didn't take it that seriously.

With lyrics and titles like *The Drinks Are On Me, But the Rest of the Night Is On You*, *Let's Have a Quickie in the Bathroom Stall*, *An Erection Is a Terrible Thing to Waste*, and *The Way You Dance Makes Me Wanna Get in Your Pants*, Jason knew they sounded juvenile, but figured at the worst, he now had a good collection of risqué poems he could use when giving romantic greeting cards to any girlfriends in the future. Or, even sing them a cappella in bed occasionally to at least get some light laughs.

Another song idea was called *Long Legged Lady*, which he teased Barbara Piotrowski saying he had written about her when he lightly sang her a sample of the chorus.

> *"Long legged lady won't ya come home with me*
> *Long legged lady, I wanna feel em round me"*

Although he had briefly imagined staging a musical revue at discos as a new promotion, he knew it was just a stupid idea and knew he'd never have the time, the expertise, or even the money to really afford to stage it. But regardless, he still ended up with a forty-page handwritten outline with over a half a dozen songs and titled it *Getting Head.*

Jason was at least satisfied he'd kept himself distracted with something that was fun to write, but after spending a month on *Getting Head*, he knew he needed to get serious about what he was going to do next.

Jan Berry was visiting Jason at Lori's apartment, and they were both talking about their future plans along with the usual favorite topics they both had in common, music and girls.

Jan had been back in the recording studio trying to record some new songs and music without his former *Jan and Dean* partner, Dean Torrance and had already told Jason about his strained relationship with Dean and was hoping to get a new band together to eventually begin performing live concerts again on his own. Jan was partially paralyzed and sometimes still spoke with difficulty or a stutter due to the car accident, but his mind was usually sharp, and Jason never had a problem communicating with him.

Jason and Jan had already talked about the irony of how one of *Jan and Dean's* biggest hit songs, *Dead Man's Curve,* had seemed to have eerily predicted Jan's own car crash.

"I should have just kept writing songs about surfing and girls," Jan lightly chuckled, "Writing a song about a car crash made it really happen somehow."

"It's f-f-freaky how sometimes life imitates art," Jan stuttered lightly, trying to talk about the coincidence, "It's like I was predicting my own future."

Jason lightly added his own example about how the hit song from the summer before, *Tush* by ZZ Top, could also have predicted his own life the past year and sarcastically sang the coincidental lyrics about how he'd been "bad and good in both Dallas, Texas, and Hollywood" just looking for some *Tush.*

"It does seem that there's always a song that seems to describe some of the things that I'm going through," Jason smiled, "It does seem freaky sometimes."

Although Jan seemed capable and coherent at times, because of some of the brain damage he'd suffered in the car accident, he did sometimes revert to acting childish, and Jason did sometimes feel he was talking with a ten-year old.

That afternoon Jan was again giggling like a ten-year-old, and Jason even felt like a ten-year-old himself, as he was joking about some of his dirty songs he'd written, and they both started joking about ideas for some other stupid songs.

Jason had always teased Jan about his obsession with Slurpee's from the chain of *7-11* stores, which was what Jan was actually going in to buy when his Corvette was stolen the day Jason had met him.

They both started to make up funny parody lyrics to Jan's biggest hit *Surf City* which Jason joked fit Jan's current obsession more than surfing or girls had in the past.

"I'm goin' to seven-eleven and gonna get me a Slurpee," Jason jokingly sang to the melody to *Surf City*, before they both continued with, "Seven-Eleven here we come!" with Jan adding, "Cause nothin' tastes better when I get really thirsty…"

"There's a song about art *imitating* your life," Jason half laughed.

"W-w-we could record and sell the *Slurpee* song as a new jingle to Seven-Eleven stores," joked Jan about parody lyrics, "We could record it as *Jan and Jason* instead of *Jan and Dean.*"

But they both always just laughed it off their funny song ideas and knew it was mainly for entertaining themselves and never took it seriously.

"Maybe someday," Jason smiled, "But music is your business and not mine, so I'd better stick with what I do best."

"Another b-b-bach-bach…," Jan tried to say.

"Bachelorette contest?" Jason finished saying for him, "No, like I said, I'm not doing the singles stuff anymore and trying to come up with something new that can attract audiences."

"My sexiest girl contest went over good in Texas, so I just need to start up some more original ideas without the *singles* angle," Jason explained.

"S-s-sexy is good," laughed Jan.

"Well, I'm going to start contacting some of the discos again," Jason added, "So I should have another beauty contest you can judge in a month or two."

"Two chicks for every boy!" Jan again lightly sang the other *Surf City* lyrics, "Just let me know when, and I'll be there."

After Jason drove Jan back to the house in Bel Aire he shared with his parents, and was driving back to Lori's apartment in Hollywood, he was loudly playing one of his current favorite songs, *Tightrope*, by the *Electric Light Orchestra* from one of his cassette tapes.

During his drive home, Jason kept rewinding the tape to that particular song, listening to all the lyrics as he continued thinking about his own current situation.

Besides thinking of different coincidences about some of the lyrics, certain songs always seemed to motivate him, and that song had lyrics he liked about someone who felt they had come to the end of their rope and was pleading for someone to *drop them down a line* to help them stay *positive* and find answers.

As Jason sang along with the lyrics, hoping that someone would *drop him down* a *line* of assistance, he realized he needed to focus fairly quickly about what he was going to do and not wait for some miracle.

He at least had a temporary apartment and a car, but with less than three thousand dollars left to his name, Jason knew that money wouldn't last him longer than four or five more months, and he needed to think about something fast for income.

It was near the end of August and Jason finally felt it was safe enough to start another new beginning, and once again remembered that *only the dead never change.*

Jason began connecting with several previous business contacts over the next few weeks, letting them know he was no longer involved with the *National Singles Register* and was branching out with a new production company.

He knew he would need a business telephone number where he could be contacted in the future knowing no one could ever reach him at the newspaper office any longer.

Annie Gaybis gave Jason the name of the answering service she used that had live operators who answered with any business name Jason chose for only fifteen dollars a month. He liked that idea and it would at least sound like he had a secretary and could print a business phone number on his new business cards.

Jason had already proven to himself with his last three promotions in Dallas, that he could be successful without the *National Singles Register* as his *"vehicle"* and just needed to get back to work on his own.

He knew his parents had always made all of the money from the newspaper anyway, and with even more discos opening up everywhere and nightlife becoming hotter than it had ever been, Jason felt if he became a full-time nightclub promoter with different parties every week and could start to make some serious money.

Jason also knew the title of hosting parties as the editor and publisher of the *National Singles Register*, and being a member of the press is what gave him his *juice* and access to not sound like just some ordinary guy promoting singles parties. He at least wanted to appear like an editor and publisher who *was just between gigs* and decided to say he was planning on publishing a new nightclub and party magazine that catered to the disco and nightlife crowds.

Jason also knew that *S.T.A.R.S.* and the *World Entertainment Club* were dead, so he eventually thought of a new name for a company.

He decided to call his new business *Nightmovers Productions* and his party club members the *Nightmovers*, which seemed appropriate and fit in with the nightclub crowd he was used to attracting.

He also knew he needed a big new gimmick to attract those crowds.

Jason had always advertised all his nightclub promotions mainly as *Singles and Celebrity Parties*, but knowing his reputation as the *Singles Guy* was now over, he needed another draw that would allow him to continue making money from the discos and nightclubs to earn a living. He also noticed that since he stopped his Hollywood and Beverly Hills promotions almost a year earlier, other promoters had picked up where he had left off, and they'd been using basically the same promotional techniques Jason had started years earlier, by staging *Bikini Contests* and something called *Wet Tee-Shirt Contests* in various discos.

Just a plain sexiest girl contest didn't even sound that original or exciting to him anymore, plus Jason knew his bachelorette contest gave the actress and models in town a chance to be a cover girl on a national publication, which was always the main attraction, so he never had a problem getting contestants. He knew he couldn't make them *cover girls* any longer and even those contests almost seemed to have become boring and old the past year.

Jason had also been thinking about all the attractive girls who weren't actresses and models and wanted to come up with something to attract all types of girls in a new contest.

He was still thinking about a new contest he could promote, and everything started coming to him at once, and suddenly pictured a contest where the girls wouldn't have to have any type of *bikini body* or *"Wet Tee Shirt"* tits, or even have to be glamourous or sexy like actresses or models.

"Long legged lady, won't ya come home with me…," Jason sang out loud to himself at what he decided was his *brilliant* new idea.

He decided he could have a contest where the girls would just show their shapely and long legs without worrying about any other of their features. A *legs contest* could attract contestants from all professions who never thought they could qualify to be in an actual beauty contest and be open to all types of *real girls* like those he attracted in Dallas instead of just actresses and models.

Jason figured that it might be at least fun to try a time or two and see if he could attract contestants at least until he thought about something better.

Chapter Eleven

Jason had brought Jan Berry with him to pick up Lita Krissan at her Malibu apartment before they drove all drove together to *Tiffany's Disco* in Marina Del Rey, where Jason was hosting his first *Nightmovers* party and legs contest.

Lita had agreed to work the door and collect money at *Tiffany's* that night after Jason learned Sandi Shore was too busy working with her mother, Mitzi, at *The Comedy Store* and wouldn't be able to work with him too often anymore.

Sandi explained that *The Comedy Store* had turned into a "gold mine" and that her mother had expanded the business by taking over the building next door that had once been Art Laboe's *Oldies but Goodies* nightclub, which more than quadrupled the seating capacity.

With most of his old circle of friends moving on to different projects, Jason mainly had to promote his first new *Nightmovers* party and legs contest by himself as he had first done in Dallas. He mainly printed up and passed out hundreds of free *VIP Nightmovers* passes, which were good for half price off the four-dollar door charge.

With a full month of in-house promotion from *Tiffany's*, displaying his posters and distributing his flyers to the hundreds of regular customers, Jason hoped to draw his usual nightclub party crowd of around two or three hundred as he had the past couple years and promoted his new contest as one that any girl could enter.

Jason was hoping to clear at least six hundred dollars from his first party and although he didn't like having to take away from his profits, he was offering a hundred dollars for first place and fifty dollars for second place in his legs contest, which was the only way he could currently attract contestants.

He'd always been able to book his parties very easily, by pitching the disco owners and managers not only the celebrity judges he'd have judging his various contests, but also the benefits of the press and media coverage he'd give them in his newspaper and other media. But without a newspaper, Jason hoped getting other press and media personalities as judges would get him the press exposure he'd gotten in the past, to still make his new *Nightmovers* parties as *famous* as his previous parties.

Jason was able to find two well-known media personalities *KHJ Radio* disc jockey Mark Elliot, and *KTTV Channel 11* news anchorman Larry Burrell, along with other celebs he advertised as *celebrity* judges including "former rock star" Jan Berry, "Hollywood modeling agent" Ron Smith, "cover girl and model" Barbara Piotrowski, and Peter Lupas, one of the stars of the old hit TV show *Mission Impossible*.

Mark Elliot also ended up giving Jason advance free advertising blurbs on Mark's radio show by mentioning was going to be a judge in what he described as "a wild new ladies legs contest," which saved Jason from putting out any extra money for cash advertising.

Larry Burrell was a news anchor on an offbeat and zany newscast called *Metro News Metro News*, that ran before Norman Lear's new hit parody soap opera *Mary Hartman! Mary Hartman!* at eleven pm each weeknight. Jason had also pitched Larry Burrell about how the Dallas news stations had run weekly short funny news segments about his parties and convinced him to bring a camera crew from *Metro News Metro News* to his first *Nightmovers* party.

In the past year, he'd already seen how his audiences and contestants always loved feeling famous for the night by seeing the television cameras rolling and had enhanced his parties. It was pretty much the same formula he began using in Dallas, and Jason knew that *disco* parties were already considered *singles* parties without having to advertise that aspect.

When Jason arrived with Lita and Jan at *Tiffany's Disco* around seven-thirty pm hoping he'd attract at least a dozen contestants for his contest, he couldn't believe there were over forty girls waiting to sign up, and there was already a long line of people waiting for the doors to open at eight pm.

Jason had decided to still use the name tags for is *"Famous Couples"* game, which always gave his promotions an additional party atmosphere, but when he saw the crowd size, he hurriedly had to add more famous couples name tags for Lita to pass out to accommodate twice the party-goers he'd expected.

As Jason began assigning each legs contestant with a number as to when he would call them out on stage, he saw that *just a legs contest* attracted a wide variety of women who were more comfortable without wearing a bikini. All of the girls liked that they just had to appear to on stage wearing either hot pants or a mini skirt and surprisingly had contestants who ranged from their early twenties to women who were over fifty years old.

"I've always thought I had great legs and have always dreamed about being in a beauty contest," Jason heard one of the older contestants jokes to another girl, "Even though I'm a grandmother, I want to show the guys I'm still sexy."

Because it wasn't billed as a *beauty contest*, Jason wanted to have something that would be entertaining to the audience to liven it up rather than just have the contestants dance around on stage and posing.

Jason knew that everyone's conversations, not only in the discos, but in almost every area of culture recently, seemed to be centered around having sex, thinking about sex, or talking about sex, more than it ever had before.

He always remembered how Telly Savalas and the other judges livened up his *Bachelorette of the Year* contest with some of their questions at *The Thunderbird* in Las

Vegas and how Bill Ballance's old radio show was so popular because of Bill's regular use of innuendoes and double-entendres.

Jason had always talked that way with his friends and the girls he knew but didn't know how it would go over to talk that way over the microphone to a live audience.

As he first did at *The Sexiest Girl in Dallas Pageant*, Jason decided to just emcee the entire contest by himself and decided to enhance his poise and personality segment by asking the contestants more personal questions.

Jason had already planned to ask the typical "Turn on and turn off's" about the men the contestants preferred but added a few more questions for some more innuendo opportunities he thought would add a little comedy and sexiness to his pageant. He extended the question-and-answer segment to include the girls' "favorite way to keep their legs in shape" and their "secret fantasies," and encouraged the contestants to give answers that would tease the men in the audience.

"Try and give cute sexy answers without really being dirty," Jason encouraged the contestants, "Innuendoes can be sexier than being too graphic."

Jason figured with the way sexual attitudes had changed in the past couple of years, men weren't turned on by women who seemed too *prudish* or too *wholesome* anyway.

The contestants seemed to like advertising their intents as well, and all began talking about funny, sexy answers they would give to Jason's questions.

By the time Jason began emceeing his legs contest at ten pm, the disco was filled beyond capacity, and the television news cameraman barely had room to move around and get the segment with his large videotape camera and needed to push his way through the crowd constantly.

Jason also knew he wanted to be more entertaining onstage and started using more innuendoes and double-entendres himself while questioning the contestants. He knew they were all old corny one-liners, but Jason knew plenty of them, and they seemed to work with the crowd who obviously already had a good buzz going by the time the contest began.

If a contestant said she was a secretary, Jason would casually ask if she took good *"Dic...Tation,"* with enough of a pause to be obvious. Or, if the contestant said she worked as a dental assistant, Jason would usually tell the guys in the audience to see that contestant after the contest if they needed some *"oral work"* done.

Jason had also given a few of the girl's suggestions for some "cute and sexy" answers for some fun back and forth banter on stage and even suggested a couple of lines from the dirty song lyrics he had written.

"Well, I always like to play a game with the guys that I meet called *Disco Dutch Treat*," another one of the contestants would tease when talking about the kind men she liked at the discos.

When Jason would innocently ask her what she meant, she'd give the punchline.

"I tell the guys if the drinks are *on them* tonight," she sexily answered, "Then the rest of the night can be *on me.*"

Most of the contestants also had fun with their own innuendoes, and one contestant teased the men in the audience that she had "*Sixty-nine different ways* she loved to keep her legs in shape," which obviously got a better response than just saying she kept her legs in shape by exercising or riding a bike.

The mostly male audience always laughed and cheered loudly at every innuendo either Jason or the contestants gave, and he felt it was the liveliest contest he had presented yet.

With so many contestants, Jason was onstage with the girls for almost two hours, but he was having fun playing the *almost* straight man to the girl's apparent comedy act or occasionally dropping his own innuendoes to always get laughs from the audience.

After he finally concluded the judging and announced the winner well after midnight, almost everyone Jason talked to afterward said it was the most entertaining contest they'd ever seen, and all wanted to know when the next legs contest would be.

Jason saw the men obviously liked the *sexy talk* more than seeing the girls just dance around in bikinis, and liked that the girls seemed more accessible to them than the girls who flaunted that they were models and actresses.

After clearing over twelve hundred dollars from the door money and bar receipts from his first *Nightmovers* party, Jason knew he had a winner was back in business in California again.

When Larry Burrell ran almost a two-minute segment the following evening on *Metro News Metro News* about the *Nightmovers* party and mainly the unique legs contest, Jason suddenly had a fun new contest that would make it easier to begin once again promoting at least bi-weekly parties again.

Success was the best medicine to erase any of his bitterness and hate he felt toward his parents but had already decided that they were both dead to him, and he never wanted to see either of them again.

He'd feel much better just considering himself an orphan from now on.

જ

The disco scene was bigger than ever and the nightclubs were packed almost every night, so simply by distributing his flyers, posters, and handing our VIP memberships to the dozens of attractive women at the various discos Jason visited almost every night, was all the advertising he currently needed to attract big crowds the nights of his parties.

Near the end of the year, Jason had presented more *Nightmovers* parties and contests in different cities and discos, including *My Place* in Beverly Hills, *Le Hot Club* in Encino, *Bootleggers* in West LA, *The Playgirl Club* in Garden Grove, and *Destiny Two* in Culver City. He also had more "Miss Legs" contests booked from the *Red Onion* and *Bobby McGee's* chain of restaurants and discos to begin in early 1977. He knew he needed variety for weekly parties, so he added a men's legs contest, different themed disco dance contests, and some other specially themed parties so he could continue having regular cash flow.

Jason's men's legs contests went over as well, if not better than his *Bachelor Contests*, and as opposed to the girl's contests, he'd still have the men show more to the women by having them dance around in their swimsuits to the screaming female audiences. He thought it was interesting that his female legs contest seemed sexier to the male audience by being *less exploitive* and just having the girls *talk sexy*, while the women wanted as much *exploitation and skin* as possible from the male contestants. Jason saw that *Women's Lib* was starting to make the women act wilder than the men, sometimes almost just to prove a point.

But there was one other thought that was always in the back of Jason's mind.

He still missed being known as an editor and publisher and was still thinking about starting up another tabloid or magazine that he could have as an additional vehicle that would go along with his *Nightmovers* parties.

Just as he had in Dallas with his eight-page insert in the *National Singles Register*, Jason could focus on the disco and nightclub party scene that was now the center of everyone's universe, plus he knew he could always get some writers and feature newsworthy interviews or stories that still would glamorize singlehood.

But this time, he'd actually make money from any singles who advertised for dates along with the other profits.

There was a song by Neil Sedaka and Elton John called *Steppin' Out* that Jason currently liked, and felt the lyrics were very appropriate for the attitude of the disco and singles crowd had about *getting some romantic action* every night.

Jason thought *Steppin' Out Magazine* sounded perfect as a name for a new publication, but toward the end of the year, Bob Segar released a song called *Night Moves*, and Jason began to think it was almost destiny that a song came out that gave his *Nightmovers Club* a personal theme song.

He decided if he could find a way in 1977 actually to start another publication, it would be *Night Moves*, the magazine for the *Nightmovers*.

Jason was confident that 1977 would be the year of his best change yet.

Chapter Thirteen

There were so many nightclubs and disco's available throughout Southern California, and far enough apart from each other, to allow Jason to sometimes sell two *Nightmovers* parties a week where he knew he could attract different audiences and contestants as not to be competition to another disco he already had booked.

"Volume Partying" is the way Jason used to describe his career to anyone who asked.

It was just after midnight, and Jason had just finished up his *Nightmovers* party at *The Brass Rail* disco in Glendale. '

The Brass Rail wasn't one of the trendy nightclubs Jason had been used to producing his parties, and none of his usual friends from Hollywood and Beverly Hills had attended his party that night. He decided to get his *Nightmovers* events more well known to a wider audience, as well as building up his bankroll to eventually have enough money to start a new magazine.

Metro News Metro News had been at *The Brass Rail* earlier to interview Jason about his upcoming parties in 1977, his *Night Moves Magazine* he had "in development," as well as what he described as a "comeback concert" he was planning for Jan Berry in the future.

During the interview, Jason had mentioned that *Nightmovers Productions* would be expanding to include a variety of different entertainment events in the coming year, along with some different beauty contests and his usual *Nightmovers* mix and match themed parties.

Jason had just collected his door money from that evening's party after announcing his legs contest winner in Glendale and was counting the cash in a booth when he heard someone yell "SURPRISE!" and looked up very surprised.

"I thought I'd surprise you this time like you did to me in New York," laughed Lori Wagner, "I just flew in from Rome a couple of days ago, and Annie Gaybis told me you were here tonight."

Jason jumped up and gave her a big hug and a kiss on the cheek before she sat down, but he also could see that Lori seemed pretty buzzed and dressed wilder and more exposed than he'd ever seen her before.

He thought she looked sexier than ever, but was completely overdressed for the crowd at *The Brass Rail*, and also stood out with both of her braless breasts almost hanging out of her sheer blouse. Jason also noticed that Lori was more animated than he'd ever seen her before, as she excitedly started explaining about her time in Rome.

"My God, Jason!" Lori began excitedly describing, "You wouldn't believe how wild and crazy the filming was in Rome and how much fun I had over there," Lori leaned over as if to whisper but still spoke with excitement.

"There was so much cocaine and booze on the movie set it was just like a big party with everyone half smashed and trying to imagine the way it really was back in ancient Rome!" she began laughing, "I mean Peter O'Toole was drunk in most of his scenes, but he was great, and Malcolm McDowell was incredible as Caligula."

"Being high on coke and booze during some of the scenes was perfect for making everyone feel that we were as degenerate as the characters we were playing," she added with another laugh, "Most of the actors kept describing it as *method acting*."

Jason had never heard Lori mention anything about cocaine before and was surprised that she had brought it up so casually and wondered if that was the reason she was acting so differently. But he didn't want to bring it up and just tried to share her enthusiasm.

"Well, you look great, and that sounds wild," said Jason, "How is your part in the movie?"

I've got a few interesting scenes", she smiled, "But Bob said some of us might go back to Rome to film a few other scenes to give me more screen time."

Jason always suspected something was going on with Lori and Bob Guccione, but he had never mentioned it and knew it was something that didn't matter any longer. Their romantic relationship had all but ended almost a year earlier, and both their personal lives were something neither of them needed to discuss.

Lori then stood up and started dancing suggestively next to Jason as she heard the song that the DJ just started spinning.

"C'mon, baby this, is *my song*, let's dance!" she said as she reached out to Jason and started singing along with the lyrics to the Bee Gees' current hit disco song, *The Nights on Broadway.*

Jason didn't want to spoil her cheerful mood as he joined her on the dance floor but was starting to feel uncomfortable seeing how buzzed and different Lori was acting that night.

As Lori continued mouthing the words to the song, she began dancing and posing seductively not only to Jason, but also as if she wanted everyone in the bar to notice her, and it appeared she wanted to put on a show for all of them.

Although he should have been happier seeing her again, Jason knew this wasn't the Lori he had known for all these years and was just anxious for that song to end.

When they finished dancing, Lori continued to sway suggestively and continue posing while they stood by the bar as she looked around the crowd in the disco.

"I don't even know any of these people here, so let's go back into Hollywood if you're done with your party," Lori suddenly suggested, "We've still got almost two hours till the other bars close, so let's go party somewhere else that's more fun!"

Jason still wanted to appear that he was happy to see her and not show Lori that he was uncomfortable with her demeanor, but he really wanted to make an excuse not to spend any more time with her that night.

"Baby, I'd love to, but I need to stay here till closing time," Jason lied, "Can we get together tomorrow?"

Jason saw that Lori's mood seemed to suddenly change, hearing his excuse, and she shook her head in disappointment.

"I do want to get together again," Jason tried to add more optimistically, "But I'm too tired to do anything else tonight and just want to go home and get some sleep."

"You're so boring," Lori sarcastically laughed with some bitterness, "You used to be so much more fun."

Lori suddenly just grabbed her purse and started to leave.

"Well, I just wanted to pop in and say hello," she said with a dismissive and flippant tone, "So let's talk tomorrow and catch up."

"*Ciao Baby!*" she waved as she just walked away towards the front door.

Jason couldn't believe Lori stopped by for only fifteen minutes, and in a way, he relieved, but was also feeling a little sad in another sense.

Lori was one person he had always hoped wouldn't change that much.

✿

Lori hadn't told Jason or Annie where she could be reached since she was back in town, and it wasn't until three days later until she stopped by the apartment without any notice.

"Surprise again," Lori smiled a little embarrassedly when Jason answered the door.

"I'm sorry if I seemed a little strange the other night," Lori tried to laugh when she first walked in the apartment, "It was probably just from all the traveling and the jet lag."

"No problem," Jason just smiled back, trying not to appear that he noticed anything different about her, "At least you were in a great mood."

As they hugged hello, Jason was glad to see that she was at least back to being the *normal Lori* and offered her some coffee as they sat down.

They then began talking about everything they had been doing since they last saw each other in New York without mentioning the night at *The Brass Rail*.

"*Let My People Come* played on Broadway for about four months, but we never had what was considered an *official* opening," Lori began explaining, "We just stayed in previews before the producers decided just to close the show, but it was still a great experience."

"Hey, at least you starred on Broadway," said Jason with encouragement, "How many people do we know who can say that."

"I'm sure it was more rewarding than my Las Vegas Strip appearance," he tried to add with a chuckle.

"That sounded so funny," Lori smiled, "I wish I could have been there."

"I still haven't even seen the video that Michael Ritz shot that night," Jason smiled, "He said the playback machine is too big to try and borrow from his Air Force base, so he's still figuring out how to show it to me."

"But I've pretty much wanted to forget about all that anyway," Jason added, "So I'm not really that interested in seeing it."

After discussing a few other recent activities, Jason also let Lori know that James Bacon's book *Hollywood is a Four-Letter Town* came out and had received great reviews in the *New York Times*.

"Jim Bacon even used your anonymous story you gave him for his book about David Cassidy's dick," joked Jason, "Plus he even included that parody you sang, *love is a long and slender thing.*"

"Well, I'm at least glad he didn't use my name," Lori smiled, "I'll have to pick up the book at the airport and try to read it when I fly back to New York."

"I did find out yesterday that I will be flying back to Italy to film some more scenes for Caligula," she cheerfully continued, "So the book can give me a few laughs during all my long flights."

"Oh, that reminds me," Lori added almost apologetically, "I also needed to let you know my lease on the apartment is up at the end of this month, and I'm not going to renew it."

"After I get back from Rome, I'm just going to stay in New York and see if I can land a part in another Broadway show," she added, "But you can just lease this apartment yourself if you want to stay here."

"I appreciate you letting me stay here this year," said Jason, "But I think I'm ready to move somewhere else and need to get my own place now."

"Well, I'm glad I was at least able to help you out for a while," Lori smiled, "But it looks like you're at least back in business again and doing well."

There was a break in the conversation before Lori got more serious.

"So, have you heard anything at all from your parents?" she asked.

"Nothing and I don't ever plan to," Jason coldly changed his tone, "I'm done with them."

"All this shit that happened was probably just a blessing," he added bitterly, "I knew last year that I wasn't going to stay at the newspaper forever, and it was my mistake for even getting involved with them in the first place."

"It's so sad that it got to that point," Lori quietly said, "They were your only family."

"I told you plenty of times that we were never that close anyway, so it's no big deal," Jason tried to add nonchalantly, "But I'm just glad it's finally over with them, and it's actually been a relief."

"I don't feel like I'm part of a close family either and still have problems with my parents at times too," Lori sighed, "Maybe it was just harder because we were both only children and never had a big family."

"Who knows, but all that shit about how important families are is a joke," Jason said, getting irritated again, "It was fine when I was a kid growing up and seemed nice at times, but I don't think we were ever meant to be a family that stayed together forever."

"I figured all that crap out when I originally moved to Las Vegas, Jason sardonically smiled, "I've made a lot of friends since then, and I feel closer to them than I ever felt with my parents."

"And I'm happier just having those friends in my life," Jason added, wanting to end the subject, "So there's really nothing left to say about it."

There were another few moments of silence before Lori spoke again.

"Well, I don't think all your friends are really your friends either," Lori quietly began changing the subject, "It's hard having real friends in this town, and I'd just be careful if I were you."

"Well, you know everyone I know," Jason smiled unconcerned, "So why would you say something like that?"

"You know, it always used to bug me when we all used to go out together," Lori started lightly, "You always ended up picking up the tab for everybody, and they never even once offered to pay or even left a tip."

"That was no big deal," Jason smiled, "Some people are just cheap, but they were my friends, and I could afford it."

"It's easy always having friends when you're paying all the time," Lori added with a little sarcasm.

"Well, I had trade-outs with a lot of restaurants," Jason said defensively, "So most of them always knew that."

"But how many of them ever offered to take you out to lunch or dinner or even pay for drinks?" Lori asked more seriously, "Can you think of once?"

"Well, I never worried about that stuff," Jason again began to get irritated with the conversation.

"Jason, I've wanted to tell you something for a long time, but I didn't want to hurt your feelings," Lori began to speak carefully, "But all of those people you think are your friends aren't what you think."

"Some of them would talk behind your back," she continued with irritation herself, "And there weren't too many of your other male friends that didn't always try to fuck me when you weren't looking."

Jason was surprised by what she was saying, but didn't say anything and just let Lori continue.

"I didn't want to start any arguments with you," she tried to half-smile, "But your supposed friends are the ones who let me know how much you were screwing around on me back when we were still together."

Jason tried to give a surprised but innocent look before she continued.

"Don't worry, it wasn't your closest friends like Annie or Mixie who'd never say anything bad about you," Lori quickly added, "But someone else who you always thought was a *great friend*, couldn't seem to wait to tell me about the other women."

Jason immediately guessed that Lori might be talking about Stan Adams.

Although he didn't like hearing about any betrayals of trust, Jason didn't try to deny anything and instead just quietly shook his head, trying to be slightly defensive.

"Well, I heard some stories about you and Bob Guccione too," Jason said defensively, "Some people just like to gossip, and you can't believe everything you hear."

"Listen, Jason, I still have great feelings for you, and I don't want a few bullshit things to spoil the memories of the times we had together," Lori tried to half-smile, "All that stuff is in the past now, and although it did hurt me then, I'm over it, and it really doesn't matter anymore."

"I just wanted to let you know to be careful about who you confide in and consider a good friend," Lori added, "Some people are just fucked up, and you shouldn't trust everyone so much."

"Well, I guess there's a few people I won't be picking up the tab for in the future," Jason tried to smile and lighten the conversation.

They were both momentarily quite again before Lori then tried to change the mood herself.

"Okay, enough of all this negative stuff," she cheerfully said, "I've got to fly back to New York tomorrow, so why don't we do something fun later."

"We can go to the *Rainbow*, just the two of us," Lori said more excitedly, "We can have a Miguel's Taco Plate or some pizza like the old days."

"I'd love to, but I have another party tonight at *The Point After* in North Hollywood," Jason said, "Why don't you come with me to the party, and we can do something afterward?"

"I don't really feel like being around a lot of people tonight," Lori said, disappointed, "I just thought it would be fun to go to the Rainbow one more time before I leave."

"Okay, I'll tell you what then," Jason suggested. "I'll just announce my contest winners earlier tonight and leave the party right after that."

"I can just hop over Laurel Canyon and can probably be back here by midnight," he cheerfully added, "So that'll leave us plenty of time to spend at the Rainbow."

"Well, I do have some things I need to pack up here from my apartment here before I fly back to New York tomorrow," Lori began considering, "And I can probably do all that while you're gone."

"Okay, that sounds good," she said more cheerfully, "I'll just go take care of that stuff and meet you back here at the apartment around midnight."

"It's a date!", Jason smiled walking Lori to the door, "We can at least have a pretend New Year's Eve toast to 1977 a few weeks early seeing you won't be here this year."

"The good old 'to having fun' toast, as usual, right?" Lori half laughed as they hugged goodbye.

"Of course!" Jason smiled, "What's more important than that?"

❧

Jason did leave his party at *The Point After* early and knew he'd have no problem being back to his apartment by midnight, as he sped over Laurel Canyon back to Hollywood.

He was still thinking about the conversation he had with Lori earlier and was disappointed about many things she said about his friends, but he was more disappointed in himself for not even trying to apologize or explain certain things she'd mentioned that afternoon.

Jason wanted to have a more positive conversation and clear the air about some of those things when they were alone at *The Rainbow*.

But when he walked into the apartment, he saw Lori had already taken all of her belongings and had only left behind a note that said, *"I'm sorry,"* she had placed on top of an old photo of them together.

She was already gone, and Jason knew they had finally said their goodbye.

Chapter Fourteen

With the lease on Lori's apartment up, Jason decided to take a break from his old crowd in Hollywood and rented a large three-bedroom furnished house in Encino with a huge back yard and swimming pool.

It cost over twice as much rent as he had ever paid before, seven hundred and fifty dollars, but he was earning almost three times as much money as well, and it was a perfect *Nightmovers* party house.

He knew it wasn't really any type of *Playboy Mansion*, but Jason figured it would be fine for the present. He also decided to rent a production office on Ventura Boulevard in Van Nuys, which he eventually planned on being a *Night Moves Magazine* office.

There were a lot of people he knew who said he should work on getting investors if he wanted to start a magazine, but Jason didn't even want to consider asking other people for money or do anything even remotely similar to the way his father had done business.

He had already seen how that situation had ended up.

Jason also knew it would take several more months before he could save enough money and figure out the business angle as far as distribution and advertising, so he would continue to say, "It's still in *development*," which was what almost everyone in Hollywood said about movies.

He knew he really didn't need a magazine to make money, but Jason still felt his title as editor and publisher of the upcoming *Night Moves Magazine* sounded more official and gave him a certain gravitas instead of just being known as a nightclub promoter. He'd also gotten away from pushing his parties as "celebrity" parties and mainly saw it was more beneficial promotion wise, to always have members of the different media as judges who gave him his free advertising and publicity.

The disco managers still liked seeing *celebrity judges* on the flyers and posters, so Jason figured besides the media, some of his close friends had enough show biz credentials to be introduced as *celebrities* at his parties.

Now that he was promoting more parties away from Hollywood and Beverly Hills, the audiences in other cities were still impressed with anyone connected with show business. Besides having Jan Berry still regularly judge his contests, Lita Krissan was beginning to produce and direct documentaries, which allowed Jason to introduce her as a *"filmmaker"* while Mixie Thompson had small roles in two major films, *Logan's Run* and the NBC television movie *Raid on Entebbe* about the Israeli rescue of hostages in Idi Aman's Uganda.

Annie Gaybis had some bigger roles in the low budget exploitation films, *Black Shampoo* and *Deep Jaws* that used titles similar to earlier box office hits, so along with Jan, Mixie, and Lita, Jason usually had at least one Hollywood personality for a celebrity judge at each party and contest. Jason was mainly satisfied that it was his promotional ideas, and not just big named celebrities, that was attracting crowds to his parties.

He actually liked the new crowd and friends he was making away from the Hollywood and Beverly Hills area that reminded him more of the *real* crowd he had in Dallas.

Jason had also always stayed in touch with Martha Bland by phone, who was his only link to the time he'd spent in Dallas, but he somehow also still felt a strong connection and attraction with her even though he hadn't seen her in over six months.

With everything about Dallas having seemingly faded, he eventually was able to fly Martha to California and stay with him for a weekend as he had once promised her. She had never been to California before, so Jason decided to spend a weekend away from the discos and bars and see some of the attractions he hadn't even experienced himself in many years and knew she'd enjoy.

Jason hadn't been to Disneyland since he was a teenager, but he knew it was almost a *must see* for someone coming to California for the first time and also took her to spend an evening on the beach in Santa Monica so she could see the ocean.

As they shared a bottle of wine on the sand and just listened to the waves as they looked up at the stars, Jason was surprised how much fun he was having just being alone with Martha, and not inside of a loud disco or nightclub as he usually was every night. He had already been surprised at how much fun he had at Disneyland enjoying all of the *kid stuff* and *kiddie rides* he'd always remembered and liked sharing the experience with someone who never had before.

Martha had also told Jason that weekend, that everything in Dallas seemed normal, and she hadn't heard anything that sounds suspicious since he'd been gone. She said even people they both knew at the discos would only ask about him occasionally.

He was surprised that with all his friends in Dallas, Martha had said no one seemed that curious or interested about why he just disappeared or what had happened to him, but it did make Jason realize again that what Edy Williams had once told him was true.

Once you get out of the limelight for too long and aren't mentioned in the media, people do forget about you fast.

Jason also figured that "no news was good news" and was just glad everything about Dallas was apparently safe for him.

The most surprising thing Martha asked during their weekend together, was when she asked Jason if he had a few lines of cocaine they could enjoy, when they were lying on the beach together the night before she was going back to Dallas.

"I don't do coke," Jason just laughed to her, "I don't remember you even bringing that up in Dallas and I didn't even know you tried it before"

"I just tried it a couple of times," Martha laughed back, "But it started getting more popular in the clubs in the last few months, and I was just wondering if you tried it yet."

"Nope, I know that it's around and know people who do it, but haven't really been that interested in it myself," Jason smiled.

"But a nurse friend did give me Vitamin B-12 shots for a while which she said was supposed to give me a boost like cocaine does," Jason added, "But since she moved out of state, I just have a couple of extra Bailey's and Coffee drinks to keep me going."

"It's no big deal, I just thought it might be fun to try with you," Martha smiled, "Everyone says it enhances everything from music to sex."

"Well, I just thought about something else we can try that might be fun," Jason smiled back at Martha, "There was a bartender I met who made me a new drink the other night he claimed he invented, and came up with a great name for it."

"It's called 'Sex on the Beach," Jason continued smiling as he pulled Martha towards him on the sand, "It might be something else you can remember about your first trip to California."

"Y'all always have a funny way to get a girl to spread her legs," Martha laughed, "But I do like your style."

Jason had fun playing a tourist guide that weekend, but he was also surprised at how passionate and romantic his reunion with Martha actually was.

"Absence makes the heart grow fonder," Martha joked when Jason brought up that fact.

He had always joked it was the other way around and that, "Absence makes the heart start to *wander*," but he was glad he had renewed his relationship with Martha and had never really said goodbye.

Jason knew it wasn't always possible to keep relationships alive forever, but it was at least fun to try at times. But he still wasn't making any plans to visit Martha in Texas, and knew if they saw each other again, it would be in California.

Just in case.

Chapter Fifteen

Jason had a big *St. Valentine's Day* party planned at a nightclub in the San Fernando Valley called *The Antique Mirror* that *Metro News! Metro News*! was excited to cover for their television broadcast that evening.

He was calling it a 1920s *"Gangster's and Gatsby"* costume party, and besides having a "Sexiest Flapper" contest, he decided even to have a live re-enactment of the *St. Valentine's Day Massacre* at the nightclub for a funny segment on *Metro News*.

Jason had also saved, kept hidden, and dragged around with him for years, the gun he'd bought from Frank Reich back in 1969, and had finally found a way to make use of it.

He decided to be the main gangster and hitman himself, for the massacre at that party.

But more than just a pistol was needed, so Jason had arranged from his old friend at *Paramount Pictures* Art Wilde, to rent a real working machine gun from a licensed gun dealer the studio worked with for their movies.

Jason had purchased rounds of blank ammunition for both his gun he had bought from Frank Reich, and the machine gun he was renting, to try and make it look as real as possible and have a fun *massacre re-enactment* for the television news that night. He also rented a gangster costume from *Western Costume* used in *The Godfather Part 2* and was happy to see everyone at the *Antique Mirror* party in 1920s costumes.

The partygoers were mainly a San Fernando Valley crowd, because most of the people he knew who lived over the hill in Hollywood and Beverly Hills considered anything past Highland Ave or the Bel-Air Gates, *"Outer Space"* and seldom came to Jason's parties in the Valley.

None of his regular girlfriends were at his *Gatsby and Gangsters Party* that night, but Jason didn't mind that he was stag, and as usual, he knew it was very unlikely that he would be sleeping alone after his party.

The girls at his *Nightmovers* party looked especially sexy that night dressed as 1920s *Flapper's*, and although there were still some girl's he had meet who claimed they were actresses, Jason knew that some of them were actresses in the low budget porno films that the San Fernando Valley was becoming famous for.

The porno industry had almost become part of the mainstream movie market, since *Deep Throat* had become such a big hit and had made millions of dollars, and Jason had become friendly with some of the girls involved in that business, and there were a few of them who even entered his contests.

Two of the actresses he was already acquainted, named Cara and Sunshine, had entered his *Sexiest Flapper Contest* at *The Antique Mirror* that night and were also excited about being featured on that evening's *Metro News* broadcast.

When the camera crew from *Metro News* showed up at the party, the reporter wanted some setup action and B-Roll shots before the re-enactment of the actual *Massacre*.

As the cameras rolled, the cameraman Dean, who Jason had met a few times when he taped other *Nightmovers* parties, directed the first action scene that Jason would be involved in.

Jason walked to the pool table inside the bar with two *sexy flappers* on each of his arms and made a wager that he could make a seemingly impossible pool shot.

When he made the shot, and the other *gangsters* started complaining it was an *unfair trick shot,* Jason pulled out his pistol and started shooting directly at them as they convincingly fell dead to the floor. That was the cue for other *gangsters* in the bar to pull out their own pistols filled with blanks, and begin shooting throughout the disco.

Everyone was having fun laughing and shooting at each other because even the blank shells' sound sounded like the real thing. Dean also wanted the cameras to show *dead bodies* falling throughout the disco and make it look as dramatic as possible.

"Cut!" shouted Dean, "That looked great, just like a real gangster shootout!"

"Now, let's shoot the big *massacre!*" Dean cheerfully added as he prepared to move his camera and lights for the next scene.

The Antique Mirror was in a shopping mall and had a brick exterior, so Jason and Dean had decided there was more room to line up the *victims* against the brick wall to be massacred outside of the nightclub. They all then went outside by the parking lot, and the licensed gun dealer gave Jason the real machine gun he would be using for the re-enactment.

The gun dealer explained to Jason that the machine gun would fire dozens of blank rounds in less than five or six seconds and had "quite a kick" and make sure he held it firmly when he pulled the trigger.

As Dean said, *"Action!"* the costumed partygoers began the re-enactment just as they had rehearsed.

The scene involved two *imposter* policemen, lining up seven other costumed gangsters who represented the *Bugs Moran Gang,* who then slowly backed away from those against the wall as Jason came into the frame of the camera holding the machine gun.

The cue for Jason to begin shooting was when one of the victims against the wall yelled out, "Hey, these guys ain't cops!"

Jason then pulled the trigger and couldn't believe the kick, sound, and the flames flying out of the barrel of the gun, as he sprayed what seemed like hundreds of bullets at the falling victims against the wall.

"Cut!" yelled Dean, "That was perfect!"

Both Jason and Dean were glad they got the shot they wanted in the first take, otherwise, there wouldn't have had enough time for Dean to get back to *KTTV* to have it broadcast on *Metro News* at eleven pm.

"You're getting to almost be a regular on our news broadcasts," smiled Dean as he packed up his gear, "I'm always anxious to see what crazy thing you come up with next."

Jason was satisfied he came up with another gimmick to get television news coverage, which also always allowed him to charge the disco owners an extra ten percent of the bar receipts for the additional publicity the bars would receive.

It was about an hour after the massacre re-enactment before Jason had also completed his *Sexiest Flapper Contest,* and he was standing outside the *Antique Mirror* having a cigarette and talking with Cara, who had been one of the contestants.

"Sorry, you didn't win tonight, but I never judge my own contests," smiled Jason, "But you look great tonight, and I would've voted for you."

"Right, Jason, how many girls do you tell that to each contest?" Cara teased, "But as long as you come to the after-hours party tonight, you can be my consolation prize."

"I told you I'd *come,* I promise," Jason told her, knowing that she'd appreciate his innuendo.

He always liked the time and energy it saved him when he was the one being "picked up" by a girl instead of the other way around, but also knew that hadn't been anything unusual for most of the guys at the discos the past couple years.

Jason saw there were always at least two or three girls who would wander around near closing time, saying, *"Wanna fuck?"* to some guy at the bar and just move on to the next one if the first guy declined.

No one at the discos ever planned on ever going home alone.

As Jason and Cara were still talking outside, a police cruiser casually drove by the parking lot in front of the *Antique Mirror,* and the police officer rolled down his window and called to them.

"Someone called in and said they heard some gunfire inside the bar earlier," said the officer, "And we got another call from someone who heard what sounded like guns or fireworks going off outside, so I just thought I'd stop by and see if everything is okay."

"It's just a party," Jason half laughed to the officer. "We were just having a little fun shooting some guns with blanks at each other."

"Okay, as long as everything's all right," the officer said as he drove off, "Have a nice night."

"Jeez, that was over an hour ago," laughed Jason, "It sure took a long time for him to see if everything was alright."

"They probably just figured it was a prank call," said Cara, "I mean, who shoots guns in a nightclub?!"

"Well, talking about shooting off my gun," Jason tried to tease Cara with another innuendo, "Where is this party that you're talking about tonight?"

It was a little after two am that same night when Jason walked into the large hillside house on *Valley Side* of the Hollywood Hills with Cara and Sunshine.

They were still dressed in their costumes, and Jason saw almost a dozen others still in costume who'd also come to the after-hours party from the *Antique Mirror.*

The stereo was blasting one of Jason's current favorite songs, *Don't Leave Me This Way* by Thelma Houston, and about ten other couples were dancing on a space set up in the living room.

So many disco songs centered around having sex, and Jason always joked to the girls that *Don't Leave Me This Way* was a perfect song to represent his *"An erection is a terrible thing to waste"* catchphrase that he sometimes still used, and always got a giggle out of them when he'd sing the title of that song when they were in bed together.

Another small group was sitting at a couch, obviously spreading thin lines of cocaine on a mirror with a razor blade.

Jason recognized one of the guys on the couch as John Holmes, who was better known as *Johnny Wadd* in a serious of famous porn movies, and guessed besides Cara and Sunshine, several other girls at that party were also probably porno actresses.

"Jason, I can't believe you haven't done coke," said Cara as they joined the others on the couch.

"I just haven't got around to it," Jason said without concern, "I just like the high I get from booze and don't like to get too loaded."

"You don't get loaded from coke," teased Cara, "It just gives you energy and enhances everything."

"I did some *'white crosses'* to keep me awake when I was in college, but I'm not really into drugs," Jason just smiled, "Bailey's and Coffee and an occasional Vitamin B-12 shot is usually all I need to keep my energy going these days."

"It also really opens up your mind and makes you think better too," said another girl sitting on the couch, "But it's definitely not addictive or a hard drug like heroin."

"You must be the last person in LA who isn't doing coke," laughed John Holmes, who had finished spreading the lines on the mirror, "Or at least the first one I've met."

"Plus, you haven't really fucked until you've fucked on cocaine," added Cara with a tempting smile.

Jason smiled himself at Cara's comment because he'd heard almost the exact words from other girl's he'd known in the past who told him, "You *haven't really fucked* till you've fucked on marijuana" or *"haven't really fucked* until you've tried it on acid."

There had already been other people who told Jason cocaine was the "best drug ever invented," and there were many others he knew who said they did coke occasionally, and they all seemed fine to him.

Jason facetiously thought to himself that it was as good as night as any to let another girl *corrupt* him, knowing he didn't need to do anything important the next day, and could sleep in just in case he got too *loaded.*

Cara snorted two lines from a rolled-up hundred-dollar bill and then handed the bill to Jason.

He snorted a line in each nostril as he saw the others do, and besides just burning a little, Jason felt like his nostrils froze up and were cold, but didn't feel anything dramatic and didn't think it had any effect on him at all.

But after only a few minutes, it actually just made him feel like the effects of the booze he drank earlier had worn off, and he was able to have more drinks at the party without getting drunk.

It wasn't until about two hours later when he was in one of the bedrooms with Cara that he realized she had been right about what she said about cocaine enhancing everything.

Especially when Sunshine also decided to join them in bed.

Jason just hoped there weren't any hidden cameras rolling anywhere because he definitely felt like he was in the middle of a scene from a *porno flick,* and tried hard to keep from laughing as he enjoyed both of Cara and Sunshine's *acting talents.*

The only real effect Jason felt from the cocaine was that it kept him awake longer to have more fun.

To him, that was a good thing.

જી

After that night with Cara and Sunshine, Jason did seem to notice even more that he probably was "the last person who wasn't doing coke in LA," and started accepting occasional *bumps* from his friends he knew who already did cocaine.

Jason saw that he never a need to buy any for himself because it seemed almost everyone he was meeting at his parties, always carried a small vial or snow seal in their pockets and didn't mind sharing a couple of bumps.

There was also a certain camaraderie with the disco crowds, and everyone knew that coke kept everyone in a good mood, and did seem to enhance the music and parties more than before.

Jason also ended up meeting Sammy Davis Jr again through a friend named Danny, who explained he was Sammy's cocaine contact and had brought Jason along to Sammy's house in Beverly Hills one time.

Sammy got a laugh when Jason reminded him how they first met at Caesars Palace at Sammy's fiftieth birthday party, and Sammy also cheerfully took out a small gold spoon and shared a couple of bumps of the coke that Danny had delivered.

There was also a certain camaraderie that seemed even to turn celebrities into immediate friends with casual acquaintances when they shared cocaine.

Danny later explained he wasn't really a full-time drug dealer and only delivered cocaine to a few Hollywood celebrities. He bragged that along with Sammy Davis Jr, who he said was good for at least "an ounce of coke a week," Danny also described how a female star of a top-rated television drama would "usually give him a blow job" each time he supplied her with not only cocaine, but with the large quantity of Quaaludes she craved.

Danny also explained he mainly delivered the cocaine to supply himself with *"free cocaine"* by being able to cut the real cocaine he was delivering to the celebrities, with a powder called *Mannitol*, and separate at least a few grams for himself each week.

Jason also thought it was a waste of money himself to pay up to a hundred dollars for such a small amount that was usually sold in grams, and would only do a couple of *bumps* when someone at one of his parties would offer him some as a friendly gesture. But he did see that cocaine had its benefits and never got him high as marijuana once had, and just kept him awake longer with a clearer mind as several Bailey's and Coffee cocktails had always accomplished in the past.

He was usually producing two parties a week, and the extra boost did seem to keep him sharp, funny, and even more entertaining when he was on stage, and Jason's *Nightmovers* parties were becoming more fun than they'd ever been before. Not just at the discos, but also at the after-hours parties he began hosting at his Encino house when the bars closed.

He always remembered how a reporter in Dallas had once joked on camera about *"How Jason's parties never end,"* and did smile to himself how that statement was actually beginning to be true that year.

Jason sometimes couldn't believe how lucky he was to have created a job for himself where he was getting paid so well to be able to make a living just having fun.

Chapter Sixteen

It was a Wednesday in early April when Sia Amiri, the owner of *My Place Disco* in Beverly Hills, called Jason at his office in Van Nuys.

"Jason, you know Harold Robbins, right?" asked Sia, "He rented the club tonight for a big birthday party for his wife and said I could invite some interesting people who were regulars at the bar to help spice up the party."

Jason had only met Harold Robbins one time and just told Sia that they were *acquainted*.

"It's an open bar, so all the liquor is free, so I thought you could also bring a few sexy girls with you," Sia lightly teased, "I know you can always manage that, right?"

Jason was suddenly glad he didn't have one of his own *Nightmovers* parties scheduled that night, and also smiled to himself that his reputation as the *go-to guy* when it came to pretty women, had gotten him an invitation to a famous Harold Robbins party.

"But it's not a press party, so don't invite any photographers," Sia added, "I hear his parties are pretty wild, and he doesn't want any crazy photos floating around out there that might get published."

Jason still didn't have a definite date for when he was starting *Night Moves Magazine* but was still mentioning it was *"in development,"* so he was still considered a member of the press.

"I'll put your name on the guestlist if you'd like to come," Sia said before lightly adding, "But remember, it's strictly a private party, so don't invite anyone else unless they got great legs or big tits."

"Well, I'll be there for sure, so just put my name on the guestlist for now," Jason said, "I've already got a date tonight with someone who's pretty sexy, but I'll make some calls and see who else I can invite."

Jason already had a date planned that night with another former "bachelorette" he had reconnected with that year, named Sheri Lynn.

Sheri had also been one of Jason's back-up singers at his *Thunderbird* show in Las Vegas, and they had a brief romantic relationship a couple of years earlier, but he had always stayed in contact with her, and they had recently renewed their casual romance.

When Jason had first met her, he thought she was British because of her accent, but learned she was from Rhodesia, South Africa and had once worked for the Prime Minister Ian Smith as part of his personal security force.

With her blond hair, pretty looks, and sweet demeanor, Jason could never picture her being a *"commando"* as she described her previous occupation. Sheri Lynn was also one of the few friends who remembered his birthday earlier that year and had bought him a crazy new wristwatch that was becoming popular in the discos.

The watch had a black face that would show the digital time and date when a button was pushed once, and then spell out a secret digital message when the button was pushed twice.

The digital message on the watch she gave him was programmed to spell out the phrase, *Your…Place…Or…Mine?* which Jason had recently enjoyed displaying to any girls who would ever ask him the time.

"It's like a futuristic James Bond type of watch," Sheri joked, "I had them program a message that I thought would fit you well."

Although Jason and Sheri had renewed their romance the past couple of months, he saw by the birthday present she gave him that she understood he wasn't looking for anything exclusive, and he liked that she was comfortable with that arrangement.

He had already known how the culture had mainly been focused on having as many orgasms a week with different partners, and love and monogamy weren't currently in vogue.

At least at the discos.

After his conversation with Sia Amiri that day, Jason decided not to bother inviting any other girls to the Harold Robbins party and wanted just to bring Sheri, knowing that she'd appreciate being his only companion that night.

He did like her, and appreciated her friendship, but he never wanted her to feel like she was just *one of the girls* he was inviting to a party.

❧

When Jason arrived with Sheri Lynn at *My Place* around ten pm, the light show and strobe lights were in full effect as the DJ was blasting the disco music to the overflow crowd. The dance floor was also completely full, and the partygoers were dancing in the aisles, as scantily dressed girls and several bare-chested men were even dancing on the tables.

It was the wildest mixture of a party crowd he'd ever seen, from well- dressed celebrities, to a couple wandering magicians, along with other circus performer types, including some dressed as clowns, and many others he'd normally only see at hardcore rock and roll bars dressed in leather.

"Now, this looks like a party!" Jason cheerfully laughed to Sheri as they tried to get to the bar.

"This certainly isn't anything like your Nightmovers parties," said Sheri, who seemed a little intimidated with the wild crowd, "It's very similar to a human zoo."

"Well, it's fun not having to worry about working or playing host at this party," Jason smiled, "Let's just drink and have fun being ordinary guests tonight."

As they walked through the wall-to-wall disco, Jason caught a glimpse of Grace Robbins drinking directly from a bottle of Dom Perignon, obviously already drunk, surrounded by a group of bodybuilders in speedos encouraging her to "*Chug* the entire bottle" as they suggestively rubbed their bodies against her.

While Jason was on the dance floor with Sheri, he also saw Sammy Davis Jr dancing next to him and briefly said hello and introduced him to Sheri.

"I promise I won't try to lift you up when I introduce you to anyone again," Jason joked to Sammy, who just smiled and gave a thumbs-up as they all continued dancing. Jason also coincidently saw the sexy television actress that Danny said "craved Quaaludes" wildly dancing with two bare-chested men, and had her blouse opened enough to expose both her own bouncing breasts.

He briefly thought about how he wouldn't mind getting a blow job from that actress himself as he briefly watched her, but Jason never wanted to flirt with anyone else when he was on an *actual date* and kept his attention focused on Sheri.

Jason also was seeing why Sia said Harold Robbins didn't want any press or photographers at the party and thought about how much *Metro News* would probably have loved having a segment of the party for their newscast. He had always heard that Robbins hosted great parties, but saw he still had a long way to go even to come close to having a party like he was hosting that night.

It wasn't until after midnight that Jason learned the party at *My Place* was just a warm-up for a bigger party that would be held at Harold Robbin's mansion *after hours.*

Jason and Sheri had just come off the dance floor when one of the bare-chested bodybuilders approached them at the bar and handed them a sealed envelope.

"You two look like you'll do," said the bodybuilder nonchalantly, "Mr. Robbin's address is inside the envelope, and you'll need to show it when you arrive, so please don't lose it or share it with anyone else."

Jason watched the bodybuilder continue to walk through the crowd and decide who else to give invitations.

"Great, we're invited to the after-party", Jason excitedly said to Sheri, "I guess he thought we looked like an attractive couple."

"That sounds lovely," Sheri said as excited as her proper and polite South African accent allowed.

Jason wanted to make sure he stayed in a party mood for a few more hours and after seeing another friend that he had shared some "comradery" with before, he borrowed his friends vile, and went into the men's room to do a couple of *bumps.*

When Jason walked out of the bathroom stall after a quick blast up each nostril, he was surprised to see Dennis Cole entering the men's room.

"Dennis, long time no see!" said Jason, glad to see him again.

All of Jason's friends who knew Dennis from years earlier couldn't believe how Dennis had "hit the jackpot" when he somehow managed to become engaged to another one of the hottest actresses on television, Jaclyn Smith from *Charley's Angels*, who was also at the party that night.

"So, are you going to the after-party at Harold Robbin's house tonight?" Jason cheerfully asked Dennis figuring he'd been invited as well.

"Are you kidding?" Dennis half-laughed, "Jaclyn would kill me if I even mentioned that party to her."

"Why would she kill you?" Jason laughed, "I thought it would be fun to go and keep the party going tonight."

Dennis tried to speak to Jason softly, so no one else in the bathroom would hear.

"Jason, it's an orgy, don't you know that?!" Dennis tried to whisper, "Harold likes seeing Grace get fucked, and that's what usually happens at the *after-parties*, and those days are over for me."

No matter how wild Jason thought he was himself, he still sometimes felt naïve about certain things.

Jason was surprised, and it wasn't what he expected, but even though he briefly thought it would be fun to poke Grace Robbins, he just wasn't an *orgy guy* and wasn't something he wanted to partake.

It just wasn't romantic to him and he still liked feeling that even his one-night stands were romantic, and at least feel like they were the only ones in each other's lives when they were together, no matter if it was for a few hours or a few months.

Jason was completely satisfied with one-on-one sex, and if another girl happened to join in for a very *rare threesome*, as it had been with Cara and Sunshine, he knew it was just something that happened spontaneously, and was just a pleasant surprise sometimes. Planned out *threesomes* or *orgies* were never anything he'd wanted to be part of being involved, especially with one of his main girlfriends like Sheri Lynn.

That attitude did make Jason sometimes realize that he was a lot more normal when it came to sex than a lot of other people he knew in Hollywood.

Sheri Lynn was only slightly disappointed, but then seemed pleased when Jason told her they wouldn't be going to the after-party because he preferred spending the rest of the night alone with her.

"That sounds even more lovely," Sheri again smiled.

That was something else Jason thought was very entertaining about Sheri.

Instead of screaming, "Oh God," "Sweet Jesus!" or "Yes! Yes!" when they were in bed together, she only softly moans the words, *"Lovely! Lovely!"* in her classy South African accent.

Jason was glad he finally had the chance to attend a Harold Robbin's party but knew it would be *lovelier* just spending the rest of the night at his house one-on-one with Sheri.

That was always romantic.

Chapter Seventeen

Jason had already met several new friends and photographers at his parties who were excited about his *Night Moves Magazine* idea that still was in development and offered to eventually work as his editorial staff.

The writers would often sit in Jason's office for hours drinking beers, smoking packs of cigarettes, occasionally snorting a bump or two of cocaine, creatively coming up with ideas for exciting stories and content that would make *Night Moves Magazine* newsworthy for its premier issue.

They would usually all lightly sing together about "working on their Night Moves" each time the Bob Segar hit song would play on the radio in Jason's office while they threw around different ideas during their brainstorming sessions.

A couple of the writers were also fairly well known and had already had many of their articles published in major national magazines, and Jason briefly considered their grandiose ideas about publishing a full-size slick magazine rather than just a tabloid.

Jason liked the idea of having a classier version of the *National Singles Register* in slick magazine format, but Jason wasn't interested in some of the writer's other ideas about articles and stories about celebrities or serious subjects.

He also wanted to get away from the usual celebrity stories like he had featured when he first started the *Singles Register* and still wanted to keep the focus on the younger trendy singles market and the disco scene. Jason thought back to his old *"Everybody is a Star"* theme and decided to just focus on more stories and photos featuring his regular party crowds from his *Nightmovers* disco promotions. His partygoers had always liked seeing their names and photos in the newspapers from the parties they attended, but aside from it being a "party' and nightlife magazine, Jason also wanted to have something else that would attract readers.

During one of their brainstorming sessions, Jason and his friends talked about the idea of having a major interview in his first issue of a famous personality that could match the famous *Playboy Magazine* interviews. He agreed that having an interview with someone very unique and newsworthy could get *Night Moves* a lot of outside press and publicity immediately.

The movie that Mixie Thompson had appeared, *Raid on Entebbe* had helped make the President of Uganda Idi Amin famous, when actor Yaphet Kotto portrayed him as a charismatic but dangerous leader who threatened world peace, and Amin had become pretty much a household name the past couple years.

Although he was often compared to a modern-day Adolph Hitler, Idi Amin was also sometimes portrayed humorously in the media as an "entertaining dictator" who seemed to like all the publicity he received from being *infamous*, and had been one of the main subjects in Johnny Carson's recent comedy monologues.

When Jason learned that even an evil dictator liked receiving press and publicity just like everyone else, he decided to try and offer Idi Amin a cover story in the premiere issue of *Night Moves* and exaggerate that his new magazine was going to be as famous as other more well-known national publications.

Jason was able to track down the phone number for the Presidential Lodge in Kampala, Uganda, and said he was calling regarding an interview "similar to those in Playboy Magazine" and immediately saw that by casually dropping the name *Playboy*, he did get access to talk to several of Amin's official government ministers.

He was also glad that most of them were fairly well-spoken in English, and he had no problem communicating.

Jason heard that some of them tried to speak privately by putting their hands over the receiver but also heard them excitedly whispering the words *"Playboy"* to someone else who was also obviously listening to the call.

While he was trying to answer all of their question's they were asking him about setting up an interview, Jason even could have sworn that one time, it sounded like Idi Amin may have taken the phone from one of his ministers asked questions himself.

That person who took the phone without introducing himself, gruffly asked questions about how the interview would be structured, or if *"His excellency Amin"* would be portrayed in a complementary and positive manner. But once during the call, Jason heard the voice ask if *"I would have"* final editing approval for what was written.

Jason thought it was cool that he may have spoken to Idi Amin and might travel to Uganda to interview him., but eventually realized he could never personally afford any grandiose plans.

It did sound like a fun idea for a brief time, just as he once thought how it would be "fun" to interview Patty Hearst, but after Jason discovered what it would cost to actually travel to Uganda to interview Idi Amin, he realized he wasn't close to being prepared to for something at that level yet.

When Jason also discovered what the cost would be for printing and publishing a slick and glossy magazine, he decided all the "barnstorming" ideas he had with his friends was probably just "cocaine talk" and something he could never afford.

Jason still had no desire to try and even consider getting investors for something he should be able to do by himself, but he still wanted to publish something without having to keep saying his magazine was *"in development"* as he'd been doing for months.

His first issue of *Night Moves* needed to be something he could afford to print and pay for himself, and Jason figured that even if he didn't make money from his magazine in the beginning, he could always expand on it later. His main goal was to at least print up his first issue as inexpensively as possible so he could show that he was really an editor and publisher again, and not even worry about selling advertising and getting distribution until he had something in his hands to show everyone.

Jason knew if worse came to worse, he could at least begin by just leaving copies of *Night Moves* at the nightclubs and discos all over Southern California, which would at least make him a member of the media again, and have an additional vehicle for he could use for all of his other promotion ideas.

Jason decided he would just try to publish a quarter-fold tabloid with a four-color cover that would have a magazine look, and just print thirty-six pages of similar content as he had with the inserts in the *National Singles Register* for his *S.T.A.R.S* and *World Entertainment Club* promotions.

Jason had *Nightmovers* parties booked until June that year and knew he couldn't take a break from promoting his parties or seriously work on publishing his first issue of *Night Moves* until the summer. He also knew by then he'd have enough money saved for printing his first issue without worrying about the additional cost.

But all the brainstorming sessions with friends in his office did make Jason think about other fresh new ideas for publicity and other ways to make more money.

There were still a lot more things he wanted to do, and knew he was just getting started.

ॐ

Ever since Jason had thought about how *Metro News! Metro News!* would have loved covering the wild party that Harold Robbins had at *My Place*, but couldn't because it was private, he'd been writing out ideas that he could pitch to *KTTV* on his yellow legal pads.

Jason knew the press he received from the television news coverage in both Dallas and Los Angeles had been great for promoting his parties, but he began thinking of something that could work hand in hand with everything he was doing that could earn some actual money instead of just publicity.

He always remembered how Van Dunn had joked in Dallas about being able to film Joe Cocker completely wasted and said how it made good TV showing the candid side of what went on at some of Jason's parties.

Jason also knew that Dean, the cameraman for *KTTV*, said he was looking forward to always hearing about something new that would be wild enough for the station to show interest in broadcasting, and Jason began thinking of a completely new idea - especially when Jason noticed how much footage Dean could shoot on videotape compared to the five-minute rolls of film that Van Dunn sparingly used for his news coverage.

The videotapes were on large cartridges that ran twenty minutes and could be viewed immediately without being developed in a lab.

Because his parties were always called "a cute filler" for a news segment that only featured a minute of highlights from his parties, Jason first suggested to Dean an entire television program that would candidly show longer highlights from various parties at the hottest discos in Southern California.

"Everyone knows that discos are the biggest thing in the world right now," Jason began pitching Dean, "And it will definitely attract the trendy and hip audience you're reaching now with your current late-night shows."

"It would be a perfect fit for the hour following *Metro News! Metro News!* and *Mary Hartman! Mary Hartman!*" Jason continued, "Just one show a week, Friday nights at midnight."

Jason saw that Dean was interested and continued with his ideas.

"We could just videotape an entire night of not just that week's different contests, but a lot of other crazy party stuff," Jason excitedly added, "We can mix in a lot of the typical partying, drinking, people trying to pick on each other and different fun things to candidly show what really goes on at a typical night in a disco."

"It sounds like it could be kind of a new and different version of *Playboy After Dark*," Dean thoughtfully smiled.

"That's what I was thinking, but instead of all the usual bullshit celebrity stuff, we'll make the partygoers and beauty contestants the stars," Jason said, "There's a lot of interesting people who aren't celebrities who come to the parties that would make funny and different interview subjects."

"Plus, besides having the audience feeling like they're actually witnessing a live disco party each week," Jason concluded his pitch, "The audience watching at home can see if they come to an upcoming *Nightmovers* party, they might be on television and be one of the stars themselves."

"Do you have a name for this proposed show?" Dean asked, appearing amused by Jason's enthusiasm.

"I want to call it the *Nightmovers Party Hour*," said Jason with a wave of his hands, 'Where the real people are the stars!"

Dean decided he liked the idea and arranged a meeting for Jason and the executives at *KTTV* the following week.

Jason saw the programming manager seemed interested while he was giving his pitch and liked that Dean added his own enthusiasm himself.

"It'll be super cheap to produce and just be like an extended version of the parties we show on the news without having to pay anyone a talent fee," Dean added to Jason's pitch, "We'll have our notice of videotaping posted at the front door and just have them sign releases before they enter the discos."

"And when all the people who come to the parties spread the word that they're going to be on TV," Jason excitedly added, "You'll already have a huge built-in audience."

"Okay, we'll give a gamble and shoot some tape *on spec* and consider it news footage for now," said the main executive in charge, "Let's see how it turns out, and if we decide to air it as a pilot and make it a series, we can talk about any long-term contracts after that."

Jason really didn't worry about making that big of fee for the television show, and didn't even know how much money a TV show was worth, but figured he'd just bring Eliot Feldman with him to any future business meetings. He also knew how much more the nightclubs and discos would pay him and the crowds he'd attract by having is parties regularly televised each week for an *upcoming* television show.

He was going to be making more money either way.

Jason and Dean decided to plan on shooting footage of the rest of the parties scheduled through June to get enough variety for the possible pilot that would be broadcast in September when the new season of *Mary Hartman! Mary Hartman!* was to begin.

The timing worked out perfectly for Jason because he already had a six-week break planned after June to lay-out and design his premier issue of *Night Moves Magazine* and have it ready to publish by August or September at the latest.

He knew he had a busy three months ahead between his parties, his magazine, and now his television pilot.

Jason still had more ideas but decided that was enough to keep him busy for now.

Chapter Eighteen

The first series of parties to be videotaped and edited into a pilot was scheduled to begin near the end of May, so Jason began planning a series of different parties and writing outlines of possible scripts on his yellow legal pads.

Jason wanted to give the TV executives plenty of variety to edit, so besides his women and men's legs contest, which were to most popular, Jason was thinking of other contests for the first pilots that would be fun for the cameras.

He decided to include a revival of his *Miss Kissable Lips* contest, revive a *Cover Girl* contest, but this time for his premier issue of *Night Moves Magazine*, and even thought of a subtle name for a boobs contest called *Miss Firm and High*, playing on the some of the lyrics in the song *Night Moves*. But Jason just laughed off the idea that many girls wanted called a *Mr. Firm and Low* contest and joked that a contest like that would never get on TV.

The Tapestry in Northridge was a new disco that had recently opened and attracted what was considered the *trendy crowd*, at least for the San Fernando Valley, but Jason already had decided that was the crowd he wanted for his *"Real People are the Stars"* concept.

Jason also decided to use Sheri Lynn as his first co-hostess during the taping that night and knew her South African accent would sound good and add a little class on television.

When Jason arrived at *The Tapestry* around eight pm, there was already a line outside waiting at the entrance to get in, and by nine pm, the disco was almost filled to capacity, as Dean began wandering around the crowd with a director *KTTV* had also hired for the pilot and began videotaping.

Jason had put together a full night of entertainment for the first taping, and besides having his *Miss Kissable Lips* contest, he also included his *Famous Couples* game, which would include the *Famous Couples Dance Contest*.

He saw a lot of his regulars running around and looking for their *famous couple's* match, that they would need to compete in the dance contest for the two-hundred-dollar cash prize. Jason was also personally interviewing many of the partygoers and contestants, hoping they'd have some interesting stories to tell about their disco experiences, mixed in with a few innuendoes here and there that could be broadcast.

One his party regulars, who everyone just called *"Big Sal,"* was lightly complaining to Jason because his *famous couples* match that he found wouldn't dance with him.

Big Sal could have been a double for the actor William Conrad who was currently very popular on a television series called *Cannon*, and those who didn't already know him personally would usually ask for his autograph. Jason also knew that Big Sal always had some cocaine on him because he'd always say, "The chicks go *crazy* for this shit!" and liked that he was still popular with the girls even after they discovered he wasn't William Conrad. He would also always have a free bump or two for Jason if he ever asked.

Jason walked with Big Sal to meet the girl who wouldn't dance with him, and saw that besides being one of the tallest girls he's seen at his parties, she was also the most stunning.

"My nametag is the *Big Bad Wolf*, and this is *Little Red Riding Hood*," Sal lightly complained to Jason, "She's my *famous couples* match, but now she won't dance with me."

Jason could see why Sal wanted to dance with her because she was probably the most attractive girl at the party and looked like she'd fit in better at one of his Beverly Hills parties. She had long blond hair and was perfectly proportioned for her height.

"Well, the *Big Bad Wolf* is the match for *Little Red Riding Hood*," Jason smiled to the tall blond, "And it is customary at these parties to at least have one dance with your famous couple match."

"No, I don't think so," the tall blond laughed, "I think the real match for Little Red Riding Hood is supposed to be the *Hunter in the Woods* who kills the Big Bad Wolf with the ax."

"So there!" she sassily teased, "I'm right, and you're wrong."

Jason laughed with her and saw her logic and figured this sexy tall blond just didn't want to dance with Sal and decided to switch nametags with him.

"Okay, Sal, she's probably right," Jason smiled as he exchanged nametags, "You can have my name tag and be *Warren Beatty* the rest of the night, so just try to find *whoever* his girlfriend is this month, and you'll be back in business."

Jason and the friends who helped him fill out the name tags at his parties always laughed about having to find out who Warren Beatty was currently dating, and had to change his female *Famous Couples* match at least once a month.

"Well, that should take care of that," Jason continued smiling to the tall blond as Sal walked away, "By the way, I'm Jason Mershon, and this is my party tonight." "Hi,

"My name is Debbie Budd," she said, holding out her hand.

Jason gave her his customary kiss on the hand instead of a handshake and looked up at her.

"Hey, how tall are you anyway?" he tried to joke, "I don't think *Little Red Riding*

Hood really matches you tonight either!"

"I'm almost six feet, but the heels make me seem taller," she smiled before teasing, "Why, are you intimidated by tall women?"

"Of course not," Jason just smiled back, "I was just curious because I'm six foot and you just seemed so much taller, but now I see it's just your high heels."

He was briefly embarrassed that he may have sounded like her height would make a difference to him and hoped he didn't sound like it did.

"What are the TV cameras doing here tonight anyway?" Debbie asked deciding to change the subject.

"We're shooting a pilot for a new television show later this year," Jason said more businesslike, "And actually, I was also looking for some pretty girls to help me out with a promo we're videotaping in about a half-hour."

Jason had already decided he wanted to continue their conversation and get to know *this one* better.

"Would you be willing to get in the shot with me while I'm taping?" he casually asked Debbie.

"What would I have to do?" she asked with slight apprehension, "I don't like talking on camera."

"Just sit next to me and look sexy," Jason smiled, "That shouldn't be a problem for you."

"Right, that sounds like a pick-up line to me," she sarcastically half laughed, "And I'm the only girl here tonight you're asking?"

Jason didn't want her to think he was just *hitting on her*, so he spoke more businesslike.

"No, but I've only found three girls so far that I think will look good on camera," he added, "And you'll be doing me a big favor if you could just sit in the shot for a few minutes."

"Actually, it's a promo for a commercial channel eleven will run this summer to promote the parties," Jason explained, "I'm just going to say a few things into the camera to make everything sound fun."

"And, I just thought having pretty girls sitting next to me would look a lot better to the audience watching at home," he tried to lightly laugh.

"Sure, I'll do it," Debbie smiled, "Just let me when you need me."

"I'll definitely let you know that!" Jason smiled back as he again kissed her hand as he walked away.

Jason actually already had three other very attractive girls for the promo taping and went to find the Dean and the director to let them know another girl would be featured in the next scene.

Jason was still focused on getting some great footage that night and knew having that *tall sexy blond* in his shots would definitely add to the visuals.

But he was also looking forward to letting her know when he needed her.

❧

Dean aimed the camera at Sheri Lynn, and the director cued her to begin the short introduction he wanted to try using for one of the opening shots.

"Welcome Ladies and Gentlemen to the *Nightmovers Party Hour*, the only television show where the *real people* are the *stars!*" Sheri said with as much excitement as she could with her polite accent, "Please welcome your host for the party, the editor and publisher of *Night Moves Magazine*, Jason Mershon!"

Jason was still planning on having the first issue of *Night Moves* available by August or September, so he wanted to make sure he got in a good plug during these early tapings he hoped would be broadcast by then.

That brief introduction was the only line they needed from Sheri that night, and the director had her repeat it more three times *"with more excitement,"* before moving to the next shot.

The director then had Dean cut to the table with Jason sitting with two girls on either side of him, gazing invitingly as he began his monologue.

Jason had written what he thought would be a funny parody of Howard Beal's "I'm Mad as Hell" rant from the hit movie *Network*, to try and make an entertaining pitch to come to his parties.

"Why are you sitting at home alone tonight watching television?" Jason asked into the camera, "Aren't you bored spending your nights watching endless reruns of Mary Hartman and nothing but continuous Cal Worthington commercials as you lie alone in bed?"

"Wouldn't you rather be here with us tonight, meeting new exciting people and having fun?" Jason continued before pausing.

That was the cue for all four girls to suggestively say, *"Yeah, yeah,* we want to have fun!" and suggestively lean in towards Jason.

"Aren't you sorry you didn't come tonight?" Jason smiled at the camera, trying to be just lightly suggestive as the girls again added their *"Yeah, yeah"* in agreement, before Jason added, "Come to the *party* I meant."

"Well, that's a lotta fun too," one of the girls smiled.

"We are having fun here," said Jason briefly to the girls before looking back to the camera, "But I'm talking to the people at home watching us on TV right now."

"There are two kinds of people out there," Jason continued, "There are the *Watchers* and there are the *Movers,* so guess what kind of person you are."

"Don't you think it's time you became a *Nightmover* instead of a *Nightwatcher?*" Jason asked seriously into the camera.

622

"If you agree with what I'm saying, then there's something I want you to do right now," said Jason trying to channel Howard Beal, "I want you to get up, stop whatever you're doing, go to your window, open it and yell out as loud as you can, 'I'm bored as Hell, and *I'm not going to take it anymore…. I want to be a Nightmover!*'"

Jason repeated the phrase again before Dean cut to close-ups of the girls and several in the audience, all repeating the same mantra how they all were *"bored as Hell, and want to be a Nightmover!"*

"Cut, that's a take!" shouted the director, "That'll be a cute promo."

"Just give me about a fifteen-minute heads up when you're ready to start the kissing contest Jason," Dean added as he began to move his lights and camera towards the dance floor.

"Do you need to use me for anything else?" Debbie asked as she stood up from the table.

"Well, I could actually use you right now," Jason teased, "I need someone to have a drink at the bar with me before we start taping again because I hate to drink alone."

Jason guessed Debbie figured he was just giving her another pickup-line but was satisfied when she agreed to join him at the bar regardless.

He also decided not to show her his usual *"Your…Place…Or…Mine?"* wristwatch that he usually always teased girls with to break the ice when he'd first meet them.

Sometimes he was pleasantly surprised when girls gave him an immediate answer to the digital question but decided not to push the button twice on his watch with Debbie yet.

Jason also knew Sheri Lynn was his actual date that night, and she'd be going home with him, but he still was able to get Debbie to give him her phone number while they sat at the bar by telling her he'd call her when the promotional spot would be broadcast on television.

He knew there was something about her he liked and wanted to make sure she'd be at another one of his parties.

Throughout the rest of the party, Jason spent most of the time interviewing different partygoers who had interesting professions and emceeing both the kissing and dance contests, while Dean taped what he called "a lot of great shots of happy people trying to get laid."

The partygoers loved that the television cameras had been taping more than they had ever before and seeing them all trying to get camera time every chance they could, Jason knew that nothing had changed.

Everyone still wanted to be famous.

Chapter Nineteen

The next taping for the television pilot was scheduled for the following Monday, at a sports bar and nightclub in Westwood called the *Jumping Frog Saloon*.

Jason was home calling several girls from the dozens of phone numbers he collected at his parties and making sure he had enough legs contestants for his *Nightmover* party *KTTV* would again be taping at that party.

He wanted to call the *tall blond* he met but had three different phone numbers with the name "Debbie" on pieces of paper he had collected and wasn't sure which number was hers.

Although he was personally interested in seeing her again, Jason also thought about how great her long legs would look on camera if he could convince her to enter his legs contest.

"Hi, is this Debbie?" Jason asked into the phone, hoping he guessed the right number to call.

When he heard her voice, he thought it might have sounded like the right "Debbie" and at least carried on the conversation hoping it was.

"You'd be a great contestant for the legs contest we're taping for the television pilot on Monday," Jason spoke through the phone, "A group of us are driving to Westwood from my house in Encino, so you wouldn't even have to drive."

"You can just meet at my house and drive with us," Jason pitched her, trying to make it sound more convenient, "And maybe we can even grab a bite to eat afterward if you want."

Jason wanted to make sure it didn't sound like he was asking her out for a date, even though he planned on it turning into one, and was glad that she agreed to drive into Westwood with him.

He just hoped the girl who was agreeing to meet him was the one he thought it was.

When Jason saw her pull up, park her car in his driveway, and walked outside to greet her, he was relieved when he saw he called the right Debbie.

"Nice car!" Jason half laughed when he greeted her, "I expected to see a girl like you driving a Corvette and not something like that."

It was probably the ugliest car Jason had ever seen and was a 1974 pale green *Chevy Vega Hatchback* with a couple of dents in the fender, and Jason tried to make light of it without being too insulting.

"Interesting color too!" Jason sarcastically added.

"Don't make fun of my *Bessie*," Debbie half laughed, "She gets me where I need to go and is all I can afford right now."

Jason then tried to convincingly explain to her that his "other friends had already left," and just the two of them would be driving to Westwood alone together and still didn't want it to appear he had planned a date with her, but was glad when she said "no problem" and didn't seem uncomfortable with the arrangement.

During the drive to Westwood, Jason found out Debbie was twenty-one years old, and that her last name was actually "Budfuloski" and usually just said "*Budd*" because it was easier to pronounce.

Jason had been briefly concerned when Debbie at first told him she was a model and thought she might be one of the *"actresses"* from the San Fernando Valley, but was relieved when she explained she only modeled part-time and was mainly "just an accountant" with an ordinary job.

He also found out she still lived with her parents in Simi Valley and had eleven brothers and sisters.

"Are they all as tall as you?" Jason tried to tease.

"Yup," she said, "There's enough of us to make a great basketball team."

Jason liked her and was surprised she didn't seem to flaunt her beauty or even realize how attractive she actually was.

He decided that even though he knew he'd be busy taping another pilot episode that night at the *Jumping Frog Saloon*, and there'd be many other girls coming that he was *friends* with, he'd try and get Debbie in as many video shots as possible.

He still wanted to get to know this *one* better.

❧

Jason was sitting at the head of a long table with a dozen girls seated along both sides as Dean was preparing to start taping and also made sure Debbie was sitting directly next to him as he began another video introduction as the director shouted, "Action," and Dean began taping.

"Well, here we are at another great *Nightmovers* party, and tonight we're at the Jumping Frog Saloon in Westwood," Jason said to the camera, "It's Memorial Day, May 31st, 1977, and I'm here with some of the sexy contestants who will be competing in another exciting *Nightmovers* beauty pageant."

He wasn't sure why he even spontaneously mentioned the date when he began speaking, because he knew the pilot wouldn't even be broadcast for several more months but figured Dean could just edit that part out.

Jason spent about ten minutes talking to the contestants while Dean was taping the girls mentioning "how they loved always meeting different guys" at the *Nightmovers* parties, "What turned them on in men," and other subjects Jason thought would look fun for editing.

During another interview segment, Jason decided just to feature Debbie alone, asked her about the upcoming legs contest, and tried to encourage her to use a sexy innuendo while Dean was taping.

"And tell me, Debbie," Jason asked while holding the microphone toward her, "What is your *favorite way* to keep those sexy long legs of yours in shape?"

Debbie had a little difficulty getting the tongue-twisting rhyme to his question right, and it took several attempts, but she finally gave the answer that Jason knew would be "sexy but cute" when editing the pilot.

"By getting an *injection*, to my *mid-section*, with a lot of *affection...*," she finally answered in a sexy voice.

"Okay, cut!" said the director after the fourth take, "That one was perfect!"

"I'm sure the audience will get that innuendo loud and clear," Dean added with a laugh.

"I can't believe you got me to say that!" Debbie also laughed with slight embarrassment, "Are you really going to use that on television?"

"Well, the show is going to run at midnight on Friday nights," said Jason, "Even Johnny Carson gets racy sometimes, so I just want to make sure the show doesnt get boring."

"Besides, everyone knows that *sex sells*!" he added with a laugh.

Jason was surprised when Debbie only finished second in his legs contest later that night, but as usual, he stayed away from judging his own contests. He already had decided to just have random *Nightmovers* partygoers be chosen to act as celebrity judges, to keep his theme of the real people being the stars, instead of actual celebrities.

After another long night of taping at the party, it wasn't until almost two am when Jason drove Debbie back to his house in Encino.

"I'm sorry you didn't win tonight," Jason said as they pulled in the driveway, "But I definitely think you had the best legs."

"But like I told you, I'm not a judge," he lightly added before casually asking, "So, do you want to come inside for a drink?"

"Sorry, but this is late for me, and I do have to work tomorrow," said Debbie as she walked to her ugly pale green Chevy Vega, "And I also don't like getting home too late while I'm living at my parent's house."

"I have a younger sister who lives there too," she added, "And I don't want to be a bad influence on her."

"Let's just see if you call me again and are still interested," Debbie added with a tease as they stood by her car, "I've heard things about you at the discos."

"Don't believe everything you hear," Jason teased back.

He was disappointed that he wasn't *getting laid* that night, but tried not to show it or be like a jerk about it, and decided to just show is *gentleman* side without seeming bothered. Jason also wanted to at least show Debbie his *romantic* side before she left, and as he took her hand again to kiss it, he sang a couple of lines from an old song he'd sometimes sing that let his dates know he was interested.

He sang in his light half-serious tone, without sounding too gushy, the opening lines to the song *I'll See You in My Dreams*, about imagining *seeing* and *holding* her as he slept that night.

Jason never felt he was just giving a line when he sang those types of songs to girls, and usually were just spontaneous and appropriate feelings he usually felt at those moments. He just happened to know a lot of songs that fit different occasions, and he'd even feel more romantic himself when he sang them.

Debbie did seem to like the song Jason sang to her and gave him an appreciative kiss and hug before she drove away.

They did have a lot of fun together that night, and Jason knew the odds were pretty good that they'd be seeing each other again.

Sheri Lynn would be back in South Africa for the next few weeks visiting her family, and Jason knew he had some free time to see Debbie again as well some other *old friends* he hadn't seen for a while.

Jason never liked missing the opportunity to meet *new friends* whenever that opportunity arose, and was fairly certain that Debbie was going to become another one.

Chapter Twenty

Jason was glad that Dean and the director said all the final tapings of the parties in June went well, and they had plenty of footage to put together a fun and entertaining one-hour pilot.

Dean made some copies for Jason of the three-quarter-inch cassette tapes with the video footage from the parties and said Jason would need to rent a three-quarter-inch video player to view the party footage for any editing ideas himself. Dean also said he and the executives would look over the footage to see how they liked it, and explained that because many employees at the television station would be on vacation in July, the full editing wouldn't begin until August.

"We'll all talk again sometime towards the end of July so just have some fun till then," said Dean.

Jason was glad he had some time off coming up himself after feeling he been going non-stop most of that year and was satisfied that he had moved on from any of his bitterness from the past and felt more successful than he ever had.

He had also decided to host an *appreciation party* for dozens of his friends and party regulars who had assisted in the television pilot and helped with his promotions, not only that year, but in the past. He scheduled a big pool party and barbecue at his house in Encino on the Fourth of July, when he knew everyone would be off work and should be able to attend.

Jason also invited some other friends from Hollywood, Las Vegas, and even invited Martha Bland to fly in from Dallas to spend the entire weekend with him. He really wanted to share his success with his closest friends and knew it would be fun having them all together at a house party rather than a disco.

After his *Fourth of July* party, Jason knew he had nothing booked except for a small concert he was helping Jan Berry promote with his new band in the middle of August. It wasn't anything huge, but Jason had gotten the manager at *Tiffany's Disco* in Marina Del Rey to agree to set up a stage on the disco floor and have Jan perform a concert on a Tuesday night, which was one of *Tiffany's* slowest nights.

At least it was giving Jan the opportunity to try and start performing live again without *Dean*, and it would also give Jason the opportunity to expand his other ideas for *Nightmovers Productions* and possibly begin promoting concerts and live shows along with his disco parties.

That concert wasn't until the middle of August, and Jason still knew he'd have a nice break after his Fourth of July party. It would also be during that break, when Jason planned to prepare his premier issue of *Night Moves Magazine*, before he needed to begin working on any editing of the *Nightmovers Party Hour* television pilot.

He was actually enjoying all the new ways he was *thinking* about making money that year.

Jason wasn't even going to worry about setting up any more parties at the discos until then, and also liked that he had a few weeks to catch up with some personal pleasures.

With the free time he now had, Jason had also been seeing Debbie Budfuloski fairly regularly since Memorial Day and had already taken her to his favorite restaurant, *Lawry's the Prime Rib*, as well to his favorite piano bars where he'd romantically sing *It Had to be You* and *Embraceable You* to her. He would still lightly change a few lyrics in those songs enough, so he didn't sound like he was overly gushy after only dating for a short time.

Jason did enjoy continuing to show his romantic side by sending Debbie a dozen roses after their first passionate night together, and another bouquet of flowers to lightly celebrate the *four-week anniversary* of the first night they'd met. He joked to her that if they stayed together long enough, he promised to send her flowers every Memorial Day, which he considered their official first date.

"And as you know." Jason smiled to Debbie, "Our first date is all on video tape so well be able to look at it and laugh someday."

But after the romantic month Jason had spent with Debbie, it was especially hard and embarrassing for him to try and explain to her that Martha Bland was flying in from Dallas for his Fourth of July party, and would be spending the entire weekend with him at his house.

"Please don't get mad and try to understand, but I invited Martha before you and I really knew each other that well," Jason tried to justify, "I've been friends with Martha for over a year, and it's just for this one weekend, I promise."

Jason saw that Debbie was surprised, but he was also surprised himself by her calm reaction.

"I'm not crazy about the idea it, but we're not married," Debbie tried smile as she just shook her head, "I know you had a life before me, so as long as it's only this weekend, I'll try to live with it."

"But I might not be too understanding if there's a next time," she added with a more serious smile.

Jason was relieved that Debbie didn't seem to be upset or at least was acting that way.

"You are such an angel," Jason said as he hugged her, "I don't want you to think I'm comfortable with this either, but I wanted to be honest with you and not have you just think I'm a jerk."

"You are a jerk sometimes!" she half laughed, "But maybe that's why I like you."

While he was still hugging Debbie, Jason attempted to lightly sing her the lyrics of a song that just suddenly popped into his head that he'd barely remembered, but knew he heard somewhere before.

"You-u-u-u-u...you're an *angel"* were the only words Jason remembered but wanted to sing at least a something that described his feelings about her at that moment.

Jason had only heard that song "about an angel" a few times on the radio years earlier, and although the song never became a hit, besides the sweet melody that always stuck in his head, he did always remember the long chorus of *"You-u-u-u"* and the *"You're an angel"* part of the song. After seeing how almost *angelic* Debbie was acting after he'd told her about Martha, he suddenly remembered that song and decided the lyrics were appropriate to remind her of his feelings, and hopefully not think he was too much of a *jerk*.

But the same time, Jason did feel somewhat like a jerk because he was still looking forward to seeing Martha again, but also decided that he'd try not to be one so obviously after that weekend.

છે

Jason had private invitations printed inside envelopes that he personally handed or mailed out to his *select* circle of friends for the Fourth of July party at his house.

Of the hundred invitations he handed out, about fifty were currently in his backyard and the pool area, and a dozen or so others were wandering inside his house either eating or mixing cocktails. Jason had bought about thirty rib-eye steaks and a few dozen chicken breasts for the barbeque and had plenty of cases of beer, a case of wine, and a good variety of hard liquor, to make sure he had something for everybody.

Big Sal and a couple of others were there to offer the *other party favors* for those who indulged, which Jason saw was a large percentage of everyone at the party.

Jason mainly liked that he had a good representation of many of his friends from both his business and personal life since 1969 together at his party all at one time.

He had invited Annie Gaybis, but she was out of town that weekend, and he had even mailed an invitation to Lori Wagner in New York, but knew already she wouldn't be attending. Jason hadn't seen or heard anything from her since that last night at the apartment in Hollywood, and the last thing he had heard about her, was that she had gotten a role in a revival of the musical *HAIR* on Broadway.

630

Although Tom Casey and Frank Reich couldn't make his party because they were both working, Victor Consuela drove in from Las Vegas along with his new girlfriend, who he described only as "a great *money maker'*, and Jason noticed that Victor was spending most of his time hanging out with Big Sal. Jan Berry was having a good time talking with several girls about his comeback concert at *Tiffany's* the next month, but Jan was also very excited about a movie that was *"in development"* about his life story and recovery from his car accident called *Dead Man's Curve*. Sheri Lynn was also back from South Africa and was floating in the pool, while other guests like Cara and Sunshine wore aprons over their bikinis and were acting as chefs at the barbecue handing out food plates.

It was late afternoon when Jason was sitting by the pool with Martha Bland, Debbie Budfuloski, Sheri Lynn and Lita Krisaan talking with Michael Ritz and Mixie about their recent wedding, and did smile to himself about how *sophisticated* all the girls at the party he'd been "intimate or romantic" with had been acting that day. They had all seemed to be getting along well with each other without showing any jealousy that he was giving most of his attention to Martha and spending the entire weekend with her.

Although he was still close with all of them, Jason hadn't said the "I love you" words with anyone since Lori Wagner, but knew that if he did, it probably would have changed his relationships with them, and felt he had too many other things going on in his life for that kind of distraction.

Jason had one of the disco DJs help him set up his stereo outside, and brought two extra speakers so Jason could blast his record collection of new and old rock and roll music, and it was while the old rock song *My Generation* by The Who was blasting through the stereo, when Martha brought up the name that their generation was now being labeled.

"First, we were all called *The Rock and Roll Generation* and then *Generation Jones*, and now they're calling us *Baby Boomers*," said Martha, "I don't remember names they ever called other generations, so they must think we're special."

Jason had read about the name *"baby boomer"* they were now calling *their generation* and it seemed to be sticking because it was now becoming a part of the vocabulary.

"We are special!" Jason just smiled as he started to sing a lyric from an old *Crosby Stills and Nash* song that he always liked called *Chicago*, about how "we can change and rearrange the world" and joked that "their generation" had actually been responsible for a lot of interesting changes.

"Well, I don't like that name," Debbie said, "It reminds me of how guy's always call girls *'baby'* all the time."

"*Our generation* has at least shown people how to have a good time," Mixie, joined in, "I know we're having more fun than our parents did."

"I know our music is a lot better," added Martha as another more current song, *Life in the Fast Lane* by The Eagles, began blasting from the stereo, "The songs today are better than my grandpa's music used to be."

"I think the music was good back in the nineteen twenties too," Jason decided to add, "And I think in some ways, the seventies are just a throwback to the roaring twenties with the way everyone likes dancing and partying so much like they did back then."

"The old speakeasy nightclubs they show in the movies were almost just like the disco's today," Lita added, "And they did seem to have the same kind of fun as we do today."

"History does tend to repeat itself," said Michael Ritz, somewhat agreeing.

"Then I guess it was kind of appropriate that I ended up having my first parties at a disco called the Speakeasy and even my Gatsby and Gangsters party at the Antique Mirror," Jason joked, "We might be just be going a cycle that repeats itself every fifty years or so when people decide to just have fun being wild and crazy."

"Yeah, but instead of bootlegging booze like they did in the twenties," added Mixie with a laugh, "Now it's cocaine!"

As if almost on cue, Big Sal walked by and offered some of his *party favors*.

Those who were interested took a *quick bump* but even though Jason usually only liked snorting cocaine at night, did a *bump* with Martha and the others at the table.

"You guys go ahead and enjoy it without me," smiled Debbie, "I tried coke and really don't like it that much, so I'm fine with just enjoying my Margarita's today."

Jason already knew that Debbie wasn't a fan of cocaine, but she also knew that coke was everywhere and wasn't bothered when everyone else did it without her.

He liked that Debby wasn't a prude or judgmental about the way everyone else had fun and was glad to see that she didn't crave cocaine the way he'd seen how other girls at the discos did.

Jason was still a little surprised how friendly Debbie had been with Martha and his other "friends" that day, and did occasionally give her a discreet hug or quick kiss when they were alone together. But although he still felt a little guilty, he was at least happy that he'd been honest with her, and did hope they'd still have a relationship once the weekend was over.

He mainly enjoyed seeing all of his closest friends there at the same time enjoying his hospitality, and was satisfied how far he'd been able to come since the previous Fourth of July, and felt nothing but positiveness about the future.

The party started to thin out by six pm, and most everyone was going somewhere to watch the fireworks when it got dark and Jason had walked most of his guests, including Debbie, to their cars when they left.

He hugged Debbie and again sang *"You-u-u-u, you're an angel"* to her, and thanked her for being "so cool" and understanding about that weekend.

"But don't forget," Debby lightly threatened, "I'm only 'cool' about it this weekend."

After the last guests left, Jason walked back into the house with Martha and it was about an hour later when they were cleaning up the house when he first noticed his watch was missing.

"Have you seen my 'Your Place or Mine' watch?" he asked Martha, "I took it off earlier when I went swimming and I could swear that I left on the dresser."

They both looked around the house and out by the pool but didn't find it.

"Damn, you don't s think someone picked it up by mistake, do you?" Jason asked.

"Well, I don't know who would have come into your bedroom and look on your dresser," said Martha with a hint of suspicion, "Are you sure all these people here today were your friends."

"Of course, they were!", Jason said not wanting to think someone had stolen it.

"Well, hopefully, you'll find it," said Martha, "But some people are just weird, and maybe you shouldn't always trust them so much or leave too many things laying around."

Jason thought that was almost exactly what Lori had once told him about "not trusting his friends so much" and he started wondering if anything else he had left "laying around" would turn up missing, and the thought of one of his friends stealing from him, made the entire day of what he felt was a great party start to feel not so great.

But it was also his last night with Martha before she was flying back to Dallas the next day, and didn't want to dwell on it that night.

"No big deal," Jason tried to lightly say, "I'm sure it'll turn up, and it's just a watch I can always replace."

"Well, besides that, this was a fun weekend," Martha said as she gave Jason a big hug and kiss, "I'm so glad I came."

"That sounds like a good catchphrase to use for my parties when they end," Jason lightly teased, "Thank you for *coming*, and I hope you're glad that you *CAME!*"

"Well, don't forget to invite me again sometime so I can *come* again," laughed Martha.

Jason usually promised he would make plans to see her again, but that night he just made a toast to "till we meet again" and left it at that. He still never liked saying goodbye thinking he wouldn't see his "friends" again and always hoped that some of his relationships could last forever.

But after Martha flew back to Dallas the next day, Jason also discovered the razor blade neckless that Annie Gaybis had given him was also missing and it bothered him more than he realized.

He knew the watch and neckless had meant something special to him because they were gifts from his friends, and knew those could never be replaced or have the same meaning to him.

But the thought of having to replace his friends was also something he never liked thinking he had to worry about.

Chapter Twenty-One

Jason was anxious to make up for the uncomfortable situation he put Debbie through over the Fourth of July, so the following weekend, he planned a romantic three days together in Las Vegas.

"I've got plenty of *juice* in Vegas," Big Sal smiled after Jason mentioned his planned trip to him, "I can get you comp'd in the best suite at *The Landmark Hotel*."

Jason had always stayed at the *MGM Grand Hotel*, but hadn't been to Las Vegas since his show at *The Thunderbird*, and also didn't have the same juice himself as when he was promoting his parties up there, or as the editor and publisher of the *National Singles Register*.

After Big Sal said the comp'd suite would be on the hotel's top floor, and near the round observation bar with the panoramic view of the city, Jason figured it would be perfect.

The only real memories Jason had about *The Landmark Hotel* was from the night he spent in the observation bar with Tommy and Alvin after his audition at the *Pussycat-A-Go-Go*, but he decided it would be romantic to spend time in that bar again with Debbie. Jason also decided to just fly with Debbie to Las Vegas, which would be more enjoyable than a boring four hour drive each way.

Tom Casey hadn't been able to attend Jason's Fourth of July party, but did pick up Jason and Debbie at the airport and drove them to the Landmark.

Tom seemed slightly irritated when Jason introduced Debbie to him as "Tom" and quickly tried to laugh off and correct Jason's introduction.

"I just go by *'Casey'* now," he lightly said, "No one calls me *'Tom'* anymore."

"But you're my friend, so you can just call me *'Officer Casey'* if you want," he sarcastically teased.

Jason thought it was funny how Tom spoke so much more like a cop these days and how much he had changed since they'd first met, but knew that he had changed himself a lot as well.

One thing that hadn't changed with Jason was that he took Debbie to see his favorite show, *Hallelujah Hollywood*, at the *MGM Grand* for what Jason guessed was probably at least the tenth time.

There was always something about the staging and music in that show that always left him feeling more romantic, and after seeing the show again, Jason felt at least that part of him hadn't changed.

That entire weekend with Debbie also was their most passionate and romantic yet, and Jason was glad that nothing was mentioned about his weekend with Martha or had changed anything between them, but there was also something different about that weekend that did make Jason start to *think*.

It had been years since he had even thought about *"The Thunderbolt"* even though he felt he'd had experienced a lot of "thunderstorms" with the dozens of girls he' met in the past couple years, but he had felt a different type of "rumbling" that weekend.

Jason also felt that Debbie was one of the nicest girls he'd met in a long time and briefly thought he needed to find the song lyrics to the *"You-u-u-u...you're an angel"* song so he could make it a personal song to her, and not one of his cliché songs like *It Had to Be You.*

Being away from everything he was involved in California also allowed Jason to talk personally with Debbie and not just about business or his upcoming parties or plans.

Debbie had asked about Jason's family, and he only vaguely explained to her that "they just didn't get along well" and were "kind of estranged," without going into the full details. She had already met Victor Consuela, but after introducing her to both Casey and Frank Reich that weekend, Jason tried to explain that he always considered his friends more his real family than his parents.

"That's too bad," Debbie said, "I'm very close with my entire family and couldn't imagine not having a relationship with them."

"It's no big deal," Jason explained nonchalantly, "I'm very happy with the way it is, and I'm not really concerned about it."

"Well, I think everybody needs to have family in their life," added Debbie, "But maybe someday it'll get better, and you can work things out together."

"Maybe...," is all Jason decoded to say back to her. Even though he wanted to act optimistic with Debbie, he knew that was something that never was going to happen.

He did feel very close with Debbie that weekend, and it was more romantic than usual, but he also hoped she'd never bring anything up about his parents again.

❧

It was the week after Jason returned from Las Vegas with Debbie when he got the phone call from Dean at *KTTV*.

"Jason, I've got some tough news for you," said Dean with a touch of regret, "The KTTV executives spent several hours going over the video footage from the parties, and although they liked some of it, they think most of it is just way too much for local television and they decided to pull the plug on the pilot."

"What's wrong with it!?" argued Jason, "The whole concept was fine with them before, what changed?"

"Unfortunately, the first tape we viewed was the men's legs contest, and they really hated that one," said Dean with a sarcastic laugh, "They said no one wanted to see bare-chested men in swim trunks dancing around and said it looked too 'Homo' for television."

"But you saw the girls screaming and grabbing at them, and it didn't look *homo* at all," Jason tried to justify, "The contestants were all *straight*, and the women loved them!"

"They said it's something the general public wouldn't want to see," said Dean, "So that got them in a negative mood right off the bat."

"And then some of them even said the kissing contest looked a little too pornographic," Dean chuckled, "I did shoot a lot of close-ups of their tongues in each other's mouths, and one girl kissed like she was going down on some guy's face, and looked like she was giving his tongue some head."

"Well, we can just edit some of that stuff that out," said Jason, "We have all the other footage."

"Well, there was another guy in the meeting who argued who cares what *turns on* a dental assistant from Woodland Hills or an accountant from Simi Valley," Dean continued, "He said the television audience just wanted to know what *turns on* Farrah Fawcett or Raquel Welsh."

"The show is supposed to be about real people and not celebrities," Jason continued trying to justify, "That's what's supposed to make it original."

"I mean a lot of them were laughing and thought some of it was funny," Dean tried to add encouragingly, "But someone else would say *'it's just too racy'* even for late night TV."

"Can't we at least edit something together to at least see the response one time?" Jason tried to convince him, "I hate to see all that footage go to waste."

"The guys we originally talked with still liked it, but the higher-ups overruled them", explained Dean, "They don't want to spend time or money even editing a complete pilot."

"Maybe you can come in and offer to pay for the editing yourself and re-pitch them," Dean tried to conclude on a positive note, "But at least for now, it's a no-go Jason."

Jason suddenly felt like the air had been let out of him because besides the extra money he was hoping the television station would pay him, he had been hyping the upcoming *Nightmovers Party Hour* show like crazy for almost three months.

He knew besides the disco owners and all his friends being disappointed they wouldn't appear on television. Jason had also planned a large segment in his first issue of *Night Moves Magazine*, to include a lot of copy featuring all the past and future television tapings.

Jason knew he had some of the dubs Dean had given him of the footage from the pilot, and just figured he'd spend some more time seeing if he could arrange to edit something entertaining to re-pitch the executives in the next couple weeks.

He wasn't giving up yet.

Chapter Twenty-Two

When Jason's phone rang less than a week after getting the bad news from Dean, he recognized Tom Casey's voice without him having mentioned it.

"Jason, this is Casey!" he spoke excitedly over the phone.

Casey sounded half-serious and half-amused when he said he had something important Jason needed to know about.

"Listen, Jason, I don't know what's going on, but an FBI agent came to my parent's house asking questions about you today," Casey half laughed, "What are you doing out there in California?!"

"Yeah, right, why would the FBI be asking about me?" Jason half-joked back, "You're not serious, are you?"

"I am serious, and I have no why they'd go to my parent's house," Casey added, more irritated than concerned.

Jason immediately thought it might be because he had used that address when Casey was still living with his parents for renewing his Nevada Driver's license when he left Las Vegas in 1972.

He had always wanted to keep his ID back then to show he was three years older but had transferred that license into his California license years earlier. Jason still had his old Sunset Boulevard address on his current driver's license and never bothered changing addresses until they were up for renewal.

"You don't think it's because of that *mistake* the clerk made about my driver's license age way back in 1969, do you?" Jason half joked.

"The FBI wouldn't waste their time on a stupid *misdemeanor* like that," Casey tried to laugh, "They only investigate federal *felony* offenses."

"But it does sound like they're investigating you about something," Casey added with light suspicion, "Are you sure you're not telling me something I should know about?"

"I haven't done anything wrong," Jason tried to laugh innocently, "It's got to be some kind of mistake."

"My dad just told the FBI agent you were a friend of mine, so they said they were going to try and contact me," Casey said more seriously, "Let me do some checking around and see what I can find out."

"I'll call you back when I get more information.", Casey said before hanging up the phone.

After that call, Jason immediately started thinking that it had to be a mistake, and Casey would be able to clear anything up.

Jason then began remembering that during the *Watergate* scandal, it was discovered that the FBI sometimes investigated people even if they hadn't committed a crime, because President Nixon had an *"Enemies List,"* which included many journalists and celebrities he wanted investigated.

There were even some celebrities that Jason knew who had joked they hoped they were on the *Nixon's Enemies List,* and could say the FBI investigated them to their other Hollywood friends. Most of them hated Nixon so much they considered it a "badge of honor" or even a "status symbol" to be on his enemies list.

Jason had never published anything derogatory about Nixon in the *National Singles Register,* and if anything, Rudy Vallee had always written only positive articles about Nixon, so Jason didn't think that was any type of possible scenario.

But he also knew he didn't do anything wrong, so hopefully, he could just laugh about it later to his friends, and joke that he was at least *important enough* to be investigated by the FBI.

Jason mainly was thinking about the busy month ahead of him and convinced himself not to worry about it or let it distract him and decided that he was just going to wait for Casey to call him back and tell him it was all a joke or some stupid mistake.

It was later that same evening and Jason was having dinner with Debbie and Big Sal at Sal's favorite hangout, *The Fireside Inn* on Ventura Boulevard. Jason also liked that restaurant because they had a piano bar, and he wanted to sing the song *I'll String Along with You* to Debbie that night.

He wanted to sing her an entire song about "an angel" instead of just that one partial *"You—u-u-u-u, you're an angel"* verse. But although he thought he might have remembered once hearing a DJ say it was a song by Paul Williams, he never saw a song called *You're an Angel* on any of Paul Williams record albums and just never followed up after that.

The song *I'll String Along with You* at least had an opening lyric about an angel, so Jason decided to sing that song to Debbie later.

While they were having dinner, Jason also joked about the crazy news he'd gotten from Casey earlier.

"So, I guess I'm part of the *'in-crowd'* now," Jason half laughed while they were all having dinner, "I hear you're not a really a big deal unless the FBI is investigating you for something."

"I've had friends who've been investigated by the feds," Sal tried to say with a straight face, "And some of them got off with only five years."

"And I hear the food in the joint really ain't that bad," Sal also tried to joke with a straight face.

"Thanks for all the encouragement," Jason sarcastically replied, "That's good to know."

"When are you supposed to talk to Casey again?" asked Debbie, slightly concerned.

"Hopefully soon," said Jason, "But I'm sure it's all just a mistake."

"The only thing I could think of that was illegal was back when I was a teenager and my friends and I would sometimes shoplift eight-track tapes," Jason smiled with a chuckle, "I never could afford to buy all the new music that was coming out in the sixties and I always wanted to have my favorite songs to play in my car, so I just lifted a few dozen of them."

"Ah, that's gotta be it!" Sal continued teasing, "They finally caught up with you."

"Ya know, sometimes the FBI just hears a rumor about someone or gets a fake tip from someone who doesn't like you," Sal tried to add with optimism, "And they are almost obligated to open up an investigation."

"But as long as you really didn't do anything wrong," Sal added reassuringly, "You shouldn't have nothing to worry about."

"I'm sure it's nothing too," said Debbie squeezing his hand before teasing, "But if it is, don't worry, baby, I'll wait for you as long as you're not sentenced to more than a year or two."

"You-u-u-u-u-u-u....!" Jason laughed back to her with his own usual, but shortened, tease.

Jason was glad that both Sal and Debbie felt the same as he did about it just being some minor mistake.

"I'm more concerned about getting the television pilot back on track," Jason decided to change the subject, "I'm still deciding if it's a good idea to print up the first issue of *Night Moves* until I know about if we're going to be able to videotape any more Nightmovers Party Hour shows."

"I haven't had a disco party in over a month and might need a new angle to get the parties going again," Jason continued, "And I'm not sure if I should spend the money to print the magazine just yet, especially if I need to put out money for trying to edit the TV pilot."

"You should just get investors," said Sal, "I might know some people."

Jason knew that Sal was Italian, and some people had mentioned that he might be connected and was involved with the *Teamsters Union*, but Jason had just kept their relationship friendly and never really talked to Sal about his personal business.

"No, I'm not interested in getting investors and would prefer just financing what I do on my own," Jason said, "I just need to sell some more ideas or parties to get some more money together."

"Let me show you something I've been selling that's been making me some extra money lately" Sal smiled as he reached down at the table for his briefcase that he always carried with him.

"Take a look at this," said Sal as he opened his briefcase and handed Jason what looked like some kind of certificate.

Jason saw that they were blank birth certificates.

"They're perfect copies, and they work like a charm," laughed Sal, "I've been selling some of these lately, especially to the actresses in Hollywood who want to shave a few years off their age."

"I get at least a hundred bucks a pop for each one I sell," Sal continued to smile, "Maybe you can make some extra money by selling some of these to all those Hollywood girls you know."

Jason was fairly positive the blank birth certificates weren't the only things Sal sold for a *hundred bucks a pop* to make some extra money, but just laughed off Sal's offer and told him he'd prefer to stick with selling what he knew best.

He also didn't want to talk about any other minor concerns about business or the FBI that night and just wanted to enjoy the rest of his evening.

After he finished dinner, had a double Courvoisier, as well as a couple of bumps in the bathroom that Sal gave him, Jason was back in a positive mood and just wanted to continue feeling that everything was going to turn out alright.

He started by going to the piano bar to sing his song about an angel to Debbie.

As Jason held Debbie's hand and lightly began singing the opening verse to, *I'll String Along with You*, about how although Debbie might not be an angel, he'd "string along with her" until an actual *angel*
   did come along.

Jason never wanted to let other things distract him when he sang his love songs.

ॐ

It was almost a week before Jason heard back from Casey.

"I ran your name through the system, and nothing came up," said Casey, "So, at least there are no outstanding warrants out for you right now."

"But I did get the FBI guy's name and talked to him," Casey added, "I tried to get some information, but he wouldn't tell me anything."

"Can't your dad find something out?" asked Jason, "He was in the FBI and should still have some *juice* with them."

"Now that my dad is retired from the Bureau, he's not in the loop anymore," said Casey, "He's just pissed that they came to the house, and he wants to stay out of this."

"But the agent I talked with said that if I hear from you, to have you to call him at his office," Casey added, "You should at least call him and find out what's going on."

Jason wrote down the FBI agent's name and phone number and decided to call him immediately to see what all this BS was about.

The operator did answer the phone *"Federal Bureau of Investigation,"* so Jason knew it wasn't a prank someone was pulling on him. He then realized he needed to act serious, but still wanted to sound unconcerned after the call was transferred to the agent.

"We don't discuss investigations over the phone, Mr. Mershon," the FBI agent spoke seriously, "And we would prefer to speak with you in person."

"But there is nothing that I've been involved with that's illegal," Jason tried to joke and lightly and convince him, "Can you at least me give me an idea about what this is all about?"

"All I can tell you is that you are currently involved in investigations in California and Nevada," the agent continued seriously.

"And you can't tell me anything?" Jason continued to argue back.

"Not over the phone, but we can arrange to interview you here at the office in Las Vegas," he continued seriously, "We can go over all the details with you then."

"So, when can come in and talk with us?" the agent added, seemingly wanting an immediate commitment, "Or we can arrange a meeting at your newspaper office if you like?"

That statement surprised Jason because he hadn't even mentioned his profession to the FBI agent.

Jason didn't want to sound guilty of anything to the agent and told him that he'd check his schedule and let him know when he'd be able to come to Las Vegas.

When the agent asked for his current home address, Jason just said he'd get back to him and hung up.

Jason felt a slight panic coming over him, hearing that the FBI was actually investigating him for what Casey said was at least a *felony*.

All he had done in California for the past year were his *Nightmovers* parties, and he hadn't done any promotions in Las Vegas for over a year and a half, but he did start getting a sick feeling in his stomach when he began to think of how the FBI agent had mentioned *"his newspaper office"* and realized it might have to do with something he thought was completely out of his life.

It had to have something to do with his parents.

Chapter Twenty-Three

Jason was stressed out enough already trying to figure how to get his television pilot, his magazine, and his parties back on schedule but was more stressed and preoccupied with the phone call he knew he was going to need to make.

He hadn't spoken or heard anything from his mother in almost a year, and as far as he knew, his father had disappeared entirely. Even though Jason never wanted to see or hear from either of them again, he knew he would have to make a phone call if he wanted information, but waited a day so he could prepare himself for having to hear that miserable voice again.

"What do you want?" he heard his mother's cold voice through the phone, "I don't want anything to do with you anymore."

Jason was glad she didn't just hang up the phone as she usually did, and had planned on trying to speak reasonably, but her immediate attitude changed his as well.

"I'm under some kind of investigation with the FBI," Jason angrily said into the phone, "I need to know what the fuck is going on!"

"Good!" she snidely said back, "That'll go along good to what they're planning for you two bastards in Texas."

"What are you talking about?!" he yelled back.

This time his mother started speaking in a bitter but satisfying voice that was getting him angrier.

"I had my attorney send an affidavit to those guys in Texas stating that anything you two did in Dallas was separate from my newspaper and I'll be willing to testify against both of you if I need to," she said in a satisfied tone, "The last thing I heard from them is that the Texas State Attorney General is working on getting an indictment against both of you for fraud, so as far as I'm concerned, both of you fuckers can enjoy rotting in prison!"

After that, she did slam down the phone.

Jason didn't even try to call her back after how crazy and hateful she still sounded and just sat there for a minute looking at the receiver before he took his phone off the hook.

He didn't want to get any calls from anyone and needed to think, but the anger that had returned and was building again towards his parents is what he was mainly thinking about, but knew just thinking of a way to destroy them both wouldn't help him, and instead began going through every scenario he could think of.

He tried to figure out if there was something about an indictment in Texas, then why did the FBI agent say he was only under investigation in California and Nevada and couldn't see how they were connected.

Besides wondering if there might be something else that he didn't know about, Jason also kept wondering how he would continue doing business with all of this hanging over his head, and kept thinking about what he should, or could do, to try and clear everything up.

It wasn't until after ten pm before Jason realized he was sitting in the dark and hadn't even bothered to turn the lights while he was sitting in silence and thinking, and it was seven am before Jason realized he'd fallen asleep on the couch and still was wearing his clothes from the day before.

Jason was sorry that he even woke up because it made him start thinking again, but at least he started remembering that he didn't do anything wrong and needed to put the phone back on the hook to make some calls.

He knew there was no way he could move forward with anything unless he was able to put his current problem behind him permanently this time.

ॐ

After Jason explained the situation with his parents to Casey over the phone, Jason added that he might come to Las Vegas to talk to the FBI agent and just tell them his side of the story and how he had done nothing wrong.

"I'll just throw them both under the bus just like they did to me," Jason told Casey with bitterness.

"I wouldn't volunteer to do anything," said Casey, "If they want you, they'll come and get you, and I wouldn't try to make it easy for them."

"Even if you're completely innocent," he lightly continued, "If for some reason they don't like you when they interview you, they can trip you up and find something to charge you with."

"That's just the way we do things in law enforcement," Casey added with a slight laugh.

"What about that shit in Texas?" Jason asked, "Could that be connected?"

"I don't know, but I'd just lie low for now," Casey tried to advise, "Don't make yourself so visible and available like you always do."

"You're out there in public too much, and it might even be better to get out of town for a while and stay out of the *limelight*," Casey suggested with a touch of sarcasm, "You're always involved with so many crazy things, and people do start to wonder about you sometimes."

Jason briefly thought about what Sal mentioned about how rumors got started if one of his *friends* might have been suspicious enough about how he managed his different projects and activities to start a rumor that may have reached the FBI.

"Maybe just disappear for a while, at least until an investigation is over that will hopefully clear anything up," Casey added more seriously.

"But wouldn't it make me look guilty of something if I just stopped everything I was doing and just disappeared?" Jason asked not liking Casey's suggestion, "I did that in Dallas once, and that's what probably got all this shit started."

"It wouldn't be breaking the law to leave," Casey added, "Because if you're not guilty of anything, and there's no warrant's out or an indictment against you yet, you're not really running or hiding from anything."

When Casey mentioned *"getting out of town for a while,"* it reminded Jason of what Jim Santini once told him after the police investigated him and after Terri had stolen the stupid television set.

Jason would have loved to be able to talk with Santini about all of this, but Jim Santini was a U.S. Congressman now and probably wouldn't even remember him.

It wasn't more than ten minutes after he hung up from Casey that he got a call from Debbie.

"Baby, I haven't been able to get hold of you for two days, are you alright?" she asked with some concern. "I was worried about you."

"Debbie, there's just too much going on right now I'm trying to get straightened out," Jason hurriedly said, "Can I just call you later?" "

Okay, but please call me," she said.

Jason felt bad rushing her, and briefly worried she might have thought he was with some other girl, but he just couldn't talk to her or worry about that right now.

He needed some better advice than to just disappear for a while, but also knew he also needed to speak with a lawyer who could advise him, and Eliot Feldman agreed to meet Jason at *Du Par's Coffee Shop* on Ventura Boulevard.

"Well, I'm pretty sure you can't be charged in California for a Texas indictment," said Eliot, "But I mainly specialize in corporate and civil law and not really up to date on some of those laws."

"So, my first advice to you is again, just stay out of Texas," Eliot added with a half serious laugh. "But it's the FBI stuff that sounds weird and your cop friend in Vegas is right, so don't volunteer to any interviews without a lawyer present."

"Okay, but how can I find out what the FBI stuff is even all about?" asked Jason.

"I can refer you to a good criminal lawyer," said Eliot, "But I'm sure he'll want a retainer, and it might get expensive."

"I don't even know what I'm supposed to be accused of yet," said Jason, "Isn't there any way for you to just find out?"

"That's what you need a criminal lawyer for," Eliot lightly replied, "Do you want his name?"

"But I'm innocent of any crime!" argued Jason, "I don't want to throw money away or make it look like I'm guilty of anything."

"Hey, all clients are innocent," Eliot sarcastically laughed, "That's who lawyers make all their money from."

Jason didn't seem to be getting anything helpful from Eliot either, and it was frustrating.

When he found out that hiring a criminal attorney would take most of the money that he'd been saving to start *Night Moves Magazine*, and that it may end up costing even more money in the future, Jason decided to wait. He spent two more days alone in his house thinking and trying to think of others he could at least talk with for support or advice but wasn't sure who he could trust to discuss everything.

He finally realized he didn't have any other real friends he could call that could help him, and would have to make any decisions himself. But the stress Jason had been feeling about his current business plans and now been overtaken by the depression he was starting to feel about everything else, and the motivation he had felt just a couple weeks earlier was now gone, and he suddenly had no desire to even continue with his plans.

Jason thought he had divorced himself from any ties with his parents but realized he couldn't have any positive future ahead of him unless he tried to erase everything that ever connected them in the past.

He knew what he needed to do.

Chapter Twenty-Four

Debbie Budfuloski was the only person Jason felt he needed and wanted to talk with about what he'd decided do, and he'd spent the last hour sitting with her at his house explaining his situation.

Jason had finally explained in detail his relationship with his parents and "how fucked up" everything had currently evolved.

"Everything just feels like it's over here and I don't see how I can do any business with all this shit hanging over my head," Jason sighed, "And it might not be safe for me here either."

"Between those guys in Dallas that are suddenly back in the picture and any bullshit with the FBI," Jason added, "who knows what'll happen if I just sit around and wait."

"Do you really think they might try to arrest you?" asked Debbie with more concern he'd heard from either Casey or Eliot.

"Nobody can tell me anything," Jason said with some bitterness, "But I think I do need to get away until I can get my head on straight and try to do something somewhere else for a while."

"I don't want to raise any suspicions, so I'm still going to help promote Jan Berry's concert at *Tiffany's* as if nothing is wrong," Jason said, "But after that, I have nothing set up and decided it's the best time to leave."

"I'm still renting my house and my car month to month, so I don't have any long-term commitments," he continued, "So, I'm going to just turn in my car, pack up some things, and fly away somewhere I can just get lost in the crowd."

"At least it'll look like I finished all my business and didn't run away from anything," Jason added with finality, "But the less anyone sees or hears anything about Jason Mershon again, the better."

Debbie didn't say anything, but Jason saw her sad and disappointed look.

"I think the safest thing for me to do right now is to just disappear without anything traceable, just in case," Jason tried to explain with logic, "And the further I can get away from anything involving my parents, the better."

"I've thought about a lot of things the past few days, and looking back, it's all just turned into a bunch of bullshit that I don't want hanging over my head anymore," Jason continued explaining with some regret, "I think I just need a fresh start somewhere as almost a new person."

"And just leave all your friends behind without a word?" said Debbie, "That doesn't seem right."

"I just want to be done with everything," Jason said with quiet bitterness. "I don't trust anyone anymore, and I'm to the point where I don't care if I see them again."

"Don't say that; you've got friends that care for you," said Debbie, "And you can always trust me."

They sat silent for at least a minute, not knowing what else to say.

"If you are going to leave town," Debbie suddenly said, "Then I'm going with you."

Jason didn't expect to hear that, but then he saw the tears in her eyes.

"I really care for you, Jason, and I don't want you to just disappear," she began crying.

That brought a change Jason wasn't expecting, and he never expected Debbie to cry over him.

"Don't you want me to come with you?" she asked, trying to wipe her tears.

"Debbie, of course, I would, but I don't know how we can make it work." he said, "I'm talking about leaving in the next couple weeks, and I don't even know how long I'll be gone."

"I can arrange something," Debbie said more optimistically, "I can just tell my parents I'm going to spend a few months with my brother out of state, and no one will even know that I went with you."

Jason did feel closer with Debbie than anyone else in his life for the past two months, but they had never even exchanged any "I love you" words together and he also couldn't believe that she would even consider just leaving everything behind as he was, and running away with him.

He couldn't picture any girl he'd known ever considering or offering anything like that and was immediately mad at himself for not realizing his actions affected someone else besides him.

"There's nothing I'd like more than you coming with me," Jason asked, hoping she was serious, "But are you sure you really want to do this?"

"It could be an adventure to see where the next road can take us," she smiled, "But no matter what happens, I'd at least like to try and find out."

"Well, it might be more like *Bonnie and Clyde* than *Romeo and Juliet*," Jason tried to laugh, "Especially if there really are federal agents looking for me."

"Couldn't you have picked a couple that doesn't die in the end?" Debbie tried to laugh with him.

"But I do want to be with you," she said again before lightly adding, "You always say I'm an angel, so let me really be your angel and help take care of you."

Jason held her close for a long time and gave her a more romantic *"You-u-u-u-u, you're an angel"* than he ever had before.

"Oh, and one more thing," Debbie smiled, "This *angel* has wheels, and I know that my *Bessie* will be our chariot that will take us anywhere we need to go."

Jason felt a warmth coming over him, realizing he had found someone who really wanted to run away with him, and somehow, he also knew she was the only person he needed in his life right now.

It did make him start to believe that Debbie really might be an angel, almost like in the song *Tightrope,* who had come to "throw him down a line" and to rescue him just like he had once wished for.

It also made Jason feel he wasn't alone anymore which made his plan sound like it might actually work.

Jan Berry's concert at *Tiffany's* was August sixteenth, and Jason wasn't really in the right frame of mind to attend, but he promised Jan he would be there. There were also very few other people that were in the right frame of mind to see Jan perform a concert that night either.

Earlier that afternoon, there was a bulletin on every radio and television station announcing that Elvis Presley had just died in Memphis. The news briefly did seem to replace Jason's problems with the sadness about Elvis dying and being the end of an important era, but Jason had still shown up at *Tiffany's* on schedule to continue to appear that he was involved with business as usual.

Jan had a tough time performing his concert that night, and the other band members had to cover several vocals that Jan had a difficult time completing, but Jason at least felt good about helping with the concert as he promised. He also felt there were only a few people he could really trust with what he was planning and was still secretive about all the details with most of them, and just told Jan he "had business away from California" for a while, but promised he'd call him and try to stay in touch.

Jason also knew with Jan's concert now completed he was satisfied that he had no other obligations to fulfill.

As he began his drive back to Encino from Marina Del Rey for what he knew would be the last time, it seemed every radio station was playing nothing but Elvis Presley songs, and each one was bringing back a particular memory to Jason, of a particular time in his life. But as he continued driving, he also knew that anything he thought had made him happy in the past no longer mattered.

Jason was still a little apprehensive and actually sad about what he was planning, but he felt that everything he had tried accomplishing the past five years, or even the past twenty-six years, were now basically as dead as Elvis Presley.

But he wanted them to be dead and knew any memories now needed to be erased and forgotten. He also knew the only way things would ever get better and completely free him from his worries, his bitterness, and especially his parents, was that like Elvis Presley, Jason Mershon would also have to die.

At least figuratively.

He just hoped he was doing the right thing and could somehow become born again into a new life.

❧

When he drove away from California with Debbie in his favorite new car, a beautiful pale green 1974 *Chevy Vega* hatchback, two days after Elvis Presley died, Jason did think it was a little ironic that on the same day as Elvis Presley's funeral, Jason Mershon and everything about his past was also being buried that day.

Jason had already seen Big Sal after saying he decided to take one of his blank birth certificates as he told Sal "Just in case," but besides Debbie, there weren't any others he told about his actual plans. He just hoped the distraction of Elvis' death and funeral would at least have everyone not notice that he was disappearing himself that day and give him time to leave town discreetly.

As Jason and Debbie drove across the California state line north on Interstate 15, the current hit song that had constantly been playing on the radio for the past several weeks from Fleetwood Mac's number one album *Rumours*, was again coincidentally playing on the *Chevy Vega's* AM radio.

Any depression Jason had felt about saying goodbye to everything was suddenly gone, and he was feeling nothing but optimism about what was ahead, as he sang along with the song, *Don't Stop* about how *yesterday was gone*, and not to stop *thinking about tomorrow.*

Jason lightly tried to convince Debbie that song was telling them both their destiny ahead, and even though he knew she hated to sing herself, he was able to coax her into joining him in singing the last chorus as they drove to their new adventure.

As Jason squeezed Debbie's hand while they sang the *oooh's,* and the lyrics about not *looking back* together, he felt an even stronger warmth coming over him, and he knew everything was going to be alright.

And, just as the song *Don't Stop* faded out, so did *Jay* and *Jason Mershon's* past life.

Jason with James Drury, star of "The Virginian" TV show and his first Bachelorette of Dallas.

Jason in Dallas 1976.

Television news reporters in Dallas were first ones to describe Jason's parties as "Gatsbyesque" or similar to those in The Great Gatsby.

Jason welcomes David Clayton-Thomas and Blood, Sweat & Tears to his first World Entertainment Club party in Dallas, 1976.

Jason tries to keep drunk superstar Joe Cocker upright at his televised World Entertainment Party at Number 3 Lift Disco, 1976.

Jason being interviewed with the City of Dallas Mayor, Robert Folsom.

Mayoral Candidate Garry Weber at Jason's World Entertainment Club Party.

Jason recruiting Bachelorette contestants, 1976.

Top left: Jason with two friends, Candy and Melanie. Top right: Jason with Martha Bland (right) and another Bachelorette at one of his parties. Bottom: Jason was always promoting the benefits of being single in the *National Singles Register* and at his parties.

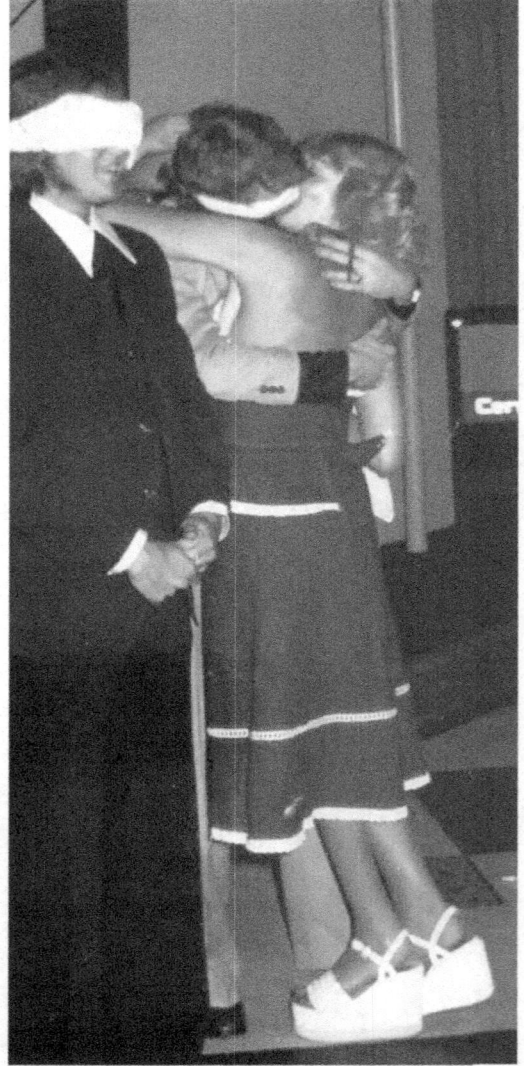

Left: Jason recreating the St. Valentine's Day Massacre for KTTV's Metro News! Metro News! on February 14, 1977. Right: The Kissing Contest for the "Nightmovers Party Hour", was the only contest where Jason decided to be involved judging. Of course, he made sure he was the first in line to judge the contestants kissing ability while the other blindfolded judges waited their turn.

Jason taping promo for the television pilot "The Nightmovers Party Hour - Where the Real People are the Stars", at the Tapestry Disco, 1977.

Jason interviewing "Legs Contest" contestant Debby Budd, for a segment of the television pilot "The Nightmovers Party Hour", May 31, 1977 at Jumping Frog Saloon, Westwood, California.

Jan Berry and Jason, 1977.

Jason interviewing "Legs Contest" contestant Debbie Budd, for

a segment of the television pilot "The Nightmovers Party Hour,"

May 31, 1977 at Jumping Frog Saloon, Westwood, California.

EPILOGUE
PREVIEW TO VOLUME TWO

It was still over a month away from the official beginning of winter, but the first snow had already fallen in the small city at the foot of Pike's Peak in the Rocky Mountains.

The local live afternoon television show *Midday* was just beginning its daily broadcast in that small city. The host, Bill Bruce, was sitting at the news desk reporting the world and national news headlines before previewing the other local stories would be featured in the next hour.

"Plans are continuing for Egyptian president Anwar Sadat to make his historic trip to Israel this month," Bill Bruce was reporting, "President Carter said he hopes the visit and face to face meeting with Prime Minister Menachem Begin will be the first steps to lasting peace in the Middle East."

"Here in the United States, the Senate is expected to vote today to cut emissions demand by increasing the gas tax for all gas-guzzling cars, with the national average for a price of gasoline now up to sixty-two cents a gallon" he continued, "In other news, in what was considered a slap in the face to anti-gay activist Anita Bryant, San Francisco elected its first openly gay mayor, Harvey Milk."

"The investigation continues into the plane crash that killed three members of the rock band Lynyrd Skynyrd, including lead singer Ronnie Van Zant," Bill Bruce switched to entertainment news, "And later in today's show, we'll be featuring a report about a new craze that is currently invading Great Britain called the *'Punk'* look."

Jason had been sitting quietly at the news desk off-camera, as he listened to him reading the news from the cue cards, and was thinking how Bill Bruce had to be the most boring host he had ever seen on television.

Besides looking like he was at least seventy years old, Bill Bruce spoke in a super slow monotone voice that was impossible to generate any excitement, and Jason wondered how he ever got a job in broadcasting.

But Jason also knew this was Colorado Springs, not Hollywood and was exactly what he had been looking for. He knew no one outside of Colorado Springs or Pueblo would even see the *Midday* show that day, and knew it was safe.

"I'd also like to mention that in the studio today, we have the sixteen finalists of a unique beauty pageant that has been getting a lot of attention here in Colorado Springs for the past month," Bill Bruce finally concluded his report, "And after our first break, we'll be speaking with the man who started the pageant, the head honcho you might say, and his name is Jason Hunter."

While Jason waited to be introduced after the commercial break, he was still pleasantly surprised about how quickly he had been to blend into this small city tucked away in the mountains, and had already made a new and well-known name for himself.

Two of Debbie Budfuloski's eleven brothers and sisters lived in Colorado Springs, and it was the first stop they made after leaving California, before Jason's original plan of hiding out in a bigger city like Chicago.

Debbie's brother, Steven, had a small apartment near downtown Colorado Springs and had been letting Jason and Debbie sleep in an unfurnished second bedroom that he wasn't using.

Jason figured it would at least give him time to stop and think about what he was going to do now.

"Colorado Springs is the last place on Earth anyone would even think of looking for you," Debbie tried to convince Jason when they first arrived, "And I'm sure no one from Texas, California or Las Vegas would even hear about anything that goes on in a small town like this."

It was only after a week in Colorado, before they both decided that seeing that had a free place to stay for a while, and didn't want to spend all their cash traveling while they figured things out, that Colorado Springs was probably the best place to stay for a while.

Their immediate concern was how to earn an income before the money Jason had run out.

Jason and Debbie had both talked about getting jobs to at least have some type of regular income to keep them going, but Jason had no idea about what kind of job he could apply without disclosing his past.

The one thing he was positive about was that he didn't want to be Jason Mershon anymore and truly wanted to become a new person. And, he wanted to divorce himself from everything and everyone that included the name, *Mershon.*

Jason also knew if he applied for a job somewhere, he'd have to show his driver's license, so if he wanted to become a new person, he needed a new driver's license with a new name.

Jason briefly thought of changing his first name to *"Dax"* after the main character in *The Adventurers* but decided he wanted to keep *"Jason"* as his first name, especially when he learned it was becoming one of the most popular baby names of the 1970s.

"Bond, Jason Bond…," Jason suggested to Debbie when they were trying to think of a new name together.

"I think it has a ring to it!" he added with a laugh.

659

"Sounds too phony," Debbie sarcastically laughed back, "That sounds as bad as your other choice, *Jason Gatsby*."

"But 'Bond' will even fit it with our song," Jason tried to justify.

On one of the last night's that they'd spent in California after they decided to run away together, Jason and Debbie had gone to a drive-in theatre to see the new James Bond movie, *The Spy Who Loved Me*, and since then, the title song *Nobody Does It Better* by Carly Simon, had become what Jason told Debbie was their first official *"our song."*

They had been throwing so many different last names to each other after they decided to stay in Colorado Springs; Jason wasn't even sure who came up with the name *"Hunter,"* but as soon as they both heard it, something about it just sounded right.

Jason had the blank birth certificate that Big Sal had given him, and he knew he'd have to come up with a good story as to why he was almost twenty-seven years old and never had a driver's license before.

Because Colorado Springs was a big military town with both Army and Air Force bases, Jason and Debbie figured out a good story to tell.

Jason would just tell the clerk at the Colorado Department of Motor Vehicles that his father had been in the military overseas for the past twenty years, and he never was in the U.S. long enough to apply for a driver's license.

He made several copies of the blank birth certificate because he knew if he made a mistake while typing, it would kill any chance he had for a new identity, and was glad he did, because he did make several mistakes when he was using the typewriter at the public library, filling out every line trying to make it look official.

Jason typed in new parents' names, new birth cities, and every other official line that needed to be filled in with what sounded legitimate. He also decided to include his real birth year of 1951, knowing that the altered driver's license he had used since 1969 showed that he'd be turning thirty years old sooner than he wanted.

Once he had one filled out perfect, he folded and unfolded the certificate several times, dampened it a little, and ran it through a clothes dryer, all trying to make it look older and worn.

Jason then applied for a new driver's license to see if his story was convincing. Less than two hours later, Jason showed Debbie his new temporary Colorado Driver's License with her brother's address, his new name, Jason James Hunter.

"Wow, when we first started dating, you were twenty- nine years old," Debbie teased, "And now I've got a twenty-six-year-old boyfriend."

"I might want one of those birth certificates when I start pushing thirty myself," she laughed.

"I can't believe how easy it was," Jason also half laughed, "They believed everything I told them."

"And now that I'm a new person," he smiled, "Hopefully, I can find a new job."

Debbie had been talking about looking for a job as an accountant, and Jason was still trying to figure out what kind of job would actually suit him best with no prior experience or job history he could show.

"Well, I know you're not that crazy about my *'Bessie'* for a car," said Debbie, "And you are going to need something to drive."

"They do give car salesmen a demo to drive when they work at a car dealership," she said, "And you are a good salesman in a lot of ways, so maybe that's something you should think about at least temporarily."

The thought of actually having to get an ordinary job was somewhat depressing after having been somewhat self-employed for so many years. Still, Jason knew he needed to start over again somewhere.

And, it would at least give him a new car to drive.

Jason found a car dealership in Denver through the want ads that were hiring and drove the seventy miles from Colorado Springs to apply in person.

"Let me ask you this," asked the dealership sales manager as he interviewed Jason, "If you bought a car from me and found out later that I made a profit of over a thousand dollars, how would you feel?"

Jason thought about it and figured out what the best answer was.

"Well, I suppose if I thought I got a good deal from you when I bought the car," said Jason, "I shouldn't feel bad about you making a profit as well."

"Everyone should realize *it's no sin to make a profit*," Jason smiled.

"Right answer!" shouted the sales manager, "That's exactly the way all of our customers should feel!"

"And I like your personality and quick thinking," he added.

Jason ended up getting hired on the spot and was surprised at how easy it had been to get a job, but he still wasn't that thrilled about the prospect of becoming just a *car salesman.*

The sales manager explained that the job paid commission only and that Jason could earn anywhere from twenty-five dollars, up to one hundred and fifty dollars for each car he sold but added that Jason would receive a car to drive as a demo as the main perk of being a car salesman.

Jason liked the prospect of having a new car to drive, but explained to the sales manager he'd need at least a week or two to get things organized in Colorado Springs before he could start.

The sales manager said that was no problem and gave Jason paperwork that needed to be filled out and brought back when he was ready to start.

Jason decided he wanted to try one last thing before taking a job that required a hundred and forty-mile round trip commute every day or having to move to Denver.

He also knew he could always make a better commission with his own product than just selling a car.

Jason saw that Colorado Springs did have a big drinking crowd, but was surprised that besides happy hours, there were no other bars that were currently featuring any special promotions. And, he saw it as a virgin city almost as he had when he moved to Dallas.

He figured trying a promotion in a small city far enough away from Hollywood, Texas, and Las Vegas that no one paid any attention, would as least be something to try once.

"It's just something I can try to make some quick money, and it's what I know how to do the best," Jason tried to add with excitement when he explained his idea to Debbie, "And most importantly, it's something we can work on together."

After Debbie agreed that it might be all right to try once just to make some extra money, but added he should still consider the car salesman job as well, Jason decided to give his idea a shot.

"We still have your car *Bessie* to get us by for now," Jason lightly added, "So let's see what happens, and if it doesn't work out, I can always take the job in Denver."

It was three days before he was supposed to start his new job in Denver as a car salesman, when Jason walked into a bar and nightclub called *The Emporium Ltd* at 118 North Tejon St. in Colorado Springs, after arranging a meeting with the owner.

He was sitting across from an older woman with grey hair, who Jason guessed was in her late fifties, who said she had recently bought out her partner and was now the only owner of the bar.

Jason wasn't sure how someone her age would react to his pitch.

"My name is *Hunter*, Jason Hunter," he said, "And I'm producing "The *Official* Miss Legs of Colorado Springs Beauty Pageant."

"I'm just looking around to see which nightclubs in the city would be a good location for one of our preliminary contests," Jason added in his businesslike tone, "If you're interested in being the first bar to host a Miss Legs Colorado Springs preliminary, you should get a ton of new business and publicity."

"Oh goodie!" she shouted with excitement, "That sounds like something fun."

"It's basically a free opportunity for you that won't cost any money upfront, and we do all the promotion," Jason casually added, "You'll just need to agree to give *Steppin' Out Productions* the door charge the night of the pageant, and twenty percent of the gross bar receipts we help generate for you."

As soon as Jason heard the next words out of the older woman's mouth, he knew he wouldn't be starting a job as a car salesman.

"How can I sign up to be first?" she agreed before Jason had to say anything else.

Now it was less than three months later. After receiving a front-page story in the Gazette Telegraph newspaper after his first preliminary at *The Emporium Ltd*, everyone in the city seemed to have heard about Miss Legs of Colorado Springs. Jason

662

had been invited on the *Midday* television to preview and promote his upcoming city finals.

The commercial break had ended, and the camera angle went wide, showing Jason sitting next to the host at the news desk.

"Well as I'm sure everyone knows, there have already been four preliminaries of the Miss Legs of Colorado Springs pageant," Bill Bruce immediately began his introduction in his monotone voice, "And here in the studio is the man himself who is producing the pageant, Jason Hunter."

"Tell me why do we have a Miss Legs contest, Jason?" Bill Bruce asked in his slow, boring voice, "Is there any particular reason, or any reason at all?"

Jason was glad that Andi Joyce, the television weather girl at that station, and who he had made a celebrity judge in one of his earlier preliminaries, had a friend in the studio that day who discreetly offered Jason a bump of cocaine right before the *Midday* show began.

He wanted to make sure he livened up his segment on the show with some excitement and energy.

"Well Bill, beauty contests are American as mom and apple pie," Jason said confidently to the host, "You've got Miss USA, Miss America, Miss Universe along with many others, and knowing that a lot of women take great pride in their legs, this gives those women an easy opportunity to compete in a beauty pageant, win some great prizes, and be recognized in the city for just showing their best assets."

"Miss Legs is just something new, different, and will definitely be the biggest and most exciting beauty pageant ever held in Colorado Springs!" Jason added with his *excited* tone.

Jason knew that now that he was being seen in Colorado Springs on television as Jason *Hunter*, as well as having already had his new name and photo featured in the local newspapers, he had succeeded in becoming born again as a new person. He knew it wasn't completely *legitimate*, but it was close enough for now.

A Baby Boomers Last Stand--A True Story of a Novel Life
from Truman to Trump, continues in Volume Two

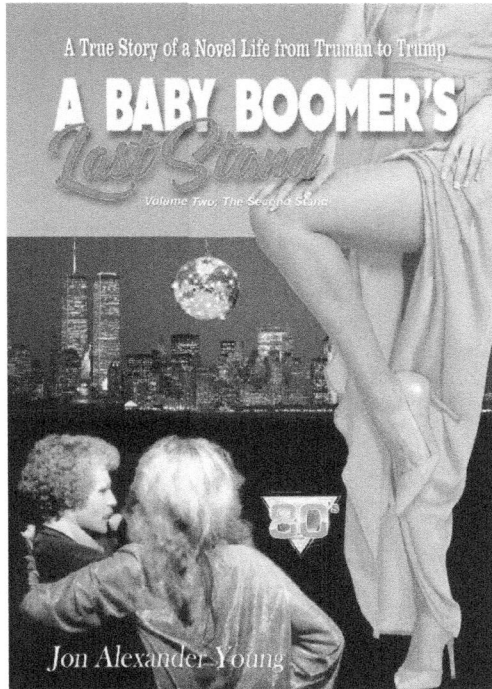

A True Story of a Novel Life from Truman to Trump

A BABY BOOMER'S
Last Stand

Volume Two: The Second Stand

Jon Alexander Young

"THE SECOND STAND"
1978-1986

Made in the USA
Las Vegas, NV
14 January 2026